Secretary of the Treasury

I0061802

Secretary of the Treasury Annual Report 1871

Secretary of the Treasury

Secretary of the Treasury Annual Report 1871

ISBN/EAN: 9783741135903

Manufactured in Europe, USA, Canada, Australia, Japa

Cover: Foto ©knipser5 / pixelio.de

Manufactured and distributed by brebook publishing software
(www.brebook.com)

Secretary of the Treasury

Secretary of the Treasury Annual Report 1871

ANNUAL REPORT

OF THE

SECRETARY OF THE TREASURY

ON THE

STATE OF THE FINANCES

FOR

THE YEAR 1871.

WASHINGTON:
GOVERNMENT PRINTING OFFICE.
1871.

TABLE OF CONTENTS.

REPORT

SECRETARY OF THE TREASURY.

TREASURY DEPARTMENT,
December 4, 1871,

SIR: The country has been prosperous during the year now closing, and the public finances have shared in the general prosperity.

During the fiscal year ending June 30, 1871, the reduction of the public debt was $94,327,764 84 The total decrease in the public debt from March 1, 1869, to December 1, 1871, was $277,211,892 16; and during the same period the annual interest charge has been reduced $16,741,436 04.

The revenues for the year 1871, and the receipts since the first of July last, show that the time has arrived when a considerable further reduction in taxes can be made, and yet leave the Government in a position to pay at least fifty millions of·dollars annually of the principal of the public debt, including the amount pledged through the sinking fund. In my annual report to Congress for 1870, I expressed the opinion that the settled policy of the country should contemplate a revenue sufficient to meet the ordinary expenses of the Government, pay the interest on the public debt, and from twenty-five to fifty millions of dollars of the principal annually. To that opinion I adhere, with even a stronger conviction that the payment annually upon the principal of the public debt should not be less than fifty millions of dollars.

Large as the revenues of the country have been during the last three years, our system of taxation has not been oppressive to individuals, nor has it in any sensible degree embarrassed the business of the country; and while relief from taxation is desirable it is yet more desirable to maintain the public credit in its present elevated position, not only as an example to other nations, but for its historical value in enabling the Government to make loans for large amounts upon favorable terms if, unhappily, in the future an exigency should require such loans to be made.

The power to negotiate a large loan at five per cent. interest, and to enter upon negotiations for the sale of bonds bearing five, four-and-a-half, and four per cent. interest, is derived entirely from the exhibition of an honest purpose on the part of the people to maintain the public faith, and the consequent ability on the part of the Government to answer that expectation by large and frequent payments upon the public debt.

The revenue from customs for the fiscal year 1871 was greatly in excess of the estimates, amounting to $206,270,408 05, against $194,538,374 44, for the preceding year. The cost of collecting this revenue was $6,560,672 61, for 1871, being three and eleven hundredths per cent., while the cost for the year 1870 was $6,237,137 25, or three and twenty hundredths per cent.

The appropriation for the collection of the customs, with the additions derived from fines, penalties, and forfeitures, exceeded the expenditures by the sum of more than eight hundred thousand dollars, and there is no doubt that the permanent appropriation will be ample for the present year, and for the next fiscal year.

The reduction of the rates of duty on the 1st of January, 1871, under the act of July 14, 1870, diminished the importation of many articles during the last six months of the year 1870, but there was consequently a large addition to the revenues for the first six months of the year 1871.

A comparison of the first six months of the calendar year 1871 with the first six months of the calendar year 1870, shows an increase of fifty-five per cent. in the quantity of tea imported, twenty per cent. in the quantity of coffee, fifty-three per cent. in the quantity of brown sugar, one hundred and twenty per cent. in the quantity of pig iron, one hundred and eighty-six per cent. in the quantity of melado, one hundred and thirty-nine per cent. in the quantity of spices, and a large increase in many other articles.

The probability is that the customs revenue for the current year will exceed that for the year 1870–'71.

The receipts from internal revenue were $143,098,153 63, being $4,048,984 29 less than the estimates presented to Congress in December last for the fiscal year ending June 30, 1871. The estimates for the current fiscal year were $126,418,000, and it is probable that the receipts will be equal to the estimates.

The net receipts for the fiscal year ending June 30, 1871, were as follows:

From customs	$206, 270, 408	05
From internal revenue	143, 098, 153	63
From sales of public lands	2, 388, 646	68
From miscellaneous sources	31, 566, 736	53
	383, 323, 944	89

The expenditures for the same period were:

For civil and miscellaneous purposes	$69, 498, 710	97
For War Department	*35, 799, 991	82
For Navy Department	19, 431, 027	21
For Indians	7, 426, 997	44
For Pensions	34, 443, 894	88
For interest on the public debt	125, 576, 565	93
	292, 177, 188	25

The miscellaneous revenues for the fiscal year ending June 30, 1871, were derived from the following sources:

Premium on sales of coin	$8, 892, 839	95
Fees from United States consuls	565, 563	24
Storage, rent, labor, &c., at custom-houses	414, 310	61
Fines, penalties, and forfeitures for violations of customs laws	952, 579	86
Fees on letters patent	620, 319	11
Tax on circulation, deposits, &c., of national banks	6, 003, 584	32
Repayment of interest by Pacific railway companies	813, 284	75
Homestead and other land fees	645, 923	17
Steamboat fees and marine-hospital tax	385, 535	16
Proceeds of sale of coin-interest on sinking and special funds	7, 701, 662	73
Judiciary—fines, penalties, and forfeitures	75, 836	30
Tax on seal-skins	101, 080	00
Reimbursement to the United States for salaries of storekeepers in internal revenue bonded warehouses.	557, 235	41
Direct tax	580, 355	37
Emolument fees	585, 887	69
Parting charges—refining gold and silver bullion	211, 721	14
Proceeds of Indian trust lands	1, 140, 120	28

*This is the net amount after deducting $8,280,093 13 repaid into the Treasury as proceeds of sales of ordnance, etc. The true expenditures were $44,080,084 95.

Accrued interest on, and proceeds of sale of, Indian trust-fund stocks, and interest on deferred payments on Indian-trust lands............................	$387,921 01
Reimbursements to the United States for moneys advanced to meet matured interest on non-paying stocks held in trust for various Indian tribes......	35,535 00
One, two, three, and five-cent coinage..............	150,000 00
Unenumerated	745,441 43
	31,566,736 53

The receipts for the first quarter of the present fiscal year were:

From customs....................................	$62,289,329 37
From internal revenue.............................	35,553,175 01
From sales of public lands........................	602,680 61
From miscellaneous sources.......................	8,753,189 61
	107,198,374 60

The expenditures for the same period, excluding payments on account of the sinking fund, were:

For civil and miscellaneous purposes...............	$16,579,732 46
For War Department..............................	12,590,653 05
For Navy Department.............................	6,513,040 93
For Indians......................................	3,404,133 42
For Pensions	8,090,698 69
For interest on the public debt	36,725,124 37
	83,903,382 92

The estimated receipts for the remaining three quarters of the present year, are as follows:

From customs....................................	$148,000,000 00
From internal revenue............................	90,000,000 00
From sales of public lands........................	2,000,000 00
From miscellaneous sources	18,000,000 00
	258,000,000 00

The estimated expenditures for the same period, excluding payments on account of the sinking fund, are:

For civil and miscellaneous purposes...............	$50,000,000 00
For War Department.............................	31,000,000 00

For Navy Department............................. $13,500,000 00
For Indians......................................   6,000,000 00
For Pensions 24,000,000 00
For interest on the public debt....................   85,000,000 00

                                                       209,500,000 00

These estimates show a balance applicable to the payment of the principal of the public debt for the fiscal year ending June 30, 1872, $71,794,991 68.

The receipts and expenditures for the fiscal year ending June 30, 1873, are estimated as follows:

RECEIPTS.

From customs.................................... $212,000,000
From internal revenue...........................   126,000,000
From sales of public lands......................   3,000,000
From miscellaneous sources......................   18,000,000

                                                       359,000,000

EXPENDITURES.

Legislative establishment........................ $3,421,812 40
Executive establishment..........................   17,443,531 38
Judicial establishment...........................   3,383,350 00
Military establishment...........................   31,422,509 88
Naval establishment..............................   18,946,088 95
Indian affairs...................................   5,445,617 97
Pensions 30,480,000 00
Public works under Treasury Dep't .. $3,104,500 00
Public works under Interior Dep't ...   244,800 00
Public works under War Dep't 14,609,662 97
Public works under Navy Dept't 1,483,100 00
Public works under Agricultural Dep't,   26,500 00
                                                       19,468,562 97

Postal service...................................   5,474,001 00
Miscellaneous....................................   11,258,325 44
Permanent appropriations 126,281,974 00
Sinking fund.....................................   22,895,930 00
Interest upon the capital of the sinking fund.......   5,783,333 00

                                                       301,705,036 99

These estimates show a balance of $57,294,963 01 applicable to the payment of the principal of the debt, in addition to the sum of $28,679,263 due on account of the sinking fund, or the sum of $85,974,226 01 in all.

In the estimates for the next fiscal year I have not included in the receipts the premium on gold which may be sold, nor in the expenditures the premium which may be paid on bonds to be purchased in currency.

In the suggestions I have the honor to make in reference to the reduction of taxes, I keep in view two important facts: first, that the ability of the nation to pay at least fifty millions annually of the principal of the public debt shall not be impaired; and, secondly, that in the change of the revenue system no violence shall be done to the business interests of the country. While I do not undertake to state precisely the causes which have contributed to the public prosperity, there is no substantial reason for questioning the truth of the statement that the last few years have been the most prosperous in the history of the country; years without example in our own affairs, and without parallel in the affairs of any other Government.

It is practicable to dispense with all revenue from internal sources except that derived from stamps, spirits, tobacco, and malt liquors. These sources should furnish for the year 1872–'73 a revenue of about one hundred and ten millions of dollars, making a reduction of taxes of sixteen millions of dollars. The revenue from customs under existing laws, and from lands and miscellaneous sources, would amount to about two hundred and thirty-three millions more, making a total revenue for that year of three hundred and forty-three millions of dollars.

The expenses of the Government, not including the amount payable on account of the sinking fund, are estimated at $273,025,773 99.

If to this sum be added fifty millions of dollars for payments on account of the public debt, including the amount due on the sinking fund, there remains a balance of about twenty millions, within which reductions may be made in the revenue from customs. This amount, added to the reductions proposed under the internal revenue laws, gives a total reduction of thirty-six millions.

In this view, I respectfully recommend to the consideration of Congress the reduction of the duties on salt to the extent of fifty per cent.; the duty on bituminous coal to fifty cents per ton; the reduction of the duty on raw hides and skins; and the removal of all duties from a large class of articles produced in other countries, which enter into the arts and manufactures of this country, and which are not produced in the United States, and the revenue from which is inconsiderable. Such a list, with the revenue derived from each article, is in course of preparation, and will be submitted to Congress.

The removal of duties from a large class of articles used in manufactures, and the reduction of the duties upon coal, furnish an opportunity for a moderate decrease in the rates of duties upon those products whose cost will be diminished by these changes.

While nothing, as the consequence of legislation, could be more disastrous to the public prosperity than a policy which should destroy or seriously disturb the manufacturing interest of the country, it is still possible, by wise and moderate changes adapted to the condition of business and labor, to reduce the rates of duties with benefit to every class of people.

The average premium on gold for the year 1868 was 39.84 per cent.; for the year 1869 it was 32.56 per cent. premium; for the year 1870 it was 14.83 per cent. premium; and for the first eleven months of the year 1871 it was 12.1 per cent. premium. The value of the paper currency of the country during the years 1869 and 1870 was apparently appreciated by the increased use of paper money in the South, but chiefly by the establishment of the credit of the United States upon a firm basis. On the first of January, 1871, the last-named fact was fully accomplished, and since that time the appreciation of the paper currency has been due wholly to the increased demand for it in the business affairs of the country. The difference between the value of paper money at the present moment and its value on the first of December, 1870, may be attributed to the latter cause, and furnishes the best means which the country has yet had for ascertaining the quantity of paper currency which can be used and its value kept at par with gold.

The result of this test concurs with what seems to me to be the best opinion upon the subject, that the amount of paper money in circulation is still so great that it cannot be maintained in value at par with coin. There are two modes of relief: One is to reduce the volume of currency, as was recommended by me in my annual report submitted to Congress in December, 1869; the other mode is to await the growth of the country, and the increasing demands of business, which in time will produce the desired result.

The chief means of securing the end sought, without a reduction in the volume of currency, would be the use of paper money upon the Pacific coast. With this object in view, steps have already been taken by this Department for the purpose of ascertaining whether it is practicable to substitute paper for coin, and I have reason to anticipate that a change may be made in the laws relating to National Banks tending to that result, which will not affect unfavorably the general character of the system.

It is my duty to call the attention of Congress to the importance of abolishing the system of shares in moieties, as far as the benefits inure to revenue officers, and other persons officially connected with the Government. This measure was recommended in my last annual report, and a statement was submitted to Congress showing the amount received by officers of customs, together with a bill increasing their salaries without any increase of appropriations from the Treasury; the sum now paid from moieties being quite sufficient to place the entire force upon a satisfactory footing in regard to pay.

During the last fiscal year the office of collector and surveyor of the port of New York each received from moieties the sum of $49,215 69, and the naval office the sum of $48,195 59.

In most of the cases the officers do not perform special services entitling them to the amounts granted, and importers and others whose acts are made the subject of investigation, complain, and, I think, with just reason, that the agents of the Government have a pecuniary interest in pursuing those charged with violations of the law. The Government ought to pay fair salaries, and rely upon the good faith of its officers for the performance of their duty. One of the difficulties which the Department has to meet, frequently is, that customs officers have an interest in proceedings for the discovery of fraud, the settlement of cases, or the prosecution of them, which is different from the real interest of the Government; and, as a necessary result, the conduct of such officers is open to suspicion, both on the part of those who are pursued by them, and the Government that they ostensibly represent.

It may be deemed expedient to leave the law as it now stands in regard to informers who are not officers, making it a penal offense for any officer to enter into an arrangement with an informer for any share of the proceeds of the information, and giving to the informer perpetual right of action for the recovery of any money or other valuable thing paid or given to an officer engaged in the discovery or prosecution of a fraud or legal wrong against the Government.

The report of the Comptroller of the Currency shows that one hundred and forty-five banks have been organized under the act approved July 12, 1871, providing for the issue of fifty-four millions of dollars of additional bank circulation, and that the sum of $22,333,900 has been issued.

By virtue of the same act, the Treasury has redeemed $22,230,000 of the three per cent. certificates then in circulation, leaving the sum of $23,490,000 now outstanding. I take the liberty of suggesting, that it appears to me to be wise to leave the distribution of the circulation authorized by said act as it now stands.

Should the States that have already received their proportion of circulation be authorized to take what may remain, only a brief period will elapse before a demand will be made from States with limited circulation for an increase. It seems prudent, therefore, to retain the balance of the fifty-four millions for distribution in those States now having a claim to it, on the basis of equality of apportionment.

The details of the subscription to the Loan show that the National Banks, have, upon the whole, acted liberally—more than a hundred millions of dollars having been subscribed for by them on their own account.

It is not unreasonable to tender to these institutions the opportunity to subscribe for bonds under the act of July 14, 1870, to an amount equal to the deposits required of them as security for circulation, and to couple that offer with a provision that, after ninety days, to the extent that the offer may be declined, other banking associations may be formed in the several States where the existing banks shall have failed to make the required subscription, and the circulation transferred from such banks to the new associations.

The banks now organized cannot justly complain, if, having an opportunity to pursue the business upon the new bonds, and declining it, other associations shall succeed to their franchises and rights.

The business of the Bureau of Engraving and Printing has been carried on with diligence during the year, and with satisfactory results.

Although some efforts have been made at counterfeiting the special papers used by the Department, they have not been successful, and the specimens captured are so crude as not to excite serious apprehensions as to ultimate success.

Since the first of July, 1869, seventy million sheets of paper have been manufactured, all of which have been accounted for on the books of the Department.

I respectfully recommend that an appropriation be made for a new issue of national bank notes. Those now in use are much worn and very successful counterfeits of several denominations have appeared.

The public building used as a custom-house, court-house, and post office, at Chicago, was destroyed by the great fire on the 8th of October last. The exterior walls remain, and the building could be repaired, but, anticipating the growth of Chicago and the magnitude of its public business, I advise the erection of a building suited to the wants of a first-class city.

It is important that a much larger piece of land should be obtained, either by addition to the present lot or by the purchase of another site. On the 18th of October last, I wrote a letter to Governor Palmer, asking him to recommend to the Legislature the passage of an act granting authority to the courts of the State of Illinois to condemn such land as might be required, in case the Government should be unable to obtain it by purchase at a reasonable price, payment to be made upon an appraisal. In every case, the site for a building erected by the Government for public uses should be large enough to separate it from all other structures, thus furnishing sufficient light for the prosecution of business, and adequate security also against fire and the depredations of lawless persons. It is hardly necessary to say, that in the existing condition of affairs at Chicago, it is important that an appropriation, available during the present fiscal year, should be made without unnecessary delay.

Since my last annual report, the Supervising Architect has completed the custom-house, court-house, and post office, at Portland, Maine; the court-house and post office at Des Moines, Iowa; the court-house and post office at Madison, Wisconsin; the appraisers' stores at Philadelphia; and the assay office at Boise City, Idaho.

It is now expected that the custom-house and post office at St. Paul, Minnesota; the marine hospital at Chicago, Illinois; the court-house and post office at Astoria, Oregon; the custom-house at Machias, Maine; the branch mint at San Francisco, California; and the custom-house at Cairo, Illinois, will be finished and ready for use by the first day of July next. At that time there will remain, in an unfinished condition, the court-house and post office at Columbia, South Carolina; the custom-house at New Orleans, Louisiana; the custom-house at Charleston, South Carolina; the court-house and post office at Knoxville, Tennessee; the custom-house and post office at Portland, Oregon; the court-house and post office at New York; the post office and independent treasury at Boston, and the custom-house and post office at Omaha, Nebraska.

The prosecution of these works—four of which are of great importance—in connection with public buildings to be erected at Chicago, and the erection of marine hospitals at Pittsburg, San Francisco, and New York, will, in my opinion, sufficiently occupy the Supervising Architect of the Treasury and the force at his command. I cannot, therefore, advise appropriations for other public buildings until some of those in process of construction shall have been completed. The points at which the erection or repair of public buildings is most needed are Hartford, Indianapolis, Cincinnati, and St. Louis.

Under an act passed at the last session of Congress, appropriating two hundred thousand dollars for the purpose of more effectually securing life and property on the coasts of New Jersey and Long Island, a careful examination of the coast and of the life-saving stations has been made by experienced officers of the revenue service. In accordance with their report, proposals were invited and accepted for the erection of fourteen new houses on the coast of New Jersey and six upon the coast of Long Island. Repairs are also making upon the old houses on the Long Island coast.

The operations of the coast survey, which are under the administrative direction of this Department, have been prosecuted with the usual energy, as will be seen from the brief report of progress made by the Superintendent, in advance of the usual detailed report, with maps, annually submitted to Congress.

The survey of the Atlantic coast is now rapidly approaching completion, that of the Gulf coast is more than half finished, and the work on the Pacific coast is being pressed forward vigorously.

The estimates submitted substantially conform to the appropriations for the present year. An increase is asked for the item of extending the triangulation across the country to the Pacific ocean, great interest having been manifested by the authorities of the States traversed in the prosecution of the work.

The business entrusted to the Light-House Board is one of the most important branches of the public service in the control of this Department, and I am able to state that it is conducted with fidelity and with reference solely to the maritime interests of the country.

The estimates made by the Light-House Board exceed the appropriations for the present year but they appear to be necessary, and I respectfully recommend them to the consideration of Congress.

Under an act of Congress, approved July 30, 1870, Dr. John M. Woodworth has been appointed Supervising Surgeon of the Marine Hospital Service. His administration is satisfactory to the Department.

The average number of hospital patients for the fiscal year ending June 30, 1870, was one thousand and sixteen, and for the year ending June 30, 1871, one thousand one hundred and ninety-eight. The total cost of the service for the first-named year was $405,624, being an average, for each patient, of $1 09 per day; and for the latter year $453,082 42, or an average of $1 04 per day.

In the first-named year the hospital tax was $168,153 70, and in the latter year it amounted to $293,592 14.

The Supervising Surgeon is of opinion that pavilion hospitals are better adapted to the successful treatment of the sick than the ordinary buildings of brick and stone, while the expenses are only one-fourth as great.

In accordance with his suggestion, I recommend an appropriation of fifty thousand dollars for the purchase of land and the construction of a pavilion hospital at Pittsburg, Pennsylvania. The present hospital is situated in the vicinity of iron mills and railways, and as it can be sold for about seventy thousand dollars, the Government will be fully reimbursed for the cost of a new hospital, while the comfort of the patients will be promoted.

An estimate has been made that the sum of fifty thousand dollars will be sufficient for the construction of a pavilion hospital on Angel Island, in the Bay of San Francisco, sufficient to accommodate one hundred and fifty patients, and I also recommend an appropriation of that amount for that purpose.

I also respectfully renew the recommendation, made heretofore, for a pavilion hospital near the city of New York sufficient for the accommodation of two hundred patients.

The Revenue Marine Service employs twenty-five steam-vessels and eight sailing vessels. In addition to these, there are two large steamers upon the Lakes, not in commission, and two schooners upon the coast condemned as not fit for duty.

Of the six large steamers upon the Lakes, four only are in commission, and as the others are not needed, I have the honor to recommend that authority be given for their sale.

During the last year four iron steamers have been built—three of two hundred and fifty, and one of three hundred and fifty tons burden. Under the existing appropriation of two hundred thousand dollars, the Department is about to issue proposals for four small iron propellers, two for the Pacific and two for the Atlantic coast.

A further appropriation of two hundred thousand dollars is needed to enable the Department to carry into effect the recommendation of the Commission, whose report was approved by the Department and submitted to Congress May 26, 1870.

The plan recommended by the Commission, when fully adopted, will effect a reduction in the expenses of this branch of the service of about five hundred thousand dollars, or about thirty-four per cent. of the whole cost. The changes proposed contemplate the use of vessels of less tonnage, and a consequent reduction in the number of men employed.

The expenses of the Revenue Marine Service for the year ending

June 30, 1871, were $1,251,984 52, against $1,138,393 31 for the preceding year. The first quarter of the present fiscal year shows a reduction in expenses of $83,201 42, as compared with the corresponding period of the preceding year.

At the date of my last report, a board of officers was in session charged with the duty of examining the officers then in active service. The report showed that five captains, ten first lieutenants, nine second lieutenants, and ten third lieutenants, were not qualified for duty. The persons found to be incompetent have been discharged, and their places have been filled by promotion and by the appointment of additional officers, after a competitive examination.

There are several officers in the service who, on account of age, are unfit for active duty. For the supply of officers in their places, and for the increase of the number of engineers, rendered necessary by the substitution of steam for sailing vessels, additional appropriations are required for the next fiscal year. This branch of the public service is, upon the whole, in a satisfactory condition.

During the third session of the 41st Congress a bill was submitted for the organization of a Mint Bureau. The bill passed the Senate but failed in the House of Representatives; though not, as I am informed, from any objection to the principles on which it was framed. I urgently recommend the passage of a similar bill at the present session of Congress. All the Mints and Assay Offices are nominally in charge of the Treasury Department; but there is not, by authority of law, any person in the Department who, by virtue of his office, is supposed to be informed upon the subject; and no one on whom the Secretary of the Treasury can officially rely for information or advice in the management of this important branch of the public business.

It is estimated that the internal commerce of the country is fifteen times as great as our external commerce, but the statistics are not trustworthy or complete; and I respectfully recommend that provision be made for obtaining such returns as will show fully the trade of the country upon the rivers, canals, lakes, and railways.

The report of Mr. Charles Bryant, Special Agent, who has had charge of the fur seal-fishery at the Islands of St. Paul and St. George, shows that the business has been conducted by the Alaska Commercial Company in substantial conformity to the terms of the contract. Mr. Bryant suggests an appropriation for the construction of a house upon each island, for the accommodation of the agents of the Government, who at present are dependent upon the company for board and shelter; and, although I am not aware that any evil has resulted from the

XVI REPORT OF THE SECRETARY OF THE TREASURY.

arrangement, it is manifest that it ought not to be continued. It is estimated that an appropriation of five thousand dollars will be sufficient for a suitable building on each island.

The agents charged with the management of the seal fishery have been detailed from the customs service. As the full number of agents authorized by law is needed upon customs business, I respectfully recommend that authority be given for the appointment of two agents and two assistant agents, and that a suitable appropriation be made for their salaries and expenses. The necessity of two agents at each island is apparent. The agents will desire to return to the States as often as once in two years; and, moreover, it is wise for the Government to have not less than four persons in its employment connected with the care of the people and the business of the islands.

Mr. Bryant also makes suggestions as to further provision for the care of the natives, which appear to me to deserve consideration.

I again call the attention of Congress to the importance of increasing the salaries of the Bureau Officers and Heads of Division in the Treasury Department.

At present there is great inequality and injustice existing. The First Comptroller receives a salary of five thousand dollars a year, while the Second Comptroller and other Bureau Officers, whose duties are hardly less important, receive only three thousand dollars. The Solicitor of the Treasury is upon a salary of three thousand five hundred dollars, while the Solicitor of Internal Revenue, whose duties are less important, receives a salary of four thousand dollars.

The Heads of Division, in the Internal Revenue, receive salaries of twenty-five hundred dollars per annum, while in every other branch of the Treasury they are selected from fourth class clerks, whose salaries are fixed by law at eighteen hundred dollars a year; although, for several years an appropriation has been made from which the Secretary of the Treasury, in his discretion, has increased the salaries in his own office to twenty-eight hundred dollars per annum.

It is not an exaggeration to say that the head of a division in charge of the loans, of the warrants, or of the sub-treasury accounts, occupies a position in which the country and the world are more concerned than in that of the Collector of Customs at New York; yet the latter officer receives more than fifty thousand dollars a year, while it is with difficulty that the former is able to secure the inadequate sum of twenty-eight hundred dollars.

The same remark might with truth be made of several Bureau Officers, and of persons in the office of the Treasurer of the United States.

In this connection, I also recommend an increase of the salary of the Supervising Surgeon of the Marine Hospitals.

· I think it my duty to speak of the provisions of the act creating the Department of Justice, by which the Solicitor of the Treasury and the Solicitor of the Internal Revenue Office are made officers of that Department. The proper and essential duty of the Solicitors is to give advice to the Secretary and Bureau officers upon questions which arise in the daily business of the Department. Under the existing system, the Attorney General is made nominally responsible, while, in fact, he ought to be exempt from all responsibility for the advice given by these officers, that, upon a reference to him of questions which may have been previously considered by them, he may be free to revise or reverse their action. These officers should receive their appointments through the Treasury Department, and be responsible to its head. It is a fundamental error in administration, to place in one of the Departments officers deriving their appointment from another Department.

Should the Attorney General transfer these officers to the Department of Justice, as appears to have been contemplated by the act, this Department would be deprived substantially of their services. I earnestly recommend the restoration of these officers to their former positions in the Treasury.

The examination of persons designated for clerical service, and for promotion in the Treasury Department, has been continued, with beneficial results; and the examination is even more exacting in its requirements than at the date of my last annual report. Means will be taken to extend the system, with such modifications as the difference of duties may suggest, but with equal efficiency, if possible, to the principal custom-houses, and to other branches of the public service under the control of this Department.

On the 28th of February last public notice was given that on the 6th of the following March books would be opened in this country and in Europe for subscriptions to the National Loan, under the act approved July 14, 1870, and the conditions on which the subscriptions would be received were also made known. All the national banks, and a large number of bankers both in this country and in Europe, were authorized to receive subscriptions. The first preference was given to subscribers to the five per cent. bonds, within the limit of two hundred millions of dollars. On the 1st of August the subscriptions amounted to sixty-five millions seven hundred and seventy-five thousand five hundred and fifty dollars, chiefly by the national banks.

II S R

Under date of July 14, 1871, a despatch was received from Hon. William A. Richardson, Assistant Secretary of the Treasury, then in London, stating that certain bankers in Europe proposed to take the remainder of the two hundred millions of five per cents. upon certain conditions. This proposition was considered and modified, and early in August an agreement was made with Messrs. Jay Cooke & Co., representing bankers in Europe and in the United States. By the terms of the agreement, the parties represented by Messrs. Jay Cooke & Co. had the right to subscribe for the remainder of the two hundred millions of said bonds, by giving notice thereof, at any time previous to the first of April next, and by subscribing for ten millions at once and for an average of at least five millions of dollars of bonds per month during the intervening time, subject to the right of the national banks to subscribe for fifty millions of dollars within sixty days from the 25th day of August.

It was also agreed that the subscriptions should all be made through national banks, and certificates of deposit therefor issued by said banks to the Secretary of the Treasury, bonds to be lodged with the Treasurer of the United States for the amount of the deposit. By a printed circular issued on the 10th of August, 1871, it was announced that national banks making or obtaining subscriptions, payable in coin, would be designated by the Secretary of the Treasury as depositaries of public money, on the usual condition of placing in the hands of the Treasurer of the United States bonds of the United States for the security of such deposits; and that, at the commencement of each month, notice would be given of the redemption of an amount of bonds equal to the amount of subscriptions in coin for the preceding month, interest to cease in ninety days from the date of such notice.

It was also stated in the circular that, as the bonds called should mature, the deposits would be drawn from the several banks proportionately.

It was further agreed that the subscribers to the loan should receive as commissions whatever might remain of the half of one per cent. allowed by law upon the two hundred millions, after paying the cost of paper for the bonds, for engraving, printing, advertising, delivery, and all other expenses of the same.

Under this agreement the books were opened in this country and in Europe, and by the last of August subscriptions were obtained for the entire amount offered.

On the first of September public notice was given that certain five-twenty bonds, to the amount of one hundred millions of dollars, of the issue of 1862, specified by number as nearly as was practicable, according to the provisions of the act of July 14, 1870, would be paid on the first of December, and that the interest would cease on that date. Of the bonds so called, more than eighty millions of dollars are now in the possession of the Department; of which amount, seventeen millions of dollars have been paid in coin, and the remainder have been received or deposited in exchange for the five per cent. bonds.

Previous to September five per cent. bonds to the amount of $62,139,550, had been issued and payment made therefor. The work of delivering the bonds subscribed for at that date is now going on, and under such circumstances as to leave no doubt that the whole business will be concluded in a brief period of time.

By the act establishing the national banking system, the Secretary of the Treasury was authorized to make them depositaries of any public money, except receipts from customs; and the act authorizing the refunding of the national debt directed the Secretary of the Treasury to give three months' notice of the payment of any bonds which, in such notice, might be specified and called for payment. In the same act it was provided that the money received for the new bonds should be used only in payment of bonds outstanding known as five-twenty bonds. The statute proceeded upon the idea that the holders of five-twenty bonds should receive three-months' interest upon their bonds after notice should be given by the Government.

As this notice could be given safely only upon subscriptions already made or secured, the general necessary result, even in case the money were paid into and held in the Treasury of the United States, would be a loss of interest for three months.

On the 1st of August last the demand for the new bonds had nearly ceased; but, by the agreement referred to, the necessary loss to, the Government incident to the refunding of the public debt was made the means of securing subscriptions to the amount of about one hundred and thirty millions of dollars.

The banks, or those represented by the banks, derived an advantage in the use of the amount of their subscriptions for three months, but this without other loss to the Government than what was incident to the negotiation of the loan under the law.

I am informed by Judge Richardson, and such is my own opinion, that the most serious obstacle in the way of negotiating the four and four-and-a-half per cent. bonds in Europe is the inadequacy of the commissions allowed. When the circular of the 28th of February last was issued, one or two leading European bankers declined to act as agents, and I am persuaded that others who accepted the agency failed to give that attention to the business which would have been bestowed upon it had the commissions corresponded more nearly to those usually received by them for the negotiation of public loans. The credit of the country is fully established in every financial centre of Europe, and the bonds of the United States can be negotiated at their market value in a larger number of cities than the bonds of any other country in the world. Under these circumstances, I think it my duty to advise such an allowance for commissions upon the four and four-and-a-half per cent. bonds as will secure the negotiation of them with the least possible delay. It needs no analysis of the subject to show that the interests of the country will be greatly promoted by the proceeding, even though the commissions should seem to be unnecessarily large. I also recommend that authority be given for the payment of interest in London. This can be done without the least cost or risk to the Government.

Returns for the fiscal year 1870–'71 show that the ocean commerce of the United States is passing rapidly into the hands of foreign merchants and shipbuilders. In the year 1860, nearly seventy-one per cent. of the foreign commerce of this country was in American ships; in 1864, it had fallen to forty-six per cent.; in 1868, to forty-four per cent.; and in 1871, it is reported at less than thirty-eight per cent.

The loss of the shipping of the United States is due chiefly to two causes—first, the destruction of American vessels by rebel cruisers during the war; and, secondly, the substitution of iron steamships for the transportation of freight and passengers upon the ocean, in place of sailing vessels and steamships built of wood.

When the war opened English builders of iron steamships had acquired considerable proficiency, and since that period the art has been carried to higher perfection in Great Britain than in any other part of the world. It is stated that the superiority of British machinery and knowledge of the business by British mechanics give an advantage over American shipbuilders equal at least to ten per cent. upon the cost of construction. They possess additional advantages in the cost of labor, the cost of iron, coal, and other materials, and in the rate of interest upon the capital employed, equal in all to about twenty per cent. more, so that the difference in favor of British shipbuilders is at least thirty per cent.

In considering the means for the restoration of our ocean commerce, two facts must be accepted: First, that it is useless to attempt to revive it with wooden ships; and, secondly, that iron ships moved by sails cannot compete with iron ships propelled by steam. Hence, the only practical questions for consideration are these: Can the construction of iron steamships be established in this country, and, if so, by what means?

The trans-ocean commerce of the United States would employ about six million tons of shipping, if each vessel made but one round voyage in a year. The value of our exports and imports has already reached the sum of nearly eleven hundred millions of dollars, and during the present decade it will exceed fifteen hundred millions of dollars annually. The annual returns for freight and passengers are about one hundred millions of dollars.

The history of the loss of our commerce, as shown in the statistics already given, renders it certain that without some efficient action on the part of the Government, the entire foreign trade of the country will soon pass into the hands of our rivals.

The monopoly of the trade between the United States and Europe by foreign merchants and shipbuilders carries with it the monopoly of shipbuilding for the entire world, and, as a consequence, the Atlantic trade, the trade of the Pacific, and the seas adjacent thereto, will be carried on in English-built steamers.

An alteration of the law by which foreign-built vessels may be admitted to American registry will furnish no adequate relief. On the contrary, the change would stimulate shipbuilding in England, while the prospect of establishing it on this continent would diminish in proportion to the prosperity of the business in the ship-yards of our rivals.

In view of the facts of our extensive coast upon the Atlantic and Pacific oceans, and our position with reference to Europe and Asia, the country ought not to be satisfied with any policy which does not look to the establishment and continuance of shipbuilding in the United States, the encouragement of our own seamen and merchants, and the control of so much, at least, of the commerce of the world as is derived from the export of our products and the importation of articles required for domestic consumption.

The removal of duties upon foreign articles used in the construction of iron steamships, or the allowance of a drawback equal to the amount of duties paid, will not, in the existing condition of things, secure the reëstablishment of the business. But were it otherwise, the removal of duties or the allowance of drawback raises practical questions of great difficulty, while any concession by an indirect process is likely in the end to prove unnecessarily expensive to the country. Several of the existing lines of European steamers were established by the aid of Government subsidies. They are still encouraged by the same means; and it is unreasonable to expect that our merchants and ship-builders can successfully compete with this formidable combination, unless they are supported by the power of their own Government.

After careful consideration of the whole subject, I am prepared to advise the passage of a law guaranteeing to persons who may employ in the foreign trade American-built first-class iron steamships of not less than two thousand tons burden each, an annual payment, for the period of five years, of the sum of thirteen dollars per ton. The subsidy should be proportionately less to vessels of lower classification.

In making this recommendation, I do not assume that there is no other practicable method of restoring our commerce, but I present it as the method which appears to me to be the most efficient and economical.

Connected with this plan, it will be wise to consider whether the ships may not be so constructed as to be available for naval purposes, and, in case of war, subject to the right of the United States to take them upon payment of their appraised value. A similar suggestion was made by the Secretary of the Navy in his report for the year 1869. They should also be required to carry the mails upon moderate terms, or in consideration of the subsidy.

The use of sailing vessels and steamers built of wood may be continued successfully in the coasting trade, the trade with the British possessions, and upon the rivers and lakes of the country; but any effort to regain our former position upon the ocean by their agency must end disastrously.

I entertain the opinion that the policy suggested will be effectual, and that in a comparatively short period our mechanics and artisans will acquire equal skill with those of England, and that we shall not only have the aid of the best machinery now in use elsewhere, but that important improvements will be made, calculated to place the country in a position of superiority.

We shall also be able to test practically the quality of American iron, which, for the purpose of shipbuilding, is represented as better than that used in Great Britain.

If it shall appear, as is claimed, that American iron is about ten per cent. better than the iron used in England, an advantage will be secured, not only in the diminished cost of the vessels, but also in the increased tonnage capacity of American ships of equal dimensions over those constructed with inferior materials.

Accepting as a truth, established by experience, that the ocean commerce of the world is to be carried on in iron steamships, we must consider and decide whether the United States shall disappear from the list of maritime nations, or whether, by a determined and practical effort, we can regain the position which we occupied previous to the late rebellion.

GEO. S. BOUTWELL,
Secretary of the Treasury.

Hon. JAMES G. BLAINE,
Speaker of the House of Representatives.

TABLES ACCOMPANYING THE REPORT.

TABLE A.—*Statement of the net receipts (by warrants) for the fiscal year ended June 30, 1871.*

CUSTOMS.

Quarter ending September 30, 1870	$57,729,473 57	
Quarter ending December 31, 1870	42,054,528 98	
Quarter ending March 31, 1871	55,277,257 73	
Quarter ending June 30, 1871	51,209,152 77	
		$206,270,408 05

SALES OF PUBLIC LANDS.

Quarter ending September 30, 1870	842,437 67	
Quarter ending December 31, 1870	510,915 28	
Quarter ending March 31, 1871	502,102 94	
Quarter ending June 30, 1871	533,190 79	
		2,388,646 68

DIRECT TAX.

Quarter ending September 30, 1870	37,260 72	
Quarter ending December 31, 1870		
Quarter ending March 31, 1871		
Quarter ending June 30, 1871	543,094 65	
		580,355 37

INTERNAL REVENUE.

Quarter ending September 30, 1870	49,147,137 92	
Quarter ending December 31, 1870	31,033,265 08	
Quarter ending March 31, 1871	28,249,835 61	
Quarter ending June 30, 1871	34,667,915 02	
		143,098,153 63

PREMIUM ON SALES OF COIN.

Quarter ending September 30, 1870	2,238,704 43	
Quarter ending December 31, 1870	1,675,451 76	
Quarter ending March 31, 1871	1,806,045 40	
Quarter ending June 30, 1871	3,172,038 36	
		8,892,839 95

TAX ON CIRCULATION, DEPOSITS, ETC., OF NATIONAL BANKS.

Quarter ending September 30, 1870	2,950,022 42	
Quarter ending December 31, 1870	69,121 87	
Quarter ending March 31, 1871	2,909,512 77	
Quarter ending June 30, 1871	74,927 26	
		6,003,584 32

REPAYMENT OF INTEREST BY PACIFIC RAILWAY COMPANIES?

Quarter ending September 30, 1870	147,510 07	
Quarter ending December 31, 1870	167,520 71	
Quarter ending March 31, 1871	138,586 39	
Quarter ending June 30, 1871	359,667 58	
		813,284 75

CUSTOMS FINES, PENALTIES, AND FEES.

Quarter ending September 30, 1870	147,063 68	
Quarter ending December 31, 1870	344,192 33	
Quarter ending March 31, 1871	240,521 21	
Quarter ending June 30, 1871	220,802 64	
		952,579 86

FEES—CONSULAR, LETTERS PATENT, STEAMBOAT, AND LAND.

Quarter ending September 30, 1870	509,538 61	
Quarter ending December 31, 1870	412,904 96	
Quarter ending March 31, 1871	427,212 52	
Quarter ending June 30, 1871	705,973 13	
		2,055,629 22

MISCELLANEOUS SOURCES.

Quarter ending September 30, 1870	$1,352,081 66	
Quarter ending December 31, 1870	8,820,224 63	
Quarter ending March 31, 1871	974,027 00	
Quarter ending June 30, 1871	1,113,129 77	
		$12,268,463 06
Total receipts exclusive of loans		383,323,944 89
Balance in Treasury June 30, 1870, (including $3,396 18 received from "Unavailable.")		149,505,867 78
		532,829,812 67

TABLE B.—*Statement of the net expenditures (by warrants) for the fiscal year ended June 30,*
1871.

CIVIL.

Congress	$5,004,820 19	
Executive	9,412,418 23	
Judiciary	3,320,018 08	
Government of Territories	281,808 74	
Sub-treasuries	304,071 78	
Surveyor General's Offices	121,144 05	
Inspiration of steam vessels	121,899 47	
Mints and assay offices	173,605 07	
Total civil list		$18,760,779 46

FOREIGN INTERCOURSE.

Diplomatic salaries	467,731 91	
Salaries of United States Consuls	414,329 13	
Office rent and other expenses of consulates	91,187 50	
Expenses under the neutrality act	450 00	
Rescuing American citizens from shipwreck	50 00	
Relief and protection of American seamen	40,257 22	
Expenses under habeas corpus act	2,942 95	
Hudson's Bay and Puget Sound Agricultural Company commission	325,000 00	
American and Mexican claims commission	27,048 65	
Capitalization of Scheldt dues	66,584 00	
Consular receipts	3,564 22	
Contingent and miscellaneous items	165,228 29	
Total foreign intercourse		1,604,373 87

MISCELLANEOUS.

Mint establishment	954,043 59
Coast Survey	735,000 00
Carrying free mail-matter	700,000 00
Light-house Establishment	2,712,668 25
Refunding excess of deposits for unascertained duties	1,787,266 59
Revenue-cutter service	1,251,984 52
Custom-house buildings	785,019 95
Furniture, fuel, &c., for custom-houses	298,983 87
Repairs and preservation of custom-houses, &c	225,869 11
Collecting customs revenue	6,560,672 01
Debenture and drawbacks under customs laws	978,358 33
Refunding duties erroneously or illegally collected	400,650 68
Marine hospital establishment	481,004 76
Distributive shares of fines, penalties, and forfeitures	488,135 55
Defending suits for captured and abandoned property	15,007 41
Unclaimed merchandise	2,487 41
Assessing and collecting internal revenue	7,075,187 17
Internal revenue allowances and drawbacks	451,203 66
Punishing violation of internal revenue laws	58,712 57
Refunding taxes erroneously or illegally collected	612,243 30
Dies, paper, and stamps	357,663 51
Public buildings and grounds in Washington	478,997 21
Mail steamship service	731,250 00
Telegraphic communication between the Atlantic and Pacific coasts	40,000 01
Deficiencies in revenue of Post Office Department	3,700,000 00
Court-houses, post offices, &c	1,523,879 22
Refunding proceeds of captured and abandoned property	730,389 78
Expenses of suits of captured and abandoned property	12,650 31
Expenses refunding national debt	332,173 04
Plates, paper, &c., office Comptroller of Currency	160,551 52
Detecting, &c., persons engaged in counterfeiting, &c	117,955 84
Refunding to Massachusetts interest on advances, war 1812–15	678,362 41
Columbian Institute for Deaf and Dumb	152,802 00
Government Hospital for the Insane	132,271 03
Capitol extension and dome	201,816 33

Repairs of public buildings in Washington	$70,429 48
Expenses of charitable institutions in Washington	55,000 00
Metropolitan Police	210,455 59
Suppression of the slave trade	7,546 77
Repayment for lands erroneously sold	43,765 49
Refunding excess of deposits for surveying public lands	22,232 66
Proceeds of swamp lands to States	9,673 00
Expenses of Eighth and Ninth Census	1,955,111 13
Surveys of public lands	564,940 76
Penitentiaries in the Territories	91,271 80
Five per cent. fund to States	23,265 90
Payment for illegal capture of British vessels and cargoes	760,728 72
Payment under relief acts	255,045 16
Unenumerated items	41,515 00

Total miscellaneous $40,116,762 90

INTERIOR DEPARTMENT.

Indians	7,426,097 44
Pensions	34,443,894 88

Total Interior Department 41,870,892 32

MILITARY ESTABLISHMENT.

Pay Department	6,146,981 79
Commissary Department	3,483,668 52
Quartermaster's Department	12,746,330 97
Ordnance Department	778,490 21
Forts and fortifications	1,287,167 46
Improvement of rivers and harbors	4,834,277 88
Military Academy	178,956 66
Medical Department	173,294 06
Freedmen's Bureau	463,240 82
National Asylum for Disabled Volunteer Soldiers	296,287 32
Bounties to soldiers	10,656,300 53
Reimbursing States for raising volunteers	2,379,246 72
Horses and other property lost in service	228,836 75
Contingencies of the Army	257,404 39
Washington and Oregon volunteers in 1855 and 1856	42,131 71
Payments under relief acts	110,887 67
Capture of Jefferson Davis	1,611 50
Bronze equestrian statue of Lieutenant General Winfield Scott	15,000 00
	44,060,084 95
Deduct proceeds of sales of ordnance, &c	8,280,093 13

Total Military Establishment 35,799,991 82

NAVAL ESTABLISHMENT.

Pay and contingent of the Navy	7,200,763 28
Marine Corps	838,791 17
Yards and Docks	2,037,542 66
Equipment and Recruiting	1,462,625 98
Navigation	404,922 34
Ordnance	574,331 02
Construction and Repairs	4,233,590 03
Steam Engineering	1,082,864 86
Provisions and Clothing	1,286,715 04
Medicine and Surgery	235,301 99
Salvage of vessels of the United States	15,000 00
Payments under relief acts	58,578 85

Total Naval Establishment	19,431,027 21
Interest on public debt	125,576,565 93
Premiums on purchase of bonds	9,016,794 74
Total expenditures, exclusive of loans	292,177,188 25
Excess of redemption over issue of loans and Treasury notes	130,735,147 18
Total net expenditures	422,912,335 43
Balance in Treasury June 30, 1871	109,917,477 24
	532,829,812 67

TABLE C.—*Statement of the redemption and issue of Loans and Treasury notes (by warrants) for the fiscal year ended June 30, 1871.*

Character of loans.	Redemption.	Issues.	Excess of redemptions.	Excess of issues.
Temporary loan, acts of February 25, 1862, (12 Statutes, 345,) March 17, 1862, (12 Statutes, 370,) July 11, 1862, (12 Statutes, 532,) June 30, 1864, (13 Statutes, 218)	$96,000 00		$96,000 00	
Certificates of indebtedness, acts of March 1, 1862, (12 Statutes, 352,) March 17, 1862, (12 Statutes, 370,) and March 3, 1863, (12 Statutes, 710)		$15,058 02		$15,058 02
Coin certificates, act of March 3, 1863, section 5, (12 Statutes, 711)	71,237,820 00	56,577,000 00	14,660,820 00	
Three per cent. certificates, acts of March 2, 1867, (14 Statutes, 558,) July 25, 1868, (15 Statutes, 183)	13,665,000 00	*140,000 00	13,665,000 00	
Treasury notes of 1857, act of December 23, 1857, (11 Statutes, 257)	5,100 00		5,100 00	
Seven-thirties of 1861, act of July 17, 1861, (12 Statutes, 259)	16,400 00		18,400 00	
Old demand notes, acts of July 17, 1861, (12 Statutes, 261,) August 5, 1861, (12 Statutes, 313,) February 12, 1862, (12 Statutes, 338)	9,750 50		9,750 50	
Legal-tender notes, acts of February 25, 1862, (12 Statutes, 345,) July 11, 1862, (12 Statutes, 532,) January 17, 1863, (12 Statutes, 822,) March 3, 1863, (12 Statutes, 710)	120,592,311 00	120,588,311 00	4,000 00	
One-year notes of 1863, act of March 3, 1863, (12 Statutes, 709)	33,300 00		33,300 00	
Two-year notes of 1863, act of March 3, 1863, (12 Statutes, 709)	16,400 00		16,400 00	
Compound-interest notes, acts of March 3, 1863, (12 Statutes, 709,) and June 30, 1864, (13 Statutes, 218)	1,324,910 00		1,324,910 00	
Seven-thirties of 1864 and 1865, acts of June 30, 1864, (13 Statutes, 218,) and March 3, 1865, (13 Statutes, 468)	165,700 00		165,700 00	
Loan of 1847, act of January 28, 1847, (9 Statutes, 118)	16,500 00		16,500 00	
Loan of 1848, act of March 31, 1848, (9 Statutes, 217)	13,300 00		13,300 00	
Texan indemnity stock, act of September 9, 1850, (9 Statutes, 447)	78,110 62		78,110 62	
Loan of 1860, act of June 22, 1860, (12 Statutes, 79)	6,973,000 00		6,973,000 00	
Oregon war debt, act of March 2, 1861, (12 Statutes, 198)	54,900 00		54,900 00	
Loan of 1863, act of March 3, 1863, (12 Statutes, 709)	150 22		150 22	
Fractional currency, acts of July 17, 1862, (12 Statutes, 592,) March 3, 1863, (12 Statutes, 711,) and June 30, 1864, (13 Statutes, 218)	30,395,713 92	31,103,900 06		708,186 14
Certificates of indebtedness of 1870, act of July 8, 1870, (16 Statutes, 197)	362 41	678,362 41		678,000 00
Five-twenties of 1862, act of February 25, 1862, (12 Statutes, 345)	36,302,750 00		36,302,750 00	
Five-twenties of March, 1864, act of March 3, 1864, (13 Statutes, 13)	525,500 00		525,500 00	
Five-twenties of June, 1864, act of June 30, 1864, (13 Statutes, 218)	23,510,550 00		23,510,550 00	
Five-twenties of 1865, act of March 3, 1865, (13 Statutes, 468)	25,708,050 00		25,708,050 00	
Consols of 1865, act of March 3, 1865, (13 Statutes, 468)	44,804,200 00		44,804,200 00	
Consols of 1867, act of March 3, 1865, (13 Statutes, 468)	23,293,550 00		23,286,750 00	
Consols of 1868, act of March 3, 1865, (13 Statutes, 468)	412,400 00	11,800 00	412,400 00	
Funded loan of 1881, acts of July 14, 1870, (16 Statutes, 272,) and January 20, 1871, (16 Statutes, 399)		59,669,150 00		59,669,150 00
Totals	399,518,728 67	268,783,681 49	191,805,541 34	61,070,394 16
Excess of redemptions			191,805,541 34	
Excess of issues				61,070,394 16
Net excess of redemptions charged in receipts and expenditures			130,735,147 18	

In comparing the foregoing table with the issues and redemptions, as shown by a comparison of the debt statements of July 1, 1870, and July 1, 1871, numerous differences will be discovered. The following notes will serve to explain them :

The actual net redemption of the temporary loan during the year was $101,000, and of three per cent. certificates, $13,660,000. To correct an error in former accounts of receipts and expenditures, $5,000 was credited as an issue in the former account, and charged as a redemption in the latter; thus making this statement vary in both these accounts from the public debt statement, into which this error was not brought.

In covering into the Treasury the receipts on account of certificates of indebtedness in former years, $18,241 77 was covered as on account of principal, when it should have been covered as on account of interest; and $3,183.75 was covered as premium, when it should have been covered as principal; thus making an actual difference in this loan account of $15,058 02 between the public debt statement and the loan account, as by the receipts and expenditures.

In the quarter ending September 30, 1868, $150 22 was covered to the credit of the *principal* of the loan of 1863, which should have been covered as *premium*; a counter entry was made in this year to correct the error, which therefore makes a difference in the account.

On the 31st of December, 1864, $12,000 was covered into the Treasury as legal tenders, and $8,000 as fractional currency. It should have been the reverse; and in order to correct this error, a counter entry was made, leaving the difference of $4,000 in this account to offset the same error in former years. The remaining difference between these two accounts, of six cents, is explained by the fact that the Treasurer of the United States was reimbursed for six cents more fractional currency than he redeemed in one quarter, and in this quarter made a deposit of this amount to correct the error.

In covering into the Treasury receipts from the loan authorized on account of the Oregon war, $54,900 was erroneously credited to the account of five-twenties of 1862. In order to correct this error, a warrant and counter warrant were issued, charging this amount to the five-twenty account and crediting it to the Oregon war account.

The amount of the Treasury notes of 1857 outstanding, as shown by the debt statement, on the 1st of July, 1870, was $2,000. During the year it was discovered that this account was erroneous by the amount of certain Treasury notes which had been twice charged as redeemed, though of course not twice paid. To correct this error the Treasury notes redeemed within the year were not deducted from the debt statement, and therefore appear in the account of receipts and expenditures as that much redemption in excess of the amount as shown by the debt statement.

In the examination of the account of the Texan indemnity loan, it was discovered that $30 62 had been covered as principal, when it should have been covered as interest; also, that $17,080 was covered as principal, which should have been covered as premium. Counter entries to correct this error have been made in this year's accounts, and therefore show a difference when compared with the debt-statement accounts, into which these counter entries do not enter.

In the examination of the account of the loans of 1847 and 1848, it was discovered that $5,500 had been charged as a redemption to the loan of 1847, which should have been charged to the loan of 1848. A counter entry was made during the year to correct this error.

In the debt statement an error of $800 was discovered, being an amount redeemed and twice deducted.

The following items have been added to the public debt statement since the 1st of July, 1870, being the amount of debt outstanding, but unascertained until subsequent to that date : Old debt, $57,665; Mexican indemnity stock, $1,104 91; bounty-land scrip, $3,975.

In October, 1868, Congress passed an act for the relief of Ober, Nanson & Co., to indemnify them for $60,000 compound-interest notes lost at sea in the steamship "Republic." This amount was paid under the relief act, but the Treasury-note account was not charged with them until recently, when, in making the examination, an error was discovered of $500 in the Loan-Branch numerical registers, (from which the public debt statement was formerly made,) by checking off two notes as redeemed against one actually paid, and the correction of which left the amount to be charged but $59,500.

December 22, 1870, a warrant was drawn charging the account of seven-thirties of 1865 with the redemption of $1,000. It was discovered, on examination of the accounts, that this warrant was for the redemption of a bond of the loan of five-twenties of 1865, and a warrant and counter warrant were issued to correct the error.

The following table exhibits the redemptions of five-twenty bonds, as shown by the public debt statement, during the fiscal year, compared with the receipts and expenditures, and the differences :

	By Public Debt Statement.	By Warrant.	Difference.
5 20's, 1862	$51,038,100	$36,362,750	$14,675,350
5-20's, March, 1864	1,262,900	525,500	737,400
5-20's, June, 1864	39,595,050	23,510,550	16,084,500
5-20's, 1865	35,676,450	25,768,050	9,908,400
Consols, 1865	90,415,800	44,804,200	45,611,600
Consols, 1867	51,355,400	23,286,750	28,068,650
Consols, 1868	3,120,400	412,400	2,708,000
			$117,793,900

Prior to the 1st of July, 1870, the bonds purchased on account of the sinking and special funds were neither deducted from the debt statement nor charged as redeemed in the loan accounts, for want of authority of law. After the passage of the act of July 14, 1870, which conferred the authority, these purchased bonds were charged to the proper loan account and deducted from the debt statement, and the amounts were credited by counter warrant to the funds from which the purchases had been made. The amount of this transfer was $117,740,000, leaving a difference of $53,900, which is explained by the paragraph in relation to Oregon war bonds, and the paragraph next above this one.

The bonds representing the difference between $117,740,000 (explained above) and the $121,429,100, amount of bonds purchased to July 1, 1870, not having been received and paid for prior to the act of July 14, 1870, and not having entered into the accounts, were treated as an actual redemption in the subsequent quarter, and therefore form a part of the redemptions by warrants, as shown in the preceding table.

TABLE D.—*Statement of net expenditures (by warrants) under direction of the customs service, for the fiscal year ended June 30, 1871.*

Expenses of collecting revenue from customs		$6,560,672 61
Repayments to importers for excess of deposits		1,787,266 59
Debentures, drawbacks, and bounties		945,441 52
Expenses revenue-cutter service		1,121,026 43
Construction of revenue cutters		130,973 88
Repairs, &c., of custom-houses, marine hospitals, and other public buildings		224,669 15
Furniture and repairs of furniture		97,281 11
Fuel and miscellaneous items		191,652 76
Construction of appraisers' store, Philadelphia		92,583 28
Distributive shares of fines, penalties, and forfeitures		488,135 55
Expenses of collecting captured and abandoned property		15,007 41
Debentures and other charges		32,916 81
Proceeds of sale of goods, &c		199.59
Payment of taxes on salaries		348 84
Preventing smuggling		968 36
Return of unclaimed merchandise		2,487 41
Refunding of money erroneously covered into the Treasury		1,757 11
Refunding duties, act March 3, 1871		488,321 37
Refunding duties under warehouse acts		581 20
Additional compensation to collectors and naval officers		262 26
Expenses of Lazaretto property, Philadelphia		0,880 68
Compensation of persons employed in insurrectionary States		6,000 81
Reliefs		13,179 40
Total		12,209,733 45
Marine hospital establishment	435,924 66	
Marine hospital at Chicago	45,080 10	
		481,004 76

LIFE-SAVING STATIONS.

Compensation to two superintendents	3,057 38	
Compensation to fifty-four keepers	10,174 46	
Contingent expenses	337 93	
Six experienced surfmen	8,544 00	
Protecting human life	15,000 00	
Life-saving apparatus, (contingent)	626 40	
		37,740 17

LIGHT-HOUSE ESTABLISHMENT.

Supplying light-houses with oil	278,574 95	
Repairs and incidental expenses	258,565 48	
Salaries of light-house keepers	398,326 28	
Salaries of boat-keepers	5,549 00	
Seamen's wages, &c	223,010 81	
Expenses of weighing, supplying losses of beacons, &c	323,075 08	
Commissions to superintendents	3,425 17	
Repairs, &c. of fog-signals	36,876 71	
Expenses of superintendents in visiting	2,365 57	
Repairs of light-houses	102,799 70	
Building and expenses of light-houses	1,042,369 33	
Total		2,674,928 08

EXPENDED ON CUSTOM-HOUSES.

In Maine	98,835 24	
In New York	89,546 78	
In Pennsylvania	166 57	
In Maryland	10,345 00	
In Virginia	10,000 00	
In South Carolina	93,124 79	
In Louisiana	86,684 25	
In Illinois	62,130 83	
In Michigan	14,262 13	
In Minnesota	113,534 55	
In Oregon	33,747 62	
In California	9,067 42	
In Ohio	5,000 00	
In Tennessee	66,091 49	
Total		692,436 67
Grand total		16,095,843 13

RECAPITULATION.

Expenses of collecting, &c	12,209,733 45
Custom-houses	602,436 67
Marine hospitals	481,004 76
Life-saving stations	37,740 17
Light-house Establishment	2,674,928 08
Total	**16,095,843 13**

TABLE E.—*Statement of net expenditures (by warrants) on account of internal revenue, for the fiscal year ended June 30, 1871.*

Expenses of assessing and collecting internal revenue	$7,075,187 17
Allowance or drawback	451,203 66
Detecting, &c., violations of internal revenue laws	58,712 57
Dies, paper, and stamps	367,663 51
Compensation of Commissioner, deputies, clerks, &c	380,922 00
Contingent expenses of office of Commissioner Internal Revenue	7,390 79
Compensation of persons employed in insurrectionary States	54,080 33
Repair of building at San Francisco	259 38
Reliefs	4,018 00
Refunding duties erroneously or illegally collected	600,165 74
Refunding money erroneously covered into the Treasury	2,947 12
Refunding surplus proceeds	130 44
Total	**9,001,680 71**

TABLE F.—*Statement of the net receipts (by warrants) for the quarter ended September 30, 1871.*

RECEIPTS.

Customs	$62,289,329 37
Sales of public lands	602,680 61
Internal revenue	35,553,175 01
Premium on sales of coin	3,613,847 47
Tax on circulation and deposits, &c., of national banks	3,175,046 38
Repayment of interest by Pacific Railroad companies	223,013 69
Customs fines, penalties, and fees	206,279 40
Consular, letters-patent, homestead, and land fees	417,224 51
Miscellaneous	1,116,878 16
Total receipts, exclusive of loans	107,198,374 60
Balance in Treasury June 30, 1871	109,917,477 24
Total	**217,115,851 84**

TABLE G.—*Statement of the net expenditures (by warrants) for the quarter ended September 30, 1871.*

CIVIL AND MISCELLANEOUS.

Customs	$4,445,530 77
Internal revenue	1,991,084 83
Diplomatic service	639,286 01
Judiciary	819,360 98
Interior (civil)	1,859,272 94
War civil	295,864 34
Treasury proper	4,820,108 90
Quarterly salaries	28,435 38
Total miscellaneous	14,898,953 15
Indians	3,404,133 42
Pensions	8,090,698 69
Military Establishment	12,590,653 05
Naval Establishment	6,513,040 93
Interest on public debt	36,725,124 37
Premiums on purchase of bonds	1,680,779 31
Total expenditures, exclusive of loans	83,903,382 92
Excess of redemption of loans over receipts	23,096,168 74
Total net expenditures	106,999,551 66
Balance in Treasury September 30, 1871	110,116,300 18
Total	**217,115,851 84**

TABLE H.—*Statement of the redemption and issue of Loans and Treasury notes (by warrants) for the quarter ended September 30, 1871.*

Character of loans.	Redemptions.	Issues.	Excess of redemptions.	Excess of issues.
Treasury notes prior to 1846, acts of October 12, 1837, (5 Statutes, 201,) May 21, 1838, (5 Statutes, 228,) March 31, 1840, (5 Statutes, 370,) February 15, 1841, (5 Statutes, 411,) January 31, 1842, (5 Statutes, 469,) August 31, 1842, (5 Statutes, 581,) and March 3, 1843, (5 Statutes, 614).	$100 00		$100 00	
Loan of 1847, act of January 28, 1847, (9 Statutes, 118).	200 00		200 00	
Seven-thirties of 1861, act of July 17, 1861, (12 Statutes, 259).	3,100 00		3,100 00	
Old demand notes, acts of July 17, 1861, (12 Statutes, 261,) August 5, 1861, (12 Statutes, 313,) February 12, 1862, (12 Statutes, 338).				
Five-twenties of 1862, act of February 25, 1862, (12 Statutes, 345).	3,449 25		3,449 25	
Legal-tender notes, acts of February 25, 1862, (12 Statutes, 345,) July 11, 1862, (12 Statutes, 532,) January 17, 1863, (12 Statutes, 822,) March 3, 1863, (12 Statutes, 710).	2,401,700 00		2,401,700 00	
Fractional currency, acts of July 17, 1862, (12 Statutes, 592,) March 3, 1863, (12 Statutes, 711,) June 30, 1864, (13 Statutes, 218).	17,775,066 00	$17,775,066 00		
One year notes of 1863, act of March 3, 1863, (12 Statutes, 709).	7,703,899 49	5,688,200 00	2,015,699 49	
Two year notes of 1863, act of March 3, 1863, (12 Statutes, 709).	4,610 00		4,610 00	
Compound-interest notes, acts of March 3, 1863, (12 Statutes, 709,) June 30, 1864, (12 Statutes, 218).	1,660 00		1,660 00	
Coin certificates, act of March 3, 1863, section 5, (12 Statutes, 711).	47,410 00		47,410 00	
Five-twenties of March, 1864, act of March 3, 1864, (13 Statutes, 13).	13,623,400 00	10,622,500 00	3,000,900 00	
Five-twenties of June, 1864, act of June 30, 1864, (13 Statutes, 218).	122,000 00		122,000 00	
Seven-thirties of 1864 and 1865, acts of June 30, 1864, (13 Statutes, 218,) March 3, 1865, (13 Statutes, 468).	2,360,000 00		2,360,000 00	
Five-twenties of 1865, act of March 3, 1865, (13 Statutes, 468).	16,300 00		16,300 00	
Consols of 1865, act of March 3, 1865, (13 Statutes, 468).	2,188,100 00		2,188,100 00	
Consols of 1867, act of March 3, 1865, (13 Statutes, 468).	7,815,800 00		7,815,800 00	
Consols of 1868, act of March 3, 1865, (13 Statutes, 468).	1,362,100 00	*400 00	1,361,500 00	
Three per cent. certificates, acts of March 2, 1867, (14 Statutes, 558,) July 25, 1868, (15 Statutes, 183).	76,050 00		76,050 00	
Texan Indemnity stock, act of September 9, 1850, (9 Statutes, 447).	4,410,000 00	†15,000 00	4,395,000 00	
Loan of 1860, Act of June 22, 1860, (11 Statutes, 79).	7,000 00		7,000 00	
Funded loan of 1881, acts of July 14, 1870, (16 Statutes, 272,) January 20, 1871, (16 Statutes, 399).	36,000 00	$2,757,350 00	36,000 00	$2,757,350 00
Loan of 1861, (1881's,) acts of July 17, 1861, (12 Statutes, 259,) and August 5, 1861, (12 Statutes, 313).		‡3,100 00		3,100 00
Totals	59,957,984 74	36,861,816 00		
Excess of redemptions			26,356,618 74	
Excess of issues			2,760,450 00	2,760,450 00
Net excess of redemptions charged in receipts and expenditures			23,096,168 74	

* Conversion of compound-interest notes.   † Conversion of 7-30's of 1864 and 1865.   ‡ Conversion of 7-30's of 1861.

* Conversion of 5-20's and Consols.   ‡ Conversion of 7-30's of 1861.

TABLE I.—*Statement of the principal of the public debt (balances) on the 1st of January of each year from 1837 to 1843, and on the 1st of July of each year from 1843 to 1871.*

Years.	Received from loans during the year.	Paid on account of loans during the year.	Excess of receipts over redemptions.	Excess of redemptions over receipts.	Principal of debt at the close of year.
1836	*$336,957 83		*$336,957 83		*$336,957 83
1837	2,992,989 15	$21,822 91	2,971,166 24		3,308,124 07
1838	12,716,820 86	5,590,723 79	7,126,097 07		10,434,221 14
1839	3,857,276 21	10,718,153 53		$6,860,877 32	3,573,343 82
1840	5,589,547 51	3,912,015 79	1,677,531 72		5,250,875 54
1841	13,659,317 38	5,315,712 19	8,343,605 19		13,594,480 73
1842	14,808,735 64	7,801,990 09	7,006,745 55		20,601,226 28
1843	12,479,708 36	338,012 64	12,141,695 72		32,742,922 00
1844	1,877,181 35	11,158,450 85		9,281,269,50	23,461,652 50
1845	None	7,536,349 49		7,536,349 49	15..925,303 01
1846	None	375,100 04		375,100 04	15,550,202 97
1847	28,872,399 45	5,596,067 05	23,276,331 80		38,826,534 77
1848	21,256,700 00	13,038,372 54	8,218,327 46		47,044,862 23
1849 {	†233,075 00				
	28,588,750 00	12,804,828 54	16,016,996 46		63,061,858 69
1850	4,045,950 00	3,655,035 14	390,914 86		63,452,773 55
1851 {	‡5,303,573 92				
	203,400 00	654,951 45	4,852,022 47		68,304,796 02
1852	46,300 00	2,151,754 31		2,105,454 31	66,199,341 71
1853	16,350 00	6,412,574 01		6,396,224 01	59,803,117 70
1854	₹13,249 48	17,574,144 76		17,560,895 28	42,242,222 42
1855	800 00	6,656⁰065 86		6,655,265 86	35,586,956 56
1856	200 00	3,614,618 66		3,614,418 66	31,972,537 90
1857	3,900 00	3,276,606 05		3,272,706 05	28,699,831 85
1858	23,717,300 00	7,505,250 82	16,212,049 18		44,911,881 03
1859	28,287,500 00	14,702,543 15	13,584,956 85		58,496,837 88
1860	20,776,800 00	14,431,350 00	6,345,450 00		64,842,287 88
1861 {	‖2,019,776 10				
	41,861,709 74	18,142,900 00	25,738,585 84		90,580,873 72
1862	529,692,460 50	96,096,922 09	433,595,538 41		524,176,412 13
1863	776,682,361 57	181,086,635 07	595,595,726 50		1,119,772,138 63
1864	1,128,834,245 97	432,822,014 03	696,012,231 94		1,815,784,370 57
1865	1,472,224,740 85	607,361,241 68	864,863,499 17		2,580,647,869 74
1866	712,851,553 05	620,263,249 10	92,588,303 95		2,773,236,173 69
1867	640,426,910 29	735,536,980 11		95,110,069 82	2,678,126,103 87
1868 {	¶1,000,000 00				
	625,111,433 20	692,549,685 88		66,438,252 68	2,611,687,351 19
		**1,000 00			
1869	238,678,081 06	261,912,718 31		23,235,637 25	2,588,452,213 94
1870	285,474,496 00	393,254,282 13		107,770,786 13	2,480,672,427 81
1871	268,820,131 49	{ 396,281,226 98			2,353,211,332 32
		{ ††3,274,051 69		130,735,147 18	
	6,953,362,681 96	††$4,603,425,401 33	2,836,804,734 21	††‖86,957,453 58	

NOTE.—This statement is from warrants, except the additions noted, viz:

* Being estimated amount of debt outstanding at this time.
† $233,075 war-bounty stock. The *issue* of this stock does not enter into the account of receipts and expenditures, because no money came into the Treasury by reason of the issue. They were issued in satisfaction of claims.
‡ $5,000,000 Texan indemnity bonds; $303,573 92 fourth and fifth instalments Mexican bonds, *issue.* Explanation same as in above note.
₹ Including $9,900 war-bounty stock, a repayment; no expenditures the same year. $51 67 interest on old funded debt, a repayment; no expenditures the same year.
‖ $2,019,776 10 discount on bonds of February 8, 1861, not charged to the loan; waiting action of Congress to make proper entry.
¶ $1,000,000 should be charged to Navy Pension fund and credited to the Navy Pension fund three per cent. certificates.
** $1,000 to be added to redemption of loan of 5-20s, June 30, 1864, being a donation of Peters.
†† $3,274,051 69 being differences between the Loan accounts, as shown by the Receipts and Expenditures and the Public Debt Statement from 1837 to 1871, awaiting action of Congress before the proper entries can be made to correct the differences which are all in the Receipts and Expenditures.

TABLE K.—*Statement of outstanding principal of the public debt of the United States on the 1st of January of each year, from 1791 to 1842, inclusive.*

Year.	Amount.	Year.	Amount.
1791	$75,463,476 52	1817	$123,491,965 16
1792	77,227,924 66	1818	103,466,633 83
1793	80,352,634 04	1819	95,529,648 28
1794	78,427,404 77	1820	91,015,566 15
1795	80,747,587 39	1821	89,987,427 66
1796	83,762,172 07	1822	93,546,676 98
1797	82,064,479 33	1823	90,875,877 28
1798	79,228,529 12	1824	90,269,777 77
1799	78,408,669 77	1825	83,788,432 71
1800	82,976,294 35	1826	81,054,059 99
1801	83,038,050 80	1827	73,987,357 20
1802	80,712,632 25	1828	67,475,043 87
1803	77,054,686 30	1829	58,421,413 67
1804	86,427,120 88	1830	48,565,406 50
1805	82,312,150 50	1831	39,123,191 68
1806	75,723,270 66	1832	24,322,235 18
1807	69,218,398 64	1833	7,001,698 83
1808	65,196,317 97	1834	4,760,082 08
1809	57,023,192 09	1835	37,513 05
1810	53,173,217 52	1836	336,957 83
1811	48,005,587 76	1837	3,308,124 07
1812	45,209,737 90	1838	10,434,221 14
1813	55,962,827 57	1839	3,573,343 82
1814	81,487,846 24	1840	5,250,875 54
1815	99,833,660 15	1841	13,594,480 73
1816	127,334,933 74	1842	20,601,226 28

TABLE L.—*Statement of outstanding principal of the public debt of the United States on the 1st of July of each year, from 1843 to 1871, inclusive.*

Year.	Amount.	Year.	Amount.
1843	$32,742,922 00	1858	$44,911,881 03
1844	23,461,652 50	1859	58,496,837 88
1845	15,925,303 01	1860	64,842,287 88
1846	15,550,202 97	1861	90,580,873 72
1847	38,826,534 77	1862	524,176,412 13
1848	47,044,862 23	1863	1,119,772,138 63
1849	63,061,858 69	1864	1,815,784,370 57
1850	63,452,773 55	1865	2,680,647,869 74
1851	68,304,796 02	1866	2,773,236,173 69
1852	66,199,341 71	1867	2,678,126,103 87
1853	59,803,117 70	1868	2,611,687,851 19
1854	42,243,222 42	1869	2,588,452,213 94
1855	35,586,956 56	1870	2,480,672,427 81
1856	31,972,537 90	1871	2,353,211,332 32
1857	28,699,831 85		

TABLE M.—*Statement of the receipts of the United States from March 4, 1789, to June 30,*

Year.	Balance in the Treasury at commencement of year.	Customs.	Internal revenue.	Direct tax.	Public lands.	Miscellaneous.
1791	....	$4,399,473 09	....	....	....	$10,478 10
1792	$973,905 75	3,443,070 85	$208,942 81	....	....	9,918 65
1793	783,444 51	4,255,306 56	337,705 70	....	....	21,410 88
1794	753,661 69	4,801,065 28	274,089 62	....	....	53,277 97
1795	1,151,924 17	5,588,461 26	337,755 36	....	....	28,317 97
1796	516,442 61	6,567,987 94	475,289 60	....	$4,836 13	1,169,415 98
1797	888,995 42	7,549,649 65	575,491 45	....	83,540 60	399,139 29
1798	1,021,899 04	7,106,061 93	644,357 95	....	11,963 11	58,192 81
1799	617,451 43	6,610,449 31	779,136 44	....	....	86,187 56
1800	2,161,867 77	9,080,932 73	809,396 55	$734,223 97	443 75	152,712 10
1801	2,623,311 99	10,750,778 93	1,048,039 43	534,343 38	167,726 06	345,649 15
1802	3,295,391 00	12,438,235 74	621,898 89	206,565 44	188,628 02	1,500,505 86
1803	5,020,697 64	10,479,417 61	215,179 69	71,879 20	165,675 69	131,945 44
1804	4,825,811 60	11,098,565 33	50,941 29	50,198 44	487,526 79	139,075 53
1805	4,037,005 26	12,936,487 04	21,747 15	21,882 91	540,193 80	40,382 30
1806	3,999,388 99	14,667,698 17	20,101 45	55,763 86	765,245 73	51,121 86
1807	4,538,123 80	15,845,521 61	13,051 40	34,732 56	466,163 27	38,550 42
1808	9,643,850 07	16,363,550 58	8,190 23	19,159 21	647,939 06	21,822 85
1809	9,941,809 96	7,257,506 62	4,094 29	7,517 31	442,252 33	62,162 57
1810	3,848,056 78	8,583,309 31	7,430 63	12,448 68	696,548 82	84,476 84
1811	2,672,276 57	13,313,222 73	2,295 95	7,666 66	1,040,237 53	59,211 22
1812	3,502,305 80	8,958,777 53	4,903 06	859 22	710,427 78	126,165 17
1813	3,862,217 41	13,224,623 25	4,755 04	3,805 52	835,655 14	271,571 00
1814	5,196,542 00	5,998,772 08	1,662,984 82	2,219,497 36	1,135,971 09	164,399 81
1815	1,727,848 63	7,282,942 22	4,678,059 07	2,162,673 41	1,287,959 28	285,282 84
1816	13,106,592 88	36,306,874 88	5,124,708 31	4,253,635 09	1,717,985 03	273,782 35
1817	22,033,519 19	26,283,348 49	2,678,100 77	1,834,187 04	1,991,226 06	109,761 08
1818	14,989,465 48	17,176,385 00	955,270 20	264,333 36	2,606,564 77	57,617 71
1819	1,478,526 74	20,283,608 76	229,593 63	83,650 78	3,274,422 78	57,098 42
1820	2,079,992 38	15,005,612 15	106,260 53	31,586 82	1,635,871 61	61,338 44
1821	1,198,461 21	13,004,447 15	69,027 63	29,349 05	1,212,966 46	152,589 43
1822	1,681,592 24	17,589,761 94	67,665 71	20,961 56	1,803,581 54	452,957 19
1823	4,237,427 55	19,088,433 44	34,242 17	10,337 71	916,523 10	141,129 84
1824	9,463,922 81	17,878,325 71	34,663 37	6,201 96	984,418 15	127,603 60
1825	1,946,597 13	20,098,713 45	25,771 35	2,330 85	1,216,090 56	130,451 81
1826	5,201,650 43	23,341,331 77	21,589 93	6,638 76	1,393,785 09	94,588 66
1827	6,358,686 18	19,712,283 29	19,885 68	2,626 90	1,495,845 26	1,315,722 83
1828	6,668,286 10	23,205,523 64	17,451 54	2,218 81	1,018,308 75	65,126 49
1829	5,972,435 81	22,681,965 91	14,502 74	11,335 05	2,329,356 14	112,648 55
1830	5,755,704 79	21,922,391 39	12,160 62	16,980 59	2,329,356 14	73,227 77
1831	6,014,539 75	24,224,441 77	6,933 51	10,506 01	3,210,815 48	584,124 05
1832	4,502,914 45	28,465,237 24	11,630 65	6,791 13	2,623,381 03	270,410 61
1833	2,011,777 55	29,032,508 91	2,759 00	394 12	3,967,682 55	470,096 67
1834	11,702,905 31	16,214,957 15	4,196 09	19 80	4,857,600 69	480,812 32
1835	8,892,858 42	19,391,310 59	10,459 48	4,263 33	14,757,600 75	759,972 13
1836	26,749,803 96	23,409,940 53	370 00	728 79	24,877,179 86	2,245,902 23
1837	46,708,436 00	11,169,290 39	5,493 84	1,087 70	6,776,236 52	7,001,444 59
1838	37,327,252 69	16,158,800 36	2,467 27	....	3,730,945 66	6,410,348 45
1839	36,891,196 94	23,137,924 81	2,553 32	755 22	7,361,576 40	979,939 86
1840	33,157,503 68	13,499,502 17	1,682 25	....	3,411,818 63	2,567,112 28
1841	29,963,163 46	14,487,216 74	3,261 36	....	1,365,627 42	1,004,054 75
1842	28,685,111 08	18,187,908 76	495 00	....	1,335,797 52	451,995 97
1843*	30,521,979 44	7,046,843 91	103 25	....	898,158 18	285,895 92
1844	39,186,284 74	26,183,570 94	1,777 34	....	2,059,939 80	1,075,419 70
1845	36,742,829 62	27,528,112 70	3,517 12	....	2,077,022 30	361,453 68
1846	36,194,274 81	26,712,667 87	2,897 26	....	2,694,452 48	289,950 13
1847	38,261,959 65	23,747,864 66	375 00	....	2,498,355 20	220,808 30
1848	33,079,276 43	31,757,070 96	375 00	....	3,328,642 56	612,610 69
1849	29,416,612 45	28,346,738 82	1	....	1,688,950 55	685,379 13
1850	32,827,082 69	39,668,686 42	....	....	1,859,894 25	2,064,308 21
1851	35,871,753 31	49,017,567 92	....	....	2,352,305 30	1,185,166 11
1852	40,158,353 25	47,339,326 62	....	....	2,043,239 58	464,249 40
1853	43,338,860 02	58,931,865 52	1	....	1,667,084 99	988,081 17
1854	50,261,901 09	64,224,190 27	....	....	8,470,798 39	1,105,352 74
1855	48,591,073 41	53,025,794 21	....	....	11,497,049 07	827,731 40
1856	47,777,672 13	64,022,863 50	....	....	8,917,644 93	1,116,190 81
1857	49,108,229 80	63,875,905 05	....	....	3,829,486 64	1,259,920 88
1858	46,802,855 00	41,789,620 96	1	....	3,513,715 87	1,352,029 13
1859	35,113,334 22	49,565,824 38	....	....	1,756,687 30	1,454,596 24
1860	33,193,248 60	53,187,511 87	....	....	1,778,557 71	1,088,530 25
1861	32,979,530 78	39,582,125 64	....	....	870,658 54	1,023,515 31
1862	30,963,857 83	49,056,397 62	....	1,795,331 73	152,203 77	915,327 97
1863	46,965,304 87	69,059,642 40	37,640,787 95	1,485,103 61	167,617 17	3,741,794 38

*For the half year from January

1871, *by calendar years to* 1843, *and by fiscal years* (*ending June* 30) *from that time.*

Year.	Dividends.	Interest.	Premiums.	Receipts from loans and Treasury notes.	Gross receipts.	Unavailable.
1791	....	....	....	$361,391 34	$4,771,342 53	....
1792	$8,028 00	....	....	5,102,498 45	8,772,458 76	....
1793	38,500 00	....	....	1,797,272 01	6,450,195 15	....
1794	303,472 00	....	....	4,007,950 78	9,439,855 65	....
1795	160,000 00	$4,800 00	....	3,396,424 00	9,515,758 59	....
1796	160,000 00	42,800 00	....	320,000 00	8,740,329 65	....
1797	80,960 00	....	....	70,000 00	8,758,780 99	....
1798	79,920 00	78,675 00	....	200,000 00	8,179,170 80	....
1799	71,040 00	....	....	5,000,000 00	12,546,813 31	....
1800	71,040 00	....	....	1,565,229 24	12,413,978 34	....
1801	88,800 00	10,125 00	....	....	12,945,455 95	....
1802	39,960 00	....	....	....	14,995,793 95	....
1803	....	....	....	....	11,064,097 63	....
1804	....	....	....	....	11,826,307 38	....
1805	....	....	....	....	13,560,693 20	....
1806	....	....	....	....	15,559,931 07	....
1807	....	....	....	....	16,398,019 26	....
1808	....	....	....	....	17,060,661 93	....
1809	....	....	....	....	7,773,473 12	....
1810	....	....	....	2,750,000 00	12,134,214 28	....
1811	....	....	....	....	14,422,634 09	....
1812	....	....	....	12,837,900 00	22,639,032 76	....
1813	....	300 00	....	26,184,135 00	40,524,844 95	....
1814	....	85 79	....	23,377,826 00	34,559,536 95	....
1815	....	11,541 74	$32,107 04	35,220,671 40	50,961,237 60	....
1816	....	68,665 16	086 09	9,425,084 91	57,171,421 82	.)..............
1817	202,426 30	267,819 14	....	466,723 45	33,333,592 33	....
1818	525,000 00	412 62	....	8,353 00	21,593,936 66	....
1819	675,000 00	....	....	2,291 00	24,605,665 37	....
1820	1,000,000 00	....	40,000 00	3,000,824 13	20,881,493 68	....
1821	105,000 00	....	....	5,000,324 00	19,573,703 72	....
1822	297,500 00	....	....	....	20,232,427 94	....
1823	350,000 00	....	....	....	20,540,666 26	....
1824	350,000 00	....	....	5,000,000 00	24,381,212 79	....
1825	367,500 00	....	....	5,000,000 00	26,840,858 02	....
1826	402,500 00	....	....	....	25,260,434 21	....
1827	420,000 00	....	....	....	22,966,363 96	....
1828	455,000 00	....	....	....	24,763,629 23	....
1829	490,000 00	....	....	....	24,827,627 38	....
1830	490,000 00	....	....	....	24,844,116 51	....
1831	490,000 00	....	....	....	28,526,820 82	....
1832	490,000 00	....	....	....	31,867,450 66	$1,389 50
1833	474,985 00	....	....	....	33,948,426 25	....
1834	234,340 50	....	....	....	21,791,935 55	....
1835	506,480 82	....	....	....	35,430,087 10	....
1836	292,674 67	....	....	....	50,826,796 08	....
1837	....	....	....	2,992,989 15	27,947,142 19	63,288 35
1838	....	....	....	12,716,820 86	39,019,382 60	....
1839	....	....	....	3,857,276 21	35,340,025 82	1,458,782 93
1840	....	....	....	5,589,547 51	25,069,662 84	37,469 25
1841	....	....	....	13,050,317 38	30,519,477 65	....
1842	....	....	....	14,808,735 64	34,784,932 89	11,188 00
1843*	....	....	71,700 83	12,470,708 36	20,782,410 48	....
1844	....	....	666 60	1,877,181 35	31,198,555 73	....
1845	....	....	....	....	29,970,105 80	28,251 90
1846	....	....	....	....	29,699,967 74	....
1847	....	....	28,365 91	28,872,399 45	55,368,168 52	30,000 00
1848	....	....	37,080 00	21,256,700 00	56,992,479 21	....
1849	....	....	487,065 48	28,588,750 00	59,796,892 98	....
1850	....	....	10,550 00	4,045,950 00	47,649,388 88	....
1851	....	....	4,264 92	203,400 00	52,762,704 25	....
1852	....	....	....	46,300 00	49,893,115 60	....
1853	....	....	22 50	16,350 00	61,603,404 18	103,301 37
1854	....	....	....	2,001 67	73,802,343.07	....
1855	....	....	....	800 00	65,351,374 68	....
1856	....	....	....	200 00	74,056,899 24	....
1857	....	....	....	3,900 00	68,969,212 57	....
1858	....	....	....	23,717,300 00	70,372,665 96	....
1859	....	....	709,357 72	28,287,500 00	81,773,965 64	15,408 34
1860	....	....	10,008 00	20,776,800 00	76,841,407 83	....
1861	....	....	33,630 90	41,861,709 74	83,371,640 13	....
1862	....	....	68,400 00	529,692,460 50	581,680,121 59	11,110 81
1863	....	....	602,345 44	776,682,361 57	889,379,652 52	6,000 01

1, 1843, to June 30, 1843.

TABLE M.—*Statement of the receipts of the United States*

Year.	Balance in the Treasury at commencement of year.	Customs.	Internal revenue.	Direct tax.	Public lands.	Miscellaneous.
1864	$36,523,046 13	$102,316,152 99	$109,741,134 10	$475,648 96	$588,333 29	$30,291,701 86
1865	134,433,738 44	84,928,260 60	209,464,215 25	1,200,573 03	996,553 31	25,441,556 00
1866	33,933,657 89	179,046,651 58	309,226,813 42	1,974,754 12	665,031 03	29,036,314 23
1867	160,817,099 73	176,417,810 88	266,027,537 43	4,200,233 70	1,163,575 76	15,037,522 15
1868	198,076,537 09	164,464,599 56	191,087,589 41	1,788,145 85	1,348,715 41	17,745,403 59
1869	158,936,082 87	180,048,426 63	158,356,460 86	ᐸ765,685 61	4,020,344 34	13,997,338 65
1870	183,781,985 76	194,538,374 44	184,899,756 49	229,102 88	3,350,481 76	12,942,118 30
1871	177,607,512 69	206,270,408 05	143,098,153 63	580,355 37	2,388,646 68	22,093,541 21
	....	2,981,260,790 71	1,631,820,461 33	27,239,672 42	191,713,472 08	229,467,039 79

*This item is an amount heretofore credited to the Treasurer

from March 4, 1789, to June 30, 1871, &c.—Continued.

Year.	Dividends.	Interest.	Premiums.	Receipts from loans and Treasury notes.	Gross receipts.	Unavailable.
1864			$21,174,101 01	$1,128,873,945 36	$1,393,461,017 57	$9,210 40
1865			11,683,446 89	1,472,224,740 85	1,805,939 345 93	6,095 11
1866			38,083,055 68	712,851,553 05	1,270,884,173 11	172,094 29
1867			27,787,330 35	640,426,910 29	1,131,060,920 56	721,827 93
						2,675,918 19
1868			29,203,629 50	625,111,433 20	1,030,749,516 52	
1869			13,755,491 12	238,678,081 06	609,621,828 27	*2,070 73
1870			15,295,643 76	285,474,496 00	696,729,973 63	
1871			8,392,839 95	268,768,523 47	652,092,468 36	*3,396 18
	$9,720,136 29	$485,224 45	168,011,700 29	7,094,541,041 38	12,325,259,628 74	2,670,451 28

as unavailable and since recovered and charged to his account.

2 S R

TABLE N.—*Statement of the expenditures of the United States from March 4, 1789, to June 30, 1871, b= calendar years to 1843, and by fiscal years (ending June 30) from that time.*

Year	War	Navy	Indians	Pensions	Miscellaneous	Premiums	Interest	Public debt	Gross expenditures	Balance in Treasury at the end of the year
1791	$632,804 03		$27,000 00	$175,813 88	$1,083,971 61		$1,177,863 03	$699,984 23	$3,797,436 78	$973,905 75
1792	1,100,702 09		13,648 85	109,243 15	4,672,604 38		2,373,611 28	693,050 25	8,962,920 00	783,444 51
1793	1,130,249 08		27,282 83	80,087 81	511,451 01		2,097,859 17	2,633,048 07	6,479,977 97	753,661 69
1794	2,639,097 59	$61,408 97	13,042 46	81,399 24	750,350 74		2,752,523 04	2,743,771 13	9,041,593 17	1,151,024 17
1795	2,480,910 13	410,562 03	23,475 68	68,673 22	1,378,920 66		2,947,059 06	2,841,639 37	10,151,240 15	516,442 61
1796	1,260,263 84	274,784 04	113,563 98	100,843 71	801,847 58		3,239,347 68	2,577,126 01	6,367,776 84	888,995 42
1797	1,039,402 46	382,631 89	62,396 58	92,256 97	1,259,422 62		3,172,516 73	2,617,250 12	8,625,877 37	1,021,809 04
1798	2,009,522 30	1,381,347 70	16,470 09	104,845 33	1,139,524 94		2,955,875 90	2,955,875 09	8,583,618 41	617,451 43
1799	2,466,946 98	2,858,081 84	20,302 19	95,444 03	1,039,391 68		2,815,651 41	1,706,578 84	11,002,396 97	2,161,867 77
1800	2,560,878 77	3,448,716 03	31 22	64,130 73	1,337,613 22		3,402,601 04	1,138,563 11	11,952,534 12	2,623,311 09
1801	1,672,944 08	2,111,424 00	9,000 00	73,533 37	1,114,768 45		4,411,830 06	2,679,876 98	12,273,376 94	3,295,391 00
1802	1,179,148 25	915,561 87	94,000 00	85,440 39	1,462,929 40		4,239,172 16	5,294,235 24	13,270,487 31	5,020,697 64
1803	822,055 85	1,215,230 53	60,000 00	62,902 10	1,842,635 76		3,949,462 36	3,306,697 07	11,258,983 67	4,825,811 60
1804	875,423 93	1,189,832 75	116,500 00	80,092 60	2,191,009 43		4,185,043 74	3,977,206 07	12,615,113 72	4,037,005 26
1805	712,781 28	1,597,500 00	196,500 00	81,854 59	3,768,598 75		2,657,114 22	4,583,960 63	13,598,309 47	3,999,388 90
1806	1,224,355 38	1,649,641 44	234,200 00	81,875 53	2,890,137 01		3,368,968 26	5,572,018 64	15,021,196 36	4,538,123 80
1807	1,288,685 91	1,722,064 47	205,425 00	70,500 00	1,697,897 51		3,369,578 48	2,938,141 62	16,292,292 99	9,643,850 07
1808	2,900,834 40	1,884,067 80	213,575 00	82,576 04	1,423,285 61		2,597,073 23	7,701,288 96	16,762,702 04	9,941,809 96
1809	3,345,772 17	2,427,758 80	337,503 84	87,833 54	1,215,803 79		2,866,074 90	3,286,279 36	13,867,226 30	3,848,056 78
1810	2,294,323 94	1,654,244 20	177,625 00	83,744 16	1,101,144 98		3,163,671 09	5,163,671 12	13,309,994 49	2,672,276 57
1811	2,032,828 19	1,965,566 39	151,875 00	75,043 88	1,367,291 40		2,585,435 57	5,414,564 43	13,592,604 86	3,502,305 80
1812	11,817,798 24	3,959,365 15	277,845 00	91,402 10	1,683,088 21		2,451,272 57	1,998,349 88	22,279,121 15	3,862,217 41
1813	19,652,013 02	6,446,600 10	167,358 28	86,989 91	1,729,635 61		3,599,455 22	7,508,668 22	39,190,520 36	5,196,542 00
1814	20,350,806 86	7,311,290 86	167,394 86	90,164 36	2,208,029 70		4,593,239 04	3,307,304 90	38,028,230 32	1,727,848 63

*For the half year from January 1, 1843, to June 30, 1843.   †Outstanding warrants.

NOTE.—This statement is made from warrants paid by the Treasurer up to June 30, 1866. The outstanding warrants are then added, and the statement is by warrants issued from that date. The balance in the treasury June 30, 1871, by this statement, is $138,019,122 15, from which should be deducted the amount deposited with the States, $28,101,044 91, leaving the net available balance, June 30, 1871, $109,917,477 24.

The statement of the Receipts and Expenditures, on account of the principal of the public debt, as per Tables M and N, shows the net receipts from the organization of the Government to June 30, 1871, to have been.. $7,094,541,041 38

The expenditures for the same period were... 4,857,434,540 51

Leaving...∴................. 2,237,106,500 87

as the amount of the principal of the public debt outstanding and unpaid on June 30, 1871.

The amount of the principal of the public debt, outstanding and unpaid, as shown by the monthly Debt Statement for July 1, 1871, and Tables I and L, is $2,353,211,332 32, showing a difference of $116,104,831 45 more outstanding by Debt Statement than by the Statement of Receipts and Expenditures. This difference is thus explained: The following stocks were issued in payment of various old debts and claims, but in the transactions no money ever came into the Treasury. On the maturity of the stock it was paid off, showing an expenditure where there had been no corresponding receipt:

Revolutionary debt of the several States, estimated.. $76,000,000 00
Mississippi stock, exact... 4,282,151 12
Louisiana purchase, exact.. 11,250,000 00
Washington and Georgetown debt to Holland, exact... 1,500,000 00
United States Bank stock,   " 7,000,000 00
Six per cent. Navy stock,   " 711,700 00
Texas purchase,   " 5,000,000 00
Mexican indemnity, fourth and fifth instalments, exact.. 303,573 92
In addition to the foregoing, the following amount is to be added, being composed of discount suffered in placing loans, interest paid and erroneously charged as principal, and various errors in settling and stating loan accounts. All of these latter and the Revolutionary debt are now being investigated, and will be explained in a future report in detail...∴... 10,057,406 41

                                                116,104,831 45

It must be borne in mind, in reading this explanation, that the errors alluded to are not such as in any manner affect the cash account of the Government, or reflect upon the integrity of former officers of the Treasury. A part of the differences has arisen from a want of knowledge and care on the part of subordinate clerks in stating loan accounts, but much the larger proportion has occurred from a want of unity, *system, and proper method* in the accounts as heretofore kept in the department. And these latter defects are partly owing to a want of sufficient legislation to enable the accounts to be properly kept. A bill was presented to Congress at its last session which was intended to supply this deficiency. It passed the House, but was not reached in the Senate. Until there is legislation, these errors and defects in the accounts must be perpetuated, and others must be made.

As an illustration of the class of differences which require legislation before they can be corrected, the two following are given: In 1850 there were $5,000,000 in bonds issued to pay Texan Indemnity. For these bonds no money was ever received, and therefore there is no entry representing them on the credit side of the account, as in ordinary loan transactions. When the stock matured it was paid out of the Treasury and charged in the loan accounts, thus erroneously reducing this account by just the amount paid. The loan of February, 1861, was sold at a discount of $2,019,776 10. Only the difference between the amount of this loan and of this discount was received into the Treasury. The loan appears in the Debt Statement at the par of the issue, but in the Receipts and Expenditures it can only appear (for want of a premium and discount account) at the actual amount of money received for the loan.

TABLE O.—*Statement of purchases of bonds from May, 1869, to September* [illegible] *currency and gold, the average cost in currency and gold of each purchase, and the average cost of all p*[illegible] *to the end of each month.*

Date of purchase.		Opening price of gold.	Principal.	Amount paid.	Currency value of interest accrued on bonds bought "flat."	Net cost.	Net cost estimated in gold.	Average rate of premium on each purchase.	Average cost in gold of each purchase.	Average rate of premium on total purchases to date.	Average cost in gold of total purchases to date.
1869.											
May	12	138½	$1,000,000	$1,155,070 00	$2,504 36	$1,152,565 64	$832,177 36	15.26	83.22		
	19	142	70,000	81,718 00		81,718 00	57,548 45	16.74	82.21		
	19	142	1,000,000	1,168,512 10		1,168,512 10	822,895 85	16.85	82.29		
	27	139½	1,000,000	1,153,581 50		1,153,581 50	826,940 14	15.36	82.69	15.84	82.72
June	3	138¼	1,000,000	1,164,058 90	711 78	1,164,770 68	842,510 43	16.48	84.25		
	10	138⅜	1,000,000	1,161,967 00		1,161,967 00	838,208 84	16.20	83.82		
	17	138¼	1,000,000	1,152,950 00		1,152,950 00	833,960 21	15.30	83.40		
	23	137⅛	1,620,000	1,870,402 50		1,870,402 50	1,364,012 76	15.46	84.20		
	26	137⅛	1,000,000	1,158,228 25		1,158,228 25	842,347 82	15.82	84.23	15.82	83.55
July	1	137½	1,000,000	1,158,098 75		1,158,098 75	842,253 63	15.81	84.22		
	3	137	3,000,000	3,496,474 00		3,496,474 00	2,552,170 80	16.54	85.07		
	9	136	3,000,000	3,518,044 00		3,518,044 00	2,586,797 06	17.27	86.23		
	14	137⅜	3,000,000	3,607,622 90		3,607,622 90	2,626,113 12	20.25	87.54		
	15	137	1,000,000	1,201,850 00		1,201,850 00	877,262 77	20.18	87.73		
	21	135⅛	3,000,000	3,600,028 80		3,600,028 80	2,664,221 12	20.00	88.81		
	28	136⅛	3,000,000	3,604,859 00		3,604,859 00	2,640,922 34	20.16	88.03		
	29	135¾	1,000,000	1,201,570 55		1,201,570 55	885,134 84	20.16	88.51	17.85	85.93
August	4	136	2,000,000	2,431,136 80		2,431,136 80	1,787,600 59	21.56	89.38		
	11	135⅛	2,000,000	2,422,038 27		2,422,038 27	1,787,482 12	21.10	89.37		
	12	135⅛	1,000,000	1,198,931 70		1,198,931 70	887,276 00	19.89	88.73		
	18	133	2,000,000	2,378,781 81		2,378,781 81	1,788,557 75	18.94	89.43		
	25	133⅛	2,000,000	2,389,539 01		2,389,539 01	1,793,275 07	19.48	89.66		
	26	133⅞	1,000,000	1,196,247 80		1,196,247 80	893,555 78	19.63	89.36	18.48	86.87
September	1	133⅜	2,000,000	2,401,991 00		2,401,991 00	1,800,930 46	20.10	90.05		
	8	136	2,000,000	2,356,000 00		2,356,000 00	1,732,352 94	17.80	86.62		
	9	135⅞	1,000,000	1,183,972 53		1,183,972 53	871,368 92	18.40	87.14		
	15	136⅜	2,000,000	2,369,639 55		2,369,639 55	1,740,782 04	18.48	87.04		
	22	137¾	2,000,000	2,337,657 62		2,337,657 62	1,697,029 12	16.88	84.85		
	23	141⅜	1,000,000	1,165,548 50		1,165,548 50	822,982 17	16.55	82.30		
	25	133⅝	3,000,000	3,537,158 16		3,537,158 16	2,647,078 14	17.91	88.24		
	29	133⅝	3,000,000	3,473,533 12		3,473,533 12	2,599,463 51	15.78	86.65	18.35	86.90
October	6	130	2,000,000	2,319,139 18		2,319,139 18	1,783,953 22	15.96	89.20		
	7	131⅛	1,000,000	1,159,945 10		1,159,945 10	884,610 18	15.99	88.46		
	7	131⅛	*153,500	178,187 69		178,187 69	135,891 47	16.08	88.53		

TABLE O.—*Statement of purchases of bonds from May, 1869, to September 30, 1871, &c.—Continued.*

Date of purchase.	Opening price of gold.	Principal.	Amount paid.	Currency value of interest accrued on bonds bought "flat."	Net cost.	Net cost estimated in gold.	Average rate of premium on each purchase.	Average cost in gold of each purchase.	Average rate of premium on total purchases to date.	Average cost in gold of total purchases to date.
1869.										
October 13	130¼	$2,000,000	$2,318,863 53		$2,318,863 53	$1,782,043 06	15.94	89.10		
20	130	2,000,000	2,314,079 00		2,314,079 00	1,780,060 77	15.70	88.00		
27	130½	1,000,000	1,152,000 00		1,152,000 00	885,302 59	15.20	88.53	17.86	87.20
November 3	130½	2,000,000	2,392,000 00		2,392,000 00	1,768,844 38	14.63	88.09		
4	128½	2,000,000	2,257,255 21		2,257,255 21	889,906 26	12.86	88.43		
4	128¾	1,000,000	1,126,243 74		1,126,243 74	891,680 39	12.68	88.99		
5	126¾	1,000,000	1,129,090 29		1,129,090 29	179,773 12	12.91	89.17		
5	126¼	*201,300	227,580 43	167 43	227,413 00	386,751 63	12.97	89.31		
10	126¼	*453,300	492,858 94	2,917 87	489,941 07	1,780,492 61	12.99	89.32		
17	127¼	2,000,000	2,259,000 00		2,259,000 00	1,775,035 35	12.95	89.02		
17	127¼	2,000,000	2,256,513 09		2,256,513 09	888,132 95	12.83	88.75		
24	127½	1,000,000	1,129,039 02		1,129,039 02	2,671,260 54	12.90	88.81	16.97	87.48
December 1	122¼	2,000,000	3,382,483 67		3,382,483 67	1,807,158 41	12.75	89.04		
2	122¼	1,000,000	2,206,992 21		2,206,992 21	901,971 06	10.35	90.36		
8	123½	2,000,000	1,102,659 61		1,102,659 61	1,818,593 78	10.27	90.20		
15	121¾	1,000,000	2,248,236 56		2,248,236 56	1,839,598 27	12.41	90.93		
16	121¼	2,000,000	2,239,710 90		2,239,710 90	919,557 94	11.98	91.98		
22	120¾	2,000,000	2,215,985 83		2,215,985 83	1,844,733 26	10.80	92.24		
29	119¾	2,000,000	2,220,427 12		2,220,427 12	1,852,285 40	11.02	92.61		
30	119¾	1,000,000	1,110,507 80		1,110,507 80	926,388 15	11.05	92.64	16.13	88.20
1870.										
January 5	119¼	2,000,000	2,246,595 03		2,246,595 03	1,876,071 01	12.33	93.80		
11	122¼	*451,700	517,400 49		517,400 49	422,367 75	14.54	93.51		
11	122¼	1,342,550	1,539,826 93	32 58	1,539,794 35	1,256,974 98	14.69	93.63		
13	122¼	2,000,000	1,141,010 09		1,141,010 09	938,137 79	14.10	93.81		
19	121¾	2,000,000	2,281,656 49		2,281,656 49	1,877,823 45	14.08	93.89		
27	122	1,000,000	1,142,872 27		1,142,872 27	936,780 55	14.29	93.08		
February 10	120¾	1,000,000	1,126,500 00		1,126,500 00	932,919 25	12.65	93.30		
11	117½	50,000	66,325 00		66,325 00	46,888 66	12.65	93.78		
24	116¼	1,000,000	1,115,764 80		1,115,704 80	948,577 94	11.57	94.86	15.94	88.53
March 2	116¼	1,000,000	1,117,488 85		1,117,488 85	950,043 06	11.75	95.04		
10	111	1,000,000	1,107,377 50		1,107,377 50	351,559 61	10.74	95.16		
17	113	1,000,000	1,067,347 35		1,067,347 35	361,574 19	6.73	96.16		
24	112¼	1,000,000	1,067,480 27		1,067,480 27	353,107 39	6.75	95.31	15.79	88.73
		1,000,000	1,060,440 34		1,060,440 34	342,613 63	6.04	94.26		

	30	111⅞	1,000,000	1,069,985 26		1,069,985 26	956,411 41	7.00	95.64	15.42	89 04
April	7	112	1,000,000	1,070,574 91		1,070,574 91	955,870 46	7.06	95.59		
	13	112⅛	1,000,000	1,073,953 37		1,073,953 37	954,625 22	7.39	95.46		
	21	113⅜	1,000,000	1,078,778 18		1,078,778 18	951,513 28	7.88	95.15		
	27	113⅞	1,000,000	1,100,490 79		1,100,490 79	966,402 45	10.05	96.64		
	30	114⅞	*345,400	390,847 25	7,826 85	383,020 40	333,423 63	10.89	96.53		
	30	114⅞	*758,800	859,029 25	18,099 70	840,929 55	732,038 78	10.82	96.47	15.10	89.36
May	5	114⅝	2,000,000	2,215,447 70		2,215,447 70	1,932,778 80	10.77	96.64		
	12	115⅞	*1,850	2,074 31	3 85	2,070 46	1,794 55	11.92	97.00		
	12	115⅜	1,000,000	1,118,370 86		1,118,370 86	969,335 52	11.84	96.93		
	19	114¾	2,000,000	2,230,611 87		2,230,611 87	1,943,888 34	11.53	97.19		
	26	114¼	1,000,000	1,108,910 71		1,108,910 71	970,600 18	10.89	97.06	14.90	89.76
June	2	114½	2,000,000	2,223,786 41		2,223,786 41	1,942,171 53	11.19	97.11		
	9	113½	1,000,000	1,109,976 64		1,109,976 64	977,952 99	11.00	97,79		
	16	113½	2,000,000	2,217,755 94		2,217,755 94	1,960,447 24	10.89	98.02		
	23	111⅝	1,000,000	1,104,612 10		1,104,612 10	989,574 11	10.46	98.96		
	30	111⅝	2,000,000	2,218,005 71		2,218,005 71	1,987,015 19	10.90	99.35	14.65	90.31
July	7	112½	1,000,000	1,107,000 00		1,107,000 00	987,290 97	10.70	98.73		
	11	115½	*690,400	758,749 60		758,749 60	659,065 88	9.90	95.46		
	11	115⅛	*1,683,150	1,848,423 98		1,848,423 98	1,605,580 00	9.82	95.39		
	14	112⅞	2,000,000	2,182,332 89		2,182,332 89	1,933,406 77	9.12	96.67		
	21	121¾	1,000,000	1,070,136 00		1,070,136 00	878,961 81	7.01	87.90		
	28	121⅝	2,000,000	2,162,085 83		2,162,085 83	1,777,665 64	8.10	88.88	14.29	90.52
August	4	121¾	1,000,000	1,085,712 21		1,085,712 21	891,755 41	8.57	89.17		
	11	116¼	2,000,000	2,191,414 93		2,191,414 93	1,885,088 11	9.57	94.25		
	18	116¾	1,000,000	1,097,329 29		1,097,329 29	939,896 61	9.73	93.99		
	25	117⅞	2,000,000	2,181,093 02		2,181,093 02	1,850,344 02	9.05	92.52	14.07	90.62
September	1	116⅜	1,000,000	1,091,038 65		1,091,038 65	937,519 78	9.10	93.75		
	8	114	3,000,000	3,272,957 77		3,272,957 77	2,871,015 58	9.10	95.70		
	15	114⅜	2,000,000	2,183,503 11		2,183,503 11	1,909,073 76	9.18	95.45		
	22	113⅞	3,000,000	3,281,789 74		3,281,789 74	2,881,922 93	9.39	96.06		
	29	113⅞	2,000,000	2,177,057 86		2,177,057 86	1,911,796 14	8.85	95.59	13.71	90.98
October	6	113	2,000,000	2,174,300 26		2,174,300 26	1,924,159 52	8.72	96.21		
	13	113⅞	2,000,000	2,170,465 37		2,170,465 37	1,906,006 91	8.52	95.30		
	20	112⅞	2,000,000	2,170,236 48		2,170,236 48	1,922,690 12	8.51	96.13		
	27	112	2,000,000	2,165,529 30		2,165,529 30	1,933,508 30	8.28	96.68	13.44	91.24
November	3	110¾	1,000,000	1,077,698 19		1,077,698 19	973,090 92	7.77	97.31		
	3	110¾	*245,850	265,173 81		265,173 81	239,434 59	7.86	97.39		
	3	110¾	*542,250	584,808 61	8 06	584,800 55	528,036 61	7.85	97.39		
	10	110⅜	1,000,000	1,072,263 90		1,072,263 90	971,473 52	7.23	97.15		
	17	113	1,000,000	1,064,972 36		1,064,972 36	942,453 42	6.50	94.25		
	25	112	1,000,000	1,065,650 15		1,065,650 15	951,473 35	6.56	95.15	13.25	91.39
December	1	110⅝	1,000,000	1,064,917 08		1,064,917 08	962,636 91	6.49	96.26		
	8	110⅝	1,000,000	1,063,854 32		1,063,854 32	961,676 22	6.38	96.17		
	15	111¼	1,000,000	1,065,972 75		1,065,972 75	958,177 75	6.60	95.82		
	22	110⅝	1,000,000	1,064,459 26		1,064,459 26	962,223 06	6.45	96.22		
	29	110¾	1,000,000	1,064,473 95		1,064,473 95	961,150 29	6.45	96.11	13.05	91.53
	1871.										
January	4	110¾	2,000,000	2,147,345 03		2,147,345 03	1,938,911 99	7.37	96.96		
	11	111	1,000,000	1,074,257 50		1,074,257 50	967,799 55	7.43	96.78		
	18	110⅝	2,000,000	2,144,457 32		2,144,457 32	1,938,492 49	7.22	96.92		

TABLE O.—*Statement of the purchases of bonds from May, 1869, to September 30, 1871, &c.*—Continued.

Date of purchase.	Opening price of gold.	Principal.	Amount paid.	Currency value of interest accrued on bonds bought "flat."	Net cost.	Net cost, estimated in gold.	Average rate of premium on each purchase.	Average cost in gold of each purchase.	Average rate of premium on total purchases to date.	Average cost in gold of total purchases to date.
January 25	110⅝	$1,000,000	$1,074,651 96		$1,074,651 96	$971,436 80	7.46	97.14	12.85	91.72
February 1	111⅛	2,000,000	2,173,985 90		2,173,985 90	1,943,227 62	8.70	97.16		
8	111⅞	2,000,000	2,175,643 46		2,175,643 46	1,946,884 53	8.78	97.34		
15	111¼	2,000,000	2,184,170 19		2,184,170 19	1,963,299 05	9.21	98.16		
21	111¼	2,000,000	2,191,633 24		2,191,633 24	1,970,007 41	9.58	98.50	12.68	91.99
March 1	110⅞	2,000,000	2,199,585 00		2,199,585 00	1,983,842 16	9.98	99.19		
8	111¼	2,000,000	2,199,570 48		2,199,570 48	1,977,142 00	9.98	98.85		
15	111⅜	2,000,000	2,191,702 96		2,191,702 96	1,967,859 00	9.58	98.39		
22	110⅞	2,000,000	2,188,826 83		2,188,826 83	1,974,139 19	9.94	98.71		
29	110¼	2,000,000	2,183,254 76		2,183,254 76	1,980,276 42	9.16	99.01	12.52	92.34
April 3	110¼	216,000	235,807 20		235,807 20	213,884 08	9.17	99.02		
5	110⅜	3,000,000	3,295,500 00		3,295,500 00	2,985,730 46	9.85	99.52		
12	110⅛	2,000,000	2,197,018 24		2,197,018 24	1,995,022 24	9.85	99.75		
19	111⅜	3,000,000	3,317,193 80		3,317,193 80	2,971,730 17	10.57	99.06		
26	110⅞	2,000,000	2,215,181 72		2,215,181 72	1,997,909 10	10.76	99.90	12.41	92.71
May 3	111⅛	2,000,000	2,221,571 71		2,221,571 71	1,999,164 64	11.08	99.96		
10	111¼	2,000,000	2,223,162 54		2,223,162 54	1,998,348 35	11.16	99.92		
17	111⅞	2,000,000	2,228,989 07		2,228,989 07	1,992,392 46	11.45	99.62		
24	111⅝	2,000,000	2,224,133 69		2,224,133 69	1,992,504 98	11.21	99.63		
31	111⅞	2,000,000	2,225,697 79		2,225,697 79	1,989,450 54	11.28	99.47	12.35	93.04
June 7	112¼	1,000,000	1,115,811 40		1,115,811 40	994,041 33	11.58	99.40		
14	112⅜	1,000,000	1,114,175 30		1,114,175 30	991,479 69	11.42	99.15		
21	112⅜	1,000,000	1,116,587 05		1,116,587 05	993,625 85	11.66	99.36		
28	113⅛	1,000,000	1,118,691 60		1,118,691 60	988,898 65	11.87	98.89	12.34	93.16
July 5	113½	1,000,000	1,132,384 49		1,132,384 49	997,695 59	13.24	99.77		
12	112⅛	1,000,000	1,122,692 96		1,122,692 96	999,059 35	12.27	99.91		
19	112½	385,600	433,278 38		433,278 38	385,136 33	12.36	99.88		
26	112¼	1,000,000	1,122,086 99		1,122,086 99	999,632 06	12.21	99.96	12.34	93.26
August 2	112⅛	162,750	182,407 63		182,407 63	162,682 39	12.08	99.96		
9	112	20,100	22,509 99		22,509 99	20,098 20	11.99	99.99		
16	112¼	1,000,000	1,122,127 56		1,122,127 56	999,668 21	12.21	99.97		
23	112¼	1,000,000	1,121,011 54		1,121,011 54	998,673 98	12.10	99.87	12.34	93.35
30	113¼	1,000,000	1,125,650 82		1,125,650 82	993,952 16	12.56	99.39		
September 6	113⅞	1,000,000	1,128,864 31		1,128,864 31	991,318 82	12.89	99.13		
13	113⅞	1,000,000	1,125,800 00		1,125,800 00	988,627 88	12.58	98.86		
20	114⅛	3,000,000	3,375,135 99		3,375,135 99	2,957,402 34	12.50	98.58		
25	115	3,000,000	3,397,836 15		3,397,836 15	2,954,640 13	13.26	98.49		
27	114½	2,000,000	2,262,400 68		2,262,400 68	1,975,895 78	13.12	98.79	12.36	93.59

TABLE O—Continued.—RECAPITULATION BY LOANS.

Date of purchase.	Principal.	Amount paid.	Currency value of interest accrued on bonds bought "flat."	Net cost.	Net cost estimated in gold.	Average rate of premium on each purchase.	Average cost in gold of each purchase.	Average rate of premium on total purchases to date.	Average cost in total gold of purchases to date.
Five-twenties of 1862	$28,759,250	$34,297,907 73	$938 14	$32,296,900 59	$26,940,669 87			$12 30	$93 68
Five-twenties of March, 1864	31,004,900	1,176,394 00	12 48	1,176,382 42	915,140 70			17 12	91 11
Five-twenties of June, 1864	30,891,200	34,144,384 00	4,024 32	34,140,360 28	28,313,076 00			12 35	93 82
Five-twenties of 1865	28,794,350	32,040,702 57	53 48	32,040,649 09	27,464,141 31			11 27	95 33
Consols of 1865	90,857,750	101,857,904 91	24,983 68	101,832,921 23	85,602,121 89			12 11	94 15
Consols of 1867	46,576,640	35,010,708 08	744 92	55,015,963 16	44,539,776 49			13 25	91 69
Consols of 1868	2,090,900	3,481,485 76	91 90	3,481,393 86	2,668,662 44			16 43	88 91
Total	231,375,300	360,015,488 55	30,848 92	259,984,639 63	216,533,577 70			12 36	93 50

☞ The public bonded debt has been reduced by the amount of these bonds, which have ceased to bear interest, and have been cancelled and destroyed. The six per cent. bonded debt has also been reduced by the amount of five per cents. issued to take their place. There have also been paid in coin, and cancelled and destroyed, other bonds to the amount of $7,009,000, which matured January 1, 1871.

NOTE.—The purchases marked (*) are "interest purchases," being the bonds bought with the proceeds of the interest collected on the bonds previously purchased.

Purchases with "accrued interest on bonds previously purchased" were discontinued July 14, 1870, date of the act authorizing the refunding of the National debt, and directing the cancellation and destruction of the bonds purchased. All purchased bonds, whether bought before or since that date, have ceased to bear interest, and the annual interest charge has been reduced by the amount of interest that would have been payable on these if they had not been redeemed.

Description			Rate of interest				
OLD DEBT. Unclaimed dividends upon debt created prior to 1800, and the principal and interest of the outstanding debt created during the war of 1812, and up to 1837.		On demand	5 and 6 per cent				$57,665 00
TREASURY NOTES PRIOR TO 1846. The acts of October 12, 1837, (5 Statutes, 201;) May 21, 1838, (5 Statutes, 228;) March 31, 1840, (5 Statutes, 370;) February 15, 1841, (5 Statutes, 411;) January 31, 1842, (5 Statutes, 469;) August 31, 1842, (5 Statutes, 581;) and March 3, 1843, (5 Statutes, 614,) authorized the issue of Treasury notes in various amounts, and with interest at rates named therein from 1 mill to 6 per centum per annum.	1 and 2 years	1 and 2 years from date.	1 mill to 6 per cent.	Par			82,075 35
LOAN OF 1842. The act of July 21, 1841, (5 Statutes, 438,) authorized a loan of $12,000,000, with interest of not exceeding 6 per centum per annum, reimbursable at the will of the Secretary of the Treasury, after six months' notice, or at any time after January 1, 1845. The act of April 15, 1842, (5 Statutes, 473,) authorized an additional sum of $5,000,000, and made the amount obtained on the loan, after the passage of the last act, reimbursable as should be agreed upon at the time of issue, either after six months' notice, or at any time not after January 1, 1863.	20 years	January 1, 1863.	6 per cent.	Par	$17,000,000 00	$8,000,000 00	6,000 00
TREASURY NOTES OF 1846. The act of July 22, 1846, (9 Statutes, 39,) authorized the issue of Treasury notes in such sums as the exigencies of the Government might require; the amount outstanding at any one time not to exceed $10,000,000, to bear interest at not exceeding 6 per	1 year.	1 year from date.	6 per cent.	Par	10,000,000 00		6,000 00

MEXICAN INDEMNITY. A proviso in the civil and diplomatic appropriation act of August 10, 1846, (9 Statutes, 94,) authorized the payment of the principal and interest of the fourth and fifth instalments of the Mexican indemnities due in April and July, 1844, by the issue of stock, with interest at 5 per centum, payable in five years.	5 years	April and July 1849.	5 per cent	Par	350,000 00	303,573 92	1,104 91
TREASURY NOTES OF 1847. The act of January 28, 1847, (9 Statutes, 118,) authorized the issue of $23,000,000 Treasury notes, with interest at not exceeding 6 per centum per annum, or the issue of stock for any portion of the amount, with interest at 6 per centum per annum. The Treasury notes under this act were redeemable at the expiration of one or two years; and the interest was to cease at the expiration of sixty days' notice. These notes were receivable in payment of all debts due the United States, including customs duties.	1 and 2 years	After 60 days' notice.	6 per cent	Par	23,000,000 00		950 00
LOAN OF 1847. The act of January 28, 1847, (9 Statutes, 118,) authorized the issue of $23,000,000 Treasury notes, with interest at not exceeding 6 per centum per annum, or the issue of stock for any portion of the amount, with interest at 6 per centum per annum, reimbursable after December 31, 1867. Section 14 authorized the conversion of Treasury notes under this or any preceding act into like stock, which accounts for the apparent over issue.	20 years	January 1, 1868		Par	23,000,000 00	28,207,000 00	2,150 00
TEXAN INDEMNITY STOCK. The act of September 9, 1850, (9 Statutes, 447,) authorized the issue of $10,000,000 stock, with interest at 5 per centum per annum, to the State of Texas, in satisfaction of all claims against the United States arising out of the annexation of the said State. This stock was to be redeemable at the end of fourteen years.	14 years	January 1, 1865	5 per cent	Par	16,000,000 00	,000,000 00	181,000 00
LOAN OF 1848: The act of March 31, 1848, (9 Statutes, 217,) authorized a loan of $16,000,000, with interest at not exceeding 6 per centum per annum, reimbursable after July 1, 1868. The Secretary of the Treasury was authorized to purchase this stock at any time,	2 years	July 1, 1868	6 per cent	Par	16,000,000 00	16,000,000 00	24,900 00

TREASURY NOTES OF 1857.

The act of December 23, 1857, (11 Statutes, 257,) authorised the issue of $20,000,000 in Treasury notes, $5,000,000, with interest at not exceeding 6 per centum per annum, and the remainder with interest at the lowest rates offered by bidders, but not exceeding 6 per centum per annum. These notes were redeemable at the expiration of one year, and interest was to cease at the expiration of sixty days' notice after maturity. They were receivable in payment of all debts due the United States, including customs duties.

LOAN OF 1858.

The act of June 14, 1858, (11 Statutes, 365,) authorised a loan of $20,000,000, with interest at not exceeding 5 per centum per annum, and redeemable any time after January 1, 1874.

LOAN OF 1860.

The act of June 22, 1860, (12 Statutes, 79,) authorised a loan of $21,000,000, (to be used in redemption of Treasury notes,) with interest at not exceeding 6 per centum per annum, redeemable in not less than ten nor more than twenty years.

LOAN OF FEBRUARY 1861, (1881's.)

1 year	60 days' notice	5 and 5½ per cent.	Par	$20,000,000 00	$20,000,000 00	$2,000 00
15 years	January 1, 1874	5 per cent	Par	20,000,000 00	20,000,000 00	20,000,000 00
10 years	January 1, 1871	5 per cent	Par	21,000,000 00	7,022,000 00	49,000 00

Description	Redeemable	Rate of interest		Payable	Amount authorized		
TREASURY NOTES OF 1861. The act of March 2, 1861, (12 Statutes, 178,) authorized a loan of $10,000,000, with interest at not exceeding 6 per centum per annum, redeemable on three months' notice after July 1, 1871, and payable July 1, 1881. If proposals for the loan were not satisfactory, authority was given to issue the whole amount in Treasury notes, with interest at not exceeding 6 per centum per annum. The same act gave authority to substitute Treasury notes for the whole or any part of loans authorized at the time of the passage of this act. These notes were to be received in payment of all debts due the United States, including customs duties, and were redeemable at any time within two years from the date of the act.	2 years 60 days	6 per cent.	Par	2 years after date 60 days after date	{ 22,468,100 00 12,896,350 00 }	35,364,450 00	3,200 00
OREGON WAR-DEBT. The act of March 2, 1861, (12 Statutes, 198,) appropriated $2,800,000 for the payment of expenses incurred by the Territories of Washington and Oregon, in the suppression of Indian hostilities in the years 1855 and 1856. Section 4 of the act authorized the payment of these claims in bonds redeemable in twenty years, with interest at 6 per centum per annum.	20 years	6 per cent.	Par	July 1, 1881	2,800,000 00	1,090,850 00	945,000 00
LOAN OF JULY AND AUGUST 1861, (1881's.) The act of July 17, 1861, (12 Statutes, 259,) authorized the issue of $250,000,000 bonds, with interest at not exceeding 7 per centum per annum, redeemable after twenty years. The act of August 5, 1861, (12 Statutes, 313,) authorized the issue of bonds with interest at 6 per centum per annum, payable after twenty years from date, in exchange for 7-30 notes issued under the act of July 17, 1861. None of such bonds were to be issued for a sum less than $500, and the whole amount of them was not to exceed the whole amount of 7-30 notes issued under the above act of July 17. The amount issued in exchange for 7-30's was $139,318,100.	20 years	6 per cent.	Par	July 1, 1881	250,000,000 00	{ 50,000,000 00 139,318,100 00 }	180,318,100 00
OLD DEMAND NOTES. The act of July 17, 1861, (12 Statutes, 259,) authorized the issue of $50,000,000 Treasury notes, not bearing interest, of a less denomination than fifty dollars and not less than ten dollars, and payable on demand by the assistant treasurers at Philadelphia, New York, or Boston. The act of August 5, 1861, (12 Statutes, 313,) authorized the issue of these notes			Par	On demand	60,000,000 00	60,000,000 00	96,505 50

in denominations of five dollars; it also added the assistant treasurer at St. Louis and the designated depositary at Cincinnati to the places where these notes were made payable. The act of February 12, 1862, (12 Statutes, 338,) increased the amount of demand notes authorized $10,000,000.

SEVEN-THIRTIES OF 1861.

The act of July 17, 1861, (12 Statutes, 259,) authorized a loan of $250,000,000, part of which was to be in treasury notes with interest at 7 3-10 per centum per annum, payable three years after date of act.

3 years	7 3-10 per cent	August 19 and October 1, 1864.	Par	$140,094,750 00	$140,094,750 00	$23,100 00

FIVE-TWENTIES OF 1862.

The act of February 25, 1862, (12 Statutes, 345,) authorized a loan of $500,000,000, for the purpose of funding the treasury notes and floating debt of the United States, and the issue of bonds therefor, with interest at 6 per centum per annum. These bonds were redeemable after five and payable twenty years from date. The act of March 3, 1864, (13 Statutes, 13,) authorized an additional issue of $11,000,000 of bonds to persons who subscribed for the loan on or before January 21, 1864. The act of January 28, 1865, (13 Statutes, 425,) authorized an additional issue of $4,000,000 of these bonds and their sale in the United States or Europe.

5 or 20 years	6 per cent	May 1, 1867.	Par	515,000,000 00	514,771,600 00	463,733,500 00

LEGAL TENDER NOTES.

The act of February 25, 1862, (12 Statutes, 345,) authorized the issue of $150,000,000 United States notes, not bearing interest, payable to bearer at the Treasury of the United States, and of such denominations as the Secretary of the Treasury might deem expedient, not less than five dollars; $50,000,000 to be in lieu of demand notes authorized by the act of July 17, 1861; these notes to be a legal tender. The act of July 11, 1862, (12 Statutes, 532,) authorized an

			Par	450,000,000 00		356,000,000 00

not more than $35,000,000 of a lower denomination than five dollars; these notes to be a legal tender. The act of March 3, 1863, (12 Statutes, 710,) authorized an additional issue of $150,000,000 United States notes, payable to bearer, of such denominations, not less than one dollar, as the Secretary of the Treasury might prescribe; which notes were made a legal lender. The same act limited the time at which Treasury notes might be exchanged for United States bonds to July 1, 1863. The amount of notes authorized by this act were to be in lieu of $100,000,000 authorized by the resolution of January 17, 1863, (12 Statutes, 822.)

TEMPORARY LOAN.

The act of February 25, 1862, (12 Statutes, 346,) authorized temporary loan deposits of $25,000,000, for not less than thirty days, with interest at 5 per centum per annum, payable after ten days' notice. The act of March 17, 1862, (12 Statutes, 370,) authorized the increase of temporary loan deposits $50,000,000. The act of July 11, 1862, (12 Statutes, 532,) authorized a further increase of temporary loan deposits to $100,000,000. The act of June 30, 1864, (13 Statutes, 218,) authorized a further increase of temporary loan deposits to not exceeding $150,000,000, and an increase of the rate of interest to not exceeding 6 per centum per annum, or a decrease of the rate of interest on ten days' notice, as the public interest might require.

CERTIFICATES OF INDEBTEDNESS.

The act of March 1, 1862, (12 Statutes, 352,) authorized the issue of certificates of indebtedness to public creditors who might elect to receive them, to bear interest at the rate of 6 per centum per annum, and payable one year from date, or earlier, at the option of the Government. The act of May 17, 1862, (12 Statutes, 370,) authorized the issue of these certificates in payment of disbursing officers' checks. The act of March 3, 1863, (12 Statutes, 710,) made the interest payable in lawful money.

FRACTIONAL CURRENCY.

The act of July 17, 1862, (12 Statutes, 592,) authorized the use of postal and other stamps as currency, and made them receivable in payment of all dues to the United States less than five dollars. The 4th section of the act of March 3, 1863, (12 Statutes, 711,)

Not less than 30 days.	After 10 days' notice.	4, 5, and 6 per cent.	Par.	150,000,000 00		90,310 00
1 year.	1 year after date.	6 per cent.	Par.	No limit.	561,753,241 00	5,000 00
	On presentation.		Par.	50,000,000 00		40,582,874 56

authorized the issue of fractional notes in lieu of postal and other stamps and postal currency; made them exchangeable in sums not less than three dollars for United States notes, and receivable for postage and revenue stamps, and in payment of dues to the United States, except duties on imports, less than five dollars; and limited the amount to $50,000,000. The 5th section of the act of June 30, 1864, (13 Statutes, 220,) authorized an issue of $50,000,000 in fractional currency, and provided that the whole amount of these notes should not exceed this sum.

LOAN OF 1863.

The act of March 3, 1863, (12 Statutes, 709,) authorized a loan of $900,000,000, and the issue of bonds with interest at not exceeding six per centum per annum, and redeemable in not less than ten nor more than forty years, principal and interest payable in coin. The act of June 30, 1864, (13 Statutes, 219,) repeals so much of the preceding act as limits the authority thereunder to the current fiscal year, and also repeals the authority altogether except as relates to $75,000,000 of bonds already advertised for.

17 years	July 1, 1881	6 per cent	Premium of 4.13	$75,000,000 00	$75,000,000 00	$75,000,000 00

ONE-YEAR NOTES OF 1863.

The act of March 3, 1863, (12 Statutes, 710,) authorized the issue of $400,000,000 Treasury notes, with interest at not exceeding 6 per centum per annum, redeemable in not more than three years, principal and interest payable in lawful money, to be a legal tender for their face value.

1 year	1 year after date	5 per cent	Par			123,067 00

TWO-YEAR NOTES OF 1863.

COIN CERTIFICATES.

The 5th section of the act of March 3, 1863, (12 Statutes, 711,) authorized the deposit of gold coin and bullion with the Treasurer or any Assistant Treasurer, in sums not less than $20, and the issue of certificates therefor in denominations the same as United States notes; also authorized the issue of these certificates in payment of interest on the public debt. It limits the amount of them to not more than 20 per centum of the amount of coin and bullion in the Treasury, and directs their receipt in payment for duties on imports.

3 F

COMPOUND INTEREST NOTES.

The act of March 3, 1863, (12 Statutes, 709,) authorized the issue of $400,000,000 Treasury notes, with interest at not exceeding 6 per centum per annum, in lawful money, payable not more than three years from date, and to be a legal tender for their face value. The act of June 30, 1864, (13 Statutes, 218,) authorized the issue of $200,000,000 Treasury notes, of any denomination not less than $10, payable not more than three years from date, or redeemable at any time after three years, with interest at not exceeding 7 3-10 per centum, payable in lawful money at maturity, and made them a legal tender for their face to the same extent as United States notes. $177,046,770 of the amount issued was in redemption of 5 per cent. notes.

TEN-FORTIES OF 1864.

The act of March 3, 1864, (13 Statutes, 13,) authorized the issue of $200,000,000 bonds, at not exceeding 6 per centum per annum, redeemable after five and payable not more than forty years from date, in coin.

FIVE-TWENTIES OF MARCH, 1864.

The act of March 3, 1864, (13 Statutes, 13,) authorized the issue of $200,000,000 bonds, at not exceeding 6 per centum per annum, redeemable after five and payable not more than forty years from date, in coin.

Description	Term	When redeemable	Rate of interest	Price	Amount authorized	Amount issued	Amount outstanding
COIN CERTIFICATES.		On demand		Par	Indefinite	442,925,000 00	19,886,300 00
COMPOUND INTEREST NOTES.	3 years	June 10, 1867, and May 15, 1868.	6 per cent, compound.	Par	400,000,000 00	17,250,000 00 / 177,045,770 00 / 22,728,390 00	708,500 00
TEN-FORTIES OF 1864.	10 or 40 years	March 1, 1874	5 per cent	Par	200,000,000 00	196,117,300 00	194,567,300 00
FIVE-TWENTIES OF MARCH, 1864.	5 or 20 years	November 1, 1869	6 per cent	Par		3,882,500 00	2,619,600 00

FIVE-TWENTIES OF JUNE, 1864.

The act of June 30, 1864, (13 Statutes, 218,) authorized a loan of $400,000,000, and the issue thereof or of bonds redeemable not less than five nor more than thirty (or forty, if deemed expedient) years from date, with interest at not exceeding 6 per centum per annum, payable semi-annually, in coin.

SEVEN-THIRTIES OF 1864 AND 1865.

The act of June 30, 1864, (13 Statutes, 218,) authorized the issue of $200,000,000 Treasury notes, of not less than $10 each, payable at not more than three years from date, or redeemable at any time after three years, with interest at not exceeding 7 3-10 per centum per annum. The act of March 3, 1865, (13 Statutes, 468,) authorized a loan of $600,000,000, and the issue therefor of bonds or Treasury notes. The notes to be of denominations not less than $50, with interest in lawful money at not more than 7 3-10 per centum per annum.

NAVY PENSION FUND.

The act of July 1, 1864, (13 Statutes, 414,) authorized the Secretary of the Navy to invest in registered securities of the United States so much of the Navy pension fund in the Treasury January 1 and July 1 in each year as would not be required for the payment of naval pensions. Section 2 of the act of July 23, 1866, (15 Statutes, 170,) makes the interest on this fund 3 per centum per annum in lawful money, and confines its use to the payment of naval pensions exclusively.

FIVE-TWENTIES OF 1865.

Description	Term	Date	Rate	Price		
FIVE-TWENTIES OF JUNE, 1864	5 or 20 years	November 1, 1869	6 per cent	Par	$125,561,300 00	$85,966,250 00
SEVEN-THIRTIES OF 1864 AND 1865	3 years	{ August 15, 1867. June 15, 1868. July 15, 1868. }	7 3-10 per cent	Par	$800,000,000 00	$29,992,500 00	452,800 00
NAVY PENSION FUND	Indefinite		3 per cent	Par	Indefinite	14,000,000 00	14,000,000 00

semi-annually, at not exceeding 6 per centum per annum, when in coin, or 7 3-10 per centum per annum in currency. In addition to the amount of bonds authorized by this act, authority was also given to convert Treasury notes or other interest-bearing obligations into bonds authorized by it. The act of April 12, 1866, (14 Statutes, 31,) construed the above act to authorize the Secretary of the Treasury to receive any obligation of the United States, whether bearing interest or not, in exchange for any bonds authorized by it, or to sell any of such bonds, provided the public debt is not increased thereby.

CONSOLS OF 1865.

The act of March 3, 1865, (13 Statutes, 468,) authorized the issue of $600,000,000 of bonds or Treasury notes in addition to amounts previously authorized; the bonds to be for not less than $50, payable not more than forty years from date of issue, or after any period not less than five years; interest payable semi-annually, at not exceeding 6 per centum per annum, when in coin, or 7 3-10 per centum per annum in currency. In addition to the amount of bonds authorized by this act, authority was also given to convert Treasury notes or other interest-bearing obligations into bonds authorized by it. The act of April 12, 1866, (14 Statutes, 31,) construed the above act to authorize the Secretary of the Treasury to receive any obligations of the United States, whether bearing interest or not, in exchange for any bonds authorized by it, or to sell any of such bonds, provided the public debt is not increased thereby.

CONSOLS OF 1867.

The act of March 3, 1865, (13 Statutes, 468,) authorized the issue of $600,000,000 of bonds or Treasury notes in addition to amounts previously authorized; the bonds to be for not less than $50, payable not more than forty years from date of issue, or after any period not less than five years; interest payable semi-annually, at not exceeding 6 per centum per annum, when in coin, or 7 3-10 per centum per annum in currency. In addition to the amount of bonds authorized by this act, authority was also given to convert Treasury notes or other interest-bearing obligations into bonds authorized by it. The act of April 12, 1866, (14 Statutes, 31,) construed the above act to authorize the Secretary of the

5 or 20 years	July 1, 1870	6 per cent	Par	332,998,950 00	332,998,950 00	242,583,150 00
5 or 20 years	July 1, 1872	6 per cent	Par	379,602,350 00	379,602,350 00	325,246,950 00

TABLE P.—*Statement of the public debt of the United States June 30, 1871—Continued.*

	Length of loan.	When redeemable.	Rate of interest.	Price at which sold.	Amount authorized.	Amount issued.	Amount outstanding.
Treasury to receive any obligation of the United States, whether bearing interest or not, in exchange for any bonds authorized by it, or to sell any of such bonds, provided the public debt is not increased thereby.							
CONSOLS OF 1868.							
The act of March 3, 1865, (13 Statutes, 468,) authorized the issue of $600,000,000 of bonds or Treasury notes in addition to amounts previously authorized; the bonds to be for not less than $50, payable not more than forty years from the date of issue, or after any period not less than five years; interest payable semi-annually, at not exceeding 6 per centum per annum, when in coin, or 7 3-10 per centum per annum, when in currency. In addition to the amount of bonds authorized by this act, authority was also given to convert Treasury notes or other interest-bearing obligations into bonds authorized by it. The act of April 12, 1866, (14 Statutes, 31,) construed the above act to authorize the Secretary of the Treasury to receive any obligation of the United States, whether bearing interest or not, in exchange for any bonds authorized by it, or to sell any of such bonds, provided the public debt is not increased thereby.	5 or 20 years	July 1, 1873	6 per cent	Par	$42,539,350 00	$42,539,350 00	$39,418,950 00
THREE PER CENT. CERTIFICATES.							
The act of March 3, 1867, (14 Statutes, 558,) authorized the issue of $50,000,000 in temporary loan certificates of deposit, with interest at 3 per centum per annum, payable in lawful money on demand, to be used in redemption of compound-interest notes. The act of July 25, 1868, (15 Statutes, 183,) authorized $25,000,000 additional of these certificates for the sole purpose of redeeming compound-interest notes.	Indefinite	On demand	3 per cent	Par	75,000,000 00	84,945,000 00	31,883,000 00

the Mexican war, or scrip, at the option of the soldiers, to bear 6 per centum interest per annum, redeemable at the pleasure of the Government, by notice from the Treasury Department. Interest ceases July 1, 1849.

CERTIFICATES OF INDEBTEDNESS OF 1870.

The act of July 8, 1870, (16 Statutes, 197,) authorized the issue of certificates of indebtedness to refund the interest paid by the State of Massachusetts on money expended by her on account of the war of 1812–'15, payable in lawful money, with four per centum interest per annum, payable semi-annually.

5 years	September 1, 1876	4 per cent	Par	678,362 41	678,362 41	678,000 00

FUNDED LOAN OF 1881.

The act of July 14, 1870, (16 Statutes, 272,) authorizes the issue of $200,000,000 at 5 per centum, $300,000,000 at 4½ per centum, and $1,000,000,000 at 4 per centum, principal and interest payable in coin of the present standard value, at the pleasure of the United States Government, after ten years, for the 5 per cents; after fifteen years, for the 4½ per cents; and after thirty years, for the 4 per cents; these bonds to be exempt from the payment of all taxes or duties of the United States, as well as from taxation in any form, by or under State, municipal, or local authority. Bonds and coupons payable at the Treasury of the United States. This act not to authorize an increase of the bonded debt of the United States. Bonds to be sold at not less than par in coin, and the proceeds to be applied to the redemption of outstanding 5-20's, or to be exchanged for said 5-20's, par for par. Payment of these bonds, when due, to be made in order of dates and numbers, beginning with each class last dated and numbered. Interest to cease at the end of three months from notice of intention to redeem. The act of January 20, 1871, (16 Statutes, 399,) increases the amount of 5 per cents to $500,000,000, provided the total amount of bonds issued shall not exceed the amount originally authorized, and authorizes the interest on any of these bonds to be paid quarterly.

	5 per cent				59,669,150 00

	2,353,211,332 32

TABLE Q.—*Statement of 30-year 6 per cent. bonds (interest payable January and July) issued to the several Pacific Railway companies, under the acts of July 1, 1862, (12 Statutes, 492,) and July 2, 1864, (13 Statutes, 359.)*

Name of company.	Amount of bonds outstanding.	Amount of interest accrued and paid up to date, as per preceding statement.	Amount of interest due, as per Register's schedule.	Total interest paid by the United States.	Repayment of interest by transportation of mails, troops, &c.	Balance due the United States on interest account, deducting repayments.	Balance of accrued interest due the United States on interest account.	Total amount of interest due the United States from Pacific Railway companies.
On July 1, 1865.								
Central Pacific	$1,258,000 00		$37,740 00	$37,740 00				$37,740 00
Kansas Pacific								
Union Pacific								
Central Branch, Union Pacific								
Western Pacific								
Sioux City and Pacific								
	1,258,000 00		37,740 00	37,740 00				37,740 00
On January 1, 1866:								
Central Pacific	2,362,000 00	$37,740 00	55,056 83	92,796 83				92,796 83
Kansas Pacific	640,000 00		6,417 53	6,417 53				6,417 53
Union Pacific								
Central Branch, Union Pacific								
Western Pacific								
Sioux City and Pacific								
	3,002,000 00	37,740 00	61,474 36	99,214 36				99,214 36

Roads.							
Western Pacific							
Sioux City and Pacific							
	11,002,000 00	235,327 04	274,879 74	510,206 78		510,206 78	510,206 78
On July 1, 1867.							
Central Pacific	4,602,000 00	257,803 37	136,534 50	424,337 87	22,849 07	401,488 80	401,488 80
Kansas Pacific	3,360,000 00	94,630 03	78,654 29	173,285 22	27,444 40	145,840 82	145,840 82
Union Pacific	5,590,000 00	117,072 74	147,820 87	265,499 61		265,499 61	265,499 61
Central Branch Union Pacific	960,000 00	10,099 74	22,408 75	32,508 49		32,508 49	32,508 49
Western Pacific	330,000 00		8,206 03	6,206 03		8,206 03	8,206 03
Sioux City and Pacific							
	14,762,000 00	510,206 78	393,630 44	903,837 22	50,293 47	853,543 75	853,543 75
On January 1, 1868.							
Central Pacific	6,074,000 00	424,337 87	145,613 83	569,951 70	20,899 07	540,052 03	540,052 03
Kansas Pacific	4,380,000 00	173,285 22	122,580 26	295,865 48	148,935 26	146,930 22	146,930 22
Union Pacific	8,100,000 00	265,499 61	210,563 28	476,061 89	249,191 98	226,809 91	226,809 91
Central Branch Union Pacific	1,280,000 00	32,508 49	30,325 50	62,833 99		62,833 99	62,833 99
Western Pacific	320,000 00	6,206 03	9,600 00	17,806 03		17,806 03	17,806 03
Sioux City and Pacific							
	20,714,000 00	903,837 22	518,681 87	1,422,519 09	428,026 31	994,492 78	994,492 78
On July 1, 1868.							
Central Pacific	7,020,000 00	569,951 70	185,041 16	755,592 86	36,949 07	718,643 79	718,643 79
Kansas Pacific	6,080,000 00	295,865 48	163,258 16	461,123 64	266,367 71	194,755 03	194,755 03
Union Pacific	12,957,000 00	476,061 89	288,593 66	764,655 75	324,853 03	243,802 72	243,802 72
Central Branch Union Pacific	1,600,000 00	62,833 99	46,974 27	109,808 26		109,808 26	109,808 26
Western Pacific	320,000 00	17,806 03	9,600 00	27,406 03		27,406 03	27,406 03
Sioux City and Pacific	1,112,000 00	19,603 76	19,603 76	19,603 76		19,603 76	19,603 76
	29,089,000 00	1,422,519 09	715,671 21	2,138,190 30	828,169 81	1,314,020 49	1,314,020 49
On January 1, 1869.							
Central Pacific	10,684,000 00	755,592 86	347,193 73	1,102,786 59	946,158 10	1,056,628 40	1,056,628 40
Kansas Pacific	6,303,000 00	645,723 09	194,599 45	645,723 09	388,406 97	277,316 12	277,316 12
Union Pacific	24,073,000 00	764,655 75	549,109 77	1,313,765 52	719,214 87	594,550 65	594,550 65
Central Branch Union Pacific	1,600,000 00	109,808 26	46,000 00	157,808 26		157,808 26	157,808 26
Western Pacific	320,000 00	27,406 03	9,600 00	37,006 03		37,006 03	37,006 03
Sioux City and Pacific	1,112,000 00	19,603 76	33,360 00	52,963 76	16 27	52,947 49	52,947 49
	50,097,000 00	2,138,190 30	1,171,862 95	3,310,053 25	1,133,706 21	2,176,257 04	2,176,257 04
On July 1, 1869.							
Central Pacific	22,789,000 00	1,102,785 59	616,429 59	1,719,216 18	72,666 99	1,646,540 19	1,646,540 19
Kansas Pacific	6,303,000 00	645,723 09	189,090 00	534,813 09	546,509 10	288,243 99	288,243 99
Union Pacific	25,998,000 00	1,313,765 52	768,104 37	2,081,860 89	906,446 11	1,175,423 78	1,175,423 78
Central Branch, Union Pacific	1,600,000 00	157,808 26	43,000 00	205,808 25	3,490 79	202,317 47	202,317 47

TABLE Q.—*Statement of 30-year 6 per cent. bonds (interest payable January and July) issued to the several Pacific Railway companies, &c.*—Continued.

Name of company.	Amount of bonds outstanding.	Amount of interest accrued and paid to date, as per preceding statement.	Amount of interest due, as per Register's schedule.	Total interest paid by the United States.	Repayment of interest est by transportation of mails, troops, &c.	Balance due the United States on interest account, deducting repayments.	Balance of accrued interest due the United States on interest account.	Total amount of interest due from the United States to the Pacific Railway companies.
On July 1, 1869.								
Western Pacific	$320,000 00	$37,006 03	$9,600 00	$46,606 03		$46,606 03		$46,606 03
Sioux City and Pacific	1,628,320 00	52,963 76	43,544 93	96,508 69		96,492 42		96,492 42
	58,638,320 00	3,310,053 25	1,674,768 89	4,984,822 14	1,529,186 26	3,455,632 88		3,455,632 88
On January 1, 1870.								
Central Pacific	$25,881,000 00	$1,719,216 18	$772,528 08	$2,491,744 26	$116,765 86	$2,374,978 40		$2,374,978 40
Kansas Pacific	6,303,000 00	634,813 89	189,090 00	1,023,903 09	631,224 39	392,678 10		392,678 10
Union Pacific	27,075,000 00	2,681,869 89	209,859 96	2,891,729 85	1,107,427 54	1,784,302 31		1,784,302 31
Central Branch, Union Pacific	1,600,000 00	205,808 26	48,000 00	253,808 26	5,301 92	248,506 34		248,506 34
Western Pacific	1,548,000 00	73,288 76	26,682 73	73,288 76		73,288 76		73,288 76
Sioux City and Pacific	1,628,320 00	96,508 69	48,849 60	145,358 29	353 13	145,005 16		145,005 16
	64,135,320 00	4,964,822 14	1,895,010 37	6,879,832 51	1,861,073 44	5,018,759 07		5,018,759 07
On July 1, 1870.								
Central Pacific	$25,881,000 00	$2,491,744 26	$770,023 58	$3,261,767 84	$164,054 13	$3,097,713 67	$155,730 40	$3,253,444 07
Kansas Pacific	6,303,000 00	1,023,903 09	189,090 00	1,212,993 09	684,359 12	528,633 97	28,717 58	557,351 55
Union Pacific	27,075,000 00	2,891,729 85	821,641 20	3,713,371 05	1,289,576 67	2,423,794 18	67,767 69	2,491,561 87
Central Branch, Union Pacific	1,600,000 00	253,808 26	46,000 00	301,808 26	7,401 92	294,406 34	17,857 43	312,263 77
Western Pacific	1,970,000 00	73,288 76	57,908 60	131,197 36		131,197 36	4,274 71	135,472 07
Sioux City and Pacific	1,628,320 00	145,358 29	48,849 60	194,207 89	396 08	193,811 81	5,154 20	198,966 01
	64,457,320 00	6,879,832 51	1,935,512 98	8,815,345 49	2,145,788 16	6,669,557 33	279,502 01	6,949,059 34
On January 1, 1871.								
Central Pacific	$25,881,000 00	$3,261,767 84	$776,430 00	$4,038,197 84	$241,638 70	$3,796,559 14	$326,995 81	$4,123,554 95
Kansas Pacific	6,303,000 00	1,212,993 09	180,090 00	1,402,083 09	768,148 66	633,934 43	56,879 25	690,813 08

On July 1, 1871.								
Central Pacific	$25,881,000 00	$4,038,197 84	$776,430 00	$4,814,627 84	$343,266 90	$4,471,360 94	$949,753 57	$4,921,114 51
Kansas Pacific	6,303,000 00	1,402,083 09	180,090 00	1,591,173 09	857,330 93	733,842 16	76,932 82	810,774 98
Union Pacific	27,236,512 00	4,530,466 41	817,095 36	5,347,561 77	*1,755,303 15	3,592,258 62	269,874 27	3,862,132 89
Central Branch, Union Pacific	1,600,000 00	340,806 26	. 48,000 00	397,808 28	9,276 92	388,531 34	46,725 32	435,256 66
Western Pacific	1,970,000 00	190,297 36	59,100 00	249,397 36	8,281 25	241,116 11	16,376 52	257,492 63
Sioux City and Pacific	1,628,320 00	243,057 49	48,840 60	291,907 09	401 88	291,506 21	23,515 13	315,020 34
	64,618,833 00	10,753,910 45	1,938,564 96	12,692,475 41	2,973,861 03	9,718,614 38	903,177 63	10,621,792 01

This amount exceeds by $14,786 12 the accounts in Register's office, owing to the fact that the warrant crediting this amount passed the Secretary's office on the 30th June, 1871, and was included in the accounts of that year in that office. This warrant did not reach the Register until the July following, and therefore does not appear in the accounts of the latter office until the next year.

TABLE R.—*Returns, by award of the United States Court of Claims, of proceeds of property seized as captured or abandoned under the act of March 12, 1863, paid from July 1, 1870, to June 30, 1871.*

Date.	To whom paid.	Amount.
July 8, 1870	Leonard Wagner	$1,499 60
July 8, 1870	Jacob Mills	1,014 56
July 8, 1870	John L. Fenwick	533 65
July 8, 1870	Mary McManus	507 28
July 8, 1870	H. W. Dorre and A. Seckendorf	887 74
July 8, 1870	Tobias Scott	253 64
July 8, 1870	Henry Steitz	3,201 15
July 19, 1870	James Heagney	2,317 98
July 19, 1870	Joseph A. Sasportas	1,807 18
July 19, 1870	John Thompson and William Robb	2,409 58
July 19, 1870	Frederick Jaeger	4,945 98
July 19, 1870	David L. Mathews	126 82
July 19, 1870	Christian Amme	887 74
July 19, 1870	William Grant	507 28
July 19, 1870	William A. Rook	2,029 12
July 19, 1870	Daniel McSwiney	253 64
July 19, 1870	Catherine Martin	873 14
July 19, 1870	Samuel S. Miller	993 42
July 19, 1870	Albert Van Dohlen	380 46
July 19, 1870	Harriet A. Chaves	2,394 36
July 19, 1870	Ellen Higgins	7,616 22
July 19, 1870	Charles Schwarz	496 71
July 19, 1870	George Ott	1,821 27
July 19, 1870	Thomas Price	993 42
July 19, 1870	Jacob Rosenfeld	3,311 40
July 19, 1870	Jacob Rosenband	6,454 51
July 19, 1870	Robert Williams	6,622 90
July 19, 1870	Bridget Logan	10,202 66
July 19, 1870	Ellen M. Kennedy	225 52
July 19, 1870	Tobias Brown	3,311 40
July 20, 1870	Margaret Mangen	1,324 56
July 22, 1870	Robert H. Barney	426 74
July 22, 1870	Moses Vanderhorst	634 10
July 22, 1870	John Burns	126 82
July 27, 1870	Martin O'Donnell	634 10
July 28, 1870	John Fitzgerald	676 59
August 1, 1870	Asa Faulkner	2,301 15
August 3, 1870	S. Alexander Smith	8,927 82
August 9, 1870	Nicholas Culliton	1,004 10
August 10, 1870	Lazarus Kohn	5,172 88
August 12, 1870	S. Alexander Smith	4,298 58
August 12, 1870	Rudolph Lobsiger	887 74
August 23, 1870	James Melvin	253 64
August 24, 1870	Ephraim Zacharias	4,801 53
August 24, 1870	August Geilfuss	4,071 20
August 27, 1870	F. Furman and G. Searight	10,421 71
September 5, 1870	John Spain	1,108 95
September 27, 1870	William M. Lowry	419 14
September 29, 1870	Antonio Ponce	5,583 73
October 1, 1870	Martin Caulfield	553 56
October 1, 1870	Francis Perry	253 64
October 11, 1870	Mary Dallas	887 74
October 13, 1870	Mina Berg	11,258 76
October 14, 1870	Warren M. Benton	34,625 79
November 28, 1870	Henry A. Eaier	19,681 92
December 1, 1870	Frederick M. Scharfer	1,570 72
December 16, 1870	B. Ogle Tayloe's executors	10,435 43
December 27, 1870	Horace B. Tebbetts	19,225 24
January 3, 1871	Erastus S. Foster	12,305 72
February 4, 1871	Isaac Bernheimer et als	186,692 36
March 4, 1871	Charles Findley	2,767 16
April 12, 1871	Warren M. Benton	1,113 21
May 9, 1871	Louis Robider	1,986 84
May 15, 1871	Hebrew Congregation	1,158 99
May 17, 1871	Michael Lynch	8,102 22
May 19, 1871	James O'Keeffe	1,655 70
May 19, 1871	Thomas R. Mills et als	123,846 36
May 25, 1871	James Kilduff	25,229 70
May 27, 1871	Frederick Schuster	45,334 84
May 27, 1871	Diedrick Muller	4,197 08
May 29, 1871	James G. Mills	7,450 65
June 5, 1871	Alfred Abrams	126 82
June 6, 1871	Alexander Stoddart	21,031 70
June 12, 1871	Ferdinand Brown	2,090 01
June 15, 1871	Christian L. Blaize	1,141 38
June 15, 1871	Robert Cattel	380 46
June 20, 1871	George F. Drew	33,114 00

TABLE R.—*Returns, by award of the United States Court of Claims, &c.*—Continued.

Date.	To whom paid.	Amount.
June 20, 1871	William D. Oliveira and Ellen M. Oliveira	$662 28
June 22, 1871	William G. Wyly and James G. Wyly	20,124 10
June 23, 1871	James McDonald	662 28
June 24, 1871	Richard Harrison	760 92
June 24, 1871	George I. Holmes	253 64
June 24, 1871	Henry Behrens	507 28
June 24, 1871	Daniel Sinclair	1,014 56
June 26, 1871	Lazarus Strauss	5,463 81
Total		730 889 78

TABLE S.—*Awards of the United States Court of Claims of proceeds of property seized as captured or abandoned, under act of March 12, 1863, decreed but not paid during the fiscal year ending June 30, 1871.*

Date of decree.	Name of claimant.	Amount awarded.
November 20, 1870	Maximilian A. Dauphin	$17,869 92
February 20, 1871	Ramon Molina	4,207 95
February 27, 1871	Philip Dzialynski and Davis Greenfield	36,076 33
March 13, 1871	Ann Worthington, administratrix	165,673 42
March 20, 1871	Michael Gordon	1,051 98
March 20, 1871	William Duggan	175 33
March 20, 1871	Terence Nugent, jr	2,273 34
March 27, 1871	Edward Laplante	112,650 25
March 27, 1871	Lewis Fried	5,491 69
March 27, 1871	Thomasine B. Hoyt and James M. Latta	8,017 33
April 10, 1871	Francis J. Ruekh	713 92
April 10, 1871	George Taylor and William Tipper	8,766 50
April 10, 1871	Henry Wurzburg and Simon Witkouski	60,138 19
April 17, 1871	Jacob Cohen	2,805 28
April 24, 1871	Lewis Ross	1,218 59
April 24, 1871	Charles and Margaret Schubert	673 50
April 24, 1871	Richard Kelly, administrator	808 20
April 24, 1871	James A. Seddon	45,300 43
April 24, 1871	Patrick Kennedy	465 13
April 24, 1871	William T. Porter	4,168 06
April 24, 1871	Charlotte M. E. Gallie	20,338 28
May 1, 1871	Michael Boley	1,227 31
May 1, 1871	Frederick Chastenet	2,968 71
May 1, 1871	Joanna Moulton	2,075 00
May 2, 1871	Lapéne and Ferré	34,368 00
May 8, 1871	Benjamin Mantoue	9,823 12
May 15, 1871	David and Thomas Harrison	54,176 97
May 15, 1871	Stephen Watson	73,638 60
May 22, 1871	Daniel Haas	12,123 00
May 22, 1871	Louis de Bebian	16,833 55
May 22, 1871	William J. Myers & Co	52,949 66
May 26, 1871	Mary A. Cherrill	1,077 60
May 26, 1871	Alexander and Hugh C. Lecky	2,293 69
May 26, 1871	Francis T. Willis	23,404 22
May 26, 1871	Ake Henry	12,345 75
May 26, 1871	James Mix	5,378 27
May 26, 1871	Rebecca A. Minor, executrix	20,481 71
May 26, 1871	Max Levy	4,863 63
May 26, 1871	James S. Rhodes, administrator	5.371 53
Total		835,283 86

REPORT OF COMMISSIONER OF INTERNAL REVENUE.

REPORT

OF

THE COMMISSIONER OF INTERNAL REVENUE.

TREASURY DEPARTMENT,
OFFICE OF INTERNAL REVENUE,
Washington, November 21, 1871.

SIR : During the fiscal year covered by the following report Hon.
C. Delano was Commissioner from July 1 to November 1, 1870, and
Hon. A. Pleasonton from January 3 to its close. During November
and December, 1870, and until January 3, 1871, I was Acting Commissioner by reason of the vacancy caused by the resignation of Mr. Delano.

I have the honor to transmit herewith the tabular statements made
up from the accounts of this office, which the Secretary of the Treasury is required to lay before Congress, as follows :

Table A, showing the receipts from each specific source of revenue
and the amounts refunded in each collection district, State, and Territory of the United States for the fiscal year ended June 30, 1871.

Table B, showing the number and value of internal revenue stamps
ordered monthly by the Commissioner, the receipts from the sale of
stamps and the commissions allowed on the same; also the number and
value of stamps for tobacco, cigars, snuff, distilled spirits, and fermented
liquors, issued monthly to collectors during the fiscal year ended June
30, 1871.

Table C, showing the territorial distribution of internal revenue from
various sources in the United States for the fiscal years ended June
30, 1864, 1865, 1866, 1867, 1868, 1869, 1870, and 1871.

Table D, showing the aggregate receipts from each collection district,
State, and Territory for the fiscal years ended June 30, 1863, 1864,
1865, 1866, 1867, 1868, 1869, 1870, and 1871.

Table E, showing the total collections from each specific source of
revenue for the fiscal years ended June 30, 1863, 1864, 1865, 1866, 1867,
1868, 1869, 1870, and 1871.

Table F, showing the ratio of receipts from specific sources to the
aggregate of all collections for the fiscal years ended June 30, 1864,
1865, 1866, 1867, 1868, 1869, 1870, and 1871.

Table G, an abstract of reports of district attorneys concerning suits
and prosecutions under the internal revenue laws during the fiscal year
ended June 30, 1871.

Table H, an abstract of seizures of property for violation of internal
revenue laws during the fiscal year ended June 30, 1871.

Table I, showing the number of proof-gallons of spirits in each collection district, State, and Territory in the United States, exclusive of
the quantity in internal revenue warehouses, May 1, 1871.

These tables exhibit the full result of the operations of this Bureau
from its organization to the present time.

The aggregate receipts from all sources, exclusive of the direct tax upon lands, and the duty upon the circulation and deposits of national banks, were, for the fiscal year 1871, $144,011,176 24. This sum includes the amounts refunded and allowed on drawbacks.

Drawbacks have been allowed on general merchandise, under section 171, act of June 30, 1864, limited by the act of March 31, 1868, amounting to $22,887 97. This amount is larger than that allowed for the fiscal year 1870, on account of the adjudication of old claims for drawback on cotton goods rendered admissible by joint resolution No. 78, approved July 14, 1870.

There was refunded during the past fiscal year, for taxes illegally assessed and collected, the sum of $617,581 07. This large increase over the year preceding was due to the adjustment of claims that had been suspended during former years, for more complete consideration ; for instance, the claim of one of the States which was embraced in the above aggregate, and amounting to $45,866, for taxes collected on dividends declared upon stock owned by the State. This was the largest claim ever allowed by the Bureau, and was referred to the Attorney General for his advice.

My estimate of the receipts for the current fiscal year under the present law is $125,000,000.

SPIRITS.

The number of distilleries (other than fruit) registered during the last fiscal year was 1, 043
Number of fruit-distilleries registered 7, 149

    Total 8, 192

Of the distilleries (other than fruit) 517 were operated during the year, and of the fruit-distilleries, 4,007.

The returns to this office for the last fiscal year show a total production in taxable gallons, from material other than fruit, of 54, 576, 446
From fruit 2, 199, 733

    Total yearly production 56, 776, 179

The following tabular statement shows the distribution of distilleries in the various States and Territories:

Statement showing the number of distilleries registered and operated during the fiscal year ended June 30, 1871.

States and Territories.	Grain.		Molasses.		Fruit.		Total number registered.	Total number operated.
	No. registered.	No. operated.	No. registered.	No. operated.	No. registered.	No. operated.		
Alabama	9	1			75	8	84	9
Arkansas	2	1			40	1	42	2
California	11	6	1		341	150	353	156
Connecticut	6	5			170	133	176	138
Delaware	1				70	67	71	67
Georgia	2	1			347	209	349	210
Idaho	2	1					2	1
Illinois	54	54			48	14	102	68
Indiana	32	26			213	56	245	82
Iowa	21	3			13		34	3
Kansas	5	3					5	3
Kentucky	262	128			673	406	935	534
Louisiana	16	2	10		1		27	2
Maine			1	1			1	1
Maryland	36	9	2		83	8	121	17
Massachusetts	2	2	8	8	54	48	64	58
Michigan	3	2					3	2
Minnesota	4	1					4	1
Mississippi	7	1			6		13	1
Missouri	36	13			129	7	165	20
Montana	2	2					2	2
Nebraska	2	2					2	2
Nevada	1						1	
New Hampshire			1		2	2	3	2
New Jersey	5	3			223	136	227	139
New Mexico	1				9	1	10	1
New York	75	18	2	2	132	86	209	106
North Carolina	18	6			1,757	1,218	1,775	1,224
Ohio	84	65			88	42	172	113
Oregon	3				5	2	8	2
Pennsylvania	180	95	2		74	47	256	142
Rhode Island			1	1			1	1
South Carolina	5				67	53	72	53
Tennessee	48	22			524	380	572	402
Texas	5				16		21	
Utah	1	1					1	1
Vermont					14	8	14	8
Virginia	50	21			1,795	864	1,845	885
Washington	4	1					4	1
West Virginia	7	2			181	55	188	57
Wisconsin	13	8					13	8
Total	1,015	505	28	12	7,149	4,007	8,192	4,524

Gallons.

The quantity of spirits in bond July 1, 1870, was 11,671,886
The quantity entered in bond for the year ended June 30, 1871, was 54,576,446
The quantity withdrawn from bond during last period, was 59,503,972
The quantity remaining in bond June 30, 1871, was...................... 6,744,360
The quantity remaining in bond July 1, 1870, as per present report, less than
quantity stated in the report for 1870, shown by corrected reports of collectors received subsequent to the publication of the report for 1870 was.. 10,572

The total quantity of spirits in the United States, not in internal revenue warehouses, on the 1st of May, 1871, was 41,185,713 proof-gallons, showing a decrease in the quantity on the market since November 15, 1870, of 4,452,580 gallons.

The receipts from spirits for the fiscal year ended June 30, 1871, were as follows:

Spirits distilled from apples, grapes, and peaches.................... $1,236,005 67
Spirits distilled from materials other than apples, grapes, and peaches. 29,921,308 48
Distilleries, per diem tax on.. 1,901,602 98
Distillers' special and barrel tax...................................... 5,683,077 31
Rectifiers 959,800 18
Dealers, retail liquor... 3,651,484 73
Dealers, wholesale liquor.. 2,151,281 06

4 F

Manufacturers of stills, (special tax)	$1,927	49
Stills or worms, manufactured	3,240	00
Stamps, warehouse, rectifiers' and wholesale liquor dealers'	758,427	00
Excess of gaugers' fees	13,693	20
Total	46,281,848	10

SURVEYS OF DISTILLERIES.

Uniformity in estimating the spirit-producing capacity of distilleries being indispensable to a just and equal assessment of the tax, a classification of distilleries has been arrived at, based upon the different kinds of material used and the modes of operating; and rules have been given for estimating the capacity of each class, which experience has shown to be equally just to the Government and the distillers.

The local surveyors having been thoroughly instructed in their duties, the expense of making surveys will be materially lessened in the future.

SPIRIT-METERS.

By the annual report for 1870, page 7, it will be seen that Tice's Sample Meters, theretofore adopted and prescribed for use in distilleries, were then being tested for the purpose of determining their utility. The period within which distillers were required to procure meters was extended from time to time until the 8th day of June, 1871, when Circular No. 96 was issued discontinuing their use.

GAUGING INSTRUMENTS.

Correctness and uniformity in the weighing and gauging of spirits are necessary to a just collection of the tax and to avoid unnecessary detention of spirits in transit. These objects can only be attained by the use of instruments of the same standard.

To accomplish these objects, in addition to the hydrometer prescribed for use in 1867, there has been adopted what is known as the "Prime and McKean's Combination Gauging Rod," which is required to be used for determining the capacity of casks.

To secure accuracy in these instruments, arrangements have been made by which all hydrometers and gauging rods are inspected and tested in this office before being sent out for use.

Internal revenue gaugers are furnished with hydrometers at the expense of the Government, but are required to supply themselves with the combination rod at their own expense.

These instruments, distributed under the present system of inspection, seem to give general satisfaction, and their accuracy and uniformity have relieved the trade of the embarrassments resulting from errors in gauging.

FERMENTED LIQUORS.

The amount of tax received on fermented liquors at $1 per barrel was, for the years—

1866	$5,115,140 49	1869	$5,866,400 96
1867	5,819,345 49	1870	6,081,520 54
1868	5,685,663 70	1871	7,159,740 20

The increase for the year 1871, as shown in the above statement, is believed to be due, in part at least, to the greater attention given to that subject by internal revenue officers during that year. ' This attention has revealed some defects in the law, which call for early remedial legislation.

TOBACCO.

The total receipts from tobacco for the fiscal year ended June 30, 1871, were $33,578,907 18. As compared with the receipts from the same source for the preceding fiscal year, the accompanying tables show the following results:

Year ended June 30, 1871, tobacco, chewing, &c., and snuff	$20,677,717 84
Year ended June 30, 1870, tobacco, chewing, &c., and snuff	19,708,780 61
Showing an increase in class 32-cents of	968,937 23
Year ended June 30, 1871, tobacco, smoking, scraps, shorts, &c	$4,882,821 83
Year ended June 30, 1870, tobacco, smoking, scraps, shorts, &c	4,591,702 81
Showing an increase in class 16-cents of	291,119 02
Year ended June 30, 1871, cigars, cheroots, &c	$6,598,173 24
Year ended June 30, 1870, cigars, cheroots, &c	5,718,780 04
Showing an increase on cigars, &c., of	879,393 20
Year ended June 30, 1871, received from sale of export stamps	$66,147 00
Year ended June 30, 1870, received from sale of export stamps	48,097 50
Increase from sale of export stamps	18,049 50
Year ended June 30, 1871, received from dealers in leaf-tobacco	$221,661 98
Year ended June 30, 1870, received from dealers in leaf-tobacco	200,205 54
Increased collection from dealers in leaf-tobacco	21,456 44
Year ended June 30, 1871, from dealers in manufactured tobacco	$970,017 96
Year ended June 30, 1870, from dealers in manufactured tobacco	929,892 64
Increased collection from dealers in manufactured tobacco	40,125 32
Year ended June 30, 1871, from special taxes of tobacco and cigar manufacturers	$162,367 33
Year ended June 30, 1870, from special taxes of tobacco and cigar manufacturers	153,248 74
Increased collection from special taxes of tobacco and cigar manufacturers	9,118 59

Showing a total increase of $2,228,199 30 over the total amount of receipts from the same sources for the preceding fiscal year.

ANNUAL PRODUCTION.

The total amount of manufactured tobacco, represented by the amount of collections for the fiscal year ended June 30, 1871, was as follows:

	Pounds.
Chewing-tobacco, snuff, &c., class 32-cents	64,617,868
Smoking-tobacco, scraps, shorts, &c., class 16-cents	30,517,636
Add to this the quantity exported	10,621,082
And excess remaining in warehouses June 30, 1871, over June 30, 1870	72,377
Giving a total product for the year, of	105,828,963

The total number of cigars, cheroots, &c., on which taxes were collected, was 1,332,844,357.

The steady and uniform increase, from month to month, in the revenues derived from manufactured tobacco, cigars, &c., since the present law went into operation, by which the mode of collecting taxes on these articles was changed from an assessment after removal from the manufactory and sale, to a prepayment, by means of suitable stamps, before the goods are removed from the place of manufacture, has fully demonstrated the superiority of the present system over the former. Fewer frauds are possible where the taxes are required to be paid at the manufactory, and before the goods are allowed to go upon the market, and where every package is required to bear upon it the evidence that the tax has been paid. But, notwithstanding the encouraging progress that has been made toward a thorough and complete collection of the revenues from this source, I am forced to the conclusion that, during the last fiscal year, much tobacco has escaped taxation through the refilling of empty stamped packages, the second use of stamps, the use of counterfeit stamps, the removal of small quantities from the place of manufacture without stamps, and stamping as class 16-cents, tobacco which, under the law, should have been stamped at the rate of 32 cents per pound.

UNIFORM RATE OF TAX.

The present law imposes on all chewing-tobacco a tax of 32 cents per pound, and the same rate on all smoking-tobacco from which any portion of the stems has been removed. But practically *all* smoking-tobacco, with slight exceptions, is claimed to be taxable only at the rate of 16 cents, and no one except the manufacturer knows or can know whether it contains all the stems which are natural to the leaf, or a less quantity. The natural leaf, cut with all the stems in, is, previous to being so cut, put through a process of sweetening, to fit it for chewing purposes, thus making it actually chewing-tobacco, though sold under the name of smoking-tobacco and stamped class 16-cents. By the manipulations of some manufacturers the fine-cut shorts, " which have passed through a riddle of 36 meshes to the square inch by process of sifting," constitute the bulk of their products and are used as chewing-tobacco, though paying a tax of only 16 cents per pound, while sweetened scraps, a product of plug manufacturers, are put up in large quantities and sold under the 16-cent tax for chewing purposes. A uniform rate of tax, while it would allow every manufacturer to manipulate his products in his own way without restrictions being placed upon his modes of manufacturing, would effectually close the door to the perpetration of fraud or the evasion of taxes by their improper classifications.

RESULTS OF A UNIFORM TAX AT DIFFERENT RATES.

From the tables presented in this report it will be seen that more than two-thirds of the manufactured tobacco which reached taxation during the last fiscal year paid the tax of 32 cents per pound, yielding four-fifths of the revenue which was collected directly from the article by stamps. Had a tax been collected at a uniform rate of 32 cents per pound on the entire product of manufactured tobacco which reached taxation during the last fiscal year, the receipts therefrom would have been $30,443,361 28. Adding to this sum the taxes collected on cigars, the special taxes of manufacturers of tobacco and cigars, of dealers in leaf, and dealers in manufactured tobacco, &c., the total receipts would have been $38,461,728 79. Similar calculations show that a uniform tax of 24 cents per pound on the same quantity would have realized the sum of $30,850,888 47, and that a uniform rate of 16 cents per pound would have realized the sum of $23,240,048 15. Thus, it will be seen that on the assumption that the same number of pounds would have reached taxation had the rate of tax been uniform, either at 16, 24, or 32 cents per pound, a uniform rate of 32 cents would have increased the revenue by the sum of $4,882,821 61, while a uniform rate of 24 or 16 cents would have diminished those receipts in the sums respectively of $2,728,018 71 and $10,338,859 03. I am aware that it is contended by those who advocate a reduction of the tax to a uniform rate of 16 cents per pound that the increased consumption which would result from such a reduction, and the greater number of pounds which would reach taxation, would nearly, if not quite, compensate for the reduction in the rate. I am unable, however, to see any well-grounded reason for such a conclusion—first, because such a reduction would have little, if any, tendency to increase the consumption of smoking tobacco, as nearly all smoking-tobacco now pays but 16 cents tax; secondly, such a reduction alone would not tend to diminish the quantity of raw or leaf tobacco consumed, for most of the leaf-tobacco sold directly to consumers is used for smoking purposes, and the motive to smoke untaxed leaf would not be removed or lessened by diminishing the tax on chewing-tobacco; thirdly, because whatever increase in consumption there might be from such a reduction in the rate must necessarily be of chewing-tobacco, of plug, twist, fine-cut, &c., and of snuff, and of these the consumption would have to be doubled, making it one hundred and twenty-eight millions of pounds, where it is now only sixty-four millions of pounds, in order to obtain the same amount of revenue as was collected the last fiscal year. Such an increase in the consumption of chewing tobacco is not to be expected.

My own opinion is, that with the tax at 24 cents, taking into account the natural increase of the revenue as shown between the collections of succeeding years, and with the advantage of some legislation hereinafter recommended, we shall be able to keep the collections on tobacco up to those under the present rates.

This recommendation, however, is made without regard to its relation to future total revenue results. If it should be the opinion of Congress that the yield of revenue from internal taxes should not be materially decreased, then, to accomplish the desirable results expected from a consolidation of the tax on tobacco, and to compensate in part to the revenue the expected large loss from the expiration of the income-tax during the current fiscal year, and the further material loss from "Articles and occupations formerly taxed but now exempt," (a rapidly decreasing item, of course,) I would advise a consolidation of the tobacco tax at 32 cents per pound.

PEDDLERS OF TOBACCO.

I am satisfied, from the evidence which has accumulated at this office, that much of the fraud above-referred-to is effected through the instrumentality of peddlers.

In order to put an end to this illicit traffic some additional legislation is required. I would, therefore, recommend that every person who sells or offers to sell manufactured tobacco, snuff, or cigars from wagons in the manner of peddlers traveling from place to place, be required to pay a special tax of fifteen, twenty-five, or fifty dollars, according as they travel with one, two, or more horses or mules, and to comply with such regulations as may be prescribed by the Commissioner of Internal Revenue.

SALE OF LEAF-TOBACCO TO CONSUMERS.

For the last three years this office has been in possession of information that a large and increasing amount of raw or leaf tobacco, in portions of the country, was being sold at retail directly to consumers without the payment of tax. Evidences of this traffic have, from time to time, been furnished by assessors and collectors, and more especially by supervisors, who, in taking transcripts from the books required by law to be kept by leaf-dealers, have reported that they find scores of pages of these books where entries were made of sales from one-half pound to four pounds each; and I am constantly in receipt of letters from manufacturers of tobacco, complaining of the injury to their business arising from such sales, and informing me that in some localities where they formerly received frequent and large orders for manufactured tobacco they now make no sales, the same parties who used to make these orders now ordering instead supplies of natural leaf from the wholesale leaf-dealers. Against this traffic, grown to such large proportions, so injurious to their business as manufacturers, and prejudicial to the interest of the Government revenue, they ask to be protected.

To this end, I would recommend that section 59 of the act of July 20, 1868, be so amended as to impose a special tax of five hundred dollars on every person who shall make a business of selling raw or leaf-tobacco to persons other than those who have paid special tax as leaf-dealers, or as manufacturers of tobacco, snuff, or cigars, or who shall sell leaf-tobacco in quantities less than twenty-five pounds, or who shall sell such tobacco directly to consumers, or for consumption without its being manufactured. And if this is not deemed sufficient, I would further recommend such a tax on the sales of such dealers in excess of $5,000 annually as would be equivalent to the tax on the same amount and value of manufactured tobacco. Such a provision of law will not only give the required protection to the manufacturer who now pays a special tax for carrying on his business, in addition to a specific tax on all his products, but it will also, I am persuaded, tend largely to increase the Government revenue from this source.

EXPORT BONDED WAREHOUSES.

In the absence of any provision of law providing for drawback on manufactured tobacco and snuff when exported, the law has provided for a system of export bonded warehouses to be established at any port of entry in the United States for the storage of manufactured tobacco and snuff intended for exportation.

Under this provision of law there are now in operation sixteen export bonded warehouses, two having been established during the last fiscal year, viz, one at the port of Mobile, Alabama, and one at Portland, Oregon, while one of those previously established at Philadelphia has been discontinued.

The quantity of tobacco, &c., stored in the several export bonded warehouses during the fiscal year ended June 30, 1871, was as follows:

	Pounds.
Fourth district, Massachusetts	1,503,867
Thirty-second district, New York	12,799,611
Second district, Pennsylvania	2,606,556
Third district, Maryland	3,060,556

	Pounds.
Third district, Virginia	2,638,529
First district, Louisiana	1,547,095
First district, California	2,158,883
First district, Oregon	64,167
Total amount	26,379,264

The quantity withdrawn for exportation from the several export bonded warehouses during the fiscal year ended June 30, 1871, was as follows:

	Pounds.
Fourth district, Massachusetts	853,724
Thirty-second district, New York	6,699,688
Second district, Pennsylvania	40,838
Third district, Maryland	218,916
Third district, Virginia	2,630,175
First district, Louisiana	10,355
First district, California	167,387
Total quantity exported	10,621,083

WITHDRAWN FOR CONSUMPTION.

The quantity withdrawn for consumption on payment of the tax, from the several bonded warehouses, for the fiscal year ended June 30, 1871, was as follows:

	Pounds.
Fourth district, Massachusetts	521,237
Thirty-second district, New York	2,464,979
Second district, Pennsylvania	2,658,736
Third district, Maryland	2,435,503
Third district, Virginia	32,784
First district, Louisiana	1,431,287
First district, California	1,930.164
First district, Oregon	24,969
Total for consumption	11,499,659

These figures show that less than half of the tobacco, &c., removed in bond from the manufactories, is actually exported. From the eight bonded warehouses established at the several ports of Philadelphia, Baltimore, New Orleans, San Francisco, and Portland, Oregon, in which were stored during the fiscal year ended June 30, 1871, 9,437,257 pounds of manufactured tobacco, only 437,495 pounds during this period were withdrawn for exportation, while 8,480,656 pounds were withdrawn for consumption on payment of the tax.

Nearly nine-tenths of all the tobacco exported from the country is shipped through the bonded warehouses at New York and Richmond, Virginia; and of this a large portion is never stored in the bonded warehouses. The shipments are made directly from the factories, the goods being carted by the warehouses, and only constructively entered therein, though the owners thereof are charged with a month's storage.

The practical operation of this system of bonded warehouses hitherto has been to give to a few individuals and firms, more particularly to the proprietors of the warehouses, the same facilities for storing tobacco without the prepayment of the tax as were given by the former system of Class B, bonded warehouses, abolished by the act of July 20, 1868.

It is my own opinion, and, so far as I have been able to ascertain, it is the opinion of manufacturers of tobacco generally, that the present system of export bonded warehouses can be entirely abolished to the interest both of the Government and of the manufacturers.

Under the present system all the tobacco bonded at the warehouse in Richmond, Virginia, is exported without ever entering the warehouse, and the same is true of much of the tobacco bonded in New York.

By abolishing the present system of export bonded warehouses, and providing for the exportation of manufactured tobacco, snuff, and cigars, as other merchandise is exported, allowing a drawback of the tax paid upon proof of landing abroad, requiring the tobacco to be loaded under the supervision of an inspector, and the tax-paid stamps to be destroyed by said officer to prevent relanding, it is believed a large portion of the expenses now incurred by the manufacturers in exporting their goods would be saved, the Government would receive the taxes on all goods when removed from the place of manufacture, all jobbers and dealers in manufactured tobacco would be placed on the same footing with regard to the traffic in tax paid goods, and the special privileges and advantages enjoyed by a few individuals and firms would be removed.

I would recommend that Congress provide that evidence of the loss at sea satisfactory to the Commissioner of Internal Revenue shall have all the force of a landing certificate for the purposes of drawback.

Other systems of exportation designed to remedy the evils of the present bonded warehouse system have been suggested; but they involve the multiplying of bonds to be taken in lieu of tax. A multiplication of such bonds would result in an increase of losses to the Government. The records of the United States courts in many sections of the country are largely occupied by suits on bonds taken for spirits and refined petroleum, under similar systems tothose proposed. In a large majority of the cases, the principals being insolvent generally before suit was brought, the sureties have either not been found on original process; or, if found, a return of no goods on final process has realized to the Government a total loss of its supposed security.

STAMPS.

Since the last annual report of the Commissioner, contracts have been made for printing revenue stamps as follows, viz: With Mr. Joseph R. Carpenter, of Philadelphia, for documentary and proprietary stamps; with the Continental Bank Note Company of New York, for printing tints for distilled spirits and tobacco stamps; with the National Bank Note Company of New York, for printing tints for beer stamps. These contracts were awarded to the lowest bidders possessing the facilities for doing the work, after due publication of advertisements for proposals in the newspapers of the various leading cities in the United States.

Important changes have been made in the materials and manner of preparing stamps in order to prevent fraudulent issues, counterfeiting, and re-use. Heretofore nearly all the issues of revenue stamps have been printed in a single color upon ordinary commercial paper furnished by the parties doing the printing. By the changes referred to, the Government provides a distinctive paper, and permits the printing of stamps upon no other, and requires that all stamps shall be printed in two or more colors.

It is well known that the revenue derived from stamps has seriously suffered through the fraudulent re-use of stamps. It has been found no difficult matter on the part of evil-disposed persons, by the use of chemicals carefully manipulated, to remove the cancellation-marks entirely without injuring the appearance of the stamps, thus enabling dishonest parties to re-use them, or to sell the same for re-use, and de fraud the Government to that extent.

It is believed that the stamps now being furnished under the contracts alluded to, cannot be tampered with. Especially is this thought to be the case with the adhesive, and tobacco, snuff, and cigar stamps printed upon chameleon paper. This paper so effectually changes its color upon the application of chemical agents employed for the restoring of stamps for re-use, as to render restoration to its original state impossible. In addition to the protection afforded by this paper, a soluble ink is used in the preparation of adhesive stamps. This ink contains the ingredients of ordinary writing ink; any acid or alkali of sufficient strength to remove the cancellation made would destroy also that portion of the stamp which is printed in the soluble ink.

By printing the stamps in two or more colors, counterfeiting, which has been largely practiced by photography, becomes impossible.

Another feature in the present issue is, that with the exception of the documentary and proprietary stamps, none are allowed to be entirely prepared by any single establishment.

The New York Bank Note Company print the tints only of certain stamps, while the Bureau of Engraving and Printing finishes and delivers them to this office, from whence they are issued to collectors.

The paper used for printing these stamps was adopted especially for that purpose by the Secretary of the Treasury, upon the recommendation of this office, and is manufactured by Messrs. Jas. M. Willcox & Co., of Glenn Mills, Pennsylvania, under Government supervision. It is not lawful for any one to manufacture this paper, or to sell or have it in possession, except by authority of the Department.

It may be added that the average cost of the present series of stamps is considerably less per thousand than that of the previous issue.

ABSTRACT OF CASES COMPROMISED.

The whole number of cases compromised, as provided under section 102, act of July 20, 1868, during the fiscal year ended June 30, 1871, was 730.

Amount of tax accepted	$349,795 12
Assessed penalty fixed by law	20,076 36
Specific penalty in lieu of fines, penalties, and forfeitures	248,626 50
Total amount received by compromises	618,497 98

ABSTRACT OF REPORTS OF DISTRICT ATTORNEYS FOR THE FISCAL YEAR 1871.

Number of indictments	4,217
Number of proceedings *in rem*	1,048
Number of other suits *in personam*	1,712
Whole number commenced	6,977
Number of convictions on indictments	1,232
Number of judgments recovered in other suits *in personam*	1,106
Number of judgments recovered in proceedings *in rem*	844
Total number of suits decided in favor of United States	3,182
Number of acquittals	258
Number of other suits *in personam* or *in rem* decided against the United States	198
Total number of suits decided against the United States	456

Number of suits settled, not prosecuted, or dismissed..................... 2,306
Number of suits pending July 1, 1871 5,676
Amount of judgments recovered in suits *in personam*, including fines, &c. $1,419,064 48
Amount collected and paid into court in suits *in personam* (including
　indictments) on account of judgments, fines, &c 594,339 97
Amount collected and paid into court as proceeds of forfeiture....:.... 145,238 51

ABSTRACT OF SEIZURES.

Seizures of property for violation of internal revenue law during the fiscal year ended June 30, 1871, were as follows:

273,757 gallons of distilled spirits, valued at........................... $339,395 70
　1,366 barrels of fermented liquors, valued at....................... 9,569 00
　2,907 pounds of snuff, valued at...................................... 887 10
281,293 pounds of tobacco, valued at 109,234 44
2,094,376 cigars, valued at 58,820 54
Miscellaneous property, valued at..................................... 397.333 36

Total value of seizures...............................;............... 915,240 14

Statement showing the gross proceeds realized from sales, during the fiscal year 1871, under section 63, act of July 13, 1866, together with expenses and amount deposited; also the per cent. of expenses to gross proceeds.

States.	Gross proceeds.	Expenses and stamps.	Amount deposited.	Per cent.
California...	$971 75	$241 45	$730 30	24.8
Connecticut..	115 86	57 95	57 91	50.0
Georgia...	504 57	344 28	160 29	68.2
Illinois..	41 58	37 76	3 82	90.8
Indiana...	159 15	16 00	143 15	10.0
Iowa...	43 99	43 99	....	100.0
Kentucky...	332 08	202 18	129 90	60.8
Maine..	7 50	7 50	....	100.0
Missouri..	1,031 55	516 94	514 61	50.1
Mew Jersey...	46 90	6 20	40 70	13.2
New York...	593 67	255 18	338 49	42.9
North Carolina.....................................	1,272 50	669 40	603 10	52.6
Ohio..	154 30	48 81	105 49	31.6
Pennsylvania.......................................	1,233 41	509 53	723 88	41.3
South Carolina.....................................	255 11	184 44	70 67	72.2
Tennessee..	170 84	48 03	122 81	28.1
Texas...	228 26	99 09	129 26	43.3
Virginia..	549 06	525 44	23 62	95.6
Wisconsin..	87 20	77 36	9 84	88.7
Total..	7,799 28	3,891 44	3,907 84	49.9

ADDITIONAL RECOMMENDATIONS.

I fully approve, and would here renew, the following recommendation made in last year's report by the then Commissioner, Mr. Delano:

The act of July 14, 1870, exempted from taxation, under schedule C, canned and preserved fish, leaving prepared mustard, sauces, sirups, jams, and jellies still liable to the stamp tax. These articles being either condiments or conserves, and generally of home or culinary production, never having been a fruitful source of revenue, and the collection of the tax thereon always attended with no inconsiderable amount of trouble and vexation, I would recommend that they hereafter be relieved from the stamp tax now imposed upon them under the clause in schedule C relating to "canned meats," &c.

There are now in the hands of collectors and United States marshals, stored in bonded warehouses and elsewhere, considerable quantities of condemned, forfeited, and abandoned tobacco, so depreciated in value that it cannot be sold for enough to pay charges and for the necessary stamps. This tobacco was manufactured under the old law; conse-quently it is unstamped. Under the present law it cannot be sold or offered for sale without first being properly stamped, and there is no provision of law under which the Commissioner of Internal Revenue can furnish stamps for it. The want of authority to furnish stamps for such tobacco, which is constantly accumulating in the hands of Government officers, has caused much embarrassment. I would therefore earnestly recommend that Congress authorize the Commissioner, upon the requi-sition of the officers having the custody and control of such tobacco, to furnish suitable revenue stamps to be attached and cancelled before the same is offered for sale.

It frequently happens that tax-paid stamps are lost from packages of spirits by unavoidable accident, without fault on the part of the persons interested, the spirits being thus exposed to seizure and detention. The present law makes no provision for re-stamping such packages, except on the re-payment of the tax. Inasmuch as the stamp is a device to protect alike the interests of the Government and the tax-payer, it is considered that authority should be given to complete that protection by re-stamping.

It was recommended last year by Mr. Commissioner Delano that Con-gress provide, by joint resolution or otherwise, for the remission of all taxes assessed on ship-builders under the fourth section of the act of March 31, 1868, as had not been collected. No action, however, was taken upon the subject, and not feeling at liberty to allow further delay, I have ordered their collection.

Section 44 of the act of June 30, 1864, gives to the Commissioner, "subject to regulations prescribed by the Secretary of the Treasury," authority to abate and refund taxes and penalties in certain classes of cases. One of these regulations (Circular 79) provides in effect that no claim or application for the refunding of taxes will be entitled to con-sideration by the Commissioner, unless it shall be filed with him either prior to August 4, 1871, (Circular 79 having been issued August 3, 1869,) or within two years from the date of the payment of the tax.

It will be observed that this simply affects the question of the con-sideration by the Commissioner of claims thus barred, but does not, it is claimed, limit any right of action upon them.

One of my predecessors, Mr. Rollins, in his report for 1868, remarks upon this subject as follows:

The authority vested in the Commissioner of Internal Revenue to refund taxes erroneously collected has been the means of preventing much expensive litigation, and has afforded speedy and inexpensive relief to many persons who have been compelled to pay more than was legally due. While a withdrawal of this authority would be productive of great hardship in many cases, I am satisfied that a statutory limitation of the time within which such claims must be presented would tend to prevent much abuse. When the legality of an assessment is not seriously questioned at the time it is made, the evidence in its support is very apt to disappear with a change in the officers of the district; and it is not then difficult for a skillful attorney to present reasons in support of a claim for refunding such as are hard to be set aside.

I would recommend that the Commissioner be prohibited from con-sidering or allowing any claim not presented within two years from the time the tax was paid; and that all claims be barred in the courts after six years from the date of payment of the tax.

Section 44 of the act of July 20, 1868, should, in my opinion, be amended by making the minimum penalty smaller, such penalty being now a fine of not less than $1,000, with not less than six months im-prisonment. The undue severity of this punishment would seem to be obvious as applied to the offenses of carrying on the business of a retail or wholesale liquor dealer, rectifier, or manufacturer of stills, "without having paid the special tax," in cases wherein no intent to defraud exists, the omission arising from ignorance of the law, or other circumstances not fraudulent, yet constituting no legal excuse under the terms of the section. The practical effect of providing so disproportionate a punishment for these offenses is to discourage complaints, defeat convictions, and induce suspensions of sentence, in many cases in which some reasonable punishment should be enforced, as well to vindicate the law as to secure future compliance with its requirements.

Section 63 of the act of July 13, 1866, (p. 31, of Compilation of 1867,) should be amended to make it apply to cases arising under any internal revenue act. As it is now, it applies only to offenses under that act of 1866, and previous act, to which it was an amendment. I would also recommend that the limitation of amount should be extended from $300 to $500, as contained in the parallel provision of the customs laws, (section 11 of act of July 18, 1866, 14 Stat. at Large, p. 180.)

I would call attention to the report of last year in relation to the subject of "direct taxes," and would renew the recommendation of early legislation for the final disposition of all lands which have been acquired and are now owned by the United States under the direct-tax laws.

COLLECTORS' ACCOUNTS.

The complaint which has heretofore existed of delay in the settlement of ex-collectors' accounts has been, it is believed, entirely removed by the operation of the regulations of this office now in force.

Prior to April, 1870, it appeared that the accounts of 61 ex-collectors had been closed, which number, however, has since been increased to 434, leaving at the present time 230 accounts still open. Of this number 115 have been placed in the hands of United States attorneys for suit on the bonds of the delinquent collectors, the residue being in course of adjustment at this office.

Respectfully,

J. W. DOUGLASS,
Commissioner.

Hon. GEORGE S. BOUTWELL,
Secretary of the Treasury.

REPORT OF THE COMPTROLLER OF CURRENCY.

REPORT

OF

THE COMPTROLLER OF THE CURRENCY.

OFFICE OF THE COMPTROLLER OF THE CURRENCY,
Washington, November 10, 1871.

SIR : In compliance with the provisions of section 61 of the National Currency Act, I have the honor to present through you to the Congress of the United States the following report for the year ending September 30, 1871 :

Since my last annual report, one hundred and fifty-five National Banks have been organized, making the total number to October 1, eighteen hundred and eighty-six. Of this number, ten banks, to-wit :

The Central National Bank of Baltimore, Maryland,
The First National Bank of Hightstown, New Jersey ;
The National Security Bank of Philadelphia, Pennsylvania ;
The Keeseville National Bank, New York ;
The Central National Bank of Hightstown, New Jersey ;
The East Chester National Bank of Mount Vernon, New York ;
The Merchant's National Bank of Newark, New Jersey ;
The National Bank of the Commonwealth of Boston, Massachusetts ;
The National Bank of Kutztown, Pennsylvania ;
The Littleton National Bank, New Hampshire,

with an aggregate capital of $1,960,000, were organized by the surrender and transfer of circulating notes for that purpose by existing National Banks, and did not increase the aggregate of bank circulation.

One hundred and forty-five banks have been organized during the year under the act approved July 12, 1870, providing for the issue of fifty-four millions of additional national bank circulation.

The names of the banks are as follows, to-wit,

	Capital.
The Second National Bank of Lawrence, Kansas	$100,000
The State National Bank of Springfield, Illinois	150,000
The German National Bank of Chicago, Illinois	250,000
The First National Bank of Palmyra, Missouri	100,000
The City National Bank of Selma, Alabama	100,000
The Loudoun National Bank of Leesburgh, Virginia	50,000
The South Bend National Bank, Indiana	100,000
The First National Bank of Lake City, Minnesota	50,000
The First National Gold Bank of San Francisco, California	1,000,000
The Citizen's National Bank of Charlottesville, Virginia	100,000
The Merchants' National Bank of Burlington, Iowa	100,000
The Hastings National Bank, Michigan	50,000
The City National Bank of Chattanooga, Tennessee	100,000
The Teutonia National Bank of New Orleans, Louisiana	200,000
The National Bank of Somerset, Kentucky	60,000

	Capital.
The First National Bank of Appleton, Wisconsin....	$50,000
The First National Bank of Santa Fé, New Mexico........	150,000
The First National Bank of Pleasant Hill, Missouri........	100,000
The First National Bank of Holly, Michigan	50,000
The Merchant's National Bank of Richmond, Virginia.....	200,000
The First National Bank of Lanark, Illinois	50,000
The Fayetteville National Bank, North Carolina...	50,000
The First National Bank of Sioux City, Iowa...........	100,000
The First National Bank of Charlotte, Michigan....... ...	50,000
The First National Bank of Franklin, Kentucky..........	100,000
The First National Bank of Niles, Michigan	100,000
The Washington National Bank, Iowa	50,000
The First National Bank of Fort Scott, Kansas	50,000
The First National Bank of Mason, Michigan	80,000
The Central National Bank of Columbia, South Carolina ...	100,000
The Citizen's National Bank of Raleigh, North Carolina....	100,000
The First National Bank of Springfield, Kentucky...,. ...	150,000
The First National Bank of Saginaw, Michigan	100,000
The Commercial National Bank of Petersburgh, Virginia...	120,000
The Boone County National Bank of Columbia, Missouri ...	100,000
The First National Bank of Boscobel, Wisconsin.........	50,000
The First National Bank of Seneca, Illinois	50,000
The State National Bank of New Orleans, Louisiana.......	500,000
The Gallatin National Bank of Shawneetown, Illinois......	250,000
The First National Bank of Osceola, Iowa	50,000
The National Bank of Jefferson, Texas	100,000
The New Orleans National Bank, Louisiana	200,000
The Farmers and Merchants' National Bank of Vandalia, Illinois	100,000
The Citizens' National Bank of Flint, Michigan	50,000
The Merchants and Farmers' National Bank of Charlotte, North Carolina...	150,000
The Winona Deposit National Bank, Minnesota,	100,000
The Lumbermen's National Bank of Stillwater, Minnesota..	50,000
The Bellefontaine National Bank, Ohio	100,000
The First National Bank of Kewanee, Illinois	75,000
The First National Bank of Sigourney, Iowa	50,000
The Union National Bank of Oshkosh, Wisconsin	100,000
The Merchants' National Bank of Dayton, Ohio	200,000
The First National Bank of St. Clair, Michigan	100,000
The Madison National Bank of Richmond, Kentucky	200,000
The Farmers' National Bank of Bushnell, Illinois	50,000
The Union National Bank of Aurora, Illinois	125,000
The First National Bank of Kankakee, Illinois	50,000
The First National Bank of Saint Peter, Minnesota	50,000
The First National Bank of Charleston, West Virginia.....	78,000
The Union National Bank of New Orleans, Louisiana	600,000
The First National Bank of Lincoln, Nebraska	50,000
The First National Bank of Albia, Iowa	50,000
The First National Bank of Cheyenne, Wyoming Territory..	100,000
The Commercial National Bank of Dubuque, Iowa	100,000
The Manufacturers' National Bank of Racine, Wisconsin...	100,000
The First National Bank of Paris, Missouri	100,000
The National Bank of Chester, South Carolina	50,000
The Farmers' National Bank of Keithsburgh, Illinois	50,000

Capital.

The Exchange National Bank of Polo, Illinois	$60,000
The First National Bank of Harrodsburgh, Kentucky	100,000
The First National Bank of Lewistown, Illinois	50,000
The First National Bank of Jefferson City, Missouri	75,000
The First National Bank of Charles City, Iowa	50,000
The First National Bank of Indianola, Iowa	50,000
The First National Bank of Cassopolis, Michigan	50,000
The First National Bank of Anamosa, Iowa	50,000
The First National Bank of Montgomery, Alabama	100,000
The First National Bank of Elkader, Iowa	50,000
The Rockford National Bank, Illinois	100,000
The National Commercial Bank of Mobile, Alabama	208,000
The National Bank of Commerce of Green Bay, Wisconsin.	100,000
The Manufacturers' National Bank of Appleton, Wisconsin.	50,000
The People's National Bank of Winchester, Illinois	75,000
The Gainesville National Bank, Alabama	100,000
The First National Bank of South Haven, Michigan	50,000
The Farmers' National Bank of Salem, Virginia	50,000
The New Orleans National Banking Association, Louisiana.	600,000
The Union City National Bank, Michigan	50,000
The First National Bank of Olathe, Kansas	50,000
The First National Bank of Allegan, Michigan	50,000
The First National Bank of St. Anthony, Minnesota	50,000
The First National Bank of Nicholasville, Kentucky	65,000
The Northern National Bank of Big Rapids, Michigan	75,000
The First National Bank of Pueblo, Colorado Territory	75,000
The National Bank of Franklin, Tennessee	60,000
The Commercial National Bank of Versailles, Kentucky	100,000
The First National Bank of Atlantic, Iowa	50,000
The Livingston County National Bank of Pontiac, Illinois..	50,000
The First National Bank of Baxter Springs, Kansas	50,000
The First National Bank of La Grange, Missouri	50,000
The First National Bank of Wyandott, Kansas	50,000
The First National Bank of Greenville, Illinois	100,000
The Second National Bank of Winona, Minnesota	100,000
The Bates County National Bank of Butler, Missouri	50,000
The National Bank of Newberry, South Carolina	50,000
The Cook County National Bank of Chicago, Illinois	300,000
The First National Bank of Brownville, Nebraska	100,000
The German National Bank of Covington, Kentucky	250,000
The National Bank of Spartanburgh, South-Carolina	60,000
The First National Bank of Grand Haven, Michigan	100,000
The First National Bank of Mason City, Illinois	50,000
The Second National Bank of Charleston, Illinois	100,000
The First National Bank of Marseilles, Illinois	50,000
The First National Bank of Tuskaloosa, Alabama	50,000
The First National Bank of Frankfort, Indiana	100,000
The Nebraska City National Bank, Nebraska	100,000
The First National Bank of Warrensburgh, Missouri	50,000
The First National Bank of Port Huron, Michigan	100,000
The Valley National Bank of St. Louis, Missouri	250,000
The Covington City National Bank, Kentucky	300,000
The National Exchange Bank of Augusta, Georgia	250,000
The First National Bank of Newnan, Georgia	125,000
The Mills County National Bank of Glenwood, Iowa	65,000

5 F

	Capital.
The Citizens' National Bank of Faribault, Minnesota	80,000
The First National Bank of Paola, Kansas	50,000
The National Bank of Rolla, Missouri	100,000
The First National Bank of St. Joseph, Michigan	50,000
The National Bank of Illinois, at Chicago, Illinois	500,000
The First National Bank of Jefferson, at Charlestown, West Virginia	50,000
The Rush County National Bank of Rushville, Indiana	100,000
The First National Bank of Marengo, Illinois	50,000
The Knoxville National Bank, Iowa	100,000
The Union National Bank of Macomb, Illinois	60,000
The First National Bank of Vincennes, Indiana	100,000
The First National Bank of Webster City, Iowa	50,000
The First National Bank of Paxton, Illinois	50,000
The First National Bank of Knobnoster, Missouri	50,000
The Meridian National Bank of Indianapolis, Indiana	200,000
The Citizens' National Bank of Peru, Indiana	100,000
The First National Bank of Tama City, Iowa	50,000
The Dixon National Bank, Illinois	100,000
The Will County National Bank of Joliet, Illinois	100,000
The National Bank of Piedmont, West Virginia	50,000
The Wellsburgh National Bank, West Virginia	100,000
The Citizens' National Bank of Niles, Michigan	50,000

The aggregate capital of the banks named is $15,996,000, and is distributed among the several States as follows:

	Capital.
Alabama, 5 banks	$558,000
Colorado, 1 bank	50,000
California, (gold,) 1 bank	1,000,000
Georgia, 2 banks	375,000
Illinois, 27 banks	2,995,000
Iowa, 16 banks	1,015,000
Indiana, 6 banks	700,000
Kansas, 6 banks	350,000
Kentucky, 9 banks	1,325,000
Louisiana, 5 banks	2,100,000
Missouri, 11 banks	1,025,000
Minnesota, 7 banks	480,000
Michigan, 17 banks	1,155,000
Nebraska, 3 banks	250,000
North Carolina, 3 banks	300,000
New Mexico, 1 bank	150,000
Ohio, 2 banks	300,000
South Carolina, 4 banks	260,000
Tennessee, 2 banks	160,000
Texas, 1 bank	100,000
Virginia, 5 banks	520,000
West Virginia, 3 banks	278,000
Wyoming Territory, 1 bank	100,000
Wisconsin, 6 banks	450,000

The total amount of currency issued under the act of July 12, 1870, to October 1, 1871, is $22,333,990, some $20,000,000 of which has been furnished to new banks, and the remainder to existing banks which had not received their full quota, or which had increased their capital to meet the growing demands of business.

The condition of the Southern States since the passage of the act has been such as to preclude the possibility of their taking any considerable portion of the circulation provided, and consequently the number of banks organized in the South is small. This fact made it possible, after the expiration of the year specified in section one of the act of July 12, 1870, to organize additional banks in the Western States, and accordingly nearly all of the really meritorious applications in those States were granted. I estimate that the Western and Northwestern States can be fully supplied and still leave from $20,000,000 to $25,000,000 for the Southern States when they are in condition to take it.

In New Orleans a disposition has been manifested to adopt the national banking system generally, and while but two new banks have been organized there, three of the old banks have reorganized as national banks, and it is understood that several others are contemplating a similar change. One obstacle in the way of such changes is the limitation fixed by the act to the amount of circulation that can be furnished to any one bank, to wit, $500,000. Quite a number of the New Orleans State banks employ a very much larger capital, and could advantageously employ a much larger circulation. The propriety of removing this restriction in certain cases is respectfully suggested.

Since my last report but one bank has been established on a gold basis—the First National Gold Bank of San Francisco—with a capital of $1,000,000. It is presumed that the success of this institution is not so flattering as to induce the organization of others of a similar character, though, in view of the obstacles and the opposition which it meets, it holds its own and is gradually winning its way into public confidence.

The tenacity with which the Pacific States adhere to a gold currency is quite notable. Whether it is equally praiseworthy, is another thing. It is not clear that those States derive any substantial benefit from the course they have pursued, and it is beginning to be manifest that the United States are not at all benefited by it. The substitution of a paper currency in California and the other gold-producing States for their present hard money would probably set free for the use of the Government and the whole country some thirty or forty millions of gold, and at the same time provide those communities with a more economical, active, and accommodating circulating medium.

I recommend that provision be made for the establishment of national banks in California and the other Pacific States upon a legal-tender basis, and that the law be so modified as to enable them to cope successfully with other banking institutions at present doing business in those States.

There is nothing especial to note in the history or management of the banks during the year. A few cases of dishonesty have occurred, but none of any magnitude. The examinations made under the provisions of section 54 of the currency act have been instrumental in developing irregular and dishonest practices in time to prevent loss to the bank in quite a number of cases, and there is no doubt of their efficacy in securing judicious management and general compliance with all the important requirements of the act.

Occasional complaint is made that national banks are in the habit of charging higher rates of interest than the laws of the several States authorize, but as the law itself provides a remedy or a penalty for usury, and places it at the disposal of the complainant, I have not felt called upon to take any official action on the subject. While nothing

will justify a bank for violating any provision of law, I desire, nevertheless, to call the attention of Congress again to the very high rates of
taxation that are imposed on national banks in most of the States. It
is asserted by bank officers, and admitted to be true, that local taxation
is so high in some of the States as to make it impossible to lend money
at legal rates without loss to the bank. It is probably true that, in some
instances, the object of the legislature in imposing these burdens is a
hostile one, intended to drive national banks out of existence, while, in
other cases, onerous taxes are imposed under the impression that the
banks are making enormous profits, and can afford to divide them with
the State. I am of opinion that the public good would justify some
limitation to the power of the States to tax the shares of national banks.
The average tax paid to the United States is $2\frac{1}{2}$ per cent. on the capital of the banks, and it seems to me that the equivalent of this tax ought
to be sufficient for the States in which the banks are located.

I recommend that the Comptroller of the Currency be clothed with
power to act in cases where the capital of a bank has been seriously
impaired by losses or otherwise, either by requiring the capital to be
made whole by assessment of the shareholders, or by requiring the
bank to wind up its affairs within a reasonable time if its capital is not
made good. Also to wind up the affairs of any bank which is not
engaged in the transaction of a legitimate and reputable business, or
which has obtained an organization through false or fraudulent representations.

I think it would have a tendency to check the circulation of counterfeit notes, if national banks were required to stamp all such notes, when
presented at the counter of the bank, with the word " counterfeit," and
I suggest the expediency of legislative provision for that purpose.

The circulation furnished to national banks has now been outstanding
for an average period of about five years, and it is being returned in
constantly increasing amounts for new notes. Since the organization of
the Bureau to September 30, the total amount returned for destruction
is $54,546,345, of which $23,948,827 were returned during the last year.
The handling of these notes involves much care and labor, and requires
an addition to the present available force of the office.

Carefully prepared tables will be found in the appendix, as follows:

1st. The number of banks, amount of capital, bonds, and circulation
in each State and Territory.

2d. The number and amount of each denomination of bank-notes issued,
redeemed, and outstanding.

3d. The number and amount of each denomination of gold bank-notes
issued and outstanding.

4th. Statement of amount and different kinds of bonds held to secure
circulation.

5th. Banks in the hands of receivers.

6th. National banks in liquidation which have deposited lawful money
to redeem their circulation, and taken up their bonds.

7th. National banks in liquidation for the purpose of consolidating
with other banks.

8th. Reserve tables.

9th. List of clerks employed during the fiscal year ending June 30,
1871.

10th. Expenditures for the fiscal year ending June 30, 1871.

SPECIE PAYMENTS.

The time when, and the means by which, specie payments may be resumed have for some years been the subject of much anxious consideration and of earnest public discussion. The problem is one of general and pervading interest, closely connected with the public welfare, and, like all questions of public importance, has called forth a great variety of opinions. Writers who have made a study of this and kindred branches of political economy, with few exceptions, agree that when in time of suspension of specie payments there has been a very considerable increase of paper money, there must be a corresponding decrease before specie payments can be safely resumed.

Assuming the paper currency to be redundant, or in excess of the normal demands of trade, the excess must be retired in order to bring the currency up to a specie standard. This redundancy has been attributed to the currency of the United States by a majority of those who have written and spoken on the subject since the year 1864, and the remedy prescribed has been "contraction."

So prevalent was this view of the case at one time that, in 1866, Congress, in obedience to what was regarded as a sound and correct principle of political economy, provided by law for a gradual withdrawal and cancellation of United States notes to the extent of four millions a month; but, owing to the funding operations of the Treasury, this provision was not carried into effect until the latter part of the year 1867, when the process of contraction was commenced. Just at this time, also, commenced a stringency in the money market, which increased in severity as contraction went on. To the people the stringency seemed to be produced by the contraction, though it is now evident that other causes conspired to aid in producing the result. The hard times, however, were generally attributed to the depletion of the money markets by the actual withdrawal of ten millions of currency in six months, and its continued reduction at the rate of four millions per month thereafter.

This opinion had all the force of conviction in the public mind, and found its appropriate expression in an act of Congress, which became a law, in February, 1868, prohibiting any further reduction of the currency, and so the matter now stands. If there is a superabundance of currency, which must be retired before a specie basis can be reached, the first step toward specie payments must be the repeal of the act of February, 1868. If public sentiment will not permit or sanction such action by Congress, it will be because the people do not wish for resumption at the expense of contraction. If this is the only road to specie payments, it remains closed by the mandate of the people.

In direct antagonism to the demand for specie payments at all hazards, and without regard to consequences, is the doctrine of a currency permanently divorced from a specie basis. It is argued, and with some degree of plausibility, that the convertibility of paper money into coin on demand, has always been an unsound element of currency, because it has never been practicable when actually required. Under any system of currency of which credit forms a part, convertibility is but little more than a name, satisfactory enough as long as the times are easy and confidence prevails, but exceedingly dangerous and mischievous when the money market is deranged, and distrust has taken the place of confidence. The conversion of paper is seldom demanded in any considerable amounts until credit is wavering, and everything is looked upon with suspicion. Then, the demand is not limited to the 25 or 30 per cent. which the banks may have in reserve. Loss of confidence, and the knowledge that provision for payment is only partial, are precursors of panics, suspensions, failures, and all the disasters incident to such a state of affairs. It is a maxim in military science that a line of fortifications is just as strong as the weakest place in it, and no stronger. So, in finance, a system is never safe that is vulnerable at any point, or under any circumstances. Panics are the weak places in all theories or systems of convertible currencies, of which credit forms a constituent element.

Absolute convertibility can be secured only by locking up the specie; and for each dollar under lock and key, issuing a paper promise to pay a dollar on demand. In this case the note is only the title to the thing, and there should not be more titles than there are things; in other words, there must not be more paper dollars than there are specie dollars. The convertibility hobby has been ridden to death. The uniform failure of all attempts to secure it should admonish bankers and financiers that there may be such a thing as progress and improvement even in banking and currency, The Bank of England may be regarded as furnishing the conditions most favorable to the convertibility theory, yet in every time of real need its charter has been disregarded, and the bank has been obliged to suspend. The history of the banks in the United States is but a series of suspensions, occurring as often as conversion was demanded.

Ultimate solvency is of far greater importance to the community than convertibility, and the liberal and judicious use of credit is of far more value in the commercial world than the instant command of gold and silver. Credit is the great element of modern progress. Notwithstanding the abuses to which it has been subjected, it has rejuvenated the world. The prosperity of the United States is, in great measure, due to this life-giving power. Currency based on actual deposits of coin would have given no opportunity for enterprise, no room for growth. Heterogeneous as the currency of this country has been, false and delusive as its promises have proved, yet the element of credit which has entered so largely into its composition has proved an inestimable benefit. Specie has not been at the bottom of this prosperity, for we have had but little of it, comparatively, and whenever the demand has been made for the redemption of currency, the banks have been obliged to suspend. We owe our welfare and progress to the liberal, and not always judicious, use of credit, more than to anything else. And particularly is this true of the last six or eight years. During that period we have had a currency based exclusively upon credit. It has held out no false promise; and, as a consequence, we have been exempt from all currency panics or disturbances.

Those who favor the views herein expressed, maintain and believe that our currency system, as at present established, is the best and safest we have ever had. They believe that the premium on gold may be gradually reduced in the next few years, as it has been in the past, until it shall become practicable to obtain coin for paper, in such reasonable amounts as may be required in trade by exchange-at rates merely nominal. They make a distinction between "convertibility by redemption," which is the generally accepted idea, and convertibility by exchange, which is their idea. This, they affirm, would bring all the benefits of resumption, without any of its attendant dangers. The plan involves the recognition of bullion dealers, who shall be entitled to regular and legitimate commissions, premiums, or profits. The assent of the public to this proposition relieves the banks and the Government from the necessity and the burden of furnishing coin for nothing. Trade would soon adapt itself to this basis, would calculate and allow these premiums or commissions, and would take out of our system a dangerous, unnecessary, and delusive element.

A theory which has found much favor in the last few years, is embodied in the proposition that "the currency should be maintained at its present volume until the industrial and commercial interests of the country shall recover from the effects of the war, and until the natural growth in population and wealth, the revival of enterprise, the increased facilities of trade, and the expansion of our borders, shall create a legitimate use for the whole amount of currency now outstanding." Just how long this will take has not been stated, and probably is not susceptible of demonstration; but the idea is a plausible one, and commends itself to popular favor, as affording an easy and gradual transition to specie payments without any of the inconveniences and hardships associated in the public mind with contraction.

The fundamental idea underlying this theory is that the conditions necessary to growth exist already. It presupposes that the country may prosper; that trade, industry, and enterprise may flourish; that labor may have a bountiful reward; that individuals and communities may grow rich and increase in wealth and substance, notwithstanding a superabundant, irredeemable, depreciated currency. If this assumption is correct, it is hardly necessary to look forward to the time when natural growth shall absorb the surplus currency, and specie payments shall come in the course of nature.

If the currency, in its present condition, is so far conducive to prosperity as to make it probable that, at no distant day, the country will actually need all the paper currency now in circulation, the inference would go far toward destroying the force of the usual arguments in favor of early resumption, as it would establish the fact that specie payments are not essential to the growth and prosperity of the country. If the assumption is not correct, the whole proposition fails; for without growth and increase in resources and trade, the currency would forever remain in excess.

Granting, however, that the business of the country is likely to attain such dimensions as to require the entire present volume of currency for its accommodation, there is another aspect of the case to be considered. When the point is reached at which the currency ceases to be redundant, the supposition is that it will rapidly appreciate to par with gold, and that gold will then resume its functions as currency. When this takes place, one of two things is likely to occur: There must be a very considerable inflation, in consequence of the addition of gold and silver to the currency, or there must be a reduction in the volume of paper money. In other words, if there shall not be inflation, there must be contraction; but it will be contraction as a consequence, not as a cause; contraction brought about by natural and self-acting causes, not by act of Congress, nor by the exercise of arbitrary power in any quarter. This would be a legitimate result, and, if it should take place, would not be liable to the same objections that are urged against contraction now.

But whether the coin shall be added to the paper, and so swell the volume of currency and produce inflation, or whether a proportion of the paper shall be retired, as the coin comes forth to take its place as a constituent part of the currency, the probabilities seem to be that, with a wise administration of the finances, paper and specie will gradually and surely, though perhaps slowly, approximate to an equality in value.

If it were possible, in considering the practicability of resumption, to distinguish between circulation and deposits, making the former paya- ble in specie, while the latter should be payable in kind, much of the difficulty and danger attendant on a return to specie payments would be removed.

Although the legal obligation to pay coin or lawful money for deposits, in the absence of any stipulation on the subject, is not disputed, yet it is probable that the banks, by concerted action, would have no diffi- culty in arranging with their customers to receive for their deposits the same kind of money deposited. This understanding is quite general between the banks and their customers, outside of two or three of the large eastern cities. If the banks in those cities would agree to settle their balances, through their clearing houses, in current funds, much of the difficulty of making deposits likewise payable in current funds would be obviated. Ordinarily those very banks pay all deposits in miscel- laneous funds, and the obligation to pay specie or lawful money only recurs to plague them when they are least able to meet the demand.

It would be practicable to place the currency on a specie basis long before it would be possible to place the entire demand liabilities of the banks on a similar footing. In New York, provision could easily be made for thirty-four millions of bank notes; but, according to estab- lished usage there, specie payments would involve provision for over $200,000,000 deposits. It is this practice which renders the finances of the country so unsteady and unreliable, to wit, the false principles which underlie the financial management of the great centers of money and trade.

If New York cannot maintain specie payments according to her own standard, they cannot be maintained successfully elsewhere for any length of time under any circumstances, and hence it is a matter of vital importance to the country at large to scrutinize carefully, not only the grounds upon which this assumed obligation is based, but also the ability of the parties to carry it into practical effect. During the last five years there have been no apprehensions in any quarter of a currency panic. That element of disaster has happily been wanting in the dis- turbances which have characterized the money market from time to time; and yet it is an admitted fact that we have more than once been upon the verge of a panic which threatened the most disastrous conse- quences. There have been not less than three occasions during the last five years in which, if the New York banks had been paying specie, according to their interpretation of specie payments, they would have been obliged to suspend from inability to pay, not their circulating notes, but their deposits; and this at a time when specie payments, if they had prevailed throughout the country, could have been maintained at every other point, as far as the currency was concerned.

To the people the establishment of the currency on a sound and sol- vent basis is the one important thing. It makes but little difference to them whether depositors in the large cities are entitled to receive specie for deposits made in currency. This is not a vital point in public esti- mation, and it may safely be left to private contract, as many other equally important questions are. The inquiry recurs, then, conceding the desirability of resuming specie payments, must all efforts in that direction be retarded and imperiled by the undertaking of a few banks, few in number, but powerful by virtue of their central position, to place deposits upon the same basis ? If any substantial interest were sacrificed, or any valuable principle violated, by the abandonment of this dogma, there might be some reason for taking the risk ; but if deposits could be made payable in kind, that is, in current funds, lawful money, or gold, as the case might be, the depositor could have no just ground of complaint, while one great obstacle to the resumption and maintenance of specie payments would be removed.

In the solution of these questions lies one of the most important problems of the day ; but, in view of the various theories advanced, it seems probable that the true solution will come only with time.

The doctrine of contraction as a means to an end for the purpose of hastening a return to specie payments, has been condemned by the people. It has been tried and rejected, and may be considered as abandoned.

The proposition to wait until the business of the country shall expand to such an extent as to require the whole volume of paper money in circulation, involves no immediate action, meets the views of the public more fully than any other plan, and is probably safer than any scheme which requires legislative interference.

It is also very evident that the undertaking, heretofore considered, to place the entire currency debt of the country on a specie basis, by the payment of deposits in coin, would be an unwise and mischievous thing, a vain and futile attempt, which would lead to panics and failures in the future as in the past. If specie payments are to be resumed, let the effort be concentrated upon the currency, and leave deposits and all other currency debts to be adjusted by private contract. As the first step in this direction, the associated banks in all cities should be required to settle balances, through their clearing-houses, in current funds.

The discrediting of national-bank currency, which is the consequence of their present regulations in this respect, is unwise and injurious, and creates a distinction between bank currency and lawful money which is unnecessary and which ought not to exist.

It would be a wise measure to provide for the extension of the national banking system wherever capital and trade may invite, withdrawing, if it should seem desirable, United States notes, as fast as bank-notes are issued.

A well-managed national bank, with a *bona fide* paid-up capital, is not a dangerous institution in any community. A deliberate, legitimate investment of capital in banking by men who, in a majority of cases, have had the sagacity, the enterprise, and the prudence to make their own money, men who are usually the most reliable members of society, can hardly be considered unwise, certainly not injurious to the interests of the people in whose midst it is made.

A national bank affords a safe place for the deposit of all the little hoards and savings which otherwise would be unemployed. It aggregates these into a fund which becomes useful and powerful in stimulating trade and enterprise.

There is reason to believe that the national banks organized during the last year in places previously without banking facilities have had no little instrumentality in helping to bear the strain that comes with every autumn. They have paid out in their several localities the currency furnished to them, while they have called out and utilized for the public good large sums of money previously distributed among and held by the people in small amounts ; and in this they have contributed to the annual supply of money required in the West, and which otherwise would have been drawn from the eastern cities.

I therefore do not hesitate to recommend that provision be made for the organization of national banks wherever they may be needed.

If, with each million of bank-notes issued, a million of legal-tenders is withdrawn, the time will come when the circulation to be redeemed will be so much larger in proportion than the funds for its redemption, that the latter must appreciate in value, while the enhanced cost of redemption will be a wholesome check upon bank issues.

If free banking is made practicable upon the basis suggested, any further increase or inflation of the currency will be rendered impossible, and every hundred thousand dollars of bank-notes so issued will have a tendency to accelerate the resumption of specie payments, while, at the same time, it will make the process gradual, and throw the responsibility and the burden upon the banks and the capital of the countrys where they legitimately belong. These are agencies which can tell with unerring certainty when and how to act, and the precise moment when it will be safe and wise to re-establish the business and finance, of the country on a specie basis.

Respectfully submitted.

HILAND R. HULBURD,
Comptroller of the Currency.

Hon. GEO. S. BOUTWELL,
Secretary of the Treasury.

APPENDIX.

Statement showing the number of banks, amount of capital, amount of bonds deposited, and circulation, in each State and Territory, on the 30th day of September, 1871.

States and Territories.	Organized.	Closed or closing.	In operation.	Capital paid in.	Bonds on deposit.	Circulation issued.	In actual circulation.
Maine	62	1	61	$9,125,000.00	$8,399,250	$8,414,346	$7,532,600 00
New Hampshire	42	....	42	4,889,000 00	4,919,000	4,835,845	4,341,695 00
Vermont	42	1	41	7,910,012 50	7,271,400	7,191,350	6,468,720 00
Massachusetts	210	3	207	88,072,000 00	65,616,750	68,233,960	57,480,866 00
Rhode Island	62	....	62	20,364,800 00	14,851,400	15,081,565	13,236,805 00
Connecticut	83	2	81	25,056,820 00	20,078,400	20,443,410	17,800,455 00
New York	318	27	291	113,140,741 00	73,545,900	83,960,388	64,018,348 00
New Jersey	58	1	57	12,580,350 00	11,371,850	11,422,575	10,032,520 00
Pennsylvania	207	9	198	51,780,240 00	45,731,750	46,327,610	40,357,046 00
Maryland	33	1	32	13,590,202 50	10,296,750	10,789,210	9,181,306 00
Delaware	11	....	11	1,528,185 00	1,453,200	1,477,875	1,303,475 .00
District of Columbia	6	3	3	1,350,000 00	1,234,000	1,471,800	1,081,570 00
Virginia	27	4	23	3,870,000 00	3,711,500	3,481,880	3,312,400 00
West Virginia	19	2	17	2,621,000 00	2,504,750	2,452,540	2,175,540 00
Ohio	140	10	130	24,349,700 00	21,401,400	22,357,655	19,338,976 00
Indiana	77	2	75	15,032,000 00	14,333,300	14,095,465	12,524,942 00
Illinois	118	3	115	17,128,000 00	15,527,200	15,245,550	13,722,825 00
Michigan	64	3	61	7,263,800 00	5,896,300	5,909,210	5,310,360 00
Wisconsin	46	5	41	3,400,000 00	3,314,550	3,539,650	3,083,257 00
Iowa	67	7	60	4,997,750 00	4,764,000	5,146,875	4,452,999 00
Minnesota	25	2	23	2,432,025 00	2,413,000	2,325,500	2,104,600 00
Kansas	12	....	12	850,000 00	785,000	741,800	649,600 00
Missouri	34	4	30	8,895,300 00	6,191,750	6,401,670	5,679,718 00
Kentucky	29	....	29	6,168,240 00	5,625,150	5,350,510	5,071,730 00
Tennessee	20	1	19	2,817,300 00	2,706,150	2,656,170	2,443,171 00
Louisiana	7	1	6	3,500,000 00	2,858,000	2,813,020	2,555,489 00
Mississippi	2	2	....	....	....	66,000	33,776 00
Nebraska	7	2	5	650,000 00	640,000	581,100	561,500 00
Colorado	4	....	4	400,000 00	404,000	383,490	358,990 00
Georgia	12	2	10	2,384,400 00	2,156,400	2,041,300	1,942,743 00
North Carolina	9	....	9	1,560,000 00	1,515,100	1,385,300	1,362,300 00
South Carolina	7	....	7	1,895,460 00	1,380,000	1,245,340	1,240,150 00
Alabama	9	1	8	916,275 00	842,150	884,100	766,783 00
Nevada	1	....	1	250,000 00	100,000	146,200	72,486 00
Oregon	1	....	1	250,000 00	250,000	136,000	135,000 00
Texas	5	....	5	625,000 00	625,000	648,300	557,500 00
Arkansas	2	....	2	200,000 00	200,000	192,500	180,000 00
Utah	2	1	1	250,000 00	150,000	176,520	132,281 00
Montana	1	....	1	100,000 00	100,000	90,000	90,000 00
Idaho	1	....	1	100,000 00	100,000	94,300	89,500 00
Wyoming	1	....	1	75,000 00	30,000	27,000	27,000 00
New Mexico	1	....	1	150,000 00	150,000	135,000	135,000 00
Fractional redemptions reported by Treasurer United States.	....	....	....	....	....	....	8 20
Total	1,884	100	1,784	462,518,601 60	365,444,350	380,609,879	322,952,030 20
GOLD BANKS.							
Massachusetts	1	....	1	300,000 00	150,000	120,000	120,000 00
California	1	....	1	1,000,000 00	500,000	375,000	375,000 00
Total	2	....	2	1,300,000 00	650,000	495,000	495,000 00

Statement exhibiting the number and amount of notes issued, redeemed, and outstanding
September 30, 1871.

	No. of notes.	Amount.
Ones:		
Issued	12, 537, 657	$12, 537, 657 00
Redeemed	5, 276, 057	5, 276, 057 00
Outstanding	7, 261, 600	7, 261, 600 00
Twos:		
Issued	4, 195, 791	8, 391, 582 00
Redeemed	1, 493, 326	2, 986, 652 00
Outstanding	2, 702, 465	5, 404, 930 00
Fives:		
Issued	28, 174, 940	140, 874, 700 00
Redeemed	3, 276, 374	16, 381, 870 00
Outstanding	24, 898, 566	124, 492, 830 00
Tens:		
Issued	9, 728, 375	97, 283, 750 00
Redeemed	933, 445	9, 334, 450 00
Outstanding	8, 794, 930	87, 949, 300 00
Twenties:		
Issued	2, 779, 392	55, 587, 840 00
Redeemed	245, 361	4, 907, 220 00
Outstanding	2, 534, 031	50, 680, 620 00
Fifties:		
Issued	433, 426	21, 671, 300 00
Redeemed	82, 972	4, 148, 600 00
Outstanding	350, 454	17, 522, 700 00
One hundreds:		
Issued	321, 163	32, 116, 300 00
Redeemed	76, 287	7, 628, 700 00
Outstanding	244, 876	24, 487, 600 00
Five hundreds:		
Issued	14, 642	7, 321, 000 00
Redeemed	6, 017	3, 008, 500 00
Outstanding	8, 625	4, 312, 500 00
One thousands:		
Issued	4, 843	4, 843, 000 00
Redeemed	4, 005	4, 005, 000 00
Outstanding	838	838, 000 00

Total amount of all denominations outstanding on the 30th day of September, 1871	322, 950, 080 00
Add for fragments of notes outstanding, lost, or destroyed, portions of which have been redeemed	1, 950 20
Total	322, 952, 030 20

Statement exhibiting the number and amount of gold bank notes issued and outstanding September 30, 1871.

	No. of notes.	Amount.
Fives:		
Issued	16, 000 }	$80, 000
Outstanding	16, 000 }	
Tens:		
Issued	10, 000 }	100, 000
Outstanding	10, 000 }	
Twenties:		
Issued	4, 000 }	80, 000
Outstanding	4, 000 }	
Fifties:		
Issued	650 }	32, 500
Outstanding	650 }	
One hundreds:		
Issued	650 }	65, 000
Outstanding	650 }	
Five hundreds:		
Issued	125 }	62, 500
Outstanding	125 }	
One thousands:		
Issued	75 }	75, 000
Outstanding	75 }	
Total amount outstanding September 30, 1871		495, 000

Statement showing the amounts and kinds of United States bonds held by the Treasurer of the United States, to secure the redemption of the circulating notes of national banks, on the 30th day of September, 1871.

Registered bonds, act of June 14, 1858	$640, 000
Registered bonds, act of February 8, 1861	3, 929, 000
Registered bonds, act of July 17, August 5, 1861	61, 488, 700
Registered bonds, act of February 25, 1862	16, 524, 850
Registered bonds, act of March 3, 1863	33, 146, 850
Registered bonds, act of March 3, 1864—5 per cent	102, 232, 450
Registered bonds, act of June 30, 1864	17, 686, 500
Registered bonds, act of July 1, 1862, July 2, 1864	15, 176, 000
Registered bonds, act of March 3, 1864—6 per cent	2, 243, 000
Registered bonds, act of March 3, 1865, 5-20—1st series	13, 286, 500
Registered bonds, act of March 3, 1865, Consols, 1865—2d series	7, 596, 550
Registered bonds, act of March 3, 1865, Consols, 1867—3d series	12, 201, 350
Registered bonds, act of March 3, 1865, Consols, 1868—4th series	2, 824, 000
Registered bonds, act of July 14, 1870. January 20, 1871—5 per cent. funded loan	77, 118, 600
Total	366, 094, 350

Statement showing the national banks in the hands of receivers, their capital, amount of United States bonds and lawful money deposited to secure circulation, amount of circulation delivered, the amount of circulation redeemed at the Treasury of the United States, and the amount outstanding, on the 30th day of September, 1871.

Name and location of bank.	Capital.	U. S. bonds on deposit.	Legal tenders deposited, as realized from sale of bonds.	Circulation delivered.	Circulation redeemed.	Circulation outstanding.
Venango National Bank, Franklin, Pa.	$300,000	....	$85,000 00	$85,000	$78,628 50	$6,371 50
Merchants' National Bank, Washington, D. C.	200,000	$50,000	180,000 00	180,000	163,829 00	16,171 00
Tennessee National Bank, Memphis, Tenn.	100,000	....	90,000 00	90,000	82,198 75	7,801 25
First National Bank, Selma, Ala ..	100,000	....	85,000 00	85,000	75,316 75	9,683 25
First National Bank, New Orleans, La.	500,000	....	180,000 00	180,000	159,510 50	20,489 50
National Unadilla Bank, Unadilla, N. Y.	120,000	....	100,000 00	100,000	91,005 25	8,994 75
Farmers and Citizens' National Bank, Brooklyn, N. Y.	300,000	....	253,900 00	253,900	229,853 00	24,047 00
Croton National Bank of the City of New York, N. Y.	200,000	....	180,000 00	180,000	164,917 65	15,082 35
First National Bank, Bethel, Conn.	60,000	....	26,300 00	26,300	20,339 50	5,960 50
First National Bank, Keokuk, Iowa	100,000	....	90,000 00	90,000	79,139 50	10,860 50
National Bank of Vicksburg, Miss	50,000	....	25,500 00	25,500	18,708 75	6,791 25
First National Bank, Rockford, Ill.	50,000	25,000	30,240 00	45,000	32,483 00	12,517 00
First National Bank of Nevada at Austin, Nev.	250,000	100,000	59,393 75	131,700	72,214 00	59,486 00
Total	2,330,000	175,000	1,385,333 75	1,472,400	1,268,144 15	204,255 85

Statement showing the national banks in voluntary liquidation that have deposited lawful money with the Treasurer of the United States to redeem their circulation, withdrawn their bonds, and been closed under the provisions of section 42 of the act; their capital, circulation issued, circulation surrendered, circulation redeemed by the Treasurer of the United States, and circulation outstanding on the 30th day of September, 1871.

Name and location of bank.	Capital.	Circulation delivered.	Circulation surrendered.	Circulation redeemed by the Treasurer of the United States.	Circulation outstanding.
First National Bank, Columbia, Mo ..	$100,000	$90,000	$78,010	$9,425 00	$2,565 00
First National Bank, Carondelet, Mo.	30,000	25,500	....	23,348 75	2,151 25
National Union Bank, Rochester, N. Y.	400,000	192,500	2,550	81,013 75	108,936 25
Farmers' National Bank, Waukesha, Wis	100,000	90,000	....	69,320 25	20,679 75
First National Bank, Bloffton, Ind	50,000	45,000	3,770	19,433 00	21,797 00
First National Bank, Jackson, Miss	100,000	40,500	....	13,515 00	26,985 00
First National Bank, Skaneateles, N. Y.	150,000	135,000	6,585	70,074 30	58,340 70
Appleton National Bank, Appleton, Wis	50,000	45,000	....	23,276 50	21,723 50
National Bank of Whitestown, N. Y.	120,000	44,500	....	16,649 00	27,851 00
First National Bank, Cedarburg, Wis	100,000	53,350	18,000	33,969 50	34,030 50
Commercial National Bank, Cincinnati, Ohio.	500,000	345,950	....	194,945 50	151,004 50
First National Bank, South Worcester, N. Y.	175,000	137,400	4,500	78,805 75	74,094 25
Nat'l Mechanics and Farmers' Bank, Albany, N. Y	350,000	314,950	48,410	142,027 75	124,512 25
Second National Bank, Des Moines, Iowa	50,000	42,500	2,200	18,642 50	21,657 50
First National Bank, Oskaloosa, Iowa	75,000	67,500	3,755	33,435 05	30,309 95
Merchants and Mechanics' Nat'l Bank, Troy, N. Y	300,000	184,750	13,900	84,174 60	86,675 40
First National Bank, Marion, Ohio	125,000	109,850	4,017	55,755 15	50,077 85
National Bank of Lansingburgh, N. Y.	150,000	135,000	12,000	62,987 65	60,012 35
Nat'l Bank of North America, New York, N. Y..	1,000,000	333,000	65,800	132,699 65	134,500 35
First National Bank, Hallowell, Me	60,000	53,350	2,500	24,986 00	25,864 00
Pacific National Bank, New York, N. Y	422,700	134,990	4,715	61,537 50	68,737 50
Grocers' National Bank, New York, N. Y.	300,000	85,250	45,810	5,208 00	34,232 00
Savannah National Bank, Savannah, Ga.	100,000	85,000	....	44,306 25	40,693 75
First National Bank, Frostburg, Md.	50,000	45,000	4,250	16,804 00	23,946 00
First National Bank, Vinton, Iowa	50,000	42,500	885	18,523 75	23,091 25
First National Bank, Decatur, Ill.	100,000	85,250	....	46,041 15	39,208 85
First National Bank, Berlin, Wis	50,000	44,000	3,923	16,447 10	23,629 90
First National Bank, Dayton, Ohio.	150,000	135,000	2,900	67,076 70	65,023 30

Statement showing the national banks in voluntary liquidation, &c.—Continued.

Name and location of bank.	Capital.	Circulation delivered.	Circulation surrendered.°	Circulation redeemed by the Treasurer of the United States.	Circulation outstanding.
National Bank of Chemung, Elmira, N. Y	$100,000	$90,000	....	$45,083 75	$44,916 25
First National Bank, St. Louis, Mo	200,000	179,990	....	88,574 50	91,415 50
First National Bank, Lebanon. Ohio	100,000	85,000	....	41,023 75	43,976 25
National Union Bank, Owego, N. Y	100,000	88,250	$5,400	200 00	82,650 00
Chemung Canal National Bank, Elmira, N. Y	100,000	90,000	3,500	33,642 15	52,857 85
National Insurance Bank, Detroit, Mich	200,010	85,000	9,500	15,500 00	60,000 00
State National Bank, St. Joseph, Mo	100,000	90,000	3,813	18,100 00	68,087 00
National Exchange Bank, Lansingburgh, N. Y	100,050	90,000	4,308	11,901 90	73,790 10
Saratoga County Nat'l Bank, Waterford, N. Y	150,000	135,000	8,000	23,200 00	103,800 00
Farmers' National Bank, Richmond, Va	100,000	85,000	8,500	....	76,500 00
First National Bank, Des Moines, Iowa	100,000	90,000	700	16,500 00	72,800 00
First National Bank, Fenton, Mich	100,000	49,500	....	9,500 00	40,000 00
National State Bank, Dubuque, Iowa	150,000	127,500	14,900	....	112,600 00
Total	6,807,710	4,484,480	387,101	1,767,655 15	2,329,723 85

Statement showing the national banks in liquidation for the purpose of consolidating with other banks, their capital, bonds deposited to secure circulation, circulation delivered, circulation surrendered and destroyed, and circulation outstanding September 30, 1871.

Name and location of bank.	Capital.	U. S. bonds on deposit.	Circulation delivered.	Circulation surrendered.	Circulation outstanding.
Pittston National Bank, Pittston, Pa	$200,000	....	(*)	....	....
Fourth National Bank, Indianapolis, Ind	100,000	$87,500	$85,700	$8,700	$77,000
Berkshire National Bank, Adams, Mass	100,000	....	(*)	....	....
First National Bank, Leonardsville, N. Y	50,000	50,500	45,000	....	45,000
National Bank of the Metropolis, Washington, D. C.	200,000	154,000	180,000	52,400	127,600
First National Bank, Providence, Pa	100,000	93,850	90,000	7,750	82,250
National Bank of Crawford County, Meadville, Pa	300,000	....	(*)	....	....
Kittanning National Bank, Kittanning, Pa	200,000	....	(*)	....	....
City National Bank, Savannah, Ga	100,000	....	(*)	....	....
Ohio National Bank, Cincinnati, Ohio	500,000	511,000	450,000	35,400	414,600
First National Bank, New Ulm, Minn	60,000	50,500	54,000	8,800	45,200
First National Bank, Kingston, N. Y	200,000	173,000	180,000	26,200	153,800
National Exchange Bank, Richmond, Va	200,000	196,300	180,000	5,180	174,820
First National Bank, Downingtown, Pa	100,000	86,000	89,500	13,000	76,500
First National Bank, Titusville, Pa	100,000	87,100	86,750	13,700	73,050
First National Bank, New Brunswick, N. J	100,000	96,700	90,000	8,800	81,200
First National Bank, Cuyahoga Falls, Ohio	50,000	37,000	45,000	12,600	32,400
Second National Bank, Watertown, N. Y	100,000	96,000	90,000	3,600	86,400
First National Bank, Steubenville, Ohio	150,000	150,000	135,000	....	135,000
First National Bank, Plumer, Pa	100,000	90,000	87,500	7,300	80,200
First National Bank, Danville, Va	50,000	41,000	45,000	8,700	36,300
First National Bank, Dorchester, Mass	150,000	131,500	132,500	20,900	111,600
National Savings Bank, Wheeling, W. Va	100,000	79,000	90,000	19,100	70,900
First National Bank, Clyde, N. Y	50,000	49,500	44,000	3,000	41,000
First National Bank, La Salle, Ill	50,000	42,000	45,000	8,600	36,400
National Bank of Commerce, Georgetown, D. C	100,000	80,000	90,000	18,800	71,200
Miners' National Bank, Salt Lake, Utah	150,000	102,000	135,000	43,200	91,800
National Exchange Bank, Philadelphia, Pa	300,000	180,000	175,750	23,400	152,350
Central National Bank, Cincinnati, Ohio	500,000	389,000	425,000	83,025	341,975
Merchants' National Bank, Milwaukee, Wis	100,000	101,500	90,000	....	90,000
Central National Bank, Omaha, Neb	100,000	....	(*)	....	....
First National Bank, Clarksville, Va	50,000	30,000	27,000	....	27,000
First National Bank, Burlington, Vt	300,000	281,000	270,000	17,100	252,900
Muskingum National Bank, Zanesville, Ohio	100,000	98,000	90,000	2,300	87,700
United National Bank, Winona, Minn	50,000	50,000	45,000	875	44,125
Clarke National Bank, Rochester, N. Y	200,000	200,000	180,000	....	180,000
First National Bank, Wellsburg, W. Va	100,000	100,000	90,000	....	90,000
First National Bank of Newton, Newtonville, Mass	150,000	115,000	130,000	27,000	103,000
Total	5,610,000	4,028,950	3,992,700	479,430	3,513,270

* No circulation.

Table of the state of the lawful-money reserve of the national banks of the United States, as shown by the reports of their condition at the close of business on the 28th day of December, 1870.

States and Territories	Number of banks	Liabilities to be protected by reserve	Reserve required: 15 per cent. of liabilities	Reserve held	Per cent. of reserve to liabilities	FUNDS AVAILABLE FOR RESERVE				Due from redeeming agents
						Specie	Legal tenders	Clearing-house certificates	Three per cent. certificates	
Maine	61	$12,980,819	$1,948,472	$2,918,395	22.5	$37,976	$1,035,756		$5,000	$1,839,663
New Hampshire	41	8,490,567	973,585	1,317,778	21.2	40,681	466,764			870,333
Vermont	41	8,491,766	1,273,764	1,746,534	21.6	62,316	643,111			959,307
Massachusetts	160	52,748,766	7,912,315	10,686,935	20.3	212,299	4,217,865		80,000	6,071,751
Rhode Island	62	19,030,351	2,852,553	3,571,786	18.7	36,720	1,350,066		185,000	2,109,980
Connecticut	81	30,062,599	4,569,389	6,852,514	18.8	66,426	2,405,642		75,000	4,290,446
New York	232	74,337,811	11,150,672	14,352,685	19.6	496,701	5,610,732		90,000	7,795,252
New Jersey	54	24,976,635	3,746,495	5,577,805	22.3	147,044	1,933,966		650,000	3,296,796
Pennsylvania	151	44,258,725	6,638,809	9,089,923	20.5	128,232	4,311,592		200,000	3,995,099
Delaware	11	2,379,527	356,929	464,903	19.5	2,848	184,258		655,000	197,797
Maryland	18	4,225,207	633,781	1,164,836	27.5	34,896	418,074		80,000	681,866
Virginia	19	6,336,926	950,539	1,154,561	18.2	75,483	520,517		30,000	558,562
West Virginia	14	4,205,179	630,777	719,751	17.1	26,361	394,081			279,315
North Carolina	6	2,470,781	370,618	460,150	18.6	29,245	269,422		20,000	161,483
South Carolina	3	1,638,328	245,749	354,188	21.6	16,612	151,700			185,876
Georgia	8	3,555,829	533,374	997,393	28.0	88,920	652,337		50,000	206,136
Alabama	3	730,689	112,633	462,233	61.5	26,766	108,123			327,344
Texas	4	1,305,605	204,841	471,739	34.5	59,089	245,939			56,770
Arkansas	2	397,208	59,581	54,886	13.8	881	98,569			25,436
Kentucky	16	4,335,859	650,370	971,795	22.4	5,680	489,976			476,139
Tennessee	17	5,115,421	767,314	1,301,490	25.4	6,830	776,381			457,279
Ohio	118	27,694,659	4,154,199	5,798,707	20.9	81,386	2,887,433		245,000	2,585,888
Indiana	69	19,677,699	2,951,655	3,705,050	18.8	10,064	2,136,242		35,000	1,394,744
Illinois	74	14,673,988	2,201,098	3,415,003	23.3	104,210	1,551,831		60,000	1,698,962
Michigan	42	7,073,099	1,060,965	1,562,665	22.1	22,853	836,091		36,000	668,721
Wisconsin	32	4,325,062	648,694	1,004,342	23.2	21,046	451,104		10,000	497,192
Iowa	45	8,737,904	1,310,686	1,999,842	22.9	60,955	1,136,010			792,877
Minnesota	18	4,644,202	696,630	892,490	19.2	18,536	470,348			403,506
Missouri	14	3,505,590	525,838	825,528	23.5	25,139	458,351		10,000	331,438
Kansas	4	1,951,649	123,833	161,418	19.6	9,256	116,670			40,820
Nebraska	3	825,554	292,747	470,925	24.1	38,37	129,761			331,308
Oregon	1	818,559	122,783	199,064	24.3	20,385	131,936			28,991
Colorado	3	1,542,522	231,378	562,188	36.4	38,37	207,650			334,152
Utah	1	296,473	44,472	74,730	25.2	12,73	45,121			25,500
Idaho	1	140,927	21,139	41,450	29.4	19,04	28,198			477
Montana	1	219,096	32,864	57,641	26.3	19,04	38,600			
Total	1,430	406,311,675	60,946,750	85,721,389	21.0	2,359,126	36,842,257		2,543,000	43,977,006

Table of the state of the lawful money reserve—Continued. CITIES, as shown by reports of the 28th of December, 1870.

Cities of redemption.	Number of banks.	Liabilities to be protected by reserve.	Reserve required: 25 per cent of liabilities.	Reserve held.	Per cent. of reserve to liabilities.	FUNDS AVAILABLE FOR RESERVE.				Due from redeeming agents.
						Specie.	Legal tenders.	Clearing house certificates.	Three per cent. certificates.	
Boston	46	$80,064,843	$20,016,211	$23,179,404	28.9	$2,184,839	$8,925,845	$51,000	$4,060,000	87,957,720
Albany	7	10,216,904	2,554,226	4,249,545	41.6	9,933	1,192,455		295,000	2,822,157
Philadelphia	30	47,689,371	11,922,343	14,196,268	29.9	933,835	4,900,673	1,930,000	5,410,000	971,760
Pittsburgh	16	13,025,519	3,756,381	4,084,065	27.2	110,027	1,855,260		375,000	1,745,779
Baltimore	13	18,651,076	4,662,769	5,451,274	29.2	193,457	2,456,089	198,000	890,000	1,783,728
Washington	3	2,550,182	637,545	661,577	26.2	44,830	985,096		195,000	142,651
New Orleans	3	3,023,331	755,833	1,084,190	35.9	32,453	956,913			94,824
Louisville	4	1,340,787	335,197	378,352	28.2	3,411	207,645		5,000	162,296
Cincinnati	5	7,682,170	1,920,542	2,365,299	30.8	51,092	1,189,200		100,000	1,025,000
Cleveland	6	5,391,853	1,348,463	1,428,756	26.5	11,464	709,000		190,000	518,292
Chicago	15	19,135,198	4,783,800	5,768,064	30.1	166,128	3,267,812		385,000	1,949,144
Detroit	3	3,623,552	905,888	1,162,415	30.4	4,697	510,286		60,000	587,432
Milwaukee	4	2,602,102	630,525	696,228	26.8	5,734	387,427		15,000	283,067
St. Louis	7	7,622,685	1,905,671	2,109,993	27.7	64,926	971,132		395,000	673,935
Leavenworth	2	877,597	219,399	223,747	25.5	1,050	110,423		10,000	102,274
Total	164	225,699,170	56,424,793	67,045,190	29.7	3,867,876	27,855,256	2,109,000	12,383,000	20,822,058
New York	54	195,097,247	48,774,312	58,802,126	30.1	16,061,406	13,825,720	18,440,000	8,475,000	

6 F

Table of the state of the lawful money reserve—Continued. STATES, *as shown by reports of the 18th of March, 1871.*

States and Territories.	Number of banks.	Liabilities to be protected by reserve.	Reserve required: 15 per cent. of liabilities.	Reserve held.	Per cent. of reserve to liabilities.	FUNDS AVAILABLE FOR RESERVE.				Due from redeeming agents.
						Specie.	Legal tenders.	Clearing-house certificates.	Three per cent. certificates.	
Maine	61	$12,839,195	$1,925,879	$2,940,796	22.1	$25,373	$905,864		$5,000	$1,814,419
New Hampshire	41	6,737,831	1,010,675	1,683,342	25.0	28,901	459,460			1,194,981
Vermont	41	9,020,437	1,353,065	1,858,309	20.6	12,914	622,159		90,000	1,103,236
Massachusetts	160	52,847,515	7,927,127	11,945,806	22.6	135,639	4,037,779		135,000	7,587,188
Rhode Island	62	18,907,385	2,821,108	3,503,311	18.6	4,185	1,337,220		75,000	2,046,906
Connecticut	81	30,754,198	4,613,129	7,498,857	24.4	116,483	1,304,547		90,000	5,141,927
New York	232	76,866,228	11,529,934	18,606,995	24.2	45,982	3,304,755		590,000	12,286,258
New Jersey	56	25,938,930	3,890,839	6,193,927	23.9	59,294	1,885,846		190,000	4,022,787
Pennsylvania	151	45,667,104	6,850,066	10,017,927	21.9	108,702	1,093,058		570,000	5,249,637
Delaware	11	2,346,806	352,021	330,373	21.8	814	172,974		80,000	274,785
Maryland	18	4,928,030	634,994	1,098,826	20.8	3,014	399,214		30,000	639,598
Virginia	22	4,237,276	635,591	1,258,344	17.9	85,384	615,171			560,789
West Virginia	14	2,715,498	407,325	687,754	16.2	42,373	346,392		20,000	298,179
North Carolina	8	1,900,540	285,081	603,297	22.2	4,337	296,227			273,733
South Carolina	4	3,968,297	595,245	567,087	26.6	16,938	156,800			331,349
Georgia	8	945,884	141,883	1,621,017	25.7	91,023	749,281		50,000	130,713
Alabama	3	1,495,136	224,270	401,399	42.4	19,295	179,461			292,567
Texas	5	1,348,136	52,217	618,444	41.4	354,428	183,397			80,739
Arkansas	5	4,370,477	730,572	50,229	14.4	1,204	42,462			6,563
Kentucky	20	4,870,477	865,306	975,201	20.0	4,414	537,342			433,445
Tennessee	18	5,768,709	4,274,674	1,275,725	22.1	55,307	600,566		185,000	619,552
Ohio	118	28,497,825	3,147,311	6,017,601	21.1	36,135	2,786,392		35,000	3,009,274
Indiana	70	20,962,071	2,560,994	4,200,378	20.0	154,86	2,100,602		25,000	1,910,168
Illinois	79	17,073,327	1,901,791	3,796,130	22.2	125,541	1,682,634		30,000	1,963,235
Michigan	49	8,011,940	1,201,791	1,969,622	24.6	32,519	893,856		25,000	1,012,947
Wisconsin	32	4,530,623	679,593	1,032,132	22.8	14,108	413,297			579,217
Iowa	48	9,898,020	1,484,703	2,166,882	21.9	58,627	1,198,998		10,000	899,197
Minnesota	19	5,038,611	755,791	661,442	17.1	16,346	429,628			415,458
Missouri	16	3,873,322	580,998	780,673	20.1	24,314	416,311		10,000	330,008
Kansas	6	1,286,277	192,942	280,381	21.8	3,040	132,221			145,360
Nebraska	3	1,922,600	288,390	482,627	25.1	9,885	113,576			359,166
Oregon	3	845,692	126,854	288,295	34.1	83,212	64,658			140,625
Colorado	3	1,516,816	227,522	420,160	27.7	21,698	129,342			269,125
Utah	1	377,600	56,640	39,173	10.4	8,412	36,261			500
Idaho	1	146,818	22,023	23,214	15.8	9,835	5,060			8,301
Montana	1	270,700	40,605	81,194	30.0	25,744	17,100			38,354
Total	1,465	423,793,830	63,569,073	95,615,960	22.6	2,420,967	35,569,817		2,945,000	55,360,156

Table of the state of the lawful money reserve—Continued. CITIES, as shown by reports of the 18th of March, 1871.

Cities of redemption.	Number of banks.	Liabilities to be protected by reserve.	Reserve required: 25 per cent of liabilities.	Reserve held.	Per cent of reserve to liabilities.	FUNDS AVAILABLE FOR RESERVE.				Due from redeeming agents.
						Specie.	Legal tenders.	Clearing-house certificates.	Three per cent. certificates.	
Boston	46	$90,627,640	$22,656,910	$26,398,176	32.7	$2,082,005	$9,138,798		$3,335,000	$11,842,373
Albany	7	10,567,433	2,641,858	4,225,435	40.0	10,529	1,150,377		265,000	2,799,529
Philadelphia	30	48,329,151	12,082,288	14,543,046	30.1	414,931	4,629,829	$1,975,000	4,910,000	2,613,286
Pittsburgh	16	15,776,242	3,944,060	4,302,391	27.3	89,205	1,906,998		380,000	1,944,188
Baltimore	13	19,716,503	4,929,126	5,554,167	28.1	115,553	2,545,549	254,000	750,000	1,889,065
Washington	3	2,751,294	687,821	833,221	30.3	52,186	446,254		160,000	174,781
New Orleans	6	4,683,031	1,170,758	1,671,090	35.6	83,038	982,216			605,766
Louisville	4	1,333,085	333,271	359,753	27.0	2,748	199,709		5,000	132,296
Cincinnati	5	8,139,351	2,034,838	2,354,065	28.9	69,976	1,034,425		120,000	1,129,664
Cleveland	6	5,646,617	1,411,654	1,766,245	31.3	3,229	705,000		130,000	928,016
Chicago	16	22,993,004	5,748,251	6,761,500	29.4	130,170	4,028,835		210,000	2,392,475
Detroit	3	4,260,701	1,065,175	1,564,074	36.7	16,575	538,749		60,000	948,750
Milwaukee	4	2,651,323	715,331	667,708	23.3	3,469	362,981		15,000	226,258
St. Louis	7	8,424,123	2,106,031	2,110,096	25.0	73,815	1,010,966		355,000	670,305
Leavenworth	2	881,982	220,495	196,052	22.2	1,164	112,005		10,000	72,283
Total	168	236,991,470	59,247,867	73,306,939	30.9	3,148,593	28,795,311	2,229,000	10,685,000	28,449,035
New York	54	229,897,516	57,474,379	65,277,854	28.4	16,181,876	24,455,978	18,370,000	6,270,000	
San Francisco	1	84,883	21,221	185,872	219.0	185,872				

Table of the state of the lawful money reserve. Continued. STATES, as shown by reports of the 29th of April, 1871.

States and Territories.	Number of banks	Liabilities to be protected by reserve.	Reserve required: 15 per cent. of liabilities.	Reserve held.	Per cent. of reserve to liabilities.	FUNDS AVAILABLE FOR RESERVE.				Due from redeeming agents.
						Specie.	Legal tenders.	Clearing-house certificates.	Three per cent. certificates.	
Maine	61	$13,162,052	$1,977,308	$2,950,340	22.4	$99,826	$1,067,580		$5,000	$1,777,934
New Hampshire	41	6,579,815	986,972	1,494,826	22.7	25,754	473,179			995,893
Vermont	41	9,076,694	1,361,504	1,874,433	20.7	41,625	668,936		85,000	1,078,872
Massachusetts	160	56,014,715	8,402,207	12,882,144	23.0	193,402	4,236,875		120,000	8,331,967
Rhode Island	62	19,501,967	2,925,295	3,797,709	19.5	37,446	1,421,136		75,000	2,264,127
Connecticut	81	32,819,683	4,921,962	8,519,704	26.0	122,334	2,431,019		90,000	5,875,831
New York	231	76,323,533	11,448,530	17,303,961	22.5	365,439	5,606,665		515,000	10,716,677
New Jersey	56	26,548,035	3,983,205	6,125,357	23.1	192,201	1,949,162		185,000	3,888,994
Pennsylvania	151	46,818,022	7,022,703	10,380,433	22.2	110,379	4,521,691		505,000	5,243,363
Delaware	11	2,580,183	387,026	539,305	20.9	2,322	208,153		80,000	248,330
Maryland	18	4,068,357	610,254	979,375	24.1	30,713	409,345		30,000	509,117
Virginia	22	7,349,810	1,102,472	1,239,233	16.9	88,500	734,641			415,992
West Virginia	15	4,434,376	665,156	749,926	16.9	24,160	392,316		10,000	323,150
North Carolina	9	2,882,309	432,340	596,318	20.7	51,821	300,292			244,205
South Carolina	9	2,084,378	312,657	664,590	31.9	27,005	284,700			351,985
Georgia	8	3,933,472	590,020	1,205,767	30.7	136,275	577,258		50,000	442,234
Alabama	5	1,010,551	151,643	321,032	31.8	22,509	169,309			129,814
Texas	5	1,998,209	299,731	1,001,054	50.1	337,211	310,384			354,059
Arkansas	2	402,370	60,356	39,165	9.7	18	27,991			10,656
Kentucky	21	5,065,430	759,813	983,804	19.4	8,401	574,634			401,249
Tennessee	18	6,308,142	931,221	1,304,945	21.0	41,510	679,148			563,987
Ohio	119	28,343,155	4,251,473	6,002,889	21.4	35,165	3,092,210		170,000	2,765,514
Indiana	70	22,562,097	3,384,315	6,037,454	22.3	180,021	2,410,352		30,000	2,417,081
Illinois	85	17,530,019	2,629,517	3,760,030	21.4	96,523	1,733,524		25,000	1,905,571
Michigan	50	8,417,364	1,262,605	2,073,117	24.6	43,787	949,695		30,000	1,050,245
Wisconsin	35	4,699,942	704,991	1,067,731	22.6	11,683	456,083		15,000	584,665
Iowa	51	5,108,630	766,294	2,250,694	22.6	56,163	1,262,351		10,000	921,870
Minnesota	19	3,746,202	561,930	999,253	19.6	14,119	448,472			536,631
Missouri	15	1,444,362	216,654	778,181	90.8	28,979	397,985		10,000	341,217
Kansas	6	2,179,715	326,957	323,671	22.4	3,925	168,437			151,299
Nebraska	4	989,407	148,411	627,816	28.8	9,640	270,167			348,009
Oregon	1	137,832	20,675	346,396	33.0	66,890	71,835			207,671
New Mexico	1	1,472,419	220,868	25,612	18.6		139,133			11,605
Colorado	3	442,249	66,337	345,130	23.4	18,463	19,668			187,594
Utah	1	36,343	5,451	70,166	15.9	49,958	4,781			500
Wyoming	1	175,207	26,281	9,933	97.3	81	19,781			5,071
Idaho	1	271,678	40,752	30,149	17.2	7,065	13,450			9,634
Montana	1			35,932	13.2	9,753	10,100			16,082
Total	1,484	436,412,072	65,461,811	98,698,874	22.6	2,504,656	38,506,554		2,040,000	55,647,695

Table of the state of the lawful money reserve—Continued. CITIES, as shown by reports of the 29th of April, 1871.

Cities of redemption.	Number of banks.	Liabilities to be protected by reserve.	Reserve required: 25 per cent. of liabilities.	Reserve held.	Per cent. of reserve to liabilities.	FUNDS AVAILABLE FOR RESERVE.				
						Specie.	Legal tenders.	Clearing-house certificates.	Three per cent. certificates.	Due from redeeming agents.
Boston	47	$84,512,926	$21,128,232	$26,225,350	31.0	$2,215,624	$9,338,385	$150,000	$2,610,000	$11,911,341
Albany	7	12,739,052	3,184,763	5,404,887	42.5	10,410	1,112,064		235,000	4,047,413
Philadelphia	30	52,217,119	13,054,280	16,444,713	31.5	379,426	7,415,965	2,365,000	4,145,000	2,140,322
Pittsburgh	16	15,985,126	3,996,282	4,343,237	27.2	76,348	2,476,303		350,000	1,440,586
Baltimore	14	20,349,778	5,087,444	5,893,622	29.0	310,068	2,936,932	182,000	690,000	1,774,622
Washington	3	2,346,137	586,534	918,561	39.2	52,210	431,815		135,000	299,536
New Orleans	6	5,359,033	1,339,756	1,887,580	35.2	154,105	1,176,320			557,155
Louisville	4	1,434,004	358,501	425,829	30.0	3,584	274,325		5,000	142,920
Cincinnati	5	8,619,602	2,154,901	2,818,026	32.7	62,420	1,360,053		105,000	1,290,553
Cleveland	6	5,450,676	1,362,669	1,653,467	30.3	2,750	705,642	9,572	90,000	845,503
Chicago	16	24,173,924	6,043,481	7,730,724	32.0	122,609	4,599,121		205,000	2,803,994
Detroit	3	3,810,323	952,581	1,346,279	35.3	1,942	673,690		60,000	610,647
Milwaukee	4	3,028,417	757,104	1,046,879	34.6	6,228	410,791		15,000	614,800
St. Louis	7	7,835,741	1,958,935	2,260,307	98.8	58,465	1,069,903		260,000	871,939
Leavenworth	2	962,747	240,687	258,270	26.8	196	186,147		10,000	61,927
Total	170	248,824,605	62,206,150	78,657,731	31.6	3,455,385	34,167,456	2,706,572	8,915,000	29,413,318
New York	54	226,873,165	56,718,291	65,709,218	29.0	11,895,172	30,834,046	18,875,000	4,105,000	
San Francisco	1	406,297	101,574	445,130	109.5	440,601	4,529			

State		$5,000				%				
Maine	$1,874,524	$5,000		$1,050,534	$24,135	22.7	$2,954,193	$1,950,134	$13,000,891	61
New Hampshire	1,247,957			478,388	14,397	5.5	1,740,722	1,024,438	6,889,591	41
Vermont	1,167,022	85,000		711,469	33,296	2.3	1,996,787	1,403,660	9,357,733	41
Massachusetts	7,792,399	110,000		4,286,978	133,708	2.0	12,297,085	8,069,597	55,130,648	160
Rhode Island	2,742,470	75,000		1,369,673	34,075	25.2	4,221,918	3,005,791	20,038,609	62
Connecticut	5,724,605	90,000		2,511,665	105,678	22.3	4,431,948	5,017,194	33,482,295	81
New York	10,570,385	465,000		1,619,781	220,254	24.5	16,935,420	11,412,331	76,081,543	231
New Jersey	4,378,463	160,000		1,996,731	99,040	21.5	6,634,234	4,058,672	27,057,812	57
Pennsylvania	5,398,204	440,000		1,407,066	99,119	21.5	10,634,991	7,050,862	47,005,744	151
Delaware	253,239	80,000		189,878	2,792	20.9	525,909	382,539	4,550,261	11
Maryland	568,458	30,000		476,016	43,211	26.5	1,117,685	635,800	4,238,669	18
Virginia	390,290			682,596	82,391	17.9	1,355,267	1,136,354	7,575,692	22
West Virginia	342,054	10,000		416,937	24,330	17.4	793,321	631,846	4,545,641	15
North Carolina	330,624			295,023	43,756	21.9	669,403	458,229	3,054,858	9
South Carolina	196,465			297,685	17,964	23.1	512,114	332,185	2,214,567	5
Georgia	466,769	50,000		509,793	77,632	28.5	1,104,194	581,177	3,874,512	8
Alabama	177,154			117,433	36,839	34.7	331,416	143,031	953,540	3
Texas	217,855			235,716	237,849	40.0	711,420	266,469	1,776,460	5
Arkansas	9,028			28,164	1,867	10.5	39,059	55,628	370,857	2
Kentucky	453,086			565,347	6,910	20.3	1,025,343	737,974	5,053,157	21
Tennessee	670,727			723,014	50,986	23.5	1,444,727	935,374	6,235,830	18
Ohio	3,479,437	165,000		3,003,275	49,901	22.4	6,697,613	4,462,390	99,882,599	119
Indiana	2,895,269	30,000		2,449,309	69,040	23.9	5,443,618	3,413,517	22,756,778	70
Illinois	2,714,967	25,000		1,728,656	97,543	24.8	4,565,566	2,763,571	18,423,808	87
Michigan	1,020,911	30,000		931,930	45,803	24.1	2,108,544	1,313,034	8,753,559	52
Wisconsin	710,482	15,000		504,810	10,970	24.5	1,241,202	759,923	5,066,142	36
Iowa	1,256,441	10,000		1,303,925	66,614	24.7	2,636,980	1,603,425	10,689,500	55
Minnesota	729,641			541,079	15,216	21.6	1,285,936	890,988	5,939,918	20
Missouri	367,399	10,000		432,275	19,943	20.9	835,617	599,702	1,363,698	17
Kansas	79,019			133,114	3,933	15.8	216,066	204,555		6
Nebraska	390,709			208,123	2,061	18.1	610,893	325,491	2,169,941	4
Oregon	176,583			63,132	6,108	33.1	321,823	143,473	969,824	1
New Mexico	5,108			10,434	52	9.9	15,594	23,657	157,713	1
Colorado	232,336			152,946	2,985	27.1	411,267	227,665	1,517,770	3
Utah	500			41,965	36,946	15.0	80,811	80,645	537,639	1
Wyoming	3,850			15,215	1,460	39.5	20,625	7,833	52,219	1
Idaho	10,172			12,103	10,435	17.9	32,710	27,431	182,876	1
Montana	13,182			20,000	32,142	22.2	65,224	44,141	294,275	1
Total	59,307,684	1,865,000		38,461,550	2,032,371	22.9	101,706,605	66,473,276	443,155,183	1,497

Table of the state of the lawful money reserve—Continued. CITIES, as shown by reports of the 10th of June, 1871.

Cities of redemption.	Number of banks.	Liabilities to be protected by reserve.	Reserve required: 25 per cent of liabilities.	Reserve held.	Per cent of reserve to liabilities.	FUNDS AVAILABLE FOR RESERVE.				
						Specie.	Legal tenders.	Clearing-house certificates.	Three per cent. certificates.	Due from redeeming agents.
Boston	48	$86,046,552	$21,511,638	$25,037,049	29.9	$1,510,266	$10,589,227		$2,490,000	$10,447,556
Albany	7	12,070,991	3,017,748	5,910,319	49.0	10,791	1,451,154		235,000	4,213,374
Philadelphia	30	56,060,396	14,015,099	17,166,352	30.6	124,149	10,386,880	$1,370,000	2,920,000	2,365,323
Pittsburgh	16	16,217,636	4,054,409	4,471,925	27.6	46,824	2,034,617		210,000	2,180,484
Baltimore	14	20,585,889	5,146,472	6,199,083	30.1	264,386	2,936,324		505,000	2,152,373
Washington	3	2,677,997	669,499	924,373	34.5	26,513	413,637	341,000	135,000	349,223
New Orleans	6	5,416,639	1,354,160	1,796,900	33.2	68,738	889,664			838,498
Louisville	4	4,604,263	401,066	445,973	27.8	2,741	309,276		5,000	128,956
Cincinnati	5	9,941,679	2,485,419	3,393,067	34.1	71,970	1,315,940		105,000	1,897,157
Cleveland	6	6,391,102	1,649,775	1,934,000	29.3	2,358	723,000		70,000	1,135,642
Chicago	16	27,585,265	6,896,316	9,670,730	35.0	99,652	5,304,849		205,000	4,061,929
Detroit	3	4,178,044	1,044,511	1,513,710	36.2	20,670	648,270		60,000	784,770
Milwaukee	4	3,234,236	808,559	1,326,683	41.0	9,836	372,559			944,538
St. Louis	7	8,238,920	2,059,555	2,657,032	32.3	31,554	940,880	22,000	185,000	1,478,498
Leavenworth	2	807,209	201,803	154,844	19.2	305	63,349		10,000	81,190
Total	171	261,964,118	65,316,029	82,602,940	31.6	2,290,753	38,382,626	1,733,000	7,135,000	33,061,561
New York	54	248,112,785	62,028,196	76,615,404	30.9	11,410,568	43,534,836	17,515,000	4,155,000	
San Francisco	1	641,831	160,458	475,552	74.1	469,904	5,648			

Table of the state of the lawful money reserve—Continued. STATES, as shown by reports of the 2d of October, 1871.

States and Territories	Number of banks	Liabilities to be protected by reserve.	Reserve required: 15 per cent of liabilities.	Reserve held.	Per cent of reserve to liabilities.	FUNDS AVAILABLE FOR RESERVE.				
						Specie.	Legal tenders.	Clearing-house certificates.	Three per cent. certificates.	Due from redeeming agents.
Maine	61	$13,431,337	$2,014,701	$2,913,698	21.7	$89,129	$1,062,632		$5,000	$1,756,937
New Hampshire	41	7,145,760	1,071,864	1,689,992	23.7	12,842	541,829			1,135,321
Vermont	41	9,820,883	1,473,132	2,039,487	20.8	36,471	725,554			1,292,462
Massachusetts	160	58,173,090	8,725,964	12,031,275	20.7	104,287	4,584,036		45,000	7,275,952
Rhode Island	62	20,884,452	3,132,668	3,938,673	20.7	39,184	1,406,796		70,000	2,462,693
Connecticut	87	31,873,666	4,781,349	6,410,584	18.9	79,900	2,501,048		30,000	3,744,638
New York	230	78,736,208	11,810,431	15,788,693	20.1	197,042	5,712,284		65,000	9,329,367
New Jersey	57	29,418,590	4,412,788	6,616,827	22.5	90,031	2,195,963		350,000	4,215,833
Pennsylvania	151	48,911,393	7,336,709	9,482,835	19.4	85,539	4,543,641		115,000	4,363,635
Delaware	11	2,952,474	442,871	609,147	22.7	2,632	227,803		290,000	358,512
Maryland	18	4,727,130	709,070	1,400,274	29.6	26,271	489,239		80,000	684,764
Virginia	23	9,102,536	1,365,380	1,565,138	17.2	74,082	807,342			683,314
West Virginia	14	4,624,075	693,611	936,372	20.3	9,352	379,917			547,103
North Carolina	9	3,556,836	533,525	641,775	18.0	27,092	321,641			293,042
South Carolina	7	2,767,305	415,096	557,432	20.1	16,687	356,610		50,000	184,135
Georgia	10	3,793,872	569,081	756,097	19.9	67,185	510,006			128,394
Alabama	7	1,228,809	184,321	194,701	15.8	15,496	137,962			41,363
Texas	5	1,673,062	280,809	710,838	38.0	70,497	241,078			199,963
Arkansas	2	362,910	54,437	74,783	20.6	1,317	31,131			42,335
Kentucky	25	6,235,890	935,384	1,240,432	19.5	8,835	554,610			860,306
Tennessee	19	6,360,281	954,042	1,716,622	22.8	20,209	663,121			513,102
Ohio	119	31,038,695	4,655,804	6,408,386	19.5	5,635	3,230,105		140,000	3,290,862
Indiana	72	23,503,793	3,525,569	4,498,964	21.6	62,001	2,444,366		25,000	2,872,019
Illinois	92	19,952,721	2,992,908	2,522,018	23.0	4,870	1,835,997		30,000	2,566,873
Michigan	57	10,292,558	1,340,284	1,311,334	22.5	1,254	1,047,915		30,000	400,233
Wisconsin	37	5,580,207	882,031	682,435	22.4	45,295	567,982		10,000	723,158
Iowa	57	11,551,699	1,732,755	2,786,435	24.1	15,766	1,276,822		10,000	450,318
Minnesota	22	4,373,404	971,807	1,646,636	25.4	20,941	359,943			1,071,129
Missouri	21	4,194,663	656,011	853,350	19.5	6,985	470,203			362,306
Kansas	9	2,504,399	254,200	373,386	22.0	9,911	169,689			196,734
Nebraska	6	1,146,408	375,660	623,722	24.9	96,028	176,677			437,640
Oregon	1	181,459	27,223	347,631	30.3	74,131	113,647			208,146
New Mexico	1	1,897,184	284,576	51,633	28.2	28,114	30,806			20,827
Colorado	4	435,448	65,317	535,902	28.8	138	135,180			325,931
Utah	1	81,966	12,295	54,902	12.6	74,131	26,268			500
Wyoming	1	212,782	31,917	32,819	40.0	333	11,053			21,408
Idaho	1	372,941	55,941	43,131	20.3	11,602	19,281			12,248
Montana	1			57,645	15.5	6,998	27,400			23,253
Total	1,536	467,619,031	70,142,834	98,946,184	21.2	1,814,922	40,139,433		1,355,000	55,636,824

Table of the state of the lawful money reserve—Continued: CITIES, *as shown by reports of the 2d day of October, 1871.*

Cities of redemption.	Number of banks.	Liabilities to be protected by reserve.	Reserve required: 25 per cent of liabilities.	Reserve held.	Per cent of reserve to liabilities.	FUNDS AVAILABLE FOR RESERVE.				
						Specie.	Legal tenders.	Clearing-house certificates.	Three per cent certificates.	Due from redeeming agents.
Boston	48	$84,152,222	$21,038,055	$22,833,508	27.1	$877,093	$9,849,550		$2,095,000	$10,013,865
Albany	7	11,794,540	2,948,635	4,258,838	36.1	8,854	1,327,697		165,000	2,757,287
Philadelphia	30	51,719,617	12,929,904	14,180,493	27.4	119,528	6,503,839	$2,415,000	2,005,000	3,137,126
Pittsburgh	16	17,240,422	4,310,105	4,874,941	28.3	40,721	2,423,254		85,000	2,325,966
Baltimore	14	20,105,539	5,026,385	5,219,198	26.0	92,712	2,821,259		265,000	2,040,227
Washington	3	2,607,335	651,834	716,433	27.5	34,113	322,974		135,000	224,346
New Orleans	7	7,751,863	1,937,971	1,755,681	22.6	116,741	999,907			639,433
Louisville	4	1,763,490	440,873	530,684	30.8	500	254,971		5,000	260,013
Cincinnati	5	13,096,639	3,274,159	4,667,921	35.6	18,359	1,944,830		100,000	2,604,732
Cleveland	6	6,560,859	1,640,215	1,905,064	29.0	7,516	987,320		35,000	843,158
Chicago	18	27,530,722	6,889,931	8,723,340	31.7	84,399	4,995,870	12,070	205,000	3,438,071
Detroit	3	5,014,904	1,253,748	1,677,096	33.6	465	637,116		60,000	970,515
Milwaukee	4	3,037,293	759,325	941,740	31.0	9,400	410,042			522,307
St. Louis	8	9,067,026	2,266,757	2,788,411	30.8	22,533	1,241,379		110,000	1,394,490
Leavenworth	2	782,901	195,725	146,240	18.7	158	84,742		10,000	51,340
Total	175	262,254,497	65,563,692	75,230,997	28.7	1,433,092	34,904,050	2,497,070	5,395,000	31,241,785
New York	54	221,937,487	55,484,371	59,151,314	26.7	8,712,131	32,044,183	17,695,000	500,000	
San Francisco	1	442,158	11,054	81,518	18.4	81,518				

Names and compensation of officers and clerks in the office of the Comptroller of the Currency during the fiscal year ending June 30, 1871.

Name.	Class.	Salary.	Period of service.
COMPTROLLER.			
Hiland R. Hulburd		$5,000	12 months.
DEPUTY COMPTROLLER.			
John Jay Knox		2,500	12 months.
CLERKS.			
Linus M. Price	Fourth class..	1,800	12 months.
J. Franklin Bates	do	1,800	Do.
Edward Wolcott	do	1,800	Do.
John D. Patten, jr	do	1,800	Do.
George W. Martin	do	1,800	Do.
John W. Magruder	do	1,800	Do.
John W. Griffin	do	1,800	Do.
John Burroughs	do	1,800	Do.
John S. Langworthy	do	1,800	Do.
Charles A. Jewett	do	1,800	Do.
Aaron Johns	do	1,800	3 months.
Edward S. Peck	do	1,800	7 months.
Charles H. Norton	Third class....	1,600	12 months.
Gordon Perkins	do	1,600	7 months 9 days.
Edward Myers	do	1,600	12 months.
C. D. F. Kasson	do	1,600	11 months.
Edward S. Peck	do	1,600	5 months.
George H. Wood	do	1,600	12 months.
Aaron Johns	do	1,600	1 month.
Fernando C. Cate	do	1,600	12 months.
Edwin C. Denig	do	1,600	4 months.
William H. Milstead	do	1,600	12 months.
Frank A. Miller	do	1,600	Do.
Henry H. Smith	do	1,600	1 month.
William A. Page	do	1,600	7 months.
John A. Kayser	do	1,600	8 months.
Albert A. Miller	do	1,600	3 months.
George McCullough	do	1,600	Do.
Dayton S. Ward	do	1,600	Do.
C. Burr Vickery	do	1,600	Do.
William A. Page	Second class ..	1,400	5 months.
John Joy Edson	do	1,400	12 months.
Charles H. Cherry	do	1,400	Do.
Charles Scott	do	1,400	Do.
William Cruikshank	do	1,400	Do.
George McCullough	do	1,400	9 months.
Albert A. Miller	do	1,400	Do.
John A. Kayser	do	1,400	4 months.
R. T. J. Falconer	do	1,400	11 months.
William D. Swan	do	1,400	8 months
Fisher A. Simkins	do	1,400	Do.
Dayton S. Ward	do	1,400	4 months.
T. Elwood Major	do	1,400	Do.
George Wallace, jr	do	1,400	Do.
W. W. Eldridge	do	1,400	Do.
Leonard Whitney	do	1,400	Do.
C. D. F. Kasson	First class....	1,200	1 month.
Horatio Nater	do	1,200	12 months.
John A. Corwin	do	1,200	20 days.
Augustus F. McKay	do	1,200	12 months.
John J. Patton	do	1,200	Do.
T. Elwood Major	do	1,200	8 months.
William D. Swan	do	1,200	4 months.
Philip T. Snowden	do	1,200	12 months.
Reuben Smith	do	1,200	5 months.
Fisher A. Simkins	do	1,200	3 months 11 days.
Charles Bradshaw	do	1,200	1 month 29 days.
Dayton S. Ward	do	1,200	2 months 15 days.
George Wallace, jr	do	1,200	4 months 24 days.
Watson W. Eldridge	do	1,200	4 months 18 days.
Leonard Whitney	do	1,200	3 months 15 days.
J. C. Jansen	do	1,200	5 months 25 days.
William Sinclair	do	1,200	5 months 8 days.
Isaac C. Miller	do	1,200	5 months 4 days.
Miss Frances R. Sprague	do	1,200	4 months 20 days.
Walter Taylor	do	1,200	3 months 21 days.
William B. Groene	do	1,200	3 months 9 days.

Names and compensation of officers, &c., in the office of the Comptroller, &c.—Continued.

Name.	Class.	Salary.	Period of service.
Alanson T. Kinney	First class	$1,200	3 months.
Edw. W. Moore	do	1,200	2 months 27 days.
Mrs. Sarah F. Fitzgerald	Female clerk	900	12 months.
Mrs. Etha E. Poole	do	900	12 months.
Mrs. Louisa A. Hodges	do	900	Do.
Mrs. Mary A. Blossom	do	900	1 month 15 days.
Mrs. Sophy C. Harrison	do	900	12 months.
Mrs. Mary L. McCormick	do	900	Do.
Mrs. Fayetta C. Snead	do	900	Do.
Mrs. Faunie M. Anderson	do	900	2 months.
Mrs. Marie L. Sturgus	do	900	12 months.
Mrs. Maggie B. Miller	do	900	10 months 10 days.
Mrs. C. F. B. Stevens	do	900	9 months 26 days.
Miss Agnes C. Bielaski	do	900	11 months.
Miss Celia N. French	do	900	12 months.
Miss Louise W. Knowlton	do	900	Do.
Miss Anna W. Story	do	900	Do.
Miss Julia M. Baldwin	do	900	Do.
Miss Christina Hinds	do	900	Do.
Miss Maggie L. Simpson	do	900	Do.
Miss Alice Wick	do	900	3 months.
Miss Josephine Hyde	do	900	Do.
Miss Eliza R. Hyde	do	900	9 months.
Miss Clara J. Fenno	do	900	12 months.
Miss Eliza M. Barker	do	900	Do.
Miss Amelia P. Stockdale	do	900	Do.
Miss Love L. Bursley	do	900	11 months 5 days.
Miss Harriet M. Black	do	900	10 months 5 days.
Miss Mary D. Massey	do	900	9 months 25 days.
Miss Margaret E. Gooding	do	900	6 months 17 days.
Miss Julia Greer	do	900	5 months 29 days.
Miss Lizzie Henry	do	900	5 months 28 days.
Miss Margaret L. Browne	do	900	5 months 26 days.
Miss Augusta Fox	do	900	5 months 20 days.
Miss Alice M. Kennedy	do	900	2 months 5 days.
Miss Nellie M. Fletcher	do	900	1 month.
William E. Hughes	Messenger	840	12 months.
Samuel Neill	do	840	Do.
Ozro N. Hubbard	do	840	Do.
Edmund E. Schreiner	do	840	Do.
Philo Burr	Watchman	720	Do.
Charles H. Bryan	do	720	10 months 15 days.
Edward Bryan	do	720	1 month 16 days.
Townsend Clement	do	720	5 months 20 days.
Andrew L. Williams	do	720	3 months 11 days.
Henry Sanders	Laborer	720	12 months.
Julius E. De Saules	do	720	Do.
Charles McC. Taylor	do	720	6 months.

Expenditures of the office of the Comptroller of the Currency for the fiscal year ending June 30, 1871.

For special dies, plates, paper, printing, &c. $160,551 52
For salaries 101,400 00

Total 261,951 52

The contingent expenses of the office were paid out of the general appropriation for contingent expenses of the Treasury Department, and as separate accounts are not kept for the different Bureaus, the amount cannot be stated.

REPORT OF FIRST COMPTROLLER.

REPORT

OF THE

FIRST COMPTROLLER OF THE TREASURY.

TREASURY DEPARTMENT,
First Comptroller's Office, October 27, 1871.

SIR: I have the honor to submit the following report of the operations of this office during the fiscal year ending June 30, 1871.

Number of warrants countersigned, entered upon blotters, and posted in ledgers, viz:

Treasury, proper	1,691
Public debt	245
Quarterly salary	1,398
Diplomatic	2,296
Customs	3,876
Internal revenue	5,941
Judiciary	1,703
War, civil	42
War, pay	3,642
War, repay	1,143
Navy, pay	1,390
Navy, repay	233
Interior, civil	1,797
Interior, pay	1,680
Interior, repay	54
Appropriation	148
Internal revenue, (covering)	3,086
Customs, (covering)	1,549
Land, (covering)	591
Miscellaneous, (covering)	4,504

Number of accounts received from the First and Fifth Auditors of the Treasury, and Commissioner of the General Land Office, revised and certified, viz:

Judiciary, embracing the accounts of United States marshals for their fees, and for the expenses of the United States courts, of the United States district attorneys, and of the commissioners and clerks of United States courts	1,718
Diplomatic and consular, embracing the accounts arising from our intercourse with foreign nations, expenses of consuls for sick and disabled seamen, and of our commercial agents in foreign countries	1,910
Public lands, embracing the accounts of the registers and receivers of land offices, and surveyors general and their deputies, and of lands erroneously sold	2,589
Steamboats, embracing the accounts for the expenses of the inspection of steamboats, and salaries of inspectors	575
Mint and its branches, embracing accounts of gold, silver, and cent coinage, of bullion, of salaries of the officers and of the expenses	125
Public Debt, embracing accounts of the United States Treasurer, and the Assistant Treasurer's accounts, for the redemption of United States stocks and notes, and for payment of interest on the public debt	781

Public printing, embracing accounts for printing, for binding, and for paper.... 72
Territorial printing, embracing accounts for printing, binding, and paper for the
   legislatures of the several Territories.................................... 14
Territorial, embracing accounts for the legislative expenses of the several Ter-
   ritories, and the incidental expenses of their government..................... 354
Congressional, embracing accounts for contingent expenses, &c., of the United
   States Senate and House of Representatives................................ 110
Collectors of internal revenue, embracing their accounts of the revenue collected,
   accounts for expenses of collecting the same, and accounts for their salaries
   and commissions, and the expenses of their offices......................... 3,952
Assessors of internal revenue, embracing accounts for their commissions and the
   expenses of levying the taxes.. 1,212
Miscellaneous, internal revenue, embracing accounts for salaries and expenses of
   supervisors, drawbacks, informers, &c.................................... 2,081
Stamp agents, embracing accounts for the sale of internal revenue stamps...... 1,646
Miscellaneous, embracing accounts for the contingent expenses of the executive
   departments at Washington, salaries of judges, marshals, district attorneys,
   &c.. 1,834
Number of letters written on official business.............................. 9,385
Number of receipts of collectors of internal revenue for tax-lists examined,
   registered, and filed 2,803
Number of official bonds examined, registered, and filed..................... 1,169
Number of requisitions examined, entered, and reported, viz:
   Diplomatic and consular.. 776
   United States marshals... 210
   Collectors of internal revenue.. 2,897

The Comptroller deems it unnecessary to give in this report a statement of the revenues received and the disbursements made, inasmuch
as the records of the Secretary's office correspond with those of the
Comptroller's, and the financial report will present the same figures and
results as would be presented by this office.

The foregoing statement of the labor performed in the office shows
that there has not been any reduction in its amount, and that it remains
as large as in former years, and requires that the force should be continued.

   I am, sir, very respectfully, your obedient servant,

                             R. W. TAYLER,
                                 Comptroller.

Hon. GEORGE S. BOUTWELL,
     Secretary of the Treasury.

REPORT OF THE SECOND COMPTROLLER

7 F

REPORT

OF

THE SECOND COMPTROLLER OF THE TREASURY.

TREASURY DEPARTMENT,
Second Comptroller's Office, September 30, 1871.

SIR : I have the honor to submit the following detailed statement of the business operations·of this office for the fiscal year ending June 30, 1871 :

The aggregate number of accounts of disbursing officers and agents which have been received, as well as those which have been finally adjusted, is as follows :

	Received.	Revised.	Amount.
From the Second Auditor	3, 639	4, 066	$198, 446, 896
From the Third Auditor	3, 748	3, 829	205, 953, 053
From the Fourth Auditor	672	684	27, 446, 171
Total	8, 059	8, 579	431, 846, 120

The above accounts have been duly entered, revised, and the balance found thereon certified to the Secretary of the Department in which the expenditure has been incurred, viz: those from the Second and Third Auditors to the Secretary of War, (excepting the accounts of Indian agents, which are certified to the Secretary of the Interior,) and those from the Fourth Auditor to the Secretary of the Navy.

Character of accounts.	Received.	Revised.	Amount.
FROM THE SECOND AUDITOR.			
Embracing accounts of disbursing officers of the War Department for collecting, organizing, and drilling volunteers.	17	17	$655, 886
Paymasters' accounts, for the pay and rations, &c., of officers and soldiers of the Army.	903	1, 300	176, 005, 231
Special and referred accounts, including National Asylum and arrears of officers' pay, &c.	749	749	2, 237, 739
Accounts of Army recruiting officers, for clothing, equipments, and bounty to recruits, &c.	239	272	967, 865
Ordnance, embracing the accounts of disbursing officers of the Ordnance Department for arsenals, armories, armaments for fortifications, arming militia, &c.	108	109	8, 633, 115
Indian Department—Accounts of Indian agents, including the pay of Indian annuities, presents to Indians, expenses of holding treaties, pay of interpreters, pay of Indian agents, &c., and the settlement of personal claims for miscellaneous services of agents and others in connection with Indian affairs.	1, 041	1, 037	6, 819, 479
Medical and hospital accounts, including the purchase of medicines, drugs, surgical instruments, hospital stores, the claims of private physicians for services, and surgeons employed under contract.	380	380	1, 132, 447
Contingent expenses of the War Department	202	202	268, 190
Freedmen's Bureau. Pay and bounty			1, 726, 944
Total	3, 639	4, 066	198, 446, 896

Character of accounts.	Received.	Revised.	Amount.
FROM THE THIRD AUDITOR.			
Quartermasters' accounts, for transportation of the Army, and the transportation of all descriptions of Army supplies, ordnance, and for the settlement of personal claims for services in the Quartermaster's Department.	2, 499	2, 540	$152, 755, 986
Commissaries' accounts, for rations or subsistence of the Army, and for the settlement of personal claims for services in the Commissary Department.	977	990	9, 587, 154
Accounts of pension agents, for the payment of military pensions, including the entries of the monthly reports of new pensioners added to the rolls, and the statements from the Commissioner of Pensions respecting the changes arising from deaths, transfers, &c., and for pension claims presented for adjustments.	152	165	34, 768, 120
Accounts of the Engineer Department, for military surveys, the construction of fortifications, for river and harbor surveys and improvements.	87	91	7, 934, 832
Accounts for the relief of freedmen and refugees	33	10	906, 911
Total..	3, 748	3, 829	205, 953, 053
FROM THE FOURTH AUDITOR.			
Quartermasters of the Marine Corps: Embracing accounts for the expenses of officers' quarters, fuel, forage for horses, attendance on courts-martial and courts of inquiry, transportation of officers and marines, supplies of provisions, clothing, medical stores, and military stores for barracks, and all incidental supplies for marines on shore.	4	5	389, 408
Accounts of paymasters of the Marine Corps, for pay and rations of the officers and marines, and servants' hire.	4	5	903, 967
Paymasters of the Navy: Accounts for the pay and rations of the officers and crew of the ship, supplies of provisions, of clothing, and repairs of vessels on foreign stations.	346	347	4, 908, 069
Paymasters at navy-yards: Accounts for the pay of officers on duty at navy-yards, or on leave of absence, and the pay of mechanics and laborers employed on the various works.	120	123	13, 071, 773
Navy agents' accounts for their advances to paymasters, purchases of timber, provisions, clothing, and naval stores.	163	165	7, 748, 831
Navy pension agents' accounts for the payment of pensions of officers and seamen, &c., of the Navy, and officers and privates of the Marine Corps.	35	39	424, 123
Total....................................	672	684	27, 446, 171
CLAIMS REVISED DURING THE YEAR.			
Soldiers' pay and bounty	18, 853	19, 417	2, 552, 690
Sailors' pay and bounty	1, 879	1, 562	377, 344
Prize money................................	1, 876	1, 934	177, 363
Contract surgeons..........................	17	17	....
Property lost in the military service, including horses lost in the military service.	359	359	55, 678
Oregon and Washington Territory war claims..............	85	85	75, 239
Of States for enrolling, subsisting, clothing, supplying, arming, equipping, paying, and transporting their troops in defense of the United States.	24	24	2, 769, 052
Subsistence	78	78	67, 705
Total..........................	23, 171	23, 476	6, 075, 076
Referred cases......................	1, 794	1, 794	....

Number of settlements for the fiscal year ending June 30, 1871................................... 6, 564
Number of accounts on hand at the commencement of the fiscal year July 1, 1870 .... 1, 262
Number of accounts on hand at the close of the fiscal year ending June 30, 1871............... 742
Number of letters written on official business.. 1, 114

Number of requisitions recorded during the year.

	War.	Navy.	Interior.
Accountable.......................................	1, 071	1, 020	837
Refunding...	963	269	61
Settlement	2, 033	342	1, 010
Transfer...	453	105	8
Total......................	4, 520	1, 736	1, 916

Number of contracts, classified as follows :

Quartermaster's Department	585
Charter-parties	1
Engineer Department	151
Indian Department	90
Freedmen's Bureau	2
Ordnance	None.
Navy Department	134
Adjutant General	122
Commissary of Subsistence	145
Total	1,230

Official bonds filed	201
Pensioners recorded	22,793

Respectfully submitted.,

J. M. BRODHEAD,
Comptroller.

Hon. GEORGE S. BOUTWELL,
Secretary of the Treasury.

REPORT OF THE COMMISSIONER OF CUSTOMS.

REPORT

OF

THE COMMISSIONER OF CUSTOMS.

TREASURY DEPARTMENT,
Office of Commissioner of Customs, September 2, 1871.

SIR: I submit herewith, for your information, a statement of the work performed in this office during the fiscal year ending June 30, 1871.

The number of accounts on hand July 1, 1870, was		135
The number of accounts received from First Auditor during year		6,013
		6,148
The number of accounts passed during the year	5,905	
The number of accounts returned during the year	44	
		5,949
The number of accounts on hand June 30, 1871		199

There was paid into the Treasury of the United States, from sources the accounts of which are settled in this office:

On account of customs	$206,270,408 05
On account of fines, penalties, and forfeitures	952,579 86
On account of steamboat inspections	223,823 70
On account of drayage, storage, &c	414,310 61
On account of marine hospital money, (from January 1, 1871)	161,711 46
On account of emolument fees	585,887 69
	208,608,721 37

And there was paid out of the Treasury:

On account of expenses of collecting the revenue from customs	$6,560,672 61
On account of excess of deposits	2,276,169 16
On account of debentures	945,441 52
On account of revenue-cutters, construction and maintenance	1,252,000 31
On account of public buildings	1,350,133 87
On account of light-houses, construction and maintenance	2,674,928 08
On account of marine hospital, care of sick seamen	437,493 86
On account of distributive shares of fines	488,135 55
On account of life-saving stations, Long Island and New Jersey	37,740 17
On account of miscellaneous accounts	73,128 00
	16,095,843 13

The number of estimates received was	2,157
The number of requisitions issued	2,129
The amount involved in said requisitions	$9,648,285 81
The number of letters received was	11,814
The number of letters written was	11,862
The number of letters recorded was	11,539
The amount involved in this statement	$234,352,850 31
The average number of clerks employed	26

CAPTURED AND ABANDONED PROPERTY.

During the past year the business in this division has been very small, having been confined principally to the settlement of accounts for legal services, under act of April 20, 1870, and to the review of work already done, the latter necessitated by the adverse claims of cotton agents in settling their accounts.

I append tabular statement of the expenditures out of appropriations, the accounts of which are settled in this office, marked A.

Statement of receipts from fines, penalties, and forfeitures, by districts, as shown by the accounts, so far as they have been received at this office, marked B.

Statement showing the transactions in bonded merchandise, marked C.

Very respectfully, your obedient servant,

W. T. HAINES,
Commissioner of Customs.

Hon. GEORGE S. BOUTWELL,
Secretary of the Treasury

A.—*Statement of expenditures out of appropriations, the accounts for which are adjusted in the office of the Commissioner of Customs.*

Title of appropriation.	Gross expenditures.	Repayments.	Net expenditures.
Expense collecting revenue from customs	$6, 627, 483 49	$66, 810 88	$6, 560, 672 61
Repayment to importers for excess deposits	2, 004, 166 96	216, 900 37	1, 787, 266 59
Debentures or drawbacks, bounties, &c	1, 026, 688 06	81, 246 54	945, 441 52
Expense of the revenue-cutter service	1, 167, 083 66	46, 057 23	1, 121, 026 43
Construction of revenue-cutters	130, 958 09	....	130, 958 09
Repairs, &c., custom-houses and other public buildings	229, 137 66	3, 268 55	225, 869 11
Furniture and repairs for public buildings	99, 148 49	1, 867 38	97, 281 11
Fuel and miscellaneous items, public buildings	203, 530 33	11, 877 57	191, 652 76
Construction of four steam revenue-cutters	3, 001 53	....	3, 001 53
Construction fire-proof appraiser's store, Philadelphia	93, 313 73	730 45	92, 583 28
Distribution of shares of fines, penalties, and forfeitures	489, 221 44	1, 085 89	488, 135 55
Expense of collecting, &c., captured and abandoned property	15, 007 41	....	15, 007 41
Debentures and other charges	32, 916 81	....	32, 916 81
Proceeds of sale of goods, wares, &c	199 59	....	199 59
Payment of taxes on salaries	348 84	....	348 84
Act to prevent smuggling, &c	968 36	....	968 36
Unclaimed merchandise	2, 487 41	....	2, 487 41
Refunding money erroneously received and covered in Treasury	1, 757 11	....	1, 757 11
Refunding duties, 4th section act March 3, 1871	488, 321 37	....	488, 321 37
Refunding duties under warehousing system	581 20	....	581 20
Additional compensation to collectors and naval officers	262 26	....	262 26
Expenses, lazaretto property, Philadelphia	8, 289 36	289 36	8, 000 00
Compensation of persons employed in insurrectionary States	6, 000 81	....	6, 000 81
Relief of Collector William Gates	5, 567 50	....	5, 567 50
Relief of Brazil Steamship Company	7, 611 90	....	7, 611 90
Total miscellaneous	12, 644, 053 37	430, 134 22	12, 213, 919 15
From which deduct the following excess of repayments:			
Preservation and protection of public buildings commenced, &c	1, 720 15	2, 920 11	
Building or purchase of such other vessels, &c	358 95	3, 344 69	
	2, 079 10	6, 264 80	4, 185 70
Total net miscellaneous	....	....	12, 209, 733 45
Custom-houses:			
Bangor, Maine	8, 462 27	4 82	8, 457 45
Machias, Maine	1, 000 00	....	1, 000 00
Wiscasset, Maine	7, 011 18	87 88	6, 923 30

A.—*Statement of expenditures of appropriations, &c.*—Continued.

Title of appropriation.	Gross expenditures.	Repayments.	Net expenditures.
Custom-houses—Continued :			
Portland, Maine..........	$84,920 74	$2,466 25	$82,454 49
Ogdensburgh, New York	701 88	51 30	650 58
Barge office, New York..........	90,400 72	1,504 52	88,896 20
Philadelphia, Pennsylvania..........	168 43	1 86	166 57
Baltimore, Maryland..........	10,345 00	....	10,345 00
Petersburgh, Virginia	12,123 52	2,123 52	10,000 00
Charleston, South Carolina..........	93,124 79	....	93,124 79
Knoxville, Tennessee..........	65,628 69	5,000 00	60,628 69
New Orleans, Louisiana..........	86,584 25	....	86,584 25
Chicago, Illinois..........	20,566 94	567 61	19,999 33
Cairo, Illinois..........	43,090 64	959 14	42,131 50
Detroit, Michigan..........	14,627 10	364 97	14,262 13
St. Paul, Minnesota..........	113,534 55	....	113,534 55
Portland, Oregon	19,173 98	....	19,173 98
Astoria, Oregon	14,573 64	....	14,573 64
San Francisco, California..........	9,067 42	....	9,067 42
Sandusky, Ohio..........	5,000 00	....	5,000 00
Knoxville, Tennessee, purchase of a site	10,250 00	....	10,250 00
Total custom-houses..........	710,355 74	13,131 87	607,223 87
From which deduct the following excess of repayment:			
Custom-house at Nashville, Tennessee..........	10 64	4,797 84	4,787 20
Total net expenditures for custom-houses..........	....	....	692,436 67
Marine Hospital Establishment..........	526,681 59	89,187 73	437,493 86
Marine hospital, Chicago..........	45,080 10	....	45,080 10
Total marine hospitals..........	571,761 69	89,187 73	482,573 96
From which deduct the following excess of repayment:			
Repairs of marine hospital, Chelsea, Massachusetts..	....	1,569 20	1,569 20
Total net expenditures marine hospitals..........	....	....	481,004 76
Life-saving stations :			
Compensation of 2 superintendents	3,068 51	11 13	3,057 38
Compensation of 54 keepers	10,200 00	25 54	10,174 46
Contingent expenses	378 12	40 19	337 93
Six experienced surfmen	8,544 00	....	8,544 00
Protecting human life	15,000 00	....	15,000 00
Life-saving apparatus, (contingencies)	626 40	....	626 40
Total life-saving expenditures..........	37,817 03	76 86	37,740 17
Light-house Establishment:			
Supplying light-houses with oil..........	327,733 82	49,158 87	278,574 95
Repairs and incidental expenses..........	343,873 42	80,303 21	263,570 21
Salaries of light-house keepers	420,425 47	22,099 19	398,326 28
Salaries of light-boat keepers..........	5,583 00	34 00	5,549 00
Seamen's wages	240,872 83	17,862 02	223,010 81
Expenses of weighing and supplying losses of beacons..........	343,606 99	20,531 91	323,075 08
Commissions to superintendents..........	3,425 17	....	3,425 17
Repairs, &c., fog-signals	41,017 54	4,140 83	36,876 71
Expenses of superintendents in visiting..........	2,669 37	313 80	2,355 57
Repairs of light-houses in 3d district..........	40,600 00	....	40,600 00
Repairs of light-houses in 10th district	37,000 00	....	37,000 00
Repairs of light-houses in 11th district	3,000 00	....	3,000 00
Repairs of light-houses in 13th district	22,199 70	....	22,199 70
Building and expenses of light-houses in the several States	1,225,303 64	182,934 31	1,042,369 33
Total Light-House Establishment	3,057,310 95	377,378 14	2,679,932 81
From which deduct the following excess of repayment:			
Reëstablishing lights on southern coast	14,063 88	19,068 61	5,004 73
Total net expenditure Light-House Establishment	....	....	2,674,928 08

A.—*Statement of expenditures of appropriations, &c.*—Continued.

RECAPITULATION.

Title of appropriation.	Gross expenditures.	Repayments.	Net expenditures.
Miscellaneous :			
Expenditures in excess	$12, 644, 053 37	$430, 134 22	
Repayments in excess	2, 079 10	6, 264 80	
Total	12, 646, 132 47	436, 399 02	$12, 209, 733 45
Custom-houses:			
Expenditures in excess	710, 355 74	13, 131 87	
Repayments in excess	10 64	4, 797 84	
Total	710, 366 38	17, 929 71	692, 436 67
Marine hospital :			
Expenditures in excess	571, 761 69	89, 187 73	
Repayments in excess		1, 569 00	
Total	571, 761 69	90, 756 93	481, 004 76
Life-saving stations	37, 817 03	76 86	37, 740 17
Light-House Establishment :			
Expenditures in excess	3, 057, 310 95	377, 378 14	
Repayments in excess	14, 063 88	19, 068 61	
Total	3, 071, 374 83	396, 446 75	2, 674, 928 08
Aggregate net expenditures			16, 095, 843 13
Total miscellaneous	12, 646, 132 47	436, 399 02	12, 209, 733 45
Total custom-house	710, 366 38	17, 929 71	692, 436 67
Total marine hospital	571, 761 69	90, 756 93	481, 004 76
Total life-saving stations	37, 817 03	76 86	37, 740 17
Total Light-House Establishment	3, 071, 374 83	396, 446 75	2, 674, 928 08
Grand total	17, 037, 452 40	941, 609 27	16, 095, 843 13

B.—*Statement of fines, penalties, and forfeitures collected at the various ports of the United States during the fiscal year ending June 30, 1871, as appears by the accounts of the officers of customs received at this office.*

District or port.	Time embraced.	Amount.
Aristook, Mo	July 1, 1870, to June 30, 1871	$2, 922 32
Bangor, Me	July 1, 1870, to Dec. 31, 1870	4, 210 00
Belfast, Me	July 1, 1870, to Dec. 31, 1870	858 00
Castine, Me	July 1, 1870, to April 30, 1871	468 50
Machias, Me	July 1, 1870, to Feb. 28, 1871	285 38
Passamaquoddy, Me	July 1, 1870, to June 30, 1871	2, 044 81
Portland and Falmouth, Me	July 1, 1870, to June 30, 1871	6, 725 46
Waldoborough, Me	July 1, 1870, to Dec. 31, 1870	24 05
Portsmouth, N. H	July 1, 1870, to June 30, 1871	1, 923 84
Vermont, Vt	July 1, 1870, to June 30, 1871	12, 550 05
Bristol and Warren, R. I	Aug. 9, 1870, to Aug. 31, 1870	74 82
Middletown, Conn	July 1, 1870, to Dec. 31, 1870	230 00
New Haven, Conn	July 1, 1870, to June 30, 1871	7, 892 02
New London, Conn	July 1, 1870, to June 30, 1871	190 00
Barnstable, Mass	November, 1870	75 47
Boston and Charlestown, Mass	July 1, 1870, to Mar. 31, 1871	24, 590 96
Edgartown, Mass	July 1, 1870, to June 30, 1871	207 14
Gloucester, Mass	July 1, 1870, to June 30, 1871	1, 049 29
New Bedford, Mass	July 1, 1870, to Mar. 31, 1871	963 88
Albany, N. Y	September and October, 1870	166 60
Cape Vincent, N. Y	July 1, 1870, to Mar. 13, 1871	2, 945 94
Champlain, N. Y	July 1, 1870, to Mar. 31, 1871	2, 298 80
Genesee, N. Y	October and December, 1870	1, 198 16
New York, N. Y	July 1, 1870, to May 31, 1871	534, 597 88
Niagara, N. Y	July 1, 1870, to Jan. 31, 1871	1, 647 72
Oswegatchie, N. Y	July 1, 1870, to Dec. 31, 1870	2, 388 52
Oswego, N. Y	July 1, 1870, to Dec. 31, 1870	446 57
Perth Amboy, N. J	July 1, 1870, to Dec. 31, 1870	395 00
Erie, Pa	July 1, 1870, to Nov. 30, 1870	81 54
Philadelphia, Pa	July 1, 1870, to Dec. 31, 1870	5, 224 50
Georgetown, D. C	July 1, 1870, to Dec. 31, 1870	145 00
Annapolis, Md	July 1, 1870, to Mar. 31, 1871	1, 229 46
Baltimore, Md	July 1, 1870, to June 30, 1871	1, 469 13
Alexandria, Va	July 1, 1870, to June 30, 1871	90 00
Cherrystone, Va	July 1, 1870, to Dec. 31, 1870	10 00
Norfolk and Portsmouth, Va	July 1, 1870, to Mar. 31, 1871	560 85
Richmond, Va	Sept. 1, 1870, to June 30, 1871	125 00
Wheeling, W. Va	July 1, 1870, to June 30, 1871	2, 618 68
Pamlico, N. C	July 1, 1870, to Mar. 31, 1871	10 00
Wilmington, N. C	July 1, 1870, to Mar. 31, 1871	607 61
Charleston, S. C	July 1, 1870, to June 30, 1871	1, 154 84
Georgetown, S. C	July 1, 1870, to Mar. 31, 1871	7, 270 92
Mobile, Ala	July 1, 1870, to June 30, 1871	1, 325 00
New Orleans, La	July 1, 1870, to Mar. 31, 1871	2, 293 01
Apalachicola, Fla	July 1, 1870, to Dec. 31, 1870	200 00
Fernandina, Fla	July 1, 1870, to Oct. 31, 1870	185 25
St. Mark's, Fla	July 1, 1870, to April 30, 1871	26 98
Brazos de Santiago, Texas	July 1, 1870, to April 30, 1871	2, 148 69
Corpus Christi, Texas	July 1, 1870, to Dec. 31, 1870	1, 510 95
Saluria, Texas	July 1, 1870, to June 30, 1871	446 67
Texas, Texas	July 1, 1870, to Mar. 31, 1871	535 74
Louisville, Ky	July 1, 1870, to Sept. 30, 1870	115 00
St. Louis, Mo	July 1, 1870, to Oct. 31, 1870	1, 642 19
Cincinnati, Ohio	July 1, 1870, to April 30, 1871	10, 801 11
Chicago, Ill	July 1, 1870, to Mar. 31, 1871	4, 159 80
Detroit, Mich	July 1, 1870, to Mar. 31, 1871	9, 930 60
Huron, Mich	July 1, 1870, to Mar. 31, 1871	5, 130 73
Michigan, Mich	July 1, 1870, to Sept. 30, 1870	43 82
Milwaukee, Wis	July 1, 1870, to Feb. 28, 1871	532 30
San Francisco, Cal	Dec. 1, 1870, to April 30, 1871	13, 101 20
Puget Sound, Wash. Ter	July 1, 1870, to Mar. 31, 1871	3, 999 50
Total	....	692, 287 25

Schedule of warehouse transactions at the several districts and ports of the United States for the year ending June 30, 1871.

Districts.	Balance of bonds from last return.	Warehoused and bonded.	Rewarehoused and bonded.	Constructively warehoused.	WAREHOUSE BONDS.					
					Increase of duties ascertained on liquidation.	Withdrawal duty paid.	Withdrawal for transportation.	Withdrawal for exportation.	Allowances and deficiencies.	Balance of bonds not due.
Albany	$2,690 00	$1,987 31		$140,970 03		$139,115 33			$1,854 70	$1,423 89
Alexandria	1,525,195 55	4,973,585 06	$63,930 57	836 85	$1 93	4,033 25	$10,909 52	$35,474 59	58 95	683,614 31
Baltimore †	7,809 33	16,056 32	3,007 71	64,227 54	126,478 63	4,831,642 34	63,739 18	844 00	491,776 59	8,493 21
Buffalo Creek	24,786 01	2,906 10	788 74	82,941 78	46 14	29,687 30	729 39	2,465 22	7,077 59	2,132 09
Belfast	38,053 67	24,855 74	2,671 44			22,063 74		2,024 59	1,070 46	24,855 74
Bangor	7,805 40	76,352 09		157 50	250 97	38,650 15			2,325 93	23,020 39
Bath	2,898 96	4,257 45		22 70		54,135 21			313 41	1,135 25
Bristol and Warren	937 91					5,707 75				916 74
Barnstable										
Boston †	4,621,938 69	3,647,450 30	9,660 42	117,110 94	42,751 01	4,550,666 42	25,753 23	9,680 89	231,176 17	3,270,176 32
Brunswick †		68,446 04	201,610 50	206,168 72		18,394 67	2,053 90	293,087 50	27 79	30,093 58
Champlain §	65,332 25	75,556 52	504,954 85	171,525 21	769 86	665,222 74	13,037 88	4,810 48	149,198 59	81,516 49
Chicago §	2,381 27	3,602 39	20,899 20	15,422 42	63 44	20 00	400 14	48,467 33	13,643 76	9,218 52
Cuyahoga	31,389 99	53,114 16	15,657 29	3,998 13	348 39	17,792 30	965 35	1,205 00	11,006 58	26,047 54
Charleston	6,889 62	1,588 60	814 47		12 59	66,468 49	269 14			2,873 72
Castine §	59,379 91		364,686 92	263,712 41	255 81	681 38		4,809 56	120,677 10	28,859 79
Cincinnati §	176 40					538,498 16				
Cairo				75,031 90		75,209 30				
Corpus Christi †	2,565 45	6,590 94	57,337 09		382 36	7,102 14		36,708 23	443 34	2,822 13
Detroit	1,888 20	2,703 72	32,328 59	582,596 69	87 07	64,860 07	17,898 76	367,151 47	4,554 35	8,659 92
Delaware §	1,544 58		31,354 61			31,419 87			1,479 68	
Dubuque			5,981 61	6,606 25						
Dunkirk					4 60	6,975 82			4,393 90	1,222 94
Evansville					157 43	1,731 73				
Erie †	605 90	67 49	2,095 40	68,321 43	60 54	70,426 20		160 79	661 98	61 68
Frenchman's Bay †	1,517 43	892 39				2,319 63			90 19	558 60
Fall River	613 58		105 81	7,183 33		7,183 35		135 39		
Fernandina				135 39						

Port										
Memphis	37,373 34		81,618 65	34,702 98	7,151 51	110,017 34			21,307 60	29,521 54
Marblehead	56,298 25	17,981 77	25,248 01	32,417 08	6,148 46	83,021 46	3,433 71	15,003 01	2,951 96	33,684 13
Minnesota§	6,274 75	313,783 60	3,289 55	1,676,872 10	2,175 65	765 25	1,676,872 10	1,885 10		
Niagara	1,324 40			32,417 08		838,137 79	21,778 04		6,749 91	36,992 71
New Haven	20,378 48	3,097 20	1,094 02	6,023 37		25,383 92	3,752 53	294 28	459 15	
Newport	19,279 85	55,692 15	2,815 00	446 94	31 06	57,486 64		1,486 24	1,069 02	12,748 45
New London	10,071 10	7,416 70	1,804 44	18,786 34		6,623 45	18,841 36	10,131 10	4,662 09	2,815 00
Newburyport§	22,943 33	588 00	1,185 52		75 77	2,549 63	815 72		678 23	23,034 21
New Bedford			20,385 48	50,174 76		52,198 24			137 50	
Norfolk and Portsmouth			154,923 04	1,578,284 36	22,718 25	1,241,568 90	1,714,614 31	51,839 73	16,008 95	2,353 05
Nashville	907,010 25	1,573,595 30		7,642 99		5,302 91			55,094 57	1,173,013 60
New Orleans‖									2,340 08	
New Albany¶										
New York. (No returns)										
Nantucket				438 16		236 55				
Oswego	9,794 75	561,434 35	174 00	51,937 95	14 10	151,164 76	461,977 50	501 60	2,840 99	5,282 60
Oswegatchie	3,736 85	28,013 64	4,896 32	12,402 74	746 63	21,145 81	12,174 74	916 10	1,648 49	9,518 91
Oregon	18,648 00	49,252 64	93,034 13	23,034 31		38,063 81		485 50	6	37,506 20
Providence	14,393 52	88,565 60	275 12	66,972 63	229 50	97,961 61	49,289 15	291 83	8,957 55	62,790 47
Passamaquoddy‖	1,099,593 52	2,776 51	989 74	1,615 70		378 16	15,056 26	710 12		490 08
Philadelphia‖	1,338,700 86	348,141 57		18,126 75	1,724,012 10	56,343 05	4,640 62	58,067 54	1,027,672 21	
Portsmouth	245,242 13	150,870 36	855,953 09	5,614 58	704 62	86,019 14	454,994 41	1,493 85	14,739 12	1,776 03
Portland and Falmouth*	2,986 32		51,101 74			354,683 90		4,638,187 18		52,485 81
Pensacola	835 95		12,608 18	18,883 80		3,457 67				
Petersburg			3,586 71	3,342 01	44 13	22,707 22	332 80	3,342 01	1,046 26	648 56
Plymouth	5,635 30		25,367 11	11,127 07		41,205 58			23,131 30	7,346 94
Pittsburgh			53,034 81	3,228 09						705 08
Puget Sound	4,262 55	2,845 82		432,924 42	154 60	2,027 99	3,228 09		1,596 99	
Perth Amboy				7,247 90		778 90	433,507 29		469 72	
Quincey			879 56	7,373 41	134 54	26,046 35			3,781 96	3,072 95
Richmond	6,556 66	10,935 69	2,965 30	44,293 19	1,089 95	352,036 44	21,996 57	52,313 64		1,873,644 72
San Francisco**	1,873,084 82	379,276 11	21,218 49	106 19	106 19	27,361 18	762 90	3,263 55	3,925 48	522 25
Salem and Beverly	11,372 60	745 60	10,019 93	2,392 49	258 90	65,928 94		24,350 67	3,177 90	9,948 97
Savannah§	42,618 36	47,988 87		2,520 50	1,175 67	2,129,649 48			143,089 33	135,746 24
St. Louis	125,567 51	1,263 20		5,614 58	246 15	12,900 90	6,220 78		971 69	1,428 65
Saluria	3,063 11			18,883 80		18,883 90				
Sandusky						2,845 82				
St. Mary's				7,503 15		34,519 34				
Selma				20,733 84	618 15	0 7,503 15			18,370 66	21,649 59
Superior	56,168 93		6,395 90	1,160,353 82	316 06	174,556 59	7,873 50	14,780 14		
Texas	61,226 93	145,855 87		17,578 80		6,660 86	278,138 79	883,846 53	2,169 31	19,269 78
Vermont	6,232 40	3,962 10	336 60	26,567 94	34 26	23,635 08		27 00		2,918 20
Wilmington	7,915 99		690 34					499 82	2,146 45	190 52
Wiscasset		13,462 34	2,238 58			60,336 31		1,155 25		16,171 31
Willamette§	37,506 20						7,873 50			
Total	**11,390,715 92**	**14,236,433 21**	**3,341,527 58**	**14,203,024 14**	**236,461 28**	**19,323,360 17**	**6,839,864 15**	**6,676,457 79**	**1,538,731 42**	**8,959,748 60**

* To February 28, 1871.   † To April 30, 1871.   ‡ To October 31, 1870.   § To May 31, 1871.   ‖ To December 31, 1870.   ¶ To January 31, 1871.   ** For the month of July, 1870.

REPORT ON THE FINANCES.

RECAPITULATION.

Balance of bonds from last return	$11, 320, 715 92	Withdrawal dutypaid	$19, 323, 360 17
Warehoused and bonded	14, 236, 433 21	Withdrawal for transportation	6, 839, 864 15
Rewarehoused and bonded	3, 341, 527 58	Withdrawal for exportation	6, 676, 457 79
Constructively warehoused	14, 203, 024 14	Allowances and deficiencies	1, 538, 7 1 42
Increase of duties ascertained on liquidation	236, 461 28	Balance of bonds not due	8, 959, 748 60
Total	43, 338, 162 13	Total	43, 338, 162 13

W. T. HAINES,
Commissioner.

OFFICE OF COMMISSIONER OF CUSTOMS, *September* 2, 1871.

REPORT OF THE FIRST AUDITOR.

REPORT·

OF

THE FIRST AUDITOR OF THE TREASURY.

TREASURY DEPARTMENT,
First Auditor's Office, September 18, 1871.

SIR: I have the honor to submit the following statement of the business transactions of this office for the fiscal year ended June 30, 1871:

Accounts adjusted.	Number of accounts.	Amounts.
RECEIPTS.		
Collectors of customs	1,546	$187,356,571 31
Collectors under steamboat act	526	204,619 92
Internal and coastwise intercourse	1	26,003 74
Mints and assay offices	23	50,765,660 22
Fines, penalties, and forfeitures	489	924,623 27
Marine hospital money collected	24	2,701 68
Miscellaneous receipts	255	57,807 99
	2,864	239,338,078 13
DISBURSEMENTS.		
Collectors as disbursing agents of the Treasury	1,194	$6,029,273 63
Official emoluments of collectors, naval officers, and surveyors	857	1,633,091 62
Excess of deposits for unascertained duties	122	1,665,653 02
Debentures, drawbacks, bounties, and allowances	90	964,215 21
Special examiner of drugs	1	417 58
Superintendents of lights	446	978,036 87
Agents of marine hospitals	507	366,373 01
Accounts for duties illegally exacted, fines remitted, judgments satisfied, and net proceeds of unclaimed merchandise paid	1,470	874,927 61
Judiciary accounts	1,895	2,624,379 11
Disbursements for revenue-cutters	421	1,058,177 64
Redemption of the public debt and the payment of interest thereon	643	602,120,163 51
California land claims	3	524 75
Inspectors of steam vessels for traveling expenses	292	31,307 21
Public printing	24	1,112,207 67
Insane Asylum, District of Columbia	6	59,350 34
Providence Hospital	12	12,000 00
Construction and repair of public buildings	800	1,581,162 07
Life-saving stations	12	10,976 68
Compensation and mileage of the members of the Senate and House of Representatives	1	435,303 59
Contingent expenses of the Senate and House of Representatives and of the several Departments of Government	438	3,214,039 04
Mints and assay offices	101	50,055,226 92
Territorial accounts	80	152,064 13
Captured and abandoned property	68	347,383 98
Salaries of the civil list paid directly from the Treasury	1,427	612,056 10
Coast Survey	19	595,514 21
Disbursing clerks for paying salaries	335	5,231,340 03
Fuel, lights &c., for public buildings	266	295,201 89
Additional compensation to collectors, &c	2	478 49
Treasurer of the United States for general receipts and expenditures	6	1,080,837,381 25
Distribution of fines, penalties, and forfeitures	154	195,143 82
Commissioner of Public Buildings	118	206,409 83
Commissioner of Agriculture	30	145,221 05
Warehouse and bond accounts	828	
Miscellaneous	1,433	9,123,470 20
	14,101	1,773,277,492 08

Reports and certificates recorded 11,426
Letters written 2,239
Letters recorded ....,.. 2,239
Powers of attorney registered and filed... 6,856
Acknowledgments of accounts written... 8,581
Requisitions answered... 365
Judiciary emolument accounts registered and filed.................................... 456
                                                                                     _____
     Total... 32,162

As the character of the business of this office has undergone no essential change since my last annual report, I am induced to adopt, in part, the language and form of that report, as applicable to this.

The preceding condensed statement of the business of this office gives so imperfect an idea of the amount of work performed, and the large responsibilities involved, that for the better understanding of the diversified character of the business, and its practical working in detail, I submit the following dissection and exhibit, as the most appropriate means of comprehending its importance and measuring its magnitude.

CUSTOMS DIVISION.

Returns are now received from 139 districts and ports. These returns are distributed as nearly equal as practicable to thirteen different desks. For the proper examination and adjustment of these accounts clerks are required who have a knowledge of the tariff laws, and are also good practical accountants. The accounts of customs are received and adjusted monthly. These accounts include the duties on imports, and duties on tonnage.

The abstracts of duties on imports in New York, Boston, Philadelphia, and San Francisco, New Orleans, Baltimore, and Portland, are very large, requiring a great amount of patient labor in comparing the entries with the tariff schedules, made up as those schedules are from the various acts of 1861, 1862, and 1864, and the several amendatory acts. In all the smaller disticts, which have no naval officer to certify the abstracts, the manifest is forwarded by the collector for each and every entry of merchandise, amounting, in districts like Portland, Vermont, Oswego, Detroit, &c., to hundreds and even thousands in a single month. These must all be examined as to the rate of duty, oath, stamp, &c., and compared with the abstract. After the abstracts are examined and the differences noted, a statement of account is made, and the collector charged with the aggregates and credited by his deposits as shown by the covering warrants.

Marine hospital duties are reported by the collectors, in separate accounts monthly, and adjusted quarterly.

The collectors of customs also render monthly accounts for expenses of collecting the revenue, which are adjusted quarterly. In these accounts are included all payments to inspectors, weighers and gangers, appraisers, revenue boatmen, contingent expenses, salary of collectors, commissions, &c. Vouchers for all these payments must be compared with the lists of appointment for the authority for payment, and examined as to correct computation, oath, &c.

Next comes the account of official emoluments, in which the collector accounts for his fees, &c., and charges his payment for clerk-hire, stationery, office-rent, &c. This account in large ports is rendered monthly, and in small ones quarterly, and adjusted yearly. Separate accounts have also to be stated in many of the districts for excess of deposits refunded, debentures paid, and expenses of the revenue-cutter service.

These are received monthly and stated quarterly. In some cases these are very large.

Monthly accounts are also received from nearly all the districts for steamboat fees and fines, penalties, and forfeitures, which are usually adjusted quarterly, and in some cases oftener.

The collectors of customs also act as disbursing agents for expenses of Marine Hospital Establishment and the Light-House Establishment, accounts for which are received monthly and quarterly and stated quarterly.

There are also many special accounts, such as payments for the salaries of janitors, and the distribution of fines and penalties. Also the cases for the refunded duties exacted in excess, tonnage duty refunded, judgment satisfied, &c.

JUDICIARY.

This division is highly important, embracing the adjustment of all judiciary accounts.

First. Accounts of United States marshals for expenses of United States courts, and for their fees for service of process, &c., in all United States cases under the fee bill of February 26, 1853, and amendments thereto. The fee bill of 1853 is general in its application to all States and Territories, but the practice of the courts in the different jurisdictions is not uniform, and hence almost every marshal has his own construction of the fee bill in making charges in his account. To adjust these accounts the closest scrutiny and thorough acquaintance with the usages and decisions of the accounting officers, a familiar acquaintance with their interpretations of the fee bill, as also the practice in the several districts, is essentially necessary. The business in the United States courts has more than doubled since the passage of the internal revenue law, the civil rights bill, and the enforcement act, and as a consequence the accounts of all officers connected with the Federal courts have assumed largely increased proportions in comparison with what they were prior to the rebellion.

Second. Accounts of district attorneys for attendance upon United States courts, and upon commissioners' examinations, for their travel and fees in all United States cases.

Third. Accounts of clerks of United States courts for their attendance, and for fees in all United States cases.

Fourth. Accounts of United States Commissioners for fees, &c.

In the examination and adjustment of all these accounts, it is necessary not only to hold the fee bill in memory, but also to be acquainted with all of the many decisions of the Attorneys General, and of the Secretary of the Interior, and to be able readily to apply the same to any charge that may be presented.

REDEMPTION AND INTEREST DIVISION.

The settlement of the accounts of the Treasurer of the United States, Assistant Treasurers, United States depositaries, and fiscal agents of the Treasury Department, for the payment of interest on the public debt and the redemption of Government obligations, funded or otherwise, is assigned to this division, and may be designated, in brief, as follows:

Registered bonds—Interest.—At the close of the present fiscal year, the amount outstanding of this class of securities, the interest of which is payable in *coin*, was $725,772,350, and in *currency*, being for bonds issued to the Pacific Railroad Companies, $64,618,832. These accounts, payments of which are made semi-annually upon schedules prepared by the Register of the Treasury, for fiscal agents, are closed and transmitted to this office for settlement within ninety days from the date of payment. In the examination of schedules, the stock being held principally by banking and other corporations, executors, administrators, and trustees of estates, and non-residents of the country, the interest of which is, in most cases, receipted by attorneys, requires careful scrutiny into the authority presented as vouchers for the receipt of dividends, and is often attended with considerable correspondence and consequent delay in the adjustment of these accounts. During the year there were seventy-six coin and twenty-six currency accounts settled, involving, in the aggregate, the sum of $48,063,987 79, to which may be included as part of the clerical labors of the division, but which does not enter into the statistics of this report, schedules examined, embracing $14,487,140 35. The number of powers of attorney and testamentary evidence of the administration of estates, received as vouchers for the receipt of interest, and which have been approved, filed, and registered, and listed for the use of fiscal agents, was six thousand eight hundred and fifty-six.

Coupon bonds—Interest. Of this class of securities outstanding at the close of the fiscal year, the interest being payable in coin, and the coupons redeemable semi-annually, amounts to $1,162,361,400. The rendition of these accounts *weekly* by the principal depositaries, and *monthly* by others, and the fact that the several issues and loans have to be kept distinct for entry upon the Register's books, with the amount of interest chargeable to each loan, imposes much additional labor upon the office, the result of which, however, is of material advantage to the Department in keeping the business of its redemptions properly posted for inspection and information. The number of this class of accounts stated was one hundred and fifty-one, amounting to $77,353,964 69, and containing four million nine hundred and eleven thousand five hundred and sixty-eight vouchers counted and canceled.

Navy pension fund.—The amount of this fund upon which the annual interest of three per cent. is paid, amounts to $14,000,000. There have been two accounts stated during the year, amounting to $400,000.

Redemption of United States stock.—The amount of certificates of the loans of 1847, 1848, 1860, Texan indemnity, and the loans of 1862, 1864, and 1865, redeemed and canceled, of which accounts have been stated, amounts, including premium and interest, to $242,253,981 01. Accounts stated, forty-five; vouchers examined, one hundred and one thousand two hundred and seventy-eight.

Floating debt.—Currency obligations, consisting of Treasury notes of various issues, certificates of indebtedness, certificates of temporary loan and interest thereon, amount to $14,657,331 89, embraced in one hundred and thirty-seven accounts, and containing twenty-two thousand six hundred and twenty vouchers.

United States obligations destroyed—consisting of old demand notes, legal-tender notes, fractional and postal currency, and gold certificates—amount to $219,379,898 18, and the number of vouchers examined, eight hundred and fifty-seven, embraced in two hundred and six accounts.

MINT ACCOUNTS AND OTHERS.

This division adjusts the accounts of the Mint of the United States, its branches, (four in number,) and assay office, New York; accounts of the governors and secretaries of the Territories; accounts for defense of suits in the Court of Claims; accounts in relation to captured and abandoned property; and salary accounts of the civil list.

The accounts of the mints and assay office are designated as bullion, ordinary, and medal accounts, and are adjusted quarterly.

The bullion accounts are voluminous, and the examination of the various accounts tedious. The abstracts of deposits, in connection with the warrants of the director or superintendent for payment, are first examined and checked, then the various accounts of the treasurer, melter and refiner, and coiner, under the following heads: "Deposit account," "gold bullion," "silver bullion," "cent bullion," "cent deposit account," "gold coinage," "silver coinage," "cent coinage," "melter and refiner's gold," "melter and refiner's silver," "melter and refiner's cent bullion," "coiner's gold," "coiner's silver," "coiner's five-cent account," "coiner's three-cent account," "coiner's bronze or one and two-cent account," "unpaid depositors," "gold coins for assay," "silver coins for assay," "unparted bar account," "silver profit and loss," "cent profit and loss," "bullion deposit profit and loss," "profit and loss," "bullion fund," "balances," and, finally, all of the above are blended in the summary statement. During the last fiscal year there were twenty-one of these accounts adjusted.

The ordinary accounts are for the incidental and contingent expenses, wages of workmen, and salaries of officers and clerks. The medal accounts are for medals manufactured for various institutions throughout the country. The accounts of the governors and secretaries of the Territories are for the contingent expenses of the executive offices, and for compensation and mileage of members, and incidental expenses of the legislative assemblies.

The accounts in relation to captured and abandoned property: These accounts are for moneys received from and disbursements for and on account of captured and abandoned property. This branch of business is drawing to a close, only three accounts received and stated during the year. The accounts for defense of suits in the Court of Claims are for expenses incurred in the defense of suits in relation to captured and abandoned property.

Salary accounts.—These are salary certificates for salaries of the Vice-President of the United States, judges of the Supreme Court, United States district judges, United States attorneys and marshals, governors and secretaries of the Territories, commissioners of claims and employés, and the officers and clerks of the United States steamboat inspection service. Some of the above are stated monthly, and others quarterly.

The whole number of accounts adjusted by this division during the year was 1,676.

WAREHOUSE AND BOND ACCOUNTS.

The act of March 28, 1854, gives to importers the privilege of storing imported goods in public or private bonded warehouses, under the supervision of customs officers, without payment of duties, for a period not exceeding three years. During this period these goods may be withdrawn at the option of the importer for consumption, on payment of duties, for transportation to other districts and ports, or for exportation out of the country.

Under the title of warehouse and bond accounts, collectors of customs are required to render accounts of all goods so stored in their respective districts, upon which the duties remain due and unpaid, with the same particularity of detail as they account for duties on goods entered for consumption.

These accounts comprise statements and vouchers, not only of all goods entered at any port, and actually placed in bonded warehouses, but also of all goods entered at such port for immediate transportation to other ports in the country, or for immediate exportation to foreign countries; such goods being considered as constructively warehoused. In these accounts are abstracts of all goods withdrawn from warehouse for consumption, transportation to other ports, or exportation to foreign countries. They contain also statements of salt withdrawn from warehouse pursuant to the provisions of the fourth section act July 28, 1866, to be taken on board vessels licensed for the fisheries, under bond, to be used in curing fish. Separate accounts are rendered of all transportation, exportation, and salt bonds taken to cover such withdrawals. Forfeited bonds delivered for prosecution are credited in these accounts to the collector, and charged to the various district attorneys. Rather more than half of the collection districts have transactions and render accounts. The rest are required to send monthly certified statements that there have been no transactions under either of these heads.

ACCOUNTS OF THE TREASURER OF THE UNITED STATES.

The magnitude of the statement will convey some idea of the labor performed in the adjustment of the accounts. The accounts of the Treasurer of the United States for the general receipts and expenditures of the Government are made up and rendered quarterly. The account current (a volume of some three hundred pages) has to be carefully compared with a certified account received from the Register, of all warrants drawn on him or in his favor during the quarter, the amount remaining unpaid and outstanding of previous quarters, and the amount of such warrants for which he claims credit as being paid, the amount of balances in the various depositories, &c. All warrants drawn on the Treasurer are paid by drafts, and he cannot receive credit for the payment of a single warrant, unless it is accompanied by its appropriate draft, properly indorsed by the payee. The examination and comparison of these drafts are intricate and laborious.

The internal revenue warrants at this time fully equal one-half of the yearly issue of warrants prior to the rebellion, many of which require the critical examination of from one to over six hundred drafts.

During the fiscal year ending June 30, 1871, six accounts of the Treasurer of the United States have been adjusted, requiring the careful examination of over 80,000 warrants and drafts; the amounts embraced in the settlement of these accounts are, for actual receipts, $1,094,073,856 29; and, for expenditures, $1,080,828,090 44.

The mileage and compensation of members of the House of Representatives are paid by the Treasurer on certificates of the Speaker of the House, which are the Treasurer's vouchers, and upon which he receives credit in the adjustment of his account as agent. This account has to be carefully compared with the journal of the Sergeant-at-Arms, who keeps the individual accounts of the members, &c.

The accounts of the Secretary of the Senate as agent for paying the compensation and mileage of Senators, and the contingent expenses of the Senate, are very intricate, owing to the irregular sessions of that body. The amount involved in the accounts adjusted during the fiscal year is $657,700 20.

SALARY ACCOUNTS.

Under this head is embraced the adjustment of the accounts (with two or three exceptions) of disbursing officers for payment of salaries to all persons in the Departments at Washington who receive a regular compensation, with some accounts also for additional clerk hire. These accounts include the pay-rolls of the Treasury, State, War, Navy, Interior, Justice, and Post Office Departments; also the accounts of the Superintendent of Weights and Measures, Clerk of the House of Representatives, Librarian of Congress, Congressional Printer, private secretaries of the President of the United States, salaries, &c., of Metropolitan police, and all the accounts of United States Coast Survey. Under this division of the work of the office is also embraced the settlement of the accounts for salaries in their offices of all United States Assistant Treasurers and United States depositaries.

CONTINGENT ACCOUNTS, ETC.,

includes the contingencies of all the Executive Departments—Treasury, War, Navy, and Interior; contingencies of the House of Representatives under different appropriations; all the accounts of the Department of Agriculture, salaries, distribution of seeds, &c., under different appropriations; all the accounts of the Commissioner of Public Buildings and Grounds, embracing repairs and preservation of all the public works in the city of Washington—about one hundred different appropriations; all the accounts of the disbursing agent for new dome, Capitol extension, enlargement of the Congressional Library, grading the public grounds around the Capitol, &c.; all the accounts of the agent, &c., for the Library of Congress, Botanic Garden, &c.—fourteen appropriations; expense of the national loan; contingent expenses of the Assistant Treasurers of the United States at New York, Boston, New Orleans, Charleston, Denver City, San Francisco, &c.; contingent expenses of the Executive Mansion; contingent expenses of Congressional Printer; accounts for repairs, &c., and for furniture for Treasury Department.

SEPARATE CLASSIFICATION OF ACCOUNTS.

The accounts settled by this division are various, and preclude any general classification. During the last fiscal year the whole number of accounts settled in this office in this branch of its business was 1,846, involving an expenditure of $4,068,262 73. The number of accounts will not diminish during the present fiscal year.

The following classification embraces the several accounts examined and settled: Construction and repairs of public buildings, furniture for public buildings, public printing, Government asylum, deaf and dumb asylum, steamboat inspectors, life-saving station, contingent expenses of United States depositories, Columbia Hospital, timber agents. Many other accounts of not less importance, that cannot well be classified, are settled.

In the recording division of the office there are employed five clerks, whose duties consist in recording the reports and certificates of the Auditor to the Comptroller of the Treasury and Commissioner of Customs, on the accounts accruing in the office and the correspondence incident thereto.

There is a large amount of miscellaneous business, much of it of great importance, requiring the highest clerical qualifications, which has no appropriate classification with any of the divisions previously described. It has its proper place in the routine of business, and is dispatched with scrupulous care.

When the Treasury Department was organized this office was created as a part of the original frame-work. Its duties were then specifically defined as the auditing branch of the Department. Its important original duties have been continued, greatly amplified, to which new and diversified duties of great importance have been added, in the long progress of legislation, as the exigencies of Government required. All of these functions are so inseparably connected with the operations of the Department proper, that they rest upon the foundation of permanency and the assurance of expansion. This connection must inevitably increase its business with the growth of the country, and the enlarged sphere of the Government precluding any expectation that the clerical force of the office can be reduced.

The clerks of the office deserve the highest commendation for their fidelity and efficiency in the performance of their respective duties, and for the scrupulous care with which they protect the interests of the Government.

I know of no higher merit of those engaged in the service of Government, and more deserving of commendation and recompense, than the faithful and efficient performance of the entire range of duty in all its delicate and responsible relations. Justice and expediency may bring this appropriately within the province of legislation as worthy of the appreciation that honors fidelity, rewards merit, and imparts moral strength to Government.

The present salaries of the clerks bear a disproportionate relation (to their prejudice) to the grade and amount of labor they perform, and the incidental responsibilities they have to assume. Beyond this, and of much greater importance in its consequences, is the total insufficiency of their salaries for the comfortable support of their families, under the most stringent economy; and the cheerless effect that it has upon their official duties, from the perplexing expedients to which they are driven by embarrassments.

I most respectfully and earnestly recommend that their condition, which is marked by humiliation and want, may be meliorated by a liberal recompense commensurate with the claims of justice and sound policy.

Most respectfully, your obedient servant,

T. L. SMITH,
First Auditor.

Hon. GEORGE S. BOUTWELL,
Secretary of the Treasury.

REPORT OF THE SECOND AUDITOR.

REPORT

OF

THE SECOND AUDITOR OF THE TREASURY.

TREASURY DEPARTMENT,
Second Auditor's Office, November 18, 1871.

SIR : I have the honor to submit herewith the annual report of this office, for the fiscal year ending June 30, 1871, showing in detail the condition of business, in each division, at the commencement of the year, its progress during the year, and its condition at the end thereof.

BOOK-KEEPERS' DIVISION.

The following statement shows the amount and nature of the work performed by this division during the year :

Requisitions registered, journalized, and posted.

On what account drawn.	Number.	Amount.
DEBIT REQUISITIONS.		
Pay.		
Advances in favor of Pay Department	71	$16, 213, 000 00
Advances in favor of Adjutant General's Department	48	213, 360 15
Advances in favor of Ordnance Department	129	1, 630, 246 87
Advances in favor of Medical Department	9	128, 000 00
Advances under direction of the Secretary of War	10	47, 132 50
Advances in favor of Indian Department	329	4, 513, 429 20
Advances under direction of the General of the Army	3	4, 000 00
Claims paid under appropriations of Pay Department	64	19, 800 96
Claims paid under appropriations of Adjutant General's Department	22	1, 796 94
Claims paid under appropriations of Ordnance Department	7	20, 809 41
Claims paid under appropriations of Medical Department	176	54, 626 44
Claims paid under appropriations in charge of Secretary of War	66	71, 724 97
Claims paid under appropriations of Quartermasters' Department	1	15 66
Claims paid under appropriations of Indian Department	985	3, 321, 280 69
Claims paid under special acts of relief by Congress	12	19, 552 55
Payments to Treasurer United States—internal revenue fund	35	47, 907 92
Payments to National Asylum for Disabled Volunteer Soldiers	12	296, 287 32
Payments to Soldiers' Home	23	93, 920 47
Total payments	2, 002	26, 701, 892 74
TRANSFER.		
Requisitions issued for the purpose of adjusting appropriations :		
Transferring amounts from appropriations found to be chargeable to such as are entitled to credit on the books of the Second Auditor's Office	18	10, 497, 991 34
Transferring amounts as above to the books of the Third Auditor's Office	353	639, 826 44
Transferring amounts as above to the books of the Register's Office	14	8, 147 95
Total transfers	385	11, 145, 965 73
Aggregate debits	2, 387	37, 847, 858 47
CREDIT REQUISITIONS.		
Deposit.		
In favor of Pay Department	24	188, 566 90
In favor of Ordnance Department	32	9, 130, 555 70
In favor of Adjutant General's Department		38 27
In favor of Medical Department	10	14, 117 66
In favor of Quartermaster's Department		14 45
In favor of Indian Department	21	426, 006 66
Total deposit	87	9, 759, 299 64

Requisitions registered, journalized, and posted—Contiuued.

On what account drawn.	Number.	Amount.
Counter.		
Requisitions issued for the purpose of adjusting appropriations :		
Transferring amounts to appropriations entitled to credit from appropriations found to be chargeable on the books of the Second Auditor's Office ..	17	$10, 519, 370 35
Transferring amounts as above from appropriations on the books of the Third Auditor's Office to the books of the Second Auditor's Office	22	94, 078 72
Transferring amounts as above from the books of the Fourth Auditor's Office to those of the Second Auditor's Office..............................	1	21, 606 00
Transferring amounts as above from the books of the First Auditor's Office to those of the Second Auditor's Office...........................	5	8, 832 97
Total counter	45	10, 643, 908 04
Aggregate credits................................	132	20, 403, 207 68
Aggregate debits and credits.......................	2, 519	58, 251, 066 15
Deducting the credits from the debits shows the net amount drawn out to be..............................	....	17, 444, 650 79
APPROPRIATION WARRANTS.		
Credits.		
In favor of appropriations of Pay Department	....	26, 073, 526 26
In favor of appropriations of Adjutant General's Department	....	472, 000 00
In favor of appropriations of Ordnance Department	....	762, 912 55
In favor of appropriations of Medical Department....................	7	108, 000 00
In favor of appropriations in charge of Secretary of War..............	....	325, 000 00
In favor of appropriations in charge of the General of the Army	....	5, 000 00
In favor of appropriations of the Quartermaster's Department............	....	1, 350, 000 00
In favor of appropriations of Indian Department	54	*13, 378, 496 01
Under special acts of relief by Congress	3	105, 412 55
Total credits.................	64	42, 580, 347 37
Debits.		
Transfer from draft and substitute fund to contingencies of the Army.....	1	150, 000 00
Transfer from "fulfilling treaty with Apaches, Kiowas, and Comanches" to appropriation for "maintenance and education of Helen and Heloise Lincoln"...........	1	5, 000 00
Transfer from "fulfilling treaty with Sioux of different tribes, including Santee Sioux, in the State of Nebraska," to appropriation for the "relief of Mrs. Fanny Kelly"	1	5, 000 00
Total debits.................	3	160, 000 00
Aggregate debits and credits	67	42, 740, 347 37
Excess of credits over debits	....	42, 420, 347 37

* Appropriations for two fiscal years are included in this amount, the appropriation warrant for the year ending June 30, 1872, amounting to $5,419,540 96, having been issued before June 30, 1871.

CONDENSED BALANCE SHEET OF APPROPRIATIONS.

	War Department.	Indian Department.
Credit.		
Balance to credit of all appropriations on the books of this office June 30, 1871.	$28, 387, 878 27	$4, 060, 042 01
Amount credited by appropriation warrant during fiscal year ending June 30, 1871.	29, 201, 851 36	13, 378, 496 01
Amount credited by deposit and transfer requisitions during same period.	19, 949, 907 40	453, 300 28
Amount credited in Third Auditor s Office to appropriations used in common by both offices.	335, 874 71	....
Total	77, 875, 511 74	17, 897, 838 30

Condensed balance sheet of appropriations—Continued.

	War Department.	Indian Department.
Debit.		
Balance to debit of appropriations on the books of this office June 30, 1870.	....	$5,000 00
Amount debited to appropriations by transfer warrants during fiscal year ending June 30, 1871.	$150,000 00	10,000 00
Amount drawn from appropriations by requisition during same period.	29,964,868 20	7,882,990 27
Amount drawn in Third Auditor's Office from appropriations used in common by both offices.	1,976,285 25	....
Balance remaining to the credit of all appropriations on the books of this office June 30, 1871.	45,784,358 29	9,999,848 03
Total	77,875,511 74	17,897,838 30

SETTLEMENTS MADE.

During the year the following settlements of a miscellaneous character were made by this division.

On what account.	Number.	Amount.
Transfer settlements for the adjustment of appropriations...................	5	$10,495,429 88
Transfers to books of Third Auditor's Office.................................	3	436,178 01
Charges and payments to officers...	2	102 96
Total..	10	10,931,710 85

SETLEMENTS ENTERED.

Paymasters	467
Recruiting...	244
Ordnance	69
Medical...	70
Treasurer United States, internal revenue fund	6
Soldiers' Home..	23
National Asylum for Disabled Volunteer Soldiers	12
Charges and credits to officers for overpayments, refundments, &c...........	352
Transfers to credit of disbursing officers on books of Third Auditor's Office.	297
Miscellaneous	69
Indian...	111

Claims, Indian	951	
Claims, War	262	
		1,213
Total number of setlements......................................		2,933
Number of certificates given to the Third Auditor's Office and the different divisions of this office...............................		1,180
Number of letters written ,...		673

PAYMASTER'S DIVISION.

The total number of accounts examined and settlements made during the year is 2,274, as follows :

Paymasters' accounts examined and reported	843
Old settlements of paymasters' accounts revised...............................	976
Charges against officers on account of double payments	283
Credits to officers for overpayments refunded	21
Miscellaneous	151
Total	2,274

The amounts involved in the above are as follows:

Paymasters' accounts $124,063,652 23
Amount of fines, forfeitures, &c., for the support of the National Asylum for Disabled Volunteer Soldiers ascertained to be due: 1st, in the
current examination of paymasters' accounts, $223,396 04 ; 2d, in
a special examination, $77,974 48 ; and 3d, in the adjustment of claims
of the heirs of deceased soldiers, $1,846 47. The amount found due
has been paid to the asylum in accordance with the act of Congress
of March 21, 1866, as follows :

August 4, 1870 .... $46,947 91
September 17, 1870 .... 11,188 59
October 6, 1870 .... 14,703 69
November 2, 1870 .... 15,816 17
December 3, 1870 .... 14,179 72
January 5, 1871 .... 57,959 61
February 1, 1871 .... 5,412 57
March 1, 1871 .... 17,443 70
April 1, 1871 .... 27,457 16
May 1, 1871 .... 21,742 47
June 1, 1871 .... 14,980 27
June 30, 1871 .... 55,385 13
                                                         ─────────   303,216 99

Amount of fines, forfeitures, &c., for the support of the Soldiers' Home,
ascertained to be due in the examination of paymasters' accounts,
and paid to said Soldiers' Home in accordance with the act of Con-
gress of March 3, 1859, as follows :
October 11, 1870 .... $27,009 33
January 10, 1871 .... 10,427 79
April 4, 1871 .... 8,527 29
May 5, 1871 .... 389 93
June 2, 1871 .... 2,281 29
June 15, 1871 .... 56 86
June 30, 1871 .... 3,632 16
                                                         ─────────   52,324 65
Amount credited to the Treasurer of the United States on account of
tax on salaries ....   41,701,85.
Amount transferred from the appropriation for "Pay of the Army" to
that for "Ordnance, ordnance stores, and supplies" on account of
deductions from the pay of officers and soldiers for ordnance and
ordnance stores, in accordance with Par. 1380, Revised Army Regulations of 1863 ....   29,134 58
Amount transferred from the appropriation for "Pay of the Army" to
that for "Support of Bureau of Refugees, Freedmen, and Abandoned
Lands," being an amount due the Freedmen's Bureau 208 50
Amount transferred from the appropriation for "Pay of the Army" to
the books of the Third Auditor's Office, on account of deductions
from the pay of soldiers for tobacco, pursuant to General Orders No.
63, War Department, Adjutant General's Office, June 11, 1867 ......   158,297 92
Amount transferred to the books of the Third Auditor's Office on
account of stoppages against officers for subsistence stores, quartermasters' stores, transportation, &c...............................   191,898 31
Amount passed to the credit of paymasters still in the service on
account of sums disbursed by them in payment of outstanding
checks of paymasters out of service...............................   2,519 61
Amount charged to officers on account of over-payments 387 18
Amount charged to officers on account of double payments 68,363 83
Amounts charged to paymasters for payments made on forged receipts   387 97
Amount credited to officers for refundment of pay drawn twice, and
for sums deposited by them to close their accounts................   5,355 51
Amount of balances found due paymasters, and paid them by requisi-
tion, to close their accounts....................................   1,319 82
Amount paid to civilians for services under reconstruction acts......   214 50
Amount credited to officers on account of refundment of erroneous
payments made to them 329 10
Miscellaneous credits 1,643 60

    Total...   124,920,956 15

Accounts of paymasters on hand June 30, 1870   3,279
Accounts of paymasters received during the year ending June 30, 1871   635

Total   3,914
Accounts of paymasters audited and reported to the Second Comptroller during
    the year   843

Accounts of paymasters remaining unsettled June 30, 1871   3,071
Draft rendezvous accounts received from the Paymaster General during the year,
    and in course of examination   30

Total number of accounts on hand June 30, 1871   3,101

Number of letters written 12,621

The number of paymasters who rendered accounts to this office during the rebellion
is 547. The accounts of 59 of these paymasters were balanced and closed prior to June
30, 1870, and 134 during the present fiscal year, making 193 paymasters whose accounts
have been finally disposed of.

Miscellaneous division.

The ordnance, medical, and miscellaneous division, and the recruiting
division were consolidated in September, 1870, and now form the miscellaneous division. The following statement shows the number of money
accounts on hand in this division at the commencement of the year ending
June 30, 1871, the number received and settled during the year, and the
number remaining unsettled at the close of the year, together with the
expenditure embraced in the settlements :

Ordnance, medical, and miscellaneous accounts on hand June 30, 1870   623
Recruiting accounts on hand June 30, 1870   976
Number of accounts received during the year   1,599
                                                                                2,368

Total   3,967
Number of accounts settled during the year   2,394

Number of accounts remaining unsettled June 30, 1871   1,573

The amounts involved in the above settlements are as follows :

Ordnance, medical, and miscellaneous :

Ordnance Department $1,433,508 93
Medical Department 218,034 80
Expended by disbursing officers out of the quartermaster's funds, not chargeable to said funds, but to certain
    appropriations on the books of this office 175,245 95
Contingencies of the Army 126,530 88
Providing for the comfort of sick and discharged soldiers   18,926 62
Expenses of military convicts 11,281 97
Bronze equestrian statue of Lieutenant General Winfield
    Scott 5,000 00
Expenses of court of inquiry held in 1868 and 1869 ......   5,000 00
Army Medical Museum 2,239 21
Expenses of the Commanding General's office 2,311 60
Contingencies of the Adjutant General's Department, at
    Department headquarters 2,517 23
Medical and Surgical History and Statistics 1,961 15
Library of the Surgeon General's office 1,028 58
Sick and wounded soldiers' fund 243 32
Medals of honor for distinguished services 142 50
Relief of Friend A. Brainard, act May 4, 1870 ....   300 00
Relief of Grenville M. Dodge, act May 6, 1870 ....   4,350 00
Relief of James M. Trotter, act June 23, 1870 ....   672 27
Relief of William H. Dupree, act June 23, 1870 ....   1 74

Relief of Lot S. Bayless, act July 11, 1870	$864 09	
Relief of Malinda Harmon, act January 21, 1871	4,696 70	
Relief of Henry H. Hoyt, act January 27, 1871	100 00	
Relief of General John C. McQniston and J. D. Skeen, act February 27, 1871	2,000 00	
Relief of Abram G. Snyder, act March 3, 1871	5,000 00	
Relief of James J. Hiles, act March 3, 1871	100 00	
Relief of W. B. Carpenter, act March 3, 1871	588 02	
Relief of William O. Sides, joint resolution February 16, 1871	130 00	
Relief of William P. Thomasson, joint resolution March 3, 1871	377 70	
		$2,023,703 26

Regular recruiting:		
Expenses of recruiting	198,435 46	
Bounties to volunteers and regulars	1,425 00	
Pay of the Army	2,061 42	
Subsistence of officers	260 40	
Pay in lieu of clothing for officers' servants	21 73	
Medical and Hospital Department	11 00	
		909,915 01

Volunteer recruiting:		
Collecting, drilling, and organizing volunteers	712,739 49	
Bounty to volunteers and regulars	33,650 00	
Draft and substitute fund	7,650 47	
Pay of 2 and 3 years' volunteers	617 50	
Pay of the Army	95 70	
Subsistence of officers	31 50	
Medical and Hospital Department	9 00	
Pay in lieu of clothing for officers' servants	1 68	
		754,795 34

Local bounty:		
Pay of 2 and 3 years' volunteers		3,930 92

Total		2,984,644 53

The registers of payments made to officers were transferred to this division August 15, 1870, since which date 1,048 paymasters' accounts have been examined for the necessary data, and 340 double payments to officers discovered and reported.

Total number of letters written, 2,286.

INDIAN DIVISION.

General report of the Indian division, for the fiscal year ending June 30, 1871:

Money accounts of agents on hand June 30, 1870	368
Property accounts of agents on hand June 30, 1870	528
Claims on hand June 30, 1870	None.
Money accounts of agents received during the year	673
Property accounts received during the year	252
Claims received during the year	969
Total	2,790

Money accounts of agents audited during the year	520
Property accounts examined during the year	203
Claims settled during the year	962
Total	1,685

Money accounts of agents on hand June 30, 1871........................   521
Property accounts on hand June 30, 1871   577
Claims on hand June 30, 1871   7

    Total number of accounts, &c., on hand June 30, 1871...........   1, 105

Amount involved in money accounts audited $5, 220, 928 91
Amount involved in claims settled 2, 973, 705 72

    Total...   8, 194, 634 63

Number of letters written 1, 417

PAY AND BOUNTY DIVISION.

The following tabular statements exhibit in detail the operation of the two branches of the pay and bounty division during the year, together with the condition of the business of the division, both at the commencement and close of the year.

Examining branch.

The three following tables show the work performed by the examining branch of this division during the year:

Claims in cases of white soldiers.

Date	Arrears of pay and original bounty.											Additional bounty, act July 28, 1866, and amendments.										
	Suspended claims.						Original claims.					Suspended claims.						Original claims.				
	No. of letters written.	Total number of claims examined.	No. rejected.	No. again suspended—additional evidence insufficient.	No. completed by additional evidence received.	Whole number examined.	No. of duplicate applications found.	No. rejected.	No. found incomplete and suspended.	No. found correct.	Whole number examined.	No. of letters written.	Total number of claims examined.	No. rejected.	No. again suspended—additional evidence insufficient.	No. completed by additional evidence received.	Whole number examined.	No. of duplicate applications found.	No. rejected.	No. found incomplete and suspended.	No. found correct.	Whole number examined.
1870.																						
July	3,680	4,699	373	1,012	429	2,714	223	467	1,019	256	1,985	2,436	2,198	76	336	220	632	478	141	682	256	1,566
August	2,935	3,810	291	1,730	354	2,384	304	281	600	241	1,436	1,570	2,836	80	580	229	839	489	15	1,076	417	1,997
September	5,228	4,502	205	1,970	660	2,835	231	242	1,010	184	1,667	3,521	2,720	150	632	465	1,247	136	244	798	295	1,473
October	2,043	4,396	365	1,370	331	2,066	190	360	634	146	1,330	1,730	2,304	392	430	389	1,141	129	143	575	316	1,163
November	1,618	5,061	300	1,711	437	2,448	380	145	2,041	67	2,633	2,646	2,776	351	722	409	1,482	398	268	482	206	1,284
December	5,082	3,604	556	1,688	374	2,618	231	292	653	68	1,186	2,625	2,233	173	772	483	1,428	178	155	332	140	805
1871.																						
January	7,333	4,726	511	1,825	569	2,905	356	255	1,079	199	1,821	3,079	2,494	137	803	389	1,329	188	192	523	262	1,165
February	4,870	4,610	468	1,945	455	2,668	164	273	592	113	1,142	2,242	1,757	293	732	446	1,471	7	103	79	97	296
March	5,717	4,703	815	2,250	450	3,515	214	264	564	146	1,188	1,689	1,275	92	870	288	1,250	4	9	8	4	25
April	5,305	4,667	666	2,233	503	3,402	179	553	464	69	1,565	966	663	84	402	161	647	2	6	13	4	16
May	4,131	3,579	670	1,636	398	2,614	223	154	533	50	965	917	629	87	366	149	602	3	6	10	5	27
June	4,772	3,336	630	1,697	302	2,529	185	101	468	53	807	930	627	114	374	119	607				4	50
Total	52,734	50,313	5,850	21,976	5,072	32,898	2,884	3,347	9,672	1,522	17,415	25,115	22,502	1,959	6,950	3,747	12,665	1,952	1,388	4,582	2,006	9,837

Claims in cases of colored soldiers, including both arrears of pay and bounties.

Date.	Original claims.					Suspended claims.				Total number of claims examined.	No. of letters written.
	Whole number examined.	No. found correct.	No. found incomplete and suspended.	No. rejected.	No. of duplicate applications found.	Whole number examined.	No. completed by additional evidence received.	No. again suspended, additional evidence insufficient.	No. rejected.		
1870.											
July	232	17	190	25	....	1,615	438	1,079	98	1,847	2,181
August	303	22	256	25	....	1,832	430	1,331	71	2,135	2,452
September	162	6	127	29	....	1,723	408	1,222	93	1,885	2,087
October	116	7	88	21	....	1,237	238	999	....	1,353	1,532
November	165	7	130	19	....	1,657	276	1,146	235	1,822	2,041
December	164	4	128	32	....	1,849	186	1,211	432	2,013	2,297
1871.											
January	215	5	183	27	....	1,454	190	911	353	1,669	1,913
February	140	11	116	13	....	869	149	625	195	1,109	1,106
March	61	3	57	1	....	1,444	288	886	270	1,505	1,624
April	85	1	73	11	....	1,278	260	869	149	1,363	1,703
May	96	2	71	23	....	1,136	209	749	178	1,232	1,417
June	126	4	111	11	....	1,274	207	870	197	1,400	619
Total	1,865	89	1,530	237	....	17,468	3,279	11,898	2,291	19,333	20,972

SUMMARY.

1870.											
July	3,783	529	1,891	653	701	4,961	1,067	3,327	547	8,744	8,297
August	3,726	660	1,932	321	793	5,045	1,013	3,560	442	8,771	6,957
September	3,302	485	1,935	515	367	5,895	1,533	3,624	448	9,107	10,836
October	2,609	469	1,297	524	319	4,444	958	2,799	687	7,053	6,049
November	4,092	280	2,661	432	718	5,587	1,122	3,579	886	9,679	6,305
December	2,155	212	1,113	419	411	5,895	1,043	3,671	1,181	8,050	10,004
1871.											
January	3,201	396	1,785	417	546	5,689	1,148	3,539	1,001	8,889	12,325
February	1,568	221	787	389	171	5,308	1,050	3,302	956	6,876	8,218
March	1,274	153	629	274	218	6,209	1,026	4,006	1,177	7,483	9,030
April	1,366	74	551	570	181	5,327	924	3,504	899	6,693	7,974
May	1,088	57	248	183	226	4,352	666	2,751	935	5,440	6,485
June	953	61	589	118	185	4,410	528	2,941	744	5,363	6,341
Total	29,117	3,617	15,418	4,862	4,846	63,031	12,098	40,823	10,003	92,148	98,821

o

Settling branch.

The three following tables show the work performed by the settling branch of this division during the year:

Claims in cases of white soldiers.

Date.	Additional bounty act, July 28, 1866.					Arrears of pay, &c., act July 22, 1861.				
	Number of claims.				Amount involved.	Number of claims.				Amount involved.
	Received.	Allowed.	Rejected.	Whole No. disposed of.		Received.	Allowed.	Rejected.	Whole No. disposed of.	
1870.										
July	3,493	586	120	706	$68,967 17	1,984	769	250	1,019	$51,980 73
August	1,410	609	100	769	70,366 06	1,660	598	139	737	78,880 62
September	899	188	80	578	51,950 00	1,195	550	177	727	75,660 03
October	728	694	71	765	78,250 87	1,039	797	140	937	99,571 82
November	903	952	54	1,006	103,208 04	1,141	599	173	772	75,113 55
December	1,043	703	83	786	75,103 04	1,269	561	112	673	79,989 92
1871.										
January	802	800	125	925	85,204 31	1,744	664	221	885	177,582 75
February	28	512	60	572	60,970 00	786	633	160	793	95,040 22
March	25	544	63	607	62,488 10	1,054	634	210	844	90,697 91
April	16	339	80	419	38,670 99	877	581	104	685	81,649 47
May	33	310	60	370	36,481 55	1,008	528	109	637	72,850 37
June	14	195	20	215	23,000 00	817	431	106	537	59,365 87
Total	9,414	6,797	921	7,718	754,763 23	14,602	7,345	1,901	9,246	1,084,283 25

Claims in cases of colored soldiers, including both arrears of pay and bounties.

Date.	Number of claims—				Amount involved.
	Received.	Allowed.	Rejected.	Whole No. disposed of.	
1870.					
July	300	470	32	502	$81,213 00
August	245	250	32	282	41,434 68
September	139	155	23	178	26,717 35
October	161	160	14	174	26,158 45
November	148	309	49	358	54,143 59
December	187	273	34	307	44,875 47
1871.					
January	187	296	34	330	51,098 72
February	55	175	22	197	29,687 67
March	71	234	19	253	37,849 92
April	103	277	40	317	42,568 94
May	95	194	25	219	38,966 33
June	140	198	49	247	34,403 82
Total	1,831	2,991	373	3,364	509,717 94

Summary.

.Date.	Number of claims—			Total No. of claims disposed of.	Amount involved.	Number of letters written.
	Received.	Allowed.	Rejected.			
1870.						
July	5,777	1,825	402	2,227	$248,160 90	5,400
August	3,343	1,517	271	1,788	190,681 46	4,273
September	2,163	1,198	285	1,493	154,322 38	4,530
October	1,928	1,651	225	1,876	203,990 14	4,400
November	2,192	1,860	277	2,137	232,465 18	4,380
December	2,499	1,537	229	1,766	199,967 42	3,319
1871.						
January	2,823	1,760	380	2,140	313,885 78	4,615
February	869	1,320	242	1,562	185,697 89	3,696
March	1,150	1,412	292	1,704	191,035 93	4,453
April	960	1,197	224	1,421	162,889 40	3,444
May	1,136	1,032	193	1,225	148,298 25	3,914
June	971	824	175	999	116,760 69	3,192
Total	25,811	17,123	3,195	20,338	2,348,164 42	49,616

Consolidated statement, showing the operation of the entire division for the fiscal year ending June 30, 1871.

Date.	Number of claims.			Whole number disposed of.	Amount involved.	Number of letters written.	Number of certificates issued.
	Received.	Allowed.	Rejected.				
1870.							
July	5,777	1,825	2,203	4,128	$248,160 90	13,697	2,062
August	3,343	1,517	1,827	3,344	190,681 46	11,230	1,293
September	2,163	1,198	1,626	2,824	154,322 38	15,366	1,938
October	1,928	1,651	1,755	3,406	203,990 14	9,449	1,479
November	2,192	1,860	2,317	4,177	232,465 18	10,679	1,522
December	2,499	1,537	2,240	3,777	199,967 42	13,323	1,645
1871.							
January	2,823	1,760	2,348	4,108	313,885 78	16,940	1,705
February	869	1,320	1,768	3,088	185,697 89	11,914	1,477
March	1,150	1,412	1,961	3,373	191,035 93	13,489	1,733
April	960	1,197	1,874	3,071	162,889 40	11,418	1,342
May	1,136	1,022	1,537	2,569	148,298 25	10,399	1,221
June	971	824	1,399	2,223	116,760 69	10,533	1,084
Total	25,811	17,123	22,955	40,078	2,348,164 42	148,437	18,571

In addition to the above there have been made in this division seventeen settlements on account of fines, forfeitures, &c., against soldiers of the regular Army, amounting to $28,957 43, paid to the treasurer of the Soldiers' Home in accordance with the act of Congress of March 3, 1859, making the total number of settlements 17,140, and the total disbursements $2,377,121 85.

Number of claims under act July 28, 1866, (white,) on hand June 30, 1870 10,040
Number of claims for arrears of pay and original bounty on hand June 30, 1870. 29,835
Number of colored claims on hand June 30, 1870 13,887

Total number of claims on hand June 30, 1870 53,762

Number of claims under act July 28, 1866, (white,) on hand June 30, 1871 7,364
Number of claims for arrears of pay and bounty (white) on hand June 30, 1871. 23,960
Number of colored claims on hand June 30, 1871 8,171

Total number of claims on hand June 30, 1871 39,495

The following statement shows the condition of the claims on hand :

Number of claims suspended, awaiting evidence to be filed by claimants or their attorneys 29,542

Number of claims under the decision of the Supreme Court in the case of United States, appellants, vs. Hosmer, awaiting further action of Congress 7,874
Number of claims ready for settlement 1,851
Number of claims unexamined June 30, 1871 228

Total 39,495

PROPERTY DIVISION.

The following statement shows the condition of business in this division :

Property returns of officers on hand June 30, 1870 63,775
Property returns of officers received during the year 9,954

Total 73,729
Property returns of officers examined during the year 39,171

Property returns of officers on hand June 30, 1871 34,558

Certificates of non-indebtedness issued to officers 1,005

Amount stopped from pay of officers for property not accounted for $766.14

Number of letters written during the year 12,685
Number of letters recorded 8,164
Number of property returns registered 9,954

DIVISION OF INQUIRIES AND REPLIES.

The work performed in the division of inquiries and replies during the year ending June 30, 1871, is as follows :

Number of inquiries on hand unanswered June 30, 1870 769

Officers making inquiry.	No. received.	No. answered.
Adjutant General	2,850	2,852
Paymaster General	4,945	4,965
Quartermaster General	260	260
Commissary General of Subsistence	50	51
Third Auditor	912	916
Fourth Auditor	23	27
Commissioner of Pensions	4,106	4,187
Other sources	7,889	4,880
Total	21,035	18,138

Inquiries on hand unanswered June 30, 1871 3,666
Corrections of records made by request of the Adjutant General 649
Rolls and vouchers copied for Adjutant General, Paymaster General, and Attorney General 923
Rolls and vouchers copied for preservation in this office 733
Rolls and vouchers partially copied and traced, for preservation in this office... 1,556
Number of letters written 3,503
Number of pages of foolscap paper used in copying 2,166

The nature and importance of the work performed by this division is indicated by the following summary of the kind of information furnished to the officers making inquiry:

To the Adjutant General.—Statements of the pay and clothing of soldiers who claim that they never received any discharge. Miscellaneous information from the muster and pay-rolls to enable the Adjutant General to perfect the records of his office.

To the Paymaster General.—Dates of enlistment, muster, and first payment of Pennsylvania volunteers, to whom that State claims to have paid advance pay. Sundry information in cases pending in the Paymaster General's Office. (The information furnished in the Pennsylvania cases has been used by the Third Auditor in adjusting claims, amounting to $648,000.)

To the Quartermaster General and Commissary General of Subsistence.—Verification of officers' signatures to receipts for Army stores to enable those Bureaus to settle claims for payment for such stores.

To the Third Auditor.—Data necessary to enable him to settle claims for horses lost in the Army. Statements as to whether the money value of stores purchased from the United States by officers has been deducted from the pay of such officers. To obtain this information the entire pay accounts of the officers concerned have to be examined.

To the Fourth Auditor.—Amount of bounty due soldiers transferred from the Army to the Navy.

To the Commissioner of Pensions.—Data necessary to enable the Pension Bureau to settle claims for pension, including copies of any evidence of marriage, relationship, &c., that may have been filed in this office.

Other sources.—Replies to miscellaneous inquiries from adjutant generals of States and other persons.

DIVISION FOR THE INVESTIGATION OF FRAUDS.

During the year 4,490 cases have been under examination, investigation, and prosecution, by this division. Briefs have been prepared in 562 cases; 454 have been finally disposed of, and 140 cases have been prepared for suit and prosecution through the various United States district courts.

The amounts recovered by suit and otherwise are as follows:

Money recovered by draft, certificate of deposit and current funds, and turned into the Treasury to be credited to the proper appropriations	$7,557 02
Amount directed to be turned over by the Freedmens' Bureau to United States paymasters to be credited to the proper appropriations, said amount having been paid to that Bureau upon claims subsequently discovered by this division to be fraudulent or erroneous	9,128 51
Amount wrongfully withheld by claim agents and secured to the proper claimants by interposition of this office and United States district courts	4,884 73
Amount of Treasury certificates and checks, issued in fraudulent cases, recovered before payment	575 65
Amount recovered on forged checks and turned over to Paymasters William B. Rochester and H. B. Reese to be credited to the proper appropriations	250 00
Amount paid by the national banks of Indiana upon forged indorsements to checks drawn upon the assistant treasurer at New York, recovered from them by the joint action of the Secretary's office and this office	15,562 79
Amount of overpayments recovered and turned over to United States paymasters for appropriate credit	2,087 29
Amount of interest recovered	326 16
Total	40,372 15

There is also on hand a bond for $1,700, payable to the United States in case certain money drawn upon forged receipts and powers of attorney is not paid over to the rightful claimants.

There áre now under examination and investigation 4,036 cases involving fraud, forgery, unlawful withholding, overpayments, &c., as follows :

Fraudulent and contested claims in cases of white soldiers, in which settlements had been made prior to notice of fraud or receipt of adverse claim...... 1,194

Fraudulent and contested unsettled claims in cases of white soldiers.......... 389

Fraudulent and contested claims in cases of colored soldiers, in which settlements had been made prior to notice of fraud or receipt of adverse claims... 557

Unsettled claims of widows of colored soldiers, involving fraud in the marriage evidence.. 234

Unsettled contested claims in cases of colored soldiers.... 265

Unsettled claims executed in Shelby County, Tennessee, in behalf of heirs of colored soldiers, all believed to be tainted with fraud...................... 1,125

Cases alleged to have been paid upon fraudulent papers, and now awaiting the action of the Court of Claims.... 72

Cases involving overpayments to United States Army officers, and in which civil actions are to be instituted... 161

Miscellaneous claims suspected of being fraudulent.... 39

    Total... 4,036

Number of claims on hand June 30, 1870......., ,.   3,370
Number of claims received during the year................................ 1,120

    Total.. 4,490
Number of claims finally disposed of during the year.... 454

Number of claims on hand June 30, 1871.... 4,036

Number of letters written... 5,059

The following is a summary of the work performed by the division since its organization :

Date.	Cases under examination.	Cases disposed of.	Amount recovered.
1869	3,143	540	$23,105 17
1870	3,044	490	24,010 28
1871	4,490	454	40,372 15

It will be oberved that the exhibit of this division indicates a largely increased amount of labor and responsibility over that of any previous year. This fact may be accounted for by the careful and rigid scrutiny, exercised by the entire office, in the examination and comparison of claims, vouchers, receipts, and paymasters' returns, and the discovery of new and bold operations of certain claim agents.

Parties implicated in pay and bounty frauds have been tried and convicted in most of the United States district courts, and great credit is due the Solicitor of the Treasury and the different United States district attorneys and marshals, for their zealous and effective co-operation in prosecuting criminal and civil suits, securing the return of money and bringing to light the schemes and practices of swindlers. Perhaps the greater benefits resulting from this action will be the repression of fraud and the prevention of future attempts to defraud the Treasury.

Obstacles are encountered in prosecuting the various frauds committed and attempted in the collection of claims adjusted by this office, owing to the absence of law regulating the fees and duties of claim agents, the doubtful construction of the thirteenth section of the act of July 4, 1864, regarding the wrongful withholding of money, the actual construction given by the courts of the act of March 2, 1863, and the bar to criminal prosecution created by the limitation act of April 30, 1790;

and I respectfully renew my request that the attention of Congress be invited to the necessity of supplying a remedy, especially by extending the time within which persons guilty of frauds may be criminally prosecuted, and by affording greater facilities and powers for the investigation and discovery of frauds, and authorizing the reimbursement of money expended by United States officers in the discharge of extra official services.

ARCHIVES DIVISION.

The work performed by this division is shown by the following statement:

Number of accounts filed in rooms of temporary deposit awaiting settlement	3,071
Number of confirmed settlements received from the Second Comptroller, verified, briefed, and transferred to permanent files:	
Paymasters	467
Indian	928
Miscellaneous	1,544
	2,939
Number of paymasters' accounts received from Paymaster General	605
Number of medical property accounts received from Surgeon General	1,626
Number of paymasters', Indian, and miscellaneous accounts verified, arranged and filed	3,544
Number of paymasters' accounts re-examined, boarded, and marked	4,032
Number of settlements withdrawn and returned to files	6,568
Number of vouchers withdrawn and returned to accounts	78,755
Number of abstracts of accounts put in book form	409
Number of duplicate vouchers examined and attached to originals	150,772
Number of mutilated rolls repaired with tracing muslin	47,418

This division is charged with the care of all the office furniture, blanks, &c., and keeps the record of payments to regiments, of which an entirely new register has been transcribed during the year.

Number of letters written	602

REGISTRY AND CORRESPONDENCE DIVISION.

Statement of work performed by the registry and correspondence division for the year ending June 30, 1871.

Number of letters received	41,517
Number of letters written	45,846
Number of letters recorded	6,078
Number of letters referred to other Bureaus	2,184
Number of dead letters received and registered	4,552
Number of licenses received and registered	566
Number of claims received, briefed, and registered	37,192
Number of miscellaneous accounts received from other offices and distributed	3,060
Number of miscellaneous vouchers received, briefed, and registered	133,998
Number of pay and bounty certificates examined, registered, and mailed	18,561
Number of pay and bounty certificates examined, registered, briefed, and forwarded to the Paymaster General, in accordance with joint resolution of April 10, 1869	9,763
Number of letters with additional evidence in the case of suspended claims, received, briefed, and registered	16,869
Number of reports calling for requisitions sent to War Department	591
Number of discharges sent to claimants and returned uncalled for	777

In addition to the above, 1,233 claims for additional bounty under act of July 28, 1866, were received after January 13, 1871, the limit fixed by the act of July 13, 1870, for filing such claims. These cannot be adjusted without further legislation by Congress.

For convenience of reference, I annex the following consolidated statement showing the various classes of accounts settled in the office, the number of each class on hand at the beginning of the year, the number received and disposed of during the year, and the number on hand at the end of the year; also the amount involved in settlements:

	On hand June 30, 1870.	Received during year.	Disposed of during year.	On hand June 30, 1871.	Amount involved in settlements.	No. of letters written.
Paymasters	3,279	665	843	3,101	$124,565,414 51	12,621
Indian agents	368	673	520	521	5,220,928 91	
Indian agents, (property)	528	252	203	577		1,417
Indian claims		969	962	7	2,073,703 72	
Bounty, arrears of pay, &c	53,762	25,811	40,078	39,495	2,346,164 42	148,437
Ordnance, medical, and miscellaneous	623				2,023,703 26	
Regular recruiting	655				202,215 01	
Volunteer recruiting	102	2,368	2,394	1,573	754,795 34	2,286
Claims for return of local bounty	219				3,930 92	
Ordnance and Quartermaster's Department, (property)	63,775	9,954	39,171	34,558		12,685
Soldiers' Home		24	24		81,282 06	
National Asylum		12	19		303,216 99	
Total	123,311	40,728	84,207	79,882	138,477,357,16	177,446

Besides the number of letters stated in the above table, there have been written 55,683 relating to the miscellaneous business of the office, making a total of 233,129.

Average number of clerks employed during the year, 265.

In addition to the foregoing, various statements and reports have been prepared and transmitted from this office, as follows:

Annual report to the Secretary of the Treasury of the transactions of the office during the fiscal year.

Annual statement of the recruiting fund, prepared for the Adjutant General of the Army.

Annual statement of the contingencies of the Army, prepared for the Secretary of War.

Annual report of balances on the books of this office remaining unaccounted for more than one year, transmitted to the First Comptroller.

Annual report of the balances on the books of this office remaining unaccounted for more than three years, transmitted to the First Comptroller.

Annual statement of the clerks and other persons employed in this office during the year 1870, or any part thereof, showing the amount paid to each on account of salary, with place of residence, &c., in pursuance of the eleventh section of the act of August 26, 1842, and resolution of the House of Representatives of January 13, 1846, transmitted to the Secretary of the Treasury.

Monthly tabular statement showing the amount of business transacted in the office during the month, and the number of accounts remaining unsettled at the close of the month, transmitted to the Secretary of the Treasury.

Monthly report of absence from duties of employés of this office with reasons therefor, transmitted to the Secretary of the Treasury.

Pay-rolls, upon which payment was made to the employés of this office, prepared semi-monthly, in duplicate.

During the past year the work of the office has been seriously delayed by reason of the reduction of its clerical force, and I earnestly recommend that it be temporarily increased to three hundred clerks, as it stood prior to July 1, 1870. In making estimates for the next fiscal year, I have felt constrained to follow the law making appropriations for the office, while convinced that the sum allowed is not sufficient.

I have believed it to be the soundest policy to employ an experienced force sufficient to close up the settlement of disbursement and other accounts growing out of the war, as rapidly as possible, until the current business of the office can be reached, and then to reduce it to such a number of clerks as may be necessary to perform the current work. An earlier reduction delays settlements and postpones the time when nothing but the current work will remain to be done.

In the annual reports of this office for the years 1864, 1865, and 1866, the subject of the early settlement of paymasters' accounts was alluded to and particularly urged, but there has been no opportunity, up to the present time, to specially facilitate their settlement.

In 1865, when such accounts, covering a disbursement of $400,000,000 were in the office unsettled, I stated that, with all the force that could then be employed, it would take *five years to settle the accounts then on hand,* and urged that a sufficient number of skilled clerks be employed to settle them in *one year,* using the following language:

"The difference in the expense between settling these accounts in five years with the present force, and settling the same in the manner proposed, is sixty-four thousand dollars. It is a large sum, but is only about one-sixth of one per cent. on the disbursements to be examined and settled, and is small compared with the probable loss to the Government through long delayed settlement, or the employment of inexperienced clerks."

The accounts referred to above, were largely increased by the heavy disbursements of 1865 and 1866, when the armies were mustered out. All the clerks possessing the requisite qualifications that could be spared from other branches of work, have been employed in the settlement of these accounts, but many of these have been from time to time necessarily withdrawn to attend to special work required by new legislation, and where the services of skilled and careful clerks were needed. During the last two years a portion of this force has been detailed to make the necessary examination of paymasters' accounts, to ascertain the amount of fines, forfeitures, stoppages, &c., and make settlements in favor of the "National Asylum for Disabled Volunteer Soldiers," and nearly one-third of the entire force has been employed in revising previous settlements and removing suspensions therein, to comply with new provisions of law in relation to the settlement of disbursing officers' accounts, and the rulings of the Comptroller.

Notwithstanding these embarrassments, the accounts of volunteer paymasters have been examined and settled, with the exception of a few who were retained in the service to pay Treasury certificates, or who have failed to close their accounts when notified of the balance due. The accounts of this latter class generally involve but small amounts, and are being prepared for suit as rapidly as possible.

But few of the accounts now remaining unsettled are either so large, or so difficult as those that have been settled, and it is believed that by an early temporary increase of the clerical force, as asked for, all paymasters' accounts on hand can be settled within a year.

It affords me great pleasure to commend the general ability, industry, and faithfulness of the gentlemen connected with this office.

In the hope that the recommendation for a temporary increase of the clerical force of the office may meet your approval, I have the honor to be, very respectfully,

E. B. FRENCH,
Auditor.

Hon. GEORGE S. BOUTWELL,
　　Secretary of the Treasury.

REPORT OF THE THIRD AUDITOR.

REPORT

OF

THE THIRD. AUDITOR OF THE TREASURY,

TREASURY DEPARTMENT,
Third Auditor's Office, August 23, 1871.

SIR : In compliance with instructions from your office, and the requirements of law, I have the honor to transmit herewith the following report of the business operations of this office for the fiscal year ending June 30, 1871 :

BOOKKEEPER'S DIVISION.

· The duties devolving upon this division are, in general, to keep the appropriation and money accounts of the office.

The annexed statement of the financial operations of the office during the fiscal year ending June 30, 1871, exhibits the amounts drawn on specific appropriations except those under direction of the Chief of Engineers of the Army, which are aggregated and entered under the general heading "Engineer Department." It also shows the repayments into the Treasury for the same period.

The average number of clerks engaged in this division during the period embraced in this report has been eight, and that number now constitutes the active force of the division.

' The amount of requisitions drawn on the Secretary of the Treasury by the Secretaries of War and of the Interior for the fiscal year ending June 30, 1871, was $63,501,843 58, as follows:

On account of Quartermaster's Department	$4,856,992 01
Incidental expenses, Qartermaster's Department	1,088,007 81
Barracks and quarters	1,184,768 12
Army transportation	6,347,509 59
Officers' transportation	32,182 87
Cavalry and artillery horses	263,448 00
Purchase of stoves	1,358 14
Clothing of the Army	923,158 25
National cemeteries	327,369 55
Keeping, &c., prisoners of war	390 00
Payment, tax on salaries	88 61
Services, Oregon and Washington volunteers	35,135 49
Pay, Oregon and Washington volunteers	6,996 22
Suppressing Indian hostilities in Minnesota in 1862	17,734 63
Minute men in Pennsylvania, Maryland, Ohio, Indiana, and Kentucky	96 38
Bureau of Refugees, Freedmen, and Abandoned Lands	462,394 72
Capture of Jefferson Davis	1,611 50
Rogue River Indian war	33,844 83
Subsistence of the Army	3,862,069 50
Pay and supplies of 100-day volunteers	6,883 98
Collecting, drilling, and organizing volunteers	756 64
Signal service	5,000 00
Claims, act March 3, 1849	197,111 75
Commutation of rations to prisoners of war in rebel States	16,000 00
Reimbursing Ohio and Indiana for expenses, &c.	100 00
* Refunding to States expenses incurred in raising volunteers	2,904,505 44

* The Honorable Secretary of the Treasury having declined payment on requisition No. 7156, dated June 30, 1871, in favor of the State of Kentucky, for the sum of $525,258 72, the amount of this requisition, (although canceled by direction of the Secretary of the Treasury,) is still retained in this report in order to exhibit the full amount of labor performed by this office during the fiscal year.

Payment to the State of Kansas	$330 00
Payment under "relief acts" to sundry persons	52,726 50
Pensions, invalid	12,340,544 11
Pensions, widows and others	21,793,380 83
Pensions, war of 1812	234,000 00
Military Academy, (sundry appropriations)	178,908 84
Relief of destitute people in the District of Columbia	7,500 00
Engineer Department, (sundry appropriations)	6,318,939 27

REPAYMENTS.

Amount of counter requisitions drawn on sundry persons in favor of the Treasurer of the United States during the fiscal year ending June 30, 1871, was $3,225,777 67, as follows:

On account of deposit	$1,531,808 48
Third Auditor's transfer requisitions	1,070,635 27
Second Auditor's transfer requisitions	613,661 41
Interior Department transfer requisitions	6,598 38
Fourth Auditor's transfer requisitions	1,025 36
War Department transfer requisitions	2,048 77

Report of business transacted in the Third Auditor's office, United States Treasury, in the fiscal year ending June 30, 1871.

Description of accounts.	Number of accounts remaining on hand June 30, 1870. Monthly and quarterly.	Number of accounts received in year ending June 30, '71. Monthly and quarterly.	Number of accounts settled in the year ending June 30, 1871.		Number of accounts unsettled June 30, 1871.	
			Monthly and quarterly.	Amount involved.	Monthly and quarterly.	Amount involved.
Quartermasters' money	94	855	665	$13,984,186 97	284	$16,362,177 60
Quartermasters' property	10,836	2,285	9,355		3,766	
Commissaries' money	1,712	2,765	3,213	5,904,744 26	1,264	973,405 39
Pension agents' money	720	930	789	32,813,334 28	861	32,658,464 89
Engineers' money	139	210	221	5,947,452 72	128	2,890,670 45
Refugees, Freedmen and Abandoned Lands money	64	42	61	1,245,280 90	45	1,334,156 83
Refugees, Freedmen and Abandoned Lands property	32	178	173		37	
Signal officers' money	1	1	2	2,880 90		
Signal officers' property	34	463	406		91	
Total	13,632	7,729	14,985	59,897,880 03	6,476	54,218,875 16
Claims for horses lost	5,531	340	540	$104,347 11	5,331	$938,364 69
Steamboats destroyed	73	12	15	263,002 23	70	604,682 11
Oregon warrants	850	176	204	49,158 83	822	65,615 19
Miscellaneous	4,041	2,335	1,352	7,868,363 44	5,024	4,140,073 80
State warrants	11	13	17	2,034,920 54	7	284,701 73
Total	10,506	2,876	2,128	10,319,792 15	11,254	6,033,437 52

QUARTERMASTER'S DIVISION.

The accounts of quartermasters cover a wide and varied range of disbursement and property accountability, embracing disbursements for barracks, quarters, hospitals, store-houses, offices, stables, forage and transportation of all army supplies, army clothing, camp and garrison equipage, the purchase of cavalry and artillery horses, fuel, forage, straw material for bedding, stationery, hired men, per diem to extra-duty men, of the pursuit and apprehension of deserters, of the burial of officers and soldiers, of hired escorts, of expresses, interpreters, spies, and guides, of veterinary surgeons and medicines for horses, of supplying posts with water, and generally the proper and authorized expenses for the movements and operations of an army not expressly assigned to any other department. The "returns" are an account of the disposition made of all property paid for by the Quartermaster's Department, (except clothing, camp and garrison equipage, which are accounted for by the Second Auditor.)

The tabular statement herewith exhibits in a condensed form the results of the labors of the force employed in this division:

| | MONEY ACCOUNTS. | | Property returns. | | SUPPLEMENTAL SETTLEMENTS. | |
	Number.	Amount involved.		Property	Money.	Amount involved.
On hand per last report, June 30, 1870.	94	$7,219,697 66	10,836			
Received during the current year.....	855	23,126,666 31	2,285	3,280	1,136	$9,810,618 85
Total......................	949	30,346,363 97	13,121	3,280	1,136	9,810,618 85
Reported during the current year.....	665	$13,984,186 97	9,355	3,280	1,136	$9,810,618 85
Remaining unsettled June 30, 1871.....	284	16,362,177 60	3,766			
Total	949	30,346,363 97	13,121	3,280	1,136	9,810,618 85

| | SIGNAL ACCOUNTS. | | | TOTAL. | |
	Property.	Money.	Amount involved.	Number.	Amount involved.
On hand per last report, June 30, 1870	34	1	....	10,064	$7,219,697 66
Received during the current year	463	1	$2,880 90	8,920	32,940,166 06
Total...............................	497	2	2,880 90	18,984	40,159,863 72
Reported during the current year	406	2	$2,880 90	14,844	$23,797,686 72
Remaining unsettled June 30, 1871...........	91		....	4,140	16,362,177 00
Total...............................	497	2	2,880 90	18,984	40,159,863 72

Number of letters sent out from the division during the year, 50,320; average number of clerks employed, 129$\frac{11}{12}$.

SUBSISTENCE DIVISION.

This division audits the accounts of all commissaries and acting commissaries of subsistence in the Army, whose duties are to purchase the provisions and stores necessary for the feeding of the Army and see to their proper distribution. These commissaries render monthly money accounts, with proper vouchers, for disbursements of the funds intrusted to them, together with a provision return, and vouchers showing the disposition of provisions and stores purchased and received during each month. These accounts are received monthly through the office of the Commissary General of Subsistence, and are, every six months, (or oftener if the officer ceases to disburse,) examined and audited in this division, and the money accounts and vouchers, together with a certified statement of their condition, referred to the Second Comptroller of the Treasury for his decision thereon. Upon their receipt back from the Comptroller, with the statement approved, the officers are then officially notified of the result of said examinations, and are called upon by this office to adjust or explain any omissions or errors that may have been discovered. The money and provision accounts, together with vouchers and papers belonging thereto, are, after examination, placed in the settled files of this division for future reference, and remain permanently in the custody of this office.

There have been received and registered during the year 2,765 money accounts of officers disbursing in the Subsistence Department, involving the expenditure of $5,957,310 68. During the same period 3,213 accounts (containing 52,132 vouchers) were audited and reported to the Second Comptroller of the Treasury, involving the expenditure of $5,904,744 26.

In connection with the above, there were received and registered during the year 1,935 provision returns, and within the same period 2,931 provision returns (containing 50,744 vouchers) were examined and adjusted.

The number of vouchers contained in the accounts examined was 102,876.

During the year 970 official letters have been written, 576 pages of differences written and copied, and 2,913 queries received and answered.

Average number of clerks engaged upon the division during the year, eight.

RECAPITULATION.

	No. of accounts.	Amounts involved.
Remaining on hand June 30, 1870	1,712	$1,920,838 97
Received during the year ending June 30, 1871	2,765	5,957,310 68
Total	4,477	7,878,149 65
Audited and reported to Second Comptroller during the year	3,213	5,904,744 26
Remaining unsettled June 30, 1871	1,264	973,405 39

Provision returns on hand June 30, 1870	1,151
Provision returns received during the fiscal year	1,935
Total	3,086
Provision returns examined during the year	2,931
Provision returns remaining on hand June 30, 1871	155

	No. of accounts.	
Money accounts on hand June 30, 1870	1,712	
Provision returns on hand June 30, 1870	1,151	
		2,863
Money accounts received during the fiscal year	2,765	
Provision returns received during the fiscal year	1,935	
		4,700
Total		7,563
Money accounts audited during the fiscal year	3,213	
Provision returns examined during the fiscal year	2,931	6,144
Total accounts on hand June 30, 1871		1,419

ENGINEER DIVISION.

This division is employed in the examination of the accounts of the officers and agents of the Engineer Department, who, under direction of the Chief of Engineers of the Army, (except the Superintendent of the Military Academy at West Point, whose disbursements are directed by the Inspector General,) disburse moneys out of various appropriations —now two hundred and forty-eight in number—made from time to time by Congress for works of a public nature, which may be classed under the following general heads, viz:

The purchase of sites and materials for, and construction and repairs of, the various fortifications throughout the United States;

Construction and repairs of roads, bridges, bridge trains, &c., for armies in the field;

Surveys on the Atlantic and Pacific coasts;

Examination and surveys of the northern and western lakes and rivers;

Construction and repairs of breakwaters;

Repairs and improvement of harbors, both on sea and lake coasts;

Improvement of rivers and purchase of snag and dredge boats for the same; and,

The expenses of the Military Academy at West Point.

The average number of clerks employed on the division for the year ending June 30, 1871, was four; and the transactions of the division for the same period are shown by the following statement, viz:

| | ACCOUNTS. | | Amounts involved. |
	Quarterly.	Monthly.	
On hand June 30, 1870	97	42	$3, 980, 095 18
Received during the year	196	14	4, 856, 027 99
Total	293	56	8, 838, 123 17
Examined during the year	166	55	5, 947, 452 72
Remaining on hand June 30, 1871	127	1	2, 890, 670 45

Supplemental settlements 23
Transfer settlements 6

STATE WAR CLAIMS DIVISION.

The duties of this division embrace the settlement, under the various acts and resolutions of Congress, of all claims of the several States for costs, charges, and expenses properly incurred by them for enrolling, subsisting, clothing, supplying, arming, equipping, paying, and transporting their troops employed by the United States in aiding to suppress the recent insurrection against the United States. Also claims on account of Indian and other border invasions.

| | ORIGINAL ACCOUNTS. | | SUSPENDED ACCOUNTS. | |
	No.	Amount.	No.	Amount.
On hand June 30, 1870	11	$1, 695, 026 07	99	
Received during the year	13	624, 596 20	17	
Total	24	2, 319, 622 27	116	
Reported during the year	17	2, 034, 920 54	30	
On hand June 30, 1871	7	284, 701 73	86	

General statement of the claims of the several States filed since July 1, 1861.

States.	Amount of claims filed by the States.	Amount paid States prior to July 1, 1870.	Amount paid to States since July 1, 1870.	Total amount paid to States prior to July 1, 1871.	Amount of unexamined claims.	Amount of suspended claims.	Total balance of unpaid claims.
Maine	$1,303,300 74	$1,120,048 75	$3,938 93	$1,024,987 68		$283,313 06	$283,313 06
New Hampshire	1,407,491 42	1,006,812 50		1,006,812 50	19,892 04	400,678 92	400,678 92
Vermont	924,673 81	779,460 60		779,460 60		125,321 17	145,213 21
Massachusetts	3,751,728 96	3,649,644 80		3,649,644 80		102,084 16	102,084 16
Rhode Island	762,611 99	757,404 19		757,404 19		5,207 80	5,207 80
Connecticut	2,255,255 94	1,727,423 36	306,604 92	2,034,038 28		221,217 66	221,217 66
New York	3,232,325 32	2,300,192 50	622,279 10	2,922,471 60		309,853 72	309,853 72
New Jersey	1,442,448 51	1,282,005 42	103,246 94	1,385,252 36		57,196 15	57,196 15
Pennsylvania	3,172,218 19	2,094,879 78	815,589 33	2,910,469 11		261,749 08	261,749 08
Delaware	3,019 20	3,019 20		3,019 20			
Maryland	23,979 72	7,162 32		7,162 32		16,817 20	16,817 20
Virginia	54,089 41	46,469 97		46,469 97		5,619 44	5,619 44
West Virginia	456,879 03	456,638 03		456,688 03		221 00	221 00
Ohio	3,206,832 77	2,738,074 98	145,304 60	2,883,379 58		255,208 74	323,443 19
Illinois	4,374,298 51	4,006,204 69	39,538 53	4,045,743 22	68,234 45	528,555 29	528,555 29
Indiana	3,530,312 41	2,464,364 73	23,255 00	2,487,619 73		1,042,692 68	1,042,692 68
Michigan	633,017 38	726,433 23		726,435 23		106,382 15	106,382 15
Wisconsin	1,141,793 81	982,144 15		982,144 15	−39,993 00	159,649 66	159,649 66
Iowa	1,071,765 94	934,624 27	17,734 63	934,624 27	27,779 42	109,362 25	137,141 67
Minnesota	443,692 71	417,937 10		435,671 73		8,020 98	8,020 98
Missouri	7,226,978 24	7,220,887 33		7,220,887 33		16,131 01	16,151 49
Kentucky	3,560,913 02	2,265,044 06	851,632 07	3,116,676 13		443,427 49	443,427 49
Kansas	12,151 04	9,360 82		9,360 82	122 09	2,990 22	2,990 22
Nebraska	45,238 84	27,560 35		27,564 35		18,239 67	18,361 76
Colorado	55,238 84	55,238 84		55,238 84			
Florida	168,606 73				68,606 73	168,606 73	168,606 73
Miscellaneous claims	67 00				67 00	67 00	67 00
Total	44,675,997 45	36,982,002 17	2,929,124 05	30,911,136 22	44,694 73	4,420,166 50	4,764,861 23

* Reported to Second Comptroller June 27, 1871.

CLAIMS DIVISION.

The duties of this division embrace the settlement of claims of a miscellaneous character, arising in the various branches of service in the War Department, growing out of the purchase or appropriation of supplies and stores for the Army ; the purchase, hire, or appropriation of water-craft, railroad stock, horses, wagons, and other means of transportation ; the transportation contracts of the Army ; the occupation of real estate for camps, barracks, hospitals, fortifications, &c. ; the hire of employyés, mileage, court-martial fees, traveling expenses, communications, &c.; claims for compensation for vessels, railroad cars, and engines, &c., lost in the military service; claims growing out of the Oregon and Washington war of 1855 and 1856, and other Indian war claims; claims of various descriptions under special acts of Congress, and claims not otherwise assigned.

The following statements show the business transacted by this division during the fiscal year ending June 30, 1871, and the condition of the business at the commencement and at the end thereof:

1.—*Miscellaneous claims.*

	Number.	Amounts claimed.	Amounts allowed.
On hand July 1, 1870................................	4,041	*$2,853,027 76	
Received during the year............................	2,335	†9,155,409 48	
Total...	6,376	12,008,437 24	
Disposed of during the year........................	1,352	‡7,868,363 44	$1,821,684 43
On hand June 30, 1871	5,024	§4,140,073 80	

* This amount is the aggregate claimed in 2,832 cases, the amounts claimed in the others (1,209) not being stated.
† This amount is the aggregate claimed in 2,190 cases, the amounts claimed in the others (145) not being stated.
‡ This amount is the aggregate claimed in 1,269 cases, the amounts claimed in the others (86) not being stated.
§ This amount is the aggregate claimed in 3,753 cases, the amounts claimed in the others (1,271) not being stated.

2.—*Oregon and Washington Indian War Claims.*

	Number.	Amounts claimed.	Amounts allowed.
On hand July 1, 1870................................	850	*$83,666 36	
Received during the year............................	176	†31,107 66	
Total...	1,026	114,774 02	
Disposed of during the year........................	204	‡49,158 83	$43,408 50
On hand June 30, 1871..............................	822	§65,615 19	

* This amount is the aggregate claimed in 439 cases, the amounts claimed in the others (411) not being stated.
† This amount is the aggregate claimed in 104 cases, the amounts claimed in the others (72) not being stated.
‡ This amount is the aggregate claimed in 136 cases, the amounts claimed in the others (68) not being stated.
§ This amount is the aggregate claimed in 407 cases, the amounts claimed in the others (415) not being stated.

3.—*Vessels, &c., lost.* (*Act March* 3, 1849.)

	Number.	Amounts claimed.	Amounts allowed.
On hand July 1, 1870	73	$740,984 34	
Received during the year	12	126,700 00	
Total	85	867,684 34	
Disposed of during the year	15	263,002 23	$136,537 92
On hand June 30, 1871	70	604,682 11	

1,530 letters have been written and 3,510 received.

HORSE CLAIMS DIVISION.

This division is engaged in settling claims for compensation for losses, sustained by officers and enlisted men, of horses and equipage while in the military service of the United States, and for the loss of horses, mules, oxen, wagons, sleighs, and harness, while in said service, by impressment or contract.

The number of claims received and docketed during the year is 330, in which the aggregate amount claimed is $75,153 48. The number settled and finally disposed of during the same period (including those received prior to as well as during the year) was 540, in which the aggregate amount claimed was $104,347 11, and on which the aggregate amount allowed was $62,193 19. There have been during the year 6,771 letters written, and 2,206 received and docketed; 3,835 claims have been examined and suspended, and 647 briefs made.

The following table presents the condition of the business of this division at the commencement and close of the year, as well as its progress through the year.

	No.	Amount.	No.	Amount.
Claims on hand July 1, 1870			5,531	$965,205 32
Claims received during the year			330	75,153 48
Claims reconsidered during the year			10	2,353 00
Total			5,871	1,042,711 80
Claims allowed during the year	395	$62,193 19		
Rejected on same		8,891 02		
Amount claimed		71,084 21		
Claims disallowed during the year	145	33,262 90		
Deduct as finally disposed of during the year			540	104,347 11
Claims on hand unsettled July 1, 1871			5,331	938,364 69

PENSION DIVISION.

The duties devolving upon this division are keeping an account with each Army pensioner of the United States, recording the name, rate, date of commencement, noting every increase, reduction, transfer, remarriage, death, and expiration, whether by limitation under existing laws, or on account of the disability having ceased. Also, keeping an account with each pension agent, (of whom there are 59,) charging him with all moneys advanced by the Government, under the several appropriations to pay pensions, receive and register the accounts as sent each month direct to this office by the agents who have disbursed the money and properly file them for settlement; examine each voucher, and enter the payment made by the agent on the roll-book opposite the pensioner's name. In addition, the act June 17, 1870, provides that every soldier who lost a limb in the service of the United States may be furnished with the artificial limb every five years, or, if he elect, may receive money commutation in lieu thereof. The bills for limbs furnished, or commutation orders in lieu thereof, as also all bills for transportation of the soldier to and from the place of fitting the limb, are paid by the several agents, and rendered in the same manner as the vouchers for payments to pensioners.

Congress, under act July 8, 1870, changed the mode of paying pensions, and authorized payments to be made quarterly instead of semiannually, as heretofore. This necessitates nearly double the amount of labor during the year, because twice as many vouchers (about 800,000) are received, examined, noted, filed, audited, and reported by settlement to the Second Comptroller for revision. The act February 14, 1871, grants pensions to the survivors of the war of 1812. Not many payments were made to this class, and reported in the accounts received during the fiscal year just closed.

The number of pensioners on the rolls at present is about 205,000; number of soldiers who receive commutation in lieu of artificial limbs, 7,707; number who receive limbs, 917; number of transportation orders approved and paid by agents, 1,116.

Amount drawn from the Treasury to pay pensions during the year ending June 30, 1871.

Invalids	$12,340,544 11
Widows and others	21,793,380 83
War of 1812, act of February 14, 1871	234,000 00
Total	34,367,924 94

Amount refunded and credited by deposit requisition.

Invalid	$416,630 54
Widows and others	472,879 17
Total	889,509 71

The difference of $4,965,152 79 between the amounts charged and the amount reported as disbursed, is in the agents' hands, to be returned and placed to the credit of the appropriation.

The following tabular statement shows the amount of business disposed of by the pension division during the year ending June 30, 1871:

	Number.	Amount involved.
Accounts on hand July 1, 1870	720	$36,958,536 73
Accounts received during the year	930	28,513,262 44
Total	1,650	65,471,799 17
Accounts reported during the year	789	$32,813,334 28
Accounts remaining unsettled June 30, 1871	861	32,658,464 89
Total	1,650	65,471,799 17

The accounts on file unsettled are divided as follows :

Accounts of 1869.. 20
Accounts of 1870.. 542
Accounts of 1871.......................:.................................... 299

Total... 861

Pensions recorded, increased, changes made, including additional for children,
of $2 per month.. 53,794
Pensions transferred... 8,281
Pension vouchers examined... 523,835
Payments entered on roll-books.. 464,569
Pages of difference and miscellaneous copied.............................. 3,382
Copies of surgeons' certificates furnished Commissioner.................. 1,179
Letters received and registered... 3,441
Letters written... 3 816

The following tabular statement exhibits the amount paid at the several agencies to pensioners, the accounts of which were received during the year ending June 30, 1871 :

State.	Agency.	Agent.	INVALIDS.		Widows and others.
			Invalid.	Artificial limbs.	
Arkansas	Fort Gibson.......	Alex'dr Clapperton.	$24 00		$851 53
Do.................	...do	George E. Webster .	1,022 73		4,338 95,
Do.................	Little Rock	James W. Demby ..	193 95		1,677 27
Do.................	...do............	James Coates......	11,539 46	$515 00	90,568 80
Connecticut........	Hartford	D. C. Rodman	120,938 02	7,552 40	318,257 61
California..........	San Francisco.....	James W. Shanklin.	25,922 42	998 00	26,220 74
District of Columbia	Washington	W. T. Collins	205,410 86	21,863 05	262,846 30
Delaware	Wilmington	Edward D. Porter .	22,868 03	1,850 00	39,044 05
Indiana	Fort Wayne	Hiram Iddings	202,305 62	5,521 10	274,907 33
Do...............	Indianapolis	C. W. Brouse	403,472 77	10,360 50	717,948 65 .
Do...............	Madison	Mark Tilton.......	130,050 54	5,308 00	273,995 59
Illinois............	Chicago	Benjamin J. Sweet.	365,537 02	14,361 50	395,597 63
Do...............	...do	D. Blakeley........	2,680 51	248 88	2,853 18
Do...............	Quincy............	B. M. Prentiss.....	174,032 43	4,500 50	252,449 29
Do...............	Springfield	William Jayne	227,414 53	7,369 96	354,081 26
Do..............	Salem	James S. Martin...	231,215 27	7,921 30	637,604 83
Iowa..............	Des Moines ...:...	Stewart Goodwell ..	91,485 24	3,229 20	195,453 34
Do...............	Fairfield	D. B. Wilson......	128,812 65	4,730 85	225,399 13
Do...............	Marion..........	Joseph B. Young ...	138,001 50	4,669 85	229,439 65
Kansas	Topeka	Charles B. Lines....	93,793 11	2,385 00	125,925 63
Kentucky..........	Lexington	A. H. Adams	44,297 42	1,150 00	193,539 45
Do...............	Louisville	Samuel McKee	109,257 43	4,050 00	388,050 09
Do...............	...do............	W. D. Gallagher ...	6,059 13	350 00	18,096 08
Louisiana..........	New Orleans.....	F. J. Kapp.........	25,789 17	1,741 00	43,606 41
Do ....:......	...do	R. H. Isabel	1,473 93	125 00	3,275 75
Maine	Augusta..........	H. Boynton........	147,652 30	8,006 50	228,017 34
Do	Bangor............	Gideon Mayo	129;886 25	5,434 25	207,048 77
Do	...do	S. B. Morrison	8,675 74	496 50	10,523 97
Do	Portland	M. A. Blanchard...	173,550 65	5,876 30	246,259 43
Massachusetts	Boston	G. C. Trumbull ...	512,295 04	27,017 06	885,999 27
Maryland	Baltimore	H. Adreon	140,287 67	7,873 80	217,163 34
Michigan	Detroit	Henry Barnes	360,713 11	14,165 91	607,826 53
Do...............	Grand Rapids.....	T. Foote	88,622 05	4,076 45	132,697 21
Missouri	Macon City	John T. Clements..	73,924 23	1,430 00	146,887 71
Do...............	...do............	W. C. Ebert	42,692 42	1,264 50	81,946 12
Do...............	St. Louis....,.....	James Lindsay	181,548 04	1,599 00	448,286 11
Minnesota	St. Paul..........	H. C. Rogers.......	106,983 70	2,757 97	158,869 02
New Hampshire ...	Concord..........	David Cross	167,436 12	1,154 33	228,217 20
Do...............	Portsmouth	D. J. Vaughan	40,519 90	2,150 00	74,341 45
New York ......:..	Albany	S. H. H. Parsons...	769,275 02	30,769 75	1,251,402 83
Do	Canandaigua.....	L. M. Drury	529,809 12	28,791 79	751,516 54
Do	Brooklyn	D. W. Haynes	60,234 22	6,784 75	113,647 09
Do	...do............	John Hall	19,423 26	1,318 10	38,593 57
Do	New York City ...	G. M. Van Buren ...	386,735 51	31,287 34	
Do	...do	W. H. Lawrence ...			570,917 46
Do	...do............	L. L. Doty			77,985 61
New Jersey........	Trenton..........	James F. Rusling...	218,217 28	14,085 10	352,763 93
North Carolina.....	Raleigh	C. H. Pelvin	10,381 87	322 70	66,237 68
Nebraska	Omaha............	E. A. Allen ...:....	14,727 39	268 00	11,781 66

State.	Agency.	Agent.	INVALIDS.		Widows and others.
			Invalid.	Artificial limbs.	
New Mexico	Santa Fé	E. W. Little	$2,470 97	$20 95	$6,865 80
Ohio	Cincinnati	William E. Davis	448,825 40	21,206 09	776,230 94
Do	Cleveland	Seth M. Barber	290,013 80	11,462 30	416,989 54
Do	Columbus	John A. Norris	268,984 17	12,750 55	531,525 95
Oregon	Oregon City	Henry Warren	2,705 96	12 20	6,648 31
Pennsylvania	Philadelphia	W. T. Forbes	1,232,562 75	57,350 17	
Do	...do	A. R. Calhoun			1,485,005 77
Do	Pittsburg	James McGregor	351,487 15	21,171 04	527,671 96
Rhode Island	Providence	Wm. H. Townsend	21,319 71	929 13	49,746 91
Do	...do	C. R. Brayton	22,298 33	2,509 20	51,123 45
Tennessee	Knoxville	D. T. Boynton	85,297 12	1,335 15	356,017 98
Do	Nashville	W. J. Stokes	37,942 75	1,372 50	182,397 30
Vermont	Burlington	J. L. Barstow	95,079 72	5,786 20	147,816 14
Do	St. Johnsbury and Montpelier.	Stephen Thomas	119,187 31	5,636 80	162,253 09
Virginia	Richmond	James T. Sutton	7,807 79	225 00	11,674 69
Do	...do	Andrew Washburn	11,820 57	1,025 00	25,190 59
West Virginia	Wheeling	J. M. Doddridge	96,275 37	4,450 00	220,053 35
Do	...do	T. M. Harris	48,307 52	2,252 10	91,152 81
Wisconsin	La Crosse	John A. Kellogg	55,799 87	1,992 20	104,057 64
Do	Milwaukee	Edward Ferguson	164,533 64	9,908 60	299,249 01
Do	Madison	Thomas Reynolds	110,147 89	6,005 35	203,381 08
Washington Ter	Vancouver	S. W. Brown	1,553 13	99 44	439 42
Total			10,421,418 55	482,110 36	17,638,341 31

The force employed in this division during the year consisted of twenty-two clerks and two copyists.

The business of this division has increased more than double, and as many of the accounts are behind in settlement, it will necessitate the addition of quite a force in order to dispatch business as promptly as it should be; this addition, however, will be made by transfer from other divisions in this office.

BOUNTY LAND DIVISION.

During the year ending 30th June, 1871, two thousand six hundred and thirty-four (2,634) bounty land claims have been examined and returned to the Commissioner of Pensions, properly certified.

Three hundred and thirty-nine (339) letters have been written on subjects connected with the division.

Nine (9) invalied pension claims, war of 1812, have been properly certified to the Commissioner of Pensions for his action.

Two thousand and ninety-nine (2,099) pension claims, war of 1812, act of Congress of February 14, 1871, have been examined and properly certified to the Commissioner of Pensions, for his action.

REFUGEES, FREEDMEN AND ABANDONED LANDS DIVISION.

The duties of this division embrace the settlement of the accounts of the agents and officers of the Bureau of Refugees, Freedmen and Abandoned Lands, for moneys expended by said agents and officers for stationery and printing, quarters and fuel, commissary stores and medical supplies, transportation, rents, repairs and building of schools and asylums, pay of superintendents of schools, clerks, agents, and officers of the bureau, telegraphing, and postage. Also incidental expenses, such as the necessary employment of colored laborers with a view to ameliorate their condition.

| | MONEY ACCOUNTS. | | No. of property accounts. |
	No.	Amount.	
On hand June 30, 1870	64	$1,879,071 47	32
Received during the year	42	700,366 26	178
Total	96	2,579,437 73	210
Reported during the year	61	1,245,280 90	173
On hand June 30, 1871	45	1,334,156 83	37

Number of letters written, 35; number of clerks employed, 2.

REGISTRY DIVISION.

To provide for the correct and prompt settlement of accounts and for the certification of the indebtedness to the United States of disbursing officers, whose accounts are audited in this office, and of persons having claims upon the Government, all such officers are required, by order of the Second Comptroller, dated March 30, 1867, to transmit direct to this office copies of their monthly accounts current, abstract of funds transferred, and return of revenue tax deducted in making payments to Government employés, within ten days after the expiration of each successive month; and further, to guard the Treasury, it is made the duty of this division to report quarterly all officers of the United States Army who have received, by transfer, funds pertaining to the Quartermaster's and Subsistence Departments and failed to account for the same within three months from the date of their receipt to the Second Comptroller, in conformity with instructions from him, dated July 21, 1869, based on the law of January 25, 1828, (4 Stat., p. 246,) which provides "that no money hereafter appropriated shall be paid to any person for his compensation who is in arrears to the United States until such person shall have accounted for and paid into the Treasury all sums for which he may be liable."

In conformity with the foregoing there have been received, acknowledged, indorsed, registered, and filed 8,306 accounts current, to wit: Commissary, 3,556; Qurtermasters', 2,829; Engineer, 1,439; Pension, 648; Bureau of Refugees, Freedmen and Abandoned Lands, 53; returns of revenue tax, abstracts of money transferred to disbursing officers, and other miscellaneous papers received, ackowledged, indorsed, recorded, and filed, 1,368; letters received, 168; letters written to officers, 255; receipts for money transferred, recorded, 3,911; queries relative to the indebtedness of officers, answered, 2,853; disbursing officers reported to the Second Comptroller as delinquent in the rendition of their accounts, 298.

COPYISTS' SECTION.

During the fiscal year ending June 30, 1871, the female copyists of this office, eight in number, have copied and compared 42,254 pages of manuscript, copied 4,758 and compared 7,690 letters, registered 827 money differences, 4,000 property differences, and 1,278 miscellaneous papers.

THE FILES.

Your attention is again respectfully invited to the urgent and constantly increasing demand for more file room in this office. The additional room referred to in my previous report as being fitted up for file purposes has been completed, and all the available space in it already filled with accounts examined during the past fiscal year. There now remains only about six hundred lineal feet of shelving available in the large file rooms of the office, which space will probably be filled before the 1st of January, 1872. These rooms, which contain the great bulk of the files of the office, are very unsuitable for the purpose, being located directly under the roof, without side windows or other proper means of ventilation. In summer they are intensely hot, while in winter they are extremely cold and uncomfortable, as they cannot be properly heated, being disconnected from the arrangements for heating other portions of the building. The rooms now occupied by part of the clerical force of this office, in the oldest portion of the eastern front of the building, are more suitable for file rooms than for clerical duty, and could be converted into file rooms as occasion and the necessities of the office require, provided other rooms be furnished for the clerks now occupying them. I have, therefore, to request that rooms capable of accommodating at least twenty clerks be assigned to this Bureau at as early a day as possible, to enable the clerks to vacate some of the rooms referred to and have them converted into file rooms. Otherwise, room for the constantly increasing files of the Bureau must be furnished in some other portion of the Department building, which would be less accessible and consequently inconvenient, and be the cause of great delay and confusion in the transaction of business.

It will be seen from the foregoing statements that the amount drawn from the Treasury through this office during the last fiscal year was $63,501,843 58, most of which ($34,367,924 94) was for pensions. The amount drawn during the previous fiscal year was $91,107,151 58. The number of money accounts of disbursing officers settled was 4,940, involving the sum of $59,897,880 03, and claims adjusted was 2,128, involving $10,319,792 15, making a total of $70,217,672 18 adjusted during the fiscal year, excluding 12,865 property and provision returns, which were adjusted, and in which were involved large disbursements made for the Army during the war. During the year the accounts of many Army officers have been closed under the provisions of the act approved June 23, 1870, to authorize the settlement of the accounts of officers of the Army and Navy for losses of funds, vouchers, and property during the war of the rebellion. It will be seen that the number of money accounts unadjusted on the 30th June, 1871, was 2,582, involving $54,218,875 16, and the number of property and provision returns was 4,049. The number of unsettled claims was 11,254, involving $6,033,-437 52, though this latter sum does not embrace all the demands against the Treasury on file, as, in a large number of claims filed, the amount claimed is not stated.

Having worked off so much of the old business of the office, and in the expectation that the business remaining on hand at the close of the fiscal year can be still further reduced, if not entirely disposed of, with the force now engaged upon the work during the present fiscal year, I believe I can safely recommend a reduction in the clerical force of this Bureau for the next fiscal year of thirty-five clerks of class one, thus effecting a saving of $42,000. But in connection with this proposed reduction I would again most earnestly call attention to recommendation in my report of last year for an increase in the salaries of the chiefs of divisions in this Bureau, and respectfully submit that the salary of the chief clerk of this office should be increased to $2,800 per annum, and that the salaries of the chiefs of the following-named divisions be increased to $2,400 each, viz: quartermasters', subsistence, pension, claims, horse claims, engineers', war of 1812 and bounty land, book-keepers', State war claims.

Seven of the above-named chiefs of division are now fourth-class clerks; the other two are third-class clerks. The proposed increase would, therefore, amount to $6,600, leaving a net saving of $35,400 on clerk-hire. The gentlemen filling these positions are necessarily called upon to perform more work than falls to the share of other clerks. I hold them to a strict accountability for the conduct and business of their respective divisions, and I respectfully submit that as the success of my proposed reduction in the force depends largely upon the ability and hearty coöperation of these gentlemen, and in view of the responsibility and importance of their duties, as well as of the fact that they will be compelled to perform much additional labor, that the interests of economy will be advanced by making the increase asked for.

In conclusion I feel it my pleasant duty to bear testimony to the general good character of the employés of this Bureau, both ladies and gentlemen, and also to the earnest and faithful manner in which they have performed their respective duties during the past fiscal year.

Respectfully submitted.

ALLAN RUTHERFORD, *Auditor.*

Hon. GEORGE S. BOUTWELL,
     Secretary of the Treasury.

REPORT OF THE FOURTH AUDITOR.

REPORT

OF

THE FOURTH AUDITOR OF THE TREASURY.

TREASURY DEPARTMENT,
Fourth Auditor's Office, September 30, 1871.

SIR: In accordance with your request, and for your observation, I herewith give you a concise statement of the business which has been transacted in this office during the fiscal year ending June 30, 1871. In making this synopsis I shall pursue the same course which I followed when submitting my last annual report, and shall exhibit the work of the office by a series of tabular statements, one for each of the divisions. These I shall present consecutively, as follows:

I.—PAYMASTER'S DIVISION, WILLIAM CONARD, CHIEF.

Statement of accounts received and settled in the Paymaster's Division from July 1, 1870, to June 30, 1871, with the amount of cash disbursed in those settled, and the number of letters received and written in relation to the same, including marine and pension accounts.

PAYMASTER'S AND MARINE ACCOUNTS.

Date.	Accounts received.	Accounts settled.	Letters received.	Letters written.	Cash disbursements.
1870:					
July	50	43	185	209	$2,428,947 92
August	32	36	276	299	1,554,045 55
September	13	14	222	226	465,499 85
October	39	29	208	213	406,295 50
November	30	32	257	256	1,056,612 73
December	17	24	133	131	1,106,002 30
1871.					
January	35	33	127	158	2,364,984 05
February	30	35	128	133	661,673 55
March	36	42	129	129	1,678,110 19
April	52	43	160	141	1,638,323 55
May	32	37	146	209	1,289,640 87
June	24	28	138	171	1,425,538 69
Total	390	396	2,111	2,277	16,075,674 75

Number of unsettled accounts on hand July 1, 1870, 19; number of unsettled accounts on hand June 30, 1871, 13; average number of clerks employed in the division, 16; number of pension accounts settled, 225; cash disbursements, $462,020 55.

Statement showing the amount disbursed at the different agencies.

PENSION ACCOUNTS.

Location.	Invalid.	Widows and orphans.	Total.
Baltimore, Maryland	$3,189 88	$7,378 39	$10,568 27
Boston, Massachusetts	35,592 21	62,854 94	98,447 15
Cincinnati, Ohio	4,562 42	14,152 27	18,714 69
Chicago, Illinois	5,914 64	7,093 91	13,008 55
Detroit, Michigan	596 73	2,011 34	2,608 07
Hartford, Connecticut	470 50	2,325 60	2,796 10
Louisville, Kentucky	1,022 65	5,493 95	6,516 60
Milwaukee, Wisconsin	415 50	1,118 53	1,534 03
New Orleans, Louisiana	2,331 15	4,327 70	6,658 83
New York, New York	46,147 71	90,793 54	136,941 25
Pittsburgh, Pennsylvania	3,543 40	7,983 97	11,527 37
Philadelphia, Pennsylvania	16,368 74	45,193 56	61,562 30
Portsmouth, New Hampshire	4,317 45	5,272 20	9,589 65
Providence, Rhode Island	1,020 34	5,198 22	6,218 56
Richmond, Virginia	2,186 14	11,468 93	13,655 07
San Francisco, California	369 70	840 00	1,208 70
St. Louis, Missouri	1,858 62	2,577 90	4,436 52
St. Paul, Minnesota	97 80	....	97 80
Trenton, New Jersey	1,290 56	6,476 84	7,767 40
Washington, District of Columbia	8,213 53	39,950 11	48,163 64
Total	139,508 65	322,511 90	462,020 55

II.—RECORD DIVISION—CHARLES COOK, CHIEF.

Statement of the correspondence of the Fourth Auditor's Office for the fiscal year ending June 30, 1871, and the work of the record division.

Date.	Letters received.	Letters written.	Letters recorded.	Letters filed.	Letters referred to other bureaus.	Letters indexed.	Names indexed and double indexed.	Number of reported accounts recorded and indexed.	Licenses registered.	Dead letters registered.	Letters written by record division.
1870.											
July..............	1,220	1,515	1,321	832	8	2,200	3,859	198	18	16	186
August............	1,354	1,580	1,641	1,057	12	1,706	3,880	103	12	9	179
September	1,131	1,456	1,587	758	30	1,081	1,988	123	6	28	122
October	1,184	1,429	1,526	926	11	3,668	6,078	69	.....	20	52
November	1,221	1,339	1,462	909	4	4,323	8,433	85	2	11	152
December	1,176	1,291	1,383	812	16	5,013	8,228	30	1	12	85
1871.											
January...........	1,181	1,617	1,641	906	18	....	....	6	11	12	90
February..........	1,142	1,387	1,060	808	21	5,290	9,181	.....	2	11	190
March.............	1,460	1,580	1,615	1,006	20	5,745	10,991	139	.....	4	158
April.............	1,208	1,725	1,506	867	11	5,223	10,424	106	5	12	74
May...............	1,227	1,273	1,324	799	20	3,427	6,206	94	1	26	82
June	1,074	1,524	1,436	787	11	2,900	4,540	282	.....	20	49
Total.........	14,578	17,716	17,502	10,467	182	40,576	73,808	1,235	58	181	1,419

Average number of clerks employed, 7½.

III.—PRIZE MONEY DIVISION—S. M. B. SERVOSS, CHIEF.

Statement of work performed by the Prize Money Division during the fiscal year ending June 30, 1871.

Date.	Prize lists.			Letters.		Claims.		Prize money.
	Number of prize lists received.	Number of prize lists made up.	Amount of prize money for distribution.	Number of letters received.	Number of letters written.	Number of claims received.	Number of claims settled.	Amount of prize money paid.
1870.								
July				246	442	332	266	$12,997 77
August		14	$21,325 36	287	382	46	40	6,053 12
September	1	14	11,860 15	242	375	41	35	2,835 92
October				279	336	41	39	5,976 63
November				243	270	360	333	15,370 35
December				238	233	91	72	4,910 81
1871.								
January				247	519	318	307	12,593 07
February				273	340	294	270	27,907 54
March				389	435	147	114	54,627 27
April				272	694	199	158	18,276 55
May				281	294	186	142	21,874 07
June	1			223	488	99	74	2,799 53
Total	2	28	33,185 51	3,220	4,808	2,154	1,850	186,222 63

Average number of clerks employed, 3¼.

IV.—GENERAL CLAIM DIVISION—A. C. ADAMSON, CHIEF.

Annual report of the General Claim Division for the fiscal year ending June 30, 1871.

Date.	Claims received.	Claims adjusted.	Am't involved.	Letters written.	No. of reports on applications for pensions.	No. of reports on applications for bounty land.	No. of reports on applications for admission to naval asylum.
On hand July 1, 1870	254						
July	131	122	$60,702 42	499	9		
August	134	150	42,434 73	485	4	1	1
September	77	153	37,220 17	483	10		1
October	124	154	15,847 89	564	21	3	
November	125	175	24,097 74	530	27	3	
December	307	162	23,478 57	555	32		2
1871.							
January	188	190	27,801 76	544	22	1	1
February	103	125	18,884 22	442	20		1
March	123	138	27,144 61	479	17		
April	138	136	18,089 12	530	16	1	2
May	115	145	19,691 34	423	18		3
June	152	193	18,626 52	519	37		
Total	1,971	1,652	334,019 09	6,053	233	9	11

Average number of clerks employed, 6¼.

V.—NAVY AGENT'S DIVISION—WILLIAM F. STIDHAM, CHIEF.

Annual report of the Navy Agent's division for the fiscal year ending June 30, 1871.

Date.	Accounts received.	Accounts settled.	Amount involved.	Letters written.	Letters received.
1870.					
July	46	43	$56,213 00	18	24
August	40	38	485,258 43	26	33
September	12	12	260,113 62	11	6
October	10	10	504,699 41	13	16
November	101	101	420,746 43	72	95
December	169	169	258,827 86	150	127
1871.					
January	100	99	315,918 62	142	136
February	25	26	731,237 97	137	140
March	18	19	441,205 66	135	143
April	39	38	1,590,086 88	128	120
May	57	57	899,004 80	115	119
June	13	16	341,000 88	103	137
Total	630	628	$6,304,992 76	1,050	1,089

ALLOTMENT ACCOUNTS.

Date.	Allotments registered.	Allotments discontinued.
1870.		
July	21	72
August	79	114
September	66	69
October	121	60
November	23	78
December	115	79
1871.		
January	94	68
February	41	75
March	139	93
April	49	108
May	34	80
June	55	133
Total	837	1,029

Statement of amount paid by Navy Agents for allotments during the year 1870.

New York	$62,837 00
Boston	36,966 50
Philadelphia	45,085 25
Washington	21,602 00
Baltimore	7,726 00
Portsmouth	7,166 00
San Francisco	2,688 00
Total	184,070 75

Accounts remaining on hand June 30, 1871, 2; average number of clerks employed, 5½; number of vouchers examined, 24,481.

VI.—BOOK-KEEPER'S DIVISION—PARIS H. FOLSOM, CHIEF.

Statement of the work performed in the Book-keeper's Division for the fiscal year ending June 30, 1871.

Date.	Cash pay requisitions.		Cash repay requisitions.		Accounts entered and balanced.	Summary statements entered.	Expenditure abstracts entered.	Appropriation accounts settled.	Letters received.	Letters written.
	No.	Amount.	No.	Amount.						
1870.										
July	140	$1,590,220 39	....	....	117	......	......	1	......	161
August	130	1,856,960 13	25	$117,547 06	146	......	......	6	85	200
September	118	1,536,634 10	17	15,712 09	28	......	......	4	120	239
October..........	153	1,827,539 86	9	47,473 60	91	......	......	......	115	249
November	79	1,285,236 33	40	537,271 00	54	......	......	......	67	59
December........	96	2,296,315 63	9	28,000 54	46	....		2	93	137
1871.										
January	138	2,067,950 50	6	99,419 50	131	......	......	......	117	164
February	107	1,371,700 56	8	240,152 40	153	44	......	1	101	145
March	135	1,554,208 07	28	919,751 84	83	25	98	24	144	167
April	110	1,375,508 92	11	37,509 38	110	37	......	18	120	158
May	99	2,772,909 17	14	16,297 99	188	55	35	1	111	150
June.............	137	1,264,177 18	12	94,027 07	78	52	30	......	123	194
Total	1,442	20,799,360 84	179	2,153,162 47	1,225	213	163	57	1,216	2,032

Internal Revenue returned and carried to that fund, $34,811 15; Navy Hospital fund returned and carried to that fund, $7,501 57; Navy Pension fund returned and carried to that fund, $58 58; average number of clerks employed, 4½.

VII.—DISBURSEMENT AND MISCELLANEOUS DIVISION—B. P. DAVIS IN CHARGE.

Statement of work performed during the fiscal year ending June 30, 1871.

Number of letters written 946
Number of dead letters registered 181
Number of licenses registered 58
Number of checks against accounts ordered 211

In addition to the above, Mr. Davis has made up various tabular statements and miscellaneous reports called for by Congress and the Secretary of the Treasury; kept the record of appointments, resignations, removals, and absences; received and distributed the stationery used by the office, and discharged the duties of disbursing clerk.

An inspection of these tables will show that a commendable amount of work has been performed during the last fiscal year, and the experience and facility of the clerks have insured that correctness and promptitude which result from familiarity with the operations required. The various chiefs of divisions are perfectly conversant with the work respectively committed to their supervision, and they have transacted it in the most satisfactory manner. I can say, as I did in my previous report, that it gives me pleasure to speak in terms of just and cordial commendation of the competent and gentlemanly clerks who compose this office. Their accord with each other, their courtesy of deportment, and the amount of work they have performed, are worthy of praise. As heretofore,

William B. Moore, esq., my chief clerk, by his constant attention to his duties, and his knowledge of them, has been of great assistance to me in the affairs of the office.

In the Paymaster's Division there have been a large number of old accounts of disbursing officers resettled, requiring unusual trouble and care, owing to the fact that in many cases their period of service was prior to the rebellion, when the laws regulating such accounts were different from those now existing. A thorough examination of all old accounts which have accumulated on the books of the office has been prosecuted, and wherever balances are found due the Government, correspondence has been entered into with the parties or their sureties, and where possible the amounts have been collected. Where this has not been done, the accounts have been prepared for suit and transmitted to the Solicitor of the Treasury

The work of the Paymaster's Division has assumed such a shape that current accounts are settled *almost immediately* upon their reception, thereby speedily detecting any errors or discrepancies, and resulting in a benefit not only to the Government, but to the disbursing officer.

The allotment business has been transferred from the Paymaster's Division to the Navy Agent's Division, and an entirely new system of checks devised to insure the proper deduction being made from the alloters' pay on board the vessels of the Navy, to offset the amounts paid on shore for the support of their families. This plan will greatly simplify the adjustment of the accounts of the paymasters and navy agents, and prevent the complications which have heretofore made them so difficult of settlement. The new system will also insure the prompt correction of an error at the time of its commission, and obviate the necessity of waiting, as heretofore, until the cruise is ended and the account of the paymaster registering the allotment is settled.

The experience of the last fiscal year has demonstrated the great value of the "adjustment appropriation account," referred to in my last annual report. Disbursements on account of the Navy necessarily assume a character different from those of any other branch of the Government, from the fact that a large portion of them are made beyond the limits of the United States, and at points remote from the Treasury. It is the practice of paymasters doing duty abroad to draw such funds as may be needed, from a single appropriation only, and to disburse them partly for the benefit of various other appropriations. That is, they borrow from one appropriation to loan to others, as the necessities of the service may require. The adjustment of these transactions devolves upon this office in the settlement of the paymaster's final account, and since his term of service is about three years, it is evident that a considerable time must elapse between the expenditure and the refunding of the amount to the proper appropriation. It has therefore frequently happened that when it was desired to thus refund the amounts involved between appropriations, transfers could not be made, because the appropriation to be drawn from was exhausted. Hence have arisen a large number of unadjusted balances. At the last settlement these transactions had reached the enormous sum of $8,948,930 04, from accounts settled mostly during the past year. Of this sum upwards of $2,500,000 cannot be returned to the appropriations from which it was borrowed, for the reason above stated. Of the remainder, upward of $2,000,000 should be adjusted upon the statement of the last appropriation adjustment account, but it may safely be said that a large portion of this cannot be transferred, on account of the present demands on the appropriation being equal to the balance on hand. Inasmuch as these balances will stand perpetually upon the ledgers of this office, unless authority by law is afforded for closing them, and since this will involve no draft of money from the Treasury, I would earnestly recommend that Congress be asked to make such provision as will authorize their final adjustment. In the future there will be no cause for this difficulty. The transactions above referred to not appearing upon the appropriation ledgers, nor upon those either of the Navy or Treasury Departments, and in order to remedy a recurrence of such a condition of accounts, I have instituted the plan of requiring a monthly detailed statement from every paymaster having funds to account for. This statement exhibits fully the source from which all funds are derived, how they were disbursed, and the exact balance on hand at the end of the month. Through it the transfers between appropriations will be effected in the same quarter of the fiscal year in which the expenditure occurs, and thus the overdrawing of any appropriation prevented.

The adoption of the plan of a full cash statement, each month, from every paymaster having public money on hand, serves to accomplish another useful purpose. Most, if not all, the defalcations which have occurred in the naval service, were accomplished through the ability of the paymaster to obtain a larger amount of funds than his rate of expenditure required. Knowing that he would not be called upon for his surplus until after the expiration of his three years' cruise and the further time necessary to pass his accounts through the accounting offices, he was tempted to use the public money for private speculation, with the hope that he could make a successful operation and return the money thus used before the day of accountability. Under the present arrangement the amount of money each paymaster has on hand is known monthly. Should his requisitions upon the Treasury appear to exceed his requirements, payment can be suspended; and upon rendering his final return the balance he should have on hand, and which he will be required to turn back into the Treasury without delay, will be definitely known.

But there is no absolute safeguard against dishonesty. Although it gives me pleasure to testify from personal acquaintance, and through official connection for a number of years, to the high character of those composing the pay corps of the Navy; and although the amount that has been lost to the Government through Navy paymasters is insignificant compared with the vast number of millions disbursed by them during and since the war, yet it is my opinion that the chances of loss to the Government should be reduced to the last possible degree by the introduction of such methods as will tend to prevent the misuse of its money by its agents.

As an important step in this direction, I would earnestly recommend that Congress enact a law authorizing the employment of not less than three persons, experts in Navy accounts, to be styled accounting agents. These persons should be attached to, and under the direction of, this Bureau. Their duties should be similar to those of the bank examiners now employed in connection with the national banks, and they should have authority to call upon any paymaster, whether on shore or upon any naval vessel, without previous notice, to exhibit his books and cash for examination. They should be paid a reasonable salary, and allowed actual traveling expenses. There is no doubt but that the small outlay thus incurred would save the Government many fold, by presenting a constant check upon any officers disposed to use its funds unlawfully, especially in those positions where remoteness from executive authority lessens the sense of direct accountability.

With the highest esteem, I have the honor to be, very respectfully, your obedient servant,

STEPHEN J. W. TABOR,
Auditor.

Hon. GEORGE S. BOUTWELL,
  Secretary of the Treasury.

REPORT OF THE FIFTH AUDITOR.

REPORT

OF

THE FIFTH AUDITOR OF THE TREASURY.

TREASURY DEPARTMENT,
Fifth Auditor's Office, Washington, November 16, 1871.

SIR: I have the honor to submit herewith the tabular statements of the operations of this office for the fiscal year ending June 30, 1871, per schedules from A to S inclusive, and also the statements of expenses of assessing and collecting internal revenue for the fiscal year ending June 30, 1870, which were not ready at the date of the last annual report. The number of accounts adjusted during the fiscal year is eighteen thousand four hundred and four, involving the sum of $820,208,679 60, and the number of letters written is eighteen thousand four hundred and thirty-six. The number of accounts adjusted for the previous fiscal year was eleven thousand nine hundred and eighty-six, and the number of letters written seven thousand two hundred and fifty-six. I take pleasure in commending the several clerks and employés of the office for uniform good deportment and general faithfulness in the discharge of their important and responsible duties.

I have the honor to be, very respectfully, your obedient servant,
J. B. MANN,
Acting Auditor.

Hon. GEORGE S. BOUTWELL,
Secretary of the Treasury.

A.—*Statement of the expenses of all missions abroad, for salaries, contingencies, and loss by exchange, from the 1st of July, 1870, to the 30th of June, 1871, as shown by accounts adjusted in this office.*

No.	Mission.	Salary.	Contingencies.	Loss by exchange.	Total.
	ARGENTINE REPUBLIC.				
1	R. C. Kirk, minister.............................	$7, 500 00	$225 75	$100 00	$7, 825 75
	AUSTRIA.				
2	John Jay, minister	12, 000 00	952 53	....	
3	J. F. DeLaplaine, secretary of legation.........	1, 800 00	....	....	
		13, 800 00	952 53	....	14, 752 53
	BELGIUM.				
4	J. R. Jones, minister	7, 500 00	560 51	....	8, 060 51
	BRAZIL.				
5	H. T. Blow, late minister......................	7, 400 00	446 92	155 19	
6	J. R. Partridge, minister......................				
7	Clinton Wright, chargé........................	4, 255 43	50 00	....	
		11, 655 43	496 92	155 19	12, 307 54
	BOLIVIA.				
8	L. Markbreit, minister........................	7, 500 00	226 40	256 50	7, 982 90

A.—*Statement of the expenses of all missions abroad, &c.*—Continued.

No.	Mission.	Salary.	Contingen- cies.	Loss by exchange.	Total.
	CHILI.				
9	J. P. Root, minister....................	$5,434 78	$113 80	$116 66	
10	J. C. Caldwell, acting minister...............	497 28	218 90	25 00	
		5,932 06	332 70	141 66	$6,406 42
	CHINA.				
11	F. F. Low, minister.......................				
12	S. W. Williams, secretary of legation.........	4,739 01	....	836 31	5,575 32
	COLOMBIA.				
13	S. A. Hurlbut, minister......................	....	....	....	
	COSTA RICA.				
14	J. B. Blair, minister........................	7,500 00	270 02	431 83	8,201 85
	DENMARK.				
15	G. H. Yeaman, late minister ....!	3,444 29	130 61	....	
16	M. J. Cramer, minister....................	6,073 37	250 09	95 60	
		9,517 66	380 70	95 60	9,993 96
	ECUADOR.				
17	E. R. Wing, minister.......................	7 500 00	702 91	935 14	9,138 05
	FRANCE.				
18	E. B. Washburne, minister....................	17,500 00	3,738 95	29 07	
19	W. Hoffman, secretary of legation.............	2,650 00	32 07	30 42	
20	F. Moore, assistant secretary of legation.......	2,000 00	....	....	
		22,150 00	3,771 02	59 49	25,980 51
	GERMAN EMPIRE.				
21	George Bancroft, minister....................	12,000 00	2,160 37	....	
22	Alexander Bliss, secretary of legation.........	3,050 83	....	....	
23	Nicholas Fish, assistant secretary of legation..	1,800 00	....	....	
		16,850 83	2,160 37	....	19,011 20
	GREAT BRITAIN.				
24	J. L. Motley, late minister...................	7,826 09	1,323 58	....	
25	R. C. Schenck, minister				
26	B. Moran, secretary of legation...............	4,556 68	2,944 11	....	
27	M. Woodhull, assistant secretary.............	....	....	....	
		12,382 77	4,267 69	....	16,650 46
	GREECE.				
28	C. K. Tuckerman, late minister...............	7,500 00	260 42	6 46	7,766 88
	GUATEMALA.				
29	S. A. Hudson, minister....., ...	11,250 00	683 90	94 52	12,028 42
	HAWAIIAN ISLANDS.				
30	H. A. Peirce, minister........................	7,500 00	101 64	....	7,601 64
	HAYTI.				
31	E. D. Bassett, minister......................	....	....	....	
	HONDURAS.				
32	Henry Baxter, minister......................	....	....	....	
	ITALY.				
33	George P. Marsh, minister....................	12,000 00	461 48	41 44	
34	G. W. Wurts, secretary of legation............	1,800 00	....	....	
		13,800 00	461 48	41 44	14,302 92
	JAPAN.				
35	C. E. DeLong, minister......................	7,404 88	638 45	476 36	
36	J. L. C. Portman, second interpreter	....	....	....	
37	J. C. Hepburn, interpreter...................	....	....	....	
		7,404 88	638 45	476 36	8,519 69
	LIBERIA.				
38	J. M. Turner, minister.......................	968 68	....	....	968 68

A.—*Statement of the expenses of all missions abroad, &c.*—Continued.

No.	Mission.	Salary.	Contingencies.	Loss by exchange.	Total.
	MEXICO.				
39	Thomas H. Nelson, minister	$12,000 00	$1,887 56		
40	P. C. Bliss, secretary of legation				
		12,000 00	1,887 56		$13,887 56
	NETHERLANDS.				
41	Hugh Ewing, late minister	3,742 18	122 80		
42	C. T. Gorham, minister	6,888 58	313 96	$5 39	
		10,030 76	435 76	5 39	11,072 91
	NICARAGUA.				
43	C. N. Riotte, minister	7,500 00	491 96		7,991 96
	PARAGUAY AND URUGUAY.				
44	J. L. Stevens, minister	11,714 48	266 43	491 42	12,472 33
	PERU.				
45	A. P. Hovey, late minister	2,500 00	102 12	93 01	
46	Thomas Settle, minister	3,085 00	194 24		
47	H. M. Brent, secretary of legation	1,500 00			
		7,085 00	296 36	93 01	7,474 37
	PORTUGAL.				
48	C. H. Lewis, minister	7,500 00	337 26	19 59	7,856 85
	RUSSIA.				
49	A. G. Curtin, minister	12,000 00	972 59		
50	E. Schuyler, secretary of legation	1,800 00			
		13,800 00	972 59		14,772 59
	SALVADOR.				
51	A. T. A. Torbert, minister	7,500 00	93 00		7,593 00
	SPAIN.				
52	D. E. Sickles, minister	12,000 00	6,543 62	911 83	
53	A. A. Adee, secretary of legation	1,800 00			
		13,800 00	6,543 62	911 83	21,255 45
	SWEDEN.				
54	C. C. Andrews, minister	7,500 00	388 09	319 66	8,207 75
	SWITZERLAND.				
55	H. Rublee, minister	7,500 00	390 37	94 31	7,984 68
	TURKEY.				
56	E. Joy Morris, ——	2,384 51	933 83	45 35	
57	W. Mac Veagh, late minister	8,056 32	1,773 69	85 76	
58	G. P. Brown, secretary of legation	3,000 00			
		13,440 83	2,707 52	131 11	16,279 46
	VENEZUELA.				
59	J. R. Partridge, late minister	1,806 65			
60	W. A. Pile, minister				
		1,806 65			1,806 65
	ALEXANDRIA.				
61	G. H. Butler, consul general		1,244 84		1,244 84
	TANGIER.				
62	F. A. Mathews, consul		800 00		800 00
	TUNIS.				
63	George H. Heap, consul		624 30		624 30
	TRIPOLI.				
64	M. Vidal, consul		746 79		746 79
		304,729 04	34,722 86	5,696 82	345,148 72
	UNITED STATES BANKERS, LONDON.				
65	Baring Bro's & Co				437,109 83
	Grand total				782,258 55

5. Final account of late minister.	16. Salary for transit to post and instructions included.
7. Salary while acting as chargé.	
9. Inclusive of transit to post.	25. No accounts received.
10. Salary while acting minister.	31. No accounts received.
11. Accounts incomplete.	32. No accounts received.
12. Salary while in charge of mission.	56. Final account of minister.
15. Final account of late minister.	59. No accounts received.

B.—Statement of consular salaries, fees, and loss by exchange for the fiscal year ending June 30, 1871.

No.	Consulate.	Salaries.	Fees.	Loss by exchange.
	A.			
1	Amoor River	$2,033 40	$57 71	$126 22
2	Algiers	1,667 10		89 42
3	Antwerp	2,767 85	3,748 43	
4	Amsterdam	1,000 00	1,219 16	
5	Aix-la-Chapelle	5,125 00	5,223 50	
6	Alexandria	6,368 00	67 97	12 36
7	Amoy	3,000 00	1,033 67	377 20
8	Apia	1,000 00	81 06	275 67
9	Aux Cayes	541 67	290 61	
10	Acapulco	2,000 00	583 85	
11	Aspinwall	2,500 00	2,533 74	
	B.			
12	Belfast	2,000 00	11,995 38	
13	Bay of Islands	1,018 29	195 44	20 57
14	Bordeaux	2,788 04	8,689 85	7 00
15	Barcelona	1,541 46	218 42	79 38
16	Batavia	582 42	439 11	6 09
17	Bremen	3,090 00	3,076 50	
18	Basle	4,000 00	6,864 00	36 09
19	Beirut	2,461 95	209 79	109 12
20	Bahia	1,000 00	1,022 59	
21	Buenos Ayres	6,808 09	4,000 40	
22	Bangkok	3,000 00	238 94	897 28
23	Brindisi	1,924 42	8 27	
24	Boulogne	1,500 00	371 53	56 81
25	Bradford	4,412 13	16,706 00	
26	Berlin	3,512 93	7,529 00	
27	Barmen	4,000 00	12,002 75	29 13
28	Birmingham	4,000 00	17,729 50	
29	Brussels	3,332 39	6,141 50	
	C.			
30	Cork	2,304 68	1,312 10	9 09
31	Calcutta	5,819 69	7,113 70	
32	Cape Town	1,000 00	403 94	50 41
33	Cadiz	1,683 42	425 95	27 20
34	Constantinople	3,000 00	522 30	189 78
35	Canea	1,000 00		100 00
36	Cyprus	1,000 00		48 75
37	Canton	5,315 09	1,798 85	562 94
38	Cape Haytien	1,872 28	1,017 20	
39	Chemnitz	2,000 00	9,311 51	
40	Carthagena	500 00	363 41	
41	Callao	3,804 35	2,619 24	
42	Coaticook	2,000 00	5,576 25	
43	Chin-Kiang	3,000 00	1,248 89	277 83
44	Clifton	2,201 61	3,742 25	
45	Ceylon	1,000 00	350 02	
	D.			
46	Dundee	2,000 00	7,067 33	3 18
47	Demerara	2,000 00	2,295 78	
48	Dresden	4,404 47	5,819 00	
	E.			
49	Elsinore	1,754 39	341 95	52 46
	F.			
50	Fort Erie	3,053 50	4,815 75	
51	Funchal	1,624 09	97 83	
52	Fayal	750 00	510 13	
53	Foochow	3,500 00	950 67	374 90
54	Frankfort-on-the-Main	4,250 00	2,709 25	20 84
	G.			
55	Genoa	1,500 00	1,531 19	
56	Glasgow	3,269 00	11,752 39	

B.—*Statement of consular salaries, fees, &c.*—Continued.

No.	Consulates.	Salaries.	Fees.	Loss by exchange.
57	Geneva	$1,500 00	$1,505 75	$5 02
58	Guayaquil	750 00	204 88	78 84
59	Gibraltar	1,500 00	846 88	....
60	Gaboon	1,551 91	91 47	....
61	Guayamas	1,000 00	872 95	....
62	Goderich	3,846 84	3,123 80	....
	H.			
63	Havana	7,000 00	20,907 98	....
64	Hong-Kong	5,581 39	8,026 75	....
65	Halifax	2,000 00	3,102 22	16 57
66	Hamburg	2,000 00	5,516 40	6 25
67	Hakodadi	3,213 49	272 14	243 42
68	Honolulu	5,300 25	6,390 77	....
69	Havre	6,000 00	3,475 14	85 27
70	Hankow	3,839 67	1,094 35	224 68
71	Hamilton	2,806 89	3,967 00	....
	J.			
72	Jerusalem	1,500 00	97 50	162 00
	K.			
73	Kingston, Jamaica	2,790 64	1,723 70	32 84
74	Kingston, Canada	1,500 00	2,143 98	....
75	Kanagawa	3,000 00	5,944 22	....
	L.			
76	Liverpool	10,540 94	41,218 43	....
77	London	8,056 33	51,240 73	....
78	Leeds	2,000 00	2,279 75	....
79	Lisbon	183 43	....	....
80	La Rochelle	1,500 00	624 50	13 13
81	Leipsic	2,812 50	7,216 50	....
82	Laguayra	1,500 00	536 61	....
83	Lahaina	1,697 79	....	....
84	Leith	3,872 84	5,357 55	....
85	Lyons	4,000 00	11,064 25	72 60
86	Leghorn	1,500 00	1,864 48	....
87	Lauthala	4,144 02	392 48	....
	M.			
88	Mayence	....	....	....
89	Manchester	3,000 00	28,903 50	....
90	Malta	1,500 00	297 17	39 33
91	Marseilles	2,500 00	3,556 24	....
92	Malaga	1,549 63	1,756 57	32 74
93	Matanzas	5,500 00	10,190 02	....
94	Munich	1,500 00	1,118 56	50 35
95	Messina	1,600 98	2,659 23	....
96	Mexico	1,000 00	691 25	....
97	Montevideo	1,178 90	2,253 03	....
98	Maranham	1,000 00	289 22	....
99	Mauritius	2,500 00	260 99	111 62
100	Montreal	14,373 30	18,700 99	....
101	Melbourne	5,766 70	2,088 57	59 70
102	Matamoras	2,000 00	2,981 63	....
	N.			
103	Nassau, N. P	2,000 00	1,636 78	3 92
104	Newcastle-upon-Tyne	2,569 91	2,596 91	1 22
105	Nantes	1,616 49	467 49	30 57
106	Nice	1,891 85	415 50	57 50
107	Nagasaki	3,000 00	674 33	358 07
108	Naples	1,125 00	938 42	19 83
109	Nuremberg	2,500 00	6,317 50	....
	O.			
110	Odessa	2,000 00	151 00	275 64
111	Oporto	750 00	140 46	47 78
112	Osaka and Hiogo	3,000 00	2,038 77	108 34
113	Omoa and Truxillo	1,000 00	59 60	....
	P.			
114	Port Stanley	1,813 89	158 11	....
115	Port Mahon	1,500 00	30 33	22 80
116	Paso del Norte	272 20	18 00	....
117	Panama	3,500 00	1,808 11	....
118	Pernambuco	2,689 03	1,187 87	113 03
119	Para	1,000 00	2,306 22	....
120	Payta	543 06	365 90	....
121	Pictou	3,489 64	2,333 29	2 45
122	Palermo	1,500 00	1,637 97	....
123	Piraeus	1,000 00	7 50	97 98
124	Prescott	5,513 20	5,176 75	28
125	Paris	7,467 39	20,776 00	171 37

B.—*Statement of consular salaries, fees, &c.*—Continued.

No.	Consulate.	Salaries.	Fees.	Loss by exchange.
126	Prince Edward Island	$1,904 63	$898 52	$17 98
127	Port Said	1,614 13	29 80	88 22
	Q.			
128	Quebec	1,724 17	.913 00	5 62
	R.			
129	Rotterdam	2,000 00	2,216 30	16 52
130	Rio de Janeiro	4,347 35	5,604 99	91 04
131	Rio Grande	750 00	483 63	....
132	Rome	2,040 04	1,785 25	32 08
	S.			
133	St. John's, N. B	4,742 75	8,441 24	3 23
134	St. Petersburg	2,000 00	798 00	160 68
135	St. Paul de Loando	750 00	47 91	
136	St. Thomas	4,347 82	1,968 17	29 80
137	St. Domingo	2,007 41	384 93	40 63
138	St. Catharine's	1,500 00	104 77	....
139	Sonneberg	4,116 34	5,558 50	....
140	Singapore	3,540 45	1,127 84	83 51
141	Santiago de Cuba	2,921 19	649 16	60 33
142	San Juan, P. R	10,048 62	9,022 69	....
143	Santiago, C. V	812 50	41 71	78 43
144	Santa Cruz	2,003 00	646 75	....
145	Stuttgart	2,000 00	3,018 25	7 96
146	Spezzia	1,500 00	10 00	98 11
147	Smyrna	2,000 00	1,533 78	71 01
148	Swatow	3,500 00	275 46	391 01
149	San Juan del Norte	2,000 00	363 81	....
150	San Juan del Sur	2,000 00	422 12	....
151	Sabanilla			
152	Stettin	1,143 53	222 53	46 35
153	Southampton	1,000 00	172 00	
154	St. Helena	1,500 00	679 06	2 96
155	St. John's, Canada			
156	Sarnia	1,500 00	1,452 50	....
157	Sheffield	7,459 68	21,293 50	....
158	Seychelles	1,467 03	58 78	20 71
159	Shanghai	6,000 00	7,412 40	....
	T.			
160	Tabasco	1,415 76	906 18	....
161	Tangier	3,456 50	6 00	100 57
162	Trieste	2,000 00	1,665 93	....
163	Tampico	1,813 86	297 95	....
164	Trinidad de Cuba	4,500 00	2,742 35	....
165	Tripoli			
166	Tunis	3,000 00	9 50	....
167	Tumbez	267 66	190 70	....
168	Tahiti	500 00	346 89	....
169	Talcahuano	1,081 52	882 61	....
170	Toronto	5,479 50	7,112 00	....
171	Tamatave	2,000 00	41 42	371 46
172	Tunstall	3,500 00	14,005 00	....
173	Turk's Island	2,579 04	608 66	....
	V.			
174	Venice	750 00	470 06	31 44
175	Valparaiso	3,000 00	2,141 60	....
176	Vienna	2,314 95	5,873 25	39 91
177	Valencia	375 00	113 46	9 38
178	Vera Cruz	3,500 00	2,228 04	....
	W.			
179	Windsor	1,500 00	2,035 25	....
180	Winnepeg	1,691 58	934 75	....
	Y.			
181	Yeddo	2,390 10	177 35	310 16
	Z.			
182	Zurich	4,092 90	7,448 75	....
183	Zanzibar	1,000 00	253 62	86 60
184	Agents to examine consular affairs	10,527 22	....	97 03

Total fees received $632,258 22
salaries paid $475,861 95
loss by exchange 8,776 68
                                                                                                484,638 63

Excess of fees over salaries and loss by exchange 147,619 59

REMARKS.

1. From April 1, 1870, to September 30, 1870, and inclusive of salary for transit.
2. Inclusive of salary for transit.
3. Inclusive of salary for transit.
5. Inclusive of consular agency.
8. From January 1, 1870, to December 31, 1870.
14. Inclusive of salary from April 1, 1869, to July 13, 1869, and for transit.
16. Returns incomplete.
18. Inclusive of consular agency.
19. Inclusive of salary of consular clerk.
21. Inclusive of allowance to H. R. Helper, per act of July 7, 1870.
23. Inclusive of salary for instruction period and transit.
25. Inclusive of expenses.
26. Inclusive of expenses.
27. Inclusive of consular agency.
28. Inclusive of consular agencies.
29. Inclusive of expenses.
30. Inclusive of salary for instruction period and transit.
31. Inclusive of salary for instruction periods.
33. Inclusive of salary for transit.
37. Inclusive of salary for instruction period and transit.
38. Inclusive of salary for instruction period and transit, and from September 1, 1869.
41. Inclusive of salary for transit.
44. Inclusive of consular agency.
48. Inclusive of expenses.
49. Inclusive of consular agencies.
50. Inclusive of consular agencies.
51. Inclusive of salary for instruction period.
54. Inclusive of salary of consular clerk and for transit.
56. Inclusive of salary, while awaiting exequatur.
60. Inclusive of part of previous year. Returns incomplete.
62. Inclusive of consular agencies, and salary for instructions and transit.
63. Inclusive of salary of consular clerk.
64. Inclusive of salary for instruction period and transits.
67. Inclusive of salary for instruction period and transit.
68. Inclusive of salary for instruction period and transits.
70. Inclusive of part of last fiscal year.
71. Inclusive of expenses.
73. Inclusive of salary for instruction period and transit.
76. Inclusive of consular agency and salary of consular clerk.
77. Inclusive of salary for instructions, transit, and awaiting exequatur
79. Returns incomplete.
81. Inclusive of salary for transit, awaiting exequatur, and of consular clerk.
83. No salary settled since January 24, 1871.
84. Inclusive of expenses.
85. Inclusive of consular agency.
87. Inclusive of reports for 1870, part of 1869 and 1866.
88. Returns incomplete.
93. Inclusive of consular agencies.
100. Inclusive of consular agencies for 1869, 1870, and 1871.
101. Inclusive of salary for instruction period, transits, and awaiting recognition.
104. Inclusive of consular agencies.
106. Inclusive of salary for instruction period and transit.
109. Expenses for clerk-hire and office-rent; suspended by Department of State.
111. Settled to December 31, 1870.
114. Inclusive of returns from January 1, 1870, and salary for transit.
116. Settled to January 16, 1871.
118. Inclusive of salary for transits and instruction period.
121. Inclusive of consular agencies.
124. Inclusive of consular agencies.
125. Inclusive of consular clerks' salaries.
126. Inclusive of first and second quarters of 1870, and salary for instruction period.
128. Inclusive of salary for instruction period and transits.
131. Accounts for second quarter of 1871 not received.
132. Inclusive of part of 1869, and salary for transit.
133. Inclusive of expenses, and consular agencies.
135. Accounts for second quarter 1871 not received.
136. Inclusive of salary for transit, and awaiting exequatur.
137. Inclusive of salary for instruction period, transit, and awaiting exequatur.
139. Inclusive of expenses.
140. Inclusive of salary for transit.
141. Inclusive of salary for instruction period and transit.
142. Inclusive of consular agencies from July 1, 1869.
143. Inclusive of salary for instruction period.
144. Inclusive of salary for instruction period and consular agency.
151. No returns.
152. Inclusive of salary for transit.
153. Accounts settled to December 31, 1870.
155. Returns included in report from Montreal.
157. Inclusive of expenses and consular agencies.
159. Inclusive of salary of consular clerks.
160. Inclusive of returns since December 2, 1868.
161. Inclusive of salary for transit.
163. Inclusive of salary for transit.
164. Inclusive of consular agencies.
165. Suspended by direction of Department of State.
167. Accounts for first and second quarters 1871 not received.
168. Accounts for first and second quarters 1871 not received.

170. Inclusive of consular agencies.
172. Inclusive of returns from October 1, 1869.
173. Inclusive of consular agencies.
176. Inclusive of salary of consular clerk.
177. Accounts suspended October 1, 1870.
181. Accounts adjusted to April 17, 1871.
182. Inclusive of consular agency.
184. Inclusive of expenses. One account suspended.

B 1.—*Expenditures on account of sundry appropriations from July 1, 1870, to June 30, 1871, as shown by adjustments made in this office.*

For interpreters to the consulates in China, Japan, and Siam $6,896 37
For salaries of the marshals of the consular courts in Japan, including that at Nagasaki, and in China, Siam, and Turkey 7,917 31
For rent of prisons for American convicts in Japan, China, Siam, and Turkey. 13,030 14
For expenses of the consulates in the Turkish dominions, namely : Interpreters, guards, and other expenses of the consulates at Constantinople, Smyrna, Candia, Alexandria, Jerusalem, and Beirut..................... 2,094 41
For expenses of cemetery at Acapulco, Mexico, and loss by exchange thereon. 1,030 00

C.—*Statement showing the amount expended by the consular officers of the United States for the relief of American seamen, the money received by said officers for extra wages, &c., and the loss by exchange incurred by them in drawing for balances due them, during the fiscal year ending June 30, 187 .*

Consulate.	Expended.	Received.	Loss by exchange.
Acapulco....................................	$712 66	$42 66	....
Alexandria..................................	101 16	....	$7 07
Algiers.....................................	3 45	....	....
Amoy.......................................	92 75	88 20	....
Amsterdam..................................	216 28	87 12	....
Ancona.....................................	3 47	....	29
Antigua....................................	55 68	36 00	....
Antwerp....................................	8 00	74 99	....
Aspinwall..................................	995 65	....	....
Aux Cayes.................................	6 00	....	....
Bahia......................................	....	74 60	....
Bangkok....................................	68 80	95 00	23 15
Barbadoes..................................	602 24	375 82	....
Barcelona..................................	75 17	....	5 53
Batavia....................................	1,493 28	485 64	88 64
Bay of Islands, New Zealand	1,600 43	812 00	12 72
Bermuda....................................	40 32	44 00	....
Bombay.....................................	22 69	26 70	....
Boulogne...................................	47 46	31 57	84
Bradford...................................	11 64	....	....
Bristol....................................	37 67	98 29	....
Buenos Ayres...............................	....	25 00	....
Cadiz......................................	656 10	268 10	37 05
Calcutta...................................	....	1,653 53	....
Callao.....................................	3,864 12	2,408 59	....
Canton.....................................	6 60	25 59	....
Cape Town..................................	1,005 65	202 34	39 29
Cardiff....................................	202 50	244 30	....
Clifton, Canada............................	6 75	....	....
Constantinople.............................	112 99	....	11 30
Cork.......................................	102 25	105 00	....
Curaçoa....................................	....	769 59	....
Demerara...................................	....	48 36	....
Dundee.....................................	12 30	....	....
Elsinore...................................	....	16 08	....
Falkland Islands...........................	1,049 89	....	....
Falmouth...................................	376 13	17 96	16 01
Fayal......................................	2,486 20	602 09	....
Fort Erie, Canada..........................	147 63	....	....
Funchal....................................	5 76	....	....
Geestemunde................................	572 44	516 95	....
Genoa......................................	146 17	138 00	....
Gibraltar..................................	163 13	247 96	....
Glasgow....................................	35 97	....	....
Guayaquil..................................	1,082 46	34 95	25 75
Halifax....................................	1,532 53	....	....
Hamburg....................................	26 00	115 08	....
Havana.....................................	458 70	1,605 89	....
Havre......................................	296 34	194 97	7 90
Hiogo......................................	....	100 00	....
ong-Kong	1,611 00	661 00	....
onolulu	3,573 25	4,199 81	....

C.—*Statement showing the amount expended by the consular officers, &c.*—Continued.

Consulate.	Expended.	Received.	Loss by exchange.
Kanagawa	$86 00	$36 00	
Kingston, Jamaica	239 04	4 86	$10 14
La Paz, Mexico	1,297 00		
Leghorn		20 00	
Leith	4 60		
Liverpool	2,116 03	3,973 55	
London	325 29	30 00	
Malaga	2,919 21	135 00	204 94
Malta		36 36	
Manchester	21 06		
Manilla	529 86	113 00	14 41
Manzanillo	119 25		
Maranham	139 75		
Marseilles	804 30	155 00	
Matanzas	170 62	405 32	
Mauritius	1,584 04	92 25	65 97
Melbourne	374 45	350 68	
Messina	50 00	20 69	
Minatitlan	57 50		
Montevideo	399 78	176 88	
Nantes		37 50	
Naples	13 22		
Nassau, Bahamas	1,701 26		12 97
Newcastle-upon-Tyne	48 40		1 66
Nice	34 20		1 49
Panama	486 50	805 00	
Para	24 10	12 50	
Paramaribo	133 98		
Paris	52 21		
Payta	4,229 89	440 00	23 71
Pernambuco	993 00	542 85	61 49
Piraeus. Greece	8 36		1 00
Puerto Cabello		320 18	
Quebec	14 00		
Riga, Russia	233 21		
Rio de Janeiro	630 18	212 99	
Rio Grande do Sul	1,545 05		
Rotterdam	66 84	115 10	
San Andres	12 65	110 00	
Santiago, Verde Islands	226 87	84 00	12 61
Seychelles	103 00	166 40	
Shanghai	655 20	814 67	
Sheffield	17 42		
Sierra Leone	65 90		
Singapore	805 46	1,050 64	
Smyrna	129 95		19 41
Southampton	68 04		
Saint Catharine, Brazil	13 13	20 00	
Saint Helena	291 48	508 47	
Saint John, New Brunswick	10 40		
Saint Thomas, West Indies	1,430 39		
Stockholm	19 81		
Swatow, China		10 55	
Sydney, Australia	131 42	23 75	
Tabasco	91 00		
Tahiti	1,815 09	306 00	142 71
Talcahuano	5,829 72	1,439 00	
Tampico	10 00		
Teneriffe		17 00	
Trieste	107 41	178 11	
Trinidad de Cuba	58 00	53 42	
Tumbez	204 25	100 00	
Turks' Islands	75 24		
Valencia	36 30	215 46	
Valparaiso	1,483 57	491 83	
Vera Cruz	19 50		
Victoria, Vancouver's Island	239 00	86 25	
Zanzibar	249 85	300 59	45 26
	61,429 29	30,729 58	883 31

RECAPITULATION.

Total amount of expenditures and loss by exchange.................................. $62,312 60
Amount of extra wages received.. 30,729 58

Excess of disbursements over receipts... 31,583 02

D.—*Statement of the number of destitute American seamen sent to the United States, and the amount paid for their passage, from the following consulates, during the fiscal year ending June 30, 1871.*

Consulate.	No. of seamen.	Amount.	Consulate.	No. of seamen.	Amount.
Acapulco	8	$80 00	Mazatlan	1	$10 00
Amsterdam	1	10 00	Messina	1	10 00
Antigua	1	10 00	Mona River	1	10 00
Aux Cayes	3	40 00	Montevideo	7	70 00
Aspinwall	53	530 00	Monrovia	1	30 00
Baracoa	1	10 00	Nassau	78	780 00
Barbadoes	37	370 00	New Castle	1	10 00
Bathurst	1	15 00	Palermo	2	20 00
Bay of Islands	2	20 00	Panama	5	50 00
Belize	3	30 00	Para	3	30 00
Bermuda	11	134 00	Paramaribo	1	10 00
Bremen	1	10 00	Pernambuco	8	80 00
Bristol	1	10 00	Plaister Cove	7	56 00
Cadiz	3	30 00	Port du Paix	2	38 00
Callao	1	10 00	Port Luis	20	1,000 00
Calcutta	2	20 00	Puerto Cabello	2	20 00
Cape Town	2	30 00	Rio de Janeiro	35	350 00
Cardenas	5	50 00	Rio Grande do Sul	7	70 00
Cardiff	2	20 00	Sagua la Grande	1	10 00
Constantinople	2	5 00	San Andres	4	40 00
Cow Bay	5	50 00	San Lucas	49	490 00
Curaçoa	1	10 00	Santiago, Cape Verde	4	75 00
Fayal	53	1,014 00	Shangbai	6	60 00
Genoa	1	12 50	Sidney	2	20 00
Gibraltar	10	100 00	Sierra Leone	3	30 00
Guadalupe	1	10 00	Singapore	4	40 00
Halifax	6	60 00	Smyrna	2	20 00
Hamilton	1	10 00	St. Croix	4	55 00
Havana	28	280 00	St. Helena	25	250 00
Havre	3	30 00	St. John's, New Brunswick	5	48 00
Hong-Kong	6	60 00	St. Thomas	36	360 00
Honolulu	23	240 00	Tahiti	3	30 00
Kanagawa	11	110 00	Taleahuana	1	10 00
Kingston, Jamaica	17	175 00	Trieste	1	10 00
La Paz	2	20 00	Trinidad	7	70 00
Liverpool	17	170 00	Turk's Island	13	130 00
Loudon	8	80 00	Vera Cruz	1	10 00
Malaga	4	40 00	Victoria, Vancouver's Island	3	30 00
Manila	1	10 00	Yarmouth	15	144 00
Mauzanilla	7	70 00	Zanzibar	6	60 00
Maraham	1	10 00			
Marseilles	1	10 00	Total	735	8,751 50
Matanzas	11	110 00			

Statement showing the amount expended by the United States consulates for expenses incurred on account of criminal seamen for the fiscal year ending June 30, 1871.

Rio de Janeiro $900 00

E.—*Statement showing the amount refunded citizens, seamen, or their representatives, directly from the United States Treasury, the several sums having been previously paid therein by consular officers, during the fiscal year ending June 30, 1871.*

William Edward MacArdle, seaman, estate of	$25 22
A. D. Bache, paymaster United States Navy	99 28
Solomon Freeman, seaman, estate of	5 32
George W. Freeman, seaman, estate of	66 67
Edwin Morey, managing owner schooner "Maria Hall"	100 03
John Furey, paymaster United States Navy	859 83
Francis Daugherty, seaman, estate of	91 80
George W. Beaman, paymaster United States Navy	117 63
William H. Smyley, late commercial agent, deceased	1,132 46
L. W. Bradley, seaman, estate of	97 92
Robert W. Allen, paymaster United States Navy	12 27
Philip E. O'Reilly, citizen, estate of	316 37
James B. Blood, seaman, estate of	23 25
J. M. Schnauffer, seaman, estate of	77 59
Ferdinand Blancke, owner of ship "William Frothingham"	225 54
Henry M. Meade, paymaster United States Navy	37 96
Thomas Edwards, seaman, estate of	112 00
Charles Wheeler, seaman, estate of	32 00
A. G. Greeley, paymaster United States Navy	28 54
Manuel (alias Frank) Sylvia, seaman, estate of	179 18
Total	3,640 86

F.—*Department accounts received and settled for the fiscal year ending June 30, 1871.*

State Department:

Expenses of Universal Exposition at Paris			$4,506 12
Publishing laws in pamphlet form			89,772 18
Proof-reading and packing			2,903 79
Extra clerk-hire			12,816 65
Copper-plate printing, books, maps, &c			3,852 70
Rescue of American citizens from shipwreck			4,534 25
Expenses under the neutrality act			5,779 22
Stationery, furniture, &c			5,000 00
Salary and expenses of British and American Joint Commission			18,007 22
Awards under convention between the United States and Peru			54,188 00
Hudson Bay and Puget Sound indemnity			325,000 00
Contingent expenses of foreign intercourse and missions abroad.	$54,877 62		
The same, approved by Department of State	20,556 44		
			75,434 06
Blank books, office-rent, &c., of consuls	41,884 66		
The same, approved by Department of State	72,340 45		
			114,225 11
			716,019 30

Interior Department:

Expenses of taking Ninth Census	$864,982 56
Expenses of taking Eighth Census	33,394 73
Taking census in Colorado	60 00
Miscellaneous and other expenses of Patent Office	117,405 16
Printing, photographing, &c., of Patent Office	34,803 28
Packing and distributing documents	7,088 24
Suppression of the slave-trade	1,589 97
	1,059,323 94

Post-Office Department:

Blank books, &c	$58,583 59
Miscellaneous expenses *	3,738 75
Ventilation of Post-Office Department building	10,000 34
	72,322 68

* Miscellaneous expenses were incurred before July 1, 1870.

G.—*Statement showing the expenses of assessing the internal revenue taxes in the several collection districts, including the salaries, commissions, and allowances of the assessors, their contingent expenses, and the compensation of assistant assessors and store-keepers, from July 1, 1870, to June 30, 1871.*

District	Gross compensation.	Tax.	Net compensation.	Clerk hire.	Stationery.	Printing and advertising.	Postage and express.	Rent of assessors.	Survey of distilleries.	Net compensation of assistant assessors.	Net compensation of store-keepers.	Tax on compensation of ass't assessors and store-keepers.	Total.
ALABAMA.													
First district*	$4,752 43	$95 48	$4,656 95	$2,700 00	$130 64	$7 50	$50 25	$278 00		$12,814 71	$593 66	$69 84	$20,360 05
Second district*	2,486 26	6 32	2,479 94	2,324 88	191 18	48 00	170 47	120 00	$27 90	13,397 64	592 76	54 37	19,483 77
Third district*	3,975 80	64 78	3,911 02	1,825 00	93 13	9 00				8,508 52		127 56	15,037 23
Total	11,214 49	166 58	11,047 91	6,849 88	414 95	64 50	220 72	398 00	27 80	34,720 87	1,186 42	251 77	54,931 05
ARIZONA.													
Arizona	2,500 00	6 32	2,493 68		32 50	27 00	15 99	300 00		2,109 01	375 53	7 97	5,353 71
ARKANSAS.													
First district	2,500 00	6 32	2,493 68	649 97	109 47	149 74	165 30	260 00		9,195 99	384 92	36 74	13,409 07
Second district	1,699 32	10 30	1,689 02	1,650 00	61 54	19 50	42 82	480 00		6,923 74		25 70	10,886 62
Third district	2,706 04	12 50	2,693 54	558 33	32 49	3 50	49 50	150 00		6,039 86		36 82	10,527 22
Total	6,905 36	29 12	6,870 24	2,853 30	203 50	172 74	257 62	890 00		22,159 59	384 92	99 26	33,802 91
CALIFORNIA.													
First district, (old)††	4,942 24	66 48	4,875 76	4,212 00	214 46		26 79	1,770 74		63,350 28	3,938 39	1,678 48	78,388 42
First district, (new)	1,000 00		1,000 00	1,249 94	35 00	17 77	48 72	510 00		8,571 78	1,210 00	50 16	12,633 21
Second district	2,160 18	29 81	2,130 37	1,490 94	93 21	127 61	117 83	190 17	32 18	7,684 95		16 03	12,511 83
Third district	2,750 66	10 65	2,740 01	1,500 00	135 00	118 55	25 99	360 00	155 91	7,656 57	645 00	52 39	13,514 22
Fourth district*	2,867 49	54 01	2,813 48	2,376 84	144 46	38 00	163 90	360 00		13,608 68	1,625 00	33 81	19,644 46
Fifth district	2,690 32	15 83	2,674 49	1,500 00	45 00	36 00	17 99	300 00	143 49	7,851 84			12,568 72
Total	16,410 89	176 78	16,234 11	12,338 72	667 33	335 93	400 32	3,620 91	321 1	108,724 10	6,818 39	1,830 87	149,460 96
COLORADO.													
Colorado	2,500 00	6 32	2,493 68	1,452 50	58 85	129 35	68 50	480 00		4,335 59		15 73	9,018 47

CONNECTICUT.													
First district	3,714 36	17 62	3,696 74	900 00	94 92	12 50	111 97	280 00	36 29	8,841 89		21 12	19,777 45
Second district	2,832 71	9 84	2,822 87	1,200 00	84 75	7 50	136 96	100 00	57 43	9,017 69		14 48	13,427 20
Third district*	1,847 86	8 39	1,839 47	950 00	43 45	14 50	60 70	300 00	9 90	4,687 84		9 56	7,905 86
Fourth district	2,398 69	6 98	2,392 41	950 00	38 35	8 25	73 66	75 00	34 00	9,325 14		15 30	12,896 81
Total	10,793 62	42 13	10,751 49	4,000 00	260 77	42 75	383 29	755 00	137 62	31,872 56	5,803 84	60 66	54,007 32
DAKOTA.													
Dakota*	3,580 07	61 80	3,518 27		84 63	6 00	46 61	210 00		1,935 16		18 54	5,800 67
DELAWARE.													
Delaware	3,061 51	16 81	3,044 70	1,375 00	98 82		77 56		127 90	10,404 89		22 47	15,123 57
DISTRICT COLUMBIA.													
District Columbia	2,345 32	8 16	2,337 16	1,725 00	72 66	49 62	10 00	420 00		8,581 56		17 47	13,196 00
FLORIDA.													
Florida	2,705 90	12 50	2,693 40	1,425 00	179 43	106 50	166 92	275 00		10,528 05		37 38	15,374 30
GEORGIA.													
First district*	2,475 88	6 32	2,469 56	1,650 00	266 96	6 50	55 00	469 02		12,387 65		39 87	17,304 69
Second district*	2,683 67	21 68	2,661 99	1,950 00	44 50	11 50	118 38	150 00	60 50	11,858 98		50 05	16,855 85
Third district*	2,726 72	10 13	2,716 39	1,930 00	168 23	23 25	162 41	332 30	60 50	19,317 04		167 36	24,670 62
Fourth district	3,000 00	8 22	2,991 78	1,800 00	105 69	7 50	77 22	350 00		13,215 07	571 00	33 59	19,113 26
Total	10,896 27	46 35	10,839 92	7,350 00	585 38	48 75	413 01	1,301 32		56,778 74	571 00	290 87	77,948 62
IDAHO.													
Idaho	2,516 36	7 13	2,509 23	248 00	16 00	69 50	17 00	600 00		5,117 91	1,532 93	41 74	10,110 57
ILLINOIS.													
First district	15,005 26	210 21	14,795 05	4,213 00	372 17	3 25	137 04	1,000 00		20,288 19	24,314 26	144 96	68,129 96
Second district*	3,339 88	63 81	3,976 07	855 00	129 55	25 15	94 36	170 00		5,674 93	825 72	14 75	11,050 78
Third district	4,987 42	72 17	4,277 01	1,300 00	43 86	90 50	129 87	180 00		6,376 45	4,398 87	18 29	19,464 90
Fourth district*	6,376 09	99 08	6,277 01	1,349 94	87 88	90 00	108 25	150 00		7,077 75	4,257 90	24 98	19,353 78
Fifth district*	10,249 38	186 27	10,063 11	1,356 00	187 44	99 43	201 92	62 85	16 15	13,552 81	10,480 08	42 94	36,215 64
Sixth district	3,951 95	53 34	3,889 61	600 00	46 96	14 90	31 34	900 00		6,471 39	1,483 76	12 71	12,749 96
Seventh district*	3,557 07	75 53	5,481 54		97 92	17 25	78 18	125 00	3 50	9,349 85	1,431 84	31 01	20,680 94
Eighth district*	6,036 83	124 18	5,912 67	1,599 99	75 40	49 10	94 98			12,071 81	7,245 34	47 02	27,049 17
Ninth district*	2,496 35	51 91	2,444 44	1,855 00	11 05		52 50	100 00	22 30	4,165 62	135 16	13 00	7,796 07

* Including items belonging to previous fiscal years not before adjusted. † Complete returns for the district not received at this office.

‡ Includes expenses of assistant assessors for fiscal year 1865 not previously reported.

G.—Statement showing the expenses of assessing the internal revenue taxes in the several collection districts, &c.—Continued.

District	Gross compensation.	Tax.	Net compensation.	Clerk hire.	Stationery.	Printing and advertising.	Postage and express.	Rent of assessors.	Survey of distillation.	Net compensation aut assessors.	Net compensation tion of store-keepers.	Tax on compensation of ass't or assessors and store-keepers.	Total.
ILLINOIS—Cont'd													
Tenth district	$1,732 39	$13 42	$1,709 17	$313 00	$48 61	$19 65	$23 79	$250 00	$52 30	$6,462 06		$14 38	$8,896 28
Eleventh district*	1,500 00	2 11	1,497 89	525 00	44 95	11 90	57 08		22 15	5,172 44		9 70	7,714 56
Twelfth district*	4,510 79	54 03	4,456 76	1,648 41	25 60	26 00	89 24	167 58	21 10	6,539 49		17 31	15,337 53
Thirteenth district*	1,568 60	5 54	1,563 06	449 94	50 06	49 00	15 21	72 00	13	6,492 13	$276 00	16 47	8,712 70
Total	67,302 23	1,011 60	66,290 63	15,477 28½	1,220 81	364 43	1,114 14	2,554 43	137 10	115,095 12	2,961 80	407 54	263,065 17
											60,810 63		
INDIANA.													
First district*	4,902 51	64 87	4,837 64	1,283 33	67 65	58 30	57 20	160 00	150 40	7,482 62	5,160 88	18 39	19,258 22
Second district*	1,892 53	11 07	1,881 46	1,149 98	79 44		19 79	101 67	129 71	5,706 48	1,154 96	11 41	10,223 19
Third district*	4,724 54	59 33	4,665 21	1,900 00	49 57	37 75	41 84	175 00	30 20	5,977 97	2,277 62	12 90	13,624 96
Fourth district*	9,047 11	110 21	8,936 90	1,749 00	64 73	26 50	39 67	120 00		4,306 63	8,729 07	19 43	23,253 60
Fifth district*	3,042 50	59 03	2,983 47	1,000 00	6 00	12 70	37 32	192 00		4,277 94	1,251 40	13 82	10,510 62
Sixth district*	3,668 14	47 52	3,620 62	1,686 13	72 15	8 40	48 50		10 60	6,688 79	379 80	15 32	12,027 61
Seventh district*	3,228 29	22 71	3,746 81	999 96	131 65	45 50	42 91	75 00	63 85	6,064 10	2,046 66	14 32	12,102 70
Eighth district*	3,228 29	64 05	4,174 24	999 96	55 27	15 65	5 00	180 00		4,666 46	1,390 37	13 15	11,501 98
Ninth district*	4,682 82	15 56	1,677 96	122 00	38 39	23 05	25 42	42 00	12 50	4,932 99	715 92	18 50	8,394 93
Tenth district	1,700 82	12 15	1,688 67	192 00	47 20	8 00	42 37	150 00		3,013 19		4 43	5,141 43
Eleventh district	1,500 00	2 11	1,497 89	435 00	38 50		81 50	150 00		3,491 84	292 00	10 97	5,986 73
Total	40,163 78	458 61	39,710 17	8,598 39	646 35	239 65	441 52	1,345 67	416 4	56,829 13	23,998 08	153 31	132,225 97
IOWA.													
First district*	2,198 06	12 67	2,185 39	720 03	61 92	21 50	45 78	110 00		5,352 98		12 30	8,497 57
Second district*	3,040 57	26 83	3,013 74	600 00	91 03	21 50	110 20	100 00	12 0	5,543 32	1,166 78	19 32	10,660 57
Third district*	3,307 54	41 17	3,296 37	642 11	127 97	21 55	83 34			6,728 19	2,277 92	18 57	13,147 45
Fourth district*	3,932 91	23 74	1,909 17	664 98	106 95	59 00	126 77	120 00	51 0	5,459 79		10 34	8,446 66
Fifth district*	1,248 63	2 11	1,246 52	458 26	118 90	46 80	12 40	120 00		4,344 08		6 99	6,397 96
Sixth district*	1,500 00		1,497 89	399 99	42 46	110 05	120 04	144 00		6,651 98		38 02	8,965 41
Total	13,227 71	108 63	13,119 08	3,485 34	549 23	280 40	498 53	594 00	63 0	34,080 34	3,446 70	105 54	56,116 02
KANSAS.													
Kansas*	2,184 12	11 95	2,172 17	1,425 00	162 78	104 85	214 50	360 00	44 9	12,163 97	994 96	27 29	17,643 13

KENTUCKY.													
First district	13,059 21	20 33	931 12	8,660 91	109 75	112 50	55 85	6 25	210 82	1,000 00	1,972 01	6 21	1,978 22
Second district*	25,771 26	51 65	10,685 42	9,701 58	92 85	150 00	20 34		83 12	1,149 99	3,887 96	75 40	3,963 36
Third district*	14,381 54	29 77	1,477 60	9,328 46	706 87	140 00	20 28	13 50	40 69	1,125 00	1,542 64	4 46	1,547 10
Fourth district*	41,806 26	44 84	25,943 42	10,351 27		170 00	21 85	9 00	176 71	1,750 01	3,379 50	30 14	3,409 64
Fifth district	34,209 03	43 03	13,135 03	12,248 99			48 00	44 50	120 52	2,499 96	6,111 90	70 43	6,181 63
Sixth district*	39,006 80	44 40	19,803 10	11,169 76	75 60	250 00	77 50	9 00	57 69	1,800 00	5,764 13	140 50	5,904 63
Seventh district*	69,219 50	134 50	41,957 90	15,083 81		430 00	99 90	12 30	199 54	2,300 00	9,136 65	200 62	9,336 67
Eighth district*	13,944 46	12 61	3,897 90	6,829 68	54 30	110 00	8 00	7 00	95 54	800 00	2,143 74	25 30	2,168 04
Ninth district*	13,416 50	20 56	4,271 64	5,517 22	167 35	350 00	57 98	7 00	104 18	658 75	2,282 38	34 82	2,317 20
Total	264,814 55	401 48	192,103 27	88,891 68	1,206 72	1,712 50	409 70	99 55	1,088 81	13,083 71	36,218 61	567 88	36,806 49
LOUISIANA.													
First district	36,840 51	93 41		21,714 39		300 00	18 84	44 50	84 91	4,075 80	4,470 03	37 97	4,508 00
Second district	17,356 57	34 71	6,451 58	12,710 76		300 00	36 39	10 00	108 33	1,724 98	2,493 66	6 32	2,499 98
Third district	14,318 88	71 25		9,078 63					198 33	2,902 36	2,493 46	6 32	2,499 78
Total	68,515 96	189 37	6,451 58	43,503 78		600 00	55 23	54 50	390 53	8,003 14	9,457 15	50 61	9,507 76
MAINE.													
First district*	9,375 00	17 15	999 00	−4,516 60		300 00	38 93	16 75	81 40	1,125 00	2,297 32	14 35	2,311 67
Second district	6,544 55	12 02		4,368 50		100 00	60 91	14 00	92 36	434 84	1,524 06	3 48	1,527 54
Third district	5,769 48	9 39		3,762 50		88 00	51 53	3 00	1 50	434 66	1,311 09	2 81	1,514 10
Fourth district	5,031 05	6 21		2,631 23		72 00	13 27	15 63	15 00	585 00	1,497 89	2 11	1,500 00
Fifth district*	5,635 04	11 36		3,389 20		100 00	29 47	14 00	49 09	375 00	1,678 48	11 61	1,690 09
Total	32,375 12	56 13	999 00	18,817 80		658 00	214 12	63 38	170 18	2,943 69	8,509 04	34 36	8,543 40
MARYLAND.													
First district	11,278 17	15 32	219 64	8,952 71		120 00	98 72	9 75	1 00	433 33	1,662 66	6 06	1,668 72
Second district	14,812 39	21 21	7,499 51	9,763 96		700 00	11 39	17 75	51 90	400 00	2,647 75	29 91	2,677 66
Third district	46,591 26	73 21	3,767 80	30,981 37			20 00	37 68	100 86	1,000 00	4,951 84	29 02	4,990 86
Fourth district	14,520 50	20 69	3,196 93	6,522 01		50 00	12 00	14 50	33 99		3,140 13	83 63	3,224 76
Fifth district*	17,900 82	19 48		9,495 76		45 00	31 88	60 25	19 12	799 98	4,131 90	63 66	4,215 56
Total	104,713 14	150 16	14,683 88	65,715 81		915 00	174 06	139 93	206 87	6,323 31	16,554 29	223 98	16,777 56
MASSACHUSETTS.													
First district*	13,166 29	14 90		8,248 72		200 00	74 03	20 12	19 72	720 00	3,883 70	78 89	3,962 50
Second district*	9,449 01	15 21	4,369 05	6,117 98		200 00	48 40	12 00	97 35	1,123 32	1,830 66	14 85	1,865 51
Third district	32,765 69	44 68	4,335 25	18,356 10		1,000 00	254 41		107 63	3,696 67	4,968 63	22 16	5,010 79
Fourth district	22,648 79	20 09	1,250 96	10,459 65		550 00	74 00	12 00	50 53	2,024 00	5,142 86	37 55	5,180 41
Fifth district	16,350 16	22 46	2,026 92	9,796 13		175 00	13 44	26 00	48 94	1,650 00	3,460 39	7 83	3,468 22
Sixth district	16,946 22	18 74		8,031 10		350 00	108 00	13 00	33 14	1,699 98	3,933 58	28 10	3,971 06

Including items belonging to previous fiscal years not before adjusted.

G.—Statement showing the expenses of assessing the internal revenue taxes in the several collection districts, &c.—Continued.

District	Gross compensation.	Tax.	Net compensation.	Clerk hire.	Stationery.	Printing and advertising.	Postage and express.	Rent of assessors.	Survey of distilleries.	Net compensation of assist-ant assessors.	Net compensation of store-keepers.	Tax on compensation of ass't assessors and store-keepers.	Total.
MASSACHUSETTS—Con.													
Seventh district	$2,403 81	$3 97	$2,399 84	$1,537 50	$23 20	$3 50	$70 18	$250 00	$4	$8,190 80		$15 36	$12,475 02
Eighth district*	2,099 67	4 17	2,095 53	1,460 00	190 33	17 75	73 45	400 00	5	8,103 32		15 34	12,345 10
Ninth district	1,803 99	3 16	1,800 83	1,060 00	50 90	19 50	93 99	200 00	36	9,961 32	$246 96	18 34	13,490 00
Tenth district*	4,085 32	52 35	4,032 97	1,475 03	84 03	24 62	0 70 29	250 00	38	10,220 56	2,465 92	20 85	18,661 64
Total	33,851 90	262 94	33,588 96	16,466 97	705 47	148 99	880 19	3,575 00	79 03	97,464 98	14,688 06	207 09	167,397 92
MICHIGAN.													
First district	4,454 66	18 01	4,436 65	1,551 00	66 35	9 50	15 00	500 00		11,294 82	1,250 96	23 92	19,124 98
Second district*	1,732 16	9 98	1,722 18	815 31	1 45	24 70	29 54	200 00		5,889 67	664 00	13 95	9,373 40
Third district*	2,716 21	62 90	2,653 31	929 97	57 86	18 25	35 65	150 00	26 5	6,636 17		12 58	10,481 71
Fourth district*	1,708 42	8 40	1,700 02	825 00	44 85	22 60	8 85	143 75		5,565 08		10 85	8,310 12
Fifth district*	1,607 02	5 59	1,601 41	825 70	138 25	14 50	55 55	155 00		7,019 83		46 35	9,810 24
Sixth district*	2,608 72	57 89	2,550 83	929 48	49 37	29 35	138 76	178 45		7,857 86		24 59	12,734 10
Total	14,827 17	162 77	14,664 40	5,876 46	358 10	119 40	283 35	1,327 20	26 5	45,263 43	1,914 96	134 24	69,833 85
MINNESOTA.													
First district*	1,722 72	13 33	1,709 39	400 00	73 69	4 50		100 00		6,382 57		17 09	8,670 15
Second district*	2,095 75	17 06	2,078 69	857 30	143 95	45 00	101 41	300 00		8,656 59	166 96	26 61	12,349 90
Total	3,818 47	30 39	3,788 08	1,257 30	217 64	49 50	101 41	400 00		15,039 16	166 96	43 70	21,020 03
MISSISSIPPI.													
First district	2,500 00	6 32	2,493 68	1,425 00	117 18		21 50	255 00		7,904 58		26 64	12,216 04
Second district*	3,108 27	26 08	3,082 19	1,750 00	190 14	61 75	47 04	300 00		15,433 30		106 51	20,872 42
Third district*	5,362 36	113 30	5,249 06	1,555 00	110 95	14 20	156 37	412 50		17,455 13	216 04	136 15	23,169 25
Total	10,970 63	145 70	10,824 93	4,730 00	424 27	75 95	224 91	967 50		40,795 01	216 04	269 30	58,258 61
MISSOURI.													
First district*	6,349 56	61 52	6,288 04	3,780 00	208 47	21 00	30 00	1,000 00		20,079 14	4,810 71	59 83	36,217 36
Second district*	1,708 24	6 62	1,701 62	875 00	298 16	63 32	232 18	180 00	123 03	7,908 75	394 00	14 71	11,711 08

Third district	3,443 19	50 07	3,309 12	1,249 97	442 23	41 60	149 73	200 00		5,435 81	526 96	12 10	10,917 46
Fourth district*	2,377 51	13 05	2,364 46	469 82	38 73	39 45	10 28	132 00		5,153 11	687 73	15 42	8,734 36
Fifth district*	3,070 65	71 46	3,603 19	1,400 82	145 90	89 45	153 54	290 30		12,873 38		62 06	19,248 49
Sixth district*	4,453 19	49 66	4,403 53	1,599 96	187 74	59 25	234 13	420 00		20,520 85	4,459 76	63 05	31,885 22
Total	22,016 34	252 38	21,763 96	9,374 75	1,321 23	313 62	809 86	2,222 30	128 05	71,971 04	10,809 16	227 17	118,713 97
MONTANA.													
Montana	3,000 00	8 42	2,991 58	1,044 06	99 80		31 40	500 00		11,060 24	1,592 66	60 01	17,319 74
NEBRASKA.													
Nebraska*	2,821 97	41 11	2,780 86	900 00	107 41	5 03	36 66	240 00	42 50	7,539 00	1,502 08	14 59	13,154 11
NEVADA.													
Nevada*	2,740 00	15 82	2,724 18	1,075 00	40 73	251 00	10 00	180 00		7,904 41		53 25	12,185 32
NEW HAMPSHIRE.													
First district	1,799 89	6 33	1,793 56	598 00	12 43	11 50	42 00	60 00		4,467 27		9 78	7,196 76
Second district	1,901 24	3 14	1,898 10	930 00	37 33	20 50	47 78	150 00		4,907 37		10 92	7,991 08
Third district	1,632 08	9 71	1,642 37	576 00	35 17	17 50	53 43	80 00	26 40	3,972 35	212 00	8 36	6,403 22
Total	5,333 21	19 18	5,334 03	2,104 00	84 93	49 50	143 21	290 00	26 40	13,346 99	212 00	29 06	21,591 06
NEW JERSEY.													
First district	1,687 93	7 60	1,680 93	939 97	28 25	11 40		150 00		11,597 48		19 35	14,369 78
Second district*	3,103 99	38 26	3,065 73	1,200 00	75 43	7 50	44 41	200 00		8,414 13		19 63	13,007 32
Third district	3,769 83	29 92	3,739 92	1,499 99	95 27	14 10	44 99	217 50	47 40	13,252 45		25 60	20,449 93
Fourth district*	3,615 83	62 58	3,553 25	1,149 99	151 92	23 80	80 25	200 00	109 80	15,298 08	1,605 32	30 24	20,510 44
Fifth district	4,105 19	14 59	4,090 60	1,108 33		36 00	9 98	125 00		20,054 26		30 60	27,575 39
Total	16,282 78	152 35	16,130 43	7,888 26	350 22	92 80	179 73	892 50	157 20	68,616 40	1,605 52	125 42	95,913 06
NEW MEXICO.													
New Mexico*	2,499 94	6 32	2,493 62	844 09	421 25	134 50	27 27	233 80		12,710 44	457 06	46 19	17,391 63
NEW YORK.													
First district* (old)	1,827 61	71 22	1,756 39	1,533 33	41 36		36 60	187 49		7,724 51	1,135 00	21 06	11,279 68
First district, (new)	1,344 44	12 52	1,344 44	1,666 67	203 76	37 50	8 59	333 33		35,040 09		43 95	39,769 38
Second district, (old)	2,635 53		2,643 01	2,400 00	132 74		3 00	749 99		17,757 14			23,685 88
Second district, (new)	1,344 45		2,344 45	2,016 67	210 77	41 80	59 72	446 69		11,035 61		88 03	15,174 39
Third district,* (old)	4,038 56	58 19	3,980 37	2,400 00	163 62		3 72	988 89		26,318 47			37,590 14
Third district, (new)	1,341 50		3,341 50	1,629 17	47 70	106 00	20 50	558 33		10,171 51	3,735 07	67 54	31,876 71
Fourth district*	2,661 18	12 80	2,648 38	4,270 50	137 39		20 00	1,041 66		23,792 25			31,855 18

* Including items belonging to previous fiscal years not before adjuste

G.—Statement showing the expenses of assessing the internal revenue taxes in the several collection districts, &c.—Continued.

District.	Gross compensation.	Tax.	Net compensation.	Clerk-hire.	Stationery.	Printing and advertising.	Postage and express.	Rent of assessors.	Survey of distilleries.	Net compensation of assistant assessors.	Net compensation of store-keepers.	Tax on compensation of ass't assessors and assistant store-keepers.	Total.
NEW YORK—Cont'd.													
Fifth district	$2,619 24	$14 31	$2,604 93	$2,662 47	$51 99	$4 00	$3 50	$466 67		$10,687 38	$24 55	$26 74	$16,505 49
Sixth district*	2,949 54	30 95	2,918 59	2,886 64	157 83	4 00	10 00	332 66		11,715 43		28 42	18,003 15
Seventh district	2,562 26	12 52	2,549 74	2,666 67	40 31			2,333 33		11,820 96		27 52	18,411 69
Eighth district	4,220 25	19 89	4,200 36	3,949 80	182 81	19 40	11 50	1,533 33		26,987 40		52 83	36,639 69
Ninth district*	4,091 40	17 94	4,073 46	3,974 97	253 66	40 50	25 69	1,140 00		22,876 94	500 82	45 84	32,943 96
Tenth district*	4,576 13	109 95	4,466 18	1,574 97	117 93	17 50	24 69	300 00		15,365 44		23 64	13,870 87
Eleventh district*	2,356 14	24 72	2,139 48	930 00	117 33	7 50	71 29	200 00		9,934 14		23 81	13,992 69
Twelfth district	1,683 34	16 32	1,339 82	1,500 00	39 48	30 54	30 00	150 00	$24 75	4,876 84		14 97	6,978 92
Thirteenth district	3,725 84	29 72	3,711 26	474 19	31 78	19 75	62 18	187 50	19 35	11,475 94		28 56	18,832 10
Fourteenth district	3,710 00	14 58	1,653 62	2,508 32	85 75	40 25	94 32	500 00	55 13	11,463 51		19 73	16,537 84
Fifteenth district*	1,500 00	11 21	3,698 69	1,875 00	60 43	17 25	31 97	400 00		4,037 37		9 53	6,125 78
Sixteenth district	1,517 65	2 99	1,497 89	540 00	11 97	24 75	30 37			3,693 89		7 10	5,629 54
Seventeenth district	1,609 53	29 62	1,514 46	1,080 00	76 65	26 25	13 86	85 00		7,165 63	63 36	18 86	11,066 70
Eighteenth district*	1,095 94	6 70	2,063 47	590 00	70 62	18 75	33 86	178 75		5,197 49		17 39	7,781 32
Nineteenth district*	1,627 94	8 50	1,667 83	642 13	46 09	1 50	39 30	125 00		5,318 19		25 48	7,808 80
Twentieth district*	2,808 94	28 54	1,619 44	750 00	111 00	19 50	89 02	125 00		7,383 31		19 87	12,231 24
Twenty-first district*	2,558 66	33 67	2,880 39	1,200 00	112 75	18 23	13 49	300 00		8,661 17	2,501 92	19 46	15,862 95
Twenty-second district*	3,215 10	32 80	2,333 12	1,722 50	91 43	28 00	72 76		2 30	9,293 18	1,741 92	18 99	17,602 43
Twenty-third district*	3,682 50	77 91	3,152 43	1,463 00	35 43	10 50	57 38	497 46	7 66	7,967 56	1,187 84	21 19	15,437 84
Twenty-fourth district*	3,167 60	7 91	3,693 70	1,780 00	51 23	12 50	55 80	125 00	6 08	4,914 22	206 96	11 20	9,221 23
Twenty-fifth district*	1,972 92	10 35	3,090 58	958 98	126 84	9 00	103 42	85 00		6,050 67		12 42	9,372 59
Twenty-sixth district*	1,908 10	32 95	1,965 01	929 97	76 09	15 50	24 70	198 09		6,132 67		13 62	9,253 00
Twenty-seventh district*	3,847 57	45 67	1,898 35	1,625 00	40 43	20 00	29 41	100 00		9,749 07	432 96	10 09	16,186 28
Twenty-eighth dist*	2,390 91	95 61	814 62	1,807 35	121 53		105 90	500 00		8,899 12	1,021 24	28 43	13,259 61
Twenty-ninth district*	6,812 45	17 74	2,345 12	2,700 00	139 12	15 50	126 44	110 34		16,942 53	7,093 47	42 11	34,117 80
Thirtieth district*	1,774 87		1,716 78	629 98	51 11		40 00	400 00		5,385 23		16 60	8,017 55
Thirty-first district*	4,252 77		1,756 96	7,066 21	570 76	43 00		67 83		51,246 36	7,831 32	110 45	71,035 91
Thirty-second district*			4,236 03										
Total	97,659 81	945 01	96,714 80	64,454 08	3,747 62	669 37	1,378 00	14,822 34	157 47	47,748 27	29,291 39	958 86	658,983 34
NORTH CAROLINA.													
First district	2,164 84	8 33	2,156 51	818 00	124 92	7 55	35 27	150 00		1,562 91		34 88	14,855 16
Second district	2,164 84	8 31	2,156 51	1,154 94	22 09	58 75	11 28	187 50		6,486 28		36 76	10,077 26
Third district	2,000 00	4 21	1,995 79	884 98	59 59	3 00	43 50	75 00	70 15	5,537 42		13 12	8,669 43
Fourth district*	3,244 43	20 54	3,223 89	1,500 00	74 32	11 00	51 14	287 50	30 00	8,821 62		31 97	18,999 41

District													
Fifth district	3,668 43	21 76	3,646 67	1,500 00	97 24	22 75	97 86	200 00	100 15	7,535 48	1,374 32	28 34	14,474 52
Sixth district	2,813 78	13 98	2,799 80	1,500 01	87 94	15 00	46 50	150 00		5,346 98	3,266 95	24 81	13,212 48
Seventh district	1,999 99	4 21	1,995 78	540 00	11 88		2 00	100 00		5,751 31	304 92	17 96	8,705 89
Total	18,056 31	81 36	17,974 95	7,897 93	477 89	118 05	287 55	1,150 00	100 15	56,041 30	4,946 39	186 64	88,994 21
OHIO.													
First district, (old)	3,375 00		3,362 41	2,811 01	54 25		20 00	900 00		16,931 43	308 00	33 20	24,387 12
First district, (new)	1,000 00	12 50	1,000 00	1,050 00	69 01	3 50	11 00	375 00		7,649 02	3,535 00	62 19	13,692 53
Second district*	12,512 05	357 71	12,512 05	1,874 00	128 87	20 15	21 79	675 00		15,640 42	12,722 46	42 21	13,557 77
Third district*	10,464 08	194 80	10,269 80	1,200 00	100 10	34 25	127 63	108 00	19 70	12,357 00	16,785 28	11 43	41,567 96
Fourth district*	5,649 08	59 59	5,589 49	1,200 00	77 89	38 00	21 79	167 50	25 10	3,263 73	6,343 24	14 55	16,697 91
Fifth district.	6,645 73	20 97	6,352 30	650 00	42 36		26 40	60 00		3,783 00	2,010 44	14 47	9,970 30
Sixth district*	5,288 63	102 33	5,184 63		42 37	34 25	68 66	100 00		4,518 80	4,507 84	17 85	15,884 01
Seventh district*	1,742 31	84 20	1,732 14	1,420 00	202 33	31 25	69 18	150 00		7,585 61	5,560 47	6 21	20,207 34
Eighth district*	5,738 31	94 40	5,643 14	600 00	19 99	34 50	4 43	100 00		4,006 43		19 92	6,478 58
Ninth district*	5,802 96	63 52	5,789 78	840 00	98 88	23 45	56 74	100 00	19 70	6,773 30	6,369 80	11 47	19,923 83
Tenth district.	4,320 26	60 45	4,789 90	1,275 00	86 06	25 25	74 60	126 75	25 10	6,093 87	2,634 96	10 87	15,312 85
Eleventh district.	2,485 11	29 43	4,955 66			23 30	10 00	60 00		5,211 86	691 78	13 62	9,885 54
Twelfth district*	1,483 21	11	1,768 48	1,898 76	18 68	19 25	116 97	125 00		6,052 36	1,948 88	16 97	14,295 55
Thirteenth district*	1,779 50	22 90	1,708 13	420 00	65 30		34 19	125 00	11 95	6,340 02	1,162 66	11 43	11,476 21
Fourteenth district*	1,716 33	12 30	1,404 50	700 00	95 30		42 70	100 80		4,632 00	408 00	8 73	7,227 22
Fifteenth district*	2,408 33	14 76	354 14	530 00	46 93	10 50	72 40	30 00	4 00	2,931 31		18 06	5,589 40
Sixteenth district*	3,385 51	14 76	2,404 60	1,500 00	165 93		43 32	130 00	32 85	4,884 59	3,264 72	11 35	10,686 26
Seventeenth district*	1,761 05	11 03	3,370 75	299 50	29 76	15 00	43 54	750 00		5,000 00	1,434 96	28 65	16,405 68
Eighteenth district.			1,750 02		160 08	12 50	31 00	100 00	24 75	9,855 85	710 96	11 63	6,738 99
Nineteenth district*					43 16					3,962 06	516 00		
Total	83,991 51	1,160 97	82,830 54	20,944 04	1,525 78	319 60	911 54	4,392 25	119 35	137,473 42	70,928 45	364 60	319,374 97
OREGON.													
Oregon	2,759 25	17 56	2,741 69	459 00	110 77	111 30	49 26	375 00	4 75	7,630 68		91 83	11,482 05
PENNSYLVANIA.													
First district, (old)*	3,569 17	36 97	3,532 20	3,066 67	20 00		2 25	600 00		16,473 40	4,634 40	57 93	23,528 92
First district, (new)	974 53	28 25	974 53	1,250 00	47 33		13 50	175 00		10,537 02	1,210 00	36 73	14,422 38
Second district*	4,313 41	28 70	4,285 34	3,450 00	104 49	15 00	7 15	600 00		19,759 09	1,307 41	51 39	29,414 06
Third district*	3,095 41	48 70	3,046 71	3,103 29	50 34		45 10	525 00		35,141 90	1,211 93	18 18	22,129 19
Fourth district*	4,827 34	61 26	4,766 08	2,908 29	111 86		11 50	600 00		24,276 95	1,075 64	38 74	31,756 32
Fifth district*	3,085 70	35 68	3,050 11	2 139 94	89 90	6 00	45 00	500 00	21 00	14,996 61	386 58	21 78	21,160 09
Sixth district*	1,913 64	44 82	1,891 50	999 95	50 45	12 00	8 35	250 00		11,259 68		21 78	11,885 59
Seventh district*	2,775 81	22 14	2,744 17	1,050 00	72 87	3 00	54 40	225 00		9,392 43	3,249 92	14 48	12,675 38
Eighth district*	3,361 98	31 31	3,332 67	1,250 00	112 16	11 60	18 10	200 00	42 84	9,259 58	4,583 19	26 70	13,320 05
Ninth district*	2,899 63	57 56	2,842 07	999 95	25 44	10 00	23 65	200 00		7,562 16	260 00	26 70	19,854 09
Tenth district*	2,519 78	51 36	2,468 52	899 97	69 74	17 50	52 01	110 00		6,450 00		11 66	11,939 14
Eleventh district*	2,407 02	25 54	2,381 48	975 02	102 17	18 25	77 32	162 50	17 25	7,364 00	962 84	18 63	10,094 29
Twelfth district*	1,956 37	24 41	1,931 96	816 67	34 99	28 00	14 94	60 00		5,343 66	1,304 20	23 17	12,073 84
Thirteenth district*													9,551 67

* Including items belonging to previous fiscal years not before adjusted.   † Complete returns for the district not received at this office.

G.—Statement showing the expenses of assessing the internal revenue taxes in the several collection districts, &c.—Continued.

District	Gross compensation.	Tax.	Net compensation.	Clerk-hire.	Stationery.	Printing and advertising.	Postage and express.	Survey of distilleries.	Rent of assessors.	Net compensation of assistant assessors.	Net compensation of store-keepers.	Tax on compensation of ass't assessors and store-keepers.	Total.
PENNSYLVANIA.—Con.													
Fourteenth district*	$2,101 18	$18 55	$2,032 63	$1,125 00	$33 45	$25 00	$13 12	$2 50	$150 00	$9,543 99	$3,100 88	$19 67	$16,074 07
Fifteenth district*	2,945 87	26 92	2,918 95	1,500 00	94 07	13 62	41 65		200 00	12,588 09	6,007 98	29 20	21,366 16
Sixteenth district*	1,873 26	19 81	1,853 45	866 61	13 21	24 10	30 75		50 00	8,626 34	10,315 66	42 77	22,148 92
Seventeenth district*	1,602 83	15 16	1,587 67	369 00	54 77	14 50	101 81		88 46	3,839 90	83 16	6 98	6,480 90
Eighteenth district*	1,782 92	16 24	1,766 68	689 97	42 62		8 50		87 50	8,153 08	400 00	19 95	11,112 36
Nineteenth district*	2,474 69	57 85	2,416 84	928 00	47 53	18 50	103 41		119 91	8,036 62	1,020 18	20 49	12,582 38
Twentieth district*	2,573 90	34 43	2,539 57	1,350 00	71 17	14 00	52 66		148 33	9,857 00	1,017 91	44 11	12,814 60
Twenty-first district*	5,351 63	74 85	5,276 78	1,200 00	88 43	9 25	76 67		41 75	8,743 39	16,788 08	44 16	32,295 83
Twenty-second dist*	4,421 35	22 21	4,399 14	1,640 99	103 35	15 00	20 97		800 00	15,024 22	4,816 88	27 63	26,881 51
Twenty-third district*	3,675 03	35 73	3,639 28	1,500 00	61 33	14 12	34 07		300 00	9,711 12	3,966 00	23 68	18,114 60
Twenty-fourth dist*	3,697 13	38 73	3,858 35	723 28	70 35				106 66	5,311 65	12,563 76	27 98	22,723 99
Total	73,649 77	868 09	72,781 68	37,016 67	1,396 02	310 99	963 01	245 62	6,590 11	261,045 11	87,465 92	737 55	463,005 13
RHODE ISLAND.													
First district*	3,478 06	13 25	3,464 81	1,901 92	42 72	24 50	33 23			14,680 89	226 96	36 73	20,375 03
Second district	1,533 44	3 78	1,529 66	690 00	11 55	16 63	18 19		200 00	5,250 36		11 30	7,716 38
Total	5,011 50	17 03	4,994 47	2,591 92	54 27	41 12	51 42		200 00	19,931 25	226 96	48 03	28,091 41
SOUTH CAROLINA.													
First district*	4,403 54	77 88	4,325 66		467 03	7 00	95 80	18 75	165 50	9,365 90	24 00	115 92	14,469 64
Second district*	2,657 20	14 15	2,643 02	249 99	2 00	14 00	17 44		240 00	8,730 95		49 92	11,657 40
Third district*	2,698 63	21 94	2,676 69	1,110 00	116 07	10 50	52 75			9,652 54		65 86	13,858 55
Total	9,759 37	114 00	9,645 37	1,359 99	585 10	31 50	165 99	18 75	405 50	27,749 39	24 00	231 00	39,985 59
TENNESSEE.													
First district	2,000 00	4 21	1,995 79	866 00	55 26	11 50	25 98	44 60	92 00	2,926 58	374 96	10 39	5,973 11
Second district	1,995 88	4 21	1,991 67	1,275 00	76 41	6 00	65 00	206 00	234 00	6,155 98	131 52	9 25	10,296 62
Third district*	2,282 74	5 16	2,277 58	1,374 98	192 51		98 00	88 50	255 00	7,029 57		11 71	11,565 16
Fourth district*	2,000 00	4 21	1,995 79		39 06	13 25	30 77		144 00	5,302 08	3,330 80	22 78	13,544 25
Fifth district*	3,616 49	38 05	3,578 44	1,800 00	101 16	47 55	42 19	24 00	330 00	11,922 64	5,304 96	30 84	23,157 94
Sixth district*	2,000 00	4 21	1,995 79	1,032 66	36 99	3 00	4 00	57 90	137 50	5,587 78	1,280 84	13 72	10,191

Seventh district*	2,011 57	2,006 79	4 78	1,125 00	24 81	20 20	21 00	96 00		4,688 57		9 76	7,982 37
Eighth district*	2,820 18	2,796 95	23 23	2,000 00	145 19	17 00	44 40	600 00		11,651 60	171 32	33 30	16,826 06
Total (TEXAS)	18,726 66	18,638 80	88 06	10,123 64	671 39	123 50	330 94	1,885 50	421 00	57,674 80	9,594 40	141 75	99,466 97
First district*	3,086 92	3,035 65	31 27	1,627 40	2 40		73 77	400 00		6,931 18		53 33	12,016 63
Second district*	2,500 00	2,493 68	6 32	1,425 00	78 65	19 50	89 76	360 00		9,381 96		35 68	13,812 48
Third district	2,391 90	2,385 58	6 32	1,325 00	406 51	111 75	73 53	400 00	52 50	12,437 74		183 89	17,064 00
Fourth district*	2,790 97¼	2,773 56	16 71	1,500 00	97 06			480 00		18,106 96		172 70	23,193 96
Total (UTAH)	10,769 09	10,708 47	60 62	5,877 40	584 62	131 25	237 08	1,640 00	52 50	46,857 84		445 54	66,089 16
Utah*	2,493 68	2,487 36	6 32	909 22	94 70	51 00	83 65	600 00	52 50	6,305 91	769 47	34 93	11,301 31
First district	1,500 00	1,497 89	2 11	41 60	21 84	8 75	79 00	187 20	34 60	3,743 42		10 17	5,579 70
Second district	1,500 00	1,497 89	2 11	161 50	53 99	14 50	98 65	62 00		2,683 06		5 43	4,607 09
Third district	1,988 80	1,974 75	14 05	544 93	47 63	33 70	60 14	200 00	34 60	7,078 66		66 29	9,940 01
Total (VERMONT)	4,988 80	4,970 53	18 27	748 03	123 56	56 95	238 79	449 20	34 60	13,505 14		81 89	20,126 80
First district*	1,748 98	1,735 24	13 74	240 00	44 92		27 75			6,067 68		21 34	8,187 59
Second district*	3,318 56	3,299 36	19 20	1,457 70	181 56	93 80	52 67	72 00		11,294 93	830 96	21 05	17,650 92
Third district*	4,317 85	4,291 72	26 13	2,199 96	194 63	110 75	177 51		183 70	8,954 37		22 04	18,622 26
Fourth district*	1,956 37	1,932 10	24 27	969 56	176 04		79 38	239 99	158 95	9,312 64		24 13	12,909 71
Fifth district	4,573 12	4,536 02	37 10	1,226 66	166 41	40 50	147 52	300 00	9 10	8,925 64	106 56	26 26	15,633 01
Sixth district*	4,492 50	4,456 03	36 47	1,500 00	307 04	33 75	236 87	191 67	16 32	12,995 01	9,130 44	32 73	27,009 77
Seventh district*	1,899 67	1,860 28	39 11	900 00	39 81	2 00	92 87	150 00		6,740 81	1,296 66	19 02	10,953 36
Eighth district*	1,500 00	1,497 89	2 11	454 99	53 81		92 66	250 00		4,963 43	180 00	9 02	7,319 08
Total (VIRGINIA)	21,207 05	21,629 58	178 47	8,958 87	1,164 22	210 80	839 06	1,203 66	363 06	69,964 51	14,147 94	176 49	118,485 70
Washington	3,000 00	2,991 58	8 42	485 00	160 99	17 00	19 05	300 00		4,924 86	865 00	10 88	9,763 48
First district*	2,673 78	2,663 11	10 67	1,200 00	106 99	22 00	29 75		16 00	6,554 89	1,034 96	8 89	11,727 70
Second district*	2,241 85	2,216 63	25 22	600 00	33 41	97 50	4 31	50 00		4,938 70	1,561 65	20 15	9,522 20
Third district	1,376 37	1,374 26	2 11	425 00	70 83	27 00	13 49	60 00		4,640 06		10 86	6,610 64
Total (WEST VIRGINIA)	6,292 00	6,254 00	38 00	2,925 00	211 23	146 50	47 55	110 00	16 00	16,153 65	2,596 61	39 90	27,760 54

* Including items belonging to previous fiscal years not before adjusted, † Complete returns for the district not received at this office,

G.—*Statement showing the expenses of assessing the internal revenue taxes in the several collection districts, &c.*—Continued.

District.	Gross compensation.	Tax.	Net compensation.	Clerk-hire.	Stationery.	Printing and advertising.	Postage and express.	Rent of assessors, &c.	Survey of distilleries.	Net compensation of assistant assessors.	Net compensation of store-keepers.	Tax on compensation of assessors and assistant store-keepers.	Total.
WISCONSIN.													
First district*	$4,985 33	$22 38	$4,963 95	$2,497 98	$111 28	$11 50	$48 76	$500 00		$13,189 42	$7,107 84	$28 55	$28,429 73
Second district*	1,743 31	10 97	1,732 34	1,375 00	109 00	22 50	130 52	104 17		6,350 86	1,606 96	11 86	11,423 03
Third district*	1,500 00	2 11	1,497 89	370 00	39 08	14 12	94 55	120 00		6,699 55		13 35	9,035 19
Fourth district*	1,500 36	13 91	1,732 45	715 00	62 41	32 35	96 74	100 00		4,298 04		17 70	7,026 99
Fifth district*	1,547 49	4 48	1,543 01	665 00	23 41	23 40	33 03	56 25		8,106 47	8,427	18 75	8,427 81
Sixth district*	1,872 27	11 63	1,860 64	540 00	124 96	19 80	189 47	240 00		7,015 73	1,606	19 32	9,990 60
Total	13,385 76	65 48	13,320 28	6,362 98	438 85	123 67	593 28	1,120 42		43,659 07	8,714 80	108 53	74,333 35
WYOMING.													
Wyoming	2,499 76	6 32	2,493 44		86 69	5 00	49 00	300 00		856 69		2 51	3,790 82

RECAPITULATION.

	Gross compensation.	Tax.	Net compensation.	Clerk-hire.	Stationery.	Printing and advertising.	Postage and express.	Rent of assessors, &c.	Survey of distilleries.	Net compensation of assistant assessors.	Net compensation of store-keepers.	Tax on compensation of assessors and assistant store-keepers.	Total.
Alabama	$11,214 49	$166 58	$11,047 91	$6,849 88	$414 95	$64 50	$220 72	$398 00	$27 90	$34,720 87	$1,186 42	$251 77	$54,931 05
Arizona	2,500 00	6 38	2,493 68		32 50	27 00	15 99	300 00		2,109 01	375 53	97	5,353 71
Arkansas	6,905 36	29 12	6,876 24	2,858 30	203 50	172 74	257 62	890 00	321 15	22,159 59	384 92	99 26	33,802 91
California	16,410 00	176 70	16,224 11	12,339 72	667 33	335 93	400 32	3,620 91		108,724 10	6,818 39	1,830 87	149,460 96
Colorado	2,500 00	42 13	2,493 68	4,000 00	58 85	129 93	68 29	480 00	137 62	31,872 56		15 73	9,018 47
Connecticut	10,793 62	61 90	10,751 49	3,518 27	260 77	43 75	383 61	755 00	127 90	1,935 16	5,803 84	60 66	54,007 32
Dakota	3,580 07	61 80	3,518 27	1,375 00	63 63	6 00	46 61	210 00		10,404 89		18 54	15,800 67
Delaware	3,061 51	16 81	3,044 70	1,425 00	98 82		77 56			8,581 56		22 47	15,138 87
District of Columbia	2,345 32	8 16	2,337 16	7,425 00	72 66	49 62	10 00	420 00	60 50	10,528 03	571 00	17 47	13,196 30
Florida	2,705 90	12 50	2,693 40	1,425 00	179 43	106 50	166 50	275 00		56,778 74	1,532 52	37 38	15,374 30
Georgia	10,886 27	46 35	10,839 80	7,385 00	585 98	48 50	413 01	600 00		5,117 91	60,810 63	290 87	77,948 82
Idaho	2,516 36	7 13	2,509 23	948 00	16 00	69 50	17 00	1,301 32	137 70	115,095 12		41 74	10,110 57
Illinois	67,302 23	1,011 60	66,290 63	15,477 28	1,220 81	364 43	1,114 14	2,554 43	416 00	56,829 13	23,998 68	407 54	963,065 17
Indiana	40,168 78	458 61	39,710 17	8,598 39	646 35	239 65	441 52	1,345 67	63 00	34,080 34	3,446 70	153 31	132,225 97
Iowa	13,227 71	108 63	13,119 08	3,485 34	549 23	290 40	498 53	594 00	44 90	12,163 97	994 96	105 64	56,116 63
Kansas	2,184 12	11 95	2,172 17	1,425 00	162 87	104 65	214 50	360 00		214 12		27 29	17,643 13
Kentucky	36,806 49	587 88	36,219 61	13,083 71	1,088 81	95 55	409 70	1,712 68	1,206 72	43,503 78	122,103 27	401 48	264,814 55
Louisiana	9,507 76	50 61	9,457 15	9,003 14	350 88	54 63	55 23	1,600 00			6,451 58	189 37	68,515 96
Maine	8,543 40	34 36	8,509 04	2,943 60	170 18	63 38	214 12	658 00		18,817 80	999 00	56 13	32,375 12

Maryland	16,777 56	223 28	16,554 28	6,323 31	206 87	139 93	174 06	915 00	79 30	65,715 81	14,683 88	150 16	104,713 14
Massachusetts	33,851 90	262 94	33,568 96	16,466 97	705 47	148 99	880 19	3,575 00	79 30	97,464 98	14,688 06	207 09	167,597 92
Michigan	14,827 17	162 77	14,664 40	5,876 40	358 10	119 40	923 35	1,327 20	26 55	45,263 43	1,914 96	134 24	69,633 85
Minnesota	3,818 47	30 39	3,788 08	1,257 00	217 64	49 50	101 41	400 00		15,039 16	166 96	43 70	21,020 05
Mississippi	10,970 63	145 70	10,824 93	4,730 00	424 27	75 95	224 91	967 50	198 05	40,795 04	216 04	269 30	58,238 61
Missouri	22,016 34	252 38	21,763 96	9,374 75	1,321 52	313 62	809 86	2,322 30		71,971 04	10,809 16	227 17	118,713 97
Montana	3,000 00	8 40	2,991 58	1,044 06	99 80		35 95	500 00		11,060 24	1,592 66	60 01	17,319 74
Nebraska	2,821 97	41 11	2,780 86	900 00	107 41	5 00	36 66	240 00	42 50	7,339 00	1,502 68	14 56	13,154 71
Nevada	2,740 00	15 82	2,724 18	1,075 00	40 73	251 00	1 00	180 00		7,904 41		53 25	12,185 32
New Hampshire	5,353 21	19 18	5,334 03	2,104 00	84 93	49 50	143 21	290 00	26 40	13,346 99	212 00	29 06	21,991 06
New Jersey	16,283 78	152 35	16,130 43	7,888 26	350 22	92 80	179 73	892 50	137 20	68,616 40	1,605 52	125 42	95,913 00
New Mexico	2,499 94	6 32	2,493 62	844 09	421 25	134 50	27 27	232 80*		12,710 44	457 66	46 19	17,321 63
New York	97,659 81	945 01	96,714 80	64,454 08	3,747 02	669 37	1,378 00	14,822 34	157 47	447,748 30	29,291 39	958 86	659,983 34
North Carolina	18,056 31	81 36	17,974 95	7,897 93	477 89	118 05	27 27	1,150 00	100 15	56,041 42	4,946 39	186 64	88,994 21
Ohio	83,991 51	1,160 97	82,830 54	20,944 04	1,525 78	319 60	911 54	4,382 25	119 35	137,473 42	70,928 45	364 60	319,374 97
Oregon	2,759 25	17 56	2,741 69	439 00	110 77	111 00	49 26	375 00	4 75	7,630 68		21 83	11,462 65
Pennsylvania	73,649 77	863 09	72,781 68	37,016 67	1,586 02	41 12	963 01	6,390 11	245 68	261,931 11	97,465 92	733 55	468,005 13
Rhode Island	5,011 50	17 03	4,994 47	2,391 92	54 27	31 50	55 42			19,931 25	226 96	48 03	28,091 41
South Carolina	9,759 37	114 00	9,645 37	1,339 99	585 10	123 50	165 99	200 00	18 75	27,749 39	24 00	231 00	39,985 50
Tennessee	18,726 86	88 06	18,638 80	10,123 64	671 39	131 25	330 94	1,898 50	42 00	57,674 74	9,594 40	141 75	99,466 97
Texas	10,769 09	60 63	10,703 47	5,877 40	384 62	51 05	283 85	1,640 00	52 50	46,857 84		443 54	66,089 16
Utah	2,493 68	6 32	2,487 36	909 22	94 70	50 95	83 65	449 20		6,305 91	769 47	34 93	11,301 31
Vermont	4,988 80	18 27	4,970 53	748 00	123 56	210 00	238 06		34 60	13,363 14		34 93	20,126 80
Virginia	21,807 05	178 47	21,628 58	8,938 87	1,164 92	146 50	839 06	1,303 06	368 08	69,954 51	14,147 94	176 49	118,485 70
Washington	3,000 00	8 42	2,991 58	485 00	160 09	19 55	47 53	110 00		4,924 80	865 00	10 88	9,763 48
West Virginia	6,292 00	38 00	6,254 00	2,225 00	211 23	123 67	583 28	110 00	16 00	16,153 65	2,596 61	39 90	27,760 54
Wisconsin	13,385 76	65 48	13,320 28	6,362 98	86 69	5 00	49 00	1,129 42		43,639 07	8,714 80	108 53	74,333 35
Wyoming	2,499 76	6 32	2,493 44					300 00		856 69		9 51	3,790 82
Grand total	762,970 77	7,839 98	755,132 49	320,936 83	22,865 18	6,107 39	14,172 50	64,294 31	4,541 95	2,341,598 65	512,898 76	8,986 49	4,042,548 06
Add amount of taxes													16,824 77
													4,059,372 83

13 F

* Including items belonging to previous fiscal years not before adjusted.

NOTE.—The districts marked "old" and "new" are those that have been consolidated, and show the amount of expenses previous and subsequent to consolidation.

NOTE.—There was refunded by distillers during the fiscal year, as pay of store-keepers, the sum of $557,235 41, which was covered into the Treasury as miscellaneous receipts. This, if not accounted for as receipts, could be deducted from the expenses, it being by law a reimbursement in form of the pay of store-keepers.

H.—*Statement showing the expenses of collecting the internal revenue taxes in the several collection districts, including the commissions, salaries, and extra allowances of the collectors ; the office expenses which are paid out of the commissions and extra allowances ; and the assessments and collections from July 1, 1870, to June 30, 1871.*

District.	Gross compensation.	Tax.	Net compensation.	Stationery and blank-books.	Postage.	Express and dep. money.	Advertising.	Tota. expense of collecting.	Expenses of administering office.	Assessments.	Collections.
ALABAMA.											
First district*	$7,032 27	$37 67	$7,894 60	$111 79	$33 37		$9 00	$8,046 43	$4,836 24	$143,313 99	$132,325 53
Second district*	10,615 95	15 72	10,600 23	116 36	202 99			10,935 30	15,596 41	115,536 53	135,724 42
Third district*	7,912 63	42 74	7,869 89	84 60	82 00		52 50	8,121 73	4,123 76	30,681 69	57,556 72
Total	26,460 85	96 13	26,364 72	312 75	318 36		61 50	27,103 46	24,556 41	295,532 23	325,606 07
ARIZONA.											
Arizona	2,976 98		2,976 98		6 00			2,982 98	476 98	13,446 54	18,027 92
ARKANSAS.											
First district*	5,520 54	12 01	5,508 53	102 07	127 67	$20 00	46 50	5,811 78	5,415 07	60,833 99	48,015 04
Second district*	7,792 91	2 11	7,790 80	106 33	114 00	63 66		8,070 90	6,133 15	47,359 53	56,547 35
Third district*	1,950 86	9 84	1,941 02		44 00	6 20		2,001 06	1,468 67	54,604 10	29,152 84
Total	15,264 31	23 96	15,240 35	208 40	285 67	69 86	46 50	15,894 74	13,036 89	162,857 62	133,715 23
CALIFORNIA.											
First district, (old)*	16,588 70	16 85	16,571 85	205 13	113 65	154 99	97 51	16,907 48	11,888 70	2,112,376 44	2,261,159 43
First district, (new)*	4,687 50		4,687 50	237 13	161 50	531 87	34 83	5,338 63	3,437 50	1,501,423 72	598,678 41
Second district*	7,115 36	47 43	7,067 93	84 35	194 50	192 68	57 50	7,940 91	7,624 17	206,439 94	229,178 73
Third district	11,049 17	100 00	10,949 17	299 07	147 05	593 31	47 00	11,745 47	7,360 00	175,557 69	145,139 75
Fourth district	9,500 77	111 93	9,388 84	252 75	331 75	593 20	119 88	10,725 58	8,169 47	247,290 11	316,692 11
Fifth district	11,820 00		11,820 00	224 74	260 48	392 20		12,817 30	8,346 00	124,629 61	100,833 05
Total	60,761 50	276 21	60,485 29	1,303 17	1,208 93	1,845 05	356 72	65,475 77	46,825 84	4,367,777 51	3,661,680 49
COLORADO.											
Colorado	10,394 56	30 22	10,364 34	66 45	81 65		139 00	10,681 65	5,652 93	57,711 17	69,993 65
CONNECTICUT.											
First district	9,139 27	24 83	9,114 44	66 31	123 00		9 40	9,337 98	3,606 89	673,241 35	643,343 19
Second district	7,307 51	10 37	7,297 14	1 00	234 52		10 75	7,553 78	3,502 09	386,033 11	376,938 54
Third district	5,046 32	19 59	5,028 73	54 99	159 00		67 60	5,329 92	1,400 00	176,952 37	154,831 98

Fourth district	6,082 36	17 82	6,064 54	55 71	155 50		18 15	6,311 72	2,253 99	245,216 92	254,317 90
Total	27,577 46	72 61	27,504 85	178 01	672 02	3 00	105 90	28,533 39	10,764 97	1,462,343 75	1,429,431 61
DAKOTA.											
Dakota*	1,737 96	3 40	1,734 56	28 61	31 00		7 50	1,808 07	250 56	6,798 00	8,091 60
DELAWARE.											
Delaware	7,756 70	28 33	7,728 37	43 08	197 80		23 55	8,021 13	2,350 00	397,465 74	446,875 10
DISTRICT OF COLUMBIA.											
District of Columbia*	6,179 20	12 56	6,166 64	65 25	96 30		58 00	6,398 95	2,029 07	261,112 27	268,575 42
FLORIDA.											
Florida*	15,306 57	76 89	15,229 68	122 34	202 67		83 10	15,714 68	9,763 77	127,517 12	126,374 42
GEORGIA.											
First district*	4,306 71		4,306 71	167 87	54 48		28 25	4,557 31	4,408 00	133,386 24	104,767 75
Second district	7,382 05	19 57	7,362 48	66 61	155 22		51 00	7,654 88	5,972 73	116,817 55	147,640 97
Third district*	8,746 66	33 60	8,713 06	93 67	108 72		6 75	8,955 40	6,987 11	158,701 74	205,536 86
Fourth district	16,928 84	151 34	16,777 50	201 77	126 22		59 00	17,315 83	9,339 90	292,192 90	288,607 04
Total	37,364 26	204 51	37,159 75	529 92	444 24		145 00	38,483 42	26,697 04	701,098 43	746,752 62
IDAHO.											
Idaho	8,006 34	31 67	7,974 67	18 75	36 49		18 00	8,079 57	3,287 55	39,101 65	61,587 23
ILLINOIS.											
First district	23,439 64	71 64	28,068 00	441 77	535 83		48 00	29,165 24	11,228 75	9,246,000 63	7,269,582 65
Second district	6,248 67	30 55	6,218 12	76 33	145 74		42 40	6,513 14	2,096 73	245,143 41	242,293 93
Third district*	10,236 33	33 98	10,200 35	71 00	162 37		10 40	10,479 70	3,316 39	658,432 44	676,413 62
Fourth district	11,696 14	33 65	11,662 49	136 93	140 50		69 75	12,042 32	3,532 00	1,156,133 92	1,219,746 69
Fifth district	17,041 97	51 98	16,989 99	89 82	225 00		58 50	17,944 98	5,676 63	2,602,131 91	2,556,906 76
Sixth district	7,716 10	18 07	7,698 03	84 24	98 74		12 70	7,944 90	2,639 63	405,012 83	374,974 90
Seventh district	11,010 83	16 88	10,993 95	108 53	232 10	33 20	51 65	11,423 31	4,171 30	798,025 15	803,238 17
Eighth district	12,208 87	32 88	12,175 99	144 46	250 00			12,613 33	4,625 01	1,193,681 73	1,093,764 60
Ninth district*	4,294 09	13 47	4,280 62	17 26	102 96		37 55	4,511 86	1,601 11	75,921 18	86,703 62
Tenth district	4,765 96	12 68	4,753 28	69 14	160 46		23 00	5,018 56	1,601 50	83,761 49	126,564 00
Eleventh district*	3,168 58	8 95	3,160 53	56 92	209 98		40 50	3,473 06	3,268 89	43,533 55	34,991 54
Twelfth district	10,090 24	25 96	10,064 28	90 14	286 98		107 72	10,555 89	4,494 98	748,356 19	776,101 74
Thirteenth district	5,223 36	7 74	5,215 62	43 03	200 00		62 50	5,530 89	4,014 38	98,877 44	116,475 56
Total	131,840 78	359 53	131,481 25	1,431 57	2,390 18	33 20	562 97	136,688 70	53,960 43	17,361,070 87	15,333,256 97

* Including items which belonged to previous fiscal years not before adjusted.

† Complete returns not received from collector.

H.—Statement showing the expenses of collecting the internal revenue taxes, &c.—Continued.

District	Gross compensation.	Tax.	Net compensation.	Stationery and blank-books.	Postage.	Express and dep. money.	Advertising.	Total expense of collecting.	Expenses of administering office.	Assessments.	Collections.
INDIANA.											
First district	$10,305 26	$10 45	$10,294 81	$196 27	$22 19		$29 75	$10,543 47	$2,156 85	$841,217 28	$768,081 08
Second district	4,777 75	10 06	4,767 69	161 97	81 00		67 00	5,087 72	1,630 40	153,168 04	119,059 93
Third district	8,711 61	5 61	8,709 00	95 49	88 73		59 90	8,953 72	5,237 48	497,503 87	497,163 60
Fourth district*	15,359 61	51 43	15,308 18	285 37	300 50	$10 00	27 50	15,922 98	3,361 66	2,143,553 87	1,814,694 99
Fifth district*	5,408 47	37 48	5,370 99	68 54	131 49		59 15	5,663 50	839 00	143,401 40	160,048 76
Sixth district	7,599 24	32 18	7,497 06	99 94	97 14		33 00	7,785 47	2,223 53	340,522 53	379,628 90
Seventh district*	8,253 87	27 19	8,226 68	118 08	59 82		59 45	8,468 37	1,756 53	412,419 43	427,511 83
Eighth district	8,362 90	36 74	8,325 46	169 86	275 00		51	8,865 51	1,996 37	543,395 33	419,269 27
Ninth district*	4,935 98	13 83	4,921 45	91 05	25 02		14 50	5,065 85	1,469 11	138,936 42	141,650 35
Tenth district*	4,111 75	8 93	4,102 82	24 63	41 80	85 92	64 55	4,328 65	1,218 13	77,888 97	87,658 34
Eleventh district*	3,948 86	5 09	3,943 77	56 17	116 28		15 00	4,136 31	2,083 04	36,257 53	35,914 63
Total	81,706 90	238 99	81,467 91	1,357 96	1,238 97	95 92	420 80	84,820 55	23,918 60	5,353,264 65	4,840,169 68
IOWA.											
First district	5,451 99	13 51	5,438 48	103 53	161 00		36 75	5,755 27	2,333 72	167,751 15	195,198 64
Second district	9,733 79	94 39	9,639 40	211 65	243 02		142 95	10,334 71	4,676 57	272,403 17	286,620 23
Third district*	10,418 04	142 20	10,275 84	273 98	365 00		50 05	11,014 89	2,534 85	366,355 27	351,578 73
Fourth district	3,765 39	8 63	3,756 76	100 75	191 39	50	58 99	4,110 03	1,889 25	60,355 27	92,513 11
Fifth district	5,185 42	2 11	5,183 31	138 66	209 37		37 99	5,361 63	2,885 04	66,967 63	95,135 45
Sixth district	12,741 19	35 93	12,705 96	173 35	256 19	41 20	103 60	13,311 53	2,042 04	64,049 90	96,733 94
Total	47,295 82	296 77	46,999 05	991 22	1,425 97	41 70	430 55	50,185 96	16,369 86	998,442 01	1,097,380 10
KANSAS.											
Kansas*	12,002 27	119 29	11,882 98	370 57	468 99		237 00	13,078 83	5,914 80	232,807 83	238,834 28
KENTUCKY.											
First district	5,623 82	10 18	5,613 64	232 05	276 00		14 70	6,166 57	2,184 32	203,011 34	206,575 31
Second district	6,952 05	10 86	6,941 19	100 31	209 42		10 00	7,335 60	3,680 14	376,517 69	317,039 16
Third district	5,044 84	8 61	5,036 23	65 97	167 40	63 82		5,278 21	1,420 00	140,604 98	138,623 22
Fourth district*	9,236 49	19 84	9,216 65	127 57	366 60	744 90	14 00	10,489 56	5,800 95	432,093 60	400,552 12
Fifth district*	13,569 99	30 14	13,539 15	448 88	132 50		119 00	14,270 17	5,836 00	2,168,537 67	2,060,535 10
Sixth district*	14,648 82	32 76	14,616 06	375 03	127 01		14 00	15,165 46	5,182 15	1,884,489 83	1,757,777 60
Seventh district*	13,305 07	39 82	13,265 25	375 54	353 90		21 50	14,056 01	6,397 20	1,292,367 93	1,242,806 83

Eighth district	126,813 23	70,312 16	1,484 10	5,253 80	15 00	808 72	160 14	78 59	4,996 81	3 26	5,000 07
Ninth district	129,359 31	119,087 83	3,575 00	5,280 65	28 50		86 32	105 16	5,655 17	5 30	5,060 47
Total	6,440,101 88	6,707,043 03	35,559 86	83,296 03	237 20	808 72	1,879 49	1,929 70	78,280 15	160 77	78,440 92
LOUISIANA.											
First district*	2,222,709 46	2,283,482 68	14,104 80	20,012 66	90 50	12 40	12 00	196 45	19,684 46	16 85	19,701 31
Second district*	117,025 30	151,067 41	12,501 40	15,732 27	46 50	200 00	75 02	76 54	15,257 89	76 41	15,334 21
Third district*	98,574 01	92,142 01	5,647 70	10,229 56	122 50	87 35	35 59	103 65	9,838 82	51 35	9,880 17
Total	2,438,308 77	2,526,692 10	32,253 90	45,974 19	259 50	299 75	122 61	376 64	44,771 06	144 61	44,915 69
MAINE.											
First district*	210,578 17	198,552 25	885 94	5,897 63	14 50		102 00	32 48	5,669 52	19 13	5,688 65
Second district*	59,714 93	53,917 09	928 10	3,393 88	38 92		117 90	58 55	3,166 30	12 25	3,178 55
Third district	56,699 25	56,974 84	894 00	3,443 39	13 50		172 34	56 58	3,191 41	9 56	3,200 97
Fourth district	56,332 22	43,000 15	717 67	3,247 39			29 14	31 98	3,174 15	12 82	3,186 97
Fifth district	43,060 01	29,436 46	1,127 86	2,894 17	15 75		59 35	27 27	2,785 25	6 55	2,791 80
Total	426,384 58	381,880 79	4,552 87	18,876 40	82 67		540 63	206 16	17,986 63	60 31	18,046 94
MARYLAND.											
First district*	111,003 13	70,679 92	1,000 00	6,291 46	31 00		167 24	161 03	5,914 44	17 75	5,933 19
Second district	287,454 00	323,300 62	2,551 80	6,765 18	38 03		143 97	115 74	6,453 29	14 15	6,467 44
Third district*	2,717,667 00	2,766,992 28	9,696 96	13,788 55	33 50		221 00	279 52	13,419 66	23 07	13,254 93
Fourth district*	180,865 51	151,603 16	2,852 40	5,571 50			40 23	87 35	5,419 53	24 39	5,443 92
Fifth district*	433,571 77	421,933 70	3,300 00	8,632 83	72 00		235 83	113 34	8,185 57	26 15	8,211 72
Total	3,732,501 43	3,736,509 68	19,400 36	41,049 98	174 53		808 27	756 98	38,204 69	105 51	39,310 20
MASSACHUSETTS.											
First district*	490,712 74	374,522 48	2,537 42	7,330 05	41 34		182 08	59 53	7,010 82	36 23	7,047 05
Second district	126,398 39	179,248 97	2,750 84	4,962 52	20 75		165 39	32 56	4,757 48	6 50	4,763 98
Third district	2,007,528 30	1,512,020 64	5,103 40	10,706 37	25 25		233 60	182 59	10,220 46	46 74	10,267 20
Fourth district	1,264,757 40	1,406,510 12	5,455 77	12,060 56	3 25		174 00	187 59	11,694 47	21 25	11,715 72
Fifth district	465,932 30	492,465 96	5,794 30	8,431 65	26 00		138 38	72 51	8,171 16	23 60	8,194 76
Sixth district	604,700 84	828,660 45	5,144 28	9,447 26			195 00	69 94	9,150 89	31 43	9,182 32
Seventh district	283,906 10	169,782 66	2,482 89	6,588 18	28 50		206 82	6 80	6,325 19	13 87	6,339 06
Eighth district*	222,047 22	964,153 64	1,396 00	6,053 60	3 50		368 13	61 70	5,696 35	24 12	5,720 47
Ninth district*	169,214 76	169,215 10	2,364 50	5,552 69	62 00	1 00	233 50	91 93	5,134 98	10 28	5,165 26
Tenth district	623,168 69	530,944 36	2,473 96	9,177 10	19 00		275 00	76 21	8,768 23	38 61	8,806 69
Total	6,258,366 76	5,917,554 38	32,403 36	80,346 24	229 59	1 00	2,071 30	841 74	76,950 08	232 63	77,292 71

* Including items which belonged to previous fiscal years not before adjusted.   † Complete returns not received from collector.

H.—Statement showing the expenses of collecting the internal revenue taxes, &c.—Continued.

District	Gross compensation.	Tax.	Net compensation.	Stationery and blank books.	Postage.	Express and dep. money.	Advertising.	Total expense of collecting.	Expenses of administering office.	Assessments.	Collections.
MICHIGAN.											
First district*	$12,978 55	$81 34	$12,897 21	$221 89	$255 03	$1 00	$50 20	$13,506 67	$4,127 80	$2,024,532 23	$2,110,545 28
Second district*	4,839 57	7 61	4,831 96	46 53	149 50	......	15 00	5,077 62	2,891 50	180,235 18	130,228 38
Third district.	4,716 80	7 51	4,709 29	65 33	178 66	2 45	35 80	4,994 61	2,763 97	106,236 93	121,679 83
Fourth district*	5,153 12	33 90	5,119 92	51 00	121 00	31 50	74 60	5,440 57	2,406 14	112,157 19	115,588 68
Fifth district.	4,570 53	2 11	4,568 42	50 80	154 87	1 00	23 10	4,823 80	2,879 05	38,873 94	107,053 00
Sixth district*	6,345 42	10 42	6,335 00	108 57	150 12	......	29 70	6,631 81	2,568 25	211,236 12	202,390 41
Total	38,623 99	142 19	38,431 80	544 14	1,009 20	35 95	232 80	40,444 08	17,636 01	2,695,291 59	2,847,485 58
MINNESOTA.											
First district*	7,847 67	37 96	7,809 71	317 05	305 49	68 50	29 50	8,561 21	5,308 12	94,924 92	87,370 56
Second district*	5,202 60	11 02	5,191 58	169 54	303 37	......	21 50	5,699 11	4,517 49	211,516 42	173,331 28
Total	13,050 27	48 98	13,001 29	486 69	608 86	68 50	51 00	14,260 32	9,825 61	306,441 34	260,701 84
MISSISSIPPI.											
First district	6,730 26	......	6,730 26	145 76	30 90	37 54	39 00	6,983 46	4,884 50	31,855 02	55,330 55
Second district*	12,993 84	......	12,993 84	185 20	147 04	1 50	13 25	13,340 83	10,862 88	104,985 57	133,000 44
Third district.	5,744 95	......	5,744 95	121 66	40 92	......	......	5,907 53	596 07	54,587 46	39,785 70
Total	25,469 05	......	25,469 05	432 62	218 86	39 04	52 25	26,231 82	16,273 45	191,428 05	228,136 69
MISSOURI.											
First district*	26,303 62	17 22	26,286 40	669 91	276 04	......	31 90	27,261 47	21,180 91	6,497,643 32	5,378,372 62
Second district*	8,435 60	22 90	8,412 70	97 30	396 51	86 87	124 40	9,146 68	6,174 59	113,715 80	88,025 61
Third district.	6,024 08	19 78	6,004 30	52 93	201 00	......	67 00	6,342 01	1,377 00	239,647 70	252,409 56
Fourth district*	6,060 27	15 68	6,044 59	98 14	163 50	......	101 88	6,422 79	1,342 00	329,903 42	258,394 79
Fifth district †	5,383 98	44 76	5,339 22	146 04	135 69	194 12	3 00	5,815 63	3,860 73	85,546 19	163,312 08
Sixth district †	22,227 96	77 11	22,150 85	381 63	502 01	19 00	158 85	23,285 45	8,781 46	1,150,672 73	551,110 45
Total	74,435 51	197 45	74,238 06	1,445 95	1,694 75	229 99	487 03	78,289 23	42,716 69	8,437,129 16	6,696,625 11
MONTANA.											
Montana*	17,958 39	74 05	17,884 34	181 25	126 40	220 67	31 09	18,517 71	12,290 79	115,555 63	107,972 59
NEBRASKA.											
Nebraska	10,514 60	......	10,514 60	84 74	66 96	......	25 00	10,691 30	5,456 35	311,732 33	210,290 02

NEVADA*........	6,435 09	93 14	6,341 95	252 26	33 70	772 07		7,493 12	6,976 94	81,597 96	96,514 41
NEW HAMPSHIRE.											
First district.....	5,121 64	14 69	5,106 95	55 09	151 26		10 00	5,338 99	1,133 49	155,936 64	162,164 08
Second district...	5,372 38	19 69	5,352 69	11 20	109 24		37 00	5,529 82	1,439 71	182,267 53	187,237 87
Third district....	3,034 42	13 26	3,021 16	57 68	168 56		48 75	3,309 41	315 00	50,237 90	51,147 22
Total.........	13,528 44	47 64	13,480 80	124 97	429 04		95 75	14,178 22	2,888 20	388,432 07	400,549 17
NEW JERSEY.											
First district....	4,894 23	12 59	4,881 64	55 87	56 00		28 00	5,006 10	2,237 82	117,139 43	142,198 35
Second district*...	7,623 34	29 11	7,594 23	76 76	221 36			7,949 36	2,492 84	494,190 62	401,741 21
Third district....	8,090 78	20 72	8,070 06	255 51	377 17		57 90	8,781 36	3,088 73	716,392 07	443,773 40
Fourth district...	6,710 64	13 60	6,697 04	255 48	154 50	77 50		7,198 12	2,590 17	384,472 60	302,365 46
Fifth district....	10,717 61	7 04	10,710 57	78 30	139 00		44 00	10,978 91	7,452 96	1,507,338 31	1,173,821 35
Total.........	38,036 60	83 06	37,953 54	721 92	947 93	77 50	129 90	39,913 85	17,862 52	3,219,383 63	2,464,029 77
NEW MEXICO........	5,970 57	6 32	5,964 25	276 25	57 45		113 50	6,417 77	3,053 90	28,567 67	34,937 26
NEW YORK.											
First district, (old)...	6,099 03	37 68	6,061 35	5 50	155 38	10 00	42 50	6,312 41	1,580 96	135,518 14	489,529 01
First district, (new)...	12,663 85	74 99	12,663 62	214 41	146 99		105 50	13,130 95	6,461 39	2,317,808 22	1,644,653 56
Second district, (old)*..	10,506 61	20 59	10,431 67	61 78	79 00		151 30	10,741 39	5,411 11	1,349,028 84	1,840,861 75
Second district, (new)...	9,117 31	16 85	15,915 72	410 50	199 69		79 68	9,806 58	7,437 07	1,530,790 68	1,135,829 91
Third district, (old)*...	13,936 31	32 41	13,834 85	591 50	125 50		53 00	16,129 12	13,779 42	659,310 52	672,583 32
Third district, (new)...	18,601 63	16 65	18,364 78	95 67	260 50	19 60	55 00	13,921 38	1,774 11	2,036,492 71	580,661 84
Fourth district*...	6,889 07	22 80	11,960 51	59 25	94 60		23 85	13,068 04	14,004 11	663,588 90	1,965,753 35
Fifth district....	11,277 36	10 85	7,960 80	49 37	325 80		146 65	11,703 22	7,957 92	1,651,981 49	644,966 54
Sixth district....	7,149 09	26 62	15,112 90	100 66	47 80		66 00	7,298 16	7,579 95	744,536 90	1,073,427 36
Seventh district*...	15,129 75	28 64	11,290 24	37 02	293 40	40 40	75 95	15,801 61	3,378 80	4,424,484 36	802,009 38
Eighth district*...	11,331 78	37 92	11,361 02	213 41	158 00	10 40	35 00	11,687 60	10,004 95	1,294,103 46	3,646,437 70
Ninth district*...	9,339 64	11 92	6,617 92	93 62	242 42	48 20	128 94	9,742 89	5,120 96	439,533 75	1,618,557 12
Tenth district....	5,645 96	49 78	6,763 07	94 01	189 96		102 00	5,970 52	4,676 85	190,131 06	763,856 48
Eleventh district...	5,801 04	24 76	10,563 59	100 67	138 02		72 25	7,090 19	2,032 89	230,245 22	205,725 54
Twelfth district...	5,924 37	4 67	7,250 43	151 40	109 02		12 75	6,460 30	2,364 19	193,483 11	280,142 76
Thirteenth district...	10,615 19	6 68	3,117 28	232 54	225 62	15 69	32 50	11,159 09	3,983 89	2,076,133 62	247,009 62
Fourteenth district...	3,975 19	9 64	2,939 96	213 21	203 10		90 00	7,622 09	2,500 35	319,607 27	1,094,694 04
Fifteenth district...	3,121 95	10 08	4,813 48	71 55	86 04			3,255 73	1,062 24	52,204 56	377,518 74
Sixteenth district*...	2,945 94		4,503 33	34 99	91 46			3,108 91	1,794 84	41,533 96	54,064 29
Seventeenth district...	4,823 52			39 61	224 70			5,134 20	3,487 16	110,618 51	48,198 12
Eighteenth district...	4,513 41			85 98	95 50			4,777 16	3,131 16	55,092 33	125,245 21
Nineteenth district.†..				62 45		7 10					101,340 63

* Including items which belong to previous fiscal years, not before adjusted.   † Complete returns not received from collector.

H.—Statement showing the expenses of collecting the internal revenue taxes, &c.—Continued.

District	Gross compensation.	Tax.	Net compensation.	Stationery and blank-books.	Postage.	Express and dep. money.	Advertising.	Total expense of collecting.	Expenses of administering office.	Assessments.	Collections.
NEW YORK—Cont'l.											
Twentieth district	$4,693 25	$7 21	$4,686 04	$24 86	$160 73		$37 25	$4,915 09	$1,575 73	$118,138 68	$119,325 03
Twenty-first district*	7,819 54	25 10	7,794 44	150 25	122 12		18 50	8,111 41	1,136 56	419,859 41	448,890 77
Twenty-second district*	10,133 03	39 27	10,093 76	73 47	279 23	$11 27	43 00	10,529 00	2,478 08	834,402 90	668,697 44
Twenty-third district	8,078 19	21 72	8,036 47	91 35	130 00		51 00	8,350 54	3,034 43	370,640 02	439,210 93
Twenty-fourth district*	8,132 67	20 68	8,111 99	83 12	257 14	12 75	26 50	8,511 68	1,557 36	680,623 75	420,488 72
Twenty-fifth district*	4,457 23	7 25	4,449 98	32 89	175 15		20 50	4,665 77	2,838 59	120,658 00	115,696 06
Twenty-sixth district*	5,379 85	8 35	5,371 50	57 59	63 04		19 95	5,528 23	2,690 79	210,170 49	190,217 71
Twenty-seventh district*	6,332 18	57 50	6,274 68	25 54	100 28		21 62	6,538 02	2,641 86	184,042 08	164,341 50
Twenty-eighth district*	9,310 10	40 21	9,269 89	43 85	177 35		35 55	9,554 55	9,310 10	533,977 25	666,905 11
Twenty-ninth district	4,284 27	13 25	4,271 02	98 25	115 48		41 00	4,539 00	1,953 15	104,372 80	93,988 51
Thirtieth district*	13,196 03	23 49	13,161 54	260 41	219 47		34 00	13,704 91	4,942 50	1,612,873 18	1,737,076 08
Thirty-first district*	7,908 64	173 77	7,734 87	151 50	306 09		11 58	8,462 93	775 69	71,313 06	89,269 27
Thirty-second district	32,654 70	37 91	32,616 79	690 40	766 90	28 12	14 40	34,121 40	25,154 70	4,490,298 82	4,464,146 31
Total	311,905 70	968 03	310,937 67	4,857 57	6,554 04	203 53	1,653 32	325,171 16	161,218 79	30,987,299 82	28,970,679 38
NORTH CAROLINA.											
First district*	6,617 52		6,617 52	48 21	138 22		18 00	6,822 95	2,270 28	39,673 37	56,889 89
Second district*	6,500 00	6 32	6,493 68	82 47	192 96		37 50	6,815 93	3,613 00	101,964 80	86,533 49
Third district	10,377 52	4 91	10,373 31	91 90	24 50		41 00	10,471 06	5,324 35	73,584 92	36,752 77
Fourth district	15,400 75	39 49	15,361 26	215 56	137 93	48 79	106 00	15,867 24	10,843 30	414,001 97	407,765 35
Fifth district*	10,372 00		10,372 00	60 64	145 13		34 00	10,651 57	7,372 00	639,472 54	627,384 36
Sixth district	8,504 27	12 69	8,491 58	62 33	88 50		40 75	8,698 85	5,850 00	248,955 20	225,329 81
Seventh district	4,700 12	10 22	4,692 90	69 52	39 25			4,811 89	3,373 66	35,973 60	28,068 35
Total	62,475 18	72 93	62,402 25	549 78	760 49	48 79	246 25	64,086 49	38,646 59	1,553,626 40	1,464,726 62
OHIO.											
First district, (old)	8,685 80	16 11	8,669 78	128 99	60 00			8,874 88	5,150 04	1,476,094 77	1,411,285 14
First district, (new)	5,392 13		5,392 13	20 80	96 00		12 00	5,510 93	2,294 49	2,065,965 88	1,521,173 59
Second district*	23,967 61	338 01	23,629 60	148 05	34 00		25 70	24,156 56	7,272 62	3,232,281 61	3,031,867 81
Third district	16,147 75	42 30	16,105 45	199 03	285 15		34 00	16,657 73	5,979 00	2,744,549 94	3,394,113 06
Fourth district	10,821 48	31 37	10,790 11	47 31	61 15		39 50	10,963 96	2,998 25	835,310 03	780,851 02
Fifth district	6,275 49	10 63	6,265 15	84 31	74 31		22 50	6,473 99	1,971 00	314,643 54	240,110 85
Sixth district*	11,311 49	23 59	11,271 62	127 03	157 96		58 75	11,618 28	4,336 07	837,448 76	751,110 31
Seventh district*	10,008 67	67	9,985 08	134 15	89 06		13 75	10,336 83	4,338 70	725,099 24	765,455 98
Eighth district	2,728 68	4 50	2,724 18	105 20	33 28		52 75	2,880 91	1,664 01	40,851 15	44,609 19
Ninth district	9,803 95	29 30	9,774 65	33 89	20 48			9,911 07	2,737 50	611,866 75	695,422 54

Tenth district, (old)*	11,177 21	22 90	11,155 01	172 79	128 20			32 95	11,511 15	3,834 96	1,133,751 10	1,109,678 62
Eleventh district*	8,337 13	25 43	8,311 70	126 49	36 95			37 50	8,537 87	2,018 84	313,146 89	415,728 76
Twelfth district	8,120 98	40 85	8,080 13	70 85	83 00			27 00	8,302 63	1,679 53	327,466 63	364,456 48
Thirteenth district	6,402 57	13 93	6,388 64	28 73	73 10			23 75	6,598 15	3,172 88	261,435 23	258,811 34
Fourteenth district	4,377 25	13 33	4,364 92	44 13	74 64			54 00	4,723 39	2,059 64	67,518 79	95,908 49
Fifteenth district*	4,511 41	9 57	4,501 84	96 67	97 52			40 50	4,667 03	1,873 07	94,957 52	102,180 49
Sixteenth district	4,479 60	9 60	4,471 49	67 67	149 01			7 00	1,699 40	1,699 00	82,626 15	98,125 56
Seventeenth district*	6,474 91	30 25	6,444 66	171 83	214 00			30 75	6,802 75	1,774 00	242,691 20	255,604 04
Eighteenth district*	10,275 32	19 55	10,255 77	181 85	177 82		60	43 12	10,701 92	6,360 66	1,537,331 17	1,003,667 37
Nineteenth district	4,243 02	6 53	4,236 49	9 25					4,473 81	1,243 78	80,935 01	91,434 05
Total	173,542 52	723 92	172,818 60	2,059 86	2,019 03	1 40		578 32	178,201 13	64,148 44	17,024,995 36	15,358,594 68
OREGON.												
Oregon	8,128 81	39 49	8,089 32	54 71	31 97	27 21		56 40	8,299 10	5,868 15	110,960 48	151,432 32
PENNSYLVANIA.												
First district, (old)*	9,229 80	13 66	9,216 14	135 29				21 60	9,386 69	5,190 17	2,196,719 72	1,819,706 13
First district, (new)	2,674 97		2,674 97	41 50					2,716 47	903 77	398,609 05	289,975 89
Second district	11,497 57	137 61	11,497 57	224 53	125 00			72 40	1,919 50	4,460 33	2,187,164 58	1,776,009 66
Third district	8,723 91	151 67	8,586 30	117 44	105 00			14 00	6,960 75	752,671 43		562,362 36
Fourth district*	13,977 27	229 73	13,825 00	256 61	300 00			53 00	14,586 68	4,705 75	1,392,336 73	1,368,098 12
Fifth district*	12,590 53	28 81	12,030 50	76 30	196 00				356,035 71	2,196 35		477,038 48
Sixth district	7,787 75	28 53	7,758 94	81 85	103 21			13 75	7,966 56	1,972 50	359,096 76	454,192 66
Seventh district*	4,866 49	25 52	4,840 97	60 19	104 00				59,619 68	1,112 39		136,131 19
Eighth district	6,124 09	23 99	6,100 81	78 65	59 60			10 50	5,070 68	1,606 00	230,064 85	351,227 90
Ninth district*	7,861 98	25 32	7,840 30	33 53	134 80				6,272 44	2,500 00	364,282 15	452,591 41
Tenth district	5,715 88	31 03	5,684 85	50 88	114 28			14 00	5,895 04	4,081 91	146,652 11	221,587 39
Eleventh district	5,898 66	33 28	5,864 86	83 41	202 00				8,079 91	737 92	166,984 07	239,805 53
Twelfth district	5,666 96	31 03	5,850 80	78 21	170 00			28 00	6,133 50	9,565 60	248,330 98	226,665 58
Thirteenth district*	4,705 78	20 87	4,684 91	52 92	136 96			88 00	6,141 17	158,427 87	58,427 03	115,686 03
Fourteenth district	5,538 09	18 37	5,327 72	92 32	152 43			59 25	4,956 60	2,164 64	134,187 64	176,132 01
Fifteenth district	6,619 95	16 83	6,603 12	83 02	161 13			45 00	5,772 31	2,954 34	297,507 23	290,988 30
Sixteenth district	5,157 40	18 62	5,141 18	47 57	200 55	63 23			8,895 75	2,258 59	138,325 87	152,137 30
Seventeenth district	4,163 32	20 29	4,143 03	43 56	117 74			16 50	5,314 71	2,095 42	56,159 91	88,777 22
Eighteenth district*	5,376 78	32 42	5,344 36	119 18	93 58			21 75	4,539 67	1,724 30	107,511 31	138,221 29
Nineteenth district	6,900 74	6 32	6,894 42	60 03	187 58				4,428 21	9,187 31	199,784 83	168,865 63
Twentieth district	8,896 52	54 57	8,845 95	193 32	391 47			20 00	7,507 31	4,125 38	187,630 31	275,050 68
Twenty-first district	11,729 85	44 83	11,684 02	105 93	221 38			13 75	12,070 93	3,895 50	685,609 00	822,550 52
Twenty-second district	11,453 52	19 30	11,434 60	171 91	161 48			6 75	1,793 79	5,251 45	1,362,556 45	1,419,363 85
Twenty-third district*	8,480 92	27 36	8,453 20	85 50	150 00			36 50	8,752 52	3,835 15	534,799 85	552,983 79
Twenty-fourth district*	9,288 72	63 36	9,223 36	89 54	257 92			14 25	9,650 43	3,385 20	363,370 69	472,463 55
Total	190,795 91	1,040 43	189,755 48	2,356 63	3,873 23	63 23		492 85	197,581 87	74,709 94	13,266,641 29	12,953,845 56

* Including items which belong to previous fiscal years not before adjusted.

H.—*Statement showing the expenses of collecting the internal revenue taxes, &c.*—Continued.

District	Gross compensation	Tax	Net compensation	Stationery and blank-books	Postage	Express and dep. money	Advertising	Total expense of collecting	Expenses of administering office.	Assessments	Collections
RHODE ISLAND.											
First district*	8,510 08	20 19	8,489 89	34 69	153 17		40 25	8,764 67	3,539 61	596,194 96	$600,603 39
Second district	3,700 32	11 72	3,688 60	36 58	43 50	$26 48	24 50	3,804 50	1,049 17	75,891 50	73,636 56
Total	12,210 40	31 91	12,178 49	71 27	196 67	26 48	64 75	12,569 57	4,598 78	672,016 46	674,439 95
SOUTH CAROLINA.											
First district*	13,032 77	40 61	12,992 16	180 28	155 95		53 75	13,422 55	6,669 95	35,417 52	49,023 26
Second district	4,603 27	18 85	4,584 42	58 83	82 75		122 05	4,866 69	2,803 66	106,904 52	115,081 90
Third district*	5,437 69		5,437 69	95 63	80 26	50	83 00	5,697 58	4,544 00	384,723 46	108,753 72
Total	23,073 73	59 46	23,014 27	334 93	318 96	50	258 80	23,986 62	14,017 61	507,045 50	272,858 88
TENNESSEE.											
First district*	8,699 35	33 43	8,665 92	49 00	92 50		22 50	8,863 55	4,844 56	93,379 30	68,159 67
Second district	6,458 28	2 08	6,456 20	37 57	50 00			6,545 55	4,810 85	85,235 88	53,819 12
Third district	7,731 97	4 21	7,727 76	79 71	50 17		5 50	7,867 55	3,920 00	77,455 48	54,463 48
Fourth district	4,320 41		4,320 41	70 04	45 00		22 50	4,457 55	2,787 94	66,028 81	61,720 15
Fifth district	3,745 43	8 42	3,737 01	132 00	167 00		17 75	8,062 43	4,745 43	361,243 59	331,521 62
Sixth district*	3,150 15	28 89	3,121 26	3 25	3 48			3,155 21	322 97	140,651 05	74,567 55
Seventh district	7,141 94	53 79	7,088 15	25 02	58 50		25 75	7,251 61	2,433 34	96,710 49	100,847 16
Eighth district	7,221 26	11 94	7,209 32	94 57	138 08		15 70	7,460 64	4,221 26	212,015 30	214,212 64
Total	52,468 79	142 76	52,326 03	490 24	604 73		109 70	53,673 46	28,086 35	1,132,719 90	955,311 39
TEXAS.											
First district*†	8,280 71	285 70	7,995 01	16 21				8,290 71		139,879 32	118,295 90
Second district*†	7,814 17	84 88	7,729 29	108 88	25 30	946 36	3 00	7,858 68	5,256 20	90,762 14	97,920 56
Third district	9,436 60	52 37	9,384 23	5 00	52 85		36 50	10,581 68	6,415 68	59,723 51	106,000 00
Fourth district*	25,466 99	464 78	25,002 21		352 20	532 65	150 05	26,506 68	11,299 54	133,107 29	134,670 66
Total	50,993 47	887 73	50,110 74	130 09	430 35	1,479 01	189 55	53,227 47	22,971 42	354,072 26	386,887 12
UTAH TERRITORY.											
Utah Territory*	26,551 09	174 88	26,376 21	263 80	200 00	222 40		27,237 52	4,601 50	36,062 47	69,877 65
VERMONT.											
First district	4,644 80	30 78	4,614 02	45 92	125 00			4,815 52		77,641 66	114,480 08

Second district*	3,993 45	15 77	3,977 68	7 30	140 45		42 50	4,176 43	149 00	79,729 77	86,988 33
Third district*	3,987 44	12 27	3,975 17		92 80		49 25	4,130 79	1,394 25	72,880 88	85,335 22
Total	12,625 69	58 82	12,366 87	53 22	358 28		91 75	13,128 94	1,543 25	230,252 31	298,603 63
VIRGINIA.											
First district*	4,893 07	31 04	4,862 03	52 78	64 08		4 00	5,013 93	5,245 69	31,809 24	27,627 33
Second district*	9,737 64	16 98	9,730 66	171 81	92 63		16 95	10,019 05	5,205 64	801,936 82	784,562 40
Third district*	12,363 87	16 51	12,367 36	229 65	164 84		27 03	12,805 36	5,439 91	2,611,004 94	2,451,723 78
Fourth district*	4,232 94	8 30	4,223 94	117 49	55 00		33 50	4,440 23	5,136 70	97,075 70	74,303 04
Fifth district†	13,606 33	106 52	13,497 83	252 21	228 81		21 00	14,106 37	5,112 44	1,891,760 10	1,636,532 70
Sixth district	6,567 06	6 43	6,560 63	311 85	253 12		35 00	7,167 01	4,119 63	1,167,837 50	168,792 11
Seventh district	4,713 93	2 69	4,711 94	115 64	155 65		36 10	5,022 52	4,919 05	97,816 89	110,576 37
Eighth district	2,939 76	15 87	2,923 89	42 18	146 50	1 80	20 25	3,146 69	478 70	39,410 83	47,008 24
Total	59,073 92	296 34	58,867 58	1,293 61	1,160 65	1 80	195 80	61,725 18	29,717 96	5,758,642 02	5,311,145 97
WASHINGTON TERRITORY.											
Washington Territory†	7,651 29		7,651 29	249 79	71 21	95 60		8,067 89	5,112 83	22,056 05	32,888 25
WEST VIRGINIA.											
First district	6,797 71	21 92	6,775 79	14 75	106 00		49 50	6,967 96	1,650 00	152,110 77	336,086 94
Second district*	6,061 11	32 04	6,029 07	3 00	101 56		20 50	6,186 17	600 00	105,079 03	140,552 94
Third district	2,626 47	8 06	2,612 41	133 21	71 86		81 73	2,913 29	1,796 87	49,163 60	37,366 61
Total	15,485 29	62 02	15,423 27	150 96	279 42		151 75	16,067 42	4,046 87	306,353 40	504,006 49
WISCONSIN.											
First district*	12,132 43	31 51	12,100 92	100 10	135 01		44 05	12,411 59	4,243 34	1,439,615 81	1,455,143 15
Second district	4,883 94	17 14	4,866 80	68 07	186 75		84 50	5,223 26	1,239 50	110,037 95	131,723 37
Third district	3,417 08	2 11	3,414 97	28 55	112 71	8 40	30 65	3,597 39	2,418 54	46,375 55	63,902 83
Fourth district*	4,332 08	17 77	4,314 31	27 06	141 00		20 30	4,520 64	1,660 00	82,883 96	95,802 16
Fifth district*	10,130 95	52 11	10,078 84	21 85	97 69	2 40	15 50	10,268 39	3,191 81	87,870 86	106,239 60
Sixth district*	10,176 96	79 89	10,097 07	25 20	112 99		40 63	10,355 78	5,239 51	132,589 28	141,896 11
Total	45,073 44	200 53	44,872 91	270 83	786 15	10 80	235 83	46,377 05	17,392 70	1,899,373 41	1,996,619 26
WYOMING TERRITORY.											
Wyoming Territory	2,936 89	11 42	2,925 47	83 76	15 00	8 75	28 25	3,072 65	286 30	9,609 41	14,563 12

NOTE.—The districts marked "old" and "new" are those that have been consolidated, and show the amount of expenses previous and subsequent to consolidation. *Including items which belong to previous fiscal years not before adjusted. †Complete returns not received from collector.

H.—*Statement showing the expenses of collecting the internal revenue taxes, &c.*—Continued.

RECAPITULATION.

District	Gross compensation	Tax	Net compensation	Stationery and blank-books	Postage	Express and dep. money	Advertising	Total expense of collecting	Expenses of administering office	Assessments	Collections
Alabama	26,460 85	36 13	26,364 72	312 75	318 36		61 50	27,153 46	24,556 41	295,532 23	325,006 67
Arizona Territory	2,976 98		2,976 98		6 00			2,982 98	476 98	13,446 54	18,027 92
Arkansas	15,254 31	23 96	15,240 35	208 40	285 67		46 50	15,894 72	13,036 89	162,857 62	133,715 23
California	60,761 50	276 21	60,485 29	1,303 17	1,208 93	89 86	356 72	65,475 37	46,825 84	4,367,777 51	3,661,680 48
Colorado Territory	10,394 56	30 22	10,364 34	66 45	81 65	1,845 05	139 00	10,631 69	5,652 93	57,711 17	69,993 65
Connecticut	27,577 46	72 61	27,504 85	178 01	672 02		105 90	28,533 56	10,764 97	1,482,343 75	1,429,431 61
Dakota Territory	1,737 96	3 40	1,734 56	28 61	31 00	3 00	7 50	1,806 07	250 56	6,798 00	8,091 60
Delaware	7,756 70	28 33	7,728 37	43 08	197 80		23 55	8,021 11	2,350 00	397,465 74	446,875 10
District of Columbia	6,179 20	12 56	6,166 64	65 25	96 50		58 00	6,398 95	2,629 07	261,112 27	266,575 42
Florida	15,306 57	76 89	15,229 68	122 34	202 67	3 00	83 10	15,714 68	9,763 77	127,517 12	126,374 42
Georgia	37,364 26	204 51	37,159 75	529 92	444 24		145 00	38,483 68	26,697 04	701,098 43	746,752 62
Idaho Territory	8,006 34	31 67	7,974 67	18 75	36 48		18 00	8,079 79	3,287 55	39,101 65	61,587 23
Illinois	131,840 78	359 53	131,481 25	1,431 57	2,820 18	33 20	562 97	136,688 70	53,960 43	17,361,070 87	15,333,256 97
Indiana	78,440 92	160 77	78,280 15	991 22	1,238 97	95 92	420 80	84,820 98	16,369 86	5,323,284 65	4,840,169 68
Iowa	47,295 82	296 77	46,999 05	929 70	1,425 07	41 70	430 55	50,185 78	35,559 86	998,442 01	1,097,380 10
Kansas	12,002 27	119 29	11,882 98	370 57	468 99		237 20	13,079 15	5,914 80	232,807 83	238,834 88
Kentucky	44,915 69	144 61	44,771 08	1,357 96	1,879 49	806 72	259 92	48,296 88	32,253 90	6,707,043 93	6,440,101 68
Louisiana	18,046 94	160 51	17,886 43	376 64	122 61	299 75	82 67	18,876 40	19,460 36	2,356,692 10	426,384 58
Maine	39,310 20	165 51	39,204 69	206 16	540 63		174 53	41,049 36	32,403 36	381,880 79	3,732,501 43
Maryland	77,202 71	252 63	76,802 71	756 98	808 27	1 00	229 39	60,346 76	17,636 61	736,509 68	6,258,366 76
Massachusetts	38,623 99	142 19	38,631 80	841 14	2,071 20	33 95	232 90	40,346 58	9,625 61	5,917,584 38	867,463 58
Michigan	13,030 27	48 98	13,020 27	544 14	1,009 30	68 50	51 06	14,965 94	46,273 69	2,695,291 39	260,701 94
Minnesota	23,469 05		25,469 05	486 69	608 86	68 04	52 25	25,231 69	12,290 79	306,441 34	228,136 69
Mississippi	74,435 51	197 45	74,238 06	432 02	618 86	329 99	487 03	78,293 75	5,456 35	139,128 05	6,696,923 11
Missouri	17,958 39	74 03	17,884 34	1,445 45	1,694 75	220 57	31 00	18,517 03	6,976 94	311,555 63	210,932 02
Montana Territory	10,514 60		10,514 60	181 25	126 40	772 07	25 00	10,691 11	81,597 20	311,732 33	400,514 41
Nebraska	6,435 09	93 14	6,480 60	84 74	66 96		95 75	7,493 08	1,732 96	81,537 96	464,027 77
Nevada	13,598 44	47 04	13,551 30	252 26	33 70	77 50	129 90	1,178 41	5,976 94	388,483 07	34,937 26
New Hampshire	38,036 60	83 06	37,953 54	194 97	493 06		113 50	39,913 77	17,962 20	3,219,383 63	28,970,879 38
New Jersey	5,970 57	66 32	5,966 23	221 92	947 93		1,653 32	6,417 36	3,053 90	28,587 67	1,468,725 62
New Mexico Territory	311,905 70		310,937 67	276 25	57 45		240 53	325,174 38	161,218 79	30,987,299 82	13,358,594 68
New York	62,475 18	968 03	310,937 67	4,857 93	6,554 04	203 53	578 32	64,090 62	38,218 50	1,553,636 40	151,432 32
North Carolina	173,542 52	72 93	62,402 25	549 78	760 49	48 79	56 40	178,201 68	64,148 14	17,084,995 36	12,953,845 56
Ohio	8,108 81	723 99	172,818 60	2,059 86	2,019 02	1 40	492 85	8,299 32	74,709 94	110,960 48	674,439 95
Oregon	190,795 91	39 49	8,089 32	55 71	31 97	27 21	64 75	197,581 38	4,568 78	13,266,641 29	272,838 83
Pennsylvania	12,210 40	1,040 43	189,755 48	2,356 65	3,873 23	63 23	258 80	12,559 56	14,017 61	672,016 46	959,311 39
Rhode Island	23,073 73	31 91	12,178 49	7 27	196 67	26 48	109 70	23,986 95	507,045 50	507,045 50	386,887 12
South Carolina	52,462 79	59 46	23,014 27	334 93	318 98	96 50	169 53	53,073 39	28,086 35	1,132,719 90	69,877 65
Tennessee	50,996 47	142 76	52,326 03	499 24	604 73			53,227 12	22,971 42	354,072 26	
Texas		887 73	50,110 74	130 09	430 35	1,479 01		27,137 65	4,601 50	36,062 47	
Utah Territory	26,551 09	174 88	26,376 21	263 69	200 00	223 40					

Vermont	12,625 69	58 82	12,566 87	53 22	358 28	....	91 75	13,198 94	1,543 25	220,252 31	988,803 63
Virginia	59,073 92	206 34	58,867 58	1,293 61	1,160 05	1 80	195 80	61,725 18	29,717 96	5,758,642 02	5,311,145 97
Washington Territory	7,651 29	....	7,651 29	249 79	71 21	95 60	....	8,067 89	5,112 83	22,056 05	32,888 25
West Virginia	15,485 44	62 02	15,423 27	150 96	279 42	....	151 75	16,067 42	4,046 87	506,353 40	504,006 49
Wisconsin	45,073 44	200 53	44,873 91	270 83	786 15	10 80	225 83	46,377 05	17,392 70	1,809,373 41	1,996,619 26
Wyoming Territory	2,936 80	11 42	2,925 47	83 76	15 00	8 75	28 25	3,072 65	286 50	9,609 41	14,563 12
Grand total	2,049,568 55	7,968 40	2,041,600 15	28,981 13	37,810 38	6,851 42	9,251 13	2,132,462 61	982,564 19	140,945,363 34	130,864,141 11

I.—*Statement of accounts of internal revenue stamp agents from April 1, 1870, to March 31, 1871.*

Dr.

To amount outstanding in agents' hands, April 1, 1870, (as per last report)...	$3,035,857 93
To amount transferred from Commissioner's account April 1, 1870, to personal accounts of match manufacturers...........................	342,612 25
To amount of stamps received from Commissioner......................	11,183,989 82
	14,562,460 00

Cr.

By amount of cash deposited with the United States Treasurer........	$10,892,024 30
*By amount allowed as commissions.................................	480,211 56
By amount of stamps returned to Commissioner......................	74,685 78
By amount allowed on affidavits of loss	10,766 85
By amount outstanding in agents' hands March 31, 1871, to be accounted for..	3,104,771 51
	14,562,460 00

Amount overpaid by agents in settlement of their accounts..........	$883 48

K.—*Statement of amounts paid for printing stamps and for stamp paper, for the Office of Internal Revenue, for the fiscal year ending June 30, 1871.*

To the Continental Bank-Note Company..............................	$255,944 99
To the American Phototype Company................................	4,628 33
To Joseph R. Carpenter	74,902 91
To Henry Skidmore..	6,623 16
To James M. Willcox & Co., (paper)	4,940 20
	347,039 59

L.—*Statement of accounts of the Commissioner of Internal Revenue for internal revenue beer stamps for the fiscal year ending June 30, 1871.*

Dr.

To amount of stamps in hands of Commissioner June 30, 1870, (as per last report)	$537,618 71
To amount of stamps received from printer.........................	7,241,666 66
To amount of stamps returned by collectors........................	42,858 83
	7,822,144 20

Cr.

By amount of stamps sent to collectors.............................	$7,571,645 00
By amount of stamps destroyed.....................................	31,972 54
By amount of stamps remaining in hands of Commissioner, to be accounted for	218,526 66
	7,822,144 20

M.—*Statement of accounts of the Commissioner of Internal Revenue for internal revenue stamps for distilled spirits, for the fiscal year ending June 30, 1871.*

Dr.

To amount of stamps in hand of Commissioner June 30, 1870, (as per last report)..	$16,310,500 00
To amount of stamps received from printer	33,412,625 00
To amount of stamps returned by collectors........................	636,275 00
	50,359,400 00

* The amount of commissions allowed to match manufacturers from April 1, 1870, to January 1, 1871, is not included herein, having been credited in the account of the Commissioner of Internal Revenue.

Cr.

By amount of stamps sent to collectors	$35,047,725 00
By amount of stamps destroyed	14,625 00
By amount of stamps remaining in hands of Commissioner, to be accounted for	15,297,050 00
	50,359,400 00

N.—*Statement of accounts of the Commissioner of Internal Revenue for internal revenue tobacco, snuff, and cigar stamps for the fiscal year ending June 30, 1871.*

Dr.

To amount of stamps in hands of Commissioner June 30, 1870, (as per last report)	$4,802,377 04
To amount of stamps received from printers	33,726,494 95
To amount of stamps returned by collectors	475,229 10
	39,004,101 09

Cr.

By amount of stamps sent to collectors	$31,964,880 72
By amount of stamps destroyed	288,239 92
By amount of stamps remaining in hands of Commissioner, to be accounted for	6,750,980 45
	39,004,101 09

O.—*Statement of accounts of the Commissioner of Internal Revenue for internal revenue stamps (adhesive) for the fiscal year ending June 30, 1871.*

Dr.

To amount of stamps in hands of Commissioner June 30, 1870, (as per last report)	$101,071 02
To amount of stamps ordered from printers	15,019,074 21
To amount of stamps returned by agents	102,024 91
To amount of discount withheld in exchange	1,921 79
	15,224,091 93

Cr.

By amount of cash deposited with the United States Treasurer	$3,649,670 62
By amount of commissions allowed	329,943 92
By amount of stamps sent to agents	10,947,500 57
By amount of stamps destroyed	291,740 12
By amount of stamps allowed on affidavits of loss	2,906 88
By amount of stamps remaining in hands of Commissioner, to be accounted for	2,329 82
	15,224,091 93

P.—*Statement of accounts of the Commissioner of Internal Revenue for internal revenue stamped foil wrappers for tobacco for the fiscal year ending June 30, 1871.*

Dr.

To amount of stamped foil wrappers received from printer, (Henry Skidmore)	$843,712 60

Cr.

By amount of stamped foil wrappers sent to collectors	$843,712 60

Q.—*Statement showing the amounts paid to certain internal revenue officers for salary and expenses; also the contingent expenses of the Office of Internal Revenue, including salary and expenses of the Special Commissioner of the Revenue, deputies, clerks, traveling expenses, &c., &c.; counsel fees, moieties and rewards, drawbacks on rum and alcohol, and taxes erroneously assessed and collected, refunded, from July 1, 1870, to July 1, 1871.*

Supervisors.	Salary.	Expenses.	Clerk-hire.	Furniture.	Rent.	Total.
E. W. Barber	$2, 255 21	$726 31	$1, 149 15	$15 00	$175 00	$4, 320 67
James R. Bayley	2, 283 08	1, 339 13	....	......	240 00	3, 862 21
Ira J. Bloomfield *	2, 488 84	932 71	1, 348 90	......	250 00	5, 020 45
John A. Bridgland *	1, 925 12	2, 960 70	1, 336 44	......	35 00	6, 257 26
Kenneth R. Cobb *	998 00	951 67	1, 005 54	......	105 33	3, 060 54
S. J. Conklin	2, 991 58	1, 002 77	1, 945 79	91 00	655 00	6, 686 14
R. G. Corwin *	271 98	20 20	135 98	......	33 34	461 50
B. R. Cowen *	2, 389 93	1, 180 48	3, 982 42	147 50	483 33	8, 183 66
Willis Drummond *	1, 824 91	889 42	749 91	......	54 17	3, 518 41
S. B. Dutcher	2, 991 58	13, 659 24	5, 634 64	32 00	1, 000 00	23, 317 46
Joe W. Dwyer	2, 991 58	2, 122 02	1, 625 78	......	129 50	6, 868 88
George W. Emery	2, 991 58	2, 446 63	1, 925 43	......	297 55	7, 661 19
I. M. Foulke	2, 991 58	2, 150 39	2, 686 00	......	1, 013 78	8, 852 65
Speed S. Fry *	1, 114 25	781 13	2, 090 90	15 00	195 00	5, 035 28
Alexander Fulton	2, 480 53	557 23	1, 725 00	20 00	....	4, 782 76
Wolcott Hamlin	2, 493 65	677 98	1, 033 68	......	24 00	4, 229 31
J. M. Hedrick *	1, 133 33	499 06	449 95	115 51	36 02	2, 233 87
Dana E. King *	1, 066 65	449 20	423 32	......	68 75	2, 007 92
W. Krzyzanowski	2, 991 58	3, 680 21	1, 890 00	......	200 00	8, 761 79
John Legro *	199 86	106 40	129 40	......	31 25	466 91
James Marr *	2, 172 24	2, 937 74	1, 341 71	......	173 00	6, 624 69
John McDonald	2, 991 68	4, 894 65	3, 359 98	260 20	720 00	12, 226 51
John O'Donnell	2, 733 21	644 24	2, 849 91	......	137 49	6, 364 85
P. W. Perry	2, 991 55	1, 885 27	1, 748 90	......	300 00	6, 925 72
Simon T. Powell *	140 11	132 21	157 13	168 52	33 75	631 72
Otis F. Presbrey	2, 991 58	1, 310 60	1, 968 69	......	570 32	6, 841 19
W. A. Simmons	2, 743 66	1, 115 27	2, 471 59	132 81	966 63	7, 429 98
N. D. Stanwood	2, 795 84	1, 129 83	1, 582 63	......	225 00	5, 733 30
W. B. Stokes *	519 17	151 60	251 39	......	52 00	974 16
Benjamin J. Sweet *	436 81	41 13	172 23	......	43 33	693 50
J. B. Sweitzer	2, 991 58	572 72	1, 425 00	......	....	4, 989 30
Alexander P. Tutton	2, 991 57	1, 002 42	1, 650 00	......	....	5, 643 99
George B. Williams *	86 82	62 16	39 13	......	....	188 11
Total	67, 460 66	53, 012 72	51, 206 42	997 54	8, 178 54	180, 855 88
Add to this amount for stationery furnished to supervisors and allowed in accounts of contractors	....	....	....	....	....	811 80
Total	....	....	....	....	....	181, 667 68

* In office a fraction of the year.

Detectives.

Name.	Salary.	Expenses.	Total.
C. C. Adams	$1,287 00	$659 60	$1,946 60
George C. Allen	1,355 31	1,020 43	2,375 74
J. N. Beach	2,197 16	1,580 35	3,777 51
Matthew Berry	366 00	332 54	698 54
Sylvanus C. Boynton	248 00	11 15	259 15
B. P. Brasher	1,727 66	1,716 52	3,444 18
E. T. Bridges	140 00	55 90	195 90
A. H. Brooks	1,332 66	619 68	1,952 34
James J. Brooks	2,405 00	506 41	2,911 41
De Witt C. Brown	451 22	244 57	695 79
John B. Brownlow	470 00	138 31	608 31
James T. Bryer	1,686 75	1,230 42	2,917 17
Willard Bullard	536 00	....	536 00
A. E. Burpee	1,862 50	1,070 21	2,932 71
Walter T. Burr	429 46	237 63	667 09
A. K. Church	225 00	155 81	380 81
D. D. Cone	48 00	41 25	89 25
John S. Delano	1,243 52	521 11	1,764 63
R. J. Easton	931 76	751 05	1,682 81
Frank E. Fowler	1,438 29	1,285 42	2,723 71
William A. Gavett	1,178 75	925 45	2,104 20
Arthur Gunther	1,559 75	2,416 25	3,976 00
Thomas Hammond, jr	1,657 66	533 43	2,191 09
A. Ward Haudy	176 00	....	176 00
Lucian Hawley	2,466 00	1,095 74	3,561 74
C. M. Horton	755 24	590 16	1,345 40
Isaac N. Hughey	432 72	7 60	440 32
D. W. Ives	430 00	45 02	475 02
William F. Keirle	512 92	....	512 92
James H. Kelly	1,328 50	666 10	1,994 60
J. J. Lamoree	2,162 01	1,573 17	3,735 18
A. N. Lewis	525 00	....	525 00
P. D. Ludington	118 80	46 95	165 75
D. H. Lyman	1,856 50	1,021 64	2,878 14
J. H. Manley	1,472 66	1,434 18	2,906 84
James M. McCauley	380 00	448 10	828 10
R. B. McPherson	400 00	570 75	970 75
Charles Parker	462 00	386 15	848 15
Henry T. Porter	65 00	133 10	198 10
W. T. Prime	212 50	142 65	355 51
A. B. Seybolt	1,401 60	1,100 10	2,501 70
J. E. Simpson	1,457 93	1,268 55	2,726 48
S. W. Thomas	557 39	691 86	1,249 25
Clifford Thomson	1,420 00	163 00	1,583 00
G. N. Timberman	73 65	17 99	91 64
Thomas Waters	371 00	466 10	837 10
William Wheaton	1,675 40	146 72	1,822.12
Total	45,490 27	28,069 12	73,559 35

Surveyors of distilleries.

Salaries	$27,166 48
Expenses	19,768 48
Total	46,934 96

14 F

Contingent expenses, salary, &c., of Special Commissioner and Commissioner's office.

Salary		$326,138 86
Tax		1,420 46
Net salary		324,718 40
Traveling expenses	$1,429 83	
Tax	15 42	
Net traveling expenses	$1,414 41	
Printing, &c	111 55	
Office furniture, &c	1,466 85	
Expressage	229 05	
Telegrams	973 00	
		4,194 86

MISCELLANEOUS EXPENSES.

Salary	$15,643 86	
Tax	259 41	
Net salary	$15,384 45	
Traveling expenses	$9,399 40	
Tax	15 92	
Net traveling expenses	9,373 48	
Expenses	$17,301 63	
Tax	48 09	
Net expenses	17,253 54	
Office furniture, rent, &c	6,901 65	
Printing, &c	13,927 45	
Stationery	31,466 88	
Expressage	20,565 45	
		114,872 90

COUNSEL FEES AND EXPENSES, MOIETIES, AND REWARDS.

Fees and expenses	$20,414 20	
Moieties	2,661 09	
Rewards	14,949 98	
		$38,025 27
		481,811 43
Drawbacks on rum and alcohol		$366,189 20
Taxes, erroneously assessed and collected, refunded		458,149 83
		824,339 03

Statement of fines, penalties, and forfeitures.

Balance on deposit to credit of the Secretary of the Treasury, July 1, 1870	$321,443 63	
Amount deposited	201,464 40	
		$522,908 03
Amount disbursed		242,658 31
Balance on deposit to the credit of the Secretary of the Treasury, July 1, 1871		280,249 72

Statement of disbursements for salaries of United States direct tax commissioners in insurrectionary districts during the fiscal year ending June 30, 1871.

State.	Salary.	Tax.	Net salary.
South Carolina...	$1, 500 00	$16 84	$1, 483 16
Mississippi...	870 65	29 03	841 62
Total..	2, 370 65	45 87	2, 324 78

Moneys refunded on lands sold for taxes and redeemed.

State.	Principal.	Interest.	Amount.
Virginia	$1, 560 00	$157 96	$1, 717 96

Moneys illegally collected in the insurrectionary districts during the fiscal year ending June 30, 1871, refunded.

Amount refunded $1,491 19

Statement of certificates issued and allowed for drawbacks on merchandise exported, as provided for under section 171 of the act of June 30, 1864, for the fiscal year ending June 30, 1871.

Number of certificates received and allowed........................... 242
Amount allowed $38, 230 54

[TABLE FOR 1870 OMITTED IN ANNUAL REPORT OF THAT YEAR.]

A.—Statement showing the expenses of assessing the internal revenue taxes in the several collection districts, including the salaries, commissions, and allowance of the assessors, their contingent expenses, and the compensation of assistant assessors and store-keepers, from July 1, 1869, to June 30, 1870.

[NOTE.—Districts marked with an asterisk not entirely completed.]

District	Gross compensation.	Tax.	Net compensation.	Clerk-hire.	Stationery.	Printing and advertising.	Postage and express.	Rent of assessor.	Net compensation of assistant assessors.	Net compensation of store-keepers.	Tax on comp. of assist'nt assess'rs & store-keepers.	Survey of distilleries.	Total.
ALABAMA.													
First district	$3,054 18	$102 70	$2,951 48	$3,000 00	$151 92	$53 50	$117 24	$375 00	$27,056 62	$463 73	$788 61		$33,514 49
Second district	3,285 03	114 23	3,170 80	2,083 24	197 03	99 25	180 61	133 75	20,969 52		526 77		27,084 45
Third district	1,285 29	26 81	1,258 48	837 50	24 15	8 00			7,304 25	2,560 39	231 52		12,128 52
Total	7,624 50	243 74	7,380 76	5,920 74	373 10	162 75	306 85	508 75	55,330 39	3,044 12	1,546 90		73,027 46
ARIZONA.													
Arizona	2,500 00	75 00	2,425 00		81 25	59 00	20 08	300 00	2,229 78		63 55		5,114 11
ARKANSAS.													
First district	4,167 64	125 09	4,042 55	1,816 65	216 98	98 49	201 10	300 00	17,472 85	860 26	453 24		25,008 78
Second district	2,561 46	78 07	2,483 39	1,950 00	130 33	73 25	91 49	357 35	11,501 64		283 42	$120 00	16,707 47
Third district	2,293 96	68 82	2,225 14		139 19	8 00	68 50	150 00	7,247 93		179 72		9,838 76
Total	9,023 06	271 98	8,751 08	3,766 65	486 42	179 74	361 09	807 35	36,222 42	860 26	916 38	120 00	51,355 01
CALIFORNIA.													
First district	4,127 46	152 25	3,975 21	6,602 70	289 77	24 99	44 41	1,259 51	26,047 29	5,896 91	870 14	16 44	44,157 23
Second district	4,243 77	162 16	4,081 35	999 95	219 07	173 29	133 33	253 56	13,511 30	594 11	398 63	296 22	21,264 38
Third district	3,001 78	100 08	2,901 70	1,500 00	82 95	116 00	75 98	360 00	12,245 24	643 21	366 99		17,925 08
Fourth district	3,337 17	116 85	3,220 32	3,082 78	175 90	124 05	203 00	500 00	19,464 12		567 49		26,770 17
Fifth district	3,631 34	131 55	3,499 79	1,500 00	170 31	54 60	82 29	300 00	12,457 64		337 47	185 11	18,249 74
Total	18,341 46	662 89	17,678 57	14,685 43	938 00	492 93	539 01	2,675 07	83,725 59	7,134 23	2,560 72	499 77	128,366 60
COLORADO.													
Colorado	2,500 00	75 00	2,425 00	1,500 00	52 97	40 25	52 00	480 00	6,199 41		177 81		10,749 63
CONNECTICUT.													
First district	3,929 66	146 46	3,783 20	900 00	107 10	18 60	152 31	290 00	11,166 39	4,310 84	261 09		20,718 44
Second district	3,626 32	131 28	3,495 04	1,200 00	54 60	10 50	257 30	100 00	9,330 88		180 86		14,448 52
Third district	2,493 10	74 64	2,418 46	999 99	59 52	12 00	109 03	300 00	7,106 75	869 22	145 93		11,874 97
Fourth district	3,042 59	106 25	2,936 34	1,000 00	101 23	8 38	85 88	75 00	10,760 44		206 37		11,967 27
Total	13,091 67	458 63	12,633 04	4,099 99	322 45	49 48	604 72	755 00	38,364 46	5,180 06	794 25		62,009 20

												Total
DAKOTA.												
Dakota	1,623 63	27 06	1,596 57		197 71	13 00	68 75	229 84	1,576 02	134 64	30 35		3,669 49
DELAWARE.												
Delaware	3,267 54	713 36	3,154 18	4,560 00	181 06	31 38	77 95		13,304 11		252 77		18,364 94
DIST. OF COLUMBIA.												
District of Columbia	3,921 03	146 03	3,775 00	1,800 00	103 36	95 50	5 00	420 00	10,334 93		201 05		16,469 67
FLORIDA.												
Florida	2,499 75	75 00	2,424 75	1,625 00	114 87	95 50	55 21	360 00	14,155 07		349 02		18,830 40
GEORGIA.												
First district	2,886 75	94 31	2,792 44	1,800 00	135 26	25 00	48 46	416 66	14,495 53		376 52	66 40	19,703 35
Second district	2,859 81	92 97	2,766 84	2,324 17	240 58	75 65	138 77	300 00	21,673 17		561 08	21 00	27,585 58
Third district	3,017 34	100 85	2,916 51	2,100 00	217 08	27 75	195 58	470 00	29,578 09	751 23	580 72	40 61	36,278 07
Fourth district	3,279 18	113 92	3,165 26	1,800 00	203 55	25 00	108 34	335 88	17,120 02	777 04	433 46		23,575 70
Total	12,043 08	402 03	11,641 05	8,024 17	796 47	153 40	491 15	1,523 37	82,656 81	1,598 27	2,191 78	128 01	107,142 70
IDAHO.												
Idaho	2,500 00	75 00	2,425 00	251 00	76 17	37 45	45 62	600 00	7,740 06	1,770 84	298 17		12,946 14
ILLINOIS.												
First district	9,069 47	407 58	8,661 89	4,141 64	391 33	29 50	314 60	1,033 33	31,395 87	26,920 50	1,200 11		72,898 66
Second district	2,970 07	98 48	2,871 59	900 00	93 87	52 75	111 89	180 00	8,849 78	1,544 60	191 50	19 35	14,393 92
Third district	3,424 76	121 92	3,303 54	1,200 96	59 94	82 81	103 67	180 00	9,714 49	1,806 99	213 41		14,458 25
Fourth district	4,044 77	156 60	3,888 17	1,389 96	166 61	30 50	271 87	150 00	9,532 37	7,036 92	252 71	68 15	22,495 25
Fifth district	7,037 63	304 92	6,732 71	1,733 00	292 95	32 25	132 25	278 99	18,732 03	13,123 44	485 60	34 00	41,145 77
Sixth district	3,508 42	125 38	3,383 04	466 00	23 50	14 50	37 00	200 00	9,656 01	2,760 12	211 24	58 00	16,574 97
Seventh district	3,551 16	126 72	3,424 44	909 89	184 31	12 00	122 21	125 00	9,738 07	2,561 92	324 64	202 30	24,135 84
Eighth district	3,993 70	149 67	3,844 03	1,499 99	272 30	47 00	252 87	106 58	14,874 49	9,384 52	375 89	14 70	30,445 58
Ninth district	1,953 87	47 68	1,906 19	900 00	114 34	3 00	73 89	110 27	4,738 49	384 12	105 81		8,806 36
Tenth district	1,915 51	45 77	1,869 74	702 00	143 67	18 50	96 58	290 25	10,813 07	184 84	206 99	28 70	14,053 87
Eleventh district	1,507 25	25 36	1,481 89	600 00	125 29	11 50	61 41	75 00	8,280 29	459 36	160 76	27 70	11,122 94
Twelfth district	3,695 68	140 30	3,754 98	1,147 08	190 40	31 35	125 97	108 00	12,463 46	3,674 88	273 31	69 20	21,563 62
Thirteenth district	1,500 00	25 00	1,475 00	499 92	85 49	27 50	14 97	72 00	9,536 43		180 38		11,780 51
Total	46,372 49	1,775 28	46,591 21	16,069 48	2,144 40	308 75	1,740 69	2,973 84	163,945 41	71,733 01	4,182 35	550 95	306,085 74

A.—Statement showing the expenses of assessing the internal revenue taxes in the several collection districts, &c.—Continued.

District	Gross compensation.	Tax.	Net compensation.	Clerk-hire.	Stationery.	Printing and advertising.	Postage and express.	Rent of assessor.	Net compensation of assistant assessors.	Net compensation of store-keepers.	Tax on comp. of assist'nt assessors & store-keepers.	Survey of distillers.	Total.
INDIANA.													
First district	$3,344 45	$121 29	$3,223 16	$983 32	$147 51	$37 75	$37 42	$160 00	$8,774 11	$4,158 00	$309 48	$137 60	$17,678 87
Second district	2,175 13	58 74	2,116 39	1,149 96	77 02	44 00	41 35	120 00	7,086 76	514 80	140 35	195 40	11,345 68
Third district	3,437 51	121 85	3,315 65	800 00	282 29	27 75	40 72	200 00	7,296 10	3,875 90	174 45		13,778 35
Fourth district	5,636 71	231 80	5,404 91	900 00	157 35	44 50	79 60	120 00	5,932 17	751 65	190 04	5 80	23,395 98
Fifth district	3,963 33	148 16	3,815 17	800 00	148 16	16 40	56 77	192 00	7,568 31	982 03	135 67	15 75	23,391 99
Sixth district	3,341 67	117 03	3,224 18	1,000 00	48 92	16 40	53 96		7,516 41		184 36	9 40	13,869 57
Seventh district	3,475 67	123 77	3,351 90	1,062 50	126 90	40 50	39 05		7,040 51	1,984 19	171 72		14,301 90
Eighth district	2,198 59	60 06	2,138 53	999 56	49 45	5 90	18 78	56 25	6,634 38	2,367 21	165 41		12,444 21
Ninth district	1,849 11	42 44	1,806 67	168 00	47 15	31 50	21 57	180 00	9,120 22	712 60	180 63	18 30	11,968 01
Tenth district	1,794 95	31 36	1,763 59	404 00	43 04	17 70	79 05	42 00	4,247 58		63 02		6,705 06
Eleventh district	1,500 00	25 00	1,475 00	500 00	120 23		177 44	150 00	6,839 41		133 75		9,243 03
Total	32,716 66	1,081 50	31,635 16	8,767 74	1,247 95	299 75	645 71	1,370 25	80,627 26	22,346 63	1,788 86	382 25	147,322 70
IOWA.													
First district	2,365 62	68 27	2,297 35	730 00	81 99	57 50	68 51	110 00	9,546 92	23 76	182 69		12,906 03
Second district	3,480 87	128 14	3,352 73	600 00	90 85	30 40	80 80	96 77	8,849 02	938 52	178 36	28 90	14,063 08
Third district	2,259 18	58 62	2,200 36	916 72	88 03	23 00	5 00		11,117 96	2,447 28	235 99		16,798 35
Fourth district	1,782 96	35 00	1,747 95	778 33	169 53	60 45	106 05	120 00	7,281 24	1,005 36	151 99	13 40	11,282 31
Fifth district	1,500 00	25 00	1,475 00	406 64	109 56	29 40	7 00	133 33	6,460 74		125 58		8,651 67
Sixth district	1,747 25	29 10	1,718 15	465 17	85 87	98 90	102 80	144 00	9,480 60		181 64		12,255 69
Total	13,135 88	344 34	12,791 54	3,896 86	625 83	489 65	370 25	604 10	52,736 68	4,414 92	1,056 45	42 30	75,962 13
KANSAS.													
Kansas	2,798 20	85 78	2,712 42	1,625 00	298 30	69 20	167 63	360 00	19,513 64	578 16	378 39	31 50	25,355 85
KENTUCKY.													
First district	1,881 50	44 14	1,837 36	1,000 00	132 57	7 25	22 12	133 30	9,088 10	1,296 45	189 12	60 45	13,567 60
Second district	1,310 44	21 84	1,288 60	1,250 00	72 99	7 00	22 93	150 00	11,085 16	10,105 98	310 45	223 30	24,205 38
Third district	1,500 00	25 00	1,475 00	1,174 19	55 70	8 00	18 98	135 62	11,026 61	2,518 72	231 76	193 10	16,605 66
Fourth district	4,754 94	167 72	4,567 22	1,766 67	217 31	20 00	83 97	321 66	13,984 51	56,339 72	231 59	185 70	77,465 76
Fifth district	4,000 00	150 00	3,650 00	1,499 96	169 69	35 00	71 00		16,444 10	17,335 41	607 68		40,905 16

District	1	2	3	4	5	6	7	8	9	10	11	12	13
Sixth district	8,348 62	367 42	7,981 20	1,555 00	252 86	30 50	105 15	250 00	14,870 71	28,407 19	567 50	127 45	53,580 06
Seventh district	5,376 37	222 94	5,153 43	2,000 00	365 61	27 25	77 96	320 00	19,897 92	86,934 15	1,526 46	2 75	113,779 07
Eighth district	2,096 84	54 84	2,042 93	800 00	110 95	26 75	3 50	110 00	8,498 14	7,465 75	236 25		19,030 34
Ninth district	1,833 49	41 66	1,791 83	753 80	161 75		54 37	330 00	6,625 39	7,483 33	211 14	436 55	17,683 77
Total	31,102 90	1,115 56	29,966 64	12,799 62	1,539 43	161 75	458 70	1,770 58	110,520 34	218,376 44	4,973 96	1,229 30	376,842 80
LOUISIANA.													
First district	3,999 98	150 00	3,849 98	4,490 60	727 82	54 50	4 87		44,541 39		1,326 19		63,455 28
Second district	2,300 00	75 00	2,425 00	1,800 00	258 23	30 50	15 96	361 84	21,671 29	9,786 12	361 04		26,562 82
Third district	1,998 63	59 96	1,938 67	1,447 33	191 06	52 75	51 40	430 03	13,493 98		333 36		17,605 22
Total	6,498 61	284 96	8,213 65	7,737 93	1,177 11	137 75	72 23	791 87	79,706 66	9,786 12	2,220 58		107,623 32
MAINE.													
First district	2,739 56	86 96	2,652 60	1,339 33	46 10	2 50	25 35	268 33	7,043 19		141 95		12,723 80
Second district	1,499 98	30 00	1,474 98	483 86	67 32	19 15	69 14	113 88	6,120 79	1,346 40	115 82		8,369 32
Third district	1,600 00	30 00	1,570 00	500 00	87 63	19 00	66 54	83 25	5,603 61		106 88		7,930 63
Fourth district	1,500 00	25 00	1,475 00	538 34	95 31	12 75	98 76	84 00	5,088 71		97 17		7,342 87
Fifth district	1,500 00	25 00	1,475 00	500 00	49 01	16 75	32 64	100 00	6,184 54		117 19		8,357 94
Total	8,839 94	191 96	8,647 98	3,381 53	345 77	70 15	342 43	649 46	30,040 84	1,346 40	579 01		44,724 56
MARYLAND.													
First district	1,598 98	34 07	1,564 91	550 00	122 44	38 09	4 82	120 00	11,101 75		206 64		13,509 01
Second district	3,000 40	95 87	2,904 53	1,513 50	148 58	30 15	17 31	700 00	11,905 61	2,995 02	291 53		20,162 75
Third district	4,934 70	197 90	4,957 90	3,223 24	149 10	30 50	39 58		34,023 29	258 98	887 53		51,491 24
Fourth district	2,047 98	59 34	1,994 94	778 33	122 78	30 50	22 97	50 00	10,960 40	5,734 08	265 43	88 10	13,782 10
Fifth district	3,326 24	116 30	3,209 94	666 67	22 33	59 50	16 04	45 00	12,415 30	5,468 81	291 64	16 55	21,920 04
Total	14,927 60	496 28	14,431 32	6,741 24	505 23	196 94	100 72	915 00	80,406 25	23,456 79	1,875 49	104 65	126,858 14
MASSACHUSETTS.													
First district	2,518 06	75 89	2,442 17	720 00	98 63	24 75	120 49	200 00	10,274 03		197 70		13,880 07
Second district	2,993 78	103 78	2,899 97	1,599 96	101 86	12 50	68 19	200 00	9,798 29	4,794 19	180 98		14,670 68
Third district	4,209 11	160 44	4,048 67	4,900 00	214 47	29 75	213 98	925 00	25,153 31	4,540 89	617 32		39,579 57
Fourth district	4,242 66	166 25	4,076 41	2,234 50	130 34	15 00	110 50	550 00	13,114 96	1,239 48	353 02		24,772 60
Fifth district	3,568 52	127 06	3,441 46	1,798 13	87 72	23 50	16 99	175 00	14,711 70	1,961 34	295 04		21,493 98
Sixth district	3,776 45	138 81	3,637 64	2,000 00	130 98	18 50	221 86	400 00	13,234 86		277 51		21,593 90
Seventh district	3,379 73	118 96	3,260 77	1,650 00	74 57	13 50	133 03	216 93	12,339 63		237 27		17,650 19
Eighth district	3,140 49	107 01	3,033 48	1,800 00	166 37	25 75	94 79	400 00	10,606 90	479 16	205 29		16,165 52
Ninth district	2,563 31	78 14	2,485 17	1,942 00	130 01	23 25	148 59	200 00	13,284 18		256 97		17,992 36
Tenth district	2,993 63	103 78	2,889 90	1,683 33	107 81	30 12	118 39	250 00	14,976 41	2,245 32	306 69		22,301 28
Total	33,385 76	1,180 12	32,205 64	18,927 92	1,242 26	216 62	1,246 22	3,516 93	137,484 18	15,260 38	2,936 79		210,100 15

A.—*Statement showing the expenses of assessing the internal revenue taxes in the several collection-districts, &c.—Continued.*

District.	Gross compensation.	Tax.	Net compensation.	Clerk-hire.	Stationery.	Printing and advertising.	Postage and express.	Rent of assessor.	Net compensation of assistant assessors.	Net compensation of storekeepers.	Tax on comp. of assist'nt assess'rs & storekeepers.	Survey of distilleries.	Total.
MICHIGAN.													
First district	$3,876 35	$147 94	$3,728 41	$1,692 00	$299 12	$20 50	$19 99	$500 00	$2,763 8?	$1,229 48	$259 59		$20,963 3?
Second district	1,962 90	44 02	1,918 88	1,083 29	285 39	24 60	81 71	200 00	10,204 4?		197 98		13,798 3?
Third district	2,095 15	54 76	2,040 39	884 91	83 47	19 25	44 30	150 00	8,530 8?		164 20		11,733 1?
Fourth district	1,708 47	39 54	1,668 93	900 00	79 73	32 30	26 73	150 00	8,039 5?		155 97		10,897 3?
Fifth district	1,500 00	25 01	1,474 99	798 92	108 32	24 30	44 67	192 44	6,737 3?		128 73		9,311 1?
Sixth district	2,906 47	92 78	2,813 69	1,146 66	138 46	51 75	147 84	181 25	14,129 6?		209 59		18,609 3?
Total	14,049 34	404 05	13,645 29	6,505 78	994 49	172 85	365 24	1,303 69	60,405 7?	1,229 48	1,175 36		84,632 60
MINNESOTA.													
First district	1,689 69	30 36	1,659 33	430 00	71 96	23 00	7 50	100 00	10,596 5?		201 70		12,898 2?
Second district	2,603 95	80 13	2,522 82	683 25	128 51	56 62	149 78	300 00	10,085 8?	693 00	199 18	$20 00	14,639 8?
Total	4,292 64	110 49	4,182 15	1,113 25	200 47	79 62	157 28	400 00	20,682 3?	693 00	400 88	20 00	27,528 10
MISSISSIPPI.													
First district	2,700 26	85 79	2,614 47	1,500 00	125 57	11 00	20 75	210 02	11,723 4?		289 93		16,205 2?
Second district	2,711 11	81 46	2,629 65	1,625 00	210 78	55 00	29 05	300 00	13,896 7?		343 96		18,736 2?
Third district	2,706 04	81 18	2,624 86	1,749 98	552 00	19 50	85 64	210 00	19,487 8?	1,227 50	309 97	54 50	26,011 8?
Total	8,117 41	248 43	7,869 98	4,874 98	888 35	85 50	135 44	720 02	45,098 1?	1,227 50	1,143 86	54 50	60,953 37
MISSOURI.													
First district	7,416 46	320 81	7,095 65	3,960 00	135 53	24 50	10 00	1,000 00	22,894 ?	5,877 62	547 23		40,998 10
Second district	1,347 68	26 41	1,321 27	712 56	224 45	98 00	222 97	140 88	10,315 ?		195 11	78 15	13,043 39
Third district	2,017 67	55 07	1,962 60	749 97	102 52	53 35	82 59	75 00	7,107 ?	118 80	136 67		10,252 19
Fourth district	2,067 07	49 21	2,017 86	628 23	42 20		85 58	121 00	10,166 ?	304 92	193 84		13,366 39
Fifth district	1,768 04	50 97	1,717 07	1,200 00	135 77	55 25	176 61	360 00	12,971 ?	2,070 75	264 93	154 15	18,840 90
Sixth district	3,621 01	135 16	3,485 85	1,699 96	339 46	28 10	175 71	420 00	21,096 ?	4,708 44	462 25	51 40	32,005 21
Total	18,237 93	637 63	17,600 30	8,950 72	979 93	189 20	753 46	2,116 88	84,551 4?	13,080 53	1,800 03	283 70	128,506 18

MONTANA.													
Montana	3,761 08	125 36	3,635 72	1,208 04	77 41		18 15	500 32	10,958 86	952 54	357 01	109 00	17,461 04
NEBRASKA.													
Nebraska	1,699 48	44 96	1,854 52	900 00	68 36	110 25	40 70	190 50	8,491 13	51 48	163 50	11 50	11,718 44
NEVADA.													
Nevada	3,073 59	99 55	2,974 04	1,264 00	241 85	43 00	18 98	260 00	11,362 54		339 70		16,164 41
NEW HAMPSHIRE.													
First district	2,051 27	52 53	1,998 74	720 00	30 94	12 75	31 50	60 50	6,733 36		128 93		9,586 63
Second district	2,642 22	82 69	2,560 13	939 50	76 94	41 88	109 85	187 50	6,196 01		119 62		10,091 81
Third district	1,503 64	25 18	1,478 46	421 00	52 78	19 75	90 84	75 00	6,700 01		127 99	12 25	8,850 09
Total	6,197 13	159 80	6,037 33	2,080 50	160 00	54 38	232 19	322 50	19,629 38		375 84	12 25	28,528 53
NEW JERSEY.													
First district	1,932 88	47 69	1,905 26	999 96	43 38	20 85	25 99	150 00	12,610 64		276 52		15,708 64
Second district	2,396 16	73 41	2,312 75	1,200 00	206 50	22 75	74 77	200 00	9,757 95		185 53	141 30	13,865 34
Third district	3,514 99	129 85	3,385 14	1,600 00	85 25	31 70	128 94	200 00	16,592 83	1,389 96	331 04	29 05	23,379 75
Fourth district	3,217 78	110 87	3,106 91	1,200 00	73 86	28 00	14 94	518 75	15,165 03		287 37	68 75	19,975 19
Fifth district	4,152 29	161 73	3,990 56	3,225 00	229 49	29 00			25,167 35		485 65		33,173 09
Total	15,224 10	523 48	14,700 62	8,224 96	637 48	103 30	244 64	1,968 75	79,293 90	1,389 96	1,529 11	239 10	106,102 01
NEW MEXICO.													
New Mexico	2,500 00	75 00	2,425 00	999 96	172 75	68 00	10 05	300 00	12,469 01	1,336 91	381 74	53 00	17,884 68
NEW YORK.													
First district	2,369 72	67 61	2,302 11	2,299 86	93 87	12 25	40 41	984 99	17,402 96		327 33		92,336 45
Second district	3,999 93	149 99	3,849 94	3,600 00	267 98	52 20	50 50	1,000 00	26,977 77	7,365 13	310 38		35,797 89
Third district	4,146 73	161 43	3,985 30	3,000 00	365 40	58 20	30 50	1,000 00	38,685 38		860 11		35,103 92
Fourth district	4,000 00	150 00	3,850 03	6,942 00	279 85	6 00	10 00	250 00	35,786 83	495 95	690 47		48,134 68
Fifth district	3,819 35	133 94	3,685 41	4,800 02	208 85	50 00	5 00	700 00	24,448 89	2,415 45	471 97		48,194 12
Sixth district	3,994 08	148 79	3,745 29	4,249 96	170 05	47 50	40 75	541 66	18,807 68		409 60		32,018 34
Seventh district	4,000 00	149 98	3,850 02	3,800 00	62 10	104 00		3,000 00	21,743 32		684 12		32,579 44
Eighth district	3,858 02	147 94	3,710 08	4,199 88	272 09	31 55	21 00	1,800 00	34,313 03	1,922 14	546 65		46,070 67
Ninth district	3,976 37	147 62	3,728 45	3,999 96	178 69	33 25	56 64	300 00	55,919 03	2,076 93	315 86		38,212 95
Tenth district	2,990 40	83 62	2,906 24	3,599 96	52 22	14 40	9 03	900 00	11,213 03	1,167 49	245 19	15 75	23,369 96
Eleventh district	1,894 98	44 74	1,850 24	1,000 00	225 83	5 00	125 80	317 00	11,913 71	388 08	315 86	3 00	13,141 05
Twelfth district	2,890 80	91 01	2,729 24	1,500 00	52 93	10 25	3 00	150 00	13,041 58		245 19		12,461 05
Thirteenth district	2,635 79	90 75	2,672 45	1,500 00	249 28		30 34	113 00	8,728 62		165 60	62 23	12,741 59
Fourteenth district	3,817 42	144 97	3,672 45	2,700 00	249 28	13 00	168 38	500 00	19,453 57		381 92		96,754 88
Fifteenth district	3,261 11	114 03	3,167 08	2,100 00	142 60	34 75	148 96	482 75	14,785 67		282 99		20,661 81

A.—*Statement showing the expenses of assessing the internal revenue taxes in the several collection districts, &c.—Continued.*

District	Gross compensation	Tax	Net compensation	Clerk-hire	Stationery	Printing and advertising	Postage and express	Rent of assessor	Net compensation of assistant assessors	Net compensation of storekeepers	Tax on coump. of assist'nt assess'rs & store-keepers	Survey of distilleries	Total
NEW YORK—Cont'd.													
Sixteenth district	$1,519 50	$23 97	$1,493 53	$600 00	$83 86	$2 50	$73 51		86,037 39		$114 17		68,290 72
Seventeenth district	1,525 37	26 26	1,499 01	318 00	63 11	10 00	29 88	$80 00	6,147 37		116 01		8,156 37
Eighteenth district	1,243 16	66 23	2,176 93	1,530 00	183 86	94 05	12 00	109 37	10,462 35		208 27		15,101 84
Nineteenth district	2,471 78	22 71	2,144 07	720 00	27 97		22 90	120 00	7,090 19		134 81		9,290 43
Twentieth district	2,135 64	56 77	2,079 41	1,477 50	110 90	43 00	10 26	130 00	10,144 82		135 25		11,238 05
Twenty-first district	3,563 50	124 03	3,439 76	1,200 00	356 32	12 00	18 66	297 98	14,805 34	$363 28	299 74	$72 32	22,508 71
Twenty-second dist.	3,410 26	120 50	3,289 76	1,800 00	75 10	7 50	17 00		10,579 40	1,865 12	217 70		16,942 84
Twenty-third district	3,634 87	131 74	3,303 13	1,500 00	155 96	25 00	50 39	504 29	33,538 05	1,774 08	282 32		21,991 72
Twenty-fourth dist.	3,095 64	131 24	2,973 21	760 00	171 75	13 00	115 42	100 00	13,373 76	2,415 60	272 01		20,127 20
Twenty-fifth district	2,969 42	67 58	2,201 84	1,044 76	133 39	15 25	82 82	87 36	6,050 52	1,875 06	137 27		10,297 10
Twenty-sixth district	2,604 28	76 08	2,528 20	999 96	77 31	21 60	71 38	175 00	11,059 30	965 92	201 18		14,977 55
Twenty-seventh dist.	2,048 50	32 40	1,996 10	1,700 00	129 48	6 35	172 59	100 00	8,059 77		154 11		11,464 45
Twenty-eighth dist.	3,335 76	116 76	3,219 17	927 21	112 17	26 00	19 24	458 33	13,815 28	1,140 48	276 46	4 05	20,490 50
Twenty-ninth dist.	3,060 77	53 02	3,007 75	1,700 00	93 78	5 00	25 00	142 50	13,592 58	2,621 52	283 46		19,419 48
Thirtieth district	6,310 08	265 48	6,044 60	2,700 00	301 88	13 50	121 50	400 00	20,338 55	9,393 94	566 82		39,312 97
Thirty-first district	1,376 02	22 95	1,353 67	800 00	54 96	10 50	192 64	90 00	6,431 03		132 28		6,932 10
Thirty-second dist.	3,501 57	141 69	3,359 68	7,441 67	1,469 22	39 00	50 50		62,410 81	7,529 48	1,330 50		82,300 56
Total	97,002 32	3,300 32	93,702 00	73,330 94	6,298 12	839 80	1,987 58	15,233 76	561,995 66	46,294 66	11,455 37	162 35	799,844 87
NORTH CAROLINA.													
First district	2,159 97	53 98	2,105 99	933 40	28 90	10 00	12 80	127 44	8,639 02		169 88		11,837 55
Second district*	1,639 20	46 08	1,793 12	1,144 91	117 26		11 00	112 50	7,453 27		145 36		10,632 06
Third district	2,164 84	54 11	2,110 73	1,060 01	47 97		20 77	72 75	4,015 51	989 84	92 29		8,317 58
Fourth district*	3,104 80	105 22	2,999 58	1,200 00	113 03		41 41	200 33	15,577 87	2,019 02	327 85	62 00	22,342 74
Fifth district*	1,573 25	46 15	1,507 10	300 00	114 35	9 50	30 62	320 00	3,031 69		60 39		5,509 58
Sixth district	2,732 02	33 32	2,649 70	1,375 00	29 15	21 50	32 60	150 00	5,039 53	1,402 77	113 32	64 25	10,755 00
Seventh district	1,999 95	50 00	1,949 95	608 66	49 11	12 00	25 00	81 86	9,389 22	1,045 44	193 94	21 08	13,170 32
Total	15,574 03	457 86	15,116 17	6,621 98	499 77	53 00	173 60	1,064 88	53,146 11	5,761 99	1,103 03	147 33	82,564 83
OHIO.													
First district	4,000 00	150 00	3,850 00	3,237 33	162 12	53 00	16 00	1,321 00	52,420 05	130 87	433 79		31,210 32
Second district	5,110 97	202 54	4,905 43	2,499 96	209 34	42 00	7 00	900 00	19,947 05	16,098 49	654 32		44,609 30
Third district	4,123 63	155 64	3,971 57	1,950 00	366 93	32 30	202 23	108 00	15,376 03	13,574 38	461 44	70 70	40,652 14
Fourth district	4,705 73	185 24	4,520 51	1,200 00	55 91	34 75	23 98	145 89	5,957 07	6,795 36	183 56		18,713 47

Fifth district	2,389 88	69 47	2,320 41	550 00	135 32	48 50	41 04	75 00	7,025 21	3,033 36	164 33	10 50	13,239 34
Sixth district	3,764 45	138 21	3,626 24	999 96	94 24	16 00	125 09	100 00	7,382 51	5,052 96	191 85	24 80	17,421 80
Seventh district	3,916 21	145 79	3,770 42	1,500 00	383 50	46 60	45 19	150 00	11,785 36	4,880 28	274 64		22,561 35
Eighth district	1,565 80	32 40	1,533 40	629 03	64 98	16 50	16 95	100 00	6,639 87	847 12	134 80	9 05	9,856 90
Ninth district	3,970 88	148 53	3,822 35	788 10	110 23	101 12	96 05	100 00	9,126 06	5,602 45	229 60	79 15	19,825 51
Tenth district	3,891 93	144 59	3,747 34	809 36	143 20	20 60	71 83		7,613 93	1,520 64	161 95		13,926 90
Eleventh district	5,609 71	230 46	5,379 25		117 80	31 25	30 00	132 00	7,639 16	879 12	153 60		14,203 58
Twelfth district	3,730 08	136 50	3,593 58	999 96	140 16	28 75	47 65	60 00	8,822 81	3,817 44	206 70		17,510 35
Thirteenth district	2,954 88	97 73	2,857 15	720 00	163 05	21 50	108 81	125 00	9,391 80	1,474 13	203 18	12 50	14,873 94
Fourteenth district	1,508 68	25 62	1,483 06	600 00	59 27	22 50	44 94	75 00	7,980 23		152 22		10,265 00
Fifteenth district	1,654 38	32 71	1,621 67	600 00	46 48	9 75	53 93	100 00	5,254 26		81 69		6,686 09
Sixteenth district	1,623 63	27 06	1,596 57	595 74	117 63	37 30	69 20	50 00	6,838 30	3,062 07	161 13	71 83	12,438 64
Seventeenth district	2,658 60	74 54	2,584 06	892 46	106 63	14 00	74 30	150 00	9,339 02	1,504 62	193 64	10 10	14,675 19
Eighteenth district	3,932 58	150 73	3,781 85	2,000 00	222 25	16 25	39 48	541 67	18,208 09	1,852 64	371 36	1 75	26,663 98
Nineteenth district	1,662 04	37 21	1,624 83	469 00	89 43	14 50	28 30	100 00	6,782 85	11 88	130 63	12 10	9,132 89
Total	62,774 08	2,184 39	60,589 69	21,040 90	2,788 47	607 17	1,141 97	4,333 56	192,529 64	75,157 81	4,564 43	302 48	358,491 69

OREGON.

Oregon	5,811 02	240 54	5,570 48	667 50	139 68	24 00	49 00	420 00	12,767 44	427 17	373 54	36 00	20,101 27

PENNSYLVANIA.

First district	3,997 13	153 97	3,843 16	4,000 00	245 07	69 15	6 05	800 00	29,768 49	8,071 94	722 78		46,803 86
Second district	3,915 02	145 32	3,769 70	3,976 33	196 90	65 50	8 90	600 00	24,131 64	2,729 95	507 82		35,478 92
Third district	3,608 04	134 51	3,473 53	3,699 98	209 37	24 50	78 85	700 00	28,923 66	5,496 67	651 32		42,606 56
Fourth district	4,015 95	154 89	3,861 06	3,900 00	298 34	117 03	12 25	600 00	34,513 59	11,089 24	851 94	4 00	54,295 51
Fifth district	3,531 18	126 53	3,404 65	2,500 00	49 63	16 33	74 98	500 00	20,537 12	908 35	403 26		27,991 06
Sixth district	2,819 60	90 97	2,728 63	1,059 96	132 85	40 00		261 65	13,961 20		264 84	18 75	18,203 04
Seventh district	4,515 11	154 56	4,360 55	1,200 00	151 82	18 22	30 45	243 74	12,977 79		244 31		18,982 57
Eighth district	2,375 83	68 77	2,307 06	1,200 00	56 54	15 25	15 44	253 89	10,097 33	2,537 86	217 10	4 00	16,537 37
Ninth district	3,468 67	123 40	3,345 27	1,200 00	130 36	16 00	20 43	362 50	13,958 04	4,304 47	308 40	36 00	23,373 07
Tenth district	1,805 08	44 36	1,760 72	999 96	58 00	16 50	30 80	200 00	9,438 96	273 24	186 61		12,778 18
Eleventh district	2,043 46	52 14	1,991 32	999 96	39 80	25 50	80 20	110 00	7,831 59		150 74		11,079 37
Twelfth district	2,408 61	70 40	2,338 21	1,083 42	177 13	10 50	240 47	100 00	9,369 17	2,799 82	207 61	70 95	16,179 67
Thirteenth district	1,772 62	38 62	1,734 00	799 98	131 01	39 00	16 72	82 92	8,260 84	1,536 48	171 16	18 00	12,618 95
Fourteenth district	2,139 70	56 97	2,082 73	1,200 00	80 07	2 00	58 00	187 50	13,227 39	3,528 36	284 57		20,366 05
Fifteenth district	2,777 07	88 83	2,688 24	1,274 00	89 13	9 75	25 83	200 00	14,400 50	7,008 60	341 33		25,696 05
Sixteenth district	1,701 41	35 05	1,666 36	733 31	126 32	22 33	11 59	56 00	13,023 99	9,437 67	340 70	21 00	25,098 57
Seventeenth district	1,773 26	34 54	1,738 72	439 50	29 33	23 00	30 19	100 00	5,065 64	704 88	103 65		8,131 26
Eighteenth district	1,744 81	33 11	1,711 70	813 34	116 53	16 00	74 46	89 58	14,843 43	1,334 52	293 44	50 00	19,049 56
Nineteenth district	2,252 76	58 49	2,194 27	995 00	64 73	37 50	29 31	120 00	9,862 86	471 24	190 86	24 75	13,799 66
Twentieth district	3,137 72	111 17	3,026 55	1,000 00	87 46	30 00	196 97	216 67	11,817 47	2,534 40	249 63	52 90	18,962 42
Twenty-first district	4,446 28	176 37	4,269 91	1,200 00	129 18	18 25	57 13	93 00	13,368 45	23,619 42	487 32	138 85	42,893 19
Twenty-second dist	4,625 72	181 28	4,444 44	2,267 00	72 03		74 35	650 00	17,632 74	5,592 34	399 78	10 00	30,762 90
Twenty-third district	3,544 39	127 21	3,417 18	1,250 00	69 55	12 25	48 52	300 00	11,713 58	5,225 22	277 26	39 75	22,076 05
Twenty-fourth dist	3,241 03	112 05	3,128 98	799 95	109 52	14 38	88 26	100 00	9,336 50	16,184 31	337 50	143 15	29,905 57
Total	71,660 45	2,373 51	69,286 94	38,491 69	2,849 67	659 44	1,310 17	6,927 45	358,081 97	115,428 93	8,193 53	632 10	593,668 41

District	Gross compensation.	Tax.	Net compensation.	Clerk-hire.	Stationery.	Printing and advertising.	Postage and express.	Rent of assessor.	Net compensation of assistant assessors.	Net compensation of storekeepers.	Tax on comp. of assist'nt assess'rs & storekeepers.	Survey of distilleries.	Total.
RHODE ISLAND.													
First district	$4,427 67	$171 37	$4,256 30	$2,123 08	$121 26	$22 87	$62 99		$15,866 78	$1,180 08	$319 99		$23,633 34
Second district	1,671 90	33 55	1,637 65	800 00	15 31	15 00	22 29		6,123 25		115 41		8,813 61
Total	6,098 87	204 92	5,893 95	2,923 03	136 57	37 87	85 28	$200 00	21,990 22	1,180 08	435 40		32,446 95
SOUTH CAROLINA.													
First district	2,293 96	68 83	2,225 14		51 44	21 75	81 66	75 00	14,523 52	702 36	424 18	$23 00	17,703 47
Second district	2,896 43	94 81	2,801 62	930 30	35 75	16 10	66 59	83 33	10,113 55		280 82		14,047 04
Third district*	4,860 23	172 62	4,687 61	1,100 00	129 86	80 30	53 21	217 20	16,096 58	353 57	407 72	21 25	22,739 28
Total	10,050 62	336 25	9,714 37	2,030 50	217 05	118 15	201 46	375 53	40,732 5	1,055 93	1,112 72	44 25	54,489 79
TENNESSEE.													
First district	1,998 00	50 00	1,943 00	1,000 00	27 72	7 50	23 54	96 00	4,077 79		78 62		7,180 35
Second district	2,000 00	50 00	1,950 00	1,500 00	94 63	24 00	70 19	267 00	9,653 -1	1,395 90	191 78		14,355 12
Third district	1,994 56	49 87	1,944 69	1,500 00	205 59		57 56	150 00	9,200 -3	966 24	186 91	150 00	14,174 91
Fourth district	2,015 34	51 30	1,964 11	505 50	134 49	4 00	23 87	96 00	8,229 -6	6,602 31	228 50		17,559 94
Fifth district	3,512 34	125 59	3,386 75	1,800 00	141 13	6 90	117 00	300 00	8,471 -3	13,998 90	469 57	61 30	34,923 11
Sixth district	2,005 38	50 26	1,955 12	1,100 00	170 51	5 30	5 25	108 33	8,563 -2	4,925 37	241 46		16,833 21
Seventh district	2,000 00	50 00	1,950 00	1,199 18	76 37	15 50	2 00	96 00	5,471 -0	394 00	111 21		9,404 15
Eighth district	3,300 41	108 27	3,192 14	2,273 31	163 11	53 85	55 43	600 00	14,062 -0	945 66	293 60		21,886 12
Total	18,826 10	535 29	18,290 81	10,877 99	1,013 54	116 75	354 86	1,713 33	73,669 5	29,426 38	1,811 74	211 30	135,676 51
TEXAS.													
First district*	5,687 59	218 32	5,469 27	1,458 34	74 60		37 50	372 90	11,456 2		297 35		18,868 73
Second district	7,332 49	273 16	7,059 33	1,500 00	135 77		53 77	371 67	10,657 49		263 41		15,777 93
Third district	2,795 33	83 86	2,711 47	1,677 42	292 35	19 00	96 36	434 28	10,410 10		256 71		15,641 33
Fourth district	2,083 36	62 50	2,020 86	1,101 90	131 36	75 55	52 34	250 00	19,949 2		507 22		23,581 73

VERMONT.													
First district	565 38	8 75	556 63	319 60	163 74	9 00	181 34	79 62	6,537 58	....	124 41	....	7,847 51
Second district	1,539 75	26 98	1,512 77	146 00	70 08	20 25	129 57	55 55	4,872 14	....	93 40	....	6,806 36
Third district*	2,126 24	60 42	2,065 82	457 90	169 08	6 00	74 11	199 43	5,380 17	....	99 63	....	8,352 51
Total	4,231 37	96 15	4,135 22	923 50	402 90	35 25	385 02	334 60	16,789 89	....	317 44	....	23,006 38
VIRGINIA.													
First district	1,401 10	23 35	1,377 75	175 00	44 74	....	11 75	66 01	7,434 82	....	138 58	28 50	9,138 57
Second district	4,677 61	177 01	4,500 60	1,933 33	327 98	39 40	102 32	....	15,004 53	1,263 42	301 80	21 00	23,192 58
Third district	3,750 50	137 52	3,612 98	2,161 63	184 59	54 50	113 70	....	10,117 70	2,081 00	223 33	20 00	18,346 10
Fourth district	1,623 63	27 07	1,596 56	879 50	134 57	10 50	94 22	208 00	7,731 70	1,898 86	172 67	23 50	12,577 41
Fifth district	4,565 15	173 15	4,392 00	1,319 80	361 81	42 50	162 25	335 22	7,465 45	743 64	153 70	....	14,822 67
Sixth district*	1,771 83	39 58	1,732 25	1,350 00	220 48	19 75	157 91	94 54	13,883 70	17,272 46	435 14	184 95	34,916 04
Seventh district	1,973 68	48 67	1,925 01	900 00	86 86	23 35	13 00	150 00	8,275 41	3,706 58	193 37	12 50	15,092 71
Eighth district	1,500 00	25 00	1,475 00	500 02	20 25	....	76 76	250 00	5,174 33	....	97 29	6 85	7,503 21
Total	21,263 50	651 35	20,612 15	9,219 28	1,381 28	190 00	731 91	1,103 77	75,087 64	26,965 96	1,715 88	297 30	135,589 29
WASHINGTON.													
Washington	3,038 46	101 92	2,936 54	600 00	125 72	13 00	26 22	299 16	4,896 24	1,090 02	163 18	106 13	10,093 03
WEST VIRGINIA.													
First district	2,659 37	87 07	2,572 30	1,200 00	127 40	51 25	41 40	....	9,634 77	609 84	188 07	17 00	14,253 96
Second district	2,825 50	89 20	2,736 30	600 00	41 44	70 62	3 40	50 00	9,152 61	3,503 97	226 63	....	16,158 34
Third district	1,500 00	25 00	1,475 00	227 00	102 37	23 75	24 10	60 00	6,334 94	....	118 71	....	8,247 16
Total	6,984 87	201 27	6,783 60	2,027 00	271 21	145 62	68 90	110 00	25,122 32	4,113 81	533 41	17 00	38,659 46
WISCONSIN.													
First district	5,067 23	207 46	4,859 77	2,500 00	171 29	7 50	116 63	500 00	14,326 09	6,221 16	336 66	51 00	28,753 44
Second district	1,827 60	41 37	1,786 23	1,250 00	135 52	11 00	141 46	150 00	8,981 81	1,275 12	183 36	9 55	13,740 69
Third district	1,500 00	25 00	1,475 00	660 00	87 82	15 50	102 13	120 00	9,174 80	330 66	175 41	....	11,965 91
Fourth district*	1,751 12	37 55	1,713 57	704 00	28 90	....	66 79	60 00	6,681 27	126 72	128 85	....	9,381 25
Fifth district	1,607 26	30 36	1,576 90	720 00	95 37	14 10	34 82	75 00	9,191 56	....	172 39	....	11,707 75
Sixth district	1,390 62	23 65	1,366 97	600 00	130 77	17 50	80 53	240 00	9,661 48	763 28	190 08	....	12,860 53
Total	13,143 83	365 39	12,778 44	6,434 00	649 67	65 60	542 36	1,145 00	58,017 01	8,716 94	1,186 75	60 55	88,409 57
WYOMING.													
Wyoming	2,840 26	85 30	2,754 96	101 64	....	10 25	....	332 66	2,688 66	....	77 27	....	5,888 17

A.—Statement showing the expenses of assessing the internal revenue taxes in the several collection districts, &c.—Continued.

RECAPITULATION.

Districts.	Gross compensation.	Tax.	Net compensation.	Clerk-hire.	Stationery.	Printing and advertising.	Postage and express.	Rent of assessor.	Net compensation of assistant assessors.	Net compensation of storekeepers.	Tax on comp. of assist'nt assessrs & store-keepers.	Survey of distilleries.	Total.
Alabama	$7,624 50	$243 74	$7,380 76	$5,920 74	$373 10	$162 75	$306 85	$308 75	$35,330 79	$3,044 12	$1,546 90		$73,027 46
Arizona	2,500 00	75 00	2,425 00		81 25	59 00	20 08	300 00	2,228 22		63 55		5,114 11
Arkansas	9,023 00	271 99	8,751 08	3,766 65	486 42	179 74	361 09	807 35	36,252 22	860 26	916 38		51,555 01
California	18,341 44	662 89	17,678 57	14,685 43	938 00	492 93	539 01	2,673 07	83,725 29	7,134 53	2,360 72	$120 00	128,366 60
Colorado	2,500 00	75 00	2,425 00	1,500 00	52 97	49 48	52 00	480 00	6,199 45		177 81	499 77	10,749 63
Connecticut	13,091 67	458 63	12,633 04	4,099 99	322 45		604 72	755 00	38,364 46	5,180 06	794 25		62,009 20
Dakota	1,623 63	27 05	1,596 57		197 71	13 38	68 75	229 84	1,376 02		30 35		3,669 49
Delaware	3,267 54	113 36	3,154 18	1,500 00	181 05	31 38	77 93		13,304 71	134 64	252 77		18,364 94
District of Columbia	3,921 03	146 03	3,775 00	1,800 00	103 36	95 50	5 00	420 00	10,334 43		201 05		16,469 67
Florida	2,499 75	75 00	2,424 75	1,625 00	114 87	133 40	55 21	360 00	14,155 57		349 02		18,830 40
Georgia	12,043 08	402 03	11,641 05	8,024 17	796 47	37 45	491 15	1,323 37	82,856 11	1,528 27	2,191 78	128 01	107,142 70
Idaho	2,500 00	75 00	2,425 00	251 00	76 17	308 75	45 62	600 00	7,740 46	1,770 84	298 17		12,946 14
Illinois	48,372 49	1,775 59	46,597 21	16,089 48	2,144 40	299 75	1,740 68	2,975 84	163,945 76	71,453 01	4,182 35	550 95	306,085 74
Indiana	32,716 66	1,081 50	31,635 16	8,767 74	1,247 93	489 65	645 71	1,370 25	80,627 56	22,346 63	1,788 98	382 25	147,328 70
Iowa	13,135 88	344 84	12,791 54	3,886 86	625 83	69 20	370 25	604 10	52,736 48	4,414 92	1,056 45	42 30	75,962 13
Kansas	2,798 20	85 78	2,712 42	1,025 00	298 30	161 75	167 63	360 00	19,513 44	578 16	378 39	31 50	25,335 85
Kentucky	31,102 20	1,115 56	29,986 64	12,799 62	1,539 43	137 75	458 70	1,770 58	110,520 94	218,376 44	4,973 96	1,229 30	376,842 80
Louisiana	8,498 61	284 96	8,213 65	3,737 93	1,177 11	70 15	72 23	791 87	79,706 46	9,786 12	2,220 58		107,623 32
Maine	8,839 94	191 96	8,647 98	3,381 53	345 57	196 94	242 43	649 46	30,040 84	1,346 40	579 01	104 65	44,724 56
Maryland	14,927 60	496 28	14,431 32	6,741 24	505 23	216 62	100 72	915 00	80,406 45	23,456 79	1,875 49		126,858 14
Massachusetts	33,385 76	1,180 12	32,205 64	18,927 92	1,242 86	172 85	1,246 22	3,516 93	137,484 18	15,260 98	2,936 79		210,100 15
Michigan	14,049 34	404 05	13,645 29	6,505 78	994 49	79 62	365 24	1,303 69	60,405 78	1,239 48	1,175 36		84,632 60
Minnesota	4,292 64	110 49	4,182 15	1,113 25	290 47	85 30	157 98	400 00	20,682 10	400 08	400 86	20 00	27,528 19
Mississippi	4,117 41	248 43	3,868 98	4,874 86	888 35	110 25	135 44	730 02	45,098 10	1,227 50	1,143 86	54 50	60,953 37
Missouri	18,237 93	527 93	17,660 00	8,350 72	979 93	43 40	753 46	2,116 86	84,351 16	13,080 53	1,800 03	283 70	128,506 18
Montana	1,761 60	125 36	1,635 72	1,208 04	68 41		18 15	560 32	10,938 36	932 54	357 01	109 00	17,460 04
Nebraska	1,899 48	49 55	1,854 52	900 00	241 85		10 98	190 50	8,491 13	51 48	163 50	11 50	11,718 44
Nevada	3,073 59	99 53	2,974 04	1,264 00	160 48		18 98	960 00	11,362 54		339 70		16,164 41
New Hampshire	6,197 10	159 50	6,037 33	2,660 50	637 48	103 30	232 19	322 50	19,629 38	1,389 96	375 84	12 25	28,528 53
New Jersey	13,524 10	523 48	13,700 62	8,224 96	172 75		244 64	1,268 75	79,293 20	1,386 91	1,529 11	239 10	106,102 03
New Mexico	2,500 00	75 00	2,425 00	999 94	68 36		10 65	300 00	12,469 31		381 74		17,884 63
New York	97,002 32	3,300 32	93,702 00	73,330 94	6,298 12	839 80	1,967 58	15,333 86	561,995 36	46,294 66	11,435 37	53 00	799,844 87
North Carolina	15,574 03	457 86	15,116 17	6,621 99	499 77	53 00	1,173 60	1,064 86	53,146 11	5,761 99	1,103 03	162 35	82,584 83
Ohio	69,774 09	2,184 39	65,599 69	21,040 98	2,788 47	607 17	1,141 97	4,333 56	192,329 54	75,427 81	4,364 44	147 33	358,401 89
Oregon	5,811 02	240 54	5,570 48	667 50	139 68	24 00	24 00	480 00	12,767 44		373 54	302 48	20,101 27
Pennsylvania	71,660 45	2,373 51	69,286 94	38,491 69	2,849 67	659 44	659 44	6,927 45	358,081 97	115,428 98	8,193 53	36 00	503,480 41
Rhode Island	6,098 87	204 92	5,893 95	2,923 08	136 57	37 87	85 28	300 00	21,990 12	1,180 08	435 40	632 10	34,446 95

Tennessee	18,826 10	535 90	18,990 81	10,877 99	1,013 54	116 75	354 80	1,713 33	73,069 55	29,428 38	1,811 74	211 30	135,676 51
Texas	17,858 77	637 84	17,260 93	5,737 68	634 08	94 55	329 97	1,428 85	52,473 68	......	1,334 69	......	77,869 72
Utah	2,441 11	56 11	2,495 00	609 00	217 05	27 00	70 41	600 00	8,708 92	491 00	258 63	......	13,207 68
Vermont	4,231 37	96 15	4,135 32	823 50	402 90	35 25	385 02	334 60	16,789 89	......	317 44	......	22,006 38
Virginia	21,963 50	651 35	20,612 15	9,219 28	1,381 98	190 00	731 91	1,103 77	75,037 64	26,963 96	1,715 88	207 30	135,589 29
Washington	3,038 46	101 92	2,936 54	2,600 00	125 72	13 00	26 22	290 16	4,896 94	1,090 02	163 18	106 13	10,093 03
West Virginia	6,984 87	201 27	6,783 60	2,027 00	271 91	145 62	68 90	110 00	25,122 32	4,113 61	533 41	17 00	38,639 46
Wisconsin	13,143 83	365 39	12,778 44	6,434 00	649 67	65 60	542 36	1,145 00	58,017 01	8,716 94	1,186 75	60 55	88,409 57
Wyoming	2,840 26	85 30	2,754 96	101 64	......	10 23	......	332 66	2,688 66	......	77 27	......	5,888 17
Grand total	709,745 42	93,438 66	686,306 76	340,949 13	34,895 98	7,208 99	17,016 65	64,616 62	3,018,658 40	723,085 40	71,668 89	5,868 57	4,898,626 72
Add amount of taxes													95,107 55
													4,993,734 27

B.—*Statement showing the expenses of collecting the internal revenue taxes in the several collection districts, including the commissions, salaries, and extra allowances of the collectors; the office expenses which are paid out of the commissions and extra allowances; and the assessments and collections from July 1, 1869, to June 30, 1870.*

[NOTE.—Districts marked with an asterisk, returns are incomplete.]

District	Gross compensation.	Tax.	Net compensation.	Stationery and blank books.	Postage.	Express and dep. money.	Advertising.	Total expenses of collecting.	Expenses of administering office.	Assessments.	Collections.
ALABAMA.											
First district	$14,211 87	$339 91	$13,871 96	$171 87	$40 41		$10 00	$14,43. 15	$6,316 38	$366,487 55	$233,676 68
Second district	22,024 92	287 76	22,337 16	222 42	334 91		75 00	22,101 30	14,015 12	324,198 22	296,718 29
Third district	20,884 15	644 88	20,239 27	136 07	49 00	$334 05	67 00	21,138 22	5,044 17	917,862 80	664,030 65
Total	57,720 94	1,272 55	56,448 39	530 36	444 32	334 05	152 00	59,17. 67	25,375 67	1,608,548 57	1,194,425 62
ARIZONA.											
Arizona	3,084 00	75 00	3,009 00		22 00		30 00	3,13. 00	584 00	20,184 36	10,891 21
ARKANSAS.											
First district	11,188 13	226 39	10,961 74	121 36	137 23	7 50	66 75	11,52. 97	6,236 12	135,591 10	146,920 31
Second district	12,908 53	212 92	12,695 61	172 92	82 03		3 00	13,16. 48	7,650 21	137,397 00	142,606 62
Third district	2,762 61	37 53	2,725 08	12 30	8 00		32 00	2,81. 91	1,675 00	33,392 25	27,626 17
Total	26,859 27	476 84	26,382 43	306 58	227 26	7 50	101 75	27,50. 36	15,561 33	306,380 35	317,153 10
CALIFORNIA.											
First district	19,137 71	200 00	18,937 71	359 82	264 90	1,227 06	9 30	19,74. 73	14,000 00	4,003,206 36	3,150,033 21
Second district	11,571 91	77 29	11,494 62	400 18	347 18		93 88	13,63. 33	12,472 88	633,697 09	399,278 71
Third district	10,342 04	22 83	10,319 21	268 70	140 44		146 50	10,89. 68	9,660 00	232,194 57	215,960 37
Fourth district	30,923 56	320 73	30,602 83	330 45	1,074 96	1,271 66	218 75	33,81. 38	21,995 50	511,946 22	572,364 19
Fifth district	16,587 84	300 39	16,287 45	606 75	204 00	1,924 86	96 33	19,41. 78	9,580 00	323,013 45	331,756 75
Total	88,563 06	921 24	87,641 82	1,935 90	2,031 30	4,423 58	564 06	97,51. 90	67,708 38	5,704,057 69	4,669,393 23
COLORADO.											

Fourth district	7,998 63	210 69	7,717 94	72 50	396 50		14 50	8,412 13	2,715 01	464,000 94	488,804 92
Total	34,453 70	823 51	33,630 19	362 10	1,102 21	3 25	138 66	36,056 67	14,083 34	2,533,705 45	2,567,489 96
DAKOTA.											
Dakota	1,737 54	27 68	1,709 86	39 69	19 91		9 75	1,810 34	184 00	9,506 63	7,917 04
DELAWARE.											
Delaware	7,923 45	204 57	7,718 88	31 65	169 23		32 75	8,157 08	2,832 00	508,062 62	484,691 37
DISTRICT OF COLUMBIA.											
District of Columbia	8,312 27	174 17	8,138 10	123 34	176 00		92 50	8,704 11	3,628 89	533,498 09	514,390 07
FLORIDA.											
Florida	10,850 20	190 92	10,659 28	172 07	124 27	119 88	68 97	11,335 39	8,541 06	180,124 13	107,181 34
GEORGIA.											
First district	10,046 90	143 90	9,903 00	123 14	72 00		6 00	10,246 04	6,169 00	289,699 00	265,856 32
Second district	15,620 66	382 17	15,238 49	176 85	266 75	5 70	111 15	16,181 11	6,795 24	303,512 29	303,065 00
Third district	11,486 70	122 84	11,363 86	118 63	148 95		30 00	11,764 28	8,029 90	250,897 46	229,734 00
Fourth district	9,675 01	4 13	9,670 88	165 19	63 30		57 00	9,980 70	8,392 49	440,060 29	322,500 52
Total	46,829 27	653 04	46,176 23	583 81	571 99	5 70	204 15	48,194 13	29,586 63	1,306,169 04	1,123,155 84
IDAHO.											
Idaho	10,440 95	120 11	10,320 84	111 72	15 75		8 00	10,576 42	5,033 00	81,522 01	58,405 47
ILLINOIS.											
First district	28,020 14	804 79	27,215 35	464 51	686 39		132 70	29,303 74	10,924 31	8,460,869 58	8,395,131 81
Second district	8,176 93	206 03	7,970 90	94 61	238 51		66 33	8,570 40	3,120 49	378,422 48	401,560 92
Third district	9,093 48	213 50	8,879 98	106 61	257 94		32 50	9,190 03	3,809 32	656,118 60	577,077 24
Fourth district	12,564 90	339 43	12,205 47	226 03	193 66		135 50	13,190 79	4,376 80	1,818,112 80	1,395,500 74
Fifth district	19,842 26	601 61	19,150 65	166 00	316 95		49 50	20,374 79	5,010 02	4,487,593 03	3,661,566 37
Sixth district	9,166 31	191 36	8,974 95	101 37	169 61			9,437 29	4,044 69	530,500 14	3,540,366 48
Seventh district	10,195 25	185 62	10,009 63	296 06	366 50		91 45	9,949 26	5,463 00	853,060 90	735,741 55
Eighth district	11,962 94	287 75	11,675 19	245 55	455 00		37 00	12,700 49	5,208 54	876,046 38	988,961 07
Ninth district	5,067 19	104 48	4,962 71	74 00	245 28		34 50	5,480 37	1,977 54	194,262 95	152,513 91
Tenth district	5,128 80	32 94	5,095 86	61 33	171 44		62 53	5,430 03	3,541 37	192,558 57	161,811 98
Eleventh district	5,825 29	55 00	5,770 29	108 17	238 50	6 25	88 00	5,959 96	2,384 03	84,124 57	80,972 15
Twelfth district	10,743 67	201 18	10,542 49	98 06	308 74		167 15	11,317 63	3,557 06	1,375,690 08	769,141 93
Thirteenth district	4,881 00	25 00	4,856 00	172 59	165 70		8 00	4,627 29	3,915 94	154,176 93	92,700 00
Total	140,068 16	3,358 69	136,709 47	2,214 97	3,808 22	6 25	904 70	147,009 30	59,852 30	21,068,736 33	18,153,046 15

15 F

B.—*Statement showing the expenses of collecting the internal revenue taxes in the several collection districts, &c.*—Continued.

District	Gross compensation.	Tax.	Net compensation.	Stationery and blank-books.	Postage.	Express and dep. money.	Advertising.	Total expense of collecting.	Expenses of administering office.	Assessments.	Collections.
INDIANA.											
First district	$9,325 40	$317 99	$9,007 41	$208 30	$10 01		$46 00	$9,589 71	$1,965 50	$266,098 49	$612,210 53
Second district	3,730 44	106 29	3,624 15	47 65	74 50		57 00	3,909 59	2,604 71	223,564 31	223,042 68
Third district	8,807 21	217 29	8,589 92	171 99	142 00		42 50	9,163 70	3,461 32	712,184 99	518,075 36
Fourth district	13,998 95	479 25	13,519 70	307 85	228 02		112 50	14,697 24	3,413 85	1,842,433 26	1,653,675 70
Fifth district	8,099 71	299 85	7,799 86	84 85	204 00		36 00	8,424 56	1,103 00	581,196 03	436,695 61
Sixth district	8,819 56	235 17	8,584 39	89 78	60 25			8,969 59	3,116 25	653,807 35	366,027 36
Seventh district	7,100 72	195 02	6,905 70	141 96	164 25		53 00	7,459 33	2,920 26	321,906 43	326,952 95
Eighth district	6,139 73	160 60	5,979 13	91 82			29 40	6,260 95	1,927 69	1,171,059 49	254,697 09
Ninth district	5,248 35	136 31	5,122 04	74 08	63 37		95 50	5,481 30	1,732 16	234,248 22	170,511 67
Tenth district	4,543 83	102 72	4,441 11	61 71	34 50		44 80	4,684 84	1,499 31	127,110 12	104,383 53
Eleventh district	5,055 29	68 38	4,986 91	286 47	261 29	$166 26	84 60	5,833 91	2,683 68	64,537 69	63,818 83
Total	82,869 19	2,308 87	80,560 32	1,546 18	1,292 39	166 26	601 30	86,475 32	25,687 73	6,053,166 38	4,950,291 31
IOWA.											
First district	6,859 19	126 05	6,733 14	238 01	207 23		47 50	7,351 93	3,335 74	523,933 89	338,087 96
Second district	7,054 74	155 67	6,899 07	226 23	325 58	5 83	67 05	7,679 43	2,941 00	342,042 93	343,772 20
Third district	6,793 97	102 05	6,691 92	260 53	429 94	3 90	17 50	7,565 84	3,752 98	535,317 15	313,002 44
Fourth district	5,036 99	73 48	4,958 51	120 24	107 17	7 47	70 00	5,431 87	2,467 45	175,244 37	148,947 85
Fifth district	5,619 49	60 38	5,559 11	118 04	133 37		33 40	5,904 30	3,411 62	136,108 21	111,948 62
Sixth district	4,675 01	41 01	4,634 00	199 31	133 36		171 60	5,179 18	2,834 75	119,332 87	117,501 51
Total	36,039 39	563 64	35,475 75	1,162 36	1,436 55	17 20	407 05	39,052 55	18,763 54	1,832,039 42	1,373,260 58
KANSAS.											

LOUISIANA.											
First district	24,378 31	200 00	24,178 31	454 08	27 50	1 60	256 30	25,117 79	19,852 95	3,285,658 92	2,750,068 50
Second district	16,998 24	29 12	16,969 12	234 27	48 14	163 00	41 00	17,484 65	10,755 16	176,749 08	146,214 91
Third district	9,629 45	132 03	9,497 42	158 77	49 37	193 21	85 75	10,116 55	8,910 50	114,496 22	71,475 04
Total	51,006 00	361 15	50,644 85	847 12	125 01	357 81	383 05	52,718 99	39,518 61	3,576,904 16	2,967,758 45
MAINE.											
First district	7,655 14	209 35	7,445 79	92 13	270 00		23 00	7,970 27	2,468 00	405,047 74	409,050 60
Second district	5,029 12	142 05	4,887 07	117 29	183 57	2 85	16 75	5,349 58	1,188 05	104,993 50	102,746 04
Third district	4,735 07	131 00	4,604 07	71 90	232 84		10 50	5,039 01	1,115 00	122,231 72	123,506 77
Fourth district	4,409 37	110 73	4,298 64	53 45	96 01		48 94	4,007 77	1,194 66	95,126 14	96,978 97
Fifth district	3,636 00	36 00	3,600 00	36 74	62 54		28 00	3,763 28	1,916 00	76,634 50	71,200 00
Total	25,464 70	629 13	24,835 57	300 81	834 36	2 85	127 19	26,729 91	7,881 71	804,033 30	803,482 38
MARYLAND.											
First district	4,422 58	120 75	4,301 83	77 51	131 23		64 98	4,695 30	1,007 50	119,804 76	97,154 61
Second district	8,623 86	248 27	8,375 59	118 84	83 97		97 75	8,924 42	2,658 41	626,187 01	578,819 65
Third district	15,597 89	303 96	15,293 93	268 26	229 50		72 75	16,228 40	8,518 93	4,545,392 79	4,177,565 28
Fourth district	5,962 60	75 18	5,887 42	123 14	59 71		125 00	6,271 30	3,458 94	278,070 40	238,198 73
Fifth district	8,498 59	178 52	8,320 07	71 53	162 30	85	79 87	8,812 29	3,927 99	549,170 36	420,107 85
Total	43,105 52	926 68	42,178 84	659 28	726 71	85	440 35	44,932 71	19,571 77	6,118,625 32	5,571,776 12
MASSACHUSETTS.											
First district	7,398 51	159 70	7,438 81	61 49	175 22		84 43	7,919 64	3,404 72	422,260 89	419,702 61
Second district	7,794 60	180 93	7,613 67	66 61	292 75		62 25	8,236 21	3,175 75	465,117 00	458,910 92
Third district	14,704 15	310 96	14,393 89	266 74	1,039 50		18 50	16,027 80	7,499 11	4,156,294 71	4,149,390 39
Fourth district	12,500 25	245 96	12,254 29	241 20	378 50		32 50	13,152 45	6,581 00	2,101,574 71	2,034,070 01
Fifth district	8,952 70	234 75	8,717 95	156 80	283 05		64 00	9,433 57	3,257 56	696,824 29	652,729 13
Sixth district	10,481 36	251 04	10,230 32	127 39	383 50		21 00	11,013 25	4,460 00	1,070,553 40	925,678 22
Seventh district	8,536 46	188 56	8,347 90	43 33	431 74	15	23 75	9,035 43	3,765 14	595,181 07	613,604 05
Eighth district	6,859 73	250 03	7,600 75	86 34	329 95		58 25	8,334 82	1,853 96	475,757 71	471,928 58
Ninth district	6,394 00	123 32	6,417 07	122 00	436 00		6 00	7,156 19	3,127 48	392,253 92	309,408 87
Tenth district	8,960 96	265 66	8,695 30	146 78	286 00		27 00	9,420 74	2,647 87	697,344 57	063,998 92
Total	93,982 86	2,210 21	91,772 65	1,319 29	4,045 21	15	414 67	99,752 18	29,778 09	10,993,190 27	10,699,430 00
MICHIGAN.											
First district	11,769 96	289 00	11,480 96	116 15	253 85		31 35	12,171 31	4,990 00	2,095,928 70	2,015,966 88
Second district	6,029 82	45 13	5,984 69	116 53	259 38		23 50	6,429 23	3,680 30	210,862 24	162,209 39
Third district	5,686 98	72 93	5,614 05	115 42	180 93		53 60	6,036 93	3,228 41	244,245 86	228,698 06
Fourth district	5,523 55	86 79	5,436 76	140 73	125 45	1 25	36 85	5,827 83	2,709 91	173,362 19	169,195 60
Fifth district	3,684 70	25 00	3,659 70	107 91	171 49	9 50	35 22	4,008 82	3,290 10	103,377 50	72,823 50
Sixth district	5,886 77	87 72	5,799 05	100 50	117 59		7 90	6,113 76	3,132 30	286,216 61	238,677 28
Total	38,581 78	606 57	37,975 21	697 24	1,108 69	10 75	188 42	40,596 68	21,031 02	3,113,993 10	2,887,570 71

First district	$8,738 48	$179 81	$8,558 67	$104 93	$153 72	$28 69	$51 50	$9,077 38	$4,142 25	$139,937 52	$145,641 44
Second district	14,878 36	178 50	14,699 86	95 21	251 76		67 25	15,295 58	7,631 25	275,709 50	340,006 21
Total	23,616 84	358 31	23,258 53	200 14	405 48	28 89	118 75	24,370 10	11,773 50	415,647 02	465,647 65

MISSISSIPPI.

First district	12,701 99	294 25	12,407 74	222 35	31 62	24 30	106 50	13,080 76	5,816 25	137,692 03	97,707 76
Second district	12,105 02	7 18	12,097 84	295 66	128 60		147 75	12,677 03	9,294 05	151,746 25	130,401 66
Third district *	7,160 52	158 21	7,002 31	314 49	139 34		33 00	7,647 35	3,498 17	121,274 17	47,736 82
Total	31,967 53	459 64	31,507 89	832 50	299 56	24 30	287 25	33,411 14	18,609 07	410,712 45	965,846 24

MISSOURI.

First district	21,701 79	221 64	21,480 15	537 98	765 70		56 37	23,061 84	16,072 13	4,715,490 27	4,590,339 97
Second district	11,316 07	148 24	11,167 83	263 28	431 17	163 36	214 15	12,384 03	9,777 90	108,289 57	124,388 10
Third district	6,296 57	188 64	6,107 93	72 33	198 05	71 00	90 75	6,722 70	1,523 65	304,748 31	278,351 07
Fourth district	5,857 45	112 74	5,744 71	208 36	255 76		43 50	6,362 07	2,602 65	410,969 94	334,587 28
Fifth district	6,886 21	118 23	6,767 98	176 78	476 51	401 94	67 45	8,006 88	4,147 93	432,368 77	211,482 45
Sixth district	9,414 12	41 48	9,372 64	372 90	649 00		246 11	10,658 13	10,650 01	976,247 45	617,861 37
Total	61,472 21	630 97	60,641 24	1,631 63	2,776 19	636 30	718 33	67,236 66	44,774 27	6,948,014 61	6,057,010 24

MONTANA.

Montana	10,692 25	70 45	10,621 80	236 82	60 96	166 35	25 00	11,181 36	9,820 25	129,261 84	64,806 63

NEBRASKA.

NEW JERSEY.											
First district	5,490 76	72 04	5,418 72	70 51	196 00		15 00	5,772 27	3,050 00	209,124 25	177,966 62
Second district	7,849 02	219 96	7,629 06	34 42	505 87		30 50	8,419 81	2,449 83	318,662 15	460,792 72
Third district	9,492 87	176 02	9,316 85	139 35	473 00			10,105 92	4,972 53	767,127 34	750,843 39
Fourth district	9,848 27	154 16	7,694 11	159 35	250 98	28 50	34 10	8,381 20	4,764 50	480,201 21	454,445 32
Fifth district	11,358 60	159 49	11,799 11	95 39	413 50		99 30	12,566 99	7,768 74	2,197,113 10	2,166,879 10
Total	42,639 52	781 67	41,857 85	499 92	1,839 35	28 50	178 90	45,185 49	22,005 60	3,972,228 05	4,010,866 15
NEW MEXICO.											
New Mexico*	2,316 95	98 12	2,288 13	239 20	92 18	2 50	105 50	2,678 63	2,111 89	70,529 69	25,316 65
NEW YORK.											
First district	8,383 22	154 38	8,228 84	213 99	217 89		41 00	8,856 03	4,333 30	593,524 45	576,247 82
Second district	17,173 01	200 00	16,973 01	376 23	163 49		50 00	17,762 72	11,725 00	2,937,124 16	2,727,562 88
Third district	17,754 59	201 25	17,553 34	748 27	616 40		188 10	19,307 36	12,729 55	2,120,198 72	2,174,381 91
Fourth district	27,819 27	200 00	27,619 27	714 42	1,221 80		412 10	30,167 90	23,488 05	3,567,339 07	3,619,579 11
Fifth district	10,224 92	239 47	9,985 45	190 83	946 80	63 00	165 45	10,830 00	4,435 52	1,051,721 79	944,923 79
Sixth district	21,798 39	256 07	21,541 42	306 23	508 10		231 65	22,844 37	15,116 19	1,209,545 54	1,833,584 73
Seventh district	11,103 01	227 07	10,875 94	107 30	172 30	8 00	19 75	11,464 26	5,411 66	1,380,053 66	1,371,721 81
Eighth district	18,917 85	200 00	18,717 85	478 21	378 00		263 35	20,037 41	14,025 51	4,027,490 33	3,583,493 06
Ninth district	12,058 86	290 51	11,768 35	180 97	253 00		125 53	12,626 38	5,127 01	2,808,586 30	1,759,617 19
Tenth district	9,736 97	178 83	9,558 09	125 28	373 47		39 50	10,275 22	5,259 27	1,353,461 30	857,935 16
Eleventh district	5,938 56	146 02	5,792 54	232 46	175 87		41 33	6,346 89	5,018 31	310,568 48	238,073 12
Twelfth district	6,853 12	132 90	6,729 92	80 68	131 61		104 13	7,105 74	3,444 04	511,917 25	398,384 88
Thirteenth district	3,370 51	78 57	5,291 94	18 75	99 88		51 00	5,593 27	2,799 10	240,490 71	185,456 42
Fourteenth district	11,010 07	288 65	10,723 42	199 76	359 80		138 50	11,614 03	4,237 68	1,447,629 78	1,406,227 84
Fifteenth district	8,651 35	228 93	8,422 42	101 07	359 80	7 70	22 75	9,250 72	3,072 88	631,379 61	630,268 57
Sixteenth district	4,421 41	110 71	4,449 35	60 14	110 13	1 75	35 50	4,753 03	1,345 84	109,266 87	106,005 52
Seventeenth district	4,303 09	71 42	4,349 99	37 58	139 12	1 50	49 98	4,641 31	1,993 00	105,510 61	97,380 28
Eighteenth district	4,614 21	43 69	6,260 29	65 95	231 95		11 25	6,673 51	4,430 38	312,018 66	274,455 60
Nineteenth district	5,181 06	69 86	4,544 35	209 11	122 37	13 87	40 62	4,958 44	2,216 34	110,580 72	111,421 13
Twentieth district	8,641 76	100 57	5,020 49	106 41	173 46	1 35	33 50	5,501 55	2,169 57	179,432 72	168,106 19
Twenty-first district	9,196 12	264 45	8,377 31	96 33	209 50		69 22	8,994 96	2,352 72	649,495 39	611,902 79
Twenty-second district	9,918 18	291 49	8,904 63	114 37	248 14		13 75	9,587 22	2,366 18	865,278 39	399,681 48
Twenty-third district	8,949 33	244 28	9,673 90	136 94	246 00		24 75	10,314 87	4,032 52	886,627 98	779,029 19
Twenty-fourth district	6,681 97	295 99	8,633 34	145 18	413 74	20 85	20 00	9,553 85	2,029 35	675,862 34	568,378 61
Twenty-fifth district	6,470 69	40 24	6,641 73	49 99	240 16		10 80	6,992 12	4,877 90	284,163 07	295,198 53
Twenty-sixth district	5,789 31	112 71	6,357 38	152 31	46 03		40 25	6,679 23	3,215 34	300,862 45	272,734 82
Twenty-seventh district	8,558 97	72 17	5,717 14	134 99	210 05		4 00	6,174 60	3,345 50	247,432 14	228,276 55
Twenty-eighth district	7,056 06	214 83	8,344 14	66 89	110 00		27 00	8,739 93	3,262 31	775,325 03	564,558 97
Twenty-ninth district	14,754 49	167 58	6,888 48	110 29	189 42	2 75	20 00	15,460 42	2,397 50	312,603 81	297,512 88
Thirtieth district	4,500 00	571 92	14,182 57	284 15	401 78		25 50	5,039 01	7,642 94	830,280 25	2,302,674 87
Thirty-first district	37,956 71	103 70	4,396 30	244 04	289 47		204 50	41,001 89	1,426 00	115,988 21	100,000 00
Thirty-second district		253 61	37,703 10	1,873 28	967 40				34,675 68	7,228,666	6,742,105 42
Total	346,347 11	6,042 82	340,304 29	7,975 40	9,608 53	119 77	2,482 71	366,533 52	200,602 69	40,210,646 36	36,417,950 36

B.—*Statement showing the expenses of collecting the internal revenue taxes in the several collection districts, &c.*—Continued.

District	Gross compensation.	Tax.	Net compensation.	Stationery and blank books.	Postage.	Express and dep. money.	Advertising.	Total expense of collecting.	Expenses of administering office.	Assessments.	Collections.
NORTH CAROLINA.											
First district	$6,679 98	$184 66	$6,494 62	$37 98	$57 82	$1 50	$15 00	$6,790 86	$1,923 67	$92,707 09	$62,743 00
Second district	6,553 55	203 21	6,350 34	135 92	92 69		61 00	6,843 16	2,035 00	140,990 11	93,632 19
Third district	3,989 00	50 00	3,939 00	140 54	16 50		2 50	4,148 04	1,989 00	47,469 13	27,356 99
Fourth district	21,564 07	610 53	20,953 54	113 53	102 93	4 50	89 00	21,874 45	7,989 06	488,860 03	419,999 86
Fifth district*	1,400 44	15 53	1,384 91	72 83				1,473 27	925 00	481,306 70	386,902 30
Sixth district	14,119 32	318 53	13,800 79	98 68	89 32	1 25	46 50	14,350 07	6,748 45	275,648 28	235,321 59
Seventh district	5,315 27	59 00	5,256 27	65 08	55 60			5,435 95	2,734 12	48,196 02	33,632 45
Total	59,620 93	1,441 46	58,179 47	663 74	407 88	7 25	216 00	60,915 80	24,274 30	1,555,029 96	1,259,598 47
OHIO.											
First district	12,206 38	209 59	11,996 79	227 70	174 00		17 50	12,625 58	7,014 62	2,663,955 74	2,365,002 87
Second district	22,665 59	740 23	21,925 36	263 34	225 98		19 25	23,173 16	6,961 07	5,244,277 96	4,844,818 80
Third district	15,630 12	411 27	15,218 85	455 11	350 74		29 50	16,465 47	6,404 65	2,730,439 13	2,373,512 15
Fourth district	11,853 30	356 81	11,496 49	78 04	86 49		39 75	12,057 49	3,717 00	1,015,363 50	976,028 19
Fifth district	6,321 21	147 31	6,173 90	191 06	83 66	75	22 50	6,619 18	2,375 00	294,478 28	254,746 13
Sixth district	11,829 40	341 13	11,488 27	228 44	143 93		21 25	12,223 02	4,006 87	1,144,051 25	951,792 74
Seventh district	11,314 52	277 10	11,037 42	203 81	133 75		55 00	11,707 68	4,772 41	1,157,476 63	1,018,314 55
Eighth district	4,966 42	109 27	4,857 15	23 37	87 53		21 00	5,101 02	1,780 98	138,410 79	137,870 99
Ninth district	12,109 74	409 34	11,700 40	107 68	218 80		55 75	12,273 17	2,923 00	1,127,732 85	1,029,322 81
Tenth district	10,852 17	273 04	10,579 13	135 43	199 02		60 25	11,257 05	4,391 47	1,185,718 91	1,108,299 51
Eleventh district	11,507 29	433 94	11,073 35	59 19	123 25		45 25	11,734 35	1,828 50	1,067,057 74	925,182 89
Twelfth district	11,248 12	393 61	10,854 51	88 41	141 40		33 50	11,492 28	2,376 00	1,042,269 81	953,523 39
Thirteenth district	7,673 94	158 35	7,515 59	106 18	104 00		28 00	7,945 52	3,506 07	434,508 04	382,526 90
Fourteenth district	4,405 55	64 70	4,340 85	73 65	65 99			4,582 20	3,111 60	115,194 79	96,851 79
Fifteenth district	4,501 09	76 20	4,424 89	100 21	142 55		29 10	4,696 88	1,977 10	155,687 91	100,108 70
Sixteenth district	4,618 31	67 30	4,551 01	137 56	287 85		36 00	4,934 42	2,272 33	177,383 55	108,178 30
Seventeenth district*	6,326 08	162 15	6,163 93	277 80	204 00		11 00	6,845 73	2,083 00	388,533 05	261,748 03
Eighteenth district*	10,039 86	178 10	9,861 76	193 29	238 08		22 65	10,456 80	5,563 02	1,383,943 12	1,262,124 83
Nineteenth district*	5,094 01	89 00	5,005 01	88 52		4 75	36 00	5,461 45	5,312 20	171,322 44	159,382 13
Total	185,163 19	4,698 53	180,264 66	3,030 79	2,873 93	5 50	563 95	191,653 36	68,277 79	21,637,764 79	19,329,275 70
OREGON.											
Oregon	16,607 99	310 52	16,297 47	110 50	74 13		163 71	16,958 33	9,397 51	247,129 58	332,159 93

PENNSYLVANIA.										
First district	13,843 41	225 81	13,617 60	231 25			70 00	14,144 66	3,868,463 03	3,318,298 32
Second district	11,781 17	208 45	11,572 72	138 05			37 71	12,096 93	1,917,550 22	2,524,427 83
Third district	11,237 33	246 26	10,137 07	348 83			55 68	11,756 76	955,225 63	1,137,040 08
Fourth district	11,214 34	122 76	11,091 58	290 11			32 50	11,788 95	1,471,590 09	1,342,439 65
Fifth district	7,486 40	156 43	7,339 92	127 32		5 50	63 30	7,785 77	595,084 16	435,016 99
Sixth district	7,601 16	186 64	7,414 53	31 95	156 10		22 98	6,031 50	651,252 09	420,231 60
Seventh district	5,737 63	148 53	5,589 12	61 88	132 66		12 82	7,072 53	307,709 07	223,765 02
Eighth district	6,908 36	211 56	6,696 80	79 56	208 99		63 40	9,843 65	330,701 07	335,222 73
Ninth district	9,415 43	258 16	9,157 29	156 50	71 77		37 90	6,371 37	736,636 27	564,165 09
Tenth district	5,944 60	128 06	6,013 32	95 09	208 30		70 75	6,410 51	403,733 55	304,137 71
Eleventh district	5,141 38	146 51	5,798 69	110 80	97 00		32 00	9,359 57	290,149 00	344,459 57
Twelfth district	6,667 16	118 88	6,748 28	173 00	284 41		58 40	4,816 68	464,670 92	334,538 40
Thirteenth district	4,509 20	76 75	4,432 45	143 32	135 36		71 25	8,398 67	195,107 42	102,783 74
Fourteenth district	5,946 06	113 27	5,892 79	84 87	296 49	43 80	38 50	8,644 29	248,252 32	235,678 86
Fifteenth district	7,579 45	162 41	7,413 79	137 04	243 50	42 70	46 15	5,680 76	470,722 76	388,371 50
Sixteenth district	5,904 61	90 90	5,413 04	203 40	184 50		26 00	4,723 76	215,917 08	138,946 65
Seventeenth district	4,321 27	91 71	4,195 02	38 64	108 12		27 00	5,574 72	111,131 73	102,971 60
Eighteenth district	5,272 59	77 37	5,195 82	120 48	193 95	90	22 00	7,300 47	173,060 80	177,259 00
Nineteenth district	6,963 75	41 91	6,849 75	245 33	293 95		73 00	7,463 98	572,473 40	980,992 74
Twentieth district	7,100 84	73 75		119 50	334 14	1 85		6,840 17	514,479 47	365,473 09
Twenty-first district	12,368 28	376 40	11,991 88	153 65	323 55	2 05	16 25	12,953 86	144,333 01	1,214,553 16
Twenty-second district	12,360 91	253 65	12,907 96	174 44	166 85	3 80	164 60	6,416 84	2,380,833 01	2,049,669 82
Twenty-third district	8,853 98	197 51	8,738 47	144 23	176 85		16 32	9,463 17	868,289 28	671,416 96
Twenty-fourth district	8,304 89	150 32	8,154 57					8,642 29	494,287 32	497,143 46
Total	193,365 64	3,864 80	189,500 84	3,494 18	4,564 49	100 60	1,037 43	292,562 34	19,348,256 50	17,361,201 46
RHODE ISLAND.										
First district	10,540 23	213 51	10,396 72	151 43	254 50		75 25	11,021 41	1,154,459 44	1,147,155 28
Second district	4,852 23	104 58	4,747 65	29 88	39 00		18 75	4,939 86	136,046 36	135,222 91
Total	15,392 46	318 09	15,074 37	181 31	293 50		94 00	15,961 27	1,290,505 80	1,282,378 19
SOUTH CAROLINA.										
First district	6,830 92	114 46	6,716 46	223 43	157 92		94 00	7,306 26	78,654 30	64,717 74
Second district	8,676 20	199 10	8,477 10	56 64	119 30		133 97	8,986 11	230,093 91	216,904 71
Third district	6,720 07	100 25	6,619 82	121 83	96 06		92 25	7,030 21	148,959 71	122,736 11
Total	22,227 19	413 81	21,813 38	401 89	373 28		390 22	23,322 58	457,707 92	405,358 56
TENNESSEE.										
First district	6,375 26	27 06	6,348 20	45 65	72 50		12 25	6,505 66	36,915 46	33,066 61
Second district	10,305 44	167 54	10,137 90	63 48	59 99		5 00	10,432 00	84,816 06	85,292 20
Third district	6,547 86	89 29	6,458 57	153 54	61 75	3 75	5 50	6,768 65	92,082 32	61,848 41
Fourth district	7,980 43	94 45	7,885 98	129 71	16 50		90 50	6,150 89	196,275 84	114,006 25
Fifth district	11,310 17	170 74	11,133 43	68 28	194 00		32 30	11,624 75	584,343 21	565,508 36
Sixth district	1,778 69	59 72	1,718 97	159 96	17 25		12 00	8,967 90	142,534 47	35,573 74

B.—*Statement showing the expenses of collecting the internal revenue taxes in the several collection districts, &c.—Continued.*

District	Gross compensation.	Tax.	Net compensation.	Stationery and blank books.	Postage.	Express and dep. money.	Advertising.	Total expenses of collecting.	Expenses of administering office.	Assessments.	Collections.
TENNESSEE—Continued.											
Seventh district	$6,400 00	$868 33	$6,331 67	$32 04	$64 50	....	$22 50	$6,539 04	$4,033 33	$90,274 48	$73,190 78
Eighth district	10,680 70	250 28	10,430 42	147 30	161 08	....	42 50	11,031 52	4,673 47	502,408 37	427,228 49
Total	61,378 53	933 41	60,445 14	818 96	647 57	$3 75	172 55	63,021 38	34,135 77	1,729,650 21	1,415,714 84
TEXAS.											
First district	4,026 05	176 11	4,026 05	142 50	42 00	5 25	....	4,215 00	5,493 32	95,431 05	57,514 95
Second district	11,034 53	....	10,858 42	144 54	38 02	12 20	58 05	11,287 33	7,439 25	71,159 86	73,238 33
Third district	8,013 57	42 37	7,971 20	105 78	36 15	299 80	149 25	8,604 05	8,118 04	109,616 68	85,843 97
Fourth district	2,860 19	65 72	2,794 47	81 16	49 33	35 00	40 00	3,065 00	1,273 39	295,393 95	434,506 90
Total	25,934 34	284 20	25,650 14	473 98	165 50	352 25	247 30	27,173 57	22,324 00	571,601 54	651,103 45
UTAH.											
Utah	5,827 22	6 18	5,821 04	164 55	124 00	145 30	57 00	6,318 67	7,013 63	133,780 79	36,898 63
VERMONT.											
First district	4,272 58	90 57	4,182 01	95 75	210 00	....	93 75	4,672 86	1,461 16	130,984 79	116,764 07
Second district	4,454 64	115 17	4,339 47	62 67	165 55	....	43 75	4,726 89	1,151 15	112,777 99	98,487 87
Third district	4,744 05	99 08	4,644 97	24 02	93 32	....	27 50	4,887 88	1,762 55	165,380 69	124,405 48
Total	13,471 27	304 82	13,166 45	182 44	467 87	....	165 00	14,286 58	4,374 86	409,142 67	339,657 42
VIRGINIA.											
First district	4,330 44	42 85	4,307 59	90 14	57 62	....	27 50	4,498 10	2,504 09	48,016 31	44,274 35
Second district	11,073 45	230 69	10,842 76	165 39	97 75	....	57 94	11,364 49	5,261 05	1,309,317 57	1,122,852 46
Third district	12,472 71	222 47	12,250 24	308 35	121 62	....	57 98	12,960 02	7,023 25	2,489,556 15	2,379,261 74
Fourth district	6,142 18	90 08	6,052 10	277 50	110 30	....	47 40	6,577 10	3,252 20	200,315 74	125,713 21
Fifth district	11,137 05	165 30	10,971 75	376 30	242 85	....	45 50	11,801 17	6,831 45	1,832,874 16	1,542,780 84
Sixth district	6,313 70	90 70	6,283 00	115 59	310 90	....	55 75	6,855 94	3,559 40	295,824 48	202,746 59
Seventh district	5,653 67	108 81	5,544 86	120 59	169 57	....	42 40	5,986 50	3,477 36	235,014 65	199,221 13
Eighth district	2,742 88	86 89	2,655 99	33 19	144 36	2 50	26 00	2,948 93	5 00	109,311 97	44,014 28
Total	59,946 08	1,037 79	58,908 29	1,487 05	1,254 97	2 50	303 07	62,993 67	30,913 50	6,520,231 03	5,661,864 60

WASHINGTON.											
Washington	9,992 72	129 52	9,863 90	189 05	110 33	314 27	98 25	10,704 62	6,362 90	70,573 67	83,272 07
WEST VIRGINIA.											
First district	7,492 00	194 65	7,297 35	67 75	135 50	......	50 60	7,745 85	2,599 00	425,350 03	388,301 17
Second district	7,116 34	240 99	6,875 45	264 81	173 23	......	45 50	7,599 88	1,296 47	477,458 93	321,065 66
Third district	2,847 76	40 67	2,807 09	138 42	97 28	......	22 50	3,105 96	1,034 38	172,767 15	44,925 30
Total	17,456 10	476 31	16,979 79	470 98	406 01	......	118 60	18,451 69	4,929 85	1,075,576 11	754,192 33
WISCONSIN.											
First district	12,637 08	350 14	12,296 94	93 06	211 86	......	55 65	12,996 65	4,634 50	1,803,428 84	1,696,272 80
Second district	5,171 11	110 92	5,060 19	76 71	178 00	......	32 32	5,458 32	1,952 75	161,100 51	165,509 42
Third district	3,943 12	25 00	3,918 12	75 74	117 15	......	30 57	4,166 58	787 04	97,742 04	83,029 73
Fourth district	4,962 84	125 01	4,767 83	63 15	210 64	......	21 15	5,187 64	1,329 00	142,803 39	129,637 03
Fifth district	5,985 93	51 53	5,934 40	186 91	163 64	79 91	53 35	6,469 74	3,893 36	122,082 50	110,411 38
Sixth district	6,180 02	25 00	6,155 02	224 17	73 00	......	9 35	6,486 69	5,078 06	98,072 98	95,037 98
Total	38,810 10	687 60	38,122 50	718 74	954 15	79 91	202 72	40,765 62	19,674 71	2,516,230 26	2,280,498 34
WYOMING.											
Wyoming	3,275 41	82 00	3,193 41	91 90	6 00	23 00	54 00	3,450 31	635 29	38,618 78	25,847 40

RECAPITULATION.

Alabama	57,730 94	1,272 55	56,448 39	530 36	444 32	324 05	152 00	59,171 67	25,375 67	1,608,548 57	1,194,425 62
Arizona	3,084 00	75 00	3,009 00	......	22 00	......	30 00	3,136 00	584 33	20,184 36	10,891 21
Arkansas	26,859 27	476 84	26,382 43	306 58	227 26	7 50	101 75	27,502 36	15,561 33	306,390 35	317,153 10
California	88,563 99	921 94	87,641 82	1,935 99	2,031 30	4,423 58	564 06	97,517 90	67,708 38	5,704,057 69	4,669,393 23
Colorado	8,931 60	62 36	8,869 24	101 28	162 50	2 00	130 50	9,267 88	8,701 25	82,531 94	73,910 34
Connecticut	34,453 17	823 31	33,630 19	362 10	1,102 21	......	138 66	36,056 67	14,083 34	2,533,705 45	2,567,489 96
Dakota	1,737 54	27 68	1,709 86	39 09	19 19	3 25	9 75	1,810 34	184 00	9,508 63	7,917 94
Delaware	7,923 45	204 57	7,718 88	31 65	169 23	......	32 75	8,157 00	2,832 00	508,062 62	484,691 37
District of Columbia	8,312 27	174 17	8,138 10	123 34	176 00	......	92 50	8,704 11	3,628 89	533,498 09	514,390 07
Florida	10,850 90	190 92	10,659 98	172 07	124 27	119 88	68 97	11,335 39	8,541 06	190,124 13	107,181 34
Georgia	46,829 27	653 04	46,176 23	583 81	571 20	5 70	204 15	48,194 13	29,386 63	1,306,169 04	1,123,155 84
Idaho	10,440 95	120 11	10,320 84	111 72	15 75	......	8 00	10,576 42	5,033 00	81,322 01	58,405 47
Illinois	140,068 16	3,358 69	136,709 47	2,214 97	3,808 52	6 25	904 70	147,002 30	59,852 30	21,062,736 33	18,153,046 15
Indiana	82,869 19	2,308 87	80,560 32	1,546 18	1,292 39	166 96	601 30	86,475 33	25,687 73	6,098,166 38	4,950,291 31
Iowa	36,039 39	563 64	35,475 75	1,162 36	1,426 55	17 50	407 05	39,052 55	18,763 54	1,373,380 42	1,375,280 58
Kansas	13,059 44	201 19	12,858 25	226 68	556 60	8 27	183 50	14,034 49	7,805 97	462,191 17	340,812 70
Kentucky	85,788 74	2,063 54	83,725 20	2,182 82	2,292 86	584 10	271 95	91,120 41	33,932 67	11,650,883 52	9,986,758 45
Louisiana	51,006 00	2,361 15	50,644 85	947 18	125 01	357 81	363 05	52,718 99	39,518 61	3,576,904 16	2,901,828 99
Maine	25,464 70	629 13	24,835 57	300 81	834 36	2 85	127 19	58,729 91	39,729 91	5,894,033 90	803,482 38
Maryland	43,105 52	928 68	41,178 84	659 98	726 71	85	440 35	44,392 71	19,571 77	6,118,635 32	5,571,776 12

B.—Statement showing the expenses of collecting the internal revenue taxes in the several collection-districts, &c.—Continued.

RECAPITULATION—Continued.

District	Gross compensation	Tax	Net compensation	Stationery and blank books	Postage	Express and dep. money	Advertising	Total expense of collecting	Expenses of administering office	Assessments	Collections
Massachusetts	$93,982 86	$2,210 21	$91,772 65	$1,319 29	$4,035 21	$0 15	$414 67	$99,752 18	$30,778 09	$10,993,190 97	$10,699,430 00
Michigan	38,581 73	606 57	37,975 21	697 24	1,108 69	10 75	188 42	40,586 98	21,031 02	3,113,933 10	2,487,570 71
Minnesota	23,618 84	358 31	23,258 53	200 14	405 48	28 89	118 75	24,370 10	11,773 50	415,647 08	425,647 65
Mississippi	31,967 53	459 64	31,507 89	832 50	299 56	24 30	287 25	33,411 4	18,609 07	416,712 45	265,846 24
Missouri	61,472 21	830 97	60,641 24	1,631 63	2,776 19	636 90	718 33	67,234 36	44,774 57	6,946,814 61	6,057,010 24
Montana	10,692 25	70 45	10,621 80	236 82	60 96	166 35	25 00	11,181 88	9,980 25	130,491 84	64,806 63
Nebraska	15,948 73	400 98	15,549 45	134 38	216 53	18 44	132 50	16,450 38	7,389 42	273,693 79	310,051 87
Nevada	12,654 60	31 86	12,622 74		101 28	599 42	566 54	13,921 14	11,017 51	220,327 31	210,910 22
New Hampshire	17,067 24	437 64	16,609 60	343 54	686 22		33 71	18,162 14	4,911 46	632,986 39	656,724 65
New Jersey	42,639 52	781 67	41,857 85	499 22	1,839 33	28 50	178 90	45,185 19	22,005 60	3,972,228 05	4,010,886 15
New Mexico	2,316 25	98 12	2,298 13	232 90	92 18	2 50	105 50	2,678 33	2,111 89	70,223 69	25,316 63
New York	346,347 11	6,042 82	340,304 29	7,975 40	9,603 88	117 77	468 71	366,533 32	200,602 69	40,216,646 36	36,417,950 70
North Carolina	59,620 93	1,441 46	58,179 47	663 74	407 88	7 25	216 00	60,915 90	24,274 30	1,555,029 96	1,259,598 47
Ohio	185,663 99	4,890 53	180,364 66	3,030 79	2,873 93	5 50	583 95	191,657 96	68,977 79	21,637,764 78	19,329,275 70
Oregon	16,607 99	310 02	16,297 47	74 13	74 13		163 71	16,556 13	9,397 51	247,129 58	332,159 93
Pennsylvania	193,392 64	3,864 80	189,500 84	3,494 18	4,564 49	100 60	1,037 43	202,366 74	93,252 74	19,348,256 80	17,361,201 46
Rhode Island	13,392 46	318 09	13,074 37	181 31	293 50		94 00	15,961 87	7,030 70	1,290,565 80	1,282,378 19
South Carolina	22,927 19	413 81	22,513 08	401 80	373 28	3 75	330 22	23,332 98	14,920 70	457,707 90	405,358 56
Tennessee	61,378 55	933 41	60,445 14	818 96	647 57		172 55	63,021 81	34,135 77	1,739,630 21	1,415,714 84
Texas	25,934 34	284 90	25,650 14	473 98	163 50	332 25	247 30	27,173 17	22,324 00	571,601 54	631,103 45
Utah	5,837 22	6 18	5,831 04	164 55	124 00	145 30	57 00	6,318 07	7,013 63	133,780 79	36,898 63
Vermont	13,411 27	304 82	13,106 45	182 44	467 87		165 00	14,286 86	4,374 86	409,142 67	339,657 42
Virginia	59,946 08	1,037 79	58,908 99	1,487 05	1,254 97	2 50	303 07	62,993 57	30,913 50	6,590,231 63	5,601,864 60
Washington	9,992 72	129 52	9,863 00	189 03	110 33	314 27	98 25	10,704 32	6,362 20	70,373 67	83,272 67
West Virginia	17,456 10	476 31	16,979 79	470 98	406 01	79 91	118 60	18,431 30	4,929 85	1,075,576 11	754,192 33
Wisconsin	38,810 10	687 00	38,122 50	718 74	954 15	23 00	202 72	40,765 22	19,674 71	2,516,230 26	2,280,498 33
Wyoming	3,275 41	82 00	3,193 41	91 90	6 00		54 00	3,450 31	635 29	38,618 78	25,847 40
Grand total	2,208,863 50	42,882 46	2,165,981 04	40,023 34	49,962 38	8,699 25	13,958 29	2,321,506 76	1,137,558 76	189,403,271 97	168,476,458 59

REPORT OF THE SIXTH AUDITOR.

REPORT

OF

THE SIXTH AUDITOR OF THE TREASURY.

OFFICE OF THE AUDITOR OF THE TREASURY
FOR THE POST-OFFICE DEPARTMENT,
October 13, 1871.

SIR: I have the honor to submit the following report of the business operations of this office for the fiscal year ending June 30, 1871. My forthcoming report to the Postmaster General will exhibit in detail all that pertains to the financial transactions of the Post-Office Department for the past fiscal year.

The work performed by the clerical force of this office can be most clearly and satisfactorily shown by divisions, and I have therefore caused each chief of division to carefully prepare a synopsis of the work performed quarterly, so far as practicable, with a view to exhibit the steady increase of the business of this Bureau, an increase which must continue with the growth of the country, and the consequent extension of mail facilities.

EXAMINING DIVISION.—DR. BENJAMIN LIPPINCOTT, PRINCIPAL CLERK.

This division receives and audits the quarterly accounts current of all post-offices in the United States. It is divided into four subdivisions, viz: the opening-room, the stamp-rooms, the examining corps proper, and the error-rooms.

1. *The opening-room.*—All returns as soon as received are opened, and, if found in order according to regulations, are entered on the register, carefully folded and tied, and then forwarded to the stamp-rooms.

The number of quarterly accounts current received each quarter of the fiscal year ending June 30, 1871, was as follows:

Third quarter, 1870.................................... 27, 738
Fourth quarter, 1870.................................. 28, 092
First quarter, 1871................................... 28, 111
Second quarter, 1871................................. 28, 615

    Total.. 112, 556

2. *The stamp-rooms.*—The quarterly returns received from the opening-room are divided alphabetically among eight stamp clerks, whose duties consist in comparing the stamp statements of the postmasters in the accounts current with their own books, and the returns made to them from the stamp division of the finance office, whence stamp orders are issued and receipts for the same received and forwarded to the stamp clerks. The returns thus approved or corrected are passed to the exam-

iners. All accounts from offices of the first and second class are passed through the various subdivisions of the office in advance of other returns, so that they may reach the chief examiner and his assistant with as little delay as possible.

The number of accounts examined and settled by the stamp clerks for each quarter of the fiscal year ending June 30, 1871, was as follows:

Third quarter, 1870.. 27, 356
Fourth quarter, 1870...................................... 27, 835
First quarter, 1871....................................... 27, 756
Second quarter, 1871...................................... 28, 378
                                                          _____
Total 111, 325

3. The examining corps proper is composed of 17 clerks, among whom the returns received from the stamp-rooms are divided by sections, each comprising several States or parts of States. The average number to each section is about 1,700. After the examination of the accounts current and the stamp account, reviewing and refooting the transcript of mails received, and examining all vouchers belonging to that portion of the work, the balance is drawn on all accounts of the 3d, 4th, and 5th classes. The returns thus examined and completed are forwarded to the registering division, to be entered upon its books.

The number of accounts examined and sent to the registering division for the fiscal year ending June 30, 1871, was as follows:

Third quarter, 1870....................................... 27, 356
Fourth quarter, 1870...................................... 27, 835
First quarter, 1871....................................... 27, 756
Second quarter, 1871...................................... 28, 378
                                                          _____
Total 111, 325

4. The error-rooms contain 6 clerks, who review and re-examine the error accounts received from the registering division, and forward to each postmaster a copy of his account, as stated by him, and as audited and corrected in this office.

The number of accounts so corrected and copied for the fiscal year ending June 30, 1871, was as follows:

Third quarter, 1870....................................... 6, 308
Fourth quarter, 1870...................................... 7, 736
First quarter, 1871....................................... 10, 116
Second quarter, 1871...................................... 7, 166
                                                          _____
Total 31, 326

Each subdivision reports weekly to the chief examiner, and monthly through that officer to the chief clerk, the progress of the work, so that the exact amount of work done by each clerk is clearly ascertained.

All vouchers relative to allowances made by the Post-Office Department for clerk hire, lights, fuel, rent, stationery, &c., at post offices of the 1st and 2d classes, are forwarded at the beginning of each quarter to the chief-examiner and his assistant for examination. A statement is then prepared showing the vouchers received, the amount allowed, and the amount suspended when found to be in excess of the allowance

On receipt of the returns from the examiners these accounts are reviewed, and the amount allowable added, and the balance drawn by the chief examiner.

The number of post-offices of the 1st and 2d classes which have received allowances for clerk hire, rent, &c., was 335.

The number of offices of the 2d class having an allowance for clerk hire only was 159.

The number of offices having an allowance for clerk hire to assist in separating the mails (independent of the number above named) was 348.

Total number of offices of all classes receiving allowances, and approved by the chief examiner, was 842.

The expense accounts of the 335 offices of the 1st and 2d classes were regularly entered by the chief examiner and his assistant on the expense register, and show quarterly the amount of vouchers received, amount allowed, and amount suspended, copies of which were forwarded to each postmaster.

Attached to the examining division is a corresponding clerk, whose duty consists in corresponding with postmasters relative to errors in their accounts current, and in making day-book entries, &c.

The amount involved in the settlement of the quarterly accounts current of postmasters during the fiscal year was as follows:

Third quarter, 1870	$4,723,683 99
Fourth quarter, 1870...................................	5,013,104 98
First quarter, 1871...................................	5,300,715 05
Second quarter, 1871......................	5,080,948 59
Total..... ..,..................................	20,118,452 61

The labors of the examining division for the fiscal year ending June 30, 1871, have been fully completed. All accounts received in proper form have been examined and passed to the registering division. At no period has the work been more perfect in all its details. Not only has there been a decided improvement in the preparation of returns by postmasters, particularly those of the 1st and 2d classes, but by judicious changes in the office the efficiency of the examining corps has been greatly increased.

REGISTERING DIVISION—F. I. SEYBOLT, PRINCIPAL CLERK.

This division receives from the examining division the quarterly accounts current of postmasters, and re-examines and registers them in books prepared for that purpose, placing each item of revenue and expenditure under its appropriate head.

Upon this division 11 clerks are employed, and during the fiscal year the following number of accounts current was received, re-examined, and registered, viz:

Third quarter, 1870.	27,342,	involving	$4,723,683 99
Fourth quarter, 1870...............	27,800,	do.	5,013,104 98
First quarter, 1871...............	27,992,	do.	5,300,715 05
Second quarter, 1871...............	28,412,	do.	5,080,948 59
Total...................	111,546,	do.	20,118,452 61

During this fiscal year, 5,287 circulars were sent to postmasters who had failed to render their quarterly returns.

The number of changes of postmasters, establishment, re-establishment, discontinuance, and change of name of post-offices reported from the appointment office during the fiscal year and noted by the registers, was as follows:

Third quarter, 1870	1,814
Fourth quarter, 1870	1,907
First quarter, 1871	2,530
Second quarter, 1871	2,443
Total	8,694

The work of this division is fully up to the requirements of the office, the quarterly accounts current received from every office having been registered to the 30th day of June, 1871, the footings and recapitulations made, and the books prepared for the registration of the accounts of the quarter closing September 30, 1871.

BOOK-KEEPER'S DIVISION—JAMES F. MAGUIRE, ACTING PRINCIPAL CLERK.

This division has in charge the ledger accounts of postmasters, late postmasters, contractors, and late contractors.

The work of this division is performed by 14 clerks, viz: One principal book-keeper, in charge of ledger of general accounts; one assistant principal in charge of ledger of warrants and deposits, cash-book, register of deposits, and all day-book entries on reports approved by the Auditor; and twelve book-keepers. The number of ledgers is 51, averaging over 575 pages each.

The number of auxiliary books posted every quarter is as follows: 11 registers of postmasters' returns, 35 pay-books, 8 journals, 3 registers of Postmaster General's drafts, 1 register of warrants, 1 stamp-journal, 1 cash-book, 1 deposit-book, 1 Auditor's draft-book, 1 money-order transfer-cash, 6 mail-messenger's registers, 6 registers of special mail service, 1 route agent's book, 1 letter-carrier's book.

Ledgers of postmasters' accounts.

Sections.	Ledgers.	Current accounts.	Late accounts.
1	4	3,475	789
2	4	3,451	564
3	4	3,567	677
4	4	4,109	783
5	5	3,782	693
6	5	4,048	1,034
7	5	3,732	920
8	4	3,525	699
Total	35	29,689	6,159

Ledgers of mail-contractors' accounts.

Section.	No. of ledger.	Current accounts.	Day-book entries journalized.	Accounts journalized from transfer sheets.
1	3	1,412	1,024	8,440
2..............................	3	1,630	1,418	8,828
3..............................	3	1,060	1,679	7,482
4..............................	3	1,153	1,735	7,841
Total......................	12	5,275	5,856	32,591

The work of this division is in excellent condition, and fully up to the regulations of the office. All postings required to be done during the fiscal year were completed in advance of the time allowed.

STATING DIVISION—WM. H. GUNNISON, PRINCIPAL CLERK.

This division has charge of the general accounts of all the postmasters in the United States, each of which is stated and balanced quarterly.

The items of the accounts of postmasters at offices of the first, second, and third classes, (from which nineteen-twentieths of the revenue of the Post Office Department is derived,) and at draft and deposit offices of the fourth and fifth classes, are obtained from the earliest records made in the office, the accounts stated and balanced within the ninety days succeeding the quarter to which the items pertain, and are handed over to the collecting division " for copy."

The remaining accounts are stated as soon as the items can be taken from the ledgers of the book-keepers, and those which show debit balances are reported to the collecting division. During the past year, all accounts showing credit balances of $10 or more to June 30, 1870, were also reported.

Accounts of late postmasters are stated during the fourth month after the quarter in which the change is reported to this office, and those showing debit balances of $1, or more, are reported to the collecting division " for copy." They are again revised before the close of the *sixth* month, and those which then show such balances are handed to the collecting division " for draft." At the close of the *eighth* month, all, except those "suspended" for special reasons, are fully stated and transferred " finally " to the collecting division.

16 F

Statement showing the number of the general accounts of present postmasters in charge of the stating division, for and during the fiscal year ending June 30, 1871, and the classification of their offices.

States and Territories.	Draft offices.		Deposit offices.		Collection offices.		Special offices.	Total number in each State and Territory.	Total number in each section.
	First, second, and third classes.	Fourth and fifth classes.	First, second, and third classes.	Fourth and fifth classes.	First, second, and third classes.	Fourth and fifth classes.	Fourth and fifth classes.		
Maine	6	4	7	105	12	674	38	846	....
New Hampshire	7	....	6	46	7	335	14	415	....
Vermont	10	4	3	59	7	358	28	469	....
Massachusetts	18	0	20	122	33	472	25	702	2,432
New York, A to S	31	4	31	271	63	1,644	260	....	2,304
Pennsylvania, A to R	8	3	30	103	38	1,977	54	....	2,209
Connecticut	9	1	12	82	14	252	32	402	....
Rhode Island	2	....	3	10	5	76	5	101	....
West Virginia	1	....	1	23	3	571	13	612	....
Wisconsin	3	1	7	83	32	908	51	1,085	2,200
North Carolina	2	....	....	22	9	759	10	802	....
South Carolina	1	....	3	10	5	334	5	358	....
Georgia	2	....	2	40	14	436	10	504	....
Alabama	3	....	3	36	5	523	12	582	2,246
California	....	....	5	29	12	480	43	569	....
Minnesota	3	....	6	19	8	598	40	674	....
Oregon	....	....	....	1	2	168	14	185	....
Kansas	1	....	5	30	16	499	124	675	....
Nebraska	1	....	....	4	5	234	50	294	....
New Mexico	....	....	....	....	2	46	1	49	....
Washington	....	....	....	2	2	91	5	100	....
Utah	....	....	....	1	3	135	5	144	....
Dakota	....	....	....	1	1	35	15	52	....
Colorado	1	....	....	2	5	97	7	112	....
Idaho	....	....	....	....	2	31	2	35	....
Montano	....	....	....	....	3	64	2	69	....
Nevada	....	....	1	1	5	48	8	64	....
Wyoming	....	....	....	....	3	21	....	24	....
Arizona	....	....	....	....	2	24	2	26	....
Alaska	....	....	....	4	....	....	....	4	3,075
Ohio	15	....	8	162	64	1,697	87	....	2,033
Illinois	7	....	13	247	85	1,273	62	1,687	....
New Jersey	2	....	13	75	23	429	24	566	2,253
Louisiana	....	....	1	7	5	211	4	228	....
Missouri	....	....	3	33	31	1,184	116	1,367	....
Tennessee	....	....	8	163	3	641	60	878	2,473
Mississippi	....	....	9	59	7	413	5	493	....
Kentucky	3	....	9	72	10	768	63	935	....
Texas	2	....	....	41	15	547	38	643	....
Arkansas	....	....	1	11	4	479	23	518	2,589
Virginia	2	....	5	65	13	1,042	33	1,160	....
New York, T to Z	2	1	4	46	12	255	41	361	....
Maryland	1	....	3	26	5	495	32	562	2,083
Delaware	1	....	1	4	1	83	2	92	....
District of Columbia	....	....	1	....	....	3	....	4	....
Indiana	10	4	9	192	32	1,053	61	1,361	....
Pennsylvania, R to Z	4	....	8	37	15	603	15	682	2,139
Iowa	15	3	14	95	18	947	51	1,143	....
Michigan	12	1	10	105	38	806	35	1,007	....
Florida	1	....	3	1	1	128	4	138	2,288
Whole number of general accounts.	....	....	....	....	....	....	....	....	30,324

Statement showing the number of changes, and the condition of the general accounts of late postmasters, for and during the fiscal year ending June 30, 1871.

Number of changes, reported to this office weekly, during the fiscal year ending June 30, 1871.	Quarters prior to third quarter, 1870.	Third quarter, 1870.	Fourth quarter, 1870.	First quarter, 1871.	Second quarter, 1871.	Total.
Changes { Discontinued		158	211	263	329	
Miscellaneous		1,339	1,575	2,268	1,860	
Established and re-established		549	403	461	999	
Accounts { Stated "Finally"		1,496	1,724			
Stated to latest dates audited				2,403	2,912	
"Suspended," stated to latest dates audited	202	70	96			
Totals	202	3,612	4,009	5,395	6,100	19,318
Deduct the number of changes classified as established and re-established, (2,412,) and accounts suspended, (368.)						2,880
Leaving the number of accounts of late postmasters settled finally, for and during the fiscal year.						16,438

Miscellaneous.

Number of credits, entries, &c.	Third quarter, 1870.	Fourth quarter, 1870.	First quarter, 1871.	Second quarter, 1871.	Total.
Credits authorized by Third Assistant Postmaster General, entered in stamp journal and general accounts.	859	545	526	549	2,479
Entries in stamp journal and general accounts, on orders from stamp clerks.	332	376	500	1,358	2,566
Entries in day-books	147	254	146	147	694
Letters written—correspondence in special cases	118	158	140	94	510
Circulars sent in answer to letters received—special cases	443	528	471	262	1,704
Reports of failures to pay indebtedness, render returns, and to qualify.	162	131	149	151	593

The foregoing description indicates partially the amount of work done by the clerks of this division. The general accounts of present and late postmasters, in charge of each of the thirteen sections thereof, are in a very satisfactory condition, and fully up to the requirements of the routine of business in this office.

COLLECTING DIVISION—E. J. EVANS, PRINCIPAL CLERK.

The duties of the collecting division are to collect all balances due from late and present postmasters and contractors throughout the United States. The average number of clerks employed is about eighteen, whose business it is to issue drafts on late postmasters and contractors, and keep a register thereof, to report to the Post-Office Department for payment all balances due to late postmasters, and keep a record of the same, to record all changes reported by the appointment office of the Post-Office Department, to record the names of postmasters becoming "late" during the fiscal year in a book kept for that purpose, to record and file away all drafts paid, to correspond with postmasters and contractors with a view to the collection of balances due the United States, to record and transmit such correspondence, to copy all postmasters' and contractors' accounts, and inclose the same in their appropriate circulars, to submit for suit the accounts of defaulting postmasters and contractors, to receive, open, and dispose of all mails arriving at the office, to prepare matter for the Biennial Register, &c.

It is proper to state, in justice to some of the gentlemen employed in this division, that their business involves a thorough knowledge of the machinery of the entire office, and much of that of the Post-Office Department, with which it is intimately associated, and that it necessitates a constant watchfulness and careful scrutiny of the various books and files from which the accounts coming before them for adjustment are made up. This is especially true of the gentlemen employed in correspondence. The number of letters written, for example, cannot adequately convey to you the amount of labor performed by them, as, in some instances, hours of investigation are required, and day-book entries made, before an intelligible letter can be written in the case. Issuing drafts, reporting balances for payment, recording changes, also require and receive great care and close application on the part of the gentlemen intrusted with these duties.

I have the satisfaction to state that the work of the division is fully up to the requirements of the Department.

Accounts of postmasters and contractors.	No.	Amount.
Accounts of postmasters becoming late during the period from July 1, 1868, to June 30, 1870, in charge of division	17,010	
Accounts of postmasters becoming late during the fiscal year:		
Quarter ending September 30, 1870	1,544	$110,763 48
Quarter ending December 31, 1870	1,811	141,342 13
Quarter ending March 31, 1871	2,508	126,019 18
Quarter ending June 30, 1871	2,205	131,889 98
Total	25,078	510,014 77
Accounts of contractors received from the pay division for collection, upon which drafts were issued:		
Quarter ending September 30, 1870	49	$7,887 08
Quarter ending December 31, 1870	57	8,665 10
Quarter ending March 31, 1871	15	4,472 78
Quarter ending June 30, 1871	27	4,069 79
Total	148	25,094 75
Drafts issued on present and late postmasters during the fiscal year:		
Quarter ending September 30, 1870	882	$110,215 90
Quarter ending December 31, 1870	1,168	120,764 50
Quarter ending March 31, 1871	1,076	141,916 63
Quarter ending June 30, 1871	939	162,552 36
Total	4,065	535,449 39
Accounts of postmasters becoming late during the fiscal year showing balances in their favor, and closed by "suspense:"		
Quarter ending September 30, 1870	485	$334 63
Quarter ending December 31, 1870	1,065	4,386 13
Quarter ending March 31, 1871	166	5,743 81
Quarter ending June 30, 1871	173	2,772 16
Total	1,889	13,236 73
Accounts of postmasters becoming late during the fiscal year showing balances due the United States, and closed by "suspense:"		
Quarter ending September 30, 1870	435	$195 64
Quarter ending December 31, 1870	148	63 96
Quarter ending March 31, 1871	12	121 45
Quarter ending June 30, 1871	1	4 84
Total	596	385 89
Accounts of postmasters becoming late during the fiscal year, showing balances due the United States, found uncollectable:		
Quarter ending September 30, 1870	92	$20,695 15
Quarter ending December 31, 1870	1	10 20
Quarter ending March 31, 1871	12	3,621 24
Quarter ending June 30, 1871	21	1,216 82
Total	126	25,543 41

Accounts of postmasters and contractors.	No.	Amount.
Accounts showing balances due late postmasters, and reported to the Post-Office Department for payment:		
Quarter ending September 30, 1870	161	$12,833 00
Quarter ending December 31, 1870	213	13,027 60
Quarter ending March 31, 1871	1,639	64,072 76
Quarter ending June 30, 1871	562	27,177 29
Total	2,575	117,110 65
Accounts of late postmasters submitted for suit:		
Quarter ending September 30, 1870	25	$20,565 98
Quarter ending December 31, 1870	20	13,859 88
Quarter ending March 31, 1871	30	15,928 36
Quarter ending June 30, 1871	17	6,118 69
Total	92	56,472 91

Letters received during the fiscal year:

Quarter ending September 30, 1870	51,505
Quarter ending December 31, 1870	53,369
Quarter ending March 31, 1871	54,534
Quarter ending June 30, 1871	59,064
Total	223,472

Letters sent during the fiscal year:

Quarter ending September 30, 1870	35,504
Quarter ending December 31, 1870	34,171
Quarter ending March 31, 1871	39,184
Quarter ending June 30, 1871	36,711
Total	145,570

Letters recorded during the fiscal year:

Quarter ending September 30, 1870	1,618
Quarter ending December 31, 1870	1,355
Quarter ending March 31, 1871	2,517
Quarter ending June 30, 1871	2,252
Total	7,742

Letters written to postmasters and others during the fiscal year:

Quarter ending September 30, 1870	1,086
Quarter ending December 31, 1870	1,315
Quarter ending March 31, 1871	1,683
Quarter ending June 30, 1871	1,642
Total	5,726

Accounts copied during the fiscal year, and sent in their appropriate circulars:

Quarter ending September 30, 1870	4,668
Quarter ending December 31, 1870	10,996
Quarter ending March 31, 1871	11,033
Quarter ending June 30, 1871	4,574
Total	31,271

Pages of post office "changes" reported by the Post Office Department during the fiscal year, recorded in the change books:

Quarter ending September 30, 1870	1,944
Quarter ending December 31, 1870	2,261
Quarter ending March 31, 1871	3,328
Quarter ending June 30, 1871	2,922
Total	10,455

Pages of Blue Book or Biennial Register prepared for publication............	1,596

Pages of stamp journal added and recapitulated:

Quarter ending September 30, 1870......................................	150
Quarter ending December 31, 1870 ....:..............	47
Quarter ending March 31, 1871...	52
Quarter ending June 30, 1871	64
Total...	313

Pages of draft register recorded :

Quarter ending September 30, 1870......................................	50
Quarter ending December 31, 1870	66
Quarter ending March 31, 1871...	58
Quarter ending June 30, 1871	52
Total...	226

Pages of book of balances recorded:

Quarter ending September 30, 1870......................................	146
Quarter ending December 31, 1870	152
Quarter ending March 31, 1871...	202
Quarter ending June 30, 1871	180
Total...	680

Pages of letter-books recorded :

Quarter ending September 30, 1870......................................	810
Quarter ending December 31, 1870	889
Quarter ending March 31, 1871...	1,047
Quarter ending June 30, 1871	1,134
Total...	3,880

LAW DIVISION—J. BOZMAN KERR, PRINCIPAL CLERK.

To this division is assigned the duty of preparing and transmitting to the Department of Justice, for suit, accounts of late postmasters and contractors who fail to pay their indebtedness to the United States upon the drafts of the Department.

The number of accounts and accompanying papers prepared for suit during the fiscal year was as follows:

In the third quarter of 1870	25 cases, involving.........		$20,565 98
In the fourth quarter of 1870	20 cases, involving.........		13,859 88
In the first quarter of 1871	30 cases, involving.........		15,928 36
In the second quarter of 1871	17 cases, involving.........		6,118 69
Total................	92 cases, involving		$56,472 91

Number of judgments obtained during the fiscal year 1871, as reported by the Department of Justice, was.........	166
Amount of collections, including interest	$46,204 30

All accounts received from the collecting division have been prepared for suit and transmitted to the Department of Justice.

FOREIGN MAIL DIVISION.—ISAAC W. NICHOLLS, PRINCIPAL CLERK.

This division has charge of the postal accounts with foreign governments, and the accounts with steamship companies for ocean transportation of the mails.

Number of accounts of each country settled during the fiscal year, and amounts involved.

Name of country.	Number of quarterly accounts.	Amount.
United Kingdom......	Five............	$1, 301, 082 44
North German Union*..................................	Two	431, 735 47
France†...	....	....
Belgium	Three..........	12, 301 63
Netherlands...	Five............	30, 216 91
Switzerland	Five............	60, 812 96
Italy	Five	38, 469 41
Total amount involved............................	....	1, 874, 618 82

*German accounts are registered and ready for settlement to date.
†Treaty expired by notification December 31, 1869. Three accounts remain unsettled; they are, however, registered and ready for settlement.

Number of duplicates registered during the fiscal year.

Received from—	3d quarter, 1870.	4th quarter, 1870.	1st quarter, 1871.	2d quarter, 1871.	Sent to—	3d quarter, 1870.	4th quarter, 1870.	1st quarter, 1871.	2d quarter, 1871.
United Kingdom........	210	186	201	249	United Kingdom	237	225	229	244
North German Union ...	106	112	132	183	North German Union ..	70	91	112	180
France..................	38	10	4	5	France..................	18	12	9	8
Belgium.................	88	77	83	105	Belgium.................	81	79	86	100
Netherlands.............	39	36	37	38	Netherlands............	41	40	43	50
Switzerland	41	38	40	43	Switzerland	41	40	43	50
Italy	37	39	37	39	Italy	41	40	43	50
West Indies.............	231	139	152	146	West Indies.............	251	145	146	159
Total received.....	790	637	686	808	Total sent.........	780	672	711	841

Amounts reported for payment on account of balances due foreign countries.

To—	Quarter ended—	Amount in gold.
United Kingdom	December 31, 1868	$18, 129 25
	March 31, 1869	28, 966 10
	June 30, 1869	26, 440 20
	September 30, 1869	24, 008 30
	December 31, 1869	28, 368 13
	March 31, 1870	19, 685 90
	June 30, 1870	15, 180 41
Total.......	....	160, 778 29
Costing in currency	....	$179, 385 22
North German Union..................................	March 31, 1870	$32, 437 49
	June 30, 1870	26, 669 91
		59, 107 40
Costing in currency	....	$66, 722 16
Belgium	September 30, 1869	$1, 325 60
	December 31, 1869	1, 353 12
	March 31, 1870	1, 430 02
	June 30, 1870	1, 149 03
	September 30, 1870	1, 369 79
		6, 627 56
Costing in currency	....	$7, 660 05
Total amount reported............................	....	$226, 513 25

Number of reports of ocean postages to the Postmaster General and amounts reported.

Third quarter, 1870.		Fourth quarter, 1870.		First quarter, 1871.		Second quarter, 1871.	
No. of reports.	Amount.	No. of reports.	Amount.	No. of reports.	Amount.	No. of reports.	Amount.
1	$6,493 39½	1	$6,839 91	1	$7,299 23	1	$1,546 27¼
1	3,264 71	1	13,901 48	1	12,579 10	1	12,720 85¼
1	1,415 53½	1	17,175 58	1	13,901 56	1	10,372 00
1	2,334 67	1	1,462 47	1	3,283 06	1	8,855 10
1	15,863 61	1	1,175 21	1	5,549 63	1	11,009 62
1	10,245 91	1	1,800 69	1	1,337 64	1	1,309 19½
1	8,766 46	1	591 73	1	6,305 30	1	5,090 61
1	4,741 24	1	7,532 32	1	1,691 94	1	9,012 38
1	131 32	1	5,628 82	1	10,172 86	·1	570 29
1	505 13	1	1,049 06	1	2,437 81	1	2,112 98
1	223 77	1	417 13	1	507 50	1	299 39
1	1,275 93	1	441 70	1	506 94	1	216 65
1	596 05	1	309 54	1	381 22	1	181 58
1	174 65	1	213 22	1	248 22	1	126 56
1	163 80	1	182 98	1	146 51	1	233 24
1	102 62	1	77 98	1	126 00	1	160 44
1	329 38	1	227 61	1	104 44	1	38 06
1	74 41	1	1,488 10	1	98 49	1	84 77
1	31 85	1	255 54			1	60 55
1	27 86	1	141 08			1	49 84
		1	1,865 59			1	28 28
		1	179 25			1	1,821 67
		1	258 14			1	491 30
		1	301 50			1	397 90
		1	328 99			1	276 17
		1	89 92			1	1,739 77¾
		1	141 50			1	561 86
		1	508 42			1	573 91
		1	68 92			1	198 60
		1	264 94			1	1,879 17
		1	331 04			1	652 22
		1	650 47			1	402 34
		1	3 70			1	189 14
						1	126 97
						1	454 75
						1	378 75
						1	548 22
						1	38 20
						1	579 71
						1	512 95
						1	536 77
						·1	174 53
						1	434 53
						1	553 80
						1	677 21
						1	23 71
20	56,762 92	33	66,889 43	18	66,677 45	46	78,421 82

Whole number of reports, 117.
Total amount reported, $268,751 62.

The following amounts have been paid in gold by the governments named:

By—	Quarter ended.	Amount in gold.
Switzerland	March 31, 1870	$1, 028 50
	June 30, 1870	1, 155 10
	September 30, 1870	1, 544 88
	December 31, 1870	1, 360 96
	March 31, 1871	1, 342 95
	Total	6, 432 39
Netherlands	December 31, 1869	$1, 151 62
	March 31, 1870	342 46
	June 30, 1870	503 73
	September 30, 1870	606 27
	December 31, 1870	772 42
	Total	3, 376 50
Italy	June 30, 1869	$1, 112 87
	September 30, 1869	670 51
	December 31, 1869	961 69
	March 31, 1870	1, 004 82
	June 30, 1870	688 72
	September 30, 1870	151 98
	December 31, 1870	941 95
	Total	5, 532 54
Total amount paid in gold		$15, 341 43

PAY DIVISION—C. HAZLETT, PRINCIPAL CLERK.

This division has in charge the settlement and payment of all accounts for transportation of the mails, including railroad companies, steamboat companies and other mail contractors, special mail carriers, mail messengers, railway postal clerks, route agents, special agents, letter carriers, and all miscellaneous payments.

To this division is also assigned the registration of all warrants and drafts countersigned by the Auditor, and the custody of the archives pertaining to all the branches of the office.

Accounts of contractors settled during the fiscal year ending June 30, 1871.

Quarter.	No.	Amount involved.
In the quarter ending September 30, 1870	6, 839	$2, 336, 582 61
In the quarter ending December 31, 1870	6, 902	2, 724, 741 92
In the quarter ending March 31, 1871	6, 870	2, 891, 316 86
In the quarter ending June 30, 1871	6, 845	3, 006, 718 44
Total	27, 456	10, 959, 359 83

Accounts of mail messengers, special, postal railway clerks, route agents, letter carriers, special agents, and miscellaneous payments.

Quarter.	No.	Amount involved.
MAIL-MESSENGER SERVICE.		
In the quarter ending September 30, 1870	2,363	$92,621 49
In the quarter ending December 31, 1870	2,432	95,950 03
In the quarter ending March 31, 1871	2,573	99,072 50
In the quarter ending June 30, 1871	2,579	101,684 22
Total	9,947	389,328 24
SPECIAL MAIL SERVICE.		
In the quarter ending September 30, 1870	1,424	$13,048 64
In the quarter ending December 31, 1870	1,580	13,549 95
In the quarter ending March 31, 1871	1,406	12,668 07
In the quarter ending June 30, 1871	1,454	12,555 31
Total	5,864	51,821 97
LETTER-CARRIERS.		
In the quarter ending September 30, 1870	1,516	$340,406 86
In the quarter ending December 31, 1870	1,534	338,297 06
In the quarter ending March 31, 1871	1,494	339,738 06
In the quarter ending June 30, 1871	1,530	335,481 25
Total	6,074	1,353,923 23
RAILWAY POSTAL CLERKS, ROUTE AND OTHER AGENTS.		
In quarter ending September 30, 1870	1,327	$305,582 49
In quarter ending December 31, 1870	1,333	319,255 74
In quarter ending March 31, 1871	1,411	341,326 23
In quarter ending June 30, 1871	1,548	355,329 87
Total	5,619	1,321,494 33
MISCELLANEOUS ACCOUNTS.		
In quarter ending September 30, 1870	173	$182,159 65
In quarter ending December 31, 1870	145	226,006 92
In quarter ending March 31, 1871	249	249,966 99
In quarter ending June 30, 1871	175	227,291 16
Total	742	885,424 72
SPECIAL AGENTS.		
In quarter ending September 30, 1870	132	$37,479 00
In quarter ending December 31, 1870	136	32,750 10
In quarter ending March 31, 1871	132	35,274 66
In quarter ending June 30, 1871	140	34,166 01
Total	540	139,669 77
Foreign mail accounts paid	166	$1,061,995 67
COLLECTION ORDERS SENT OUT TO POSTMASTERS.		
In the quarter ending September 30, 1870	21,640	$536,727 13
In the quarter ending December 31, 1870	23,411	650,194 48
In the quarter ending March 31, 1871	23,808	755,843 86
In the quarter ending June 30, 1871	23,500	735,265 95
Total	92,559	2,678,031 42

Warrants issued by the Postmaster General, passed and registered during the fiscal year.

Quarter.	Number.	Amount of disbursements.	Amount of transfers.
Quarter ending September 30, 1870	1,440	$2,114,641 87	$234,374 01
Quarter ending December 31, 1870	1,473	1,782,652 82	396,655 51
Quarter ending March 31, 1871	1,692	1,884,413 24	330,000 00
Quarter ending June 30, 1871	1,485	1,998,312 85	365,173 99
Total	6,090	7,780,020 78	1,326,203 51

Drafts issued by the Postmaster General, passed and registered during the fiscal year.

Quarter.	Number.	Amount of disbursements.	Amount of transfers.
Quarter ending September 30, 1870	3, 811	$579, 239 48	$70, 010 88
Quarter ending December 31, 1870	3, 922	611, 178 60	81, 415 17
Quarter ending March 31, 1871	5, 474	691, 550 07	122, 416 10
Quarter ending June 30, 1871	4, 494	653, 930 60	91, 229 49
Total	17, 701	2, 535, 898 75	365, 071 64

Report of the archives clerk.

Quarter.	Reports recei and filed.	Postmasters' acc nnts received and	Receipts for drafts received and filed.	Certificates of deposit received and filed.
Third quarter, 1870	5, 251		3, 520	1, 363
Fourth quarter, 1870	5, 395		3, 617	1, 173
First quarter, 1871	7, 166		5, 028	1, 371
Second quarter, 1871	5, 979	13, 192	4, 135	1, 639
Total	23, 791	13, 192	16, 300	5, 546

MONEY-ORDER DIVISION—JOHN LYNCH, PRINCIPAL CLERK.

This division was organized less than seven years ago, with but three clerks assigned thereto to perform its duties. At this time the work requires forty-seven clerks and assorters, which force, in consequence of the large increase anticipated during the current fiscal year, contingent upon an international money-order system with the United Kingdom of Great Britain and Ireland, will be entirely inadequate to perform the work. Some idea of the multifarious and responsible duties connected with this division may be formed by taking into consideration the fact that the past year shows money orders issued amounting in the aggregate to over forty-two millions of dollars, at an average of a little over nineteen dollars per order.

The division is sub-divided into five sections: the registers, examiners, deposit drafts and transfers, checkers and assorters, the work being divided as equitably as possible between the clerks.

To this division belongs the auditing of postmasters' money-order accounts, and the collection of balances due from late postmasters; and in this connection it affords me much pleasure to state that, up to this time, there has not been a failure to collect such balances.

The money-order accounts of all postmasters at money-order offices have been audited to June 30, 1871.

Number of money-order statements received, examined, and registered during the fiscal year ending June 30, 1871.

Quarter.	Number.	Amount.
Third quarter, 1870	26, 748	
Fourth quarter, 1870	28, 977	
First quarter, 1871	26, 748	
Second quarter, 1871	26, 748	
Total	109, 221	$83, 920, 276 10

Number of paid money orders received, examined, checked, and filed.

Quarter.	Number.
Third quarter, 1870	426, 187
Fourth quarter, 1870	530, 591
First quarter, 1871	610, 362
Second quarter, 1871	554, 941
Total	2, 122, 081

Number of certificates of deposit received, compared, and entered.

Quarter.	Number.	Amount.
Third quarter, 1870	23, 990	$6, 077, 213 39
Fourth quarter, 1870	31, 570	8, 065, 128 99
First quarter, 1871	36, 799	8, 426, 439 76
Second quarter, 1871	33, 277	7, 787, 518 37
Total	125, 636	30, 356, 300 51

Number of transfers and re-transfers entered.

Transfers.	Quarter.	Number.	Total.	Amount.	Total.
	Third quarter, 1870	1, 228		$144, 908 73	
	Fourth quarter, 1870	1, 319		148, 138 09	
	First quarter, 1871	1, 455		140, 548 75	
	Second quarter, 1871	1, 395	5, 397	125, 390 89	$558, 986 46
Re-transfers	Third quarter, 1870	68		18, 214 25	
	Fourth quarter, 1870	65		10, 524 94	
	First quarter, 1871	75		132, 858 07	
	Second quarter, 1871	81	289	72, 908 86	234, 506 12
	Total		5, 686		793, 492 58

Number of money orders returned for correction.

Quarter.	Number.
Third quarter, 1870	1, 008
Fourth quarter, 1870	1, 217
First quarter, 1871	2, 572
Second quarter, 1871	2, 006
Total	6, 803

Number of drafts entered.

Quarter.	Number.	Amount.
Third quarter, 1870	1, 692	$909, 077 14
Fourth quarter, 1870	1, 829	1, 016, 597 86
First quarter, 1871	1, 855	1, 001, 180 00
Second quarter, 1871	1, 972	923, 393 00
Total	7, 348	3, 850, 238 00

Having thus, with as much brevity as is consistent with the complex nature of the subject, explained the organization and practical working of my Bureau, I cannot close this report without expressing my high sense of the efficiency of the chief clerk, Mr. McGrew, the heads of divisions, and, indeed, of the employés generally under my charge.

I have the honor to be, very respectfully,

J. J. MARTIN, *Auditor.*

Hon. GEORGE S. BOUTWELL,
        Secretary of the Treasury.

REPORT OF TREASURER OF THE UNITED STATES.

REPORT

OF

THE TREASURER OF THE UNITED STATES

TREASURY OF THE UNITED STATES,
Washington, October 31, 1871.

SIR : Another year has made its round, and has brought with it the obligation, on my part, to make a statement to you of the condition of the Treasury of the United States, as it was at the close of the fiscal year which ended with the 30th day of June, 1871. Full tables are appended hereto, that will exhibit to you more readily and clearly than could be done through mere verbal statements, the money transactions and the general movement of the office during said fiscal year.

In addition, I desire to make a statement in regard to my own action during the past season, and some suggestions bearing upon the interest of the public service in the future.

NEGOTIATION OF NEW LOAN ABROAD.

Under authority of your commission I have visited, during the past season, the principal cities of Great Britain, and of Belgium, Holland, Prussia, Saxony, Baden, Bavaria, Würtemberg, Austria, Bohemia, Switzerland, and France, " for the purpose of aiding in the negotiation of the new loan." In compliance with your written instructions, I called " upon the agents appointed by the Government, with a view to ascertain the steps already taken by them," in regard to the negotiation of the loan, and made to them " such suggestions as seemed expedient to place the subject in a favorable light before the European public." With the same object in view, I called upon our embassadors and ministers, and upon our consuls and commercial agents, and upon many bankers and financial men, in the countries named. Through this intercourse with all kinds of persons, who were well informed upon such subjects, I learned that the time for placing our new loan was an unfavorable one for its success in the European money markets. It was too late, and too soon.

Had Congress given you the authority to negotiate this loan before the breaking out of the late war that France made upon Germany, it would have been all taken at once at that time. But later the bonds of several other governments were in these markets, and were offered at rates much more favorable to the purchaser than those authorized by Congress for the negotiation of our loan. Prominent among these was the new French five per cent. loan. This loan of the French Republic was finally disposed of at a rate that netted the borrower less than eighty cents on the dollar. The singular feature in its negotiation was, that it was largely taken by the late enemies of the French, the Germans. Germany had theretofore, next to our own country, been our principal reliance for the disposal of our stocks; and there was every hope that but for this French interference, that country would have alone absorbed all our stocks that were offered for sale. Under these existing circumstances, it was hardly to be supposed that the German people could then be induced to take our loan, when they could, at the same time, purchase *five thousand dollars*, face value, of the French bonds, bearing the same rate of interest as ours, for *less money* than would purchase *four thousand dollars*, face value, of the bonds of the United States. But notwithstanding this disparity between the prices of the two stocks, in consequence of the credit of our Government standing so high in the money markets of Europe, and especially in those of Germany, our loan, although netting the holder more than one-fifth less in interest, would have been taken in preference to the French, but for the fact that it was generally understood by the German people that, inasmuch as the proceeds of the French loan were to be paid to their governments, their rulers would consider the subscription to such loan, by their subjects, an act of patriotism. It was, moreover, generally understood that the German Empire would, if need be, enforce, in favor of its subjects, the punctual payment of the interest, and the repayment of the principal of the loan at the maturity of the bonds. Another circumstance unfavorable to us was, that the French government allowed to its agents, for negotiating its loan, at least two per cent. on the net proceeds realized from it, while you were authorized to allow to your agents an amount that would yield to them only one-quarter of one per cent. In addition to these advantages in favor of the French, they had in circulation five per cent. treasury-notes that had not matured; these the government agreed to take in payment for subscriptions to its loan, allowing the purchasers' unaccrued interest on these notes to their maturity.

An almost insuperable difficulty in the way of the negotiation of our loan was this low rate of commissions that it was provided to allow your agents for the disposing of the stock. With a single exception, and in that case he disagreed with the other members of his firm, every banker and business man with whom I conversed on the subject gave it as his opinion that one-quarter of one per cent. was altogether too small a compensation for the services to be rendered and the risks to be incurred. It was generally insisted that, inasmuch as other governments allowed at least two per cent. for like services, ours would, under any circumstances, be compelled to allow the same rate of compensation, before any considerable amount of the stock could be negotiated. It is known to you that the house of Hope & Co. of Amsterdam—a house that has loaned much money to our Government, commencing with our revolutionary war—refused to act as your agent on that account. A member of the firm said to me that their house had never worked for such a pitiful compensation. It was frequently intimated that many who had accepted agencies had done so for the honor it conferred on them, and not because they had hoped to succeed in disposing of any considerable part of the loan. These facts, and others as discouraging, I reported to you by letters at various times and places. Luckily, you were not disheartened by my reports, but you sent your able assistant, Judge Richardson, to Europe, with several million dollars' worth of the bonds. On his arrival in London, I, then being at Frankfort-on-the-Main, immediately put myself in communication with him, and suggested to him a plan by which the whole amount of the five per cent. loan could probably be placed. He advised me of another plan that he had devised, which, with alterations suggested by you, has succeeded, and which, I am now satisfied, was the very best thing to be done. It is certainly a source of gratulation that, by your own and Judge Richardson's adroit management, all obstacles were removed, and the loan was disposed of at a day much earlier than I, who had been and looked over the whole ground, had supposed it possible. It is, therefore, not to be wondered at that even our friends at home should have disbelieved in what is now known to be an accomplished fact.

The enemies of the Government are not even now satisfied, and would perhaps be equally dissatisfied, whether the loan was or was not taken. While yet in Europe, and after the loan had been taken, I noticed that American newspapers very unfairly criticised your action in regard to this loan; some insisting that you had "not placed the loan, or any part of the loan;" that you had "spent a round million in fruitless advertisements, in fees to useless agents, and in sending superannuated Treasury clerks on junketing tours to Europe;" and that the whole had ended in "a disastrous failure." Others conceded that the loan might perhaps be taken; but if it was, it had been hawked about Europe in a manner disgraceful to the American people "for six months;" while "the finance minister of the French Republic, emerging bruised, bleeding, and dismembered from one of the most calamitous wars in history, succeeded in placing a loan of equal amount in hardly more than the same number of hours."

The first cavilers are now silenced by the fact known to all well-informed persons, that all the five per cent. stocks offered by you have been taken, and that the Government has now none for sale. The other grumblers will probably never have the fairness to inform the readers of their papers that while you realized the face value of one hundred cents on the dollar on your new five per cent. loan, the French government received less than eighty cents on such value; and that for the eighty cents that government will be obliged to pay, at the maturity of its bonds, more than a quarter more money than it received, and in the mean time pay for the eighty cents the same rate of interest that our Government will pay on the par value that it received for its bonds of one hundred cents to the dollar. It was to me a most gratifying fact that the credit of our Government wherever I heard it spoken of, in all parts of Europe, stood unchallenged. Everybody conceded that we had both the ability and the disposition to pay all our debts. The rapidity with which you have been enabled to pay and reduce our national indebtedness is the controlling cause of this unbounded confidence that our Government will always remain faithful to its promises.

Other governments that have a financial standing have supplied their needs, and, like our own, are now out of the way, and surplus capital has again aggregated in the money markets of Europe. Under these changed circumstances, it is believed that if Congress will vest you with larger discretionary powers in regard to the compensation to be allowed to agents and other expenses attending the negotiation, and if it will authorize the interest to be paid in the country, and in the coin of the country, where the bonds may be purchased and held, the remaining loans of four and a half per cent. and four per cent., already authorized by Congress, can soon, unless untoward circumstances again intervene, be disposed of in Europe at par. I found that the most serious objection that Europeans made to our stocks was that the holder of them could not calculate exactly what dividend he would receive when the interest fell due. The rate of exchange of Europe with this country fluctuates so much, from time to time, that the amount the holder of our bonds will receive for the periodical interest due thereon will be sometimes more and sometimes less than he expected, and rarely the amount specified in the bond. This creates ill-feeling, and a jealousy on the part of the holder of our stock that his banker does not deal fairly by him; and the banker who, perhaps, bought and sold this very stock, becomes disgusted with the explanation he is constantly called upon to make in regard to the discrepancies in the amount of interest that he pays or carries to the credit of his customers. Rather than be thus annoyed, he makes up his mind in future to have nothing more to do with our stocks.

Who of our people can borrow money at home on his paper, having the interest and principal payable at his own distant home? Would a New York capitalist loan money to the Mexican Republic, were its credit ever so good, at the same rate of interest, if the interest and principal were made payable in the city of Mexico, that he would were both these payments to be made in the city of New York? The difference in the *amount* of interest to be paid on our bonds held in Europe would be comparatively *small*, whether paid at home or abroad. The saving in the *rate* of interest to be paid on moneys borrowed abroad would be *great*. The annoyance to the foreign bondholder would cease. Our stock would become the favorite one in the European money markets, and then there would be little or no danger that it would be thrown back upon our own markets in seasons of commercial revulsions. This last consideration our merchants and business men, who have innocently suffered by such return of our stocks from Europe, will understand and appreciate.

Many of our people object to making the interest on our loans payable in a foreign country, alleging as a reason that it lowers the dignity of the nation. Were it not true that, if there is any loss of dignity in money transactions, it occurs at the borrowing of the money, and not with the payment of the interest thereon, it might be worth the while for our legislators to go into the calculation of the commercial value of national dignity. In the present financial condition of our country, it can ill afford to pay an extra percentage to save itself from an imaginary loss of national dignity. While upon this subject, it just occurs to me that those of our people who are so very sensitive on this subject, and who are so anxious to sustain the dignity of the nation abroad, could find a much surer way to carry out their views and accomplish their end if they would insist that the representatives of the nation in foreign countries, who are commissioned to look after its interest and sustain its honor, should be paid a compensation on which they could subsist their families, and live decently, if not respectably. Most of our embassadors in Europe are obliged to draw largely upon their private resources, in order to sustain our national dignity abroad. With the consuls it is much worse. I found them without a habitation, "browsing around," having their offices in garrets, with stairs leading to them so steep that it was difficult to ascend them. On expostulating with one of these officers, in the capital of a highly commercial country, he informed me that he was not able to do otherwise. In order that he might keep out of debt, he was obliged to leave his family in America, and himself live in the most economical way; that he was determined to avoid the faults of his unfortunate predecessors, for whose unpaid debts he was yet being constantly dunned. What was worse, the creditors believed that the debts were the debts of the nation, and not of the individual consuls. I do not know how this strikes others, but I must confess that, as an American citizen, I felt ashamed. And yet I am sure I should not entertain such a feeling if the interest of our debt owned in Europe were made payable there. I must be excused for urging these views, for I feel a conviction that if they are carried out there will, for some time to come, be saved millions of dollars annually.

A LIBEL REFUTED.

On my return from Europe I was shown, in a New York newspaper, an infamous libel upon the Treasury Department generally, and upon me in particular. It was headed in double-leaded lines and large capital letters, " Leak in the Treasury—Millions of dollars abstracted—Mysteries brought to light—List of warrants drawn and not accounted for—Wholesale destruction of ledgers—Prodigious disclosures of fraud." It then goes on to state that " it is now positively known that every Department of the Government is reeking with corruption, and that millions of the public money have been abstracted from the Treasury." " In order to take out this money, it was entered as against the Treasurer, under the pretense that it was needed for disbursements, but it has never been accounted for." It alleges that " certain officers in the Bureaus of the First Comptroller and First Auditor were long privy to these transactions, but such was Spinner's influence with Congress, and such his power with the party leaders, whom he supplied liberally with funds, that they feared to expose the facts. The officers of the Treasury have made every effort to prevent this information from reaching the public, and upon being questioned upon the subject stoutly deny the truth of it. But the number, date, and amount of every warrant drawn for the money are known, and this bold fror⁺ of partisan and office-holding brass will not avail. The facts are but two plain and irrefutable, and it is only to be feared that they are only the beginning of numerous and greater peculations, particularly in the Navy and War Departments of the Government, and that a large portion of the whole FOUR HUNDRED AND TWENTY MILLIONS OF DOLLARS EXPENDED annually by the Government, will turn out to have been expended for the benefit of the gigantic ring of radical swindlers which centers in Washington City." And then asks, " What was done with the $3,000,000 which were drawn from the Treasury? No record of this vast amount appears on the books." Then, after preaching a homily to the Secretary of the Treasury for not reporting the facts, and quoting from laws that make it his duty " to lay before Congress an accurate statement and account of the receipts and expenditures of all the public moneys," it proceeds with a " STARTLING ARRAY OF DAMNING FIGURES, being a list of warrants for money drawn by Francis E. Spinner, and not accounted for." Here follows a list of sixty-one warrants, fifty-six of which are tolerably accurately described, except that the name of the payee is forged in every instance. The list is in the following form ; the items are taken promiscuouly :

Number of warrant.	Date.	In whose favor drawn.	Amount.
3455	Sept., 1867	F. E. Spinner	$2,932 37
1153	Aug., 1867	F. E. Spinner	12,835 00
4451	Aug., 1867	E. E. Spinner	78,044 60
4679	Nov., 1867	F. E. Spinner	20,000 00
841	July, 1868	F. E. Spinner	300,000 00
1517	July, 1868	F. E. Spinner	127,679 28

There are described in the same table fifty-five other warrants, that are each specified by *number, date and amount*, with the name of "F. E. SPINNER" *repeated in every one of them*, under the head of " In whose favor drawn," as above. An examination has been made in the various Bureaus of the Department of the books and records, and of the warrants themselves, fifty-six of which have been found, with dates and amounts tolerably correct, except a few typographical errors, and that in making up the table the numbers in twenty consecutive items were slid up one line. But they were so accurately described that they were easily found. In every one of these the name of the payee has been knowingly and maliciously falsified and forged. Five of the pretended warrants are fictitious. None such exist. The first warrant in the table, and as stated in the copy, is No. 3455 for $2,932 37, and is payable to "*Treasurer U. S. on ac. Internal Rev., as a receipt from Tax on Salaries*," and not to "*F. E. Spinner*." There are thirty-three others in this list, in amounts varying from $126 72, No. 33, to $105,594 22, No. 951, and all made payable in like manner. All these thirty-four warrants, being more than half the number specified in the whole list, have the same history.

It was the invariable practice of the War Department, when an income tax on the salaries was retained from the pay of its officers and employés, to make requisitions quarterly on the Treasury Department for the amount of the aggregate salaries, *less the income tax*, in favor of a disbursing officer, who drew the money and paid the salaries less the tax; and then to make another requisition for the gross amount of the tax that was withheld. On these last-named requisitions warrants were issued in form like the one first above described. All the thirty-four above mentioned were of this precise character and tenor. Certificates of deposit in triplicate were issued immediately on the receipt of each warrant for the amounts specified in each warrant respectively, one copy for the War Department, one for the Commissioner of Internal Revenue, and one for the Secretary of the Treasury. On the receipt of each of these certificates, the Secretary of the Treasury caused covering warrants to be issued for the respective amounts claimed, by which the money was carried into the Treasury of the United States, to the account of internal revenue receipts of tax on salaries. Every one of the thirty-four amounts named in the list as having been paid to " F. E. Spinner," was so treated, and so placed in the Treasury, as appears upon all the books; and each amount had been accounted for to, and passed upon as correct, by the First Auditor, and the audit had been confirmed and finally settled in my account by the First Comptroller of the Treasury, and his letters verifying the fact of such settlement, except for a single item hereinafter mentioned, embracing the whole list of fifty-six warrants described in the list, and which were found, had been in my possession, some of them for over one year, and all the others for over two years, before these infamous charges were published by the falsifier, who, from his evident access to the books and papers of the Department, must have known all these facts when he invented his wholesale lies. But all that has been said in regard to these thirty-four tax warrants is a simple statement of the routine of the business of the Department when moneys are transferred from one account or appropriation to another. In reality, no money was handled or passed into or out of the Treasury on any one of these thirty-four warrants and their complementary covering warrants. They simply accomplished the transfer of the several amounts specified in each from accounts of appropriations for the War Department to the credit of internal revenue for receipts from tax on salaries. The money either still remains in the Treasury, or it has been drawn out on other money warrants, to satisfy the creditors and pay the debts of the United States.

Eleven other of the warrants specified in this libelous article, instead of being payable to the order of " *F. E. Spinner,*" as is charged, are made payable to the order of the " *Treasurer U. S., to the credit of C. C. Jackson, Paymaster U. S. Navy.*" No. 1153, for $12,835, the second one in the foregoing table, is one of these. Every one of these eleven warrants was credited for the full amount on the day on which the proper drafts that were issued on them came back from the office of the Register of the Treasury. All these moneys have since been drawn out on Paymaster Jackson's checks. No money passed out of the Treasury on any one of these eleven warrants; they simply effected transfers on the books, from appropriations made for the Navy, to the agency account of a naval disbursing officer, to be used for payments on account of the Navy, and to be accounted for to the proper accounting officer by the *paymaster who disbursed the money, and not by me.* I showed to the satisfaction of the proper Auditor and Comptroller that the transfer had been made; and it being found that the paymaster had received the money, my charges were necessarily allowed in the settlement of my accounts.

Four other warrants, specified in the list as being payable to the order of "*F. E. Spinner,*" read, " Pay to Treasurer U. S. to the credit of Brvt. Brig. Genl. G. W. Balloch, Chief D. O. Bureau of Refugees, &c.," and state that their amounts are from an "appropriation" for "Support of Bureau Refugees, Freedmen, and Abandoned Lands." All that was said in regard to the eleven warrants for credit of Paymaster Jackson is equally applicable to these four, that were, in accordance with the directions contained therein, placed to the credit of General Balloch.

Seven other warrants specified in the list as being payable to " *F. E. Spinner,*" are made payable severally as follows: No. 4679, for $20,000, reads, " Pay to Treasurer U. S., to the credit of Lieut. L. B. Norton, 30th Inf'y, and Disbursing Officer Signal Dptm't." This is the fourth in the above list.

No. 841, for $300,000, is a war warrant that reads, " Pay to Brvt. Brig. Genl. Charles H. Tompkins, Deputy Quartermaster General, New Orleans, La.," and the draft for the amount is drawn on the " Ass't Treasurer U. S., New Orleans, La." The draft bears the indorsement, " To be deposited to my official credit with Ass't Treas'r U. S., at N. Orleans, Charles H. Tompkins, Brv't Br'g. Gen'l & Dep. Q. M. Gen'l." This is the fifth in the list. Neither my own name, private or official, nor that of my office, appears anywhere in or on this warrant, or in or on the draft that was issued on it. The date, number, and amount are correctly stated; all else is a deliberate forgery and lie.

No. 3113, for $30,000, reads, " Pay to Treasurer United States, to the credit of B't L't Col. F. W. Taggard, U. S. A., Must'g and Disb'g Off'r." The direction on this warrant is to place with United States Treasurer at Washington $20,000, and $5,000 with each of the assistant treasurers at New York and at St. Louis, to the credit of Colonel Taggard. It was so placed, as appears by the indorsements upon the three drafts that were issued upon the warrant upon the three offices named.

No. 5183, for $20,000, reads: " Pay to Assistant Treasurer New York City $10,000, Treasurer U. S. $10,000; both to the credit of Bt. Lt. Col. Geo. McGown, Disb'g Officer Adj't Gen'l's Office, Washington, D. C." Both the amounts were so placed, as appears by the indorsements on the draft attached to the warrant.

No. 4451, for $78,044 60, reads: " Pay to Treasurer U. S., to be deposited to the credit of Honl. O. H. Browning, Secretary of the Interior, in trust for various Indian tribes, as principal and interest on certain heretofore unpaid Missouri State bonds," "being part of the amount found due to State of Missouri, on settlement of her ac. for militia expenses during the rebellion." The amount was so credited. This is the third described in the table.

No. 5088, for $3,500, is a prize case, with which the Treasurer has nothing whatever to do. The custody of all prize money belongs to the Assistant Treasurer by law of Congress. The warrant reads, "Pay to Assistant Treasurer U. S., Washington, D. C., to be held subject to such order as may be made in relation thereto by the Dist. Court of U. S. for the Dist. of Columbia;" and states that it is "Due Prize Steamer Gov'r A. Morton." The draft bears the indorsement, "Credited as within directed, L. R. Tuttle, Ass't Treasurer U. S.," dated December 19, 1867.

No. 4553, for $635, reads, "Pay to Treasurer U. S., to be deposited to the credit of Griesenz Smither, Altheim, county of Oberamth, Kingdom of Würtemberg, Germany." On June 11, 1868, the First Comptroller, by an order in writing upon the face of the warrant, directed the amount to be paid to "Leopold V. Bierwith, consul general of Würtemberg, at New York, as attorney in fact of the heirs of Griesenz Smither," and on the next day it was so paid, as appears from Mr. Bierwith's receipt on the draft that is attached to the warrant on file.

Fifty-five warrants of the sixty-one described in the charge that the money payable thereon had not been accounted for are now explained. Besides the five alleged ones that exist only in the fertile imagination of the willful falsifier, but one, No. 1517, the last in the foregoing list, remains. This, instead of being payable to "F. E. Spinner," as is falsely stated, reads, "Pay to the Treasurer of the United States, as a special deposit, subject to the direction of the Secretary of the Treasury, by letter, one hundred and twenty-seven thousand six hundred and seventy-nine dollars and twenty-eight cents, due the State of West Virginia on settlement." The statement is made on the warrant that it is for "reimbursing West Virginia for militia expenses during the rebellion." Payment was for a time withheld on this warrant, on the request of the Secretary of the Interior, until the question of the State's liability for non-payment of interest on Old Virginia stocks held by him in trust for various Indian tribes should be settled. The legal officer of the Government gave an opinion against the State's liability, whereupon the Secretary of the Treasury directed me by letter "to send draft for the amount of $127,679 28 in favor of William E. Stevenson, governor of West Virginia, at Wheeling, W. Va." The draft for the whole amount was paid to Governor Stevenson on the 13th of July, 1869, as appears by his official indorsement upon the draft attached to the original warrant, on file in the office of the Register of the Treasury. My charge for the payment of this warrant was audited, passed to my credit, and settled in the second quarter of 1869, as appears by the letter of the First Comptroller in this office, dated March 7, 1871.

The name of "F. E. Spinner" is repeated sixty-one times in the descriptive table of warrants, published in the newspaper article, as the payee in that number of described warrants, when, in truth and in fact, as is herein shown, he is not the payee in any one of them. And I will add, that no warrant was ever issued payable to "F. E. Spinner" at any time, either before or since I came into this office, for any amount or for any purpose whatever.

It is further charged, in the same article, that "the books are not kept by double entry, and that a number of the account-books have been allowed to be destroyed." When I came into the office, more than ten years ago, I had the manner of keeping the books changed from single to double entry, and increased the number, so as to make them checks on each other. The books have been so kept up to this time.

Again, it is charged that "a large number of ledgers are missing." This is equally, with all the other charges, false. Every book of accounts that I found in the office in 1861, and every one that has been opened since, is now in the office. The whole series, by years, in every division, is complete and in perfect order, of which fact any one wishing to know may satisfy himself by personal inspection. Again, it is charged that "six cart-loads of account-books were permitted to be mutilated and then taken out of the Treasury building to be sold for paper stock; and that nothing now remains of them but the two boxes full of the red leather labels, which were torn off of them with the intention of destroying them by fire." This charge, like all the others, has just enough truth in it to give plausibility to a deliberate lie. The *immaterial* facts stated are *true*, and all the *material ones* are *utterly false*. There was a number of books of printed forms, procured by a former administration of the Department, and needlessly bound, being principally "Steamboat inspectors' certificates" and "Western river pilots' licenses"—the latter long since obsolete, and the former soon to become so. Neither could be used bound up in a book, but must be cut out for use. It was ordered, for economy's sake, that the covers be taken off from all these books, the blanks that could be used for their designed purpose to be so used, and the remainder for other office purposes; and the covers to be used for other needed books. A few other books of forms, that are now obsolete and useless for the purposes for which they were prepared, have been treated in a like manner. A few small books of naval paymasters' returns, that were in duplicate in the office of the Fourth Auditor, and of no earthly use to the Department or any one else, have also been taken to pieces and the material used for needed purposes. The labels were saved for use. Now, this wholesale falsifier must have known, from the labels and from the paper that he saw, that neither had ever belonged to "ledgers" or to any other "books of accounts," and he knew that, with the exception of the *duplicate* "paymasters' returns," not one of them had ever been used for any purpose whatever, and that not a written word or figure, nor a stroke of a pen, had ever been made in any one of the books that he speaks of as "books of accounts."

This charge of the destruction of "six cart-loads of account-books," like the one that I had taken on warrants made payable to "F. E. Spinner" moneys amounting to $3,103,057 63, and for which I have not accounted, is, I hope, sufficiently disproved by the foregoing simple statement of facts, the truth of which can be verified by any one who may choose to examine the records and papers that are accessible in the various offices of the Department to which they properly belong. The charge that I "arrived in England on the 20th of May, and proceeded to Baden, where he [I] parted with his [my] companions and disappeared," is in perfect keeping with all the rest. The whole article from the beginning all the way through to the ending, so far as any material fact is concerned, is an unmitigated lie, and was so known to be by its getters-up when it was invented, penned, and published.

These statements have been made particularly full and much in detail, because it was the only way that a negative could be proved. Each item has therefore been taken up separately and by itself, the warrants by their numbers and the amounts of money payable thereon, and the books by their kinds and titles; so that any one so disposed may be able to look up all the books and papers referred to, and thus satisfy

himself that each and every distinct charge made has not only been dis-
proved, but that it was made by the libeler with the full knowledge, at
the time of making it, that it was a deliberate and atrocious falsehood.

General charges against my official conduct, or against the management of the office given me in charge, I have never noticed. These
charges were, however, made so maliciously specific, that even fair-
minded men who did not know me nor the facts, nor the characters of
those who published them, might be led to believe that there might be
some foundation of truth in them.

It had been said of municipal officials of a northern city, that "they
do not deny the charges of robbery of the public money made against
them." There is reason to believe that, taking advantage of my absence in a foreign land, these false charges against the Treasury Department that originated in the organ of the "Ring" in that city,
whose editor is one of its members in the senate of the State, were
"back-fire" and "stop-thief" dodges, and made with a view to draw attention from themselves and their "stealings," and that they might say,
"Why should we deny general charges of official dishonesty, when an
official of the National Government, who is charged more specifically
with greater wrong-doing, makes no denial?"

These were motives that induced me to swerve from the general rule,
to give no heed to slanders and libels.

Another reason was, because I hold that the people have a right not
only to *believe*, but to *know*, that their servants who administer their
public affairs, or who have the custody and disposition of their money,
are faithful and honest.

When I first entered public life, more than forty years ago, I made it
a law to myself never to do an official act that I was not willing everybody should see me do. This rule I have never broken in a single
instance, and so long as God continues to give me the strength to adhere,
I never will break it. I have now held this office for more than ten
years, and in that time have perhaps had such opportunities, and what
would to some have been such temptations, for making money, as have
rarely been put within the reach of any man. I might easily have
become rich by speculations in stocks by my knowledge of the Government's intentions in advance of others. I have never used this
knowledge for my own or the interest of any other person. Since I
have been in the office I have never engaged in any speculations nor in
any business whatever. I have given my whole time and attention,
night and day, to the utter neglect of my own, to the care of the public's business and interest; and in consequence thereof am now, at that
age that is the time allotted to man in this world, as poor in pecuniary
things as I was on the day I came into this office. I have but little to
leave to my children, save an honest reputation, and that it is my purpose to keep and protect, and, if necessary, to defend, even to the extent
of appealing to the criminal courts of the country, for the conviction of its
libelers. I have never taken, nor permitted others to take, from the Treasury a single cent, nor any greater amount, except by authority of law.
If there are wrongs in this office, or here in the Department, or if there
have been any since I have been in it, I am in entire ignorance of them,
and feel quite sure that none other except such as have been officially
reported, and whereon the parties implicated have been pursued, and
when caught were convicted and punished, have existed, or do now
exist.

It may be doubted which does the most to undermine confidence in
our republican institutions—permitting thieving officials to escape pun-

ishment, or the apathy with which the public mind receives infamous charges against trusted public officers.

SECURITIES DEPOSITED BY INSURANCE COMPANIES.

The laws of the State of New York require (2 Revised Statutes, page 771) that before any foreign life insurance company can do business in that State, there shall be filed in the insurance department of the State the certificate of "the chief financial officer" of the State by whose laws such company is incorporated, that there is deposited with him in trust, for the benefit of the policy-holders of the company, one hundred thousand dollars in stocks or securities.

In order to avail itself of the privileges of this act and of similar enactments in other States, the National Life Insurance Company of the United States of America, incorporated by the Congress of the United States, and having its office in this District, deposited in this office one hundred thousand dollars in United States bonds, for which the Treasurer issued the certificate required by the laws of the State of New York, which certificate was accepted as sufficient by the insurance department of that State. The form of the certificate thus given is in words and figures as follows, to wit:

TREASURY OF THE UNITED STATES, *Washington, D. C.*:

I, F. E. Spinner, do hereby certify that I am Treasurer of the United States, and that the National Life Insurance Company of the United States of America, a corporation chartered by Congress, located at Washington, in the District of Columbia, has heretofore deposited in this office stocks of the United States, amounting in par value to not less than the sum of one hundred thousand dollars. And I do hereby further certify that such securities are now held by me in this office, as such Treasurer aforesaid, in my official capacity, on deposit and in trust for the benefit of all the policy-holders of said company, and to enable said company to comply with the laws of the various States in order to do business therein. And I further certify that I am satisfied that the said stocks and securities are worth one hundred thousand dollars and upwards. Said deposit was made in this office on the 12th day of August, A. D. 1868, and has ever since that period remained at all times intact for the full amount of one hundred thousand dollars in the stocks and securities above specified.

In witness whereof I have hereunto set my hand and caused my official seal to be affixed at the Treasury Department on this 31st day of December, A. D. 1870.

F. E. SPINNER. *Treasr. U. S.*

Certificates of similar purport have been given by the Treasurer for use in other States. Some time in April last the $100,000 in United States bonds were withdrawn and one hundred and ten thousand dollars, par value, in United States four per cent. coupon certificates of indebtedness of 1870, issued to the State of Maine for advances made during the war of 1812, were substituted therefor. These certificates are payable to bearer, and are not assigned to the Treasurer, the evidence of the purposes for which they are held being the letter that accompanied and which is on file with them.

After this deposit had been made, the National Capitol Life Insurance Company, another corporation in this District incorporated by Congress, deposited for the same purpose promissory notes amounting to $102,000, secured by deeds of trust on unincumbered real estate, valued, by appraisers appointed by the insurance department of the State of New York, at $247,000. This real estate has been conveyed to the Treasurer of the United States, in his official capacity, and to his successors in office, in trust for the policy-holders of said company, by a deed of trust, executed by the trustee and grantors of the above-mentioned deeds of trust. Policies of insurance amounting to $26,000, on the improvements on this property, have been assigned to the Treasurer as trustee, and filed with the other papers in his office. For these deposits a certificate in accordance with the facts stated was given by the Treasurer, to be filed in the insurance department of the State of New York.

It is proper that the facts should be stated that payment of the above-mentioned notes is promised, as appears from their tenor, when and as the same may be required by a vote of the directors of the company, the notes being payable to the order of the company. The deeds being merely collateral to the notes, it would seem that the Treasurer cannot dispose of the property for the benefit of the policy-holders until there shall have been default in the payment of the notes. As payment of the notes can be demanded only by the directors, the Treasurer would seem to be unable to make any sale for the benefit of the policy-holders in case of a failure of the company to meet its engagements, without the co-operation of the board of directors.

In addition to the difficulties already enumerated, the taking of these trusts by the Treasurer was extra-official, there being no law of the United States requiring him to take or hold securities for the purposes as above stated. It is therefore doubted whether the securities held by the Treasurer, in trust for the two before-mentioned insurance companies, could be made available in the manner that was contemplated by the legislatures of the States that enacted the laws for the protection of its policy-holding citizens.

Strongly impressed with the conviction that all corporations that by their charters are authorized to have money transactions should be compelled to give ample security for the faithful performance of all their obligations, I would most respectfully suggest that Congress be asked to so amend the acts of incorporation under which the two above-named insurance companies were created as to compel each of them to deposit, in lieu of their present unauthorized securities, at least one hundred thousand dollars in the new five per cent. bonds of the Government, with the Treasurer of the United States, and assigned to him in trust for the benefit of the policy-holders of said companies respectively, in case default should be made by them in paying their legal liabilities to said policy-holders.

In this connection it may perhaps not be inopportune to suggest the propriety of having established by law of Congress a governmental bureau to have charge of the affairs of all kinds of insurance companies and associations, in the same manner as the Comptroller of the Currency now has charge of the affairs of all the banks that issue paper money in the United States.

At the meeting of the national insurance convention, held in the city of New York, in May last, N. D. Morgan, esq., president of one of the largest insurance companies in that city, said:

The reasons why I would prefer a national bureau to the present State supervision are patent to every officer of our present companies.

Life insurance, to be successful, should not be confined to one locality. The business of a company should be extended over as great an extent of territory as possible, in order to equalize, as far as may be, the rate of mortality among its members in seasons of epidemics. A company doing an extended business in the city of New York, and in all the large cities of the United States, would hardly be affected in case of a plague raging in one of those cities, while the others are exempt; the income from the exempt district compensating for any excessive claims from the infected one. It is therefore important that the largest liberty to transact business throughout the whole country should be accorded to our life insurance companies.

Under the present system of State legislation it is very difficult for our companies to so extend their business. Restriction after restriction is thrown up against the work of the insurance agent throughout the length and breadth of the land, as though the business involved some terrible harm to the public, instead of the life-giving stream of joy and gladness that it is to the widow and the orphan.

This, to enable the work to go on as it should and would were matters different, should be remedied by the creation by Congress of an insurance bureau, to which every company in the country should report, to enable it to transact business outside of the State where located. The filing of such report, and with such deposit in the bureau as is now demanded by our own State laws, and with satisfactory evidence of solvency as the laws of Congress might demand, should secure to such reporting companies certificates of authority to transact business within any State of the Union, without regard to any State or municipal laws whatever.

Mr. Morgan's views in regard to life insurance companies are equally, applicable to fire, and, to some degree, to marine insurance companies. From personal intercourse, and through written communications with other officers of leading insurance companies, I have become satisfied that the better class of these companies would favor a law creating a bureau of national insurance companies, and that would provide for a deposit in stocks of the General Government, with the Treasurer of the United States, pledged for the security of the policy-holders of such companies.

The president of one of the leading and largest life insurance companies in the United States has written me the information that the assets of all the fire, marine, and life insurance companies, doing business in the United States, amount to four hundred and twenty million dollars; and that the amounts at risk in these companies amount to twenty-five hundred million dollars; being greater in amount than the whole national debt. He says, in view of the hope that a national bureau will be created, that "it is impossible to contemplate these stupendous aggregates and their vast annual accumulations, laden, as they all are, with the trusted elements of material welfare and human happiness, without anxious desire to anticipate future developments."

The establishment of such a national bureau would bring confidence to the insured, and would add large numbers to the millions of our people who now have a pecuniary interest in the stability of these useful and benevolent institutions. In addition, the creation of such a bureau would create a home market for a large amount of our new stocks bearing a less rate of interest than is now paid on the old United States stocks; thus conferring the double benefit of assurance from loss to many and partial exemption from taxation to all our citizens.

NATIONAL BANKS.

The delays of banks in making their semi-annual returns, and in the payment of duty referred to in my last annual report, have increased during the last fiscal year. Most of the national banks pay the tax due from them promptly, within the time specified by law, and treat this requirement as they do other obligations against their respective institutions. But there are other banks that have been carelessly, if not willfully, habitually negligent in making their returns and paying the duty due from them to the Government. A number of the banks did not pay the duty due on the 1st day of July until some time during the months of September and October. The following banks, at the date hereof, have made no reports of the amounts of duty due from them on the 1st of July last, nor have they made any payment of the duty: First National Bank of Kansas City, Missouri; Miners' National Bank of Utah, Salt Lake City, Utah; First National Bank of Utah, Salt Lake City, Utah. The two last-named banks have recently been merged into one institution.

For the protection of the Treasury against the growing evil, I would most respectfully renew the recommendation made in my last annual report, that a percentage upon such duty be added to it for every ten days' delay in payment after the expiration of the one month's time now allowed by law. Legal enactments, giving authority to this Office to add one per cent. to the duty due from banks for every ten days' delay after the time fixed by law for its payment, would seem to be the most effective measure to insure prompt payments of the duty.

"GOLDEN RULE" LOSS.

My attention has been called to a New York newspaper article, extending through five solid columns of *The Sun* of August 23, 1871. The authors have displayed much ingenuity in the relation of the story to weave such a fabric of fiction that it should seem to be truth.

The false theory attempted to be proved by this article is, that the steamer "Golden Rule," with *six hundred and eighty souls on board*, and carrying money belonging to the Treasury of the United States, *in transitu* from the Treasury at Washington to the assistant treasurer at San Francisco, was, on June 30, 1865, *at 3.40 in the night, during thick weather*, purposely run on the Roncador Reef, with a view to the robbery of the money, and that a million dollars in amount was actually stolen by the captain of the steamer and another party named ; that the safe was recovered broken open ; that it was forwarded by one of the parties in charge of the money to Washington, but that it never reached its destination, being thrown overboard on the way.

Without discussing the probability of two men conspiring, for the purpose of a possible gain, to run the vessel on a reef in the open Caribbean Sea, in the night-time, thereby endangering their own lives and those of nearly seven hundred other persons, many of whom were women and children; and without going into the testimony presented soon after the loss to the Department, that made it appear pretty clearly that the running of the vessel on the reef was purely accidental, and that the money was lost in the ocean, I hope now, in a simple statement, to overthrow every false inference drawn from the long circumstantial statements that are presented to prove that the amount of a million of dollars was stolen, and that it was not lost and totally destroyed in and by the action of the ocean.

First, then, the crushed safe did come to the Treasury and was repeatedly examined by myself and others, in company with old sea-captains and other experts, and it was the opinion of nearly all that the safe was broken by being jammed between the steamer and the rocks. Then, again, nearly all the money that was in the safe, except the million dollars in question, floated on shore, and, except a few bills, has been recovered by the Treasury. The million dollars was not in "greenbacks," as is alleged, but consisted of one thousand time-notes of one thousand dollars each, payable three years after date, with compound interest. These notes bore date May 15; were received by the Treasurer May 16; and left this office May 18. The "Golden Rule" left New York May 20, and was wrecked May 30, 1865. These notes were in regular and unbroken sequence of numbers, being from No. 5001, letter A, to 5500 ; and from No. 5001, letter B, to 5500 ; both numbers, in each case, inclusive. Both the numbers and letters appear on this kind of notes both on the upper and on the lower half of every note. Compound-interest notes were issued from Nos. 1 to Nos. 9850, repeated on each of the letters A, B, C, and D, aggregating $39,400,000.

All this immense amount, except the one thousand notes in question, and seventeen other notes scattered promiscuously through the whole series, have been presented at the Treasury, and have been paid. Not a single note of the one thousand notes of the numbers and letters above mentioned, that left this office for transportation to San Francisco, has ever been presented for payment. Of the thirty-eight thousand four hundred other notes of the same kind, that were issued at the same time, and before and after the time that the one thousand notes in question were issued, *all but seventeen notes have been redeemed*. The part of the story that this million of dollars was used by the alleged thieves, who, it is stated, were poor at the time of the wreck, are rich now, and in possession of valuable farms and stocks in the State of Maryland, is simply absurd. Had this property been bought with these notes, they would long since have been presented for payment.

A suggestion is thrown out that the numbers of the notes were changed, or rather that other notes, with other numbers, were exchanged for the notes in question by the collusion of the then Register of the Treasury with the thieves. Such a course would have been impracticable, if not impossible, and could have been of no earthly use to the supposed conspirators if it could have been done. The first note presented would have been detected, and that, too, whether the numbers were altered or not, or whether other notes with other numbers were put in their stead. If altered to or exchanged for a note of another number under 9850, the highest number issued, it would, of course, have been a *duplicate*, and there would have been no place for its register on the books. If changed to or for a higher number than the one named, it would have shown an *over-issue*, which it is now known does not exist. As no duplicate nor any number higher than 9850 has ever been presented, this false theory falls with the others. To show the utter impossibility of either being done, or that the notes in question were redeemed in any other way, it is only necessary to state that all money, these notes included, is received from the Bureau of Engraving and Printing by the Treasurer, is receipted for by him, and is then covered into the Treasury by warrant. They can only be paid out on warrants. When redeemed by the Treasurer they are carefully counted, and then cut in two parts longitudinally, thus showing both the letters and numbers of the notes on each half. The lower halves are then sent to the office of the Secretary of the Treasury, and the upper halves to the office of the Register of the Treasury. In each of these offices they are counted; and if found to be correct and agreeing in all the offices, the Treasurer is then reimbursed for the amount by warrant in his favor.

In the offices of the Secretary and of the Register, books of registry for the entire issue of these compound-interest notes were prepared, having the letters and the numbers printed in regular sequence from the first to the last number that was ever issued. These half-notes, after being so counted in these two offices, are then registered respectively in these two separate books of registry. Neither of these offices knows of the other's action unless they disagree with the Treasurer's count. In such case each reports to the Treasurer separately. These two books of registry are now found to agree, and they both show that all the notes, of this kind that have ever been issued, amounting to thirty-nine million four hundred thousand dollars, have been presented and paid, except the one thousand notes in question, and the seventeen other notes before mentioned, that have, as yet, not been presented for redemption. All the blanks opposite their appropriate letters and numbers respectively are filled up with the date on which each individual note was redeemed. The one thousand numbers representing the notes sent by the "Golden Rule" to San Francisco, running in their sequence through quite a number of pages in the books, remain a blank on all the registers. After waiting over six years and not a single one of these known notes appearing, the Comptroller of the Treasury has, after a thorough and searching investigation, wisely directed to treat them like notes certified to have been destroyed, and has thus had them taken out of the cash account; and thus has most undoubtedly correctly settled this vexed matter forever, or until that time at least when one of these notes shall be resurrected from the grave where it has been buried for over six years.

OUTSTANDING LIABILITIES.

Governments, like individuals, should follow the golden rule, and do as they would be done by. Ours, of all others, being of the citizens, should set an example of honesty to the citizens. The withholding of an honest debt is morally but little, if any, better than outright stealing. There is due from the Government money, in various amounts, to individuals, principally for unclaimed interest on United States stocks, that has been accumulating from year to year, until, in the aggregate, it amounts to quite a considerable sum. Formerly no employé of the Treasury Department was allowed to give any information that would lead to a demand for the payment of these debts. The consequence was that sharpers would, by some means, at times succeed in ascertaining some of the amounts, and the names of the persons to whom the money was due. If through city directories, or by any other means, they succeeded in ascertaining their post-office address, they would write to the parties direct; if not, then they would insert an advertisement in the "personal" of a New York newspaper, stating that "if the following-named persons will address C. A. B., box 6857, New York post-office, stating where they may be found, they will learn something greatly to their pecuniary advantage;" after which follows a long list of names. These will be recognized in this office as creditors of the Government. If the creditor gets half the money due him from the Government he is lucky. Through these means the indebtedness of the Government for these unclaimed amounts has gradually decreased, but, instead of going to the persons to whom it belonged, half at least has gone into the pockets of sneaks, who obtained the information of the indebtedness surreptitiously.

Some three years since, with the consent of the then Secretary of the Treasury, I directed letters to be written to all persons having amounts standing to their credit on the books of this office, whose address could be ascertained, informing them of such fact, and the amount of money subject to their order. Comparatively but few were reached in this way, and very many of these amounts still remain unpaid. It is therefore recommended that Congress be asked to pass a law directing the Treasurer, or other proper officer of the Treasury Department, to advertise in newspapers published in the cities of New York and Washington, at the end of each year, a list of the names of all persons to whom the Government has been indebted for more than six months next preceding the making of such list, stating the amount of said indebtedness; and that lists of the same shall be posted in conspicuous places in the offices of the Treasurer and the Assistant Treasurers of the United States for public inspection. Provision should be made in the law for the retention of a percentage from the amount, when paid, to defray the expenses of advertising. .

AUDIT OF ACCOUNTS.

The lack, need, and want of a proper officer in the Treasury Department to review, adjust, and finally settle the agency accounts of the Treasurer and the Assistant Treasurers, and Designated Depositaries, and of the Post-Office accounts that are now finally passed upon by the Auditor of the Post-Office Department, are seriously felt.

All other accounts, civil or military, or of whatever branch of the public service, are finally passed upon, adjusted, and settled by either the First or the Second Comptroller of the Treasury. Neither of the Comptrollers has any legal authority to review, decide upon, or in any manner control in the two kinds of accounts above named. The final settlement and the correct payment of these accounts should be under the supervision of a Comptroller, or other proper officer designated for that purpose. As matters now stand, in regard to the two classes of accounts named, this office is not only inconvenienced and imperiled, but it has great responsibilities thrown upon it that do not attach in other cases, and ought not in those named.

It is feared that through the loose, irregular, and anomalous manner in which these accounts are settled and paid, sooner or later, the Government will suffer serious losses. A loss to the Post-Office Department some years since, supposed to have been caused by the collusion of the then postmaster in the city of New York and an officer of the Treasury Department, and the recent loss to the Government through an agency account, would probably have been avoided had there been a proper officer of the Treasury Department to review the adjustment and the settlement of these classes of accounts, and decide upon the sufficiency of the receipts given in payment therefor.

It is suggested that the office of a Third Comptroller be created, to take all these accounts and their final settlement in charge; or that they be given, like all other accounts, for adjustment, settlement, and evidence of correct payment of the draft or check issued thereon, in charge of one of the present Comptrollers of the Treasury.

SALARIES OF EMPLOYÉS.

Attention is most respectfully called to what was said in the report from this office of the last and of former years, in regard to the inadequacy of the compensation allowed by law to the employés of the office. But for the temporary relief granted by the kindness of Congress, for the last two years, to the officers, it would not have been possible to have secured the services of persons competent to the proper discharge of required duties.

But in my opinion many of the clerks employed in this office deserve, and in justice should receive, like consideration as the officers. I would especially call attention to the tables that appear in the report of the last year relative to the more perfect organization of the *personnel* of the Treasury of the United States.

CONCLUSION.

Without the least intention or desire to throw blame upon any other officer, it is due to the officers of the Treasury that the emphatic declaration should be made, that for the defalcation of an officer belonging to another Department of the Government, neither this office, nor any one employed in it, is in any way responsible, as will be clearly made to appear, should a legal investigation of the whole matter, which is desired on my part, ever be made.

The fiscal year has ended without the loss of a single cent to the Treasury by the act, or by the negligence, of any employé in this office. For this and for other escapes from loss, I hope that I am truly thankful and grateful to that Power that has now again, as in the past, shielded me from personal harm, and the nation from consequent pecuniary loss.

I have the honor to be, very respectfully,

F. E. SPINNER,
Treasurer of the United States.

Hon. GEORGE S. BOUTWELL,
Secretary of the Treasury.

APPENDIX.

A.—GENERAL TREASURY.

I.—RECEIPTS AND EXPENDITURES.

1.—*Receipts and expenditures by warrants.*

The books of the office were closed June 30, 1871, after the entry of all moneys received and disbursed on authorized warrants within the fiscal year, as follows:

Cash, Dr.

Balance in Treasury from last year		$149,502,471 60
Received, formerly credited as unavailable		3,396 18
Received from Loans	$420,020,626 90	
Received from Customs	206,270,408 05	
Received from Internal Revenue	143,098,153 63	
Received from Lands	2,388,646 68	
Received from War	22,837,092 04	
Received from Navy	3,203,648 42	
Received from Interior	814,678 91	
Received from Miscellaneous	32,765,226 89	
Total receipts for fiscal year		831,398,481 52
		980,904,349 30

Cash, Cr.

Paid on account of Public Debt	$684,919,114 51
Paid on account of the Army	58,637,083 86
Paid on account of the Navy	22,634,675 63
Paid on account of Interior	42,685,571 23
Paid on account of Treasury proper	24,259,851 98
Paid on account of Customs	17,037,452 40
Paid on account of Treasury, Interior	5,479,247 54
Paid on account of Internal Revenue	9,128,164 23
Paid on account of Diplomatic	1,661,068 22
Paid on account of Quarterly Salaries	708,748 84
Paid on account of War, (civil branch)	924,386 11
Paid on account of Judiciary	2,911,507 51
Total expenditures for fiscal year	870,986,872 06
Balance in Treasury at close of fiscal year	109,917,477 24
	980,904,349 30

NOTE.—The above includes transfers between appropriations and repayments.

2.—*Warrants.*

The receipts, as stated in the foregoing table, were carried into the Treasury by 11,323 covering warrants, which is 477 less than were issued during the preceding year, but an increase of 331 over the year previous to that.

The payments were made on 25,711 authorized warrants, for the payment of which there were issued 31,759 drafts on the Treasury and the various branches thereof. In these two last-mentioned items there was an increase over the number issued during the preceding year of 407 warrants and of 5,805 drafts.

18 F

3.—Counter-warrants and Repayments.

The counter-warrants were issued on account of the—

Army	$12,287,957 39	
Navy	1,886,757 26	
Interior	104,874 99	
Loans	150,537,362 99	
Civil and Miscellaneous	222,803 85	
		$165,039,756 48
Public Debt Revenue counter-warrants	6,872,108 71	
Diplomatic Revenue counter-warrants	426,680 80	
		7,298,789 51
Total of counter and Revenue counter-warrants		172,338,545 99

The repay covering warrants, representing repayments of unused moneys and proceeds of sales of stores, amounted to $14,266,256 68.

NOTE.—Repay covering warrants represent repayments of money advanced to disbursing officers, and proceeds of sales of stores, both of which are credited to the appropriations from which the moneys were advanced.

Transfer and counter-warrants represent moneys which have been advanced from one appropriation and expended on account of another. The moneys are afterwards charged to the proper appropriations on transfer-warrants, and credited back on counter-warrants to the appropriations from which they were advanced. These warrants are now issued only in the settlement of old accounts arising during the war.

Revenue counter-warrants represent revenues expended before being covered into the Treasury. Such moneys are afterwards covered into the Treasury by Revenue counter-warrants, and charged on regular pay-warrants to the officers by whom they have been expended. As shown above, warrants of this kind were issued during the last fiscal year on account of the Public Debt and Diplomatic Expenses only. The Public Debt Revenue counter-warrants represent interest which accrued on the Sinking Fund, and which was expended in the purchase of United States Stocks for that fund by the Treasurer as custodian of the fund, without being first covered into the Treasury. The amounts were afterwards carried into the Treasury by Revenue counter-warrants, and charged to the Treasurer on Public Debt pay warrants. The Diplomatic Revenue counter-warrants represent moneys received by consular officers for fees, &c., and expended for expense authorized by law. This course is necessitated by the distance of those officers from the Treasury.

4.—Receipts and Expenditures by warrants, less counter and transfer warrants.

Receipts:

On account of Loans		$269,619,897 09
On account of Internal Revenue		143,098,153 63
On account of Miscellaneous		25,107,000 35
On account of Lands		2,388,646 68
On account of Army		10,549,134 65
On account of Navy		1,316,891 16
On account of Customs		206,270,408 05
On account of Interior		709,803 92
Total cash receipts for which certificates of deposit were issued		659,059,935 53
Add Revenue counter-warrants		7,298,789 51
		666,358,725 04
Deduct repayments of moneys		14,266,256 68
Receipts, agreeing with Secretary and Register		652,092,468 36
Add amount received from unavailable:		
From Depositary, St. Croix	$2,199 73	
From Depositary, Tallahassee	679 66	
From Depositary, Olympia	516 79	
		3,396 18
Add counter-warrants and repayments		179,306,013 16
Balance held from last year		149,502,471 60
Total as before		980,904,349 30

Expenditures:

On account of Public Debt	$527,509,642 81
On account of Army	46,404,856 88
On account of Navy	20,739,342 73
On account of Interior	42,555,316 48
On account of Treasury	24,199,432 31
On account of Customs	16,914,749 97
On account of Treasury, Interior	5,478,408 38
On account of Internal Revenue	9,100,987 34
On account of Diplomatic	1,205,338 20
On account of Quarterly Salaries	706,257,35
On account of War, (civil branch)	924,386 11
On account of Judiciary	2,909,607 51

Total payments by drafts	698,648,326 07
Add Revenue counter-warrants	7,298,789 51
	705,947,115 58
Deduct repayments of moneys	14,266,256 68
Expenditures, agreeing with Secretary and Register	691,680,858 90
Add transfer-warrants and repayments	179,306,013 16
Cash Balance in Treasury at close of the year	109,917,477 24
Total as before	980,904,349 30

5.—Receipts and Expenditures by Ledger.

The actual Receipts during the fiscal year, as per Cash Ledger, were as follows:

Cash, Dr.

Cash Ledger Balance June 30, 1870		$150,096,911 02
Semi-annual Bank Duty	$5,999,876 33	
Bonds, 6 per cent., 5-20s	16,800 00	
Bonds, 5 per cent., 1881	61,238,300 00	
Captured and Abandoned Property	27,500 00	
Certificates of Indebtedness of 1870	678,362 41	
Conscience Money	8,749 51	
Coin Certificates	56,577,000 00	
Customs	206,274,518 99	
Fractional Currency	31,103,900 00	
Fines and Penalties	974,793 91	
Indian Trusts	1,144,011 87	
Internal Revenue	143,117,903 25	
Internal and Coastwise Intercourse	26,097 39	
Interest, 5 per cent. loan of 1881	16,247 47	
Public Land Sales	2,406,494 32	
Miscellaneous Revenue	5,794,818 52	
Legal-Tender Notes, new issue	120,588,311 00	
Profits on Coinage	226,368 51	
Premium on Coin, &c	8,902,760 84	
Patent Fees	620,780 70	
Real Estate Direct Tax	587,165 57	
Treasury Notes, Seven-Thirties	292,237 05	
Temporary Loan	125,000 00	
Navy, (repayments)	1,257,961 69	
Miscellaneous, (repayments)	1,757,440 67	
War, (repayments)	11,469,646 60	
Total Net Receipts		661,233,046 60
Received, formerly credited as unavailable:		
From Depositary, St. Croix	2,199 73	
From Depositary, Tallahassee	679 66	
From Depositary, Olympia	516 79	
		3,396 18
		811,333,353 80

Cash, Cr.

The actual expenditures, as per Cash Ledger, were as follows:

Public Debt	$527,509,642 81
War proper	46,404,856 88
War, civil branch	924,386 11
Navy	20,739,342 73
Interior	42,555,316 48
Quarterly Salaries	706,257 35
Judiciary	2,909,607 51
Customs	16,914,749 97
Treasury proper	24,199,432 31
Treasury, Interior	5,478,408 38
Diplomatic	1,205,338 20
Internal Revenue	9,109,987 34
Total actual expenditures	698,648,326 07
Balance of cash in Treasury	112,685,027 73
	811,333,353 80
Total cash balance at the close of the year	112,685,027 73
This balance consists of gold and silver	98,448,116 75
Other lawful money	14,236,910 98
Total cash	112,685,027 73
Deduct cash not covered by warrants	2,767,550 49
Balance, as per Warrant Ledger, see above	109,917,477 24

The cash balance, as per Ledger, after all the cash accounts had been received from the various offices constituting the Treasury and entered upon the books, was—

Cash, Dr.

Ledger balance from old account	$150,096,911 02
Cash receipts during the year, as above	661,233,046 60
Received from unavailable	3,396 18
Total	811,333,353 80

Cash, Cr.

Payments during the year, as above	$698,648,326 07
Balance in cash to new account	112,685,027 73
Total	811,333,353 80

6.—Segregated Receipts and Expenditures by Warrants.

Receipts:

Public Debt.

On account of Legal-Tender Notes	$120,588,311 00
On account of Fractional Currency	31,103,900 06
On account of Coin Certificates	56,577,000 00
On account of 3 per cent. Certificates	140,000 00
On account of Certificates of Indebtedness of 1870	678,362 41
On account of Consols of 1867	11,800 00
On account of Refunding of Loan of 1881	59,669,150 00
On account of Sinking Fund	851,373 62
Total on account of Public Debt	269,619,897 09

Customs:

On account of Customs	206,270,408 05

Internal Revenue:

On account of Internal Revenue... $143,098,153 63

Lands:

On account of Lands.. 2,388,646 68

War:

On account of Quartermaster General's Department..	$156,877 15
On account of Incidental Expenses	103,022 53
On account of Clothing the Army....................	346,287 21
On account of Subsisting the Army..................	394,982 52
On account of Barracks and Quarters	195,176 30
On account of Cavalry and Artillery Horses	48,212 61
On account of Army Transportation	1,459,261 68
On account of Pay of Two and Three Years' Volunteers	91,501 14
On account of Pay of Militia and Volunteers	250,963 30
On account of Expenses of Recruiting...............	15,898 14
On account of Pay and Subsistence of Military Academy...	436,762 42
On account of Ordnance and Ordnance Stores.......	8,286,131 70
On account of Arsenals, War Department	14,835 20
On account of Officers' Transportation	1,234 14
On account of Heating and Cooking Stoves.........	1,443 92
On account of Improving Harbors and Lakes.......	86,394 50
On account of Forts and Fortifications	36,352 74
On account of Collecting and Drilling Volunteers...	16,675 99
On account of National Armories...................	629,094 72
On account of Subsistence of Officers	47,860 93
On account of Pay, &c., of the Army...............	294,093 86
On account of Bridge Trains and Equipage.........	3,586 64
On account of Rivers and Harbors	290 92
On account of Medical and Hospital Department....	84,969 68
On account of Expenses under Reconstruction Acts .	123,208 60
On account of Arms for Volunteers and Regulars....	2,716 16
On account of Commutation of Rations to Prisoners.	36 00
On account of Bounty under Act of 28th July, 1866.	24,992 00
On account of Forage for Officers' Horses.........	6,148 34
On account of Pay in lieu of Clothing..............	216,297 92
On account of Military Survey, &c..................	5,638 04
On account of Arming and Equipping Militia........	240,984 04
On account of Pay to Disabled Soldiers for Clothing not drawn	424,180 24
On account of Draft and Substitute Fund	2,000,000 00
On account of Bounty to Volunteers, Widows, and Others...	6,790,950 40

Total on account of War..................................... 22,837,092 04

Navy:

On account of Clothing for the Navy	389,928 24
On account of Pay of the Navy	1,264,494 91
On account of Provisions for the Navy..............	30,089 82
On account of Ordnance and Ordnance Stores.......	93,201 96
On account of Navy Hospital Fund	80,933 15
On account of Contingent, Navy	15,137 13
On account of Navy-yards	85,642 53
On account of Contingent, Yards and Docks........	90,699 97
On account of Clothing, Marine Corps..............	21,530 61
On account of Navigation	19,292 16
On account of Equipment of Vessels...............	152,625 77
On account of Construction and Repairs............	275,153 73
On account of Civil Estimate......................	537 84
On account of Equipment and Repairs	1,454 00
On account of Steam Machinery	171,307 98
On account of Pay of the Marine Corps	1,382 62
On account of Fuel for the Navy...................	14 19
On account of Naval Asylum	641 75
On account of Contingent, Marine Corps............	471 56
On account of Transportation for Marine Corps.....	281 25

On account of Navy Pension Fund	$420,875 24	
On account of Prize Cases, (Navy)	6,201 14	
On account of Medicine and Surgery	17,026 20	
On account of Magazines, Navy	6,345 38	
On account of Nautical Almanac	2,365 91	
On account of Naval Observatory	9,719 53	
On account of Bounty to Seamen	4,845 30	
On account of Naval Hospital, &c	998 46	
On account of Surveying Service, (Navy Department)	10,867 93	
On account of Nautical Instruments	22,344 13	
On account of Indemnity for Lost Clothing	5,061 40	
On account of Naval Stations	2,176 63	
Total on account of Navy		$3,203,648 42

Interior:

On account of Fulfilling Treaties with Indians	267,465 87	
On account of Army Pensions to Invalids	88,059 49	
On account of Pensions to Widows	266,703 69	
On account of Contingencies, Indian Department	1,396 89	
On account of Annuities to Indian Tribes	96,393 57	
On account of Navy Pension Fund	6,615 45	
On account of Incidental Expenses, Indian Service	23,796 64	
On account of Trust Fund, Interior	1,568 72	
On account of Interpreters	183 35	
On account of Subsistence of Indians	10,328 27	
On account of Civilization of Indians	52,118 59	
On account of Superintendents and Indian Agents	48 38	
Total on account of Interior		814,678 91

Miscellaneous:

On account of Consular Fees	570,634 00
On account of Premium on Sale of Gold	13,117,403 63
On account of Premium on Transfer Drafts	370,117 03
On account of Profits on Coinage	2,928,285 45
On account of Coinage of 1, 2, 3, and 5 Cent pieces	100,000 00
On account of Fines, Penalties, and Forfeitures	1,045,886 97
On account of Homestead and Other Fees	634,708 71
On account of Letters-Patent	620,319 11
On account of Locating Military Bounty-Land Warrants	12,304 47
On account of Locating Agricultural College Land-Warrants	14,213 31
On account of Salaries of Store-Keepers, (Internal Revenue)	561,060 67
On account of Surveying Services	44,931 96
On account of Emolument Fees	531,029 30
On account of Steamboat Fees	251,083 06
On account of Extension Treasury Building	40,079 97
On account of Furniture and Repairs	16,471 50
On account of Transportation, &c., Act July 2, 1864	775,742 26
On account of Services of United States Officers	277,906 56
On account of Expenses of United States Courts	23,660 57
On account of Collecting Revenue from Customs	59,363 86
On account of Collecting Internal Revenue	122,095 72
On account of Sale of Indian Lands	1,024,040 60
On account of Interest, Miscellaneous	511,911 25
On account of Light-House Service, &c	371,249 67
On account of Public Buildings	68,419 34
On account of Outstanding Liabilities	35,719 84
On account of Revenue-Cutter Service	49,460 19
On account of Expenses of National Loan	12,054 60
On account of Branch Mints, &c	33,859 91
On account of Relief and Protection American Seamen	19,263 93
On account of Expenses of Attorney General's Office	5,262 48
On account of Detecting Counterfeiters	4,922 39
On account of Blank Books and Stationery	12,943 39

On account of Miscellaneous and Contingent Expenses $81,020 79
On account of Indian Trust-Fund Bonds 336,453 25
On account of Public Printing and Binding 22,252 12
On account of Salaries of Solicitor's Office 17,419 24
On account of Labor, Drayage, and Storage 74,328 65
On account of Weighing Fees 65,329 09
On account of Indian Lands 156,381 27
On account of Incidental Expenses, Treasury Department 36,614 10
On account of Expenses of Inspectors 653 49
On account of Contingent Expenses, &c., Act August 6, 1846 .... 19,373 40
On account of Additional Clerks, &c., Act August 6, 1846 .... 34,298 94
On account of Marine Hospital Establishment 254,080 64
On account of Conscience Fund, &c 8,521 89
On account of Wages of Seamen, &c 15,795 53
On account of Sale of Old Material 19,104 77
On account of Deaths on Shipboard, &c 2,686 36
On account of Records from General Land Office 3,933 42
On account of Rebate of Interest, &c 4,035 21
On account of Captured and Abandoned Property ... 27,800 00
On account of Repayment to Importers, &c 49,063 64
On account of Direct Tax, August 5, 1861, June 7, 1864 586,532 06
On account of Prize Cases, &c 36,838 01
On account of Semi-Annual Duty on Circulation 6,003,584 32
On account of Legislation in Territories 9,980 72
On account of Copyright Fees 7,280 01
On account of Extra Compensation 22,729 13
On account of Excess of Deposits 214,922 62
On account of Debentures and Drawbacks 81,246 54
On account of Bureau of Medicine and Surgery 182 03
On account of Bureau of Yards and Docks 120 44
On account of Bureau of Ordnance, &c 258 99
On account of Tax on Seal Skins, Act July 1, 1870 .. 101,080 00
On account of Discount on Stocks held by United States 39,017 50
On account of Contingent Expenses, Foreign Intercourse 5,704 00
On account of Contingent Expenses, Two Houses of Congress 8,315 78
On Account of Contingent Expenses, Taking the Eighth Census 5,797 35
On account of Expenses of Loan 70,000 00
On account of Sale of Government Property 38,524 00
On account of Sinking Fund, (Counter-Warrant) 150,253,038 04
On account of Miscellaneous Sources 185,234 26

Total on account of Miscellaneous $183,165,956 70

Total receipts per warrant 831,398,431 52

Expenditures:

Quarterly Salaries:

On account of United States Courts $443,867 72
On account of Inspectors Steam-Vessels 114,813 19
On account of Governors, &c 150,067 93

Total on account of Quarterly Salaries $708,748 84

Diplomatic:

On account of Ministers and Consuls 1,030,336 56
On account of Foreign Intercourse 553,902 82
On account of Relief and Protection of Seamen 76,828 84

Total on account of Diplomatic 1,661,068 22

Judiciary:

On account of United States Courts................	$2,911,507 51	
Total on account of Judiciary................................		$2,911,507 51

Customs:

On account of Light-Houses..........................	3,634,819 25
On account of Collecting Revenue...................	7,129,538 45
On account of Relief..................................	13,179 40
On account of Revenue Cutter Service..............	1,294,032 81
On account of Public Buildings	1,390,246 36
On account of Refunding Duties	3,557,941 72
On account of Captured and Abandoned Property...	17,694 41

Total on account of Customs........................	17,037,452 40

Treasury Proper:

On account of Assistant Treasurers and Depositaries.	1,141,823 65
On account of National Loan	3,337,726 42
On account of Executive Department...............	50,525 48
On account of Smithsonian Institution..............	39,000 00
On account of Navy Department and Coast Survey, &c.................................	879,851 72
On account of Relief of Sundry Persons............	179,845 28
On account of Telegraphing	40,000 01
On account of Expenditures of Post-Office Department...	5,808,340 33
On account of Outstanding Liabilities	69,439 05
On account of Illegal Captures	760,748 72
On account of United States Court of Claims.	54,594 46
On account of the Agricultural Department.........	184,600 00
On account of Salaries of Governors, &c	148,487 70
On account of Salaries of Inspectors of Steam-Vessels.	42,208 88
On account of Public Buildings and Grounds........	2,253,314 49
On account of Return of the Proceeds from Captured and Abandoned Lands............................	730,909 78
On account of Treasury Department	2,460,718 79
On account of Legislative Department..............	3,332,239 09
On account of State Department...................	167,759 75
On account of Public Printing......................	1,851,397 67
On account of Commissioner of Mining Statistics....	11,500 00
On account of Refunded to States......	678,362 41
On account of Miscellaneous........................	24,906 64
On account of Refunding Taxes, &c..............	1,144 80
On account of Southern Claims Commission.........	10,106 86

Total on account of Treasury Proper	24,259,851 98

Treasury, Interior:

On account of Repayment for Lands................	53,438 49
On account of Metropolitan Police...................	216,924 93
On account of Interior Department and Post Office..	1,446,744 20
On account of Erection of Buildings................	659,358 31
On account of Salaries and Fees of Registers and Receivers......................................	351,233 20
On account of Suppression of Slave Trade...........	5,956 80
On account of Surveying, &c.................	742,200 70
On account of Expenditures of the Eighth Census and Ninth Census	1,959,584 87
On account of Relief to Sundry Persons.............	10,463 74
On account of 5 per cent. Fund, (for lands in Minnesota)	23,265 90
On account of Law Libraries for Territories.........	10,076 40

Total on account of Treasury, Interior.....................	5,479,247 54

Internal Revenue:

On account of Assessment and Collection............. $8,000,499 08
On account of Detecting Frauds...................... 60,250 19
On account of Refunding Duties, &c 1,067,414 96

    Total on account of Internal Revenue.... .... $9,128 164 23

Public Debt:

On account of Interest on Temporary Loan.......... 69 76
On account of Interest on Certificates of Indebted-
  ness 13,360 02
On account of Interest on Three Per Cent. Certificates. 1,484,017 29
On account of Interest on Navy Pension Fund...... 420,000 00
On account of Interest on Treasury Notes of 1857.... 562 96
On account of Interest on Seven-Thirties of 1861 .... 80 29
On account of Interest on One and Two Year Notes
  of 1863.... .... 3,191 30
On account of Interest on Compound Interest Notes. 63,035 58
On account of Interest on Oregon War Debt........ 55,620 00
On account of Interest on Ten-Forties of 1864....... 9,767,480 44
On account of Interest on Five-Twenties........... 48,238,812 22
On account of Interest on Consols of 1865, 1867, and
  1868 .... 44,569,891 90
On account of Unclaimed United States Interest.... 671,307 46
On account of Unclaimed Pacific Railroad Interest.. 1,380 00
On account of Unclaimed Interest on Loan of 1848.. 747 00
On account of Unclaimed Interest on Loan of 1858.. 994,055 00
On account of Unclaimed Interest on Loan of 1860.. 315,149 98
On account of Interest on Loan of 1861, (1881s)..... 12,507,619 50
On account of Interest on Loan of 1863, (1881s)..... 4,513,034 45
On account of Interest on Pacific Railroad Stock.... 3,986,475 75
On account of Temporary Loan 101,000 00
On account of Coin Certificates 71,237,820 00
On account of Three Per Cent. Certificates.......... 13,805,000 00
On account of Treasury Notes of 1857............... 5,100 00
On account of Seven-Thirty Notes.................. 210,252 25
On account of Old Demand Notes 9,750 50
On account of Certificates of Indebtedness.......... 3,546 16
On account of Legal-Tender Notes.................. 120,600,311 00
On account of Fractional Currency.................. 30,407,713 92
On account of One and Two Year Notes of 1863...... 49,700 00
On account of Compound Interest Notes............ 1,324,910 00
On account of Texan Indemnity Stock 78,110 62
On account of Oregon War Debt..... .... 54,900 00
On account of Loan of 1863, (1881s).............. 150 22
On account of Five-Twenties 127,573,500 00
On account of Consols of 1865, 1867, and 1868....... 144,903,400 00
On account of Loan of 1847........................ 16,500 00
On account of Loan of 1848........................ 61,850 00
On account of Loan of 1860........................ 6,973,000 00
On account of Premium Account................... 26,387,823 39
On account of Sinking Fund, Principal............. 3,842,300 00
On account of Sinking Fund, Premium............. 407,606 28
On account of Sinking Fund, Interest 159,926 64
On account of Special Fund, Principal............. 8,219,350 00
On account of Special Fund, Premium............. 922,533 32
On account of Special Fund, Interest.............. 57,169 31

    Total on account of Public Debt.............................. 684,919,114 51

Interior:

On account of Indian Department 7,880,997 72
On account of Navy Pensions....................... 406,648 57
On account of Army Pensions....................... 34,397,924 94

    Total on account of Interior 42,685,571 23

War, civil branch :

On account of War Department......................	$592,275 45	
On account of Public Buildings and Grounds	332,110 66	
Total on account of War, civil branch..........................		$924,386 11

War, proper :

On account of Horses Lost in Service, Relief, &c..	1,267,702 57	
On account of Secretary of War.....................	3,694,387 45	
On account of Commissary General..................	3,737,072 02	
On account of Quartermaster General...............	15,441,366 38	
On account of Paymaster General...................	16,631,210 35	
On account of Adjutant General....................	9,488,037 32	
On account of Surgeon General....................	258,263 73	
On account of Ordnance	1,681,044 31	
On account of Inspector General /	193,959 99	
On account of Engineers, (fortifications, &c.).......	6,244,039 74	
Total on account of War proper..............................		58,637,083 86

Navy :

On account of Pay of the Navy.....................	8,428,772 96	
On account of Equipment and Recruiting...........	1,621,109 55	
On account of Provisions and Clothing	1,703,853 59	
On account of Navigation	449,913 94	
On account of Construction and Repairs	4,510,812 60	
On account of Miscellaneous.......................	313,770 00	
On account of Ordnance	674,872 97	
On account of Steam Engineering	1,226,839 84	
On account of Yards, Docks, &c	2,218,914 49	
On account of Prize Money	208,946 26	
On account of Marine Corps.......................	865,524 10	
On account of Relief, &c..........................	78,640 25	
On account of Medicine and Surgery.:.............	332,705 08	
Total on account of Navy.......		22,634,675 63
Total amount of Pay-Warrants for fiscal year.................		870,986,872 06

NOTE.—The above receipts and expenditures exceed those reported by the Secretary and Register by the amount of repayments and of counter and transfer warrants issued during the year. The titles of appropriations and of sources of receipts are also, in some instances, stated differently than by those officers.

II.—BALANCES AND OVERDRAFTS.

Balances and overdrafts to the credit and debit of the Treasurer of the United States, June 30, 1871.

	Balances.	Overdrafts.
Treasurer, Washington	$16,819,617 56	....
Assistant Treasurer, New York......................	56,466,616 16	....
Assistant Treasurer, Boston........................	4,878,314 55	....
Assistant Treasurer, Philadelphia...................	6,382,460 20	....
Assistant Treasurer, Charleston....................	260,404 57	....
Assistant Treasurer, St. Louis.....................	1,314,829 13	....
Assistant Treasurer, New Orleans..................	1,793,526 05	....
Assistant Treasurer, San Francisco.................	3,963,869 23	....
Assistant Treasurer, Baltimore.....................	2,618,786 97	....
Depositary, Buffalo................................	203,008 07	....
Depositary, Chicago...............................	1,277,209 54	....
Depositary, Cincinnati.............................	852,045 11	....
Depositary, Louisville	....	$163,310 10
Depositary, Pittsburgh	615,280 24	....
Depositary, Mobile................................	215,329 57	....
Depositary, Santa Fé..............................	....	39,093 54
Depositary, Oregon City...........................	28,666 14	....
Depositary, Olympia	48,653 08	....
Depositary, Tucson................................	....	245 18

	Balances.	Overdrafts.
National Banks	$7,197,115 04	
United States Mints	7,954,885 48	
Suspense Account		$2,940 14
Balance as per Ledger		112,685,027 73
Total	112,890,616 69	112,890,616 69
Of the above balance there is in coin		98,448,116 75
And in currency		14,236,910 98
Total		112,685,027 73

III.—DISBURSING OFFICERS' BALANCES.

Balances to the credit of Disbursing Officers of the United States, June 30, 1871.

Treasurer of the United States		$1,348,111 10
Assistant Treasurer, Boston	$756,228 18	
Assistant Treasurer, New York	6,166,568 34	
Assistant Treasurer, Philadelphia	1,220,127 04	
Assistant Treasurer, Charleston	73,356 68	
Assistant Treasurer, St. Louis	1,255,705 53	
Assistant Treasurer, New Orleans	649,442 13	
Assistant Treasurer, San Francisco	2,017,802 57	
Assistant Treasurer, Baltimore	212,017 68	
With Assistant Treasurers		12,351,248 15
Depositary, Buffalo	179,796 63	
Depositary, Chicago	930,808 91	
Depositary, Cincinnati	226,869 34	
Depositary, Louisville	523,648 59	
Depositary, Pittsburgh	228,563 39	
Depositary, Mobile	112,814 13	
Depositary, Santa Fé	313,973 15	
Depositary, Oregon City	1,438 00	
Depositary, Olympia	1,022 75	
Depositary, Tucson	23,174 23	
With Depositaries		2,542,109 12
With National Bank Depositaries		4,480,912 41
Total amount in all offices to credit of Disbursing Officers		20,722,380 78

IV.—TRANSFERS OF FUNDS.

To facilitate payments at points where the moneys were needed for disbursements, transfer-letters, transfer-orders, and bills of exchange were issued during the fiscal year, as follows:

2,116 letters on National Banks	$37,112,273 82
526 transfer-orders on National Banks	6,770,000 00
51 bills of exchange on Collectors of Customs	203,000 00
1,044 transfer-orders on Assistant Treasurers and Depositaries	222,523,131 37
3,737 transfers, amounting to	266,608,405 19
Of which amount there was in coin	33,473,178 18
And in currency	233,135,227 01
Total	266,608,405 19

V.—UNAVAILABLE FUNDS, JUNE 30, 1871.

Currency:

First National Bank, Selma, Alabama	$59,978 07
Venango National Bank, Franklin, Pennsylvania	217,391 38
Total amount with National Banks	277,369 45

Deficit at New Orleans, (Whitaker's)...................... $668,566 86
Deficit at Louisville, Kentucky, (stolen).................... 9,000 00
Deficit at Louisville, Kentucky, (Bloomgart's) 11,083 52
Deficit at Santa Fé, (J. L. Collins's)...................... 30,603 03
Deficit at Olympia, Washington Territory, (Jos. Cushman's) 1,637 18

    Total with Assistant Treasurers and Depositaries................. $720,890 59

    Total unavailable currency 998,260 04

Coin:
United States Branch Mint, Charlotte, North Carolina..... $32,000 00
United States Branch Mint, Dahlonega, Georgia 27,950 03
United States Depositary, Galveston, Texas...............   778 66

    Total coin 60,728 69

    Total amount of unavailable funds 1,058,988 73

VI.—NATIONAL BANK DEPOSITARIES.

The business transactions between the Treasury and National Banks as depositaries
have been for the fiscal year as follows:
Balance brought from last year's account $8,483,549 79
Receipts during the last fiscal year..................................   99,525,759 52
Receipts during the last fiscal year for fractional currency...........   2,367,925 03

    Total..   110,377,234 34

Payments during the last fiscal year...............................   103,180,119 30
Balance due the United States 7,197,115 04

    Total...   110,377,234 34

Payments through expresses at Government expense................   6,770,000 00
Payments without expense to the Government......................   96,410,119 30

    Total..   103,180,119 30

VII.—OUTSTANDING LIABILITIES.

Amount covered into the Treasury to July 1, 1870 .... $207,643 96
And in the last fiscal year 34,331 23

    Total...   241,975 19

There has been paid to various parties entitled to receive the same to
    July 1, 1871...   35,632 41
Unclaimed balance remaining in the Treasury.....................   206,342 78

    Total..   241,975 19

VIII.—CONSCIENCE FUND.

Amounts received from various persons from December, 1863, to July 1,
    1870 .... $117,397 84
And in the last fiscal year 8,749 51

    Total amount received since November 30, 1863.................   126,147 35

IX.—OPEN ACCOUNTS.

With Assistant Treasurers   18
With Designated Depositaries..   12
With United States Mints...   10
With National Bank Depositaries...   155
With Disbursing Officers...   102
Impersonal accounts...   91
                                                            388

B.—POST OFFICE DEPARTMENT.

I.—RECEIPTS AND EXPENDITURES.

The receipts and expenditures on account of the Post Office Department, for the fiscal year, were as follows:

Cash, Dr.

Balance brought forward from last year's account		$804,193 73
Received at Washington, District of Columbia	$60,320 05	
Received at New York, New York	5,622,937 32	
Received at Philadelphia, Pennsylvania	413,459 23	
Received at Boston, Massachusetts	465,283 42	
Received at St. Louis, Missouri	152,456 01	
Received at San Francisco, California	198,708 66	
Received at Charleston, South Carolina	73,291 06	
Received at New Orleans, Louisiana	127,777 69	
Received at Baltimore, Maryland	127,188 11	
Received at Cincinnati, Ohio	5 00	
Received at Chicago, Illinois	1,271 33	
Received at Pittsburgh, Pennsylvania	1,135 69	
Received at Buffalo, New York	25 00	
Received at Mobile, Alabama	578 78	
Received at Santa Fé, New Mexico	804 02	
Received at Tucson, Arizona	167 10	
First National Bank, Galveston, Texas	3,626 33	
First National Bank, Knoxville, Tennessee	305 12	
First National Bank, Leavenworth, Kansas	1,450 08	
First National Bank, Milwaukee, Wisconsin	10,212 94	
First National Bank, Nashville, Tennessee	812 00	
First National Bank, Portland, Oregon	02	
First National Bank, Portsmouth, New Hampshire	100 00	
First National Bank, Richmond, Virginia	1,681 41	
First National Bank, St. Paul, Minnesota	30 00	
First National Bank, Springfield, Illinois	138 22	
First National Bank, Wilmington, Delaware	140 00	
Second National Bank, Detroit, Michigan	7 00	
Atlanta National Bank, Atlanta, Georgia	1,130 20	
Indianapolis National Bank, Indianapolis, Indiana	121 00	
Merchants' National Bank, Cleveland, Ohio	1,270 39	
Merchants' National Bank, Little Rock, Arkansas	704 15	
Merchants' National Bank, Portland, Maine	1,184 00	
Merchants' National Bank, Savannah, Georgia	3,347 62	
San Antonio National Bank, San Antonio, Texas	39 75	
Total receipts during the year		7,271,708 70
Total		8,075,902 43

Warrants were issued on the various offices for the payment of the aggregate amounts as follows:

Cash, Cr.

On Washington, D. C.	$354,941 63
On New York, New York	4,679,802 19
On Philadelphia, Pennsylvania	450,290 68
On Boston, Massachusetts	463,897 27
On Saint Louis, Missouri	394,438 71
On San Francisco, California	562,983 39
On New Orleans, Louisiana	481,342 14
On Charleston, South Carolina	191,839 03
On Baltimore, Maryland	195,026 74
First National Bank, Galveston, Texas	3,389 02
First National Bank, Springfield, Illinois	412 20
	7,778,363 00
Balance, Cash on hand to new account	297,539 43
Total	8,075,902 43

II.—APPROPRIATIONS FROM TREASURY FOR POST OFFICE DEPARTMENT.

Moneys included in the above receipts were drawn from the Treasury on account of the Post-Office that were not receipts of the Post-Office Department, but were appropriated for its use by Congress, as follows :

For Mail-Steamship service between San Francisco, Japan, and China:

July 12, 1870, paid Treasury warrant No. 846	$125,000 00	
October 8, 1870, paid Treasury warrant No. 1281	125,000 00	
January 6, 1871, paid Treasury warrant No. 22	125,000 00	
April 3, 1871, paid Treasury warrant No. 482	125,000 00	
		$500,000 00

For free mail-matter, Act March 3, 1847, and March 3, 1851 :

January 7, 1871, paid Treasury warrant No. 23	$350,000 00	
April 3, 1871, paid Treasury warrant No. 483	350,000 00	
		$700,000 00

For Mail-Steamship service between the United States and Brazil :

September 10, 1870, paid Treasury warrant No. 1164	$37,500 00	
December 12, 1870, paid Treasury warrant No. 1539	37,500 00	
March 20, 1871, paid Treasury warrant No. 405	37,500 00	
June 12, 1871, paid Treasury warrant No. 768	37,500 00	
		$150,000 00

For Mail-Steamship service between San Francisco and the Sandwich Islands :

July 27, 1870, paid Treasury warrant No. 933	25,000 00	
October 19, 1870, paid Treasury warrant No. 1320	18,750 00	
January 14, 1871, paid Treasury warrant No. 52	18,750 00	
April 15, 1871, paid Treasury warrant No. 533	18,750 00	
		$81,250 00

For Supplying the Deficiency in the Revenue of the Post-Office Department :

August 5, 1870, paid Treasury warrant No. 1024	1,000,000 00	
October 26, 1870, paid Treasury warrant No. 1344	500,000 00	
January 7, 1871, paid Treasury warrant No. 23	450,000 00	
April 4, 1871, paid Treasury warrant No. 491	250,000 00	
April 28, 1871, paid Treasury warrant No. 599	500,000 00	
June 30, 1871, paid Treasury warrant No. 881	1,000,000 00	
		$3,700,000 00

For Preparation of the Post Office Directory, Act March 3, 1871 :

March 30, 1871, paid Treasury warrant No. 457		1,200 00
Total amount received from Government......................		5,132,450 00

III.—RECEIPTS AND PAYMENTS BY POSTMASTERS.

Receipts by postmasters, on account of postage on letters, newspapers, and pamphlets, registered letters, emoluments, &c., disbursed by the Post Office Department without being paid into the Treasury, but afterwards carried into and out of the Treasury by warrant, were as follows :

For quarter ended September 30, 1870	$3,862,940 78
For quarter ended December 31, 1870................................	4,111,199 16
For quarter ended March 31, 1871	4,218,871 54
For quarter ended June 30, 1871...................................	4,311,394 78
Total	16,504,406 26

IV.—TOTAL RECEIPTS AND EXPENDITURES, (INCLUDING AMOUNTS RECEIVED AND PAID BY POSTMASTERS.)

Cash, Dr.

Balance from last year...		$804,193 73
From postmasters and others.......................	$2,139,258 70	
From Treasury on warrants to supply deficiencies of Post-Office Department..........................	3,700,000 00	

From Treasury on warrants for subsidies to steam-
ships $1,431,250 00
From Treasury on warrant for preparation of Post-
Office Directory 1,200 00
                                                                          $7,271,708 70
For amount received and paid by postmasters .... ·16,504,406 26

    Total 24,580,308 69

Cash, Cr.

Paid on 6,058 Post-Office warrants 7,778,363 00
Received and paid by postmasters.................. 16,504,406 26
Balance to new account 297,539 43
                                                                          24,580,308 69

C.—NATIONAL BANKS.

I.—NUMBER OF NATIONAL BANKS.

On the 30th June, 1870, the number of National Banks that had deposited securities
of the United States with this office preliminary to their organization was 1,698
The number of new banks organized during the last fiscal year was 141

    Total number of banks June 30, 1871..................................... 1,839

The number of banks that had paid duty and deposited securities for their cir-
culating notes was, on the 30th June, 1871..................................... 1,788
Failed prior to June 30, 1870, and securities sold............................... 12
Failed prior to June 30, 1870, and securities in part still held 3
Failed in last fiscal year.....:.. 0
Banks having no circulation, securities withdrawn.............................. 12
In liquidation; money deposited to redeem circulation and securities withdrawn
prior to June 30, 1870.....:.. 11
In liquidation; money deposited and securities withdrawn in last fiscal year.... 13

    Number of banks organized.. 1,839

The whole number of banks in voluntary liquidation and of those consolidated
with others on June 30, 1870, was 66
Number gone into liquidation in last fiscal year................................. 13

    Number in voluntary liquidation and consolidated..................... 79

II.—NEW NATIONAL BANKS.

The following National Banks were organized during the fiscal year:
    The Kidder National Gold Bank of Boston, Massachusetts.
    The Baxter National Bank of Rutland, Vermont.
    The National Bank of Springfield, Missouri.
    The National Bank of Maysville, Kentucky.
    The Merchants and Planters' National Bank of Augusta, Georgia.
    The People's National Bank of Norfolk, Virginia.
    The Farmers' National Bank of Stanford, Kentucky.
    The Monmouth National Bank of Monmouth, Illinois.
    The First National Bank of Gallatin, Tennessee.
    The Second National Bank of Lebanon, Tennessee.
    The Corn Exchange National Bank of Chicago, Illinois.
    The First National Bank of Brodhead, Wisconsin.
    The First National Bank of Shelbina, Missouri.
    The Moniteau National Bank of California, Missouri.
    The First National Bank of Columbia, Tennessee.
    The National Bank of Menasha, Wisconsin.
    The Salem National Bank of Salem, Illinois.
    The Citizens' National Bank of Alexandria, Virginia.
    The First National Bank of Sterling, Illinois.
    The Jacksonville National Bank of Jacksonville, Illinois.
    The Fayette National Bank of Lexington, Kentucky.
    The First National Bank of Ottawa, Kansas.
    The First National Bank of Watseka, Illinois.

The First National Bank of Decatur, Michigan.
The First National Bank of Tuscola, Illinois.
The First National Bank of Chariton, Iowa.
The First National Bank of Schoolcraft, Michigan.
The Iowa National Bank of Ottumwa, Iowa.
The National Bank of Pulaski, Tennessee.
The First National Bank of Richmond, Kentucky.
The First National Bank of Evansville, Wisconsin.
The Muskegon National Bank of Michigan.
The First National Bank of Lapeer, Michigan.
The Second National Bank of Lawrence, Kansas.
The State National Bank of Springfield, Illinois.
The German National Bank of Chicago, Illinois.
The First National Bank of Palmyra, Missouri.
The City National Bank of Selma, Alabama.
The First National Bank of Hightstown, New Jersey.
The Loudoun National Bank of Leesburg, Virginia.
The South Bend National Bank of South Bend, Indiana.
The First National Bank of Lake City, Minnesota.
The First National Gold Bank of San Francisco, California.
The Citizens' National Bank of Charlottesville, Virginia.
The National Security Bank of Philadelphia, Pennsylvania.
The Merchants' National Bank of Burlington, Iowa.
The Hastings National Bank of Hastings, Michigan.
The City National Bank of Chattanooga, Tennessee.
The Teutonia National Bank of New Orleans, Louisiana.
The National Bank of Somerset, Kentucky.
The First National Bank of Appleton, Wisconsin.
The First National Bank of Santa Fé, New Mexico.
The First National Bank of Pleasant Hill, Missouri.
The First National Bank of Holly, Michigan.
The Keeseville National Bank of Keeseville, New York.
The Merchants' National Bank of Richmond, Virginia.
The First National Bank of Lanark, Illinois.
The Fayetteville National Bank, Fayetteville, North Carolina.
The First National Bank of Sioux City, Iowa.
The First National Bank of Charlotte, Michigan.
The Central National Bank of Hightstown, New Jersey.
The First National Bank of Franklin, Kentucky.
The First National Bank of Niles, Michigan.
The Washington National Bank of Washington, Iowa.
The First National Bank of Fort Scott, Kansas.
The First National Bank of Mason, Michigan.
The Central National Bank of Columbia, South Carolina.
The Citizens' National Bank of Raleigh, North Carolina.
The First National Bank of Springfield, Kentucky.
The First National Bank of Saginaw, Michigan.
The Commercial National Bank of Petersburgh, Virginia.
The Boone County National Bank of Columbia, Missouri.
The First National Bank of Boscobel, Wisconsin.
The East Chester National Bank of Mt. Vernon, New York.
The First National Bank of Seneca, Illinois.
The State National Bank of New Orleans, Louisiana.
The Gallatin National Bank of Shawneetown, Illinois.
The First National Bank of Osceola, Iowa.
The National Bank of Jefferson, Texas.
The New Orleans National Bank of New Orleans, Louisiana.
The Farmers and Merchants' National Bank of Vandalia, Illinois.
The Citizens' National Bank of Flint, Michigan.
The Merchants and Farmers' National Bank of Charlotte, North Carolina.
The Winona Deposit National Bank of Winona, Minnesota.
The Lumbermen's National Bank of Stillwater, Minnesota.
The Bellefontaine National Bank of Bellefontaine, Ohio.
The First National Bank of Kewanee, Illinois.
The First National Bank of Sigourney, Iowa.
The Union National Bank of Oshkosh, Wisconsin.
The Merchants' National Bank of Dayton, Ohio.
The First National Bank of St. Clair, Michigan.
The Madison National Bank of Richmond, Kentucky.
The Farmers' National Bank of Bushnell, Illinois.

The Union National Bank of Aurora, Illinois.
The First National Bank of Kankakee, Illinois.
The First National Bank of St. Peter, Minnesota.
The First National Bank of Charlestown, West Virginia.
The Union National Bank of New Orleans, Louisiana.
The Central National Bank of Baltimore, Maryland.
The First National Bank of Lincoln, Nebraska.
The First National Bank of Albia, Iowa.
The First National Bank of Cheyenne, Wyoming Territory.
The Commercial National Bank of Dubuque, Iowa.
The Manufacturers' National Bank of Racine, Wisconsin.
The First National Bank of Paris, Missouri.
The National Bank of Chester, South Carolina.
The Farmers' National Bank of Keithsburgh, Illinois.
The Exchange National Bank of Polo, Illinois.
The First National Bank of Harrodsburgh, Kentucky.
The First National Bank of Lewistown, Illinois.
The First National Bank of Jefferson City, Missouri.
The First National Bank of Charles City, Iowa.
The First National Bank of Indianola, Iowa.
The First National Bank of Cassopolis, Michigan.
The First National Bank of Anamosa, Iowa.
The First National Bank of Montgomery, Alabama.
The First National Bank of Elkader, Iowa.
The Rockford National Bank of Rockford, Illinois.
The National Commercial Bank of Mobile, Alabama.
The Merchants' National Bank of Newark, New Jersey
The National Bank of Commerce of Green Bay, Wisconsin.
The Manufacturers' National Bank of Appleton, Wisconsin.
The People's National Bank of Winchester, Illinois.
The Gainesville National Bank of Gainesville, Alabama.
The First National Bank of South Haven, Michigan.
The Farmers' National Bank of Salem, Virginia.
The New Orleans National Banking Association of New Orleans, Louisiana.
The Union City National Bank of Michigan.
The National Bank of the Commonwealth, Boston, Massachusetts.
The First National Bank of Olathe, Kansas.
The First National Bank of Allegan, Michigan.
The First National Bank of St. Anthony, Minnesota.
The First National Bank of Nicholasville, Kentucky.
The Northern National Bank of Big Rapids, Michigan.
The First National Bank of Pueblo, Colorado.
The National Bank of Franklin, Tennessee.
The Commercial National Bank of Versailles, Kentucky.
The First National Bank of Atlantic, Iowa.
The Livingston County National Bank of Pontiac, Illinois.
The First National Bank of Baxter Springs, Kansas.
The First National Bank of Lagrange, Missouri.

III.—NATIONAL BANKS THAT HAVE FAILED.

The First National Bank of Attica, New York, 1865.
The Merchants' National Bank of Washington, D. C., 1866.
The First National Bank of Medina, New York, 1867.
The Tennessee National Bank of Memphis, Tennessee, 1867.
The First National Bank of Newton, Newtonville, Massachusetts, 1867.
The First National Bank of New Orleans, Louisiana, 1867.
The First National Bank of Selma, Alabama, 1867.
The National Unadilla Bank of Unadilla, New York, 1868.
The Farmers and Citizens' National Bank of Brooklyn, New York, 1868.
The Croton National Bank of the city of New York, N. Y., 1868.
The First National Bank of Bethel, Connecticut, 1868.
The First National Bank of Keokuk, Iowa, 1868.
The National Bank of Vicksburgh, Mississippi, 1868.
The First National Bank of Rockford, Illinois, 1869.
The First National Bank of Nevada, Austin, Nevada, 1869.
Whole number failed, 15.
The National Security Bank of Boston, Massachusetts, has assumed the circulation of the First National Bank of Newton, at Newtonville, Massachusetts.

19 F

IV.—NATIONAL BANKS IN VOLUNTARY LIQUIDATION.

1.—*Before July 1, 1870.*

The First National Bank of Columbia, Missouri.
The First National Bank of Carondelet, Missouri.
The Farmers' National Bank of Waukesha, Illinois.
The First National Bank of Jackson, Miss.
The First National Bank of Cedarburg, Wisconsin.
The National Bank of Lansingburgh, New York.
The Appleton National Bank of Appleton, Wisconsin.
The First National Bank of Oskaloosa, Iowa.
The Commercial National Bank of Cincinnati, Ohio.
The First National Bank of South Worcester, New York.
The First National Bank of Marion, Ohio.

2.—*In the last fiscal year.*

The First National Bank of St. Louis, Missouri.
The Chemung Canal National Bank of Elmira, New York.
The Central National Bank of Omaha, Nebraska.
The First National Bank of Clarksville, Virginia.
The First National Bank of Burlington, Vermont.
The First National Bank of Lebanon, Ohio.
The National Exchange Bank of Lansingburgh, New York.
The Muskingum National Bank of Zanesville, Ohio.
The United National Bank of Winona, Minnesota.
The First National Bank of Des Moines, Iowa.
The Saratoga County National Bank of Waterford, New York.
The State National Bank of St. Joseph, Missouri.
The First National Bank of Fenton, Michigan.

The whole number that have deposited money and withdrawn their securities is 24.

V.—REDEMPTION OF CIRCULATING NOTES OF NATIONAL BANKS FAILED AND IN LIQUIDATION.

Names of Banks.	Redeemed to July 1, 1870.	Redeemed in fiscal year.	Total Redemptions.
First National Bank, Attica, New York..	$40,188 00	$709 50	$40,897 50
First National Bank of Nevada, Austin, Nevada	11,682 25	45,031 75	56,714 00
Appleton National Bank, Appleton, Wis.	1,828 00	15,648 50	17,476 50
National Mechanics and Farmers' Bank, Albany, New York......................	....	114,527 75	114,527 75
First National Bank, Berlin, Wisconsin..	....	14,147 10	14,147 10
First National Bank, Bluffton, Indiana..	....	15,433 00	15,433 00
First National Bank, Bethel, Connecticut.	18,415 00	1,924 50	20,339 50
Farmers and Citizens' National Bank, Brooklyn, New York.................	213,062 50	10,690 50	223,753 00
First National Bank, Columbia, Mo..	9,355 00	70 00	9,425 00
First National Bank, Carondelet, Mo..	22,224 50	1,124 25	23,348 75
First National Bank, Cedarburg, Wis..	4,709 00	19,260 50	23,969 50
Commercial National Bank, Cincinnati, Ohio ....:..	27,706 00	125,739 50	153,445 50
First National Bank, Decatur, Illinois...	....	33,741 15	33,741 15
First National Bank, Dayton, Ohio......	....	51,676 70	51,676 70
First National Bank, Des Moines, Iowa..	....	....	....
National Insurance Bank, Detroit, Mich.	....	....	....
Second National Bank, Des Moines, Iowa.	....	15,142 50	15,142 50
National State Bank, Dubuque, Iowa....	....	....	....
National Bank of Chemung, Elmira, New York..............................	....	36,083 75	36,083 75
Chemung Canal National Bank, Elmira, New York	....	17,342 15	17,342 15
First National Bank, Frostburgh, Maryland...........................	....	16,804 00	16,804 00

V.—REDEMPTION OF CIRCULATING NOTES, ETC.—Continued.

Names of Banks.	Redeemed to July 1, 1870.	Redeemed in fiscal year.	Total Redemptions.
Venango National Bank, Franklin, Pennsylvania.............................	$78,248 50	$380 00	$78,628 50
First National Bank, Fenton, Michigan..	....	....	....
First National Bank, Hallowell, Maine...	....	19,486 00	19,486 00
First National Bank, Jackson, Miss ...	1,601 75	11,913 25	13,515 00
First National Bank, Keokuk, Iowa.....	72,621 50	6,518 00	79,139 50
First National Bank, Lebanon, Ohio.....	....	27,523 75	27,523 75
The National Bank, Lansingburgh, New York.............................	2,382 80	45,104 85	47,487 65
National Exchange Bank, Lansingburgh, New York.............................	....	501 90	501 90
First National Bank, Marion, Ohio......	3,783 40	39,671 75	43,455 15
First National Bank, Medina, New York.	35,062 25	1,744 50	36,806 75
Tennessee National Bank, Memphis, Tenn.	79,619 00	2,579 75	82,198 75
Croton National Bank of the city of New York, New York.....................	154,985 90	7,531 75	162,517 65
National Bank of North America, New York, New York.....................	....	109,299 65	109,299 65
Pacific National Bank, New York, New York...............................	....	54,537 50	54,537 50
Grocers' National Bank, New York, New York...............................	....	5,208 00	5,208 00
First National Bank, New Orleans, La...	155,411 00	4,099 50	159,510 50
National Union Bank, Owego, New York.	....	200 00	200 00
First National Bank, Oskaloosa, Iowa...	3,452 95	23,182 10	26,635 05
National Union Bank, Rochester, New York...............................	....	69,513 75	69,513 75
First National Bank, Rockford, Illinois..	19,755 00	9,228 00	28,983 00
First National Bank, Selma, Alabama...	70,667 50	4,649 25	75,316 75
First National Bank, South Worcester, New York.............................	9,558 00	59,247 75	68,805 75
First National Bank, St. Louis, Missouri.	....	64,274 50	64,274 50
Savannah National Bank, Savannah, Georgia..............................	....	32,806 25	32,806 25
First National Bank Skaneateles, New York...............................	....	52,174 30	52,174 30
State National Bank, St. Joseph, Mo....	....	....	....
Merchants and Mechanics' National Bank, Troy, New York................	....	67,674 60	67,674 60
National Unadilla Bank, Unadilla, New York...............................	88,347 00	2,658 25	91,005 25
National Bank, Vicksburgh, Mississippi..	16,744 00	1,964 75	18,708 75
First National Bank, Vinton, Iowa......	....	11,523 75	11,523 75
National Bank, Whitestown, New York ..	....	16,649 00	16,649 00
Merchants' National Bank, Washington, D. C..................................	159,379 75	4,449 50	163,829 25
Farmers' National Bank, Waukesha, Wis.	53,186 25	16,134 00	69,320 25
Saratoga County National Bank, Waterford, New York.....................	....	....	....
Total............................	1,353,976 80	1,307,527 00	2,661,503 80

NOTE.—The above total is $2,198 25 less than that given for the same item under the title "Redemptions," the difference being the amount of notes of the First National Bank of Newton, Newtonville, Massachusetts, redeemed and destroyed by the Treasury, but for which it was afterward reimbursed, upon the consolidation of that bank with another.

VI.—CIRCULATING NOTES OF NATIONAL BANKS FAILED AND IN LIQUIDATION OUTSTANDING.

First National Bank, Attica, New York	$3, 102 50
First National Bank of Nevada, Austin, Nevada	72, 986 00
Appleton National Bank, Appleton, Wisconsin	27, 523 50
National Mechanics and Farmers' Bank, Albany, New York	152, 012 25
First National Bank, Berlin, Wisconsin	25, 929 90
First National Bank, Bluffton, Indiana	25, 797 00
First National Bank, Bethel, Connecticut	5, 960 50
Farmers and Citizens' National Bank, Brooklyn, New York	30, 147 00
First National Bank, Columbia, Missouri	2, 565 00
First National Bank, Carondelet, Misssouri	2, 151 25
First National Bank, Cedarburg, Wisconsin	48, 030 50
Commercial National Bank, Cincinnati, Ohio	192, 504 50
First National Bank, Decatur, Illinois	51, 508 85
First National Bank, Dayton, Ohio	80, 423 30
First National Bank, Des Moines, Iowa	89, 300 00
National Insurance Bank, Detroit, Michigan	75, 500 00
Second National Bank, Des Moines, Iowa	25, 157 50
National State Bank, Dubuque, Iowa	90, 000 00
National Bank of Chemung, Elmira, New York	53, 916 25
Chemung Canal National Bank, Elmira, New York	69, 157 85
First National Bank, Frostburgh, Maryland	23, 946 00
Venango National Bank, Franklin, Pennsylvania	6, 371 50
First National Bank, Fenton, Michigan	49, 500 00
First National Bank, Hallowell, Maine	31, 364 00
First National Bank, Jackson, Mississippi	26, 985 00
First National Bank, Keokuk, Iowa	10, 860 50
First National Bank, Lebanon, Ohio	57, 476 25
The National Bank, Lansingburgh, New York	75, 512 35
National Exchange Bank, Lansingburgh, New York	85, 190 10
First National Bank, Marion, Ohio	62, 377 85
First National Bank, Medina, New York	3, 193 25
Tennessee National Bank, Memphis, Tennessee	7, 801 25
Croton National Bank of the city of New York, New York	17, 482 35
National Bank of North America, New York, New York	157, 900 35
Pacific National Bank, New York, New York	75, 737 50
Grocers' National Bank, New York, New York	34, 232 00
First National Bank, New Orleans, Louisiana	20, 489 50
National Union Bank, Owego, New York	82, 650 00
First National Bank, Oskaloosa, Iowa	37, 109 95
National Union Bank, Rochester, New York	120, 436 25
First National Bank, Rockford, Illinois	16, 017 00
First National Bank, Selma, Alabama	9, 683 25
First National Bank, South Worcester, New York	84, 094 25
First National Bank, St. Louis, Missouri	115, 715 50
Savannah National Bank, Savannah, Georgia	52, 193 75
First National Bank, Skaneateles, New York	76, 240 70
State National Bank, St. Joseph, Missouri	86, 187 00
Merchants and Mechanics' National Bank, Troy, New York	103, 175 40
National Unadilla Bank, Unadilla, New York	8, 994 75
National Bank, Vicksburgh, Mississippi	6, 791 25
First National Bank, Vinton, Iowa	30, 091 25
National Bank, Whitestown, New York	27, 851 00
Merchants' National Bank, Washington, D. C	16, 170 75
Farmers' National Bank, Waukesha, Wisconsin	20, 679 75
Saratoga County National Bank, Waterford, New York	48 000 00
Total outstanding	2, 812, 175 20

Total circulation, $5,473,679; redeemed, $2,661,503 80; outstanding, $2,812,175 20.

VII.—DEPOSITS MADE AND BALANCES REMAINING TO CREDIT OF NATIONAL BANKS FAILED
AND IN LIQUIDATION.

Names of banks.	Deposits to redeem notes.	Balance remaining.
First National Bank of Attica, New York	$44,000 00	$3,102 50
First National Bank of Nevada, Austin, Nevada	59,393 75	2,679 75
Appleton National Bank, Appleton, Wisconsin..........	45,000 00	27,523 50
National Mechanics and Farmers' Bank, Albany, New York..	266,540 00	152,012 25
First National Bank, Berlin, Wisconsin	40,077 00	25,929 90
First National Bank, Bluffton, Indiana................	41,230 00	25,797 00
First National Bank, Bethel, Connecticut	26,300 00	5,960 50
Farmers and Citizens' National Bank, Brooklyn, New York..	253,900 00	30,147 00
First National Bank, Columbia, Missouri..............	11,990 00	2,565 00
First National Bank, Carondelet, Missouri.............	25,500 00	2,151 25
First National Bank, Cedarburg, Wisconsin	72,000 00	48,030 50
Commercial National Bank, Cincinnati, Ohio	345,950 00	192,504 50
First National Bank, Decatur, Illinois.................	85,250 00	51,508 85
First National Bank of Dayton, Ohio	132,160 00	80,423 30
First National Bank, Des Moines, Iowa................	89,300 00	89,300 00
National Insurance Bank, Detroit, Michigan...........	75,500 00	75,500 00
Second National Bank, Des Moines, Iowa..............	40,300 00	25,157 50
National State Bank, Dubuque, Iowa	90,000 00	90,000 00
National Bank of Chemung, Elmira, New York........	90,000 00	53,916 25
Chemung Canal National Bank, Elmira, New York......	86,500 00	69,157 85
First National Bank, Frostburgh, Maryland........	40,750 00	23,946 00
Venango National Bank, Franklin, Pennsylvania	85,000 00	6,371 50
First National Bank, Fenton, Michigan	49,500 00	49,500 00
First National Bank, Hallowell, Maine................	50,850 00	31,364 00
First National Bank, Jackson, Mississippi	40,500 00	26,985 00
First National Bank, Keokuk, Iowa	90,000 00	10,860 50
First National Bank, Lebanon, Ohio....................	85,000 00	57,476 25
National Bank, Lansingburgh, New York ....,....	123,000 00	75,512 35
National Exchange Bank, Lansingburgh, New York	86,692 00	85,190 10
First National Bank, Marion, Ohio....................	105,833 00	62,377 85
First National Bank, Medina, New York...............	40,000 00	3,193 25
Tennessee National Bank, Memphis, Tennessee	90,000 00	7,801 25
Croton National Bank of the city of New York, N. Y....	180,000 00	17,482 35
National Bank of North America, New York, New York.	267,200 00	157,900 35
Pacific National Bank, New York, New York	130,275 00	75,737 50
Grocers' National Bank, New York, New York.........	39,440 00	34,232 00
First National Bank, New Orleans, Louisiana...........	180,000 00	20,489 50
National Union Bank, Owego, New York...............	82,850 00	82,650 00
First National Bank, Oskaloosa, Iowa..................	63,745 00	37,109 95
National Union Bank, Rochester, New York	189,950 00	120,436 25
First National Bank, Rockford, Illinois.................	30,240 00	1,257 00
First National Bank, Selma, Alabama ....:........,.....	85,000 00	9,683 25
First National Bank, South Worcester, New York.......	152,900 00	84,094 25
First National Bank, St. Louis, Missouri	179,990 00	115,715 50
Savannah National Bank, Savannah, Georgia...........	85,000 00	52,193 75
First National Bank, Skaneateles, New York...........	128,415 00	76,240 70
State National Bank, St. Joseph, Missouri ....,...	86,187 00	86,187 00
Merchants and Mechanics' National Bank, Troy, New York...	170,850 00	103,175 40
National Unadilla Bank, Unadilla, New York..........	100,000 00	8,994 75
National Bank, Vicksburg, Louisiana	25,500 00	6,791 25
First National Bank, Vinton, Iowa....................	41,615 00	30,091 25
National Bank, Whitestown, New York	44,500 00	27,851 00
Merchants' National Bank, Washington, District Columbia...................................,.........	180,000 00	16,170 75
Farmers' National Bank, Waukesha, Wisconsin.........	90,000 00	20,679 75
Saratoga County National Bank, Waterford, New York..	48,000 00	48,000 00
Total......	5,388,612 75	2,727,108 95

VIII.—SECURITIES HELD IN TRUST FOR NATIONAL BANKS.

1.—*To assure the redemption of circulating notes of National Banks, June 30, 1871.*

Registered United States bonds, 6 per cent. coin	$204,911,750
Registered United States bonds, 5 per cent. coin	139,385,800
Registered United States bonds, 6 per cent. currency	15,586,000
Coupon United States bonds, 5 per cent. coin	2,000
Amount, June 30, 1871	359,885,550
Amount received in last fiscal year	$75,938,100
Amount withdrawn in last fiscal year	58,331,100
	17,607,000
Amount held June 30, 1870	342,278,550
Total	359,885,550

2.—*To assure Public deposits with National Bank Depositaries, June 30, 1871.*

Registered United States bonds, 6 per cent. coin	$7,891,300
Registered United States bonds, 5 per cent. coin	4,752,200
Registered United States bonds, 6 per cent. currency	909,000
Coupon United States bonds, 6 per cent. coin	942,500
Coupon United States bonds, 5 per cent. coin	1,041,500
Personal bonds	330,000
	15,866,500
Amount withdrawn in last fiscal year	$3,804,500
Amount received in last fiscal year	3,268,500
Amount held June 30, 1870	16,402,500
On the 30th June, 1870, the number of Banks, Depositaries of the United States, was	148
Number discontinued in last fiscal year	2
	146
Number designated and reinstated in last fiscal year	13
Number of Depositaries, June 30, 1871	159

3.—*Statement by Loans of United States bonds held in trust for National Banks.*

Registered bonds.	Rate of interest.	When redeemable.	Amount.
Act of—			
June 14, 1858	5 per cent. coin....	January 1, 1874...	$640,000
February 8, 1861	6 per cent. coin....	December 31, 1880.	3,913,000
July 17 and August 5, 1861....	6 per cent. coin....	June 30, 1881	62,777,300
February 25, 1862	6 per cent. coin....	April 30, 1867.....	36,650.950
March 3, 1863	6 per cent. coin....	June 30, 1881.....	34,047,050
March 3, 1864	5 per cent. coin....	February 28, 1874.	104,581,750
March 3, 1864	6 per cent. coin....	October 31, 1869 ..	2,259,500
June 30, 1864	6 per cent. coin.....	October 31, 1869 ..	25,399,200
March 3, 1865, 5-20s	6 per cent. coin....	October 31, 1869 ..	19,649,100
March 3, 1865, Consols, 1865....	6 per cent. coin....	July 1, 1870	10,306,050
March 3, 1865, Consols, 1867....	6 per cent. coin....	July 1, 1872	15,105,900
March 3, 1865, Consols, 1868....	6 per cent. coin....	July 1, 1873	2,695,000
July 14, 1870, and January 20, 1871	5 per cent. coin....	May 1, 1881........	38,916,250
July 1, 1862, and July 2, 1864...	6 per cent. currency	January, 1895–'98.	16,495,000
COUPON BONDS.			
Act of—			
February 8, 1861	6 per cent. coin....	December 31, 1880.	12,000
July 17 and August 5, 1861....	6 per cent. coin....	June 30, 1881	183,500
February 25, 1862	6 per cent. coin....	April 30, 1867.....	141,500
March 3, 1863	6 per cent. coin....	June 30, 1881	211,000
March 3, 1864	5 per cent. coin....	February 28, 1874.	1,043,500
June 30, 1864 .....•.	6 per cent. coin....	October 31, 1869...	86,000
March 2, 1861	6 per cent. coin....	July 1, 1881.......	41,000
March 3, 1865, 5-20s	6 per cent. coin....	October 31, 1870 ..	60,000
March 3, 1865, Consols, 1865....	6 per cent. coin....	July 1, 1870.......	159,500
March 3, 1865, Consols, 1867....	6 per cent. coin....	July 1, 1872.......	48,000
Personal bonds held for public deposits			330,000
Total securities			375,752,050

4.—*Receipts and withdrawals of United States bonds held for circulation in fiscal year.*

Loan.	Received.	Withdrawn.
Amount held for circulation July 1, 1870	$342,278,550	
June 14, 1858		$25,000
June 22, 1860		35,000
March 2, 1861		16,000
February 8, 1861	521,000	374,000
July 17 and August 5, 1861	4,478,050	1,981,250
February 25, 1862	944,350	21,693,150
March 3, 1863	1,959,550	1,878,150
March 3, 1864, Teu-forties	12,981,700	5,309,850
March 3, 1864, Five-twenties	1,000	480,000
June 30, 1864	818,700	10,019,100
July 1, 1862, and July 2, 1864, Pacific Railroad Company.	68,000	2,222,000
March 3, 1865, Five-twenties.	1,096,100	7,098,200
March 3, 1865, Consols 1865	3,529,450	5,131,350
March 3, 1865, Consols 1867	10,435,450	1,976,050
March 3, 1865, Consols 1868	2,232,000	92,000
July 14, 1870, and January 20, 1871, Funded Loan 1881.	36,852,750	
Amount bonds on hand June 30, 1871		359,885,550
	418,216,650	418,216,650

5.—*Receipts and withdrawals of United States bonds held for Public deposits in fiscal year.*

Loan.	Received.	Withdrawn.
Amount bonds on hand July 1, 1870......................	$16,072,500	....
March 2, 1861....................................	16,000	....
February 8, 1861................................	5,000	....
July 17 and August 5, 1861	53,100	$60,400
February 25, 1862...............................	60,000	541,150
March 3, 1863...................................	81,900	106,100
March 3, 1864, Ten-forties	262,000	293,850
March 3, 1864, Five-twenties	....	200,000
June 30, 1864	100,000	123,000
July 1, 1862, and July 2, 1864, Pacific Railroad Company.	50,000	56,000
March 3, 1865, Five-twenties	7,000	368,500
March 3, 1865, Consols 1865......................	198,450	1,021,500
March 3, 1865, Consols 1867......................	371,550	931,000
March 3, 1865, Consols 1868......................	....	103,000
July 14, 1870, and January 20, 1871, Funded Loan 1881..	9,062,600	....
Amount bonds held June 30, 1871...................	....	15,536,500
	19,341,000	19,341,000

6.—*Coupon Interest.*

Payment of coin interest on coupon bonds held in trust amounted to $145,735, made by the issue of 173 coin drafts.

IX.—EXAMINATION OF SECURITIES.

The number of banks that have complied with the 25th section of the National Currency act, by causing an examination of their securities, during the fiscal year is 972, being only about one-half of the whole number of banks.

X.—SEMI-ANNUAL DUTY.

1.—*Semi-annual Duty paid to the Treasurer by National Banks, under section* 41 *of National Currency act, during the year preceding January* 1, 1871.

For the term of six months preceding July 1, 1870:
On circulation $1,471,715 00
On deposits... 1,370,391 72
On capital.. 189,965 56
                                                                        $3,032,072 28

For the term of six months preceding January 1, 1871:
On circulation 1,469,666 41
On deposits... 1,324,088 54
On capital.. 191,633 11
                                                                        2,985,388 06

Total Duty for the year... 6,017,460 34
Amount of unpaid Duty of Banks in liquidation, January 1, 1871...... 3,932 52

2.—*Comparison of duties for* 1870 *and* 1871.

Amount of Duty received in year preceding January 1, 1871.......... $6,017,460 34
Amount of Duty received in year preceding January 1, 1870.......... 5,830,887 86

Increase of duty 186,572 48

XI.—DUTIES REFUNDED.

Duties refunded to national banks in fiscal year under resolution approved March 2, 1867.

Terms.	On uncollect-ed checks.	On undivided profits.	Totals.
For six months preceding—			
July 1, 1865............................	....	$7 32	$7 32
January 1, 1866	$79 86	9 69	89 55
July 1, 1866............................	150 18	113 10	263 28
January 1, 1867	231 06	135 80	366 86
July 1, 1867............................	178 38	132 17	310 55
January 1, 1868	208 59	168 77	377 36
July 1, 1868...........................	220 21	237 70	457 91
January 1, 1869	300 84	196 14	496 98
July 1, 1869...........................	187 87	247 92	435 79
January 1, 1870	....	80 12	80 12
	1,556 99	1,328 73	2,885 72

D.—UNITED STATES PAPER CURRENCY.

I.—ISSUED, REDEEMED, AND OUTSTANDING TO JULY 1, 1871.

Old Demand Notes.

Denominations.	Issued.	Redeemed.	Outstanding.
Five Dollars	$21,800,000	$21,763,605 75	$36,394 25
Ten Dollars	20,030,000	19,995,744 25	34,255 75
Twenty Dollars	18,200,000	18,174,144 50	25,855 50
Totals.........................	60,030,000	59,933,494 50	96,505 50
Deduct discounts for mutilations			2,118 00
Total amount actually outstanding.............................			94,387 50

Legal-Tender Notes, new issue.

Denominations.	Issued.	Redeemed.	Outstanding.
One Dollar	$28,351,348	$22,800,488 40	$5,550,859 60
Two Dollars	34,071,128	26,417,778 35	7,653,349 65
Five Dollars.......................	101,000,000	63,942,257 00	37,057,743 00
Ten Dollars	118,010,000	68,473,893 75	49,536,106 25
Twenty Dollars....................	102,920,000	55,374,338 00	47,545,662 00
Fifty Dollars	30,055,200	23,478,612 50	6,576,587 50
One Hundred Dollars	40,000,000	28,925,565 00	11,074,435 00
Five Hundred Dollars..............	58,986,000	51,258,525 00	7,727,475 00
One Thousand Dollars.............	155,928,000	146,843,700 00	9,084,300 00
Totals......................	669,321,676	487,515,158 00	181,806,518 00
Deduct discounts for mutilations..................................			88,906 50
Total amount actually outstanding			181,717,611 50

Legal-Tender Notes, series of 1869.

Denominations.	Issued.	Redeemed.	Outstanding.
One Dollar	$25,700,000	$709,240 30	$24,990,759 70
Two Dollars.......................	31,024,000	1,011,093 20	30,012,906 80
Five Dollars.........................	32,140,000	36,116 50	32,103,883 50
Ten Dollars	67,320,000	211,760 00	67,108,240 00
Twenty Dollars.....................	50,440,000	54,309 00	50,385,691 00
Fifty Dollars	30,200,000	58,950 00	30,141,050 00
One Hundred Dollars	28,720,000	28,600 00	28,691,400 00
Five Hundred Dollars...............	34,800,000	150,000 00	34,650,000 00
One Thousand Dollars	54,800,000	45,000 00	54,755,000 00
Totals	355,144,000	2,305,069 00	352,838,931 00
Deduct for new notes not put in circulation.......................			178,645,449 00
			174,193,482 00
Deduct discounts for mutilations..................................			074 00
Total amount actually outstanding......................			174,193,108 00

Legal-Tender Notes, new issue and series of 1869.

Denominations.	Issued.	Redeemed.	Outstanding.
One Dollar	$54,051,348	$23,509,728 70	$30,541,619 30
Two Dollars......................	65,095,128	27,428,871 55	37,666,256 45
Five Dollars	133,140,000	63,978,373 50	69,161,626 50
Ten Dollars	185,330,000	68,685,653 75	116,644,346 25
Twenty Dollars....................	153,360,000	55,428,647 00	97,931,353 00
Fifty Dollars	60,255,200	23,537,562 50	36,717,637 50
One Hundred Dollars	68,720,000	28,954,165 00	39,765,835 00
Five Hundred Dollars.............	93,786,000	51,408,525 00	42,377,475 00
One Thousand Dollars.	210,728,000	146,888,700 00	63,839,300 00
Totals......................	1,024,465,676	489,820,227 00	534,645,449 00
Deduct for new notes not yet put in circulation.....................			178,645,449 00
Amount below which there can be no reduction			356,000,000 00
Deduct discounts for mutilations..................................			89,280 50
Total amount actually outstanding			355,910,719 50
New Issue, less discount, outstanding..............................			181,717,611 50
Series of 1869, less discount, outstanding..........................			174,193,108 00
Total as above...			355,910,719 50

TREASURER. 29)

One-Year Notes of 1863.

Denominations.	Issued.	Redeemed.	Outstanding.
Ten Dollars	$6,200,000 00	$6,176,319 00	$23,681 00
Twenty Dollars	16,440,000 00	16,378,634 00	61,366 00
Fifty Dollars	8,240,000 00	8,219,045 00	20,955 00
One Hundred Dollars	13,640,000 00	13,617,875 00	22,125 00
Total	44,520,000 00	44,391,873 00	128,127 00
Deduct for unknown denominations			90 00
			128,037 00
Deduct discounts for mutilations			237 00
Total amount actually outstanding			127,800 00

Two-Year Notes of 1863.

Denominations.	Issued.	Redeemed.	Outstanding.
Fifty Dollars	$6,800,000 00	$6,775,087 50	$24,912 50
One Hundred Dollars	9,680,000 00	9,660,410 00	19,590 00
Total	16,480,000 00	16,435,497 50	44,502 50
Deduct discounts for mutilations			152 50
Total amount actually outstanding			44,350 00

Two-Year Coupon Notes of 1863.

Denominations.	Issued.	Redeemed.	Outstanding.
Fifty Dollars	$5,905,600 00	$5,899,747 50	$5,852 50
One Hundred Dollars	14,484,400 00	14,473,300 00	11,100 00
Five Hundred Dollars	40,302,000 00	40,298,000 00	4,000 00
One Thousand Dollars	89,308,000 00	89,285,000 00	23,000 00
Total	150,000,000 00	149,956,047 50	43,952 50
Deduct for unknown denominations			10,500 00
			33,452 50
Deduct discounts for mutilations			2 50
Total amount actually outstanding			33,450 00

Compound-Interest Notes.

Denominations.	Issued.	Redeemed.	Outstanding.
Ten Dollars..........................	$23, 285, 200 00	$23, 153, 343 00	$131, 807 00
Twenty Dollars	30, 125, 840 00	29, 925, 777 00	200, 063 00
Fifty Dollars........................	60, 824, 000 00	60, 559, 770 00	264, 280 00
One Hundred Dollars	45, 094, 400 00	44, 941, 770 00	152, 630 00
Five Hundred Dollars...............	67, 846, 000 00	67, 797, 500 00	48, 500 00
One Thousand Dollars...............	39, 420, 000 00	39, 403, 000 00	17, 000 00
Total	266, 595, 440 00	265, 781, 160 00	814, 280 00
Deduct discounts for mutilations			480 00
Total amount actually outstanding			813, 800 00
Outstanding June 30, 1870			2, 191, 190 00
Redeemed within the fiscal year			1, 377, 390 00
Outstanding as above			813, 800 00

Fractional Currency, First Issue.

Denominations.	Issued.	Redeemed.	Outstanding.
Five Cents...........................	$2, 242, 889 00	$1, 201, 371 44	$1, 041, 517 56
Ten Cents............................	4, 115, 378 00	2, 838, 847 66	1, 276, 530 34
Twenty-Five Cents...................	5, 225, 696 00	4, 153, 584 60	1, 072, 111 40
Fifty Cents..........................	8, 631, 672 00	7, 607, 806 26	1, 023, 865 74
Total...........................	20, 215, 635 00	15, 801, 609 96	4, 414, 025 04
Deduct discounts for mutilations.................................			13, 849 54
Total amount actually outstanding...............................			4, 400, 175 50

Fractional Currency, Second Issue.

Denominations.	Issued.	Redeemed.	Outstanding.
Five Cents...........................	$2, 794, 826 10	$2, 081, 054 97	$713, 771 13
Ten Cents............................	6, 176, 084 30	5, 230, 369 26	945, 715 04
Twenty-Five Cents...................	7, 648, 341 25	6, 876, 342 88	771, 998 37
Fifty Cents..........................	6, 545, 232 00	5, 758, 560 17	786, 671 83
Total...........................	23, 164, 483 65	19, 946, 327 28	3, 218, 156 37
Deduct discounts for mutilations.................................			9, 354 82
Total amount actually outstanding..............................			3, 208, 801 55

Fractional Currency, Third Issue.

Denominations.	Issued.	Redeemed.	Outstanding.
Three Cents........................	$601,923 90	$505,250 81	$96,673 09
Five Cents........................	657,002 75	516,967 91	140,034 84
Ten Cents........................	16,976,134 50	15,358,774 35	1,617,360 15
Fifteen Cents, (specimens).........	1,352 40	1 65	1,350 75
Twenty-Five Cents...............	31,143,188 75	29,409,813 23	1,733,375 52
Fifty Cents........................	36,735,426 50	34,706,685 10	2,028,741 40
Total........................	86,115,028 80	80,497,493 05	5,617,535 75
Deduct discounts for mutilations...			87,100 87
Total amount actually outstanding................................			5,530,434 88

Fractional Currency, Fourth Issue, First Series.

Denominations.	Issued.	Redeemed.	Outstanding.
Ten Cents	$13,013,000 00	$7,928,592 71	$5,084,407 29
Fifteen Cents	2,912,616 00	1,847,995 47	1,064,620 53
Twenty-Five Cents................	19,788,000 00	11,318,878 37	8,469,121 63
Fifty Cents	9,576,000 00	7,584,387 80	1,991,612 20
Total........................	45,289,616 00	28,679,854 35	16,609,761 65
Deduct discounts for mutilations................			2,728 80
Total amount actually outstanding			16,607,032 85

Fractional Currency, Fourth Issue, Second Series.

Denominations.	Issued.	Redeemed.	Outstanding.
Fifty Cents	$17,024,000	$6,300,604 25	$10,723,395 75
Deduct discounts for mutilations................................			134 75
Total amount actually outstanding................................			10,723,261 00

Fractional Currency—Résumé.

Denominations.	Issued.	Redeemed.	Outstanding.
Three Cents........................	$601,923 90	$505,250 81	$96,673 09
Five Cents	5,694,717 85	3,799,394 32	1,895,323 53
Ten Cents	40,280,596 80	31,356,583 98	8,924,012 82
Fifteen Cents........................	2,913,968 40	1,847,997 12	1,065,971 28
Twenty-Five Cents	63,805,226 00	51,758,619 08	12,046,606 92
Fifty Cents	78,512,330 50	61,958,043 58	16,554,286 92
Total........................	191,808,763 45	151,225,888 89	40,582,874 56
Deduct discounts for mutilations................			113,168 78
Total amount actually outstanding................			40,469,705 78
On the above-stated amount there was held in the office at the close of business, June 30, 1871			4,413,150 00
Leaving the actual circulation at........................			36,056,555 78

II.—LEGAL-TENDER NOTES ISSUED DURING FISCAL YEAR.

One Dollar	$17,480,000
Two Dollars	16,992,000
Five Dollars	12,560,000
Ten Dollars	29,400,000
Twenty Dollars	26,680,000
Fifty Dollars	9,600,000
One Hundred Dollars	120,000
Five Hundred Dollars	34,800,000
One Thousand Dollars	54,800,000
	202,432,000

III.—NEW LEGAL-TENDER NOTES ON HAND NOT YET PUT IN CIRCULATION.

One Dollar	$10,000,449
Two Dollars	11,900,000
Five Dollars	20,700,000
Ten Dollars	39,500,000
Twenty Dollars	30,045,000
Fifty Dollars	13,100,000
One Hundred Dollars	14,500,000
Five Hundred Dollars	11,500,000
One Thousand Dollars	27,400,000
Total	178,645,449

IV.—FRACTIONAL CURRENCY ISSUED DURING FISCAL YEAR.

Ten Cents	6,407,000
Fifteen Cents	354,400
Twenty-Five Cents	10,594,500
Fifty Cents	13,748,000
	31,103,900

V.—SPECIMEN FRACTIONAL CURRENCY.

There has been received from the sale of the various kinds of fractional currency, for specimens, with faces and backs printed on separate pieces of paper, and mostly pasted on cards, as follows :

Up to July 1, 1870	$14,683 26
During the last fiscal year	378 69
Total amount sold	15 061 95

VI.—CURRENCY OUTSTANDING AT THE CLOSE OF EACH FISCAL YEAR FOR THE LAST TEN YEARS.

June 30, 1862 :

Old Demand Notes	$51,105 235 00
Legal-Tender Notes, new issue	96,620,000 00
Total	147,725,235 00

June 30, 1863 :

Old Demand Notes	$3,384,000 00
Legal-Tender Notes, new issue	387,646,589 00
Fractional Currency, first issue	20,192,456 00
Total	411,223,045 00

June 30, 1864:

Old Demand Notes	$789,037 50
Legal-Tender Notes, new issue	447,300,203 10
Compound-Interest Notes	6,060,000 00
One-Year Notes of 1863	44,520,000 00
Two-Year Notes of 1863	16,480,000 00
Two-Year Coupon Notes of 1863	111,620,550 00
Fractional Currency, first issue	14,819,156 00
Fractional Currency, second issue	7,505,127 10
Total	649,094,073 70

June 30, 1865:

Old Demand Notes	$472,603 50
Legal-Tender Notes, new issue	431,066,427 99
Compound-Interest Notes	191,721,470 00
One-Year Notes of 1863	8,467,570 00
Two-Year Notes of 1863	7,715,950 00
Two-Year Coupon Notes of 1863	34,441,650 00
Fractional Currency, first issue	9,915,408 66
Fractional Currency, second issue	12,798,130 60
Fractional Currency, third issue	2,319,589 50
Total	698,918,800 25

June 30, 1866:

Old Demand Notes	$272,162 75
Legal-Tender Notes, new issue	400,780,305 85
Compound-Interest Notes	172,369,941 00
One-Year Notes of 1863	2,151,465 50
Two-Year Notes of 1863	5,209,522 50
Two-Year Coupon Notes of 1863	1,078,552 50
Fractional Currency, first issue	7,030,700 78
Fractional Currency, second issue	7,937,024 57
Fractional Currency, third issue	12,041,150 01
Total	608,870,825 46

June 30, 1867:

Old Demand Notes	$208,432 50
Legal-Tender Notes, new issue	371,783,597 00
Compound-Interest Notes	134,774,981 00
One-Year Notes of 1863	794,687 00
Two-Year Notes of 1863	396,950 00
Two-Year Coupon Notes of 1863	134,252 50
Fractional Currency, first issue	5,497,534 93
Fractional Currency, second issue	4,975,827 08
Fractional Currency, third issue	18,001,261 01
Total	536,567,523 02

June 30, 1868:

Old Demand Notes	$143,912 00
Legal-Tender Notes, new issue	356,000,000 00
Compound-Interest Notes	54,608 230 00
One-Year Notes of 1863	458,557 00
Two-Year Notes of 1863	188,402 50
Two-Year Coupon Notes of 1863	69,252 50
Fractional Currency, first issue	4,881,091 27
Fractional Currency, second issue	3,924,075 22
Fractional Currency, third issue	23,922,741 98
Total	444,196,262 47

June 30, 1869:

Old Demand Notes	$123,739 25
Legal-Tender Notes, new issue	356,000,000 00
Compound-Interest Notes	3,063,410 00

One-Year Notes of 1863	$220,517 00
Two-Year Not s of 1863...	84,752 50
Two-Year Coupon Notes of 1863......................................	42,502 50
Fractional Currency, first issue......................................	4,605,708 52
Fractional Currency, second issue	3,528,163 65
Fractional Currency, third issue	23,980,765 19
Total..	391,649,558 61

June 30, 1870 :

Old Demand Notes	$106,256 00
Legal-Tender Notes, new issue......................................	289,145,032 00
United States Notes, series of 1869..................................	66,854,968 00
Compound-Interest Notes..	2,191,670 00
One-Year Notes of 1863	160,347 00
Two-Year Notes of 1863..	56,402 50
Two-Year Coupon Notes of 1863......................................	37,202 50
Fractional Currency, first issue......................................	4,476,995 87
Fractional Currency, second issue	3,273,191 03
Fractional Currency, third issue	10,666,556 52
Fractional Currency, fourth issue	21,401,341 00
Total..	398,430,562 48

June 30, 1871 :

Old Demand Notes	$96,505 50
Legal-Tender Notes, new issue......................................	181,806,518 00
United States Notes, series of 1869..................................	174,193,482 00
Compound-Interest Notes	128,037 00
One-Year Notes of 1863..	44,502 50
Two-Year Notes of 1863..	33,452 50
Two-Year Coupon Notes of 1863......................................	814,280 00
Fractional Currency, first issue	4,414,025 04
Fractional Currency, second issue...................................	3,218,156 37
Fractional Currency, third issue	5,617,535 75
Fractional Currency, fourth issue	27,333,157 40
Total..	397,699,652 06

VII.—COMPARATIVE STATEMENT OF TOTAL OUTSTANDING FOR THE LAST TEN YEARS.

Outstanding June 30, 1862...	$147,725,235 00
Outstanding June 30, 1863...	411,223,045 00
Outstanding June 30, 1864...	649,094,073 70
Outstanding June 30, 1865...	698,918,800 25
Outstanding June 30, 1866...	608,870,825 46
Outstanding June 30, 1867...	536,567,523 02
Outstanding June 30, 1868...	444,196,262 47
Outstanding June 30, 1869...	391,649,558 61
Outstanding June 30, 1870...	398,430,562 48
Outstanding June 30, 1871...	397,699,652 06

E.—REDEMPTIONS.

1.—REDEMPTION AND DESTRUCTION OF MONEYS AND SECURITIES DURING FISCAL YEAR.

Old Demand Notes	$9,750 50
Legal-Tender Notes, new issue......................................	118,380,297 00
Legal-Tender Notes, series of 1869..................................	2,208,014 00
One-Year Notes of 1863..	32,310 00
Two-Year Notes of 1863..	11,900 00
Two-Year Coupon Notes of 1863......................................	3,750 00
Compound-Interest Notes..	1,377,390 00
Fractional Currency, first issue.....................................	62,974 83
Fractional Currency, second issue....................................	55,034 66

Fractional Currency, third issue	$5,049,020 77
Fractional Currency, fourth issue, first series	18,932,079 41
Fractional Currency, fourth issue, second series	6,300,604 25
Coin Certificates	25,278,000 00
Coin Certificates, series of 1870	46,505,000 00
Discounts on above	45,333 76
Total amount destroyed as money	224,251,459 18
Notes of National Banks, broken and in liquidation	1,361,815 00
	225,613,274 18
Statistically destroyed	354,971,835 72
Balance on hand July 1, 1871	915,133 74
Total amount for fiscal year	581,500,243 64

Cash Account, Dr.

Balance from last year	1,035,064 51
Amount received during the year	224,086,194 65
	225,121,259 16

Contra, Cr.

Amount destroyed during the year	224,206,125 42
Balance on hand July 1, 1871	915,133 74
Discounts on same	45,333 76
Notes of National Banks, broken and in liquidation	1,361,815 00
	226,528,407 92
Statistical matter destroyed during the year	354,971,835 72
	581,500,243 64

Destroyed as money during the fiscal year	$224,251,459 18	
As per last Report	1,430,956,658 49	
		1,655,208,117 67
Destroyed statistically during the year	354,971,835 72	
As per last Report	2,383,285,109 52	
		2,738,256,945 24
Total		4,393,465,062 91
Certificate of indebtedness as per last Report, (nothing during the year)		592,905,350 26
National Bank Notes destroyed during the year	$1,361,815 00	
As per last Report	1,302,180 00	
		2,663,995 00
Total amount destroyed to July 1, 1871		4,989,034,408 17
Total of all destroyed during the year		$580,585,109 90
Before		4,408,449,298 27
		4,989,034,408 17

II.—DISCOUNTS ON MUTILATED CURRENCY.

1.—*Discounts for missing parts of mutilated currency destroyed to July 1, 1871.*

On Old Demand Notes	$2,118 00
On Legal-Tender Notes, new issue	88,906 50
On Legal-Tender Notes, series of 1869	374 00
On One-Year Notes of 1863	237 00
On Two-Year Notes of 1863	152 50
On Two-Year Coupon Notes of 1863	2 50
On Compound-Interest Notes	480 00
On Fractional Currency, first issue	13,849 54
On Fractional Currency, second issue	9,354 82
On Fractional Currency, third issue	87,100 87
On Fractional Currency, fourth issue, first series	2,728 80
On Fractional Currency, fourth issue, second series	134 75
	205,439 28
On moneys redeemed, but not destroyed	10,092 11
Total discounts from the beginning	215,531 39

2.—*Discounts by years.*

These discounts were made for the amounts and in the years as follows:

In the year 1863....	$615 27
In the year 1864....	11,393 93
In the year 1865....	13,108 09
In the year 1866....	17,813 36
In the year 1867....	24,767 69
In the year 1868....	31,671 54
In the year 1869....	38,543 56
In the year 1870....	44,622 43
In the year 1871....	32,995 52
	215,531 39

3.—*Discount Account.*

On moneys destroyed to July 1, 1871		$205,439 28
On moneys destroyed to July 1, 1870		160,105 52
Discounts for last fiscal year		45,333 76
Discounts on moneys redeemed but not destroyed up to July 1, 1870	$22,430 35	
On moneys on hand July 1, 1871	10,092 11	
		12,338 24
Total amount of discounts for fiscal year		32,995 52
Amount discounted before July 1, 1870		182,535 87
Amount of discounts for last fiscal year		32,995 52
Total of all discounts up to July 1, 1871, as above		215,531 39

III.—DESTRUCTION OF PAPER MONEY.

1.—*Number of notes destroyed.*

There have been destroyed, since the commencement of the rebellion, papers representing moneys as follows:

Old Demand Notes:

Five Dollars	4,352,817½
Ten Dollars	1,999,618½
Twenty Dollars	908,767
Total number of notes destroyed	7,261,203

Legal-Tender Notes:

One Dollar	22,827,894½
Two Dollars	13,218,406
Five Dollars	12,791,843½
Ten Dollars	6,848,534
Twenty Dollars	2,769,195
Fifty Dollars	469,608
One Hundred Dollars	289,275
Five Hundred Dollars	102,518
One Thousand Dollars	146,844
Total number of notes destroyed	59,464,118

Legal-Tender Notes, series of 1869:

One Dollar	709,379
Two Dollars	505,632
Five Dollars	7,224
Ten Dollars	21,181
Twenty Dollars	2,716
Fifty Dollars	1,179
One Hundred Dollars	286
Five Hundred Dollars	300
One Thousand Dollars	45
Total number of notes destroyed	1,247,942

One-Year Notes of 1863:

Ten Dollars	617,635
Twenty Dollars	818,938
Fifty Dollars	164,382
One Hundred Dollars	136,179
Total number of notes destroyed	1,737,134

Two-Year Notes of 1863:

Fifty Dollars	135,503
One Hundred Dollars	96,605
Total number of notes destroyed	232,108

Two-Year Coupon-Notes of 1863:

Fifty Dollars	117,995
One Hundred Dollars	144,733
Five Hundred Dollars	80,596
One Thousand Dollars	89,285
Total number of notes destroyed	432,609

Compound-Interest Notes:

Ten Dollars	2,315,348
Twenty Dollars	1,496,295½
Fifty Dollars	1,211,199
One Hundred Dollars	449,418
Five Hundred Dollars	135,595
One Thousand Dollars	39,403
Total number of notes destroyed	5,647,258½

Fractional Currency, First Issue:

Five Cents	24,057,855
Ten Cents	28,410,510
Twenty-Five Cents	16,637,853
Fifty Cents	15,224,105
Total number of notes destroyed	84,330,323

Fractional Currency, Second Issue:

Five Cents	41,660,463
Ten Cents	52,341,827
Twenty-Five Cents	27,512,513
Fifty Cents	11,520,696
Total number of notes destroyed	133,035,499

Fractional Currency, Third Issue:

Three Cents	16,846,964
Five Cents	10,348,118
Ten Cents	153,802,547
Fifteen Cents	11
Twenty-Five Cents	117,751,880
Fifty Cents	69,487,106
Total number of notes destroyed	368,236,626

Fractional Currency, Fourth Issue, First Series:

Ten Cents	79,291,993
Fifteen Cents	12,322,049
Twenty-Five Cents	45,278,342
Fifty Cents	15,170,982
Total number of notes destroyed	152,063,366

Fractional Currency, Fourth Issue, Second Series:
Fifty Cents, (all during fiscal year)...................................... 12,601,478

    Total number of notes destroyed............................. 12,601,478

Coin Certificates:
Twenty Dollars 44,015
One Hundred Dollars... 110,096
Five Hundred Dollars.. 17,542
One Thousand Dollars.. 59,793
Five Thousand Dollars... 64,552
Ten Thousand Dollars.. 2,500

    Total number of notes destroyed.............................. 298,498

Coin Certificates, series of 1870:
Five Hundred Dollars.. 3,116
One Thousand Dollars.. 7,606
Five Thousand Dollars... 3,272
Ten Thousand Dollars.. 2,371

    Total number of notes destroyed.............................. 16,365

Notes of National Banks in liquidation:
One Dollar 46,636
Two Dollars... 15,502
Five Dollars.. 283,639
Ten Dollars... 63,085
Twenty Dollars.. 16,438
Fifty Dollars... 1,823
One Hundred Dollars... 1,174

    Total number of notes destroyed.............................. 428,297

2.—*Number of notes of each kind destroyed during the fiscal year.*

Old Demand Notes.. 1,184
Legal-Tender Notes, new issue... 12,807,607
Legal Tender Notes, series of 1869...................................... 1,201,081
One-Year Notes of 1863 1,640
Two-Year Notes of 1863.. 183
Two-Year Coupon-Notes of 1863... 31
Compound-Interest Notes 12,651½
Fractional Currency, first issue.. 407,039
Fractional Currency, second issue....................................... 410,940
Fractional Currency, third issue.. 21,339,840
Fractional Currency, fourth issue, first series 105,257,622
Fractional Currency, fourth issue, second series 12,601,478
Coin Certificates 13,548
Coin Certificates, series of 1870 15,116

    Total 154,069,960½
National Bank Notes 219,840

    Total 154,289,800½
Number as per last report... 672,743,022

    Total number to July 1, 1871.............................. 827,032,822½

IV.—DESTRUCTION ACCOUNT.

Statement of face-value of money destroyed since 1861.

Old Demand Notes.. $59,935,612 50
Legal-Tender Notes.. 487,604,064 50
Legal-Tender Notes, series of 1869...................................... 2,305,443 00
One-Year Notes of 1863 .... 44,392,200 00
Two-Year Notes of 1863.. 16,435,650 00
Two-Year Coupon-Notes of 1863... 149,966,550 00
Compound-Interest Notes... 265,781,640 00
Fractional Currency, first issue 15,815,459 50

Fractional Currency, second issue	$19,955,682 10
Fractional Currency, third issue	80,584,593 92
Fractional Currency, fourth issue, first series	28,682,583 15
Fractional Currency, fourth issue, second series	6,300,739 00
Coin Certificates	428,213,900 00
Coin Certificates, series of 1870	49,234,000 00
Total destroyed, as money	1,655,208,117 67
Total destroyed, statistically	2,738,256,945 24
National Bank Notes	2,663,995 00
Certificates of Indebtedness canceled and destroyed	592,905,350 26
Total amount destroyed to July 1, 1871	4,989,034,408 17

V.—REDEMPTION ACCOUNT.

Statement of redemptions of moneys since the beginning.

Moneys destroyed before July 1, 1870		$1,430,956,658 49
Moneys destroyed within the fiscal year		224,206,125 42
Discounts on same		45,333 76
Total		1,655,208,117 67
Broken National-Bank Notes before July 1, 1870	$1,302,180 00	
During fiscal year	1,361,815 00	
		2,663,995 00
Certificates of Indebtedness before July 1, 1870, (nothing since)		592,905,350 26
Statistical matter before July 1, 1870	2,383,285,109 52	
During fiscal year	354,971,835 72	
		2,738,256,945 24
Total amount destroyed to July 1, 1871		4,989,034,408 17
Balance on hand, but not destroyed		915,133 74
Total amount redeemed to July 1, 1871		4,989,949,541 91

VI.—REDEMPTIONS AND DISCOUNTS.

Amounts paid, discounts, and amounts retired to July 1, 1871.

Old Demand Notes.

Denominations.	Amount paid.	Amount discounted.	Total amount retired.
Five Dollars	$21,763,605 75	$481 75	$21,764,087 50
Ten Dollars	19,995,744 25	440 75	19,996,185 00
Twenty Dollars	18,174,144 50	1,195 50	18,175,340 00
Total	59,933,494 50	2,118 00	59,935,612 50

Legal-Tender Notes, new issue.

Denominations.	Amount paid.	Amount discounted.	Total amount retired.
One Dollar	$22,800,488 40	$27,406 60	$22,827,895 00
Two Dollars	26,417,778 35	19,033 65	26,436,812 00
Five Dollars	63,942,257 00	16,960 50	63,959,217 50
Ten Dollars	68,473,893 75	11,446 25	68,485,340 00
Twenty Dollars	55,374,338 00	9,562 00	55,383,900 00
Fifty Dollars	23,478,612 50	1,787 50	23,480,400 00
One Hundred Dollars	28,925,565 00	1,935 00	28,927,500 00
Five Hundred Dollars	51,258,525 00	475 00	51,259,000 00
One Thousand Dollars	146,843,700 00	300 00	146,844,000 00
Totals	487,515,158 00	88,906 50	487,604,064 50

Legal-Tender Notes, series of 1869.

Denominations.	Amount paid.	Amount discounted.	Total amount retired.
One Dollar	$709,240 30	$138 70	$709,379
Two Dollars	1,011,093 20	170 80	1,011,264
Five Dollars	36,116 50	3 50	36,120
Ten Dollars	211,760 00	50 00	211,810
Twenty Dollars	54,309 00	11 00	54,320
Fifty Dollars	58,950 00	....	58,950
One Hundred Dollars	28,600 00	....	28,600
Five Hundred Dollars	150,000 00	....	150,000
One Thousand Dollars	45,000 00	....	45,000
Totals	2,305,069 00	374 00	2,305,443

One-Year Notes of 1863.

Denominations.	Amount paid.	Amount discounted.	Total amount retired.
Ten Dollars	$6,176,319	$31	$6,176,350
Twenty Dollars	16,378,634	126	16,378,760
Fifty Dollars	8,219,045	55	8,219,100
One Hundred Dollars	13,617,875	25	13,617,900
Unknown	90	....	90
Totals	44,391,963	237	44,392,200

Two-Year Notes of 1863.

Denominations.	Amount paid.	Amount discounted.	Total amount retired.
Fifty Dollars	$6,775,087 50	$62 50	$6,775,150
One Hundred Dollars	9,660,410 00	90 00	9,660,500
Totals	16,435,497 50	152 50	16,435,650

Two-Year Coupon Notes of 1863.

Denominations.	Amount paid.	Amount discounted.	Total amount retired.
Fifty Dollars	$5,899,747 50	$2 50	$5,899,750
One Hundred Dollars	14,473,300 00	....	14,473,300
Five Hundred Dollars	40,298,000 00	....	40,298,000
One Thousand Dollars	89,285,000 00	....	89,285,000
Unknown	10,500 00	....	10,500
Totals	149,966,547 50	2 50	149,966,550

Compound-Interest Notes.

Denominations.	Amount paid.	Amount discounted.	Total amount retired.
Ten Dollars..............................	$23,153,343	$137	$23,153,480
Twenty Dollars..........................	29,925,777	133	29,925,910
Fifty Dollars	60,559,770	180	60,559,950
One Hundred Dollars...................	44,941,770	30	44,941,800
Five Hundred Dollars....................	67,797,500	....	67,797,500
One Thousand Dollars..................	39,403,000	....	39,403,000
Totals	265,781,160	480	265,781,640

Fractional Currency, First Issue.

Denominations.	Amount paid.	Amount discounted.	Total amount retired.
Five Cents...............................	$1,201,371 44	$1,521 31	$1,202,892 75
Ten Cents	2,838,847 66	2,203 34	2,841,051 00
Twenty-Five Cents.......................	4,153,584 60	5,878 65	4,159,463 25
Fifty Cents	7,607,806 26	4,246 24	7,612,052 50
Totals...............................	15,801,609 96.	13,849 54	15,815,459 50

Fractional Currency, Second Issue.

Denominations.	Amount paid.	Amount discounted.	Total amount retired.
Five Cents......	$2,081,054 97	$1,968 18	$2,083,023 15
Ten Cents	5,230,369 26	3,813 44	5,234,182 70
Twenty-Five Cents......................	6,876,342 88	1,785 37	6,878,128 25
Fifty Cents..............................	5,758,560 17	1,787 83	5,760,348 00
Totals..........................	19,946,327 28	9,354 82	19,955,682 10

Fractional Currency, Third Issue.

Denominations.	Amount paid.	Amount discounted.	Total amount retired.
Three Cents	$505,250 81	$158 11	$505,408 92
Five Cents...........................	516,967 91	437 99	517,405 90
Ten Cents	15,358,774 35	21,480 35	15,380,254 70
Fifteen Cents, (specimens)......	1 65	....	1 65
Twenty-Five Cents	29,409,813 23	28,156 77	29,437,970 00
Fifty Cents	34,706,685 10	36,867 65	34,743,552 75
Totals..........................	80,497,493 05	87,100 87	80,584,593 92

Fractional Currency, Fourth Issue, First Series.

Denominations.	Amount paid.	Amount discounted.	Total amount retired.
Ten Cents	$7,928,592 71	$606 59	$7,929,199 30
Fifteen Cents	1,847,995 47	311 88	1,848,307 35
Twenty-Five Cents	11,318,878 37	707 13	11,319,585 50
Fifty Cents	7,584,387 80	1,103 20	7,585,491 00
Totals	28,679,854 35	2,728 60	28,682,583 15

Fractional Currency, Fourth Issue, Second Series.

Denominations.	Amount paid.	Amount discounted.	Total amount retired.
Fifty Cents	$6,300,004 25	$134 75	$6,300,139 00

VII.—DESTRUCTION OF NOTES OF NATIONAL BANKS IN LIQUIDATION.

1.—*Notes destroyed, by denominations.*

Denominations.	Amount paid.	Amount discounted.	Total amount retired.
One Dollar	$46,597 30	$38 70	$46,636 00
Two Dollars	30,989 50	14 50	31,004 00
Five Dollars	1,418,003 25	191 75	1,418,195 00
Ten Dollars	630,811 50	38 50	630,850 00
Twenty Dollars	328,753 00	7 00	328,760 00
Fifty Dollars	91,147 50	2 50	91,150 00
One Hundred Dollars	117,400 00	....	117,400 00
Totals	2,663,702 05	292 95	2,663,995 00

2.—*Destruction Account.*

Total amount destroyed during the year	$1,361,594 15
As per last Report	1,302,107 90
Total from the beginning	2,663,702 05
Discounts during fiscal year	$220 85
As per last Report	72 10
	292 95
Total destruction to July 1, 1871	2,663,995 00

F.—STATISTICAL DESTRUCTIONS.

I.—DESTRUCTION OF STATISTICAL MATTER DURING FISCAL YEAR.

Coin Certificates, series of 1870:

Five Hundred Dollars	$344,000
One Thousand Dollars	1,276,000
Five Thousand Dollars	3,700,000
Ten Thousand Dollars	2,700,000
	8,080,000

Legal-Tender Notes, series of 1869 :

One Dollar	$1,414,484
Two Dollars	1,399,544
Five Dollars	993,040
Ten Dollars	2,646,000
Twenty Dollars	1,322,240
Fifty Dollars	400,000
One Hundred Dollars	240,000
Five Hundred Dollars	600,000
One Thousand Dollars	1,200,000
	10,215,308

Fractional Currency, Fourth Issue, First Series :

Ten Cents	97,314 00
Fifteen Cents	26,100 00
Twenty-Five Cents	750,558 75
	873,972 75

Fractional Currency, Fourth Issue, Second Series :

Fifty Cents	280,000

Loan of 1858 :

Five Thousand Dollars	405,000

Five-Twenties of 1862 :

Fifty Dollars	300
One Hundred Dollars	500
Five Hundred Dollars	1,500
One Thousand Dollars	3,166,000
Ten Thousand Dollars	130,000
	3,298,300

Ten-Forties of 1864 :

One Thousand Dollars	45,000
Ten Thousand Dollars	220,000
	265,000

Loan of July and August, 1861, (1881s) :

Fifty Dollars	27,950
One Hundred Dollars	225,300
Five Hundred Dollars	1,215,500
One Thousand Dollars	4,666,000
Five Thousand Dollars	100,000
	6,234,750

Five-Twenties of June, 1864 :

Fifty Dollars	37,150
One Hundred Dollars	334,100
Five Hundred Dollars	2,186,500
One Thousand Dollars	12,772,000
	15,329,750

Five-Twenties of 1865 :

Fifty Dollars	$1,900
One Hundred Dollars	194,400
Five Hundred Dollars	600,000
One Thousand Dollars	2,782,000
	3,578,300

Consols of 1867 :

Fifty Dollars	745,350
One Hundred Dollars	2,614,100
Five Hundred Dollars	596,000
One Thousand Dollars	3,349,000
	7,304,450

Certificates of Indebtedness :

One Thousand Dollars	720,000

One-Year Notes of 1863 :

Twenty Dollars	160

Two-Year Notes of 1863 :

One Hundred Dollars	$400	
One Thousand Dollars	2,000	
		2,400

Pacific Railway Registered Bonds :

One Thousand Dollars	320,000	
Five Thousand Dollars	1,145,000	
Ten Thousand Dollars	2,560,000	
		4,025,000

Special Accounts :

Fifty Dollars	6,300	
One Hundred Dollars	53,100	
Five Hundred Dollars	81,500	
One Thousand Dollars	952,000	
Five Thousand Dollars	2,050,000	
Ten Thousand Dollars	130,790,000	
		133,932,900

Five per cent. Registered Bonds—Funded Loan of 1880 :

Fifty Dollars	17,500	
One Hundred Dollars	340,000	
Five Hundred Dollars	1,650,000	
One Thousand Dollars	1,100,000	
Five Thousand Dollars	5,250,000	
Ten Thousand Dollars	10,500,000	
		18,857,500

4½ per cent. Registered Bonds—Funded Loan of 1885 :

Fifty Dollars	15,000	
One Hundred Dollars	80,000	
Five Hundred Dollars	275,000	
One Thousand Dollars	1,600,000	
Five Thousand Dollars	4,000,000	
Ten Thousand Dollars	8,000,000	
		13,970,000

Four per cent. Registered Bonds—Funded Loan of 1900 :

Fifty Dollars	15,000	
One Hundred Dollars	55,000	
Five Hundred Dollars	275,000	
One Thousand Dollars	1,300,000	
Five Thousand Dollars	3,500,000	
Ten Thousand Dollars	8,000,000	
		13,145,000

Five per cent. Registered Bonds—Funded Loan of 1881:

Fifty Dollars	$218,250	
One Hundred Dollars	549,100	
Five Hundred Dollars	5,750,000	
One Thousand Dollars	11,029,000	
Five Thousand Dollars	24,695,000	
Ten Thousand Dollars	43,040,000	
		$85,281,350

4½ per cent. Registered Bonds—Funded Loan of 1886:

Fifty Dollars	110,000	
One Hundred Dollars	280,000	
Five Hundred Dollars	1,550,000	
One Thousand Dollars	5,200,000	
Five Thousand Dollars	5,500,000	
Ten Thousand Dollars	8,000,000	
		20,640,000

5 per cent. Coupon Bonds—Funded Loan of 1881:

One Hundred Dollars	$450,700 00	
Five Hundred Dollars	686,000 00	
One Thousand Dollars	6,204,000 00	
		7,340,700 00
Internal Revenue Stamps		1,191,994 97
Total for fiscal year		354,971,835 72
Amount as per last Report		2,383,285,109 52
Total to July 1, 1871		2,738,256,945 24

II.—NUMBER OF NOTES DESTROYED DURING FISCAL YEAR ON STATISTICAL ACCOUNT.

Coin Certificates, series of 1870	2,980
Legal-Tender Notes, series of 1869	2,656,376
Fractional Currency, fourth issue, first series	4,149,375
Fractional Currency, fourth issue, second series	560,000
Loan of 1858	81
Five-Twenties of 1862	3,193
Ten-Forties of 1864	67
Loan of July and August, 1861, (1881s)	9,929
Five-Twenties of June, 1864	21,229
Five-Twenties of 1865	5,964
Consols of 1867	45,589
Certificates of Indebtedness	720
One-Year Notes of 1863	8
Two-Year Notes of 1863	6
Pacific Railway Registered Bonds	805
Special Accounts	15,261
5 per cent. Registered Bonds, Funded Loan 1880	10,250
4½ per cent. Registered Bonds, Funded Loan 1885	4,850
4 per cent. Registered Bonds, Funded Loan 1900	4,200
5 per cent. Registered Bonds, Funded Loan 1881	41,628
4½ per cent. Registered Bonds, Funded Loan 1886	15,200
5 per cent. Coupon Bonds, Funded Loan 1881	12,083
Total number for fiscal year	7,559,794
Number as per last Report	30,653,095
Total number of notes to July 1, 1871	38,212,889

G.—COIN CERTIFICATES.

I.—RECEIPTS AND REDEMPTIONS OF ALL ISSUES.

Coin Certificates of all issues received from Printing Bureau, exclusive of amount destroyed statistically:

Twenty-Dollar Notes	$960, 160
One-Hundred-Dollar Notes	13, 445, 700
Five-Hundred-Dollar Notes	29, 004, 000
One-Thousand-Dollar Notes	110, 008, 000
Five-Thousand-Dollar Notes	523, 040, 000
Ten-Thousand-Dollar Notes	225, 000, 000
Total	901, 457, 860

Cash destructions of all issues:

Twenty-Dollar Notes	$880, 300
One-Hundred-Dollar Notes	11, 009, 600
Five-Hundred-Dollar Notes	10, 329, 000
One-Thousand-Dollar Notes	67, 399, 000
Five-Thousand-Dollar Notes	339, 120, 000
Ten-Thousand-Dollar Notes	48, 710, 000
Total	477, 447, 900
Redeemed, but not destroyed	2, 212, 700
	479, 660, 600

Amount on hand	$401, 910, 960	
Amount outstanding	19, 886, 300	
		901, 457, 860

II.—COIN CERTIFICATES, OLD SERIES.

Denominations.	Received from Printing Bureau.	Amount on hand.	Issued.
20s	$960, 160	$160	$960, 000
100s	11, 645, 700	800	11, 644, 900
500s	9, 004, 000	4, 000	9, 000, 000
1, 000s	60, 008, 000	8, 000	60, 000, 000
5, 000s	323, 040, 000	40, 000	323, 000, 000
10, 000s	25, 000, 000		25, 000, 000
Total	429, 657, 860	52, 960	429, 604, 900

Denominations.	Issued.	Redeemed.	Outstanding.
20s	$960, 160	$880, 300	$79, 700
100s	11, 644, 700	11, 009, 600	635, 300
500s	9, 000, 000	8, 772, 000	228, 000
1, 000s	60, 000, 000	59, 792, 000	208, 000
5, 000s	323, 000, 000	322, 760, 000	240, 000
10, 000s	25, 000, 000	25, 000, 000	
Total	429, 604, 900	428, 213, 900	1, 391, 000
Deduct amount on hand redeemed but not destroyed			252, 200
Total old series outstanding			1, 138, 800

III.—COIN CERTIFICATES, SERIES OF 1870.

Denominations.	Received from Printing Bureau.	Amount on hand.	Issued.
100s	$1,800,000	$1,720,000	$80,000
500s	20,000,000	17,256,000	2,744,000
1,000s	50,000,000	38,972,000	11,028,000
5,000s	200,000,000	178,660,000	21,340,000
10,000s	200,000,000	165,250,000	34,750,000
Total	471,800,000	401,858,000	69,942,000

Denominations.	Issued.	Redeemed.	Outstanding.
100s	$80,000	....	$80,000
500s	2,744,000	$1,558,000	1,186,000
1,000s	11,028,000	7,606,000	3,422,000
5,000s	21,340,000	16,360,000	4,980,000
10,000s	34,750,000	23,710,000	11,040,000
Totals	69,942,000	49,234,000	20,708,000
Deduct amount redeemed but not destroyed			1,960,500
Total series of 1870 outstanding			18,747,500

IV.—TOTAL REDEMPTIONS OF COIN CERTIFICATES.

At Washington $625,280
At Boston 15,139,020
At New York 451,244,320
At Philadelphia 712,720
At Charleston 248,920
At New Orleans 771,420
At St. Louis 440,620
At San Francisco 1,040
At Baltimore 9,520,520
At Buffalo 82,980
At Chicago 346,080
At Cincinnati 316,300
At St. Paul 9,000
At Louisville 115,620
At Mobile 86,760

Total amount of redemptions since first issue $479,660,600

V.—MOVEMENT OF COIN CERTIFICATES.

Washington Office Notes:
Received from Printing Bureau $3,200,000
Redeemed and destroyed $3,193,200
On hand, (as statistical samples) 800
                                                                    3,194,000
Outstanding of Washington issue 6,000

New York Office Notes:
Sent to New York previous to June 30, 1870 450,810,000
Sent to New York during fiscal year 58,890,000

Total amount sent to New York 509,700,000
Remaining on hand at New York June 30, 1871, never issued. 10,198,000

Total issued from New York Office 499,502,000
Total redeemed of New York issue 479,621,700

Outstanding of New York issue 19,880,300

Total outstanding as per Public Debt statement, July 1, 1871 19,886,300

VI.—ISSUES AND REDEMPTIONS BY FISCAL YEARS.

Issued:

From November 13, 1865, to June 30, 1866, inclusive	$98,493,660
From July 1, 1866, to June 30, 1867, inclusive	109,121,620
From July 1, 1867, to June 30, 1868, inclusive	77,960,400
From July 1, 1868. to June 30, 1869, inclusive	80,663,160
From July 1, 1869, to June 30, 1870, inclusive	76,731,060
From July 1, 1870, to June 30, 1871, inclusive	56,577,000
Total issued	499,546,900

Redeemed:

From November 13, 1865, to June 30, 1866, inclusive	$87,545,800	
From July 1, 1866, to June 30, 1867, inclusive)	101,295,900	
From July 1, 1867, to June 30, 1868, inclusive	79,055,340	
From July 1, 1868, to June 30, 1869, inclusive	65,255,620	
From July 1, 1869, to June 30, 1870, inclusive	75,270,120	
From July 1, 1870, to June 30, 1871, inclusive	71,237,820	
Total redeemed		479,660,600
Total outstanding as per books of this office		19,886,300

VII.—ON HAND, REDEEMED, AND OUTSTANDING.

1.—*Coin Certificates on hand at New York.*

On hand at New York, July 1, 1870	$7,885,000
Sent to New York during fiscal year	58,890,000
Total	66,775,000
Less amount issued during year	56,577,000
On hand July 1, 1871, (never issued)	10,198,000
On hand, redeemed July 1, 1871, but not returned to Washington	252,000
Total on hand at New York, as per statement of Assistant Treasurer at New York	10,450,000

2.—*Redemptions.*

Redemptions for the fiscal year amounted to	$71,237,820
Outstanding July 1, 1871, per Public Debt statement	19,886,300
Total	91,124,120

NOTE.—Up to August 1, 1869, redemptions were made at the offices of the various Assistant Treasurers and depositaries, but subsequent to that date redemptions were made only at the office of the Assistant Treasurer, New York. All the redemptions for the fiscal year were made at the New York Office.

3.—*Coin Certificates, all issues, outstanding, by denominations.*

Twenty-Dollar Notes	$78,100
One-Hundred-Dollar Notes	690,700
Five-Hundred-Dollar Notes	1,238,500
One-Thousand-Dollar Notes	3,109,000
Five-Thousand-Dollar Notes	4,660,000
Ten-Thousand-Dollar Notes	10,110,000
Total amount outstanding	19,886,300
Balance outstanding, as per public debt statement July 1, 1870	34,547,120
Issued during fiscal year	56,577,000
Total as above	91,124,120

VIII.—RÉSUMÉ.

Amount received from Printing Bureau, exclusive of amount destroyed statistically..	$901,457,860
Amount on hand	401,910,960

Amount issued..		499,546,990
Amount redeemed and destroyed..	$477,447,900	
Amount redeemed, but not destroyed....................................	2,212,700	
Total amount redeemed at close of fiscal year....................		479,660,600
Total amount outstanding close of fiscal year....................		19,886,300

H.—THREE PER CENT. CERTIFICATES.

I.—RECEIPTS AND REDEMPTIONS.

Received from Printing Bureau		$160,000,000
Redeemed and destroyed...................................	$53,200,000	
Destroyed statistically	1,980,000	
		55,180,000
		104,820,000
On hand, Washington and New York..		72,935,000
Outstanding as per Public Debt statement, July 1, 1871..............		31,885,000

II.—MOVEMENT OF THREE PER CENT. CERTIFICATES.

Sent to Assistant Treasurer, New York..		$93,000,900
Redeemed	$53,200,000	
On hand, New York..	7,915,000	
		61,115,000
Outstanding, as above...		31,885,000

I.—TEMPORARY-LOAN CERTIFICATES.

Outstanding 4 per cents:		
Payable at the Cincinnati Office............................	$75,000 00	
Total of 4 per cents		$75,000 00
Outstanding 5 per cents:		
Payable at the Washington Office	405 00	
Payable at the New York Office	500 00	
Payable at the Philadelphia Office........................	800 00	
Total of 5 per cents		1,705 00
Outstanding 6 per cents:		
Payable at the Washington Office........................	255 00	
Payable at the Philadelphia Office.......................	2,200 00	
Payable at the Cincinnati Office.........................	1,400 00	
Total of 6 per cents		3,855 00
Total of all kinds outstanding............................		80,560 00
Recapitulation by Offices:		
Payable at the Washington Office........................	$660 00	
Payable at the New York Office..........................	500 00	
Payable at the Philadelphia Office.......................	3,000 00	
Payable at the Cincinnati Office.........................	76,400 00	
Total amount outstanding.................................		$80,560 00

K.—CERTIFICATES OF INDEBTEDNESS.

I.—ISSUED, REDEEMED, AND OUTSTANDING.

Old series issued:

Numbers 1 to 153,662 of $1,000	$153,662,000 00
Numbers 1 to 14,500 of $5,000	72,500,000 00
Numbers 15,001 to 31,010 of $5,000	80,050,000 00
Numbers 31,111 to 69,268 of $5,000	190,790,000 00
Numbers 1 to 13 of various amounts	1,591,241 65

Total of first series issued	498,593,241 65

New series issued:

Numbers 1 to 15,145 of $1,000	$15,145,000	
Numbers 1 to 9,603 of $5,000	48,015,000	
Total of second series issued		63,160,000 00
Total amount issued		561,753,241 65

*Redeemed to July 1, 1871	$561,748,241 65	
Outstanding, as per debt statement	5,000 00	
		$561,753,241 65

Five certificates of the denomination of $1,000 are outstanding, two of which are caveated.

II.—PRINCIPAL AND INTEREST PAID.

Total amount of interest paid to July 1, 1871	$31,157,108 61
Principal paid as above stated	561,748,241 65
Total principal and interest paid to July 1, 1871	592,905,350 26

L.—TREASURY NOTES OF 1861.

Issued:

46,076 of Fifty Dollars	$2,303,800
44,958 of One Hundred Dollars	4,495,800
13,665 of Five Hundred Dollars	6,832,500
8,836 of One Thousand Dollars	8,836,000
113,535 of all denominations	22,468,100

Redeemed:

46,041 of Fifty Dollars	$2,302,050
44,944 of One Hundred Dollars	4,494,400
13,665 of Five Hundred Dollars	6,832,500
8,836 of One Thousand Dollars	8,836,000
113,486 of all denominations	22,464,950

Outstanding:

35 of Fifty Dollars is	$1,750	
14 of One Hundred is	1,400	
49 of all denominations is		3,150
Total redeemed and outstanding		22,468,100

This account agrees with the books of the Register. The Secretary's books show $50 more outstanding.

---

* No redemptions during fiscal year.

M.—SEVEN-THIRTIES OF 1861 AND OF 1864 AND 1865.

I.—CONVERSIONS AND REDEMPTIONS.

1.— *Conversions and redemptions during fiscal year by series and denominations, and in gross amounts during former years.*

Seven-Thirties of 1861 :

26 Fifties	$1,300
18 One Hundreds	1,800
5 Five Hundreds	2,500
1 One Thousand	1,000
Redeemed during the fiscal year	6,600
Redeemed previous to July 1, 1870	140,065,050
Total amount redeemed	140,071,650
Outstanding July 1, 1871	23,100
Total original issue	140,094,750

First series, August 15, 1864 :

246 Fifties	$12,300
174 One Hundreds	17,400
13 Five Hundreds	6,500
1 One Thousand	1,000
Redeemed during the fiscal year	37,200
Redeemed previous to July 1, 1870	299,827,450
Total amount redeemed	299,864,650
Outstanding July 1, 1871	127,850
Total original issue	299,992,500

Second series, June 15, 1865 :

172 Fifties	$8,600
176 One Hundreds	17,600
24 Five Hundreds	12,000
9 One Thousands	9,000
Redeemed during the fiscal year	47,200
Redeemed previous to July 1, 1870	330,817,250
Total amount redeemed	330,864,450
Outstanding July 1, 1871	135,550
Total original issue	331,000,000

Third series, July 15, 1865 :

548 Fifties	$27,400
412 One Hundreds	41,200
45 Five Hundreds	22,500
3 One Thousands	3,000
Redeemed during fiscal year	94,100
Redeemed previous to July 1, 1870	198,716,500
Total amount redeemed	198,810,600
Outstanding July 1, 1871	189,400
Total original issue	199,000,000

21 F

2.—Recapitulation of all the issues converted and redeemed.

992 Fifties	$49,600
780 One Hundreds	78,000
87 Five Hundreds	43,500
14 One Thousands	14,000
Redeemed during the fiscal year	185,100
Redeemed previous to July 1, 1870	969,426,250
Total amount redeemed	969,611,350
Outstanding July 1, 1871	475,900
Total	970,087,250

II.—OUTSTANDING.

1.—Statement by series and denominations of Seven-Thirties of 1861 and of 1864 and 1865 outstanding June 30, 1871.

Seven Thirties of 1861 :

70 Fifties	$3,500
66 One Hundreds	6,600
6 Five Hundreds	3,000
10 One Thousands	10,000
Total	23,100

First series, August 15, 1864 :

753 Fifties	$37,650
517 One Hundreds	51,700
53 Five Hundreds	26,500
12 One Thousands	12,000
Total	127,850

Second series, June 15, 1865 :

252 Fifties	$12,600
389½ One Hundreds	38,950
96 Five Hundreds	48,000
36 One Thousands	36,000
Total	135,550

Third series, July 15, 1865 :

1,023 Fifties	$51,150
852½ One Hundreds	85,250
54 Five Hundreds	27,000
26 One Thousands	26,000
Total	189,400

2.—Recapitulation of the four series combined outstanding.

2,098 Fifties	104,900
1,825 One Hundreds	182,500
209 Five Hundreds	104,500
84 One Thousands	84,000
Total	475,900

N.—RETIREMENT OF FIVE-TWENTY BONDS.

I.—FIVE-TWENTY BONDS PURCHASED DURING FISCAL YEAR.

Loan.	Coupon.	Registered.	Total.	Premium paid.	Accrued interest paid.
5-20s of 1862	$2,144,450	$8,565,900	$10,710,350	$979,352 40	$126,890 02
5-20s of March, 1864...	....	230,000	230,000	24,799 45	1,440 08
5-20s of June, 1864 ...	7,790,450	3,479,100	11,269,550	1,016,855 17	141,869 06
5-20s of 1865	11,200,700	4,855,800	16,056,500	1,472,382 63	183,951 10
Consols of 1865.......	27,927,600	8,112,750	36,040,350	3,357,293 50	479,156 47
Consols of 1867.......	14,521,450	2,333,250	16,854,700	1,554,241 64	230,737 07
Consols of 1868.......	176,700	39,500	216,200	21,586 62	3,352 89
	63,761,350	27,616,300	91,377,650	8,426,511 41	1,167,396 69

II.—FIVE-TWENTY BONDS PURCHASED FROM MAY 11, 1869, (THE DATE OF THE FIRST PURCHASE,) TO JULY 1, 1871.

Loan.	Coupon.	Registered.	Total.	Premium paid.	Accrued interest paid.
5-20s, 1862........	$2,623,150	$23,225,500	$25,848,650	$3,166,058 54	$291,238 .10
5-20s, March, 1864.	....	982,400	982,400	169,230 80	12,360 83
5-20s, June, 1864..	19,351,800	8,682,850	28,034,650	3,456,506 16	339,316 64
5-20s, 1865	16,457,700	10,474,400	26,932,100	3,012,107 90	317,753 64
Consols, 1865.....	66,746,250	17,405,450	84,151,700	10,152,879 96	1,108,737 52
Consols, 1867.....	36,779,650	9,102,400	45,882,050	6,088,403 59	619,629 14
Consols, 1868.....	2,490,700	484,500	2,975,200	489,364 11	39,906 87
Total........	144,449,250	70,357,500	214,806,750	26,534,551 06	2,728,942 74

III.—FIVE-TWENTY BONDS CONVERTED INTO THE FUNDED LOAN OF 1881 DURING FISCAL YEAR.

Loan.	Coupon.	Registered.	Total.
5-20s, 1862..................	$650,000	$24,729,100	$25,379,100
5-20s, March, 1864	....	380,500	380,500
5-20s, June, 1864...............	812,450	10,914,200	11,726,650
5-20s, 1865..................	959,750	8,006,750	8,966,500
Consols, 1865	1,842,800	5,646,150	7,488,950
Consols, 1867...............	1,792,100	3,726,650	5,518,750
Consols, 1868........	21,700	187,000	208,700
Total..................	6,078,800	53,590,350	59,669,150

IV.—FIVE-TWENTY BONDS RETIRED TO JULY 1, 1871.—PURCHASES AND CONVERSIONS.

Loan.	Coupon.	Registered.	Total.
5-20s, 1862................................	$3,273,150	$47,954,600	$51,227,750
5-20s, March, 1864	....	1,362,900	1,362,900
5-20s, June, 1864.........................	20,164,250	19,597,050	39,761,300
5-20s, 1865...............................	17,417,450	18,481,150	35,898,600
Consols, 1865............................	68,589,050	23,051,600	91,640,650
Consols, 1867............................	38,571,750	12,829,050	51,400,800
Consols, 1868............................	2,512,400	671,500	3,183,900
Total............................	150,528,050	123,947,850	274,475,900

V.—COST OF PURCHASED FIVE-TWENTIES.

1.—*Statement of purchase of Five-Twenty Bonds, showing their net cost in gold and currency, the average gold cost of each purchase, and the average gold cost of all the purchases made prior to the end of each month, from May, 1869, to July 1, 1871.*

Date of purchase.	Principal.	Net cost.		Av. gold cost of a $100 bond.	Av. gold cost of total purchase to date.
May 12, 1869............	$1,000,000	$1,152,565 64	$832,177 36	83.22	....
May 19, 1869............	70,000	81,718 00	57,548 75	82.21	....
May 19, 1869............	1,000,000	1,167,512 10	822,895 85	82.29	....
May 27, 1869............	1,000,000	1,553,581 50	826,940 14	82.69	82.72
June 3, 1869............	1,000,000	1,164,770 68	842,510 43	84.25	....
June 10, 1869............	1,000,000	1,161,967 00	838,208 84	83.82	....
June 16, 1869............	1,000	1,155 00	835 44	83.54	....
June 17, 1869............	1,000,000	1,152,950 00	833,960 21	83.40	....
June 23, 1869............	1,620,000	1,870,402 50	1,364,012 76	84.20	....
June 26, 1869............	1,000,000	1,158,228 25	842,347 82	84.23	83.55
July 1, 1869............	1,000,000	1,158,098 75	842,253 63	84.22	....
July 3, 1869............	3,000,000	3,496,474 00	2,552,170 80	85.07	....
July 9, 1869............	3,000,000	3,518,044 00	2,586,797 06	86.23	....
July 14, 1869............	3,000,000	3,607,622 90	2,626,113 12	87.54	....
July 15, 1869............	1,000,000	1,201,850 00	877,262 77	87.73	....
July 21, 1869............	3,000,000	3,600,028 80	2,664,221 12	88.81	....
July 28, 1869............	3,000,000	3,604,859 00	2,640,922 34	88.03	....
July 29, 1869............	1,000,000	1,201,570 55	885,134 84	88.51	85.93
Aug. 4, 1869............	2,000,000	2,431,136 80	1,787,600 59	89.38	....
Aug. 11, 1869............	2,000,000	2,422,038 27	1,787,482 12	89.37	....
Aug. 12, 1869............	1,000,000	1,198,931 70	887,276 00	88.73	....
Aug. 18, 1869............	2,000,000	2,378,781 81	1,788,557 75	89.43	....
Aug. 25, 1869............	2,000,000	2,389,539 01	1,793,275 07	89.66	....
Aug. 26, 1869............	1,000,000	1,196,247 80	893,555 78	89.36	86.87
Sept. 1, 1869............	2,000,000	2,401,991 00	1,800,930 46	90.05	....
Sept. 8, 1869............	2,000,000	2,356,000 00	1,732,352 94	86.62	....
Sept. 9, 1869............	1,000,000	1,183,972 53	871,368 92	87.14	....
Sept. 15, 1869............	2,000,000	2,369,639 55	1,740,782 04	87.04	....
Sept. 22, 1869............	2,000,000	2,337,657 62	1,697,029 12	84.85	....
Sept. 23, 1869............	1,000,000	1,165,548 50	822,982 17	82.30	....
Sept. 25, 1869............	3,000,000	3,537,158 16	2,647,078 14	88.24	....
Sept. 29, 1869............	3,000,000	3,473,533 12	2,599,463 51	86.65	86.90
Oct. 6, 1869............	2,000,000	2,319,139 18	1,783,953 22	89.20	....
Oct. 7, 1869............	1,000,000	1,159,945 10	884,610 18	88.46	....

1.—*Statement of purchase of Five-Twenty Bonds, &c.*—Continued.

Date of purchase.	Principal.	Net cost.	Net cost estimated in gold.	Av. gold cost of a $100 bond.	Av. gold cost of total purchase to date
Oct. 7, 1869	$153,500	$178,187 69	$135,891 47	89.33	....
Oct. 13, 1869	2,000,000	2,318,883 53	1,782,043 06	89.10	....
Oct. 20, 1869	2,000,000	2,314,079 00	1,780,060 77	89.00	....
Oct. 21, 1869	1,000,000	1,152,000 00	885,302 50	88.53	....
Oct. 27, 1869	2,000,000	2,292,600 00	1,761,844 38	89.09	87.20
Nov. 3, 1869	2,000,000	2,257,255 21	1,768,662 26	88.43	....
Nov. 4, 1869	1,000,000	1,126,843 74	889,906 21	88.99	....
Nov. 4, 1869	1,000,000	1,129,090 29	891,680 39	89.17	....
Nov. 5, 1869	201,300	227,413 00	179,773 12	89.31	....
Nov. 5, 1869	433,000	489,241 07	386,751 83	89.32	....
Nov. 10, 1869	2,000,000	2,259,000 00	1,780,492 61	89.02	....
Nov. 17, 1869	2,000,000	2,256,513 69	1,775,035 35	88.75	....
Nov. 17, 1869	1,000,000	1,129,039 02	888,132 95	88.81	....
Nov. 24, 1869	3,000,000	3,382,483 67	2,671,260 54	89.04	87.48
Dec. 1, 1869	2,000,000	2,206,992 21	1,807,158 41	90.36	....
Dec. 2, 1869	1,000,000	1,102,659 61	901,971 06	90.20	....
Dec. 8, 1869	2,000,000	2,248,236 56	1,818,593 78	90.93	....
Dec. 15, 1869	2,000,000	2,239,710 90	1,839,598 27	91.98	....
Dec. 16, 1869	1,000,000	1,118,412 34	919,557 94	91.96	....
Dec. 22, 1869	2,000,000	2,215,985 83	1,844,733 26	92.24	....
Dec. 29, 1869	2,000,000	2,220,427 12	1,852,285 40	92.61	....
Dec. 30, 1869	1,000,000	1,110,507 80	926,388 15	92.64	88.20
Jan. 5, 1870	2,000,000	2,246,595 03	1,876,071 01	93.80	....
Jan. 11, 1870	451,700	517,400 49	422,367 75	93.51	....
Jan. 11, 1870	1,342,550	1,539,794 35	1,256,974 98	93.63	....
Jan. 13, 1870	1,000,000	1,141,010 09	938,137 79	93.81	....
Jan. 19, 1870	2,900,000	2,281,555 49	1,877,823 45	93.89	....
Jan. 27, 1870	1,000,000	1,142,872 27	936,780 55	93.68	88.55
Feb. 10, 1870	1,000,000	1,126,500 00	932,919 25	93.30	....
Feb. 11, 1870	50,000	56,355 00	46,888 66	93.78	....
Feb. 24, 1870	1,000,000	1,115,764 80	948,577 94	94.86	88.00
Feb. 24, 1870	1,060,000	1,117,488 85	950,043 66	95.04	....
March 2, 1870	1,000,000	1,107,377 50	951,559 61	95.16	....
March 10, 1870	1,000,000	1,067,347 35	961,574 19	96.16	....
March 17, 1870	1,000,000	1,067,480 27	953,107 39	95.31	....
March 24, 1870	1,000,000	1,060,440 34	942,613 63	94.26	....
March 30, 1870	1,000,000	1,069,985 26	956,411 41	95.64	89.04
April 7, 1870	1,000,000	1,070,574 91	955,870 46	95.59	....
April 13, 1870	1,000,000	1,073,953 37	954,625 22	95.46	....
April 21, 1870	1,000,000	1,078,778 18	951,513 28	95.15	....
April 27, 1870	1,000,000	1,100,490 79	966,402 45	96.64	....
April 30, 1870	345,400	383,020 40	333,423 63	96.53	....
April 30, 1870	758,800	840,929 55	732,038 78	96.47	89.36
May 5, 1870	2,000,000	2,215,447 70	1,932,778 80	96.64	....
May 12, 1870	1,850	2,070 46	1,794 55	97.00	....
May 12, 1870	1,000,000	1,118,370 86	969,335 52	96.93	....
May 19, 1870	2,000,000	2,230,611 87	1,942,888 34	97.19	....
May 26, 1870	1,000,000	1,108,910 71	970,600 18	97.06	89.76
June 2, 1870	2,000,000	2,223,786 41	1,942,171 53	97.11	....
June 9, 1870	1,000,000	1,109,976 64	977,952 99	97.79	....
June 16, 1870	2,000,000	2,217,755 94	1,960,447 24	98.02	....
June 23, 1870	1,000,000	1,104,612 10	989,574 11	98.96	....
June 30, 1870	2,000,000	2,218,005 71	1,987,015 19	99.35	90.31
July 7, 1870	1,000,000	1,107,000 00	987,290 97	98.73	....
July 11, 1870	690,400	758,749 60	659,065 88	95.46	....
July 11, 1870	1,683,150	1,848,423 98	1,605,580 00	95.39	....
July 14, 1870	2,000,000	2,182,332 89	1,933,406 77	96.67	....

1.—*Statement of purchase of Five-Twenty Bonds, &c.*—Continued.

Date of purchase.	Principal.	Net cost.	Net cost estimated in gold.	Av. gold cost or a $100 bond.	Av. gold cost of total purchase to date.
July 21, 1870	$1,000,000	$1,070,136 00	$878,961 81	87.90	
July 28, 1870	2,000,000	2,162,085 83	1,777,665 64	88.88	90.52
Aug. 4, 1870	1,000,000	1,085,712 21	891,755 41	89.17	
Aug. 11, 1870	2,000,000	2,191,414 93	1,885,088 11	94.25	
Aug. 18, 1870	1,000,000	1,097,329 29	939,896 61	93.99	
Aug. 25, 1870	2,000,000	2,181,093 02	1,850,344 02	92.52	90.62
Sept. 1, 1870	1,000,000	1,091,038 65	937,519 78	93.75	
Sept. 8, 1870	3,000,000	3,272,957 77	2,871,015 59	95.70	
Sept. 15, 1870	2,000,000	2,183,503 11	1,909,073 76	95.45	
Sept. 22, 1870	3,000,000	3,281,789 74	2,881,922 93	96.06	
Sept. 29, 1870	2,000,000	2,177,057 86	1,922,690 12	95.59	90.98
Oct. 6, 1870	2,000,000	2,174,300 26	1,924,159 52	96.21	
Oct. 13, 1870	2,000,000	2,170,465 37	1,906,006 91	95.30	
Oct. 20, 1870	2,000,000	2,170,236 48	1,922,690 12	96.13	
Oct. 27, 1870	2,000,000	2,165,529 30	1,933,508 30	96.68	91.24
Nov. 3, 1870	1,000,000	1,077,698 19	973,090 92	97.31	
Nov. 3, 1870	245,850	265,173 81	239,434 59	97.39	
Nov. 3, 1870	542,250	584,800 55	528,036 61	97.39	
Nov. 10, 1870	1,000,000	1,072,263 90	971,473 52	97.15	
Nov. 17, 1870	1,000,000	1,064,972 36	942,453 42	94.15	
Nov. 25, 1870	1,000,000	1,065,650 15	951,473 35	95.15	91.39
Dec. 1, 1870	1,000,000	1,064,917 08	962,636 91	96.26	
Dec. 8, 1870	1,000,000	1,063,854 32	961,676 22	96.17	
Dec. 15, 1870	1,000,000	1,065,972 75	958,177 75	95.82	
Dec. 22, 1870	1,000,000	1,064,459 26	962,223 06	96.22	
Dec. 29, 1870	1,000,000	1,064,473 95	961,150 29	96,11	91.53
Jan. 4, 1871	2,000,000	2,147,345 03	1,938,911 99	96.96	
Jan. 11, 1871	1,000,000	1,074,257 50	967,799 55	96.78	
Jan. 18, 1871	2,000,000	2,144,457 32	1,938,492 49	96.92	
Jan. 25, 1871	1,000,000	1,074,651 96	971,436 80	97.14	91.72
Feb. 1, 1871	2,000,000	2,173,985 90	1,943,227 62	97.16	
Feb. 8, 1871	2,000,000	2,175,643 46	1,946,884 53	97.34	
Feb. 15, 1871	2,000,000	2,184,170 19	1,963,299 05	98.16	
Feb. 21, 1871	2,000,000	2,191,633 24	1,970,007 41	98.50	91.99
March 1, 1871	2,000,000	2,199,585 00	1,983,842 16	99.19	
March 8, 1871	2,000,000	2,199,570 48	1,977,142 00	98.85	
March 15, 1871	2,000,000	2,191,702 96	1,967,859 00	98.39	
March 22, 1871	2,000,000	2,188,826 83	1,974,139 19	98.71	
March 29, 1871	2,000,000	2,183,254 76	1,980,276 42	99.01	92.24
April 3, 1871	216,000	235,807 20	213,884 08	99.02	
April 5, 1871	3,000,000	3,295,500 00	2,985,730 46	99.52	
April 12, 1871	2,000,000	2,197,018 24	1,995,022 24	99.75	
April 19, 1871	3,000,000	3,317,198 80	2,974,730 17	99.06	
April 26, 1871	2,000,000	2,215,181 72	1,997,909 10	99.90	92.71
May 3, 1871	2,000,000	2,221,571 71	1,999,164 64	99.96	
May 10, 1871	2,000,000	2,223,162 54	1,998,348 35	99.92	
May 17, 1871	2,000,000	2,228,989 07	1,999,322 46	99.62	
May 24, 1871	2,000,000	2,224,133 69	1,992,504 98	99.63	
May 31, 1871	2,000,000	2,225,697 79	1,989,450 54	99.47	93.04
June 7, 1871	1,000,000	1,115,811 40	994,041 33	99.40	
June 14, 1871	1,000,000	1,114,175 30	991,479 69	99.15	
June 21, 1871	1,000,000	1,116,587 05	993,625 85	99.36	
June 28, 1871	1,000,000	1,118,691 60	988,898 65	98.89	93.16

(

2.—*Statement by loans, showing net cost in currency and gold of bonds purchased, and average gold cost of all the purchases to July 1, 1871.*

Loan.	Principal.	Net cost.	Net cost estimated in gold.	Average cost in gold of total purchase to date.
5-20s, 1862.............	$25,848,650	$29,013,770 40	$24,056,506 41	$93 97
5-20s, March, 1864......	982,400	1,151,618 32	893,379 70	90 94
5-20s, June, 1864.......	28,034,650	31,487,131 84	26,172,134 94	93 36
5-20s, 1865.............	26,932,100	29,944,154 42	25,614,598 47	95 11
Consols, 1865	84,151,700	94,279,596 28	78,854,619 65	93 70
Consols, 1867	45,882,050	51,969,708 67	41,874,089 06	91 26
Consols, 1868	2,975,200	3,464,472 21	2,643,765 75	88 86
Total............	214,806,750	241,310,452 14	200,109,093 98	93 16

O.—COUPON INTEREST.

I—COIN COUPONS.

1.—*Coupon interest paid in coin during the fiscal year, by loans and denominations.*

Number of coupons of each loan.	Denominations.	Amount.	Total.
Loan of 1858 :			
28,471	Twenty-Five Dollars...	....	$711,775 00
Loan of 1860 :			
1,245.....................	Twenty-Five Dollars...	....	31,125 00
Loan of Feb. 8, 1861, (1881s)			
10,247.....................	Thirty Dollars..........		307,410 00
Oregon War Debt :			
383.....................	Three Dollars..........	$1,149 00	
821.....................	Six Dollars	4,926 00	
3,310.....................	Fifteen Dollars........	49,650 00	
5.....................	Fractional.............	15 00	
			55,740 00
Loan of July and August, 1861, (1881s) :			
7,098.....................	One Dollar and Fifty Cts.	10,647 00	
31,795.....................	Three Dollars..........	95,385 00	
59,328.....................	Fifteen Dollars........	889,920 00	
106,851.....................	Thirty Dollars.........	3,205,530 00	
			4,201,482 00
Five-Twenties, 1862 :			
174,501.....................	One Dollar and Fifty Cts.	261,751 50	
448,692.....................	Three Dollars...........	1,346,076 00	
282,012.....................	Fifteen Dollars........	4,230,180 00	
554,168.....................	Thirty Dollars........	16,625,040 00	
11.....................	Fractional............	24 06	
			22,463,071 56
Loan of 1863, (1881s):			
3,076.....................	One Dollar and Fifty Cts.	4,614 00	
10,668.....................	Three Dollars..........	32,004 00	
12,540.....................	Fifteen Dollars........	188,100 00	
39,123	Thirty Dollars..........	1,173,690 00	
4.....................	Fractional.............	62 45	
			1,398,470 45

1.—*Coupon interest paid in coin during the fiscal year, &c.*—Continued.

Number of coupons of each loan.	Denominations.	Amount.	Total.
Ten-Forties of 1864:			
6,029......................	Two Dollars & Fifty Cts.	$15,072 50	
20,209......................	Five Dollars............	101,045 00	
54,388......................	Twelve Dollars and Fifty Cents..........	679,850 00	
92,135......................	Twenty-Five Dollars...	2,303,375 00	
2,162......................	Fractional.............	4,805 00	
			$3,104,147 50
Five-Twenties of June, 1864:			
6,401......................	One Dollar and Fifty Cts.	9,601 50	
30,584......................	Three Dollars..........	91,752 00	
31,181......................	Fifteen Dollars........	467,715 00	
78,277......................	Thirty Dollars.........	2,010,310 00	
			2,917,378 50
Five-Twenties of 1865:			
1,264......................	One Dollar and Fifty Cts.	1,896 00	
40,170......................	Three Dollars..........	120,510 00	
73,253......................	Fifteen Dollars........	1,098,795 00	
218,499......................	Thirty Dollars.........	6,554,970 00	
			7,776,171 00
Consols of 1865:			
126,019......................	One Dollar and Fifty Cts.	189,028 50	
252,735......................	Three Dollars..........	758,205 00	
171,854......................	Fifteen Dollars........	2,577,810 00	
293,290......................	Thirty Dollars.........	8,798,700 00	
1,310......................	Fractional.............	19,535 00	
			12,343,278 50
Consols of 1867:			
200,455......................	One Dollar and Fifty Cts.	300,682 50	
401,426......................	Three Dollars..........	1,204,278 00	
216,850......................	Fifteen Dollars........	3,252,750 00	
372,531......................	Thirty Dollars.........	11,175,930 00	
1,008......................	Fractional.............	11,039,00	
			15,944,679 50
Consols of 1868:			
23,445......................	One Dollar and Fifty Cts.	35,167 50	
59,675......................	Three Dollars..........	179,025 00	
22,934......................	Fifteen Dollars........	344,010 00	
42,278......................	Thirty Dollars.........	1,268,340 00	
22......................	Fractional.............	39 00	
			1,826,581 50
Seven-Thirties of 1861:			
2......................	Three Dollars and Sixty-Five Cents,....	7 30	
2......................	Eighteen Dollars and Twenty-Five Cents...	36 50	
			43 80

2.—*Recapitulation by Loans.*

Title of Loans.	No. of Coupons.	Amount.
Loan of 1858	28,471	$711,775 00
Loan of 1860	1,245	31,125 00
Loan of February, (1881s)	10,247	307,410 00
Oregon War Debt...................................	4,519	55,740 00
Loan of July and August, 1861, (1881s).............	205,072	4,201,482 00
Five-Twenties of 1862.............................	1,459,384	22,463,071 56
Loan of 1863, (1881s).............................	65,411	1,398,470 45
Ten-Forties of 1864...............................	174,923	3,104,147 50
Five-Twenties of June, 1864.......................	146,443	2,917,378 50
Five-Twenties of 1865.............................	333,186	7,776,171 00
Consols of 1865...................................	845,208	12,343,278 50
Consols of 1867...................................	1,192,270	15,944,679 50
Consols of 1868...................................	148,354	1,826,581 50
Seven-Thirties of 1861............................	4	43 80
Total	4,614,737	73,081,354 31

II.—CURRENCY COUPONS.

There were also paid in currency six hundred and sixty-eight coupons of twenty dollars each, from Certificates of Indebtedness of 1870, amounting to $13,360.

P.—TRUST FUNDS.

There remain in the custody of the Treasurer, held by the Secretary of the Treasury in trust for the Smithsonian fund, six per cent. stocks of the State of Arkansas that matured in 1868, amounting, at their par face-value, interest excluded, to $538,000.

There are also held special deposits in sealed packages, the contents and value of which are unknown.

Q.—PAYMENTS BY CHECKS ON OTHER OFFICES.

There were drawn during the year transfer-checks on Assistant Treasurers as follows:

Currency Checks:

45,930 on New York for.....................	$42,114,780 64	
2,785 on Boston for........................	2,933,691 19	
2,523 on Philadelphia for..................	1,321,139 86	
663 on New Orleans for....................	1,095,501 04	
130 on San Francisco for..................	334,096 74	
52,031 Currency Checks, amounting to.............................		$47,799,209 47

Coin checks:

2,392 on New York for......................	6,376,092 83	
133 on Boston for........................	28,743 25	
320 on Philadelphia for..................	83,504 69	
3 on New Orleans for......	11,250 00	
7 on San Francisco for..................	4,106 99	
2,855 Coin Checks, amounting to..................................		6,503,697 76
54,886 checks, coin, and currency..............................		54,302,907 23

R.—EMPLOYÉS.

I.—CHANGES IN EMPLOYÉS OF THE TREASURER'S OFFICE DURING FISCAL YEAR.

Total force of the Treasurer's Office, June 30, 1870		372
Number of persons deceased during the fiscal year	3	
Resigned during the same period	28	
Transferred during the same period	1	
Discharged during the same period	12	
	44	
Number of persons appointed during the same period	18	26
Total force of Treasurer's Office, June 30, 1871		346

II.—SALARIES PAID.

The amount disbursed for salaries to the above number of employés during the fiscal year was as follows:

On regular roll	$170, 621 64
On temporary roll	232, 358 19
Total payments during the year	402, 979 83
Less income tax retained from salaries, (for the month of July, 1870, only)	358 99
Net amount paid for salaries	402, 620 84

S.—OFFICIAL CORRESPONDENCE.

LETTERS RECEIVED AND TRANSMITTED DURING FISCAL YEAR.

Received by mail, containing money	31,730
Received by mail, containing no money	41, 104
Received by express, money packages	37, 194
Total received	110, 028
Transmitted by mail, manuscript letters	5, 857
Transmitted by mail, printed forms filled in	99, 951
Transmitted by mail, drafts payable to order	31, 759
Transmitted by express, money packages	29, 009
Total transmitted	166, 576

T.—RECEIPTS AND DISBURSEMENTS OF ASSISTANT TREASURERS OF THE UNITED STATES FOR THE FISCAL YEAR.

NEW YORK.

Balance at close of business, June 30, 1870 .... $91,732,179 57

RECEIPTS.

On account of Customs.	$147,239,142 55	
On account of Internal Revenue	9,778,669 14	
On account of Miscellaneous........................	91,204,305 90	
On account of Transfers.............................	156,350,278 43	
On account of Patent Fees	34,314 35	
On account of Coin Certificates.....................	56,577,000 00	
On account of Temporary Loans	140,000 00	
On account of Post-Office Department.	5,633,526 91	
On account of Disbursing Officers' Accounts..........	121,108,415 98	
On account of Bullion Fund..........................	2,998,688 81	
On account of Assay, Ordinary Expense Account.....	140,313 98	
On account of Interest, Coin.........................	85,105,748 04	
On account of Interest, Notes........................	2,589,397 96	
		678,899,802 05
		770,631,981 62

DISBURSEMENTS.

On account of Treasury Department	489,940,208 03	
On account of Post-Office Department................	5,900,264 83	
On account of Disbursing Officer's Account	117,751,237 43	
On account of Bullion Fund	2,684,916 92	
On account of Assay, Ordinary Expense Account.....	124,743 24	
On account of Interest, Coin.........................	85,084,600 68	
On account of Interest, Notes........................	2,589,397 96	
		704,075,369 09

Balance at close of business, June 30, 1871 .... 66,556,612 53

BOSTON, MASSACHUSETTS.

Balance June 30, 1870 .... $7,976,296 58

RECEIPTS.

On account of Customs, (coin)........................	$22,614,529 48	
On account of Patent Fees............................	30,733 55	
On account of Sales of Internal Revenue Stamps......	880,184 60	
On account of Transfers..............................	25,819,746 87	
On account of Miscellaneous.........................	1,965,588 13	
On account of Interest Account, Registered	7,769,563 45	
On account of Post-Office Department................	468,283 42	
On account of Disbursing Officers' Accounts..........	12,718,660 75	
		72,267,290 25
		80,243,586 83

DISBURSEMENTS.

On account of Treasury Drafts.......................	28,054,877 01	
On account of Transfers..............................	16,252,971 45	
On account of Interest Account, Registered..........	7,770,793 45	
On account of Interest Account, Coupon.............	8,942,020 98	
On account of Post-Office Department................	467,013 11	
On account of Disbursing Officers' Accounts..........	11,394,459 49	
		72,882,135 49

Balance June 30, 1871 .... 7,361,451 34

PHILADELPHIA, PENNSYLVANIA.

Balance on hand July 1, 1870 .... $7,204,013 87

RECEIPTS.

On account of Customs..............................	$7,207,329 92	
On account of Internal Revenue Tax.................	377,570 21	
On account of Internal Revenue Stamps..............	1,109,475 90	
On account of Transfers............................	19,926,354 71	
On account of Patent Fees	14,242 05	
On account of Semi-Annual Duty	317,462 47	
On account of Post-Office Department...............	438,450 23	
On account of Disbursing Officers..................	10,982,723 85	
On account of Interest Funds.......................	4,181,140 82	
On account of Miscellaneous........................	4,669,302 97	
		$49,224,062 13
		56,428,076 00

DISBURSEMENTS.

On account of Treasury Drafts and G. T..............	29,457,629 40	
On account of Post-Office Drafts	476,286 31	
On account of Disbursers' Checks....................	9,928,925 67	
On account of Interest Checks......................	8,347,720 50	
		48,210,561 88

Balance on hand at close of business, June 30, 1871................... 8,217,514 12

The amount of Fractional Currency redeemed during the fiscal year was $3,335,034 71.

BALTIMORE, MARYLAND.

Balance turned over by John L. Thomas, jr., late United States Depositary, to Peter Negley, Assistant Treasurer United States, August 1,
1870 .... $4,072,830 44

RECEIPTS.

On account of Disbursing Officers..................	$1,849,029 00	
On account of Internal Revenue....................	845,504 72	
On account of Customs.............................	7,158,824 00	
On account of Gold Sales and Premiums.............	3,735,453 32	
On account of Transfers...........................	2,712,678 50	
On account of Post Office Department..............	128,529 26	
On account of Currency Redemption.................	54,572 03	
On account of Patent Fees.........................	560 00	
On account of Miscellaneous	103,885 60	
		16,589,036 43
		20,661,866 87

DISBURSEMENTS.

On account of Disbursing Officers' Checks..........	1,754,817 18	
On account of Drafts	3,419,767 63	
On account of Gold Sales..........................	3,327,843 25	
On account of Interest on Public Debt—Gold.........	1,694,501 47	
On account of Interest on Public Debt—Lawful Money..	46,230 00	
On account of Transfers	7,749,908 59	
On account of Five Per Cent. Notes and Interest....	1,141 50	
On account of Three Per Cent. Temporary Loan Interest.	124,300 00	
On account of Currency Redemption.................	50,231 03	
		18,168,740 65

Balance June 30, 1871 .... 2,493,126 22

SAN FRANCISCO, CALIFORNIA.

Balance June 30, 1870 ....$11,911,537 16

RECEIPTS.

On account of Customs	$7,539,675 93	
On account of Internal Revenue Tax	4,077,406 50	
On account of Sales of Land	448,490 12	
On account of Patent Fees	8,340 80	
On account of Various Sources	539,106,53	
	$12,613,019 88	
On account of Transfer of Funds	5,120,000 00	
On account of Public Depositors, including post-office	20,716,552 49	
	25,836,552 49	
		38,449,572 37
		50,361,109 53

DISBURSEMENTS.

On account of War	4,798,253 92	
On account of Navy	1,909,732 69	
On account of Interior	710,294 06	
On account of Customs	938,150 30	
On account of Treasury	966,053 43	
On account of Internal Revenue	217,631 67	
On account of Miscellaneous	32,878 52	
On account of Judiciary	61,465 65	
On account of Redemption Public Debt	34,283 50	
	9,668,743 74	
On account of Transfer of Funds	10,752,000 00	
On account of Public Depositors, including post-office	21,888,642 38	
	32,640,642 38	
		42,309,386 12

Balance June 30, 1871 .... 8,051,723 41

NEW ORLEANS, LOUISIANA.

RECEIPTS.

On account of Transfers	$8,080,000 00
On account of Customs	6,654,320 25
On account of Internal Revenue	2,140,283 88
On account of Disbursing Officers	9,840,712 97
On account of Post-Office Department	432,777 69
On account of Miscellaneous	2,584,199 43
Total	29,732,294 22

DISBURSEMENTS.

On account of Disbursing Officers	$9,883,979 99
On account of Post-Office Department	479,155 56
On account of Treasurer of the United States, General Account	13,452,597 05
On account of Legal-Tender Notes Redeemed	6,063,000 00
On account of Fractional Currency Redeemed	579,500 00
On account of Interest	106,071 00
Total	30,564,303 60

ST. LOUIS, MISSOURI.

Balance June 30, 1870 .... $3,548,403 14

RECEIPTS.

On account of Transfers	$6,276,751 81	
On account of Duties	2,084,646 80	
On account of Revenue	3,791,360 04	
On account of Postal	416,833 19	
On account of Officers	9,474,963 72	
On account of Miscellaneous	2,178,072 55	
		24,222,628 11
Total..		27,771,031 25

DISBURSEMENTS.

On account of Treasurer's Drafts........................	12,971,800 94	
On account of Post-Office Warrants	463,515 62	
On account of Disbursing Officers	8,933,553 19	
On account of Coin Sales.............................	1,410,351 34	
On account of Coin Interest and Drafts................	1,233,765 53	
On account of Miscellaneous	27,156 64	
		25,040,143 26
Balance June 30, 1871		2,730,887 99

CHARLESTON, SOUTH CAROLINA.

Balance on hand July 1, 1870. .... $381,496 25

RECEIPTS.

On account of Customs (Coin)...........................	$169,034 58	
On account of Internal Revenue	610,870 92	
On account of Miscellaneous............................	1,148,574 85	
On account of Disbursing Officers	1,094,587 90	
On account of Post-Office Department...................	173,391 06	
On account of Interest on Public Debt	6,629 00	
		3,203,088 31
Total		3,584,584 56

DISBURSEMENTS.

On account of Treasury Drafts, &c...................	1,864,961 31	
On account of Disbursing Officers' Checks.................	1,128,276 74	
On account of Post-Office Warrants	189,314 50	
On account of Interest on Public Debt	6,074 00	
		3,188,626 55
Balance on hand July 1, 1871............................		395,958 01
Fractional Currency received		$230,000 00
Fractional Currency redeemed		81,891 19

U.—RECEIPTS AND DISBURSEMENTS OF DESIGNATED DEPOSITARIES OF THE UNITED STATES FOR THE FISCAL YEAR.

CHICAGO, ILLINOIS.

Balance June 30, 1870	$2,726,654 41
Receipts	16,251,758 13
Total	18,978,412 54
Disbursements	$16,543,792 82
Balance June 30, 1871	2,434,619 72
Total	18,978,412 54

ST. LOUIS, MISSOURI.

Balance June 30, 1870	$1,895,833 35
Receipts	21,128,873 71
Total	23,024,707 06
Disbursements	$22,071,343 57
Balance June 30, 1871	953,363 49
Total	23,024,707 06

LOUISVILLE, KENTUCKY.

Balance June 30, 1870	$110,057 25
Receipts	4,249,351 17
Total	4,359,408 42
Disbursements	$4,413,420 64

BUFFALO, NEW YORK.

Balance June 30, 1870	$302,042 92
Receipts	3,765,682 91
Total	4,067,725 83
Disbursements	$3,858,793 79
Balance June 30, 1871	208,932 04
Total	4,067,725 83

PITTSBURGH, PENNSYLVANIA.

Balance June 30, 1870	$689,258 76
Receipts	5,054,931 71
Total	5,744,190 47
Disbursements	$5,117,655 00
Balance June 30, 1871	626,535 47
Total	5,744,190 47

SANTA FÉ, NEW MEXICO.

Balance June 30, 1870	$253,119 10
Receipts	2,902,389 38
Total	3,155,508 48
Disbursements	$2,869,007 66
Balance June 30, 1871	286,500 82
Total	3,155,508 48

OLYMPIA, WASHINGTON TERITORY.

Balance June 30, 1870	$45,763 60
Receipts	222,061 82
Total	267,825 42
Disbursements	$201,894 69
Balance June 30, 1871	65,930 73
Total	267,825 42

OREGON CITY, OREGON.

Balance June 30, 1870	$6,991 09
Receipts	48,724 97
Total	55,716 06
Disbursements	$19,236 46
Balance June 30, 1871	36,479 60
Total	55,716 06

TUCSON, ARIZONA.

Balance June 30, 1870	$51,128 17
Receipts	24,854 07
Total	75,982 24
Disbursements	$61,449 13
Balance June 30, 1871	14,533 11
Total	75,982 24

REPORT OF THE REGISTER OF THE TREASURY.

22 F

REPORT

OF

THE REGISTER OF THE TREASURY.

TREASURY DEPARTMENT,
Register's Office, October 30, 1871.

SIR: I have the honor to submit herewith my annual report of business transacted in this Bureau during the fiscal year ending June 30, 1871.

It will be observed that the amount of work performed in the various divisions does not differ widely from the amount performed in the previous year, and the clerical force will average about the same throughout the year.

The refunding of a part of the public debt has added to the labor of the loan branch, and should success continue to attend your efforts to accomplish that purpose, I shall be under the necessity of asking for an increase of clerks in that division of this office.

It affords me pleasure to bear testimony to the general good conduct and efficiency of those who are employed in the public service in this Bureau.

The chiefs of division, and the general organization of the office, remain the same as at the date of my last annual report.

The report of business transacted is submitted under the different divisions into which the office is divided.

DIVISION OF RECEIPTS AND EXPENDITURES.

The work of this division has been materially increased by the act of July 12, 1870, which provides that unexpended balances of annual appropriations shall only be applied to the payment of expenses properly made within the year, as it necessitates a duplication of accounts on both the personal and appropriation ledgers in all cases, except the appropriation be permanent or indefinite.

The following statement exhibits the work of the division for the year:

The number of warrants issued during the year for civil, diplomatic, miscellaneous, internal revenue, and public debt expenditures, was	19,032
In the preceding year	17,679
Increase	1,353
The number of warrants issued for receipts from customs, lands, direct tax, internal revenue, and miscellaneous sources, was	10,024
In the preceding year	9,561
Increase	463
The number of warrants issued for payments and repayments in the War, Navy, and Interior (Pension and Indian) Departments, was	7,977
In the preceding year	9,927
Decrease	1,950

The number of journal pages required for the entry of accounts relating to the civil, diplomatic, internal revenue, miscellaneous; and public debt receipts and expenditures, was.. 4,027
In the preceding year.. 4,017

Increase 10

The number of drafts registered was 29,186
In the preceding year... 29,735

Decrease... 549

The number of certificates furnished for the settlements of accounts was..... 9,537
In the preceding year... 6,814

Increase 2,723

The number of accounts received from the offices of the First and Fifth Auditors, and Commissioner of the General Land Office, was 20,984
In the preceding year... 20,775

Increase 209

The work of compiling the receipts and expenditures of the Government is being kept up as far as the settlement of the public accounts will permit. The manuscript for the fiscal year ending June 30, 1869, will be ready for the printer by the 1st of December next.

A large proportion of the duties of this division consists in furnishing information, and preparing statements and reports on calls made from your office and the several Bureaus of the Departments, and from Congress.

LOAN DIVISION.

The total amount of coupon and registered bonds issued during the year was $213,842,586 41. The number of bonds was 61,233.

The amount of bonds redeemed, as shown by the books of this office, was.. $216,520,312 41
Including amount which, in process of auditing and settling the accounts, had not reached this office at the close of the fiscal year.... 63,179,450 00
Exchanges... 49,807,300 00
Transfers 96,572,362 00

Making total amount canceled.................................... 426,079,424 41

The following statement shows the number of cases, number and amount of registered and coupon bonds issued and canceled during the fiscal year:

Statement showing the number of cases and number and amount of registered and coupon bonds issued and cancelled during the fiscal year ending June 30, 1871.

LOANS.	DIRECT ISSUES			EXCHANGES			TRANSFERS			TOTAL ISSUE
	No. of cases.	Bonds issued.	Amount.	No. of cases.	Bonds issued.	Amount.	No. of cases.	Bonds issued.	Amount.	Amount.
1847										
1848										
1850, Texan indemnity										
1855				13	159	$795,000 00	39	287	$1,427,000 00	$2,222,000 00
1860				1	1	1,000 00	11	28	124,000 00	125,000 00
1861, February 8				82	169	327,000 00	187	423	1,284,000 00	1,611,000 00
Oregon war							6	48	24,000 00	94,000 00
1861, July 17				451	1,734	5,377,850 00	730	2,341	6,952,800 00	12,330,650 00
1862				156	419	1,152,000 00	671	3,474	13,082,290 00	14,243,500 00
1863				244	720	1,691,150 00	365	1,066	3,158,050 00	4,849,200 00
1864, 5-20's							18	49	146,000 00	146,000 00
1864, 10-40's				445	1,610	7,911,600 00	805	2,907	11,260,950 00	19,172,550 00
1-64, June 30				136	487	1,977,010 00	307	1,373	5,782,850 00	7,759,900 00
1865				115	494	5,064,100 00	380	2,271	7,643,950 00	12,708,050 00
Consols of 1865				486	1,890	7,985,750 00	840	4,275	14,282,150 00	22,819,150 00
Consols of 1867				815	3,236	14,508,200 00	1,243	4,963	14,262,150 00	24,262,150 00
Consols of 1868	14	38	$11,800 00	276	744	2,934,500 00	203	505	1,522,400 00	4,456,900 00
Pacific Railroad	2	18	161,512 00				1,237	2,626	14,935,512 00	15,697,034 00
Compous, 1870, July 8	2	679	678,362 41							678,362 41
Funded, 1881, 5 per cent	824	21,890	66,602,250 00	18	65	82,100 00	8	39	112,500 00	66,796,850 00
Grand total	842	22,625	67,453,924 41	3,238	11,733	49,807,360 00	7,062	26,675	96,572,362 00	213,849,586 41

Statement showing the number of cases and number and amount of registered and coupon bonds, &c.—Continued.

LOANS.	REDEMPTIONS. No. of cases.	Bonds cancelled.	Amount.	CANCELED. EXCHANGES. No. of bonds.	Amount.	TRANSFERS. No. of bonds.	Amount.	TOTAL CANCELED. Amount.
1847	1	1	$1,000 00					$1,000 00
1848	1	22	10,800 00					10,800 00
1850, Texan indemnity								
1858	34	2,342	6,966,000 00	795	$795,000 00	297	$1,427,000 00	2,222,000 00
1860				1	1,000 00	28	124,000 00	7,091,000 00
1861, February 8				327	327,000 00	494	1,284,000 00	1,611,000 00
Oregon war						48	24,000 00	24,000 00
1861, July 17	146	8,788	28,384,100 00	8,398	5,377,650 00	2,979	6,952,800 00	12,330,650 00
1862	16	207	893,400 00	3,616	1,152,050 00	5,658	13,082,200 00	42,616,300 00
1863				2,554	1,691,150 00	1,164	3,159,050 00	4,849,200 00
1864, 5-20's	111	11,120	27,113,300 00	13,866	7,911,600 00	49	146,000 00	1,039,400 00
1864, 10-40's	110	10,539	24,725,450 00	2,752	1,077,050 00	4,062	11,260,950 00	10,172,550 00
1864, June 30	111	44,831	80,203,200 00	6,257	5,064,100 00	1,871	5,782,850 00	34,873,207 00
1865	85	35,612	45,323,800 00	14,541	7,085,750 00	2,622	7,643,950 00	37,433,500 00
Consols of 1865	29	1,306	2,806,900 00	32,315	14,508,200 00	7,034	14,334,000 00	103,022,950 00
Consols of 1867				7,094	2,934,500 00	6,704	14,282,150 00	74,114,150 00
Consols of 1868						758	1,522,400 00	7,355,800 00
Pacific Railroad						3,380	14,935,512 00	14,935,512 00
Coupons, 1870, July 8								362 41
Funded, 1881, 5 per cent.	1	1	362 41	97	82,100 00	20	112,500 00	104,600 00
Grand total	645	114,769	216,520,312 41	92,613	49,807,300 00	37,167	96,572,362 00	362,899,974 41
Amount redeemed which had not reached Register's office			63,179,450 00					

NOTE AND COUPON DIVISION.

The following is a detailed statement of the work performed in this division during the fiscal year, viz :

Of United States Treasury notes (upper halves) there were counted, assorted, arranged, registered, and examined as follows, viz :

	Notes.	Value.
One-year 5 per cent. Treasury notes :		
Act March 3, 1863	1,640	$32,310
Two-year 5 per cent. Treasury notes :		
Act March 3, 1863	185	11,900
Two-year 5 per cent. "coupon" Treasury notes :		
Act March 3, 1863	30	3,750
Total number 5 per cent. Treasury notes	1,855	47,960
Coupons attached	27	
Three-year compound-interest notes :		
Act March 3, 1863	311	13,000
Act June 30, 1864	11,140	1,304,380
Total compound-interest notes	11,451	1,317,380
Gold certificates :		
Act March 3, 1863, 29,913 certificates		$74,512,000

The whole number of notes and certificates received during the year was 43,219, amounting to $75,877,340.

The whole number of five and six per cent. interest notes (whole) received from the Comptroller, counted, verified, and delivered to the United States Treasurer, was 12,305, amounting to $365,350.

Of United States seven-thirty coupon Treasury notes there were received, counted, assorted, arranged, registered, examined, and compared, as follows, viz :

	Coupons.	Notes.	Value.
Act July 17, 1861	....	49	$6,500
Act June 30, 1864, and March 3, 1865 :			
First series, August 15, 1864		464	43,100
Coupons attached	312		
Second series, June 15, 1865		373	44,450
Coupons attached	195		
Third series, July 15, 1865		1,003	95,500
Coupons attached	564		
Total seven-thirty notes	1,071	1,889	189,550

The whole number of seven-thirty coupon Treasury notes received during the year was 1,889, amounting to $189,550, with 1,071 coupons attached, the same having been arranged, registered, examined, and compared with the records of the division, properly filed, and deposited in a files-room.

The total number of coupons of the various loans counted, assorted, and arranged numerically, was 4,283,704.

The total number of coupons registered was 5,087,608.

The total number of coupons examined and compared was 10,597,947.

All the redeemed coupons are received in this division, requiring a large portion of the clerical force to complete the necessary arrangements for their final disposition. After being registered and carefully compared, they are packed in boxes, which are labeled, designating the number, denomination, and kind of coupons. A schedule of the con-pons, by report, is prepared, designating the number of each denomination, loan, when due, the amount of each, and the aggregate of the whole.

The number of exchanged and redeemed bonds received, scheduled, entered in blotters, and registered upon the numerical records, was as follows, viz:

Of the loan of July 17 and August 5, 1861, 9,809 bonds, amounting to $6,081,150, with 219,948 coupons attached, amounting to $4,097,511.

Of the loan of June 30, 1864, 21,229 bonds, amounting to $15,329,750, with 636,796 coupons attached, amounting to $13,818,184 10.

Of the loan of March 3, 1865, 5,964 bonds, amounting to $3,578,300, with 187,667 coupons attached, amounting to $3,374,368 50.

Of the consols of 1865, 109,481 bonds, amounting to $60,787,350, with 3,283,808 coupons attached, amounting to $54,869,040.

Of the consols of 1867, 45,589 bonds, amounting to $7,304,450, with 1,551,123 coupons attached, amounting to $7,452,072.

These bonds, after a careful examination and comparison with the records, are delivered to a committee authorized to receive them for destruction.

NOTE AND FRACTIONAL CURRENCY DIVISION.

The work of this division has materially increased during the last year, as will appear from the following statement showing the number of notes and amount of fractional currency, Treasury notes, and national-bank notes (of such national banks as are broken or gone into voluntary liquidation) counted, examined, canceled, and destroyed, by burning, during the year, viz:

Denomination.	No. of notes.	Amount.
Postal currency	400,000	$62,000 00
Fractional currency, second issue	800,000	91,300 00
Fractional currency, third issue	20,824,000	5,072,100 00
Fractional currency, fourth issue	116,800,000	24,598,000 00
Legal-tender notes	12,677,376	114,127,200 00
Legal-tender notes, series 1869	1,103,408	2,076,170 00
Demand notes	998	8,360 00
National-bank notes	231,819	1,299,229 40
Total	152,837,601	147,334,359 40

Discounted money record kept, but not counted, in this division.

Postal currency	$974 83
Fractional currency, second issue	934 76
Fractional currency, third issue	88,720 77
Fractional currency, fourth issue	10,253 76
Legal-tender notes	190,948 35
Legal-tender notes, series 1869	17,608 15
Total	309,440 62

The number of notes counted this year was	152,837,601
The number of notes counted last year was	115,277,138
Showing an increase of	37,560,463

The amount of the notes counted this year was	$147,334,359 40
The amount of the notes counted last year was	118,116,960 50
Showing an increase of	29,217,398 90

TONNAGE DIVISION.

The tonnage of the country, as compared with that of 1870, is as follows:

	1870.		1871.	
	Vessels.	Tons.	Vessels.	Tons.
Registered, (foreign trade)	2, 942	1, 516, 800	2, 721	1, 425, 142
Enrolled and licensed, (home trade)	26, 056	2, 729, 708	26, 930	2, 857, 465
Total	28, 998	4, 246, 508	29, 651	4, 282, 607

The tonnage in "home trade" has increased 126,622 tons, and the tonnage in "foreign trade" has fallen off 91,822 tons. Stated according to the various classes of vessels, the comparison is as follows:

	1870.		1871.	
	Vessels.	Tons.	Vessels.	Tons.
Sailing-vessels	17, 534	2, 363, 086	17, 298	2, 286, 155
Steam-vessels	3, 524	1, 075, 095	3, 567	1, 087, 637
Barges	1, 530	240, 411	1, 472	260, 343
Canal-boats	6, 410	567, 915	7, 314	648, 472
Total	28, 998	4, 246, 507	29, 651	4, 282, 607

Of the total steam tonnage of the country, amounting to 1,087,637 tons, only 5 per centum is regularly employed in foreign trade.

There appears to have been a total increase during the year ending June 30, 1871, of 604 vessels—34,800 tons.

The sailing tonnage has decreased 78,231 tons; the steam tonnage has increased 12,442 tons; the barge tonnage has increased 19,932 tons; and the canal tonnage has increased 80,557 tons.

SHIP-BUILDING.

The ship-building of the country, for 1870 and 1871, is as follows:

	1870.		1871.	
	Vessels.	Tons.	Vessels.	Tons.
Sailing-vessels	816	146, 340	756	97, 176
Steam-vessels	290	70, 620	302	87, 842
Barges	162	29, 736	229	46, 822
Canal-boats	350	30, 256	468	41, 386
Total	1, 618	276, 953	1, 755	273, 226

The total ship-building, during the year ending June 30, 1871, appears to have been 3,727 tons less than during the preceding year, but there have been 137 more vessels built. This is due to the falling off in the building of large vessels for the foreign trade, and to the increase in the building of barges and canal-boats.

There has been a great falling off in the building of sailing-vessels, and an increase in the building of steam-vessels. The steam tonnage built has been designed almost exclusively for "home trade."

The tonnage built within the limits of the various grand divisions into which the country is divided is as follows :

	TONNAGE BUILT.	
	1870.	1871.
Atlantic and Gulf Coast	170, 116	150, 683
Pacific Coast	12, 720	3, 923
Northern lakes	37, 258	44, 377
Western rivers	56, 859	72, 139

The iron ship-building of the country during the past year has been very small in comparison with the iron ship-building of England, which amounted to 256,824 tons in the year 1870. Yet there has been a larger tonnage built in this country than during any previous year, since the termination of the war, as shown by the following table:

Iron vessels built in the United States from 1867 to 1871 inclusive.

	TONNAGE BUILT.				
	1867.	1868.	1869.	1870.	1871.
Sailing-vessels	None	None	1, 039	679	2, 067
Steam-vessels	None	2, 801	3, 545	7, 602	13, 412
Total	None	2, 801	4, 584	8, 281	15, 479

The iron vessels built have been designed almost exclusively for home trade. There have been two iron steamers built on the lakes and four on the western rivers.

The superiority of iron over wood as a building material for steam-vessels seems to have been well established.

THE FISHERIES.

The number of vessels and tonnage engaged in the " cod and mackerel " and " whale fisheries " during the years 1868, 1869, 1870, and 1871 is as follows:

	1868.		1869.		1870.		1871.	
-	Vessels.	Tons.	Vessels.	Tons.	Vessels.	Tons.	Vessels.	Tons.
Cod and mackerel fisheries	2, 220	83, 686	1, 714	62, 704	2, 292	91, 460	2, 426	92, 865
Whale fisheries	328	71, 343	311	70, 202	299	67, 954	249	61, 490

Our cod and mackerel fisheries exhibit a fair degree of prosperity, the tonnage thus employed being larger than during any year since the repeal of the bounty on the cod-fishery act of July 28, 1866, and in lieu thereof the substitution of a drawback on imported salt used in curing both mackerel and cod-fish.

The following statement exhibits the tonnage employed in the cod and mackerel fisheries belonging in each State:

State.	Tons.	Per cent.
Massachusetts	63,399	67.8
Maine	22,758	25
Connecticut	3,597	3.8
New York	1,830	2
New Hampshire	934	1
Rhode Island	408	0.4
Total	92,866	100

The district of Gloucester is most extensively engaged in this occupation; her cod and mackerel fleet amounting to 548 vessels, 28,569 tons, showing an increase of 97 vessels, 5,093 tons, since June 30, 1870. There appears to be a gradual decline in our tonnage employed in the whale-fishery. The entire whaling tonnage of the country is owned at the following ports:

Ports.	Vessels.	Tons.
New Bedford	187	51,442
New London	22	3,877
Barnstable	20	1,939
Edgartou	5	1,854
Salem and Beverly	5	785
Nantucket	5	729
San Francisco	3	602
Sag Harbor, N. Y.	2	261
Total	249	61,469

It appears that 84 per cent. of the total tonnage employed in whale-fishery hails from New Bedford.

REVISION OF THE LAWS RELATING TO THE REGISTRATION, ENROLLMENT, AND LICENSING OF VESSELS.

Our registration and enrollment laws now in force are substantially the enactments of December 31, 1792, and February 28, 1793. It seems to be very desirable that certain changes should be introduced, both in regard to the method of documenting vessels and in the forms of our records of title. Great improvements can also be made in the manner of keeping marine accounts and transmitting returns of the same to this Department, thus enabling us to preserve more accurately the distinctions as to customs districts, and also as to the home and foreign trade.

BOOKS AND BLANKS.

During the year ending June 30, 1871, there were issued from this office to collectors of customs, upon requisitions, 1,404 blank-books and 118,159 blank forms. There were received from the Congressional Printer 1,130 books and 78,000 blank forms.

The plan of furnishing these supplies to the custom-houses of the country from this office has proved to be highly successful both as a measure of economy and as a means of securing uniformity in the work at the custom-house and in the returns made to the office.

During the past year complete lists have been made of all the documented vessels of the United States, referring to the records of this Bureau. This has been found to be a practical necessity of the current work.

An alphabetical list of the ports of entry, ports of delivery, and hailing ports of vessels has also been prepared, showing the State and customs district in which each port is situated, together with a full geographical description of the limits of each port and district.

I remain, with great respect, yours, &c.,

JOHN ALLISON,
Register.

Hon. GEORGE S. BOUTWELL,
    Secretary of the Treasury.

Statement of the number of persons employed in each district of the United States for the collection of customs, during the fiscal year ending June 30, 1871, with their occupation and compensation, per act of March 3, 1849.

District, number of persons, and occupation.	Agg. compensation.	District, number of persons, and occupation.	Agg. compensation.
AROOSTOOK, MAINE.		**BATH, MAINE.**	
1 collector	$1,500 00	1 collector	$3,000 00
1 deputy collector	1,460 00	1 deputy collector, inspector, weigher,	
4 deputy collectors	4,380 00	gauger, and measurer	1,500 00
1 special inspector	1,460 00	1 inspector, weigher, gauger, and measurer	1,500 00
2 inspectors	1,460 00	2 inspectors	2,920 00
		1 inspector	1,096 00
MACHIAS, MAINE.		1 inspector	858 00
1 collector	1,828 89	1 inspector	600 00
1 deputy collector	1,095 00	1 inspector	500 00
1 deputy collector	912 50	1 inspector	350 00
4 inspectors	2,920 00	1 inspector	316 00
		1 inspector	237 00
FRENCHMAN'S BAY, MAINE.			
		PORTLAND AND FALMOUTH, MAINE.	
1 collector	900 48	1 collector	6,400 00
1 special deputy collector	1,200 00	3 deputy collectors	9,000 00
1 deputy collector	730 00	1 clerk	1,500 00
3 deputy collectors	1,300 00	2 clerks	2,800 00
1 inspector	1,095 00	2 clerks	2,400 00
1 inspector	500 00	1 clerk	1,300 00
1 United States officer	360 00	2 clerks	2,000 00
		1 clerk	1,100 00
BANGOR, MAINE.		1 clerk	900 00
		1 surveyor	4,500 00
1 collector	2,920 00	1 deputy surveyor	2,500 00
1 deputy collector	1,800 00	1 superintendent of warehouses	1,500 00
1 deputy collector	1,140 00	2 storekeepers	2,920 00
1 deputy collector and weigher	1,095 00	3 storekeepers	3,842 50
1 inspector	1,470 00	1 appraiser	3,000 00
1 inspector	912 00	1 assistant appraiser	2,500 00
2 inspectors	2,190 00	1 examiner	1,800 00
1 temporary inspector	800 00	2 weighers, gaugers, and measurers	4,000 00
1 occasional inspector	378 00	1 occasional weigher, &c	3,430 04
1 weigher, gauger, and measurer	1,342 00	3 inspectors	4,380 00
1 night-watchman	730 00	15 inspectors	19,162 50
1 janitor	430 00	9 inspectors	9,855 00
		2 inspectors	1,460 00
CASTINE, MAINE.		1 inspector	626 00
		8 temporary inspectors	2,870 00
1 collector	2,024 12	2 boatmen	1,460 00
1 special deputy collector and inspector	1,460 00	1 porter, appraiser's office	426 00
1 deputy collector and inspector	912 50	1 porter, custom-house	550 00
3 deputy collectors and inspectors	3,285 00	1 marker, &c	729 00
1 special inspector	1,400 00		
1 superintendent of warehouses	519 00	**KENNEBUNK, MAINE.**	
1 temporary weigher and measurer	94 56	1 collector	166 45
		1 inspector	600 00
BELFAST, MAINE.		3 inspectors	468 00
		1 inspector	120 00
1 collector	1,786 36		
1 deputy collector and inspector	1,460 00	**YORK, MAINE.**	
1 deputy collector, inspector, weigher, gauger, and measurer	1,500 00	1 collector	264 09
1 deputy collector, inspector, &c	1,247 40	1 inspector	100 00
1 deputy collector, inspector, weigher, gauger, and measurer	500 00	**PASSAMAQUODDY, MAINE.**	
1 deputy collector, inspector, &c	400 00	1 collector	3,195 42
1 temporary inspector	200 00	1 surveyor	502 54
		1 deputy collector and inspector	2,000 00
WALDOBOROUGH, MAINE.		1 deputy collector and inspector	1,460 00
		2 deputy collectors and inspectors	2,190 00
1 collector	2,811 68	1 deputy collector and inspector	987 50
1 deputy collector, inspector, weigher, measurer, and gauger	1,361 34	1 deputy collector and inspector	730 00
1 deputy collector, inspector, &c	1,337 00	1 deputy collector and inspector	912 50
1 deputy collector, inspector, &c	1,236 15	1 inspector	650 00
1 deputy collector, inspector, &c	1,225 00	3 inspectors	3,285 00
1 deputy collector, inspector, &c	921 00	1 inspector	366 00
1 deputy collector, inspector, &c	892 50	1 inspector	912 50
1 deputy collector, inspector, &c	851 11	1 inspector	1,095 00
1 deputy collector, inspector, &c	369 01	1 aid to the revenue	1,825 00
		2 aids to the revenue	400 00
WISCASSET, MAINE.		1 aid to the revenue	730 00
		1 watchman	484 00
1 collector	1,047 93	2 watchmen	912 50
2 deputy collectors and inspectors	2,190 00	1 watchman	360 00
1 deputy collector and inspector	866 00	1 boatman	71 00
1 special inspector	66 00	1 boatman	

Statement of the number of persons employed for the collection of customs, &c.—Continued.

District, number of persons, and occupation.	Agg. compensation.	District, number of persons, and occupation.	Agg. compensation.
PORTSMOUTH, N. H.		**SALEM AND BEVERLY, MASS.—Continued.**	
1 collector	$1,166 25	1 inspector	$1,000 00
1 surveyor	482 05	1 inspector	723 00
1 deputy collector and inspector	1,460 00	1 inspector	400 00
1 deputy collector and inspector	250 00	1 boatman	480 00
1 inspector, weigher, gauger, and measurer	1,500 00	1 boatman	300 00
3 inspectors	4,380 00	1 janitor	480 00
1 inspector	650 00	1 watchman	20 00
1 porter and watchman	400 00		
		MARBLEHEAD, MASS.	
VERMONT, VT.		1 deputy collector and inspector	912 50
1 collector	2,500 00	1 deputy collector and inspector	300 00
1 deputy collector	2,000 00	1 inspector	1,460 00
1 deputy collector	1,800 00	1 inspector	730 00
1 deputy collector	1,600 00	1 boatman	100 00
2 deputy collectors	2,900 00	1 collector, from February to June 30	129 01
5 deputy collectors	6,000 00		
2 deputy collectors	2,200 00	**BOSTON AND CHARLESTOWN, MASS.**	
4 deputy collectors	4,000 00		
2 deputy collectors	1,000 00	1 collector	6,400 00
1 deputy collector	900 00	1 auditor	3,500 00
1 deputy collector	800 00	2 deputy collectors, at $3,000	6,000 00
1 deputy collector	600 00	1 cashier	3,000 00
5 deputy collectors	2,750 00	1 assistant cashier	2,000 00
1 deputy collector	500 00	2 clerks	4,400 00
3 deputy collectors	2,737 50	5 clerks	10,000 00
1 customs clerk	1,200 00	1 clerk	1,900 00
1 customs clerk	913 00	3 clerks	5,400 00
1 inspector	1,095 00	7 clerks	11,900 00
1 inspector	1,000 00	6 clerks	9,000 00
1 inspector	730 00	24 clerks	33,600 00
1 inspector	500 00	8 clerks	10,400 00
21 inspectors, at $912 50 each	19,162 50	6 clerks	7,200 00
1 inspector	760 00	7 clerks	7,700 00
12 inspectors, at $608 each	7,296 00	2 clerks	2,000 00
1 inspector	90 00	1 messenger	1,200 00
11 tallyboys, at $182 50 each	2,007 50	4 assistant messengers	3,000 00
4 tallyboys, at $47 50 each	190 00	6 assistant messengers	4,212 00
2 night watchmen, at $730 each	1,460 00	1 engineer	1,100 00
1 night watchman	670 00	1 assistant engineer	702 00
1 revenue boatman	684 00	2 deputy coll'rs, Hingham & Cohasset	1,400 00
1 revenue boatman	450 00	59 inspectors	86,140 00
1 porter	600 00	29 temporary inspectors	37,047 50
		50 night inspectors	54,750 00
NEWBURYPORT, MASS.		1 superintendent of warehouses	1,800 00
1 collector	2,061 00	2 storekeepers, paid by Government	2,920 00
1 surveyor	507 00	20 storekeepers, paid by merchants	29,200 00
1 inspector	250 00	3 assistant storekeepers, paid by merchants	2,400 00
1 deputy collector and inspector	1,095 00	2 assistant storekeepers, paid by merchants	2,104 00
1 weigher, gauger, and measurer	1,095 00	11 weighers	22,000 00
1 inspector	1,095 00	4 gaugers	5,940 00
		4 measurers	5,940 00
GLOUCESTER, MASS.		15 foremen to weighers and gaugers	15,000 00
1 collector	3,000 00	15 foremen to measurers	15,000 00
1 surveyor	1,100 00	4 revenue boatmen	3,650 00
1 deputy collector	1,500 00	1 revenue-boat messenger	1,095 00
1 clerk	1,000 00	125 laborers	34,375 00
2 inspectors	2,920 00	20 laborers	10,530 00
2 inspectors	2,190 00	1 naval officer	5,000 00
2 inspectors	1,460 00	1 deputy naval officer	2,500 00
2 inspectors	600 00	1 deputy naval officer	2,000 00
1 janitor	300 00	5 clerks	9,000 00
1 keeper of building	225 00	4 clerks	6,400 00
1 boatman	360 00	1 clerk	1,500 00
7 weighers and measurers	250 00	1 clerk	1,200 00
7 storekeepers, paid by importers		1 messenger	800 00
		1 surveyor	4,500 00
SALEM AND BEVERLY, MASS.		1 deputy surveyor	2,500 00
1 collector	1,566 72	1 clerk	1,800 00
1 deputy collector and inspector	1,460 00	1 clerk	1,500 00
1 inspector and clerk	1,460 00	1 clerk	1,400 00
1 surveyor	790 53	1 clerk	850 00
1 weigher and gauger	1,500 00	1 general appraiser	3,000 00
6 inspectors	6,570 00	2 appraisers	6,000 00
		2 assistant appraisers	5,000 00
		2 clerks	4,000 00

Statement of the number of persons employed for the collection of customs, &c.—Continued.

District, number of persons, and occupation.	Agg. compensation.	District, number of persons, and occupation.	Agg. compensation.
BOSTON AND CHARLESTOWN, MASS.—Con.		PROVIDENCE, R. I.—Continued.	
4 clerks	$7,200 00	3 inspectors, weighers, gaugers, &c	$4,500 00
4 clerks	6,400 00	1 inspector, weigher, gauger, &c	1,500 00
5 clerks	7,000 00	2 inspectors, coastwise	1,460 00
1 clerk	1,100 00	2 inspectors, foreign	2,092 00
7 laborers	5,976 25	3 inspectors	788 00
1 laborer	950 00	1 inspector, permanent	460 00
1 laborer	850 00	1 inspector, Pawtuxet	1,095 00
PLYMOUTH, MASS.		1 inspector, East Greenwich	500 00
		1 messenger and storekeeper	1,200 00
1 collector	1,048 78	1 storekeeper	730 00
1 inspector	1,095 00	1 boatman at Pawtuxet	600 00
1 inspector	600 00	1 appraiser	1,581 51
1 inspector	400 00	1 messenger in appraiser's office	75 00
1 inspector	300 00		
1 inspector	200 00	BRISTOL AND WARREN, R. I.	
BARNSTABLE, MASS.		1 collector	309 61
		1 inspector	1,095 00
1 collector	1,993 00	1 inspector	250 00
1 deputy collector and inspector	1,095 00	2 temporary inspectors	204 00
1 deputy collector and inspector	900 00	1 gauger	132 00
2 deputy collectors and inspectors	1,500 00	1 weigher	52 00
1 deputy collector and inspector	800 00	1 boatman	216 00
1 deputy collector and inspector	500 00	1 storekeeper	24 00
1 deputy collector and inspector	400 00		
1 inspector	400 00	NEWPORT, R. I.	
1 aid to the revenue	300 00		
1 clerk	300 00	1 collector	1,090 16
1 boatman	150 00	1 superintendent of lights	68 47
1 keeper custom-house	350 00	1 agent of marine hospital	09
		1 deputy collector	1,200 00
FALL RIVER, MASS.		4 permanent inspectors	2,910 00
1 collector	2,087 89	1 inspector	600 00
1 deputy collector, inspector, weigher,		1 inspector	300 00
gauger, and measurer	1,606 78	1 inspector	200 00
1 permanent inspector, weigher, and		4 occasional inspectors	1,272 00
measurer	1,500 00	1 measurer	243 37
1 temporary inspector, &c	174 00	1 boatman, &c	500 00
2 temporary night-inspectors	345 00		
1 weigher, gauger, and measurer	1,078 48	STONINGTON, CONN.	
NEW BEDFORD, MASS.		1 inspector, Stonington	400 00
		1 inspector, Mystic	500 00
1 collector	2,377 00	1 surveyor, Pawcatuck	150 00
1 deputy collector and inspector	1,460 00	1 boatkeeper, Stonington	144 00
1 inspector	1,460 00	1 collector	792 57
1 inspector, gauger, weigher, and measurer	1,460 00		
1 inspector	1,000 00	NEW LONDON, CONN.	
1 inspector	300 00		
1 inspector	125 00	1 collector	3,335 77
1 inspector	120 00	1 clerk	1,800 00
2 inspectors	160 00	2 inspectors	1,000 00
1 clerk, aid to revenue	1,000 00	1 inspector	200 00
1 boatman	600 00	1 inspector, weigher, gauger, and	
		measurer	893 49
EDGARTOWN, MASS.			
1 collector	730 02	MIDDLETOWN, CONN.	
1 deputy collector and inspector	1,350 00	1 collector	1,504 61
1 deputy collector and inspector	1,095 00	1 deputy collector and inspector	1,080 72
1 temporary inspector	600 00	1 inspector at Hartford	542 00
1 temporary inspector	500 00	1 inspector, Saybrook	70 00
1 temporary inspector	500 00	1 storekeeper, Hartford	100 00
1 night inspector	600 00	1 watchman	600 00
1 night inspector	730 00		
1 revenue boatman	420 00	NEW HAVEN, CONN.	
		1 collector	3,400 00
NANTUCKET, MASS.		1 deputy collector	2,000 00
1 collector	707 14	2 inspectors and clerks	3,000 00
1 deputy collector and inspector	600 00	2 weighers, measurers, and gaugers	3,000 00
1 inspector	600 00	1 inspector	1,277 50
2 temporary inspectors	12 00	1 inspector	1,186 25
5 temporary inspectors	60 00	1 inspector	1,005 00
		1 inspector	760 00
PROVIDENCE, R. I.		1 night-watchman	1,095 00
1 collector	3,000 00	1 boatman and night-watchman	650 00
1 deputy collector, inspector, and measurer	1,500 00	1 night-watchman	400 00
		1 messenger and porter	500 00

Statement of the number of persons employed for the collection of customs, &c.—Continued.

District, number of persons, and occupation.	Agg. compensation.	District, number of persons, and occupation.	Agg. compensation
NEW HAVEN, CONN.—Cont'd.		**NEW YORK CITY, N. Y.—Cont'd.**	
1 laborer	$626 00	10 assistant appraisers	$30,000 00
1 inspector	72 00	25 examiners	62,500 00
1 inspector	60 00	1 clerk to general appraisers	2,500 00
1 inspector	48 00	2 examiners	4,400 00
		10 examiners	20,000 00
FAIRFIELD, CONN.		14 examiners	25,200 00
		2 examiners	3,200 00
1 collector	1,721 62	7 examiners	10,500 00
1 inspector	1,500 00	1 examiner of marble	1,500 00
1 inspector	200 00	4 clerks	5,600 00
1 inspector	125 00	38 clerks	45,600 00
1 night inspector	126 00	1 clerk	1,100 00
		5 clerks	5,000 00
SAG HARBOR, N. Y.		8 messengers	7,200 00
		2 openers and packers	2,347 50
1 collector	527 70	85 openers and packers	79,815 00
1 deputy collector	800 00	1 naval officer	5,000 00
1 surveyor	693 80	3 deputies	7,500 00
1 inspector	180 00	1 auditor	2,500 00
1 inspector	120 00	1 chief clerk	2,500 00
1 inspector	15 00	8 clerks	17,600 00
		2 clerks	4,050 00
NEW YORK CITY, N. Y.		17 clerks	30,600 00
		19 clerks	30,400 00
1 collector	6,400 00	12 clerks	16,800 00
1 assistant collector	5,000 00	5 clerks	6,000 00
1 auditor	7,000 00	3 messengers	3,900 00
1 assistant auditor	4,000 00	1 messenger	800 00
1 secretary to collector	3,000 00	1 surveyor	4,500 00
1 chief clerk	3,000 00	4 deputy surveyors	10,000 00
1 cashier	5,000 00	4 clerks	6,000 00
1 assistant cashier	3,500 00	5 clerks	7,000 00
8 deputy collectors	24,000 00	4 clerks	5,200 00
3 clerks	9,000 00	3 messengers	2,700 00
1 clerk	2,800 00	1 porter	720 00
9 clerks	22,500 00		
11 clerks	24,200 00	**ALBANY, N. Y.**	
31 clerks	62,000 00		
35 clerks	63,000 00	1 surveyor	4,024 52
1 clerk	1,700 00	1 deputy surveyor and inspector	1,460 00
32 clerks	51,200 00	1 clerk	480 00
44 clerks	61,600 00		
44 clerks	66,000 00	**CHAMPLAIN, N. Y.**	
67 clerks	80,400 00		
28 clerks	28,000 00	1 collector	2,500 00
9 clerks	8,100 00	1 deputy collector and cashier	1,800 00
34 clerks	27,200 00	1 deputy collector and clerk	1,600 00
1 clerk	750 00	1 deputy collector and clerk	1,200 00
1 clerk	600 00	1 deputy collector and inspector	1,000 00
3 messengers	4,428 50	8 deputy collectors and inspectors	7,200 00
1 superintendent	2,400 00	4 inspectors	3,000 00
2 ushers	2,200 00	1 boatman	300 00
2 carpenters	2,355 00	1 temporary deputy inspector	736 66
1 engineer	1,500 00	1 temporary deputy inspector	562 50
4 firemen	2,880 00	6 temporary inspectors	3,125 00
8 watchmen	8,000 00	1 night watchman	562 50
4 Sunday watchmen	520 00	1 female inspector	382 50
13 porters	9,360 00		
249 inspectors	363,540 00	**OSWEGATCHIE, N. Y.**	
7 inspectresses	7,605 00		
1 captain of night-inspectors	1,600 00	1 collector	2,563 84
2 lieutenants night-inspectors	2,400 00	1 special deputy collector	1,800 00
116 night inspectors	127,020 00	2 deputy collectors and clerks	3,000 00
19 weighers	47,500 00	1 deputy clerk and inspector	1,500 00
8 gaugers	16,000 00	5 deputy inspectors	4,000 00
1 assistant collector, Jersey City	2,000 00	2 inspectors	2,400 00
1 inspector, Troy	1,461 00	2 inspectors	2,190 00
1 surveyor, Troy	250 00	4 temporary inspectors	3,317 50
97 storekeepers	141,620 00	1 inspector	730 00
1 assistant storekeeper	1,000 00	1 watchman	650 00
9 inspectors for measuring vessels	13,140 00	1 inspectress	276 00
1 measurer of marble	2,000 00		
1 superintendent, Castle Garden	2,030 00	**CAPE VINCENT, N. Y.**	
2 inspectors, Castle Garden	2,920 00		
1 storekeeper, Castle Garden	1,460 00	1 collector	2,500 00
1 assistant storekeeper, Castle Garden	1,000 00	1 deputy collector and inspector	1,500 00
1 appraiser	4,000 00	1 deputy collector and inspector	1,200 00
1 appraiser at large	3,000 00	9 deputy collectors and inspectors	8,100 00
		4 inspectors	3,645 00
		2 temporary inspectors	1,332 00

Statement of the number of persons employed for the collection of customs, &c.—Continued.

District, number of persons, and occupation.	Agg. compensation.	District, number of persons, and occupation.	Agg. compensation.
OSWEGO, N. Y.		**PERTH AMBOY, N. J.**	
1 collector	$4,513 27	1 collector	$1,925 24
1 deputy collector	2,000 00	1 deputy collector	1,200 00
1 clerk and deputy collector	1,400 00	4 inspectors	1,631 00
1 deputy collector and inspector	1,460 00	1 inspector	730 00
2 clerks	2,266 66	2 inspectors	1,200 00
1 clerk	1,233 33	15 boatmen	1,272 75
1 clerk	1,200 00	1 clerk	323 00
1 clerk	730 00		
1 clerk	900 00	**LITTLE EGG HARBOR, N. J.**	
5 inspectors	5,475 00		
3 inspectors	2,475 00	4 inspectors	1,875 00
1 inspector	273 00	2 boatmen	1,074 00
2 inspectors	1,375 00	1 collector	250 00
1 temporary inspector	51 00		
3 deputy collectors	2,002 50	**GREAT EGG HARBOR, N. J.**	
1 janitor	547 50		
1 superintendent warehouse	1,460 00	1 collector	626 75
6 store-keepers	4,380 00	1 inspector	527 50
		1 boatman	423 00
GENESEE, N. Y.			
		BRIDGETON, N. J.	
1 collector	2,500 00		
1 deputy collector	1,800 00	1 collector	630 45
6 deputy collectors	4,392 00	1 deputy collector	75 00
7 inspectors	6,812 50	1 deputy collector	60 00
1 clerk	900 00		
		BURLINGTON, N. J.	
NIAGARA, N. Y.			
		1 collector	634 62
1 collector	2,500 00		
1 deputy collector and inspector	1,800 00	**PHILADELPHIA, PA.**	
1 deputy collector and inspector	1,500 00		
6 deputy collectors and inspectors	5,475 00	1 collector, (9 months)	4,455 00
1 deputy collector and inspector	687 50	1 collector, (3 months)	1,500 00
3 deputy collectors and inspectors	1,650 00	2 deputy collectors	6,000 00
1 special inspector	1,460 00	1 cashier	2,500 00
1 temporary inspector	730 00	1 assistant cashier	1,800 00
1 temporary inspector	667 50	2 clerks	3,600 00
3 deputy collectors	2,737 50	1 clerk, at $2,500 per annum	302 19
1 clerk	900 00	2 clerks	3,200 00
1 deputy collector	540 00	9 clerks	10,630 00
1 female examiner	546 50	11 clerks	13,297 31
1 deputy collector and watchman	1,200 00	1 clerk, at $1,200 per annum	655 43
1 deputy collector and watchman	912 50	1 assistant collector, Camden, N. J.	1,500 00
4 inspectors	3,650 00	1 messenger at custom-house	912 50
2 inspectors	1,460 00	1 porter	912 50
1 inspector	150 00	1 fireman	912 50
2 temporary inspectors	130 00	2 night watchmen	1,947 00
1 temporary inspector	52 00	1 surveyor at Chester	500 00
		54 day inspectors	78,752 00
BUFFALO CREEK, N. Y.		11 temporary inspectors	15,892 00
		2 temporary inspectors	232 00
1 collector	2,500 00	1 temporary inspector	112 00
1 deputy collector	2,000 00	1 messenger to inspectors	912 50
1 deputy at Grand Trunk Railway	1,460 00	1 captain night inspectors	1,460 00
4 deputy collectors	4,485 00	1 lieutenant night inspectors	1,200 00
2 deputy collectors	2,009 50	30 night inspectors	32,431 00
1 cashier	1,800 00	7 temporary inspectors	7,599 00
4 clerks	4,830 00	2 temporary inspectors	174 00
1 inspector	1,460 00	1 temporary inspector	24 00
20 inspectors	21,900 00	1 United States weigher	2,000 00
1 inspector	424 00	1 clerk	1,500 00
1 janitor	600 00	3 assistant weighers	3,600 00
1 fireman	600 00	6 beamsmen	6,570 00
1 watchman, U. S. depository	834 00	4 temporary beamsmen	4,371 00
		1 foreman to laborers	912 50
DUNKIRK, N. Y.		2 gaugers	2,970 00
		1 temporary gauger	1,485 00
1 collector	1,579 46	1 measurer	1,485 00
1 special deputy collector	912 50	1 assistant measurer	210 00
3 inspectors	2,015 00	1 inspector at Lazaretto	500 00
		1 inspector at Marcus Hook	547 50
NEWARK, N. J.		1 inspector at Bristol	547 50
		1 naval officer	5,000 00
1 collector	927 27	1 deputy naval officer	2,500 00
1 deputy collector	1,460 00	2 clerks	3,200 00
1 inspector	1,460 00	2 clerks	2,800 00

23 F.

Statement of the number of persons employed for the collection of customs, &c.—Continued.

District, number of persons, and occupation.	Agg. compensation.	District, number of persons, and occupation.	Agg. compensation.
PHILADELPHIA, PA.—Continued.		**BALTIMORE, MD.—Continued.**	
4 clerks	$5,200 00	5 clerks	$4,452 71
1 messenger	912 50	1 clerk	1,583 32
1 surveyor	5,239 23	7 clerks	8,400 00
1 deputy surveyor	2,500 00	1 superintendent	1,166 68
1 clerk	1,500 00	3 messengers	1,931 37
1 clerk	1,400 00	2 porters	1,825 00
1 clerk, at $1.300 per annum	650 00	45 inspectors	59,580 00
1 admeasurement clerk	1,460 00	1 inspectress	863 31
2 admeasurement clerks	2,190 00	1 inspector, Havre de Grace	400 00
1 marker	912 50	Special day inspectors during the year	3,136 00
1 measurer	912 50	1 captain of watch	1,460 00
1 general appraiser	3,000 00	1 lieutenant of the watch	1,200 00
1 clerk	1,384 44	6 watchmen	6,570 00
1 messenger	912 50	40 night inspectors	39,279 00
1 local appraiser	3,000 00	Special night inspectors during the year	3,711 00
2 assistant appraisers	5,000 00	1 secret aid to the revenue	1,095 00
1 examiner	1,800 00	1 weigher	1,905 83
2 examiners	3,000 00	1 measurer	1,500 00
2 examiners	2,800 00	2 gaugers	3,000 00
1 clerk	1,600 00	2 markers	1,825 00
3 clerks	4,200 00	1 messenger, (barge office)	912 50
9 packers	9,033 75	1 clerk-to weigher	1,400 00
1 watchman	821 25	1 clerk to weigher	1,200 00
1 laborer	821 25	1 messenger to weigher	821 25
1 messenger	912 50	Laborers in weigher's department during the year	29,868 43
1 store-keeper of the port	1,499 50	13 assistant weighers	15,534 79
1 clerk to store-keeper	1,361 96	2 assistant measurers	2,190 00
1 first foreman	892 50	1 superintendent public stores	1,800 00
1 second foreman	912 50	1 clerk and store-keeper	1,657 51
1 day watchman	912 50	1 clerk	1,200 00
1 night watchman	912 50	1 foreman	200 00
1 marker	890 12	4 porters	4,469 75
1 sampler	1,000 00	1 messenger	1,095 00
1 superintendent warehouses	1,600 00	1 engineer	1,000 00
9 assistant store-keepers	13,124 00	1 fireman	912 50
1 store-keeper	296 00	21 store-keepers private bonded warehouses, paid by proprietors private bonded warehouses	27,740 00
2 store-keepers	732 00	1 general appraiser	3,000 00
1 clerk for weigher's books	1,400 00	1 clerk	1,400 00
4 bargemen	3,650 00	2 local appraisers	6,000 00
1 special examiner of drugs	1,000 00	1 clerk	1,800 00
ERIE, PA.		4 examiners	6,000 00
1 collector	1,000 00	4 clerks	5,600 00
1 deputy collector and inspector	1,450 00	1 clerk	1,200 00
1 deputy collector and inspector	766 00	1 foreman openers and packers	1,200 00
1 temporary inspector	777 00	4 openers and packers	4,015 00
1 temporary inspector	396 00	4 porters	3,683 00
1 temporary inspector	476 00	1 messenger	912 50
1 temporary inspector	327 00	1 deputy naval officer	2,500 00
1 temporary inspector	240 00	1 clerk	1,800 00
PITTSBURGH, PA.		1 clerk	1,600 00
1 surveyor	1,400 00	5 clerks	4,125 00
1 surveyor's clerk	900 00	1 clerk	1,013 33
1 messenger and watchman	638 75	1 messenger	912 50
DELAWARE, DEL.		1 deputy surveyor	2,500 00
1 collector	2,408 48	1 clerk	1,495 99
4 deputy collectors and inspectors	3,480 00	1 clerk	1,500 00
2 inspectors	1,375 00	1 aid to surveyor	1,460 00
1 messenger	365 00	1 clerk	1,314 00
4 revenue boatmen	1,280 00	1 clerk	485 68
1 storekeeper	400 00	1 messenger	912 50
BALTIMORE, MD.		**ANNAPOLIS, MD.**	
2 deputy collectors	5,533 33	1 collector	1,189 77
1 deputy collector at Havre de Grace	1,200 00	1 surveyor	258 55
1 auditor	1,011 11	1 surveyor	52 08
1 cashier	2,500 00	1 temporary inspector	45 00
1 assistant cashier	1,800 00	1 boatman	33 00
1 clerk	1,849 99	1 boatman	15 00
8 clerks	13,817 56	2 boatmen	160 00
3 clerks	3,935 53	2 laborers	12 00
4 clerks	5,699 99	**TOWN CREEK, MD.**	
		1 surveyor	150 00

Statement of the number of persons employed for the collection of customs, &c.—Continued.

District, number of persons, and occupation.	Agg. compensation.	District, number of persons, and occupation.	Agg. compensation.
EASTERN MARYLAND.		**ALBEMARLE, N. C.—Continued.**	
1 deputy collector	$1,460 00	2 boat-hands	$480 00
1 deputy collector	1,200 00	1 coast-inspector	365 00
1 collector	1,200 00	**PAMLICO, N. C.**	
GEORGETOWN, D. C.		1 collector	1,694 84
1 collector	1,307 61	1 deputy collector	1,460 00
2 deputy collectors and inspectors	2,400 00	2 deputy collectors and inspectors	2,920 00
1 inspector	1,200 00	1 deputy collector and inspector	730 00
1 deputy inspector	200 00	2 boatmen	600 00
1 laborer	600 00	1 inspector	360 00
		2 revenue boatmen	600 00
ALEXANDRIA, VA.		**BEAUFORT, N. C.**	
1 collector	731 20		
1 deputy collector	1,500 00	1 collector	1,374 50
2 inspectors	2,160 00	1 inspector	774 00
1 janitor	600 00	1 gauger	4 74
		4 inspectors, (temporary)	357 00
RICHMOND, VA.		4 watchmen	372 00
1 collector	2,575 38	1 boatman	300 00
1 deputy collector	1,800 00		
3 inspectors	4,380 00	**WILMINGTON, N. C.**	
1 clerk	1,460 00	1 collector	2,500 00
1 janitor	912 50	1 deputy collector	2,000 00
1 watchman	730 00	1 clerk	1,500 00
		8 inspectors	9,100 00
YORKTOWN, VA.		1 weigher, gauger, &c	666 00
1 collector	693 73	1 messenger and store-keeper	1,111 00
1 deputy collector and inspector	1,338 00	4 boatmen	1,440 00
1 special deputy collector	780 00	**GEORGETOWN, S. C.**	
PETERSBURGH, VA.		1 collector	694 95
		1 inspector	1,095 00
1 collector	620 33	2 boatmen	1,200 00
1 deputy and clerk	1,800 00		
1 inspector	1,460 00	**CHARLESTON, S. C.**	
1 janitor	147 58		
1 porter and messenger	532 50	1 collector	6,410 00
		1 deputy collector	2,200 00
NORFOLK AND PORTSMOUTH, VA.		2 clerks	3,200 00
		1 clerk	1,500 00
1 collector	3,163 50	2 clerks	2,800 00
1 deputy collector	1,800 00	1 clerk	1,300 00
2 clerks	3,000 00	5 day inspectors	7,300 00
8 inspectors	11,680 00	2 day inspectors	2,856 00
2 night inspectors	2,190 00	1 day inspector	1,216 00
1 watchman	862 50	2 temporary inspectors	240 00
1 messenger	600 00	5 night inspectors	4,562 50
4 boatmen	1,920 00	1 night inspector	860 00
1 measurer	407 88	2 temporary inspectors	150 00
1 weigher	696 02	2 watchmen	1,460 00
		2 watchmen	1,300 00
CHERRYSTONE, VA.		2 weighers, measurers, and gaugers	1,992 92
1 collector	1,106 39	2 storekeepers	2,355 00
1 deputy collector and inspector	1,460 00	4 messengers and porters	3,060 00
1 deputy collector and inspector	791 00	4 boatmen	2,920 00
2 revenue boatmen	694 00	2 appraisers	3,000 00
2 revenue boatmen	139 50		
1 revenue boatman	300 00	**BEAUFORT, S. C.**	
		1 collector	1,271 72
WHEELING, W. VA.		1 deputy collector and inspector	213 06
1 surveyor	1,206 41		
1 watchman	600 00	**SAVANNAH, GA.**	
PARKERSBURGH, W. VA.		1 collector	4,000 00
		1 deputy collector	2,500 00
1 surveyor	350 00	1 auditor	2,000 00
		1 book-keeper	1,800 00
ALBEMARLE, N. C.		1 clerk	1,600 00
		4 clerks	6,000 00
1 collector	1,301 53	1 clerk	1,200 00
1 deputy and clerk	1,000 00	1 clerk	1,000 00
1 deputy collector	1,460 00	2 appraisers	3,000 00
1 deputy collector	1,095 00	1 appraiser's clerk	1,500 00

Statement of the number of persons employed for the collection of customs, &c.—Continued.

District, number of persons, and occupation.	Agg. compensation.	District, number of persons, and occupation.	Agg. compensation.
SAVANNAH, GA.—Continued.		**MOBILE, ALA.**	
11 inspectors	$16,060 00	1 collector	$6,250 00
7 temporary inspectors	7,665 00	1 deputy collector	2,500 00
1 weigher and gauger	1,500 00	1 cashier	3,000 00
20 night-watchmen	18,250 00	1 auditor	1,800 00
1 store-keeper	900 00	1 clerk	1,575 00
1 assistant store-keeper	1,095 00	1 clerk	375 00
1 janitor	1,000 00	1 admeasurer	1,460 00
4 boatmen	2,880 00	1 superintendent	1,460 00
1 appraiser's porter	360 00	7 inspectors	3,300 00
1 surveyor	1,000 00	10 inspectors	6,561 00
1 surveyor's clerk	1,200 00	1 clerk, weigher, gauger, &c	1,800 00
		2 night inspectors	2,190 00
BRUNSWICK, GA.		1 bargeman	600 00
		1 night watchman	1,095 00
1 collector	3,000 00	1 temporary watchman	150 00
9 deputy collectors and inspectors	9,191 00	1 day watchman	1,005 00
1 inspector	1,092 00	1 messenger, (3 months)	150 00
6 boatmen	2,520 00	1 temporary clerk	864 00
		Sundry inspectors	1,860 00
ST. MARY'S, GA.			
		PEARL RIVER, MISS.	
1 collector	1,327 67		
1 deputy collector	1,324 00	1 collector	256 00
2 boatmen	238 33	1 deputy collector	360 00
		2 oarsmen	720 00
FERNANDINA, FLA.			
		VICKSBURGH, MISS.	
1 collector	1,280 52		
1 deputy collector and inspector	1,460 00	1 collector	500 00
1 inspector	730 00		
1 inspector	315 00	**NATCHEZ, MISS.**	
1 boatman and porter	420 00		
3 boatmen	1,080 00	1 collector	529 80
1 boatman	37 00		
		NEW ORLEANS, LA.	
ST. JOHN'S, FLA.			
		1 collector	6,400 00
1 deputy and inspector	1,460 00	3 deputy collectors	9,000 00
2 inspectors	2,190 00	1 auditor	3,000 00
4 boatmen	1,440 00	1 cashier	2,500 00
		1 assistant cashier	2,000 00
ST. AUGUSTINE, FLA.		1 entry clerk	2,500 00
		2 clerks	4,000 00
1 collector	534 87	16 clerks	23,800 00
2 inspectors	2,920 00	6 clerks	10,200 00
4 boatmen	1,440 00	9 clerks	14,400 00
		7 clerks	10,500 00
KEY WEST, FLA.		1 clerk	1,400 00
		2 clerks	2,600 00
1 collector	2,793 23	3 clerks	3,600 00
1 special deputy collector	1,460 00	1 clerk	1,100 00
3 inspectors	2,636 00	1 clerk	720 00
2 clerks	1,852 00	1 messenger	1,100 00
4 boatmen	1,440 00	2 messengers	2,000 00
		2 messengers	1,800 00
ST. MARK'S, FLA.		1 messenger	800 00
		1 messenger	500 00
1 collector	1,144 00	1 engineer	1,460 00
3 deputy collectors and inspectors	4,380 00	1 carpenter	1,460 00
6 boatmen	2,160 00	7 laborers	7,665 00
		8 watchmen	7,300 00
APALACHICOLA, FLA.		65 inspectors	104,900 00
		23 river inspectors	25,185 00
1 collector	1,200 00	40 night inspectors	43,800 00
1 deputy collector	1,460 00	21 boatmen	15,120 00
4 boatmen	1,200 00	1 superintendent	2,500 00
4 officers revenue-cutter "Petrel"	5,496 00	1 clerk	1,500 00
Seamen and boys	3,360 00	19 store-keepers	27,740 00
6 light-house keepers	3,120 00	2 chief laborers	2,000 00
		12 laborers	8,640 00
PENSACOLA, FLA.		2 messengers	1,000 00
		2 weighers	4,000 00
1 collector	3,060 00	9 deputy weighers	13,500 00
2 deputies	2,190 00	2 gaugers	3,000 00
4 inspectors	4,380 00	1 measurer	1,500 00
1 inspector	1,460 00	1 clerk	1,500 00
4 boatmen	1,440 00	41 laborers	27,060 00

Statement of the number of persons employed for the collection of customs, &c.—Continued.

District, number of persons, and occupation.	Agg. compensation.	District, number of persons, and occupation.	Agg. compensation.
NEW ORLEANS, LA.—Continued.		**BRAZOS DE SANTIAGO, TEX.**	
1 messenger	$660 00	1 collector	$4,500 00
1 general appraiser	3,000 00	1 deputy collector and cashier	2,500 00
2 appraisers	6,000 00	1 deputy collector and book-keeper	2,500 00
1 assistant appraiser	2,500 00	1 deputy collector and entry clerk	2,000 00
6 clerks	10,200 00	1 bond clerk	2,000 00
6 clerks	10,200 00	1 clerk and inspector	1,600 00
1 sampler	1,500 00	1 storekeeper, weigher, gauger and	1,800 00
2 chief laborers	2,000 00	measurer.	
18 laborers	16,200 00	1 messenger	600 00
3 messengers	2,160 00	1 deputy collector and inspector	2,400 00
1 clerk	1,400 00	1 deputy collector and inspector	2,000 00
1 naval officer	5,000 00	1 deputy collector and inspector	1,327 78
1 deputy naval officer	2,500 00	1 boatman	480 00
2 clerks	4,000 00	1 inspectress	1,095 00
4 clerks	7,200 00		
1 clerk	1,500 00	**PASO DEL NORTE, TEX.**	
2 clerks	2,400 00		
1 messenger	720 00	1 collector	2,000 00
1 surveyor	4,500 00	1 special deputy collector	1,500 00
1 special deputy surveyor	2,500 00	3 deputy collectors	4,500 00
2 clerks	3,600 00	4 deputy collectors	4,000 00
1 clerk	1,500 00	1 deputy collector	300 00
3 clerks	3,600 00	1 clerk and inspector	1,000 00
1 clerk	1,000 00	6 mounted inspectors	7,665 00
2 clerks	1,440 00		
1 clerk	1,095 00	**MEMPHIS, TENN.**	
6 messengers	3,960 00		
		1 surveyor	4,160 05
TÉCHÉ, LA.		1 clerk	1,200 00
		1 messenger	600 00
1 collector	845 05	1 special inspector	548 00
5 inspectors	5,600 00		
		NASHVILLE, TENN.	
GALVESTON, TEX.			
		1 surveyor	2,212 53
1 collector	4,718 00		
1 deputy collector and clerk	2,000 00	**PADUCAH, KY.**	
1 deputy collector and clerk	1,800 00		
5 clerks	8,000 00	1 surveyor	386 85
2 deputy collectors and inspectors	3,000 00		
1 weigher and gauger	1,500 00	**LOUISVILLE, KY.**	
1 surveyor	1,000 00		
8 day inspectors	11,680 00	1 surveyor	3,000 00
4 night inspectors	5,840 00	1 appraiser	650 00
2 store-keepers	2,920 00	1 customs clerk	1,500 00
1 assistant store-keeper	1,252 00	1 inspector	1,460 00
1 night watchman	1,095 00	1 recording clerk	1,100 00
1 messenger	730 00	1 clerk	163 33
1 porter	730 00	1 clerk and inspector	912 50
6 boatmen	5,400 00		
1 boatman	600 00	**PORTLAND AND JEFFERSONVILLE.**	
SALURIA, TEX.		1 porter	720 00
1 collector	4,002 73	**CINCINNATI, OHIO.**	
1 surveyor	600 00		
1 deputy collector	1,500 00	1 surveyor	3,000 00
1 deputy collector	501 36	1 deputy surveyor	2,000 00
1 deputy collector	1,331 52	1 book-keeper	1,500 00
2 inspectors	2,920 00	1 weigher, gauger, &c	1,460 00
2 mounted inspectors	2,920 00	1 clerk	1,252 00
1 inspector	600 00	1 clerk	1,000 00
1 store-keeper	860 00	5 store-keepers	2,904 16
1 store-keeper	268 34	1 janitor	480 00
1 store-keeper	335 00	1 appraiser	1,091 66
1 boatman	600 00		
1 porter and messenger	240 00		
CORPUS CHRISTI, TEX.		**CUYAHOGA, OHIO.**	
1 collector	1,500 00	1 collector	2,500 00
1 special deputy collector and clerk	1,659 79	7 deputy collectors	8,570 00
1 clerk	1,500 00	1 deputy collector	480 00
6 deputy collectors and inspectors	8,760 00	1 deputy collector	300 00
2 inspectors	2,920 00	2 lumber inspectors	2,920 00
3 inspectors	505 00	1 weigher and gauger	912 50
8 mounted inspectors	10,628 00	3 clerks	3,612 50
2 store-keepers	1,110 00	1 watchman	912 50
1 porter	420 00	1 porter and watchman	730 00

Statement of the number of persons employed for the collection of customs, &c.—Continued.

District, number of persons, and occupation.	Agg. compensation.	District, number of persons, and occupation.	Agg. compensation.
SANDUSKY, OHIO.		**NEW ALBANY, IND.**	
1 collector	$2,200 00	1 surveyor	$514 38
1 deputy collector	1,000 00		
3 deputy collectors	1,812 00	**EVANSVILLE, IND.**	
3 temporary clerks	150 00	1 surveyor	3,349 85
		1 clerk	1,000 00
MIAMI, OHIO.		1 storekeeper	495 85
1 collector	2,500 00	1 appraiser	750 00
2 deputy collectors	2,800 00		
4 inspectors	1,972 00	**CHICAGO, ILL.**	
1 messenger	300 00	1 collector	4,648 79
		1 deputy collector and clerk	2,832 88
DETROIT, MICH.		1 deputy collector and clerk	1,774 73
1 collector	2,900 00	1 deputy collector and clerk	1,500 00
1 special deputy and clerk	2,250 00	1 deputy collector and clerk	1,300 00
1 deputy and clerk	1,500 00	1 deputy collector and clerk	1,000 00
1 deputy and clerk	1,400 00	1 surveyor	300 00
1 inspector	1,400 00	1 auditor	1,774 73
3 inspectors	3,900 00	1 cashier	1,400 00
2 inspectors	2,000 00	4 clerks	5,200 00
1 inspector	912 50	1 clerk	250 00
2 inspectors	1,600 00	1 appraiser	2,192 93
1 inspector	300 00	2 inspectors	2,920 00
3 inspectors	60.00	9 inspectors	11,497 50
1 inspector	120 00	4 inspectors	4,380 00
1 inspector	90 00	1 inspector	266 00
23 inspectors	13,597 88	4 inspectors	3,120 00
1 inspectress	360 00	1 inspector	183 00
3 deputy collectors	1,208 00	2 watchmen	1,825 00
1 porter and messenger	900 00	1 porter	600 00
4 inspectors*	4,000 00	1 laborer	600 00
		1 special inspector	1,460 00
HURON, MICH.		1 store-keeper	1,200 00
1 collector	2,500 00	1 store-keeper	1,277 50
1 special deputy collector	2,000 00	1 store-keeper	738 00
1 cashier and book-keeper	1,500 00	1 store-keeper	547 50
1 bond and entry clerk	1,200 00	1 store-keeper	378 00
1 marine clerk	1,095 00	1 store-keeper	255 00
1 general clerk	1,095 00		
1 deputy in charge of Grand Trunk Crossing	1,460 00	**GALENA, ILL.**	
4 inspectors†	4,380 00	1 surveyor	624 64
4 inspectors at Grand Trunk Crossing	4,380 00	1 clerk	500 00
1 inspector at Grand Trunk Crossing	821.25		
1 deputy at Great Western Crossing	912 50	**QUINCY, ILL.**	
1 night deputy at Great Western Crossing	720 00	1 surveyor	521 66
1 inspectress at Great Western Crossing	240 00	**CAIRO, ILL.**	
4 special inspectors	3,650 00	1 surveyor and acting collector	3,276 85
1 watchman and porter	730 00	1 inspector	939 00
1 deputy collector at Bay City	1,095 00		
1 deputy collector at St. Clair	800 00	**ALTON, ILL.**	
1 deputy collector at Marine City	800 00	1 surveyor	372 47
1 deputy collector at East Saginaw	600 00		
1 deputy collector at Algonac	420 00	**MILWAUKEE, WIS.**	
1 deputy collector at Alpena	360 00	1 collector	2,900 00
1 deputy collector at Lexington	180 00	2 deputy collectors	3,000 00
1 deputy collector at Sand Beach	160 00	3 inspectors	3,285 00
2 inspectors at Toronto, Ontario‡	2,372 50	2 deputy collectors	600 00
1 inspector at Stratford, Ontario‡	1,460 00	1 deputy collector	200 00
		1 deputy collector	150 00
SUPERIOR, MICH.		1 deputy collector	600 00
1 collector	2,900 00	1 janitor	910 00
10 deputy collectors	6,051 00	1 appraiser	677 75
2 aids to revenue	1,704 00		
1 special inspector	459 00	**DULUTH, WIS.**	
		1 surveyor	448 40
MICHIGAN, MICH.			
1 collector	2,852 39		
1 deputy collector	1,114 13		
19 deputy collectors	5,012 57		

* Paid by the Great Western Railway.   † Paid by the Grand Trunk Railway through custom-house.

Statement of the number of persons employed for the collection of customs, &c.—Continued

District, number of persons, and occupation.	Agg. compensation.	District, number of persons, and occupation.	Agg. compensation.
DUBUQUE, IOWA.		**SAN FRANCISCO, CAL.**—Continued.	
1 surveyor	$542 80	3 watchmen	$3,240 00
1 janitor	600 00	1 janitor	1,080 00
		1 deputy collector, *ex officio* store-keeper	3,000 00
BURLINGTON, IOWA.		3 clerks	2,600 00
		5 clerks	9,000 00
1 surveyor	431 05	2 messengers	2,160 00
		2 watchmen	2,160 00
ST. LOUIS, MO.		1 superintendent	1,200 00
		7 laborers	7,560 00
1 surveyor and acting collector	6,000 00	6 temporary laborers	4,752 00
1 clerk and special deputy	2,800 00	9 store-keepers	14,782 50
1 clerk and deputy	2,100 00	2 appraisers	6,000 00
2 clerks and deputies	3,222 25	2 assistant appraisers	5,000 00
1 clerk	1,700 00	1 examiner	2,250 00
1 clerk	1,500 00	1 examiner	2,000 00
1 clerk	1,200 00	1 examiner of drugs	2,000 00
1 appraiser	2,025 00	1 clerk	1,700 00
2 inspectors	2,920 00	1 messenger	1,200 00
1 porter	950 00	1 superintendent laborers	1,080 00
1 porter	800 00	5 laborers	5,400 00
		3 temporary laborers	2,376 00
ST. JOSEPH, MO.		1 surveyor	4,000 00
		1 deputy surveyor	3,000 00
1 surveyor	262 00	1 deputy surveyor	2,500 00
		1 clerk	1,800 00
PUGET SOUND, WASHINGTON TER.		1 messenger	1,080 00
		3 district officers	5,400 00
1 collector	3,400 00	29 inspectors	45,240 00
1 deputy collector	2,500 00	5 temporary inspectors	6,760 00
1 deputy collector	1,800 00	1 night inspector	1,560 00
1 clerk	1,600 00	1 night inspector	1,400 00
6 inspectors	8,760 00	17 night inspectors	20,400 00
1 inspectress	550 00	5 temporary night inspectors	6,000 00
1 watchman	900 00	1 inspectress	912 50
4 boatmen	3,600 00	2 inspectors, Mexican frontier	2,400 00
		6 inspectors	6,000 00
OREGON, OREG.		7 inspectors	4,200 00
		1 inspector	300 00
1 collector	3,038 82	4 weighers	8,000 00
1 deputy collector	1,800 00	1 gauger	2,000 00
1 deputy collector	1,500 00	6 laborers	6,000 00
1 inspector	1,200 00	30 temporary laborers	37,400 00
1 inspector	900 00	2 boarding officers	3,200 00
5 temporary inspectors	5,000 00	6 bargemen	6,480 00
Sundry temporary inspectors	252 00	1 naval officer	4,500 00
		1 deputy naval officer	3,125 00
WILLAMETTE, OREG.		1 cashier	2,200 00
		1 clerk	2,100 00
1 collector	2,047 19	2 clerks	3,750 00
1 deputy collector	1,500 00	1 clerk	1,800 00
1 deputy collector	1,350 00	1 clerk	1,750 00
1 appraiser	1,400 00	3 clerks	1,600 00
1 clerk	187 50	1 messenger	1,080 00
1 weigher and gauger	516 66	1 captain revenue service	2,500 00
1 inspector	881 25	1 lieutenant revenue service	1,800 00
1 inspector	572 70	1 lieutenant revenue service	1,500 00
1 porter and messenger	413 33	1 lieutenant revenue service	1,200 00
Sundry temporary inspectors	380 00	1 chief engineer	1,800 00
Sundry temporary laborers	218 40	1 assistant engineer	1,500 00
		1 assistant engineer	1,200 00
SAN FRANCISCO, CAL.		1 special agent	2,920 00
		1 special agent	2,190 90
1 collector	6,000 00		
1 auditor	3,625 00	**ALASKA.**	
2 deputy collectors	6,000 00		
1 cashier	3,000 00	No report.	
1 clerk	3,000 00		
3 clerks	6,600 00	**MINNESOTA, MINN.**	
4 clerks	8,000 00		
4 clerks	7,500 00	1 collector	2,500 00
12 clerks	21,600 00	1 deputy collector	1,200 00
3 clerks	4,800 00	1 special deputy collector, clerk, and	
1 deputy collector, San Diego	3,000 00	inspector	1,277 50
1 deputy collector, Vallejo	1,500 00	2 inspectors	1,333 00
3 messengers	3,240 00	3 mounted inspectors	3,285 00

Statement showing the amount of moneys expended for collecting the revenue from customs at each custom-house in the United States previous to June 30, 1871, not heretofore reported, per act of March 3, 1869.

District or port.	Period reported.		Amount.
	From—	To—	
Aroostook, Me	July 1, 1870	Mar. 31, 1871	$8,173 28
Passamaquoddy, Me	July 1, 1870	Mar. 31, 1871	18,134 29
Machias, Me	July 1, 1870	Feb. 28, 1871	2,833 92
Frenchman's Bay, Me	April 1, 1870	Sept. 30, 1870	3,340 24
Bangor, Me	April 1, 1870	Mar. 14, 1871	17,705 20
Castine, Me	July 1, 1870	Mar. 31, 1871	6,540 84
Belfast, Me	April 1, 1870	Mar. 14, 1871	7,427 26
Waldoborough, Me	July 1, 1870	Feb. 12, 1871	5,223 36
Wiscasset, Me	July 1, 1870	Dec. 31, 1870	1,665 41
Bath, Me	Feb. 22, 1870	Dec. 31, 1870	9,300 92
Portland and Falmouth, Me	July 1, 1870	Mar. 31, 1871	67,124 31
Saco, Me	Sept. 1, 1869	Mar. 18, 1870	1,618 31
Kennebunk, Me	July 1, 1870	Dec. 31, 1870	546 50
York, Me	July 1, 1870	Mar. 31, 1871	978 61
Portsmouth, N. H	July 1, 1870	Mar. 31, 1371	7,304 47
Vermont, Vt	July 1, 1870	June 30, 1871	99,079 30
Newburyport, Mass	April 1, 1870	Mar. 31, 1871	6,404 65
Gloucester, Mass	April 1, 1870	Dec. 31, 1870	10,936 00
Salem and Beverly, Mass	April 1, 1870	June 30, 1871	10,415 29
Marblehead, Mass	July 1, 1870	Dec. 31, 1870	1,930 80
Boston and Charlestown, Mass	April 1, 1870	Dec. 31, 1870	442,318 31
Plymouth, Mass	July 1, 1870	Mar. 31, 1871	2,755 95
Barnstable, Mass	July 1, 1870	Dec. 31, 1870	4,459 58
New Bedford, Mass	July 1, 1870	Mar. 31, 1871	6,734 97
Fall River, Mass	July 1, 1870	Mar. 31, 1871	4,842 19
Edgartown, Mass	July 1, 1870	Mar. 31, 1871	4,729 32
Nantucket, Mass	July 1, 1870	Mar. 31, 1871	1,272 48
Providence, R. I	April 1, 1870	Dec. 31, 1870	16,556 94
Bristol and Warren, R. I	July 1, 1870	April 4, 1871	1,468 91
Newport, R. I	July 1, 1870	Mar. 31, 1871	5,638 77
Stonington, Conn	July 1, 1870	June 30, 1871	1,511 63
New London, Conn	July 1, 1870	June 30, 1871	5,442 40
Middletown, Conn	July 1, 1870	Dec. 31, 1870	1,510 72
New Haven, Conn	July 1, 1870	Mar. 31, 1871	17,159 05
Fairfield, (Bridgeport,) Conn	Jan. 1, 1870	Mar. 31, 1871	3,046 09
Sag Harbor, N. Y	July 1, 1870	Mar. 31, 1871	860 76
New York, N. Y	May 1, 1870	Feb. 28, 1871	1,711,954 26
Albany, N. Y	April 1, 1870	Mar. 31, 1871	7,601 19
Champlain, N. Y	July 1, 1870	Mar. 31, 1871	21,700 01
Oswegatchie, N. Y	July 1, 1870	June 30, 1871	30,124 38
Cape Vincent, N. Y	July 1, 1870	Mar. 13, 1871	13,455 31
Oswego, N. Y	July 1, 1870	April 30, 1871	42,817 85
Genesee, N. Y	April 1, 1870	Mar. 31, 1871	19,795 19
Niagara, N. Y	July 1, 1870	Sept. 30, 1870	25,819 97
Buffalo Creek, N. Y	April 1, 1870	Mar. 31, 1871	49,196 05
Dunkirk, N. Y	April 1, 1870	Mar. 31, 1871	3,548 64
Newark, N. J	April 1, 1870	Dec. 31, 1870	2,703 46
Perth Amboy, N. J	July 1, 1870	....(*).....	....
Little Egg Harbor, N. J	July 1, 1870	Sept. 30, 1870	1,362 70
Great Egg Harbor, N. J	July 1, 1870	Dec. 31, 1870	906 06
Burlington, N. J	July 1, 1870	June 30, 1871	232 38
Bridgeton, N. J	July 1, 1870	June 30, 1871	438 19
Philadelphia, Pa	July 1, 1870	Dec. 31, 1870	583,386 03
Erie, Pa	July 1, 1870	Mar. 31, 1871	5,711 34
Pittsburgh, Pa	July 1, 1870	Mar. 31, 1871	4,907 03
Delaware, Del	April 1, 1870	Mar. 31, 1871	8,495 38
Baltimore, Md	April 1, 1870	Mar. 31, 1871	343,779 41
Annapolis, Md	April 1, 1870	....(*).....	....
Town Creek, Md *	......	....	....
Eastern District, Md	July 1, 1870	Mar. 7, 1871	2,725 56
Georgetown, D. C	July 1, 1870	Mar. 31, 1871	3,815 84
Alexandria, Va	July 1, 1870	Mar. 31, 1871	3,400 74
Tappahannock, Va	Nov. 1, 1869	June 30, 1870	495 28
Richmond, Va	Jan. 1, 1870	Dec. 31, 1870	9,950 11
Yorktown, Va	July 1, 1870	Mar. 31, 1871	1,937 26
Petersburgh, Va	April 1, 1870	June 30, 1870	979 16
Norfolk and Portsmouth, Va	Jan. 1, 1870	Dec. 31, 1870	21,717 51
Cherrystone, Va	July 1, 1870	Mar. 20, 1871	2,261 06
Wheeling, W. Va	July 1, 1870	June 30, 1871	1,015 27
Parkersburgh, W. Va	July 1, 1870	June 30, 1871	370 84
Albemarle, N. C	July 1, 1870	....(*).....	....
Pamlico, N. C	July 1, 1870	....(*).....	....
Beaufort, N. C	July 1, 1870	Mar. 31, 1871	3,047 27
Wilmington, N. C	July 1, 1870	....(*).....	....

* No report.

Statement showing the expenses of collecting the revenue from customs, &c.—Continued.

District or port.	Period reported.		Amount.
	From—	To—	
Georgetown, S. C	April 1, 1870	June 30, 1870	$1, 445 50
Charleston, S. C	July 1, 1870	Jan. 6, 1871	27, 220 64
Beaufort, S. C *	Oct. 1, 1866	Mar. 3, 1867	3, 121 81
Savannah, Ga	Jan. 1, 1870	Mar. 31, 1870	18, 327 64
Brunswick, Ga	July 1, 1870	Dec. 31, 1870	7, 355 54
Saint Mary's, Ga	July 1, 1870	Mar. 31, 1871	2, 373 48
Fernandina, Fla	July 1, 1870	Dec. 31, 1870	4, 046 97
Saint John's, Fla	July 1, 1870	Mar. 31, 1871	4, 691 29
Saint Augustine, Fla	July 1, 1870	Mar. 31, 1871	3, 695 76
Key West, Fla	July 1, 1870	Sept. 30, 1870	7, 231 82
Saint Mark's, Fla	July 1, 1870	Mar. 31, 1871	4, 807 00
Apalachicola, Fla	July 1, 1870	Dec. 31, 1870	3, 508 52
Pensacola, Fla	April 1, 1870	Dec. 31, 1870	9, 126 64
Mobile, Ala	April 1, 1870	Dec. 31, 1870	41, 990 24
Selma, Ala †			
Pearl River, Miss †			
Vicksburgh, Miss	April 1, 1870	Jan. 29, 1871	777 54
Natchez, Miss	July 1, 1870	Mar. 31, 1871	399 55
New Orleans, La	July 1, 1870	June 30, 1870	555, 211 31
Teche, La	Oct. 1, 1869	Dec. 31, 1870	4, 833 20
Texas, Tex	Nov. 1, 1869	Mar. 31, 1871	85, 756 72
Saluria, Tex	April 1, 1870	Mar. 31, 1871	14, 088 74
Corpus Christi, Tex	April 1, 1870	Mar. 31, 1871	32, 663 15
Brazos de Santiago, Tex	April 1, 1870	Mar. 31, 1871	52, 497 70
Paso del Norte, Tex	Mar. 1, 1870	Dec. 31, 1870	8, 865 06
Memphis, Tenn	July 1, 1870	Dec. 31, 1870	2, 795 72
Nashville, Tenn	July 1, 1870	Sept. 30, 1870	143 63
Paducah, Ky	Oct. 24, 1865	Mar. 4, 1867	124 03
Louisville, Ky	April 1, 1870	Mar. 31, 1871	11, 583 00
Cincinnati, Ohio	July 1, 1870	June 30, 1871	76, 541 65
Cuyahoga, Ohio	April 1, 1870	Mar. 31, 1871	19, 021 08
Sandusky, Ohio	July 1, 1870	Mar. 31, 1871	3, 014 88
Miami, Ohio	July 1, 1870	Mar. 31, 1871	7, 750 65
Detroit, Mich	April 1, 1870	Mar. 31, 1871	40, 834 45
Huron, Mich	April 1, 1870	Mar. 31, 1871	36, 813 97
Superior, Mich	April 2, 1870	Dec. 31, 1870	8, 469 79
Michigan, Mich	July 1, 1870	Mar. 31, 1871	5, 838 63
New Albany, Ind	Oct. 1, 1869	.... (†)	
Evansville, Ind	July 1, 1870	Dec. 31, 1870	848 27
Chicago, Ill	July 1, 1870	Mar. 31, 1871	50, 008 92
Galena, Ill	July 1, 1870	June 30, 1871	910 49
Peoria, Ill	July 1, 1869	Mar. 12, 1870	244 03
Quincy, Ill	April 1, 1870	Mar. 1, 1871	504 65
Alton, Ill	July 1, 1870	June 30, 1871	553 28
Cairo, Ill	April 1, 1870	June 30, 1871	5, 340 67
Milwaukee, Wis	Jan. 1, 1870	Feb. 28, 1871	15, 397 41
Minnesota, Minn	July 1, 1870	Mar. 31, 1871	7, 724 76
Dubuque, Iowa	July 1, 1870	Dec. 31, 1870	536 12
Burlington, Iowa	July 1, 1869	June 30, 1870	846 33
Keokuk, Iowa	July 1, 1870	Dec. 31, 1870	339 97
Saint Louis, Mo	July 1, 1870	June 30, 1871	73, 979 45
Montana and Idaho	April 1, 1870	Sept. 30, 1870	800 00
Alaska, Alaska	Jan. 1, 1870	June 30, 1870	8, 202 54
Wrangel Island, Alaska	Jan. 1, 1869	.... (†)	
Puget Sound, Wash	June 1, 1870	Dec. 31, 1870	13, 134 33
Oregon, Oreg	July 1, 1869	June 30, 1870	18, 231 02
San Francisco, Cal	Feb. 21, 1870	June 30, 1870	130, 325 55
Total			5, 179, 862 15

* The report for this period was not included in statement for period ending March 31, 1870; no report received since that date.

† No report.

Statement showing the amount of moneys expended for the revenue-cutter service at each custom-house in the United States previous to June 30, 1871, not heretofore reported, per act of March 3, 1869.

District.	Period reported.		Amount.
	From—	To—	
Passamaquoddy, Me	July 1, 1870	Mar. 31, 1871	$10, 338 96
Castine, Me	July 1, 1870	Mar. 31, 1871	18, 011 09
Belfast, Me	Jan. 1, 1870	June 30, 1870	49 46
Waldoborough, Me	April 1, 1870	June 30, 1871	1, 738 99
Bath, Me	April 1, 1870	......(†)	
Portland and Falmouth, Me	July 1, 1870	June 30, 1871	48, 106 29
Portsmouth, N. H	July 1, 1870	Dec. 31, 1870	855 65
Boston and Charlestown, Mass	April 1, 1870	Mar. 31, 1871	58, 294 71
Plymouth, Mass	July 1, 1870	Dec. 31, 1870	303 00
New Bedford, Mass	Mar. 1, 1870	Mar. 31, 1871	24, 437 28
Edgartown, Mass	July 1, 1870	June 30, 1871	1, 635 12
Providence, R. I	April 1, 1870	Dec. 31, 1870	492 66
Newport, R. I	July 1, 1870	Mar. 31, 1871	25, 801 05
New London, Conn	July 1, 1870	Mar. 31, 1871	16, 860 10
New Haven, Conn	July 1, 1870	July 30, 1870	50 50
Sag Harbor, N. Y	July 1, 1870	Mar. 31, 1871	909 00
New York, N. Y.	April 1, 1870	Mar. 31, 1871	118, 351 76
Oswegatchie, N. Y	July 1, 1870	June 30, 1871	5, 615 85
Oswego, N. Y	July 1, 1870	June 30, 1871	24, 600 44
Buffalo Creek, N. Y.	July 1, 1870	June 30, 1871	4, 177 91
Philadelphia, Pa.	Jan. 1, 1870	June 30, 1871	5, 174 75
Erie, Pa	July 1, 1870	Dec. 31, 1870	15, 305 84
Delaware, Del	April 1, 1870	Mar. 31, 1871	55, 638 52
Baltimore, Md	April 1, 1870	Mar. 31, 1871	105, 211 75
Richmond, Va.*	May 1, 1865	Aug. 4, 1865	2, 452 40
Norfolk and Portsmouth, Va	April 20, 1870	June 30, 1870	382 46
Pamlico, N. C	April 1, 1870	June 30, 1870	7, 556 42
Beaufort, N. C.†			
Wilmington, N. C.	April 1, 1870	June 30, 1870	8, 419 43
Georgetown, S. C	Jan. 1, 1870	Dec. 31, 1870	4, 574 22
Charleston, S. C	July 1, 1870	June 30, 1871	20, 900 62
Savannah, Ga	Jan. 1, 1870	June 30, 1870	16, 513 35
Fernandina, Fla	July 1, 1870	June 30, 1871	16, 027 32
Key West, Fla.‡	July 1, 1870	Mar. 31, 1871	10, 931 40
Apalachicola, Fla.	July 1, 1870	Feb. 28, 1871	12, 555 46
Mobile, Ala	Jan. 1, 1870	Mar. 31, 1871	49, 733 20
New Orleans, La	Jan. 1, 1870	June 30, 1870	22, 612 48
Texas, Tex	Jan. 12, 1870	Oct. 1, 1870	21, 454 69
Saluria, Tex.†	Jan. 1, 1870		
Brazos de Santiago, Tex.†	Oct. 1, 1869		
Cuyahoga, Ohio	April 1, 1870	Sept. 30, 1870	14, 177 08
Detroit, Mich	July 1, 1870	Mar. 31, 1871	27, 440 45
Chicago, Ill	Oct. 1, 1869	Mar. 31, 1871	595 00
Milwaukee, Wis	July 1, 1870	Feb. 28, 1871	20, 207 13
Alaska, Alaska	July 1, 1870	Dec. 31, 1870	20, 917 11
Puget Sound, Wash	June 1, 1870	Mar. 31, 1871	35, 761 91
Oregon, Oreg.†			
San Francisco, Cal	Feb. 21, 1870	Sept. 30, 1870	99, 001 85
Total	....	....	834, 174 66

* The report for this period was not included in statement ending March 31, 1870; no report received since that date.   † No report.

‡ The report for 4th quarter 1870 not yet received, and not included in above period.

Statement of revenue collected from the beginning of the Government to June 30, 1871, from the following sources.

(By calendar years to 1843, and subsequently by fiscal years.)

Years.	Customs.	Internal revenue.	Direct taxes.	Postage.	Public lands.	Dividends and sales of bank stock and bonds.	Miscellaneous.	Net revenue.	Loans and treasury notes, &c.	Total receipts.
From Mar. 4, 1789, to Dec. 31, 1791	$4,399,473 09	$208,942 81					$19,440 10	$4,418,913 10	$5,791,112 56	$10,210,025 75
1792	3,443,070 85	337,705 70		$11,020 51		$8,028 00	9,918 65	3,669,960 31	5,070,806 46	8,740,766 77
1793	4,255,306 56	274,089 62		29,478 49		38,500 00	10,390 37	4,652,923 14	1,067,701 14	5,720,624 28
1794	4,801,065 28	337,755 36		29,400 84	$4,636 13	303,472 00	23,729 37	5,431,904 87	4,609,196 78	10,041,101 65
1795	5,588,461 26	475,289 60		72,909 84	83,540 60	160,000 00	5,917 97	6,114,534 59	3,305,268 20	9,419,802 79
1796	6,567,987 94	575,491 45		64,500 00	11,963 11	1,240,000 00	16,566 14	8,377,529 65	362,800 00	8,740,329 65
1797	7,549,649 65	644,357 95		39,500 00		385,220 00	30,379 29	8,688,720 99	70,135 41	8,758,916 40
1798	7,106,061 93	779,136 44	$734,223 97	41,000 00		79,920 00	18,692 81	7,900,495 80	308,574 27	8,209,070 07
1799	6,610,449 31	809,396 55	534,343 38	78,500 00		71,040 00	45,187 56	7,546,813 31	5,074,646 53	12,621,459 84
1800	9,080,932 73	1,048,643 43	206,565 44	79,500 00	443 75	71,040 00	74,712 10	10,848,749 10	1,602,435 04	12,451,184 14
1801	10,750,778 93	621,898 89	71,879 20	35,000 00	167,726 06	88,590 00	266,149 15	12,935,330 95	10,125 00	12,945,455 95
1802	12,438,235 74	215,179 69	50,198 44	11,427 96	188,628 02	1,327,560 00	177,905 86	14,995,793 95	5,597 36	15,001,391 31
1803	10,479,417 61	50,941 29	21,882 91	26,500 00	165,675 69		115,318 18	11,064,097 63		11,064,097 63
1804	11,098,565 33	21,747 15	21,763 86	21,342 50	487,526 00		112,375 53	11,826,307 38	9,532 64	11,835,840 02
1805	12,936,487 04	20,101 45	34,732 56	41,117 67	540,193 80		19,039 80	13,560,693 20	123,814 94	13,689,508 14
1806	14,667,698 17	13,051 40	19,159 21	3,614 73	765,245 73		10,004 19	15,559,931 07	48,897 71	15,608,828 78
1807	15,845,521 61	8,210 73	7,517 31		466,163 27		34,935 69	16,398,019 26		16,398,019 26
1808	16,363,550 58	4,044 39	12,448 68	37 70	647,939 06		21,802 35	17,062,661 93	1,882 16	17,062,544 09
1809	7,296,020 58	7,430 63	7,517 31		442,252 33		23,638 51	7,773,473 12	2,759,992 25	12,144,266 53
1810	8,583,309 31	2,295 95	12,448 68	85,039 70	696,548 82		84,476 84	9,384,214 28	8,309 05	14,431,838 14
1811	13,313,222 73	4,903 06	7,666 66	35,000 00	1,040,237 53		60,068 52	14,423,529 09	12,837,900 00	22,639,032 76
1812	8,958,777 53	4,755 04	859 22	45,000 00	710,427 78		41,125 47	9,801,132 76	26,184,435 00	40,534,844 95
1813	13,224,623 25	1,662,984 82	3,805 52	135,000 11	835,655 14		236,571 00	14,340,409 95	23,377,911 79	50,961,237 60
1814	5,998,772 08	4,678,059 07	2,219,497 36	19,787 74	1,135,971 09		119,399 81	11,181,625 16	35,264,320 78	50,171,421 82
1815	7,282,942 22	5,124,708 31	2,162,673 41	29,371 91	1,287,959 28		150,282 74	15,696,916 82	9,494,436 16	33,833,592 33
1816	36,306,874 88	2,678,100 77	4,253,635 09	20,070 00	1,717,985 03	202,428 30	123,994 61	47,676,985 66	734,542 59	34,605,663 37
1817	26,283,348 49	955,270 20	1,834,187 04		1,991,226 06	525,000 00	80,389 17	33,099,049 74	8,765 62	21,593,936 66
1818	17,176,385 00	229,593 63	264,333 36	71 32	2,606,564 77	675,000 00	31,547 71	21,585,171 04	2,291 00	19,373,760 72
1819	20,283,608 76	106,260 53	83,650 78	6,465 95	3,274,422 78	1,000,000 00	57,027 10	24,603,314 37	3,040,824 13	20,881,493 68
1820	15,005,612 15	69,027 63	31,586 82	516 91	1,635,871 61	105,000 00	54,872 49	17,840,669 55	5,000,324 00	24,605,665 37
1821	13,004,447 15	67,665 71	29,349 05	602 04	1,212,966 46	297,500 00	152,072 52	14,573,379 72		19,573,761 94
1822	17,589,761 94	34,242 17	20,961 56	110 69	1,803,581 54	350,000 00	452,355 15	20,232,427 94		20,232,427 94
1823	19,088,433 44	34,663 37	10,337 71		916,523 10	350,000 00	141,019 15	20,540,666 26	5,000,000 00	20,540,666 26
1824	17,878,325 71	25,771 35	6,201 96	469 56	984,418 15	367,500 00	127,603 60	19,381,212 79	5,000,000 00	24,381,212 66
1825	20,098,713 45	21,589 93	2,330 85	300 11	1,216,090 56	402,000 00	129,982 25	21,840,858 02		26,840,858 02
1826	23,341,331 77	19,885 68	6,638 76	101 00	1,393,784 09	420,000 00	94,289 52	25,260,434 21		25,260,434 21
1827	19,712,283 29	17,451 54	2,626 90	20 15	1,495,845 26	455,000 00	1,315,621 83	22,966,363 96		22,966,363 96
1828	23,205,523 64		2,218 81		1,018,308 75		65,106 34	24,763,629 23		24,763,629 23

Statement of revenue collected from the beginning of the Government to June 30, 1871, from the following sources—Continued.

(By calendar years to 1843, and subsequently by fiscal years.)

Years	Customs	Internal revenue	Direct taxes	Postage	Public lands	Dividends and sales of bank stock and bonus	Miscellaneous	Net revenue	Loans and treasury notes, &c.	Total receipts
1829	$22,681,965 91	$14,502 74	$11,335 05	$86 60	$1,517,175 13	$490,000 00	$112,561 95	$24,827,627 38		$24,827,627 38
1830	21,922,391 39	12,160 62	16,980 59	55 13	2,329,356 14	490,000 00	73,172 64	24,844,116 51		24,844,116 51
1831	24,224,441 77	6,933 51	10,506 01	561 02	3,210,815 48	490,000 00	583,563 03	28,526,820 82		28,526,820 82
1832	28,465,237 24	11,630 65	6,791 13	244 95	2,623,381 03	659,000 00	99,276 16	31,865,561 16		31,865,561 16
1833	29,032,508 91	2,759 00	394 12		3,967,682 55	610,285 00	334,796 67	33,948,426 25		33,948,426 25
1834	16,214,957 15	4,196 09	19 80	100 00	4,857,600 69	586,649 50	128,412 32	21,791,935 55		21,791,935 55
1835	19,391,310 59	10,459 48		893 00	14,757,600 75	569,280 83	696,279 13	35,430,087 10		35,430,087 10
1836	23,409,940 53	370 00	4,263 33	10 91	24,877,179 86	328,674 67	2,209,891 32	50,826,796 08		50,826,796 08
1837	11,169,290 39	5,493 84	1,687 70		6,776,236 52	1,375,965 44	5,562,190 32	24,890,864 69	$2,992,989 15	27,883,853 84
1838	16,158,800 36	2,467 27			3,081,939 47	4,512,102 22	2,517,252 42	26,303,361 74	12,716,820 86	39,019,382 60
1839	23,137,924 81	2,553 32	755 22		7,076,447 35		1,265,068 91	30,023,966 68	3,857,276 21	33,681,242 69
1840	13,499,502 17	1,682 25			3,292,285 58	1,774,513 80	874,662 28	19,442,646 08	5,589,547 51	25,032,193 59
1841	14,487,216 74	3,261 36			1,365,627 42	672,769 38	331,285 37	16,860,160 27	13,639,317 38	30,519,477 65
1842	18,187,908 76	495 00			1,335,797 52	56,912 53	383,895 44	19,965,009 25	14,808,735 64	34,773,744 89
1843 (to June 30)	7,046,843 91	103 25			2,059,939 80		286,235 09	8,231,001 16	12,551,409 19	20,782,410 43
1843–44	26,183,570 94	1,777 34			2,077,022 30	5,000 00	1,075,419 70	29,320,707 78	1,877,847 95	31,198,555 73
1844–45	27,528,112 70	3,517 12			2,694,452 48		384,201 78	29,941,853 90		29,941,853 90
1845–46	26,712,667 87	2,897 26			2,498,355 20		289,950 13	29,699,967 74		29,699,967 74
1846–47	23,747,864 66	375 00			2,498,355 20		186,467 91	26,437,403 16	28,900,765 36	55,338,168 52
1847–48	31,757,070 96	375 00			3,328,642 56	4,340 39	577,775 99	35,096,699 21	21,293,790 00	59,796,892 96
1848–49	28,346,738 82	375 00			1,688,959 55	34,834 70	676,424 13	30,731,077 50	29,075,815 48	59,796,892 96
1849–50	39,668,686 42				1,859,894 25	8,955 00	2,064,308 21	43,592,886 88	4,056,500 00	47,649,388 86
1850–51	49,017,567 92				2,352,305 30		924,932 60	52,555,039 33	207,822 92	52,762,704 25
1851–52	47,339,326 62				2,043,239 58	250,943 51	463,228 06	49,846,815 60	46,300 00	49,893,115 00
1852–53	58,931,865 52				1,667,084 99	1,021 34	853,313 00	61,423,730 31	16,372 50	61,500,102 81
1853–54	64,224,190 27				11,497,049 07	31,466 78	1,105,352 74	73,800,341 40	1,950 00	73,802,291 40
1854–55	53,025,794 21				8,917,644 93		827,731 40	65,350,574 68	800 00	65,351,374 68
1855–56	64,022,863 50				8,917,644 93		1,116,190 81	74,056,699 24	200 00	74,056,899 24
1856–57	63,875,905 05				3,513,715 87		1,259,920 88	68,965,312 57	3,900 00	68,969,212 57
1857–58	41,789,620 96				1,756,687 30		1,352,029 13	46,655,365 96	23,717,300 00	70,372,665 96
1858–59	49,565,824 38				1,778,537 71		1,454,596 24	52,761,599 83	28,996,857 72	81,758,557 30
1859–60	53,187,511 87				870,658 54		1,088,530 25	36,034,599 89	20,786,808 00	76,841,407 83
1860–61	39,582,125 64				152,203 77		1,023,515 21	41,476,299 49	41,895,340 74	83,371,640 13
1861–62	49,056,397 62		1,795,331 73		167,617 17		904,011 00	51,907,944 63	529,760,860 50	581,609,805 12
1862–63	69,059,642 40	109,741,134 10	1,485,103 61		588,333 29	3,735,794 37	49,621,064 94	74,446,157 55	814,925,494 98	889,373,652 51
1863–64	102,316,152 99	209,464,215 25	475,648 96		996,553 31		26,503,183 79	302,742,354 22	1,130,709,452 85	1,393,451,907 17
1864–65	84,928,260 60	309,226,813 42	1,200,573 09		665,031 03		128,733,397 76	323,092,785 92	1,482,840,464 00	1,805,933,250 82
1865–66	179,046,651 58		1,974,754 12		1,163,575 76		42,624,852 50	619,646,647 91	651,065,430 91	1,270,712,078 82
1866–67	176,417,810 88	266,027,537 43	4,200,233 70					490,634,010 27	640,426,910 29	1,131,060,920 56

1867–'68	164,464,599 56	191,087,589 41	1,788,145 85	....	1,348,715 41	....	46,949,033 09	405,638,083 32	625,111,433 20	1,030,749,516 52
1868–'69	180,048,426 63	158,356,460 86	1,765,685 61	....	4,020,344 34	....	†27,754,900 50	370,945,817 94	238,678,081 06	609,623,899 00
1869–'70	194,538,374 44	184,899,756 49	229,102 88	....	3,350,481 76	....	28,237,762 06	411,255,477 63	285,474,496 00	696,729,973 63
1870–'71	206,270,408 05	143,098,153 63	560,355 37	....	2,388,646 68	....	30,986,381 16	383,393,944 89	266,768,523 47	653,092,468 36

* $1,458,782 93 deducted from the aggregate receipts, as per account of the Treasurer, No. 76,922.

† $2,070 73 added, being net amount paid by depositories previously deducted as unavailable.

Statement of expenditures from the beginning of the Government

[The year 1867, and subsequent, are from the account of warrants on the Treasurer

Years.	Civil list.	Foreign inter-course.	Miscellaneous.	Military service.	Pensions.
From Mar. 4, 1789, to Dec. 31, 1791	$757,134 45	$14,733 33	$311,533 83	$632,804 03	$175,813 88
1792	380,917 58	78,766 67	194,572 32	1,100,702 09	109,243 15
1793	358,241 08	89,500 00	24,709 46	1,130,249 08	80,087 81
1794	440,946 58	146,403 51	118,248 30	2,639,097 59	81,399 24
1795	361,633 36	912,685 12	92,718 50	2,480,910 13	68,673 22
1796	447,139 05	184,859 64	150,476 14	1,260,263 84	100,843 71
1797	483,233 70	669,788 54	103,880 82	1,039,402 66	92,256 97
1798	504,605 17	457,428 74	149,004 15	2,009,522 30	104,845 33
1799	592,905 76	271,374 11	175,111 81	2,466,046 98	95,444 03
1800	748,688 45	395,288 18	193,636 59	2,560,878 77	64,130 73
1801	549,288 31	295,676 73	269,803 41	1,672,944 08	73,533 37
1802	596,981 11	550,925 93	315,022 36	1,179,148 25	85,440 39
1803	526,583 12	1,110,834 77	205,217 87	822,055 85	62,902 10
1804	624,795 63	1,186,655 57	379,558 23	875,423 93	80,092 80
1805	585,849 79	2,798,028 77	384,720 19	712,781 28	81,854 59
1806	684,230 53	1,760,421 30	445,485 18	1,224,355 38	81,875 53
1807	655,524 65	577,826 34	464,546 52	1,288,685 91	70,500 00
1808	651,107 80	204,009 83	427,124 98	2,900,834 40	82,576 04
1809	712,465 13	166,306 04	337,032 62	3,345,772 17	87,833 54
1810	703,994 03	81,367 48	315,783 47	2,294,323 94	83,744 16
1811	644,467 27	264,904 47	457,919 66	2,032,828 19	75,043 88
1812	826,271 55	347,703 29	509,113 37	11,817,798 24	91,402 10
1813	780,545 45	209,941 01	738,949 15	19,652,013 02	86,989 91
1814	927,424 23	177,179 97	1,103,425 50	20,350,806 86	90,164 36
1815	852,247 16	290,892 04	1,755,731 27	14,794,294 22	69,656 06
1816	1,208,125 77	364,620 40	1,416,995 00	16,012,096 80	188,804 15
1817	994,556 17	281,995 97	2,242,384 62	8,004,236 53	297,374 43
1818	1,109,559 79	420,429 90	2,305,840 82	5,622,715 10	890,719 90
1819	1,142,180 41	284,113 94	1,640,917 06	6,506,300 37	2,415,939 85
1820	1,248,310 05	253,370 04	1,090,341 85	2,630,392 31	3,203,376 31
1821	1,112,292 64	207,110 75	903,718 15	4,461,291 78	242,817 25
1822	1,158,131 58	164,879 51	644,985 15	3,111,981 48	1,948,199 40
1823	1,058,911 65	292,118 56	671,063 78	3,096,924 43	1,780,588 52
1824	1,336,266 24	5,140,099 83	678,942 74	3,340,939 85	1,499,326 59
1825	1,330,747 24	371,666 25	1,046,131 40	3,659,914 18	1,308,810 57
1826	1,256,745 48	232,719 08	1,110,713 23	3,943,194 37	1,556,593 83
1827	1,228,141 04	659,211 87	826,123 67	3,938,977 88	976,138 86
1828	1,455,490 58	1,001,193 66	1,219,368 40	4,145,544 56	850,573 57
1829	1,327,069 36	207,765 85	1,566,679 66	4,724,291 07	949,594 47
1830	1,579,724 64	294,067 27	1,363,624 13	4,767,128 88	1,363,297 31
1831	1,373,755 99	298,554 00	1,392,336 11	4,841,835 55	1,170,665 14
1832	1,800,757 74	325,181 07	2,451,202 04	5,446,034 88	1,184,422 40
1833	1,562,758 28	955,395 88	3,198,091 77	6,704,019 10	4,589,152 40
1834	2,030,601 60	241,562 35	2,082,565 00	5,696,189 38	3,364,285 30
1835	1,905,551 54	774,750 28	1,549,396 74	5,759,156 89	1,954,711 32
1836	2,110,175 47	533,382 65	2,749,721 60	12,169,226 64	2,882,797 96
1837	2,357,035 94	4,603,905 40	2,932,428 93	13,682,730 80	2,672,162 45
1838	2,688,708 56	1,215,095 52	3,256,860 68	12,897,224 16	2,156,057 29
1839	2,116,982 77	987,667 92	2,621,340 20	8,916,995 80	3,142,750 51
1840	2,736,769 31	683,278 15	2,575,351 50	7,095,267 23	2,603,562 17
1841	2,556,471 79	428,410 57	3,505,999 09	8,801,610 24	2,388,434 51
1842	2,905,041 65	563,191 41	3,307,391 55	6,610,438 02	1,378,931 33
1843, (to June 30)	1,222,422 48	400,506 04	1,579,724 48	2,908,671 95	839,041 12
1843-'44	2,454,958 15	636,079 66	2,554,146 05	5,218,183 66	2,032,008 99
1844-'45	2,360,632 79	702,637 22	2,639,470 77	5,746,291 28	2,400,788 11
1845-'46	2,532,232 92	400,292 55	3,769,758 42	10,413,370 58	1,811,097 56
1846-'47	2,570,338 44	405,079 10	3,910,190 61	35,840,030 33	1,744,883 63
1847-'48	2,647,802 87	448,593 01	2,554,455 37	27,687,334 21	1,228,496 48
1848-'49	2,865,196 91	6,903,996 72	3,111,140 61	14,558,473 26	1,328,867 64
1849-'50	3,027,454 39	5,990,858 81	7,025,450 16	9,687,024 58	1,866,886 02
1850-'51	3,481,219 51	6,256,427 16	8,146,577 33	12,161,905 11	2,293,377 22
1851-'52	3,439,923 22	4,196,321 59	9,867,926 64	8,521,506 19	2,401,858 78
1852-'53	4,265,861 68	950,871 30	12,246,335 03	9,910,498 49	1,756,306 20
1853-'54	4,621,492 24	7,764,812 31	13,461,450 13	11,722,282 87	1,232,665 00
1854-'55	6,350,875 88	997,007 26	16,738,442 29	14,648,074 07	1,477,612 33
1855-'56	6,452,256 93	3,642,615 39	15,260,475 94	16,963,160 51	1,296,229 63
1856-'57	7,611,547 27	999,177 65	18,946,189 01	19,159,150 87	1,309,115 81
1857-'58	7,314,990 04	1,300,506 70	17,947,951 70	25,679,121 63	1,219,768 30

to *June* 30, 1871, *under the following appropriate heads.*

issued ; all previous years are from the account of warrants paid.]

Indians.	Naval establishment.	Net ordinary expenditures.	Public debt, including principal and interest.	Total.	Balances in the Treasury at the end of each year.
$27,000 00	$570 00	$1,919,589 52	$5,287,949 50	$7,207,539 02	$973,905 75
13,648 85	53 02	1,877,903 68	7,263,665 99	9,141,569 67	783,444 51
27,282 83	....	1,710,070 26	5,819,505 29	7,529,575 55	753,661 69
13,042 46	61,408 97	3,500,546 65	5,601,578 09	9,302,124 74	1,151,924 17
23,475 68	410,582 03	4,350,658 04	6,084,411 61	10,435,069 65	516,442 61
113,563 98	274,784 04	2,531,930 40	5,835,846 44	8,367,776 84	888,995 42
62,396 38	382,631 89	2,833,590 96	5,792,421 82	8,626,012 78	1,021,899 04
16,410 09	1,381,347 76	4,623,223 54	3,990,294 14	8,613,517 68	617,451 43
20,302 19	2,858,081 84	6,480,166 72	4,506,876 78	11,077,043 50	2,161,867 77
31 22	3,448,716 03	7,411,369 97	4,578,369 95	11,989,739 92	2,623,311 99
9,000 00	2,111,424 00	4,981,669 90	7,291,707 04	12,273,376 94	3,295,301 00
94,000 00	915,561 87	3,737,079 91	9,539,004 76	13,276,084 67	5,020,697 64
60,000 00	1,215,230 53	4,002,824 24	7,256,159 43	11,258,983 67	4,825,811 60
116,500 00	1,189,832 75	4,452,858 91	8,171,787 45	12,624,646 36	4,037,005 26
196,500 00	1,597,500 00	6,357,234 62	7,360,889 79	13,727,124 41	3,999,388 99
234,200 00	1,649,641 44	6,080,209 36	8,989,884 61	15,070,093 97	4,538,123 80
205,425 00	1,722,064 47	4,984,572 89	6,307,720 10	11,292,292 99	9,643,850 07
213,575 00	1,884,067 80	6,504,338 85	10,260,245 35	16,764,584 20	9,941,809 96
337,503 84	2,427,758 80	7,414,672 14	6,452,554 16	13,867,226 30	3,848,056 78
177,625 00	1,654,244 20	5,311,082 28	8,008,904 40	13,319,986 74	2,672,276 57
151,875 00	1,965,566 39	5,592,604 86	8,009,204 05	13,601,808 91	3,502,305 80
277,245 00	3,959,365 15	17,829,498 70	4,449,622 45	22,279,121 15	3,862,217 41
167,358 28	6,446,600 10	28,082,396 92	11,108,123 44	39,190,520 36	5,196,542 00
167,394 86	7,311,290 60	30,127,686 38	7,900,543 94	38,028,230 32	1,727,848 63
530,750 00	8,660,000 25	26,953,571 00	12,628,922 35	39,582,493 35	13,106,592 88
274,512 16	3,908,278 30	23,373,432 58	24,871,062 93	48,244,495 51	22,033,519 19
319,463 71	3,314,598 49	15,454,609 92	25,423,036 12	40,877,646 04	14,989,465 48
505,704 27	2,953,695 00	13,808,613 78	21,296,201 62	35,104,875 40	1,478,526 74
463,181 39	3,847,640 42	16,300,273 44	7,703,926 29	24,004,199 73	2,079,992 38
315,750 01	4,387,900 00	13,134,530 57	8,628,494 28	21,763,024 85	1,198,461 21
477,005 44	3,319,243 06	10,723,479 07	8,367,093 62	19,090,572 69	1,681,592 24
575,007 41	2,224,458 98	9,827,643 51	7,848,949 12	17,676,592 63	4,237,427 55
380,781 82	2,503,765 83	9,784,154 59	5,530,016 41	15,314,171 00	9,463,922 81
429,987 90	2,904,581 56	15,330,144 19	16,568,393 76	31,898,538 47	1,946,597 13
724,106 44	3,049,083 86	11,490,459 94	12,095,344 78	23,585,804 72	5,201,650 43
743,447 83	4,218,902 45	13,062,316 27	11,041,082 19	24,103,398 46	6,358,686 18
760,624 88	4,263,877 45	12,653,695 65	10,003,668 39	22,656,764 04	6,668,286 10
705,084 24	3,018,786 44	13,296,041 45	12,163,438 07	25,459,479 52	5,972,435 81
576,344 74	3,3 8,745 47	12,660,490 63	12,383,867 78	25,044,358 40	5,755,704 79
622,262 47	3,239,428 03	13,229,533 33	11,355,749 22	24,585,281 55	6,014,539 75
930,738 04	3,856,183 07	13,864,067 90	16,174,378 22	30,038,446 12	4,502,914 45
1,352,419 75	3,956,370 29	16,516,388 77	17,840,300 29	34,356,698 06	2,011,777 55
1,802,980 93	3,901,356 75	22,713,755 11	1,543,543 38	24,257,298 49	11,702,905 31
1,003,953 20	3,956,260 42	18,425,417 25	6,176,565 19	24,601,082 44	8,892,858 42
1,706,444 48	3,864,9:9 06	17,514,950 28	58,191 00	17,573,141 56	26,749,803 96
4,615,141 49	5,807,718 23	30,868,164 04	....	30,868,164 04	46,708,436 00
4,349,036 19	6,646,914 53	37,243,214 24	21,822 91	37,265,037 15	37,327,252 09
5,504,191 34	6,131,580 53	33,849,718 08	5,605,720 27	39,455,438 35	36,891,196 94
2,528,917 28	6,182,294 25	26,496,948 73	11,117,987 42	37,614,936 15	33,157,503 68
2,331,794 86	6,113,896 89	24,139,920 11	4,086,613 70	28,226,533 81	29,963,163 46
2,514,837 12	6,001,076 97	26,196,840 29	5,600,689 74	31,797,530 03	28,685,111 08
1,199,099 68	8,397,242 95	24,361,336 59	8,575,530 94	32,936,876 53	30,521,979 44
578,371 00	3,727,711 53	11,256,508 00	861,596 55	12,118,105 15	39,186,284 74
1,256,532 39	6,408,199 11	20,650,108 01	12,991,902 84	33,642,010 85	36,742,829 62
1,539,351 35	6,297,177 89	21,895,309 61	8,595,039 10	30,490,4 8 71	36,194,274 81
1,027,693 64	6,455,013 92	26,418,459 59	1,213,823 31	27,632,282 90	38,261,959 65
1,430,411 30	7,900,635 76	53,801,569 37	6,520,851 74	60,322,421 11	33,079,276 43
1,252,296 81	9,408,476 02	45,227,454 77	15,427,688 42	60,655,143 19	29,416,612 45
1,374,161 55	9,786,705 92	39,933,542 61	16,452,880 13	56,386,422 74	32,627,082 69
1,663,591 47	7,904,724 66	37,165,990 09	7,438,728 17	44,604,718 26	35,871,753 31
2,829,801 77	8,820,5*1 38	44,049,949 46	4,426,154 83	48,476,104 31	40,158,353 25
3,043,576 04	8,918,842 10	40,389,954 56	6,322,654 27	46,712,608 83	43,338,860 02
3,880,494 12	11,067,789 53	44,078,156 35	10,498,905 30	54,577,061 74	50,261,901 09
1,550,339 55	10,790,096 32	51,142,138 42	24,330,980 66	75,473,119 08	48,591,073 41
2,772,990 78	13,327,095 11	56,312,097 72	9,852,678 24	66,164,775 96	47,777,672 13
2,644,263 97	14,074,834 64	60,333,836 45	12,392,505 12	72,726,341 57	49,108,229 80
4,355,683 64	12,651,694 61	65,032,559 76	6,242,027 61	71,274,587 37	46,802,855 00
4,978,266 18	14,053,264 64	72,291,119 70	9,771,067 04	82,062,186 74	35,113,334 22
3,490,534 53	14,690,927 90	66,327,405 72	17,351,237 20	83,678,642 92	33,193,248 60
2,901,121 54	11,514,649 83	60,010,062 58	17,045,013 07	77,055,075 65	32,979,530 78
2,865,481 17	12,387,156 52	62,537,221 62	22,850,141 46	85,387,363 08	30,963,857 83
2,327,948 37	42,640,353 09	456,379,896 81	109,287,461 27	565,667,358 08	46,965,304 87
3,152,032 70	63,261,235 31	694,004,575 56	205,811,335 69	899,815,915 27	36,523,046 13
2,629,975 97	85,704,963 74	811,283,679 14	484,257,435 72	1,295,541,114 86	134,433,738 44
5,059,360 71	122,617,434 07	1,214,349,195 43	692,084,135 94	1,906,433,331 37	33,933,657 89
3,295,729 32	42,925,662 00	385,954,731 43	753,389,350 52	1,139,344,081 95	165,301,654 76
4,642,531 77	31,034,011 04	202,947,537 42	890,132,117 85	1,093,079,655 27	198,076,537 09
4,100,682 32	25,775,502 72	229,915,088 11	379,974,882 03	1,069,889,970 74	158,936,682 87
7,042,923 06	20,000,757 97	190,496,354 95	394,281,641 16	584,777,996 11	183,781,985 76
3,407,938 15	21,780,229 87	164,421,507 13	538,486,335 73	702,907,842 86	149,502,471 60
7,426,997 44	19,431,027 21	157,583,827 58	534,097,031 32	691,680,858 90	109,914,081 06

1871, $3,396 18 should be deducted as unavailable during the year.

Statement of outstanding principal of the public debt of the United States on the 1st of January of each year, from 1791 to 1842, inclusive; and on the 1st of July of each year, from 1843 to 1871, inclusive.

January 1, 1791	$75, 463, 476 52
1792	77, 227, 924 66
1793	80, 352, 634 04
1794	78, 427, 404 77
1795	80, 747, 587 39
1796	83, 762, 172 07
1797	82, 064, 479 33
1798	79, 228, 529 12
1799	78, 408, 669 77
1800	82, 976, 294 35
1801	83, 038, 050 80
1802	80, 712, 632 25
1803	77, 054, 686 30
1804	86, 427, 120 88
1805	82, 312, 150 50
1806	75, 723, 270 66
1807	69, 218, 398 64
1808	65, 196, 317 97
1809	57, 023, 192 09
1810	53, 173, 217 52
1811	48, 005, 587 76
1812	45, 209, 737 90
1813	55, 962, 827 57
1814	81, 487, 846 24
1815	99, 833, 660 15
1816	127, 334, 933 74
1817	123, 491, 965 16
1818	103, 466, 633 83
1819	95, 529, 648 28
1820	91, 015, 566 15
1821	89, 987, 427 66
1822	93, 546, 676 98
1823	90, 875, 877 28
1824	90, 269, 777 77
1825	83, 788, 432 71
1826	81, 054, 059 99
1827	73, 987, 357 20
1828	67, 475, 043 87
1829	58, 421, 413 67
1830	48, 565, 406 50
1831	39, 123, 191 68
1832	24, 322, 235 18
1833	7, 001, 698 83
1834	4, 760, 082 08
1835	37, 513 05
1836	336, 957 83
1837	3, 308, 124 07
1838	10, 434, 221 14
1839	3, 573, 343 82
1840	5, 250, 875 54
1841	13, 594, 480 73
1842	20, 601, 226 28
July 1, 1843	32, 742, 922 00
1844	23, 461, 652 50
1845	15, 925, 303 01
1846	15, 550, 202 97
1847	38, 826, 534 77
1848	47, 044, 862 23
1849	63, 061, 858 69
1850	63, 452, 773 55
1851	68, 304, 796 02
1852	66, 199, 341 71
1853	59, 803, 117 70
1854	42, 242, 222 42
1855	35, 586, 956 56

July	1,	1856	$31,972,537 90
		1857	28,699,831 85
		1858	44,911,881 03
		1859	58,496,837 88
		1860	64,842,287 88
		1861	90,580,873 72
		1862	524,176,412 13
		1863	1,119,772,138 63
		1864	1,815,784,370 57
		1865	2,680,647,869 74
		1866	2,773,236,173 69
		1867	2,678,126,103 87
		1868	2,611,687,851 19
		1869	2,588,452,213 94
		1870	2,480,672,427 81
		1871	2,353,211,332 32

Payments of judgments rendered by the Court of Claims, from July 1, 1870, to June 30, 1871.

To whom paid.	Date.	Nature of claim.	Amount.
M. Otterbourg	July 19, 1870	Not stated	$818 48
E. H. Gruber and M. D. Whittridge	Aug. 27, 1870	......do	620 77
A. H. Wilson	Aug. 30, 1870	......do	13,071 89
J. C. Frémont	Feb. 20, 1871	......do	18,000 00
John P. Barger	April 12, 1871	......do	1,664 79
D. Buckley	June 6, 1871	......do	300 00
Total			34,475 93

Statement exhibiting the amount of tonnage of the United States annually, from 1789 to 1871, inclusive; also the registered, enrolled, and licensed tonnage employed in steam navigation in each year.

Year ending—	Registered sail tonnage.	Registered steam tonnage.	Enrolled and licensed sail tonnage.	Enrolled and licensed steam tonnage.	Total tonnage.
	Tons.	Tons.	Tons.	Tons.	Tons.
Dec. 31, 1789	123,893		77,669		201,562
1790	346,254		132,123		274,377
1791	362,110		139,036		502,146
1792	411,438		153,019		564,457
1793	367,734		153,030		520,764
1794	438,863		189,755		628,618
1795	529,471		218,494		747,965
1796	576,733		255,166		831,899
1797	597,777		279,136		876,913
1798	603,376		294,952		898,328
1799	662,197		277,212		939,409
1800	559,921		302,571		972,492
1801	632,907		314,670		947,577
1802	560,380		331,724		892,104
1803	597,157		352,015		949,172
1804	672,530		369,874		1,042,404
1805	749,341		391,027		1,140,368
1806	808,265		400,451		1,208,716
1807	848,307		420,241		1,268,584
1808	759,054		473,542		1,242,596
1809	910,059		440,222		1,350,281
1810	984,269		449,515		1,424,748
1811	768,852		463,650		1,232,502
1812	760,624		509,373		1,269,997
1813	674,853		491,776		1,666,629
1814	674,633		484,577		1,159,210
1815	854,295		513,833		1,368,128
1816	800,760		571,459		1,372,219

Statement exhibiting the amount of tonnage, &c.—Continued.

Year ending—	Registered sail tonnage.	Registered steam tonnage.	Enrolled and licensed sail tonnage.	Enrolled and licensed steam tonnage.	Total tonnage.
	Tons.	*Tons.*	*Tons.*	*Tons.*	*Tons.*
Dec. 31, 1817	800,725	....	590,187	....	1,399,912
1818	606,089	....	619,096	....	1,225,185
1819	612,930	....	647,821	....	1,260,751
1820	619,048	....	661,119	....	1,280,167
1821	619,896	....	679,062	....	1,298,958
1822	628,150	....	696,549	....	1,324,699
1823	639,921	....	671,766	24,879	1,336,566
1824	669,973	....	697,580	21,610	1,389,163
1825	700,788	....	699,263	23,061	1,423,112
1826	737,978	....	762,154	34,059	1,534,191
1827	747,170	....	833,240	40,198	1,620,608
1828	810,810	....	889,355	39,418	1,741,392
1829	650,143	....	556,616	54,051	1,909,709
1830	575,056	1,419	552,248	63,053	1,191,776
1831	619,575	877	613,827	33,568	1,267,847
1832	686,809	181	661,827	90,633	1,439,450
1833	749,462	545	754,819	101,305	1,606,151
1834	857,098	340	778,995	122,474	1,758,907
Sept. 30, 1835	885,481	340	816,645	122,474	1,824,940
1836	897,321	454	839,226	145,102	1,822,103
1837	809,343	1,104	932,576	153,661	1,896,684
1838	819,801	2,791	982,416	190,632	1,995,640
1839	829,096	5,149	1,062,445	199,789	2,096,479
1840	895,610	4,155	1,082,815	198,154	2,180,764
1841	945,057	746	1,010,599	174,342	2,130,744
1842	970,658	4,701	892,072	224,960	2,092,391
June 30, 1843	1,003,932	5,373	917,804	231,494	2,158,603
1844	1,061,856	6,909	949,060	265,270	2,280,095
1845	1,088,680	6,492	1,002,303	319,527	2,417,002
1846	1,123,999	6,287	1,090,192	341,606	2,562,084
1847	1,235,682	5,631	1,198,523	399,210	2,839,046
1848	1,344,819	16,068	1,381,332	411,823	3,154,042
1849	1,418,072	20,870	1,453,459	441,525	3,334,016
1850	1,540,769	44,429	1,468,738	481,005	3,535,454
1851	1,663,917	62,390	1,524,915	521,217	3,772,439
1852	1,819,774	79,704	1,075,456	563,536	4,138,440
1853	2,013,154	90,520	1,789,238	514,098	4,407,010
1854	2,238,783	95,036	1,887,512	581,571	4,802,902
1855	2,440,091	115,045	2,021,625	655,240	5,212,001
1856	2,401,687	89,715	1,796,888	583,362	4,871,652
1857	2,377,094	86,873	1,857,964	618,911	4,940,842
1858	2,499,742	78,027	2,550,067	651,363	5,049,808
1859	2,414,654	92,748	1,961,631	676,005	5,145,038
1860	2,448,941	97,296	2,036,990	770,641	5,353,868
1861	2,340,020	102,608	2,122,589	774,596	5,539,813
1862	2,177,253	113,908	2,224,449	596,465	5,112,165
1863	1,892,899	133,215	2,660,212	439,755	5,126,081
1864	1,475,376	106,519	2,550,690	853,816	4,986,401
1865, old admeasurement	1,022,465	69,539	1,794,372	630,411	3,516,787
1865, new admeasurement	482,110	28,469	730,695	338,720	1,579,994
1866, old admeasurement	341,619	42,776	443,635	114,269	942,299
1866, new admeasurement	953,018	155,513	1,489,194	770,754	3,368,479
1867, old admeasurement	182,203	32,593	95,869	36,307	346,972
1867, new admeasurement	1,187,714	165,522	1,646,820	957,458	3,957,514
1868, old admeasurement	33,449				33,449
1868, new admeasurement	1,310,344	221,939	1,808,559	977,476	4,318,309
1869	1,352,586	213,252	1,651,182	890,316	4,107,336
1870	1,324,256	192,544	1,847,156	882,551	4,246,507
1871	1,244,228	180,914	1,950,742	906,723	4,282,607

Statement exhibiting the number and tonnage of registered, enrolled, and licensed vessels in the United States on the 30th of June, 1871.

States.	Registered.		Enrolled.		Licensed under 20 tons.		Total.	
	Vessels.	Tons.	Vessels.	Tons.	Vessels.	Tons.	Vessels.	Tons.
Maine	423	238,385.89	1,793	152,145.00	531	6,491.69	2,747	397,022.58
New Hampshire	11	8,586.37	47	3,937.28	15	170.66	73	12,694.31
Vermont			23	5,889.51			23	5,889.51
Massachusetts	782	352,032.78	1,822	158,451.99	323	3,696.04	2,847	514,180.81
Rhode Island	16	3,533.37	147	40,669.84	47	567.39	210	44,770.60
Connecticut	55	14,122.25	484	64,399.26	189	2,535.63	728	81,057.14
New York	797	585,801.65	6,856	912,655.36	619	7,029.87	8,272	1,505,486.88
New Jersey	51	7,022.22	706	77,633.83	247	2,896.45	1,004	87,552.50
Pennsylvania	102	40,045.96	2,911	366,607.74	180	2,127.66	3,193	417,781.36
Delaware	2	770.91	130	15,231.39	28	334.38	160	16,336.68
Maryland	98	32,815.80	1,474	107,916.57	460	5,468.85	2,032	14C,201.22
District of Columbia	7	331.54	321	23,243.24	53	613.99	381	24,188.77
Virginia	17	1,527.63	483	25,265.68	525	5,304.47	1,025	32,097.78
North Carolina	32	4,896.80	66	4,527.00	175	1,941.53	273	11,365.33
South Carolina	20	4,324.24	81	5,938.70	88	959.93	189	11,222.87
Georgia	31	11,276.73	36	4,391.98	18	159.72	85	15,828.43
Florida	54	7,524.02	84	7,155.92	106	1,100.18	244	15,780.12
Alabama	7	5,267.14	153	17,141.12	68	694.26	228	23,102.52
Mississippi			91	2,962.64			91	2,962.64
Louisiana	64	30,031.31	356	66,606.76	245	2,340.35	665	98,978.42
Texas	31	8,947.93	108	11,397.81	164	1,745.04	303	22,090.78
Tennessee			60	12,787.18	3	31.08	63	12,818.26
Kentucky			59	17,912.87			59	17,012.87
Missouri	10	1,692.18	235	101,508.26	2	10.87	247	103,211.31
Iowa			70	5,503.65	10	141.72	80	5,645.37
Minnesota			128	19,867.32	11	191.62	139	20,058.94
Wisconsin	1	90.41	243	40,075.23			244	40,165.64
Illinois	1	494.99	792	115,763.37	28	361.10	821	116,619.46
Indiana			63	9,224.05	2	34.00	65	9,258.05
Michigan	4	760.39	676	121,455.18	138	1,789.18	818	124,004.75
Ohio	10	1,819.03	1,087	161,760.42	51	677.64	1,148	164,267.09
West Virginia			108	13,768.74	10	132.36	118	13,901.10
California	133	41,509.92	604	89,315.95	189	2,414.68	926	133,300.55
Oregon	2	1,611.30	39	7,579.63	1	18.97	42	9,209.90
Washington Ter	40	10,859.34	34	13,484.15	24	209.24	98	24,552.73
Alaska			6	372.75			6	372.75
Nebraska			4	717.46			4	717.46
Total	2,721	1,425,142.10	22,380	2,805,274.83	4,550	52,190.55	29,651	4,282,607.48

SUMMARY.

	Vessels.	Tons.	Vessels.	Tons.	Vessels.	Tons.	Vessels.	Tons.
The Atlantic and Gulf coasts.	2,510	1,362,745.46	14,654	1,590,099.94	3,817	43,579.51	20,981	2,996,424.91
The Northern lakes.	22	5,011.40	5,243	703,856.16	248	3,160.28	5,513	712,027.84
The Pacific coast	175	54,040.56	683	110,752.48	10	2,642.89	1,072	167,435.93
The Western rivers	14	3,344.68	1,800	400,566.25	271	2,807.87	2,085	406,718.80
Total	2,721	1,425,142.10	22,380	2,805,274.83	4,550	52,190.55	29,651	4,282,607.48

Statement exhibiting the number and tonnage of sailing vessels, steam vessels, barges, and canal boats in each customs district of the United States on June 30, 1871.

States.	Sailing vessels.		Steam vessels.		Barges.		Canal-boats.		Total.	
	No.	Tonnage.	No.	Tonnage.	No.	Tonnage.	No.	Tonnage.	No.	Tonnage.
Maine	2,694	379,454.72	53	17,567.86					2,747	397,022.58
New Hampshire	68	12,235.09	5	459.22					73	12,694.31
Vermont	8	493.33	6	4,760.64			9	635.54	23	5,889.51
Massachusetts	2,768	486,835.81	79	27,345.00					2,847	514,180.81
Rhode Island	177	17,360.76	33	27,403.84					210	44,770.60
Connecticut	661	52,644.17	55	26,396.15	7	1,455.27	5	561.55	728	81,057.14
New York	3,250	660,005.70	844	377,018.66	407	85,365.11	3,771	374,077.41	8,272	1,505,466.88
New Jersey	763	47,717.14	80	20,871.42	30	3,368.18	131	15,595.76	1,004	87,552.50
Pennsylvania	860	131,613.48	412	97,617.26	175	35,466.94	1,746	153,083.68	3,193	417,781.36
Delaware	135	8,828.50	17	6,825.84	6	432.38	2	249.96	160	16,336.68
Maryland	1,416	77,450.32	100	37,986.35			516	30,764.55	2,032	146,201.22
Dist. Columbia	79	1,992.20	25	5,295.38	26	832.22	249	16,068.97	381	24,488.77
Virginia	830	18,428.67	61	5,253.42	15	1,258.61	119	7,156.88	1,025	32,097.78
North Carolina	249	8,725.33	20	2,464.78	4	175.22			273	11,365.33
South Carolina	165	7,439.05	24	3,700.80					189	11,222.87
Georgia	57	11,625.35	28	4,203.08					86	16,688.40
Florida	214	10,895.03	30	4,885.09					244	15,780.12
Alabama	82	7,087.67	50	11,650.59	96	4,364.26			228	23,103.52
Mississippi	66	1,219.33	11	1,411.02	14	332.29			91	2,962.64
Louisiana	430	32,720.54	208	64,370.22	18	1,687.66			665	98,978.42
Texas	248	12,241.56	36	7,815.16	19	2,034.06			303	22,090.78
Tennessee			63	12,818.26					63	12,818.26
Kentucky			54	15,555.70	5	2,357.17			59	17,912.87
Missouri	1	2.66	167	72,465.67	74	29,988.04	5	754.94	247	103,211.31
Iowa			34	3,147.36	46	2,498.01			80	5,645.37
Minnesota			62	10,863.93	77	9,195.01			139	20,058.94
Wisconsin	200	25,376.67	44	14,788.97					244	40,165.64
Illinois	339	63,598.80	155	19,291.69	102	13,076.06	225	20,652.91	821	116,619.46
Indiana			49	8,222.66	16	1,035.39			65	9,258.05
Michigan	433	40,347.39	280	50,780.88	105	23,876.46			818	124,004.75
Ohio	291	53,680.81	203	52,069.04	118	29,647.92	536	28,869.32	1,148	164,267.09
West Virginia			79	10,667.66	39	3,233.44			118	13,901.10
California	720	75,352.39	143	49,886.78	63	8,061.38			926	133,300.55
Oregon	5	749.77	31	8,125.55	6	334.58			42	9,209.90
Washing'n Ter.	74	21,661.79	22	2,843.73	2	47.21			98	24,552.73
Alaska	6	372.75							6	372.75
Nebraska			4	717.46					4	717.46
Total	17,249	2,284,855.48	3,567	1,087,637.14	1,472	260,343.09	7,314	648,471.47	29,651	4,282,607.48

SUMMARY.

Atlantic and Gulf coasts.	14,604	1,918,675.13	1,672	604,518.65	636	100,672.75	4,069	372,558.38	20,981	2,996,424.91
Northern lakes.	1,662	267,153.38	682	149,467.59	132	31,208.47	3,037	264,198.40	5,513	712,027.84
Pacific coast	803	98,136.70	196	60,856.06	71	8,443.17			1,072	167,435.93
Western rivers.	227	2,190.57	1,017	272,794.84	633	120,018.70	208	11,714.69	2,085	406,718.80
Total	17,249	2,284,855.48	3,367	1,087,637.14	1,472	260,343.09	7,314	648,471.47	29,651	4,282,607.48

TREASURY DEPARTMENT, REGISTER'S OFFICE,
                    October 30, 1871.

                                                            JOHN ALLISON, *Register.*

REPORT OF THE SOLICITOR OF THE TREASURY.

REPORT

OF

THE SOLICITOR OF THE TREASURY.

DEPARTMENT OF JUSTICE,
OFFICE OF THE SOLICITOR OF THE TREASURY,
Washington, D. C., November 23, 1871.

SIR: I have the honor to transmit herewith seven tabular statements, exhibiting the amount, character, and results of the litigation under the direction of this office for the fiscal year ending June 30, 1871, so far as the same are shown by the reports received from the United States attorneys for the several districts. These tables embrace, respectively:

1. Suits on custom-house bonds.

2. Suits on transcripts of accounts of defaulting public officers, excepting those of the Post-Office Department, adjusted by the accounting officers of the Treasury Department.

3. Post-Office suits, embracing those against officers of the Post-Office Department, and cases of fines, penalties, and forfeitures for violation of the postal laws.

4. Suits for the recovery of fines, penalties, and forfeitures under the customs revenue and navigation laws.

5. Suits in which the United States is interested, not embraced in the other classes.

6. Suits against collectors of customs and other agents of the Government, for refund of duties and acts done in the line of their official duty.

7. A general summary or abstract of all the other tables.

An examination of this summary will show that the whole number of suits commenced within the year was 2,116, of which

276 were of class 1, for the recovery of	$1,014,824 09
94 were of class 2, for the recovery of	3,606,661 06
193 were of class 3, for the recovery of	69,950 09
518 were of class 4, for the recovery of	7,452,209 98
610 were of class 5, for the recovery of	460,955 79
425 were of class 6.	
Making a total sued for, as reported, of	12,604,601 01

Of the whole number of suits brought, 493 were decided in favor of the United States; 24 were adversely decided; 387 were settled and dismissed; in 9, penalties were remitted by the Secretary of the Treasury; leaving 1,203 still pending. Of those pending at the commencement of the year, 566 were decided for the United States, 183 were decided adversely, and 1,142 were settled and dismissed. The entire number of suits decided or otherwise disposed of during the year was 2,804; the whole amount for which judgments were obtained, exclusive of decrees *in rem*, was $1,188,469 17, and the entire amount collected from all sources was $1,289,929 06.

The following tables exhibit a comparative view of the litigation of the last year and the next preceding one:

Date.	In suits commenced during the fiscal years ending June 30, 1870, and June 30, 1871.								
	Aggregate sued for.	Aggregate in judgment for the United States.	Collected.	Decided for the United States.	Decided against the United States.	Settled and dismissed.	Remitted.	Pending.	Total number of suits brought.
June 30, 1870	$5, 367, 007 44	$73, 388 24	$231, 884 71	388	11	261	32	1176	1868
June 30, 1871	12, 604, 601 01	280, 410 97	586, 271 76	493	24	387	9	1203	2116

Date.	In suits commenced prior to the fiscal years ending June 30, 1870, and June 30, 1871.					Proceedings in all suits.			
	Aggregate of judgments in old suits.	Decided for the United States.	Decided against the United States.	Settled and dismissed.	Collections in old suits.	Total number of suits disposed of.	Whole number of judgments in favor of the United States.	Whole amount of judgments.	Whole amount collected.
June 30, 1870	$199, 004 92	123	83	422	$245, 140 66	1320	511	$272, 393 16	$477, 025 37
June 30, 1871	908, 058 20	566	183	1142	703, 657 30	2804	1059	1, 158, 469 17	1, 289, 929 06

I have to remark that the suit of the United States against the Nashville and Chattanooga Railroad Company, brought in the middle district of Tennessee prior to the fiscal year, was during the year compromised by the Secretary of War, under the act of Congress approved March 3, 1871, the United States receiving bonds of the said company to the amount of $1,000,000, secured by mortgage on the road, &c., in settlement of the suit. This amount is, however, not included in this report as a collection.

I am, very respectfully,

E. C. BANFIELD,
Solicitor of the Treasury.

Hon. GEORGE S. BOUTWELL,
Secretary of the Treasury.

No. 1.—*Report of suits on custom-house bonds instituted during the fiscal year ending June 30, 1871, in the several United States courts, and of proceedings had during said period in suits which were instituted prior thereto.*

SUMMARY.

Judicial districts.	Number of suits.	In suits brought during the fiscal year. Aggregate sued for.	Aggregate in judgment.	Collections.	Decided for the United States.	Decided against the United States.	Settled, dismissed, &c.	Pending.	In suits commenced prior to the fiscal year. Judgment in old suits.	For the United States.	Against the United States.	Settled, &c.	Collections in old suits.	Whole number of suits disposed of.	Whole number of judgments for United States during the year.	Total judgments during the year.	Total collections during the year.
Maine	1	$180 00					1					2		3			
Massachusetts	1						1					1		1			
Rhode Island								1					$563 10				$563 10
New York, northern district	230	952,298 86				1	90	139				204		300			
New York, southern district									4,752 24	5		9		57	5	4,752 24	
New York, eastern district									7,565 21	48					48	7,565 21	
Pennsylvania, eastern district	5	4,135 00			1		1	4						1			
Maryland	9	17,784 90	$300 00	$300 00			1	7						2	1	300 00	300 00
Georgia									77,600 63	23			1,360 54	23	23	77,600 63	1,360 54
Alabama, middle district																	
Louisiana	22	20,338 17	495 19	256 89	2		6	14	176,265 25	30	1		416 50	46	32	176,760 44	673 39
Tennessee, western district	1	7,766 46						1			8			1			
Illinois, northern district	3	5,939 70						3	31,631 82	1					1	31,631 82	
Michigan, eastern district	3	6,411 00						3									
California									203 00	2				2	2	203 00	
Total	276	1,014,884 09	795 19	556 89	3	1	100	172	298,018 15	109	9	216	2,340 14	438	112	298,813 34	2,897 03

No. 2.—Report of suits on Treasury transcripts other than post-office cases, instituted during the fiscal year ending June 30, 1871, in the several United States courts, and of proceedings had during said period in suits which were instituted prior thereto.

SUMMARY.

Judicial districts.	Number of suits	Aggregate sued for	Aggregate in judgment	Collections	For the United States	Against the United States	Settled, dismissed, &c.	Remitted	Pending	Judgment in old suits	For the United States	Against the United States	Settled, &c.	Collections	Whole number of suits disposed of	Whole number of judgments in favor of United States	Total judgments	Total collections
Maine	1								1						1			
New Hampshire																		
Massachusetts																		
Rhode Island																		
Vermont																		
Connecticut	1	$639 84			1		1		1	$112 43	1		1	$1,184 49	1	1	$112 43	$1,184 49
New York, northern district	1	100,000 00							1	311 64	1			4,954 57	1	1	311 64	4,954 57
New York, southern district	5	1,060,113 25							5						2			
New York, eastern district	2	30,000 00	$15,000 00		1				1						1	1	15,000 00	
New Jersey	2	32,145 99		$2,400 00	1				2	15,000 00	4			12,500 00	6	4	15,000 00	14,900 00
Pennsylvania, eastern district	2	9,019 43					1		1	8,311 28	1			16,429 92	3	3	8,311 28	16,429 92
Pennsylvania, western district	3	30,633 85	35,016 53	534 16	3										3	3	35,016 53	534 16
Delaware										2,435 58	1			2,435 58	1	1	2,435 58	2,435 58
Maryland	4	108,818 82					1		1	2,190 15	3						2,190 15	
Virginia, eastern district	5	94,336 32	51,366 43		3				1	90,076 90	4			91,400 00	7	7	141,443 33	91,400 00
Virginia, western district	2	217,394 33			3				5									
West Virginia	2	32,547 37							2									
District of Columbia																		
North Carolina		50,399 92																
South Carolina		50,643 40																
Georgia	2	26,366 22							2	5,156 31	1			5,156 31	1	1	5,156 31	5,156 31
Florida, northern district	2								2	20,000 00	1		1		2	1	20,000 00	
Florida, southern district	2								2									
Alabama, northern district																		

Alabama, middle district	260,453 32	3		643 19										643 10	1			12,976 30
Alabama, southern district	5,745 57	1			366 25				3,335 98	1		3,335 98		3,335 28	1			
Mississippi, northern district	70,689 76	3			386 99				50,000 00			50,000 00		50,000 00	1			20,000 00
Mississippi, southern district	8,865 51	2													2			
Louisiana	51,754 00	2																
Texas, eastern district	9,203 54	3																
Texas, western district	261,306 62	3																
Arkansas, eastern district	216,196 27	2												2,605 39	1			304 39
Arkansas, western district	38,028 05	1		386 99					2,605 30	1		2,605 39						28,814 16
Tennessee, eastern district	1,037 08	5							92,937 22	3		92,937 22	1	03,324 21	4			366 25
Tennessee, middle district	134,675 40	2			321 75				40,471 38	2		40,471 38	1	40,471 38	2			54,396 99
Tennessee, western district	333,575 55	3							4,481 57	1		4,481 57		19,908 31	2			2,381 47
Kentucky	21,658 70	1																
Ohio, northern district	84,528 06	4													1			1,595 65
Ohio, southern district	40,617 65	3																321 75
Indiana	14,539 39	1		15,426 74														
Illinois, northern district	8,235 83	1																
Illinois, southern district	36,386 09	2																
Michigan, eastern district	7,353 01	1																
Michigan, western district					321 75													
Wisconsin, eastern district	1,164 94	1			1,164 94		1		1,164 94	1		1,164 94	1					1,164 94
Wisconsin, western district	17,730 51	2																
Missouri, eastern district	26,187 65	5		929 20	156 23		1		156 23	2			1	929 20	2			156 23
Missouri, western district																		9,184 86
Iowa																		11,435 17
Minnesota	7,222 61	1																11,000 00
Kansas																		
California			4					1										
Oregon																		
Nevada																		
Nebraska																		
New Mexico	64,103 64	1																
Utah	20,961 38																	
Washington Territory									355 53	1		335 53		355 53	1			
Colorado																		
Dakota																		
Arizona																		
Idaho	10,663 84	1																
Montana																		
Wyoming																		
Total	3,606,661 06	94		118,769 08	5,330 32		12	7	75	337,780 66	26	7	10	285,732 96	96	02	38	456,549 74	291,083 28

No. 3.—*Report of post-office suits instituted during the fiscal year ending June 30, 1871, in the several United States courts, and of proceedings had during said period in suits which were instituted prior thereto.*

SUMMARY.

Judicial districts.	Number of suits.	In suits brought during the fiscal year.								In suits commenced prior to the fiscal year.					Whole number of suits disposed of.	Whole number of judgments in favor of the United States.	Aggregate judgments.	Aggregate collections.
		Aggregate sued for.	Aggregate in judgment.	Collections.	For the United States.	Against the United States.	Settled, &c.	Remitted.	Pending.	Judgment in old suits.	For the United States.	Against the United States.	Settled, &c.	Collections.				
Maine	2		$1,189 00	$1,184 00	2					$9 01	1				3	3	$1,189 01	$1,184 00
New Hampshire	1		100 00	100 00	1										1	1	100 00	100 00
Massachusetts	3	$215 78	5 00		1		1		2	500 00				$500 00	2	1	5 00	500 00
Connecticut	3		25 00	222 79	2				1						3	2	25 00	222 79
New York, northern district	9			25 00	7										7	7		25 00
New York, southern district	1									33,021 98							33,046 98	
New York, eastern district																		
New Jersey	3	230 18	260 30	146 09	2		1			1,493 79	1			164 47	4	1	1,493 79	164 47
Pennsylvania, eastern district	3	2,880 40	146 09		1		1		2						4	3	146 09	1,306 30
Pennsylvania, western district	15	429 94	457 92	457 92	9	1			5	848 28	1			848 28	14	13	1,788 32	
Delaware										140 00	1			140 00	1	1	140 00	140 00
Maryland	9	7,520 39	940 04	1,804 78	8				1	9,118 65	27			1,956 25	9	8	1,756 76	1,804 78
Virginia, eastern district	3	31 63	1,756 76		1				1						29	28	9,118 65	1,956 25
Virginia, western district	1	1,320 34																
West Virginia	1	165 89	206 89						1	344 83	4			255 69	5	5	551 72	255 69
North Carolina	6	58 36	103 83	103 83	5				2	3,315 70	9			371 34	14	14	3,419 53	371 34
South Carolina	5	2,092 73	933 16		3				1	1,936 16	4			894 96	7	7	2,869 32	998 79
Georgia	3	167 35	149 22		2				1	8,105 79	13			1,079 82	15	15	8,255 01	1,202 01
Florida, northern district										561 64				10,202 01	5	5	1,985 58	10,202 01
Alabama, northern district	1	525 68								385 30								
Alabama, middle district	5	2,900 84	2,206 05	1,343 65	1				4	319 88	1			350 00	2	2	2,591 35	1,693 05
Alabama, southern district														228 78	2	2	319 88	228 78
Mississippi, northern district	13	4,795 78	4,004 93		7				6	1,328 96	2				12	12	5,333 89	
Mississippi, southern district	12	4,840 40	3,458 14		5				7	1,575 11	5				10	10	5,033 25	
Louisiana	6	2,018 25							6	71 11	1			71 11	1	1	71 11	71 11
Texas, eastern district	9	7,918 67				1			8	237 31	2			237 31	2	2	237 31	237 31

Texas, western district	2	420 69			2	420 69	4		6	334 46			6	1,334 46	754 35	754 35
Arkansas, eastern district	4					94 10	1	1	1	213 37			1	213 37	213 37	213 37
Arkansas, western district	2	94 10		105 12	2		1	10	3	304 57		105 12	3	409 69	290 95	396 07
Tennessee, eastern district								1	4	341 86			7	341 86	825 82	825 82
Tennessee, middle district	1	8,461 78	624 49		3	8,461 78	7	3	8	2,141 01		624 49	11	765 50	810 52	810 32
Tennessee, western district	10	160 22		192 47	1	160 22	1	1	1	66 07			1	66 07	122 40	122 40
Kentucky	1		1,118 06									1,118 06		1,118 06	996 27	1,168 74
Ohio, northern district	3	2,711 04	100 00	2,774 97				3				2,201 51		100 00		
Ohio, southern district	3	1,134 23	2,201 51	25 00			4	1		8,936 63		1,298 33		1,738 14	1,586 90	4,371 87
Indiana	4		1,298 33	25 00				3				25 00		1,288 13		25 00
Illinois, northern district	4		25 00					3		8,666 76				8,691 76	7,329 78	7,354 78
Illinois, southern district								3								
Michigan, eastern district	3	323 90	1,350 03	147 19			2	2	2	10,212 94		1,350 03	2	10,212 94	10,212 94	10,212 94
Michigan, western district	4	701 29		112 84			7		9				9			
Wisconsin, eastern district	10	277 93								331 08				331 08	27 45	174 64
Wisconsin, western district	1	50 39			1		2	5					5		303 75	416 59
Missouri, eastern district	2	920 04			2		1	1							159 54	159 54
Missouri, western district	8	1,776 99	371 94		5	2,678 56		2		2,678 56	1	371 94		3,050 50	1,025 58	1,025 58
Iowa	1															
Minnesota		3,983 01		397 55		397 55	3	1		397 55				397 55	500 00	500 00
Kansas	3	1,033 96		539 48	1	1,539 48	1	1		1,539 48	2		2	1,539 48	500 00	604 02
California	1		1,302 02									1,302 02			804 02	
Oregon	2	1,144 71				1,461 76	1	1		1,461 76	1		4	2,785 78	804 02	263 17
Nevada						468 00	1	1		468 00	1		1	2,468 00	263 17	
New Mexico	1	6,643 20		551 23		693 03	1	1		693 03	1		1	693 03		551 23
Utah																
Nebraska																
Colorado																
Dakota												551 23				
Montana																
Wyoming																
Total	193	69,950 09	24,570 91	9,321 88	99	3	9	92	134	104,800 26	1	44,098 47	246	233	129,371 17	53,420 35

No. 4.—Report of suits for fines, penalties, and forfeitures under the customs revenue laws, &c., instituted during the fiscal year ending June 30, 1871, in the several United States courts, and of proceedings had during said period in suits which were instituted prior thereto.

SUMMARY.

Judicial districts.	In suits brought during the fiscal year:									In suits brought prior to the fiscal year.					Whole number of suits disposed of.	Whole number of judgments in favor of United States.	Aggregate judgments.	Aggregate collections.
	Number of suits.	Aggregate sued for.	Aggregate in judgment.	Collections.	For the United States.	Against the United States.	Settled, &c.	Remitted.	Pending.	Judgment in old suits.	For the United States.	Against the United States.	Settled.	Collections.				
Maine	18	$177,500 00	$1,528 00	$1,265 36	6		2		10	$3,359 80	11	1	10	$6,759 80	30	17	$4,887 80	$8,025 16
New Hampshire													4	1,697 50	5	1		1,697 50
Massachusetts	31	4,815,104 62	16,679 62	16,017 30	7		2		22		1		4	17,605 07	14	8	16,679 62	33,692 37
Rhode Island	1	4,828 65							1				2		2			
Vermont	23			3,787 39	10				10				13	7,686 14	30	23		11,473 52
Connecticut	6	4,000 00	1,600 00	5,420 25	3		2	1	2	1,340 00	13		1		4	9	2,940 00	5,420 25
New York, northern district	18	2,370,028 71	50 00	4,242 41	10		1		9					660 64	12	22	50 00	4,903 05
New York, southern district	86	5,158 00	350 00	495,309 04	2		40	1	34	100 00	1		41	103,232 17	106	2	450 00	598,541 25
New York, eastern district	26		500 00	710 00	1		12	2	14	727 35	12				14	1	1,227 35	710 00
New Jersey	2	1,000 00		1,485 00		1	2		1	2,342 00	2				2		2,342 00	1,485 00
Pennsylvania, eastern district	5	500 00		3,917 47	1				1						4	1		3,917 47
Pennsylvania, western district	2														1			
Delaware																		
Maryland	9	40,000 00	350 00	100 00	5		1	1	3		5		1		7	5	350 00	100 00
Virginia, eastern district	1	500 00													2			
Virginia, western district																		
West Virginia																		
District of Columbia																		
South Carolina	1	16,000 00	50 00		1				40						1	1	50 00	
Georgia	40		1,000 00				2		5	2,100 00			1	7,270 92	11	6	3,100 00	7,270 92
Florida, northern district	8	1,000 00			1				1					5,504 00		1		5,504 00
Florida, southern district	2				1													
Alabama, northern district																		
Alabama, middle district																		
Alabama, southern district																		
Mississippi, northern district										1,800 00	3		3	700 00	3	3	1,800 00	700 00

Mississippi, southern district	93	10,500 00	200 00	5,067 16	6		3	1	93		1	71	2	245 00	84	7	200 00	187,731 22	245 00
Louisiana	13	2,050 00	400 00	400 00	4		1	1	3		3	2		182,664 06	21	7	400 00	400 00
Texas, eastern district	33							1	17									
Texas, western district	1								1									
Arkansas, eastern district											1				1			
Arkansas, western district	2					2			1		1		2		2			
Tennessee, eastern district	2				1				2				3		3	2		912 90	912 90
Tennessee, middle district				50 00	1							1	3	912 90	4	2	50 00	2,539 24
Tennessee, western district	1	1,000 00	50 00	50 00	9			1		550 00	2	4	2	2,539 24	12	11	600 00	5,049 63
Kentucky	5	300 00	3,552 00	3,552 00	43		2		3		8	2	3	1,497 63	15	51	3,552 00	5,502 00
Ohio, northern district	3		6,996 00	4,502 00			1			4,550 00	1	3		1,000 00	59	1	11,546 00	15,000 00
Ohio, southern district	11									15,000 00	1		4		1	1	15,000 00	
Indiana	53																	
Illinois, northern district									3						36			
Illinois, southern district	4											32		80 00				80 00	80 00
Michigan, eastern district																		
Michigan, western district																		
Wisconsin, eastern district	15	2,740 00	1,470 00	15,334 36	9		1		5		1	1			11	9	1,470 00	15,334 36
Wisconsin, western district	2								1		1	1			2			
Missouri, eastern district																		
Missouri, western district																		
Iowa																		
Minnesota																		
Kansas	1	1,000 00							1		1				1	1		
California																		
Oregon																		
Nevada																		
Nebraska																		
New Mexico																		
Utah																		
Washington Territory																		
Colorado																		
Dakota																		
Arizona																		
Idaho																		
Montana																		
Wyoming																		
Total	518	7,452,209 98	34,825 62	561,159 77	129	13	74	9	293	31,860 15	67	48	171	340,055 07	511	196	66,694 77	901,214 84

No. 5.—*Report of miscellaneous suits instituted during the fiscal year ending June 30, 1871, in the several United States courts, and of proceedings had during said period in suits which were instituted prior thereto.*

SUMMARY.

Judicial districts.	Number of suits.	In suits brought during the fiscal year.							In suits brought prior to the fiscal year.					Whole number of suits disposed of.	Whole number of judgments in favor of United States.	Total judgments.	Total collections.
		Aggregate sued for.	Aggregate in judgment	Collections.	For the United States.	Against the United States.	Settled, &c.	Pending.	Judgment in old suits.	For the United States.	Against the United States.	Settled, &c.	Collections.				
Maine	1	$1,500 00						1	$200 00	1							
New Hampshire	1	1,200 00						1									
Massachusetts	1		$1,052 00	$1,650 00	14								$335 25	15	15	$1,252 00	$336 25
Rhode Island	17	2,761 40						3									
Vermont			15 00													15 00	
Connecticut	3	2,150 40						3				3		2	2		
New York, northern district	15	5,221 40	1,650 00	120 15	3			40	1,290 00	2	1	2	1,509 70	5	5	2,850 00	3,159 70
New York, southern district	62	75,333 81	2,170 00	147 00	10		22	2	5,494 95	4			1,619 20	20	14	7,664 95	1,739 35
New York, eastern district	9	5,500 00						2	26,775 88	2			50 00	26	2	26,775 88	647 00
New Jersey	2	2,900 00	2,400 00	2,550 00	6		1	2	27,226 41	1	1	1		1	1	27,226 41	
Pennsylvania, eastern district	9	2,360 00						9	2,047 16	1			2,047 16	8	7	4,447 16	4,597 16
Pennsylvania, western district	17	3,500 00						2		6		1	326 80	1			326 80
Delaware		3,500 00			15		6		9,288 50	1			100 00				100 00
Maryland	23	32,435 99	19,710 00		8	3			9,288 50					21	21	28,998 50	
Virginia, eastern district	2	10,000 00	1,415 11	27 52				9	1,010 50	1	1	1		2	1	1,010 50	27 52
Virginia, western district								2	100 00	1			1,000 00	15	9	1,515 11	1,000 00
West Virginia														1			
District of Columbia																	
North Carolina	4	3,300 00	3,300 00		13			1	5,560 00	4				8	7	8,860 00	
South Carolina	24	18,925 00	2,751 40	45 75	17	3	2	9	1,018 57	1		1		16	13	3,769 97	45 75
Georgia	43	47,642 78	1,590 00		1		1	34	100 00	1				10	8	1,690 00	
Florida, northern district	3	16,281 30	500 00		1			1						2	1	500 00	
Florida, southern district	1		100 00		1								6,721 78	1	1	100 00	6,721 78
Alabama, northern district	1			100 00													100 00
Alabama, middle district																	
Alabama, southern district	1	500 00			2			1									
Mississippi, northern district	2	10,000 00	1,100 00									2	2,000 00	2	2	1,100 00	2,000 00

District														
Mississippi, southern district	2						2	27						
Louisiana	7	10,443 31					7							
Texas, eastern district	29		2,125 00	329 20	2	27	22			2,125 00		2	29	100 00	329 20
Texas, western district							1							
Arkansas, eastern district	2	30 00	105 00	329 20	27	22	14			105 00	329 20		3	27	
Arkansas, western district	30		2,590 00				4			2,930 00			30	1,105 00	5,342 63
Tennessee, eastern district	1	1,000 00		32 00			8	1,000 00		2,509 00		1	5		
Tennessee, middle district	1	30 00	2,509 00	85 88			4	360 00		1,106 00		4	19	6,117 20	2,208 20
Tennessee, western district	102	1,000 00	1,106 00	39 00			1			210 00		1	5	1,286 50	1,637 19
Kentucky	5		210 00	25 00						37,653 83		2	6	1,460 00	3,047 40
Ohio, northern district	4	420 00	37,653 83		10		1			75 00		30	15	42,293 83	39 00
Ohio, southern district	19	300 00	75 00		1		4	780 00		50 00		17	9	855 00	25 00
Indiana	9		50 00				1					1	1	50 00	
Illinois, northern district	1	2,800 00	180 00	100 00			3	5,245 30		180 00		7	1	5,245 30	100 00
Illinois, southern district	3	136 80	1,360 95	831 95		2	1	250 00		1,360 95		6	5	430 00	1,647 20
Michigan, eastern district	6		200 00	200 00				1,275 25		200 00		7	4	2,645 20	900 00
Michigan, western district	4	60 00				1	5					4	1	900 00	
Wisconsin, eastern district	3						4							
Wisconsin, western district	7	27,000 00	5,500 00	423 80	2	5	2	14,000 00		5,500 00		10	55	19,500 00	933 80
Missouri, eastern district	8	2,300 00	1,216 00		4	3	4	13,225 00	825 25	1,216 00		16	2	14,441 00	
Missouri, western district	3		30 00		3			4,000 00		30 00		4	7	4,030 00	
Iowa														
Minnesota	49	4,300 00	5,476 88	437 15	46	1	5	1,570 00	500 00	5,476 88		55	52	7,046 88	2,107 87
Kansas	6	150 00	100 00	100 00	1		3	4,048 00		100 00		2	7	4,148 00	100 00
California	7		2,725 00	2,668 50	7					2,725 00		7		2,725 00	2,668 50
Oregon									1,670 72					
Nevada							52							
Nebraska	55	52,000 00			1	1						6		211 26	
New Mexico								136 26						
Washington Territory	3		75 00		2		2		136 26	75 00		4	3	136 26	136 26
Colorado	1											2	1	211 26	
Dakota														
Arizona	2	2,000 00					2							
Idaho	5				5		5					1			
Montana	1	300 00	300 00		1					300 00		1	1	300 00	
Wyoming														
Total	610	462,955 79	101,450 17	9,902 90	249	7	53	301	135,589 98	80	8	40	31,410 66	437	329	237,040 15	41,313 56

No. 6.—*Report of suits against collectors of customs and other officers, instituted during the fiscal year ending June 30, 1871, in the several United States courts, and of proceedings had during said period in suits which were instituted prior thereto.*

SUMMARY.

Judicial district.	In suits brought during the fiscal year.				In suits commenced prior to the fiscal year.			Whole number of suits disposed of.	Whole number of judgments for United States during the year.
	Number of suits.	Decided for the United States.	Settled, dismissed, &c.	Pending.	For the United States.	Against the United States.	Settled, &c.		
New Hampshire								1	1	
Massachusetts	16			16	1			1	1
Vermont	8			2			1	1	1
New York, northern district	3		2	1				0	
New York, southern district	389	1	139	249	147	105	702	1,094	148
New Jersey	1			1					
Pennsylvania, eastern district	6		2	4				2	
Florida, northern district						1		1	
Alabama, southern district					2	1		3	2
Ohio, southern district	4			4		1		1	
Illinois, northern district	1			1		2		2	
Michigan, eastern district	1		1					1	
Missouri, eastern district	1			1					
California	1			1					
Total	425	1	144	280	150	111	704	1,110	151

No. 7.—*Statistical summary of business arising from suits, &c., in which the United States is a party, or has an interest, under charge of the Solicitor of the Treasury, during the fiscal year ending June 30, 1871.*

Suits brought during the fiscal year ending June 30, 1871.

Judicial districts.	Suits on Treasury transcripts.		Post-office suits.		Fines, penalties, and forfeitures under the customs revenue laws.		Suits on custom-house bonds.		Suits against collectors of customs and other officers of the United States.	Amount of the costs in favor of the United States.	Miscellaneous suits.		Total amount reported sued for.	Total amount reported in judgments in favor of United States.	Total amount reported collected.
	No.	Amount.	No.	Amount.	No.	Amount.	No.	Amount.	No.	Amt.	No.	Amount.			
Maine	1	$639 84	2	$215 78	18	$177,500 00	1				1	$1,500 00	$179,000 00	$2,717 00	$2,449 36
New Hampshire			1								1	1,200 60	1,200 00	100 00	100 00
Massachusetts	1	100,000 00	3		31	4,815,104 62	1	$180 00	16		17	2,761 40	4,818,046 02	17,731 62	16,017 30
Rhode Island	5	100,113 25	3		1	4,838 65							4,828 65		
Vermont					23								3,205 62	1,615 00	3,797 39
Connecticut	6	1,060,000 00	3		6				2		3	2,350 00	109,221 40	1,705 00	7,293 04
New York, northern district	3	30,000 00	9		18	4,009 00					15	5,221 40	109,221 40	2,545 00	4,387 56
New York, southern district	3	30,000 00	1		86	2,370,028 71	1	952,268 86	3		62	5,333 81	4,437,744 63	500 00	495,456 08
New York, eastern district					26	5,158 00	230		389		2	5,500 00	40,658 00	15,600 00	710 00
New Jersey	3	32,145 99	3	230 18	5						9	2,900 00	35,376 17	2,660 00	6,435 50
Pennsylvania, eastern district	3	32,019 43	3	2,880 40	2	1,000 00			1		2	360 00	35,063 79	146 09	4,063 55
Pennsylvania, western district	3	30,633 85	15	429 94	5	500 00	5	4,135 00	6		17	3,500 00		55,666 57	992 08
Delaware															
Maryland	1	106,816 82	9	7,520 39	9	40,000 00	9	17,784 90			23	32,435 99	206,360 10	3,121 87	2,232 30
Virginia, eastern district	4	94,936 32	3	31 63	9	500 00						10,000 00	104,567 13	51,366 43	
Virginia, western district	5	217,394 33	1	1,320 34	3								216,067 67		
West Virginia	2	32,547 37	1	165 89	1								32,713 96	206 89	
District of Columbia															
North Carolina	2	50,399 92	6	58 36	1	16,000 00					4	3,300 00	53,758 28	3,403 83	103 83
South Carolina	2	50,643 40	5	2,099 73	40						24	13,883 00	71,561 13	3,734 56	45 75
Georgia, northern district	2	26,366 22	3	167 35	8						43	47,642 78	91,176 35	1,739 22	
Florida, southern district					2		1				3	16,281 30	16,281 30	1,500 00	
Alabama, northern district			1	525 68							1			100 00	100 00
Alabama, middle district	3	260,453 32	5	2,900 84	93							500 00	1,025 66	2,906 05	1,343 65
Alabama, southern district	1	15,745 57			13								263,354 16		
Mississippi, northern district	3	70,689 76	13	4,795 78	12	10,500 00					1	10,000 00	15,745 57	5,748 12	
Mississippi, southern district	2	8,865 51	12	4,640 40	6	2,650 00	22	29,338 17			2	1,000 00	76,485 54	3,558 14	
Louisiana	3	51,754 09	6	2,018 25	9						7		24,285 91	695 19	5,324 05
Texas, eastern district	3	9,893 54	0	7,918 67	0						3	10,443 31	86,603.82	812 21	729 20
Texas, western district	2	261,396 62	9		33						29		17,812 21	2,525 00	
Arkansas, eastern district	1	216,196 27	2	430 69	1						2	30 00	261,396 62	105 00	5,354 05
Arkansas, western district	1	315 68	4								30		216,646 96	2,500 00	315 08

No. 7.—Statistical summary of business arising from suits, &c.—Continued.

Judicial districts.	Suits brought during the fiscal year ending June 30, 1871.						In suits brought prior thereto.					Whole number judgments returned in favor United States during the year.	Total of suits disposed of.	Whole amount judgments rendered in favor of United States during the fiscal year ending June 30, 1871.	Whole amount collections from all sources during the fiscal year ending June 30, 1871.
	Decided for the United States.	Decided against the United States.	Settled, dismissed, &c.	Remitted.	Pending.	Total number suits commenced.	Amount judgments in all old suits this year.	Decided for the United States.	Decided against the United States.	Settled, dismissed, &c.	Amount reported collected in all old suits this year.				
Maine	8	1	3		11	22	$3,359 81	12	1	12	$6,719 80	20	36	6,076 81	9,209 16
New Hampshire	1				1	2	200 00	1		5	50	2	7	100 00	1,797 50
Massachusetts	22		3		43	68		3		6	16,411 32	25	34	17,931 62	34,458 62
Rhode Island				1		1				3			3		563 10
Vermont	12		2	1	12	27	1,319 43	13		1	7,690 14	15	42	2,955 00	11,473 52
Connecticut	8		4		3	13	340 00	2		14	1,159 70	10	13	3,017 43	8,862 74
New York, northern district	25		291		17	47	33,923 57	6		5	3,464 33	31	44	41,473 57	7,851 89
New York, southern district	11	1			468	773	35,355 17	166	106	949	108,426 74	177	1,526	32,755 17	604,142 82
New York, eastern district	10		12	1	17	30	35,627 41	52		2	9	53	74	53,627 41	710 00
New Jersey	2		3	2	5	18	17,647 16	3		1	14,311 63	13	24	19,707 46	21,146 63
Pennsylvania, eastern district	28	1	6		23	23	8,311 29			2	16,256 72	6	17	3,457 37	20,820 28
Pennsylvania, western district			1		8	37	10,136 78	10			5,548 29	38	15	65,803 35	1,940 36
Delaware							3,586 08	1		1		3	39	3,586 08	2,575 58
Maryland	22	1	9		20	51	2,290 15	4		1	2,775 55	3	4	6,119 02	3,229 30
Virginia, eastern district	4		1		4	10	99,195 55	31	1	2	94,356 25	28	36	150,561 98	94,359 25
Virginia, western district					6	6						35	39		
West Virginia	1				2	3	344 83	4			27 03	5	5	551 72	667 03
District of Columbia															
North Carolina	8		2		4	12	8,875 70	13		1	94 96	21	24	12,279 53	998 79
South Carolina	16	3	3		13	32	8,054 73	5			8,150 74	21	24	6,689 29	8,396 49
Georgia	9				77	88	90,962 73	38	1	4	6,118 86	47	49	92,701 95	16,718 66
Florida, northern district	2		2		6	11	24,085 58	11			16,787 42	13	21	25,585 58	12,787 42
Florida, southern district	2		3		1	1						2	2		100 00
Alabama, northern district	1				2	8	385 30	1			350 00				
Alabama, middle district					7	8	2,119 88		2		2,228 78	2	4	2,591 35	1,693 65
Alabama, southern district	10		9		8	18	1,328 96	5	1		12,176 30	15	10	2,119 88	2,928 78
Mississippi, northern district	7		2	1	102	109	4,910 39	6		71	245 00	13	15	7,077 08	12,976 39
Mississippi, southern district	8			1	33	51	226,336 36	33	11	2	203,151 67	41	13	227,031 55	245 00
Louisiana	31	12			28	74		5			237 31	36	131	2,525 00	208,475 73
Texas, eastern district					4	4							53		966 51
Texas, western district	2		2		5	7	2,334 46	7		1	754 35	9	10	2,439 46	754 35
Arkansas, eastern district															

No. 7.—Statistical summary of business arising from suits, &c.—Continued.

Suits brought during the fiscal year ending June 30, 1871.

Judicial districts	Suits on Treasury transcripts No.	Amount	Post-office suits No.	Amount	Fines, penalties, and forfeitures under the customs revenue laws No.	Amount	Suits on custom-house bonds No.	Amount	Suits against collectors of customs and agents or officers of the United States No.	Amt.	Miscellaneous suits No.	Amount	Total amount reported sued for.	Total amount reported in judgments in favor of United States.	Total amount reported collected.
Tennessee, eastern district	5	$38,028 05	2	$94 10							1	$1,000 00	$39,122 15	$105 12	$105 12
Tennessee, middle district	2	1,057 40									1	30 00	1,087 40		32 00
Tennessee, western district	3	134,675 55			2						102	114,274 00	265,177 79	3,133 49	644 00
Kentucky	1	333,575 70	4	8,461 72	2						5	1,000 00	334,575 70	1,106 06	475 99
Ohio, northern district		21,658 00	10		1	$1,600 00	1	$7,766 46			4		21,818 29	1,378 82	2,799 97
Ohio, southern district	1	84,592 65	3	160 22	5	300 00					19	420 00	85,948 65	38,190 82	3,577 00
Indiana	2	49,617 39	4		3				4		9	4,300 00	56,928 43	20,317 07	25 00
Illinois, northern district	4	14,539 83	1	2,711 04	11		3	5,939 70			1		21,613 76	25 00	4,923 75
Illinois, southern district	3	36,386 01	4	1,134 23					1		3	2,800 00	11,035 09	7,176 00	821 95
Michigan, eastern district	1		4	323 90			3	6,411 00			6	136 60	42,933 81	1,360 95	200 00
Michigan, western district	1		4	701 29					1		4		60 00	200 00	
Wisconsin, eastern district	2	1,164 94	3	50 39							3	60 00	1,164 94		1,164 94
Wisconsin, western district	1	17,730 51	4	277 93									45,054 41	3,500 23	147 19
Missouri, eastern district		26,787 65		920 04					1		7	27,000 00	29,688 94	3,495 23	692 87
Missouri, western district				1,776 99							8	2,200 00	50 39	30 00	
Iowa	1	7,222 61									3		8,142 65	5,848 82	
Minnesota													4,477 93	1,570 00	
Kansas					15	2,740 00			1		49	4,200 00	4,666 99	2,725 00	
California			3	3,983 01	2						6	150 00	3,983 01		
Oregon				1,144 71							7		1,144 71		
Nevada				1,033 96									117,137 60		
Nebraska	4	64,103 64									55	52,000 00			437 15
New Mexico	1	20,961 38			1	1,000 00					3		21,961 38	1,302 02	15,434 36
Utah														75 00	2,668 50
Washington Territory											1		19,309 04	300 00	75 00
Colorado													300 00		
Dakota											2				
Arizona											5				
Idaho											1				
Montana	1	10,665 84	1	8,643 20								300 00			551 23
Wyoming															
Total	94	3,606,661 06	193	69,950 09	518	7,452,209 98	276	1,014,894 09	425		610	460,935 79	12,604,601 01	290,410 97	586,271 76

No. 7.—*Statistical summary of business arising from suits, &c.*—Continued.

| Judicial districts. | Suits brought during the fiscal year ending June 30, 1871 | | | | | In suits brought prior thereto | | | | | | Whole number judgments in favor of United States returned during the year. | Total of suits disposed of. | Whole number judgments rendered in favor of United States during the year ending June 30, 1871. | Whole amount collections from all sources during the fiscal year ending June 30, 1871. |
	Decided for the United States.	Decided against the United States.	Settled, dismissed, &c.	Remitted.	Pending.	Total number suits commenced.	Amount judgments reported in all old suits this year.	Decided for the United States.	Decided against United States.	Settled, dismissed, &c.	Amount collected in all old suits this year.				
Tennessee, eastern district	2				6	8	$104 57	1		1	$230 95	3	4	$409 69	$396 07
Tennessee, middle district			1		4	5	341 86	4		2	85 82	4	12	341 86	825 82
Tennessee, western district	15				97	112	8,354 60	12	1	1	30,573 11	97	98	11,448 07	3,323 11
Kentucky	4		1		1	7	246 07	2	2	3	4,570 69	6	10	1,332 00	30,573 75
Ohio, northern district	15	3	1		10	17	1,250 00	4	5		56,599 24	19	22	136,319 04	5,513 99
Ohio, southern district	11		2		9	33	98,127 22	11	1	10	3,491 37	22	51	53,064 52	57,015 23
Indiana	17		1		4	18	30,198 01	11	1	8	1,825 63	18	29	55,438 46	6,778 34
Illinois, northern district	15		2		4	21	36,113 39	13	2	2	8,491 00	13	25	11,537 06	5,074 63
Illinois, southern district	1				15	69	13,912 06	9	1	2	1,900 00	14	16	11,976 00	8,953 43
Michigan, eastern district	51		3		1	9	4,895 25	3			825 25	60	70	2,645 20	5,923 75
Michigan, western district	7		1			3	1,875 00	3	4	1	10,112 94	10	17	23,412 94	10,647 20
Wisconsin, eastern district	1		2		12	18	25,212 94	3				4	7		10,412 94
Wisconsin, western district			1		7	93	14,000 00	11	32	2	27 45	8	51	19,500 00	164 94
Missouri, eastern district	4		1		2	4	13,556 08	1			863 75	24	29	17,051 31	1,496 62
Missouri, western district	13	2	1		7	3	4,000 00	1			9,244 40	4	5	4,030 00	9,344 40
Iowa	3		3		1	57					13,576 30				11,435 17
Minnesota					3	23	4,248 56				00 00	57	63	10,097 38	14,213 45
Kansas	46		1		6	9	4,251 00	9	1	1		13	15	5,891 00	15,434 36
California	10				12	3		3		1		7	9	2,725 00	3,168 50
Oregon	7		1		1	2						2	2		
Nevada	1				2	60	397 55	1			363 17	4	6	2,785 78	263 17
Nebraska	1				1		1,483 76	3			304 02	2	8	1,539 48	804 02
New Mexico			3		57		1,539 48			1					

REPORT OF THE SUPERVISING ARCHITECT.

REPORT

OF

THE SUPERVISING ARCHITECT OF THE TREASURY.

TREASURY DEPARTMENT,
OFFICE OF THE SUPERVISING ARCHITECT,
November 17, 1871.

SIR: I have the honor to submit the following report of the progress of the various works, with the construction, repair, or improvement of which this office has been charged, and also of the condition of the public property under its supervision, together with some recommendations in regard thereto.

Since the date of my last report, the only new buildings that have been commenced are the court-house and post-office at Columbia, South Carolina, and the custom-house and post-office at Machias, Maine. Work has been resumed on the custom-house at New Orleans, Louisiana, St. Paul, Minnesota, and the marine hospital at Chicago, Illinois, and has been continued on the custom-houses at Charleston, South Carolina; Knoxville, Tennessee; Cairo, Illinois; Omaha, Nebraska; Portland and Astoria, Oregon; the branch mint at San Francisco, California; the court-house and post-office at New York, and the post-office and treasury building at Boston, Massachusetts.

The custom-house at Portland, Maine; the court-houses and post-offices at Des Moines, Iowa; Portland, Maine; and Madison, Wisconsin; appraiser's stores at Philadelphia, Pennsylvania; and the assay office at Boise City, Idaho, have been completed, furnished, and are now occupied. The custom-houses at Alexandria, Virginia; Detroit, Michigan; New Bedford and Newburyport, Massachusetts; Newark, New Jersey; Portsmouth, New Hampshire; and the court-houses and post-offices at Windsor and Rutland, Vermont; and the marine hospital at Chelsea, Massachusetts, have been thoroughly repaired and remodeled, and are now in good condition. The old custom-house at Charleston, South Carolina, for the repair of which a special appropriation was made, has been refitted, and is now occupied. The addition to, and the remodeling of the custom-house and post-office at Baltimore, Maryland, is now in progress. Repairs, more or less, have been made on the following buildings, viz: Marine hospitals at Key West, Florida, and St. Louis, Missouri; and the custom-houses at Bath and Bangor, Maine; Boston and Barnstable, Massachusetts; Buffalo, New York; Cleveland, Ohio; Eastport, Maine; San Francisco, California; Cincinnati, Ohio; Erie, Pennsylvania; Galveston, Texas; Mobile, Alabama; New York, New York; Norfolk, Virginia; Oswego, New York; Pensacola, Forida; Pittsburgh, Pennsylvania; Philadelphia, Pennsylvania; Providence, Rhode Island; St. Louis, Missouri; Wilmington, North Carolina; the court-houses and post-offices at Boston, Massachusetts; Indianapolis, Indiana; New York, New York; and the marine hospitals at Cleveland, Ohio; Detroit, Michigan; and Portland, Maine.

The following appropriation was made at the last session of Congress, viz:

That the Secretary of the Treasury be, and he is hereby, authorized and directed to cause to be constructed a suitable building, fire-proof, at Trenton, New Jersey, for the accommodation of the post-office, United States circuit and district courts, pension, and internal revenue offices; and for this purpose there is hereby appropriated, out of any money in the Treasury not otherwise appropriated, one hundred thousand dollars, to be expended under the direction of the Secretary of the Treasury, who shall cause proper plans and estimates to be made, so that no expenditure shall be made or authorized for the full completion of said building beyond the amount herein appropriated.

Under the authority conferred by this act, offers of sites for the building were solicited by advertisement. After a full examination, it was found that a suitable lot could not be obtained for less than $45,000. As the appropriation expressly stipulated that no expenditure should be made or authorized for the full completion of the building beyond the sum of $100,000, and as it was so manifestly impossible to erect such a building as the act required for $55,000, (the balance that would remain after paying for the site,) no further action could be taken by the Department, even payment of the bills for advertising being estopped by the provisions of the act itself, they are still unpaid. This result was anticipated by this office, and vindicates the opinions uniformly expressed by me, that the building could not be erected for the sum it was proposed to appropriate. In this connection I desire to again call attention to the fact that it is impossible to reduce the cost of work below its intrinsic value by limitations on appropriations. Such limitations operate, as in the present instance, as a practical repeal of the appropriation, if respected, or in applications for deficiencies if ignored or evaded. No other result ever has been or ever can be obtained. If it were possible to reduce the market value of labor and materials by legislation, the object sought for could undoubtedly be attained, but not otherwise.

I would also, in this connection, call attention to the appropriation for the construction of the court-house and post-office at Columbia, South Carolina. An appropriation of $75,000 was made on the 3d of March, 1869, for the commencement of work without any other limitation than that a suitable site should be given by the citizens. Under this authority plans were prepared and approved by the Secretary of the Treasury, Secretary of the Interior, and Postmaster General, as required by law, for a building, the estimated cost of which was $285,161. This appropriation was afterward carried to the surplus fund under the operation of the act of July 5, 1870, in regard to unexpended balances. The following appropriation was subsequently made, viz:

That the appropriation made March 3, 1869, having been covered into the Treasury, the Secretary of the Treasury be, and he is hereby, authorized and directed to cause to be constructed upon the site already given to and owned by the United States, a suitable building, fire-proof, at Columbia, South Carolina, for the accommodation of the post-office and United States circuit and district courts; and for this purpose there is hereby appropriated out of any money in the Treasury, not otherwise appropriated, seventy-five thousand dollars, to be expended under the direction of the Secretary of the Treasury, who shall cause proper plans and estimates to be made, so that no expenditure shall be made or authorized for the full completion of said building beyond the amount herein appropriated.

The original plans contemplated a first-class granite building, three stories in height. These plans have been necessarily abandoned, and the foundation laid for a plain brick building of the same general ground-plan and dimensions, though but two stories in height, and which will be entirely inadequate for the accommodation of the officers for whose use it is intended, for the proper transaction of the public business, and unsatisfactory to the citizens of Columbia, who gave the property under the assurance that a suitable edifice would be erected; and it will be not only discreditable in itself as a Government building, but conspicuously so, in comparison with the magnificent though unfinished State-house in its immediate vicinity. I cannot too strongly recommend the repeal of the limitation on the cost of this building before the completion of the foundation.

The custom-house at Machias, Maine, will be completed within the amount of the appropriation, but by diminishing the durability of the structure, a light galvanized iron cornice and tin roof having been substituted for the granite cornice and slate roof contemplated by the original design. This saving has been made at the expense of true economy, and with the certainty that both roof and cornice will need renewal within a comparatively short time.

No action has been taken in regard to the new custom-house, court-house, and post-office at St. Louis, Missouri, for which an appropriation of $300,000 was made July 15, 1870, and renewed on April 20, 1871, that sum being entirely insufficient for the purpose. The building now occupied was erected at a time when labor and material were much cheaper than at present, and cost $321,987 08; it is entirely too small, is cheaply and poorly constructed, and is in every way unsuitable for the wants of the Government, as I have reported heretofore. To erect a building within the limit of the present appropriation would be but a waste of money. A new building is undoubtedly needed at St. Louis, but should not be commenced unless the Government can afford to spend the amount necessary to produce the proper result.

The work on the custom-house at St. Paul, Minnesota, which was suspended by the limitations placed on the cost of the building in the act of April 20, 1870, has been resumed, (the limitation having been repealed by the act of March 3, 1871,) and is now well advanced. The progress has been, on the whole, satisfactory; the work is of superior quality; and the cost has been less than the amount of any responsible proposal that could be obtained under advertisement. It is expected that the building will be inclosed during the present season, and be completed at an early date, and within the amount of the appropriation. This building would have been finished and occupied during the present year but for the legislation referred to. Charges were made by one Thomas M. Newson, who alleged that the contract for granite had been awarded without competition, and at extravagant rates, and that he, Newson, was both able and willing to furnish granite of equal quality, at much lower prices than were paid the contractor, viz, 65 cents per cubic foot, delivered at the site of the building without any allowances whatever. Although these charges were fully investigated by a committee of Congress, of which Hon. J. C. Churchill was chairman, and although their report entirely vindicated the action of this office, it is gratifying to be able to state that the report is also fully sustained, under oath, by no less a person than Mr. Newson himself, who, since that date, entered into a contract for granite with the Light-House Board, giving bond for the faithful performance thereof, which he subsequently declared, under oath, he was unable to fulfill, though awarded to him at much higher rates than those paid by this office. In his affidavit he states that he had no quarry, but owned land on which granite existed in large quantities and from which he expected to obtain it with very little expense of stripping or cost of opening; that, upon trial and working, the rock on the outside of the quarry proved fractious, and that every piece was spoiled by splitting; that after the quarry was fully opened he found it impossible to quarry stone for less than one dollar per foot; that he had entered into a contract to furnish and deliver at $1 25 per foot; but that, so delivered, its net cost to him would be $2 10 per foot; that to comply with his contract would involve a loss of $23,000, which would be ruinous to himself and others, and that he based his bid on the opinion of other persons, having himself no knowledge of the business.

This case is worthy of record as a specimen of the kind of evidence on which the charges against the management of this office have been based, and as an illustration of the correctness of the statement made in my last report, "That bonds are unnecessary in contracting with honorable and responsible men, and utterly worthless as a protection against rogues and shysters; thus placing the honest, *bona fide* bidder at the mercy of the dishonest and irresponsible one."

Work on the marine hospital at Chicago, Illinois, which was suspended at the same time and under the same conditions as at St. Paul, was resumed early last spring. It has been pushed forward with great energy, and will be finished at an early day, and would have been completed within the amount of the original estimates and the limitations of law but for the damage done to the building during the suspension of the work and the loss of material and increase in prices caused by the late fire, which the superintendent estimates at $14,060 50. The only result attained by the suspension of work on these buildings has been the complete vindication of this office against the charges made, a demonstration that its estimates were correct and its prices low, and a direct increase in cost to the Government.

In my last report I expressed the opinion that no expenditure on the custom-house at New Orleans, Louisiana, could make it a suitable, convenient, or creditable building. Since then much labor and time have been expended in the preparation of plans for its completion. It gives me great pleasure to report that the work of completing it is progressing in a satisfactory manner, and that alterations and improvements have been made that, while materially reducing the cost of finishing the building, have at the same time greatly increased its convenience, and they certainly do not detract from, if they do not improve, its external appearance. The first or basement story is now nearly completed. As the business of the port is steadily increasing, I would strongly recommend that an appropriation for the completion of the building be made without any further delay. It will, when finished, though devoid of beauty, be a permanent and substantial structure, and will accommodate all the branches of the public service.

The progress of work on the court-house and post-office in New York City has been not only gratifying but its cost has been kept within the amount of the estimates. The first story is now nearly completed. An idea of the immense amount of work that has been done may be formed from the following statement of materials used, and labor expended, to the present time, viz: 2,476,960 bricks; 15,701 barrels cement; 144,087 feet cube granite; 2,689 yards rubble masonry; 5,206,443 pounds of wrought and cast iron. And the magnitude of the undertaking, from the fact that there are now engaged at Dix Island 1,002 persons in the preparation of the granite alone, of whom 704 are employed in cutting the granite for the Government, and 298 in quarrying the stock and otherwise for the contractors. Three hundred and twenty-seven thousand one hundred and sixty-nine and one-half days' labor have already been expended in cutting and boxing the granite after it has been quarried; and it is estimated that three hundred thousand days' labor will be required to complete that branch of the work alone. The fidelity and capacity that have been exhibited by the superintendent, the Hon. Calvin T. Hulburd, cannot be overestimated or too highly praised. I see no reason whatever to doubt that the building will be completed within the limit fixed by law.

The nature of the soil required that the foundations for the New York post-office should be laid at a depth of 33 feet below the level of the sidewalk, and that sheet-piling should be used to the entire depth, while at Boston the same result was attained at a depth of 19 feet, and without any unusual precautions. The latter building is therefore much further advanced than the former, the second story being nearly completed. The progress of this work is highly gratifying to the Department, and in the highest degree creditable to the superintendent, Gridley J. F. Bryant, esq., though he has been considerably delayed by the legal proceedings referred to in my last report, which were found necessary to procure the additional property required, the lot originally purchased being inadequate for the site of the building. These questions have, however, been satisfactorily adjusted by the condemnation of the property at its appraised value, under a special act of the State of Massachusetts, all other attempts to procure the property at a fair price having failed. For this result the Government is mainly indebted to the untiring energy and perseverance of the postmaster, Gen. W. L. Burt. No further delay in the prosecution of the work is anticipated; and should the expectations of this office be realized, the building will be ready for occupancy by the Post-Office Department during the summer of 1872.

The progress of the work on the branch mint at San Francisco, California, has been satisfactory, and it will, unless any unforeseen obstacle should occur, be completed during the ensuing season. The estimates for this building, as for all others on the Pacific coast, were prepared on the basis of disbursements in coin. The Department having, however, decided that all payments must be made in currency, the amount of the appropriation must be increased accordingly. With this addition, the estimates will, it is believed, be found correct, and the work be finished at an early day, and as soon as the necessary machinery for the building can be completed, for which an appropriation must be obtained. This building has been designed as an earthquake-proof as well as fire-proof structure, and no pains spared to make it as permanent and substantial as possible. It is believed that success has been attained. The management of the superintendent, W. P. O. Stebbins, esq., has been highly creditable to him, and satisfactory to the Department.

The management and progress of the work on the custom-house at Astoria, Oregon, have been satisfactory; and had a sufficient appropriation been made, the building could have been inclosed during the past season. The cost of the work has been materially reduced, and, should no unforeseen difficulty occur, it will be finished for $10,000 less than originally estimated.

The progress of the work on the custom-house at Portland, Oregon, has been unsatisfactory, great trouble having been experienced in obtaining stone, the contractor being unable to fulfill his contract within the time specified, being neither conversant with the business nor possessed of the necessary capital to prosecute the work in a proper manner. The result is a fair illustration of the results of awarding contracts to the lowest bidder, irrespective of their ability. These difficulties have been in part, at least, overcome, and there is no good reason why the building should not be completed at an early day.

Great difficulty has been experienced in obtaining the services of competent mechanics at Knoxville, Tennessee, and considerable annoyance and embarrassment has been thereby caused to the Department. The marble of which the exterior of the building is erected justifies the expectations formed in regard to it, both as regards quality and cost. The building will be, when completed, one of the most substantial and permanent owned by the Government.

Work on the custom-house at Omaha, Nebraska, is progressing as rapidly as the limited appropriation permits, the first story being nearly completed. In this connection I desire to call attention to the impossibility of completing the building within the amount of appropriation, according to the original plans, which contemplated a three-story building, with an attic, and which were prepared under the direction of, and approved by, the Secretary of the Treasury, Secretary of the Interior, and Postmaster General, in accordance with law. The restrictions subsequently imposed will compel the completion of the building as a two-story structure. This will not furnish sufficient room for the proper transaction of the public business, and will necessitate an extension at no distant day, and at a greatly increased cost. It is not probable that another public building will be needed in the State of Nebraska for many years to come; and I cannot too urgently recommend that the present building should be constructed of sufficient capacity to meet the wants of the public service.

The resumption of work on the custom-house at Charleston, South Carolina, has proved an undertaking of unusual difficulty, many of the plans having been destroyed during the war, as well as a large portion of the valuable material that was intended for its construction. A large amount of marble work, some completed, and the remainder in various stages of completion, was stored on the premises and at the quarry at Hastings, New York. Much of it was seriously damaged and has required great care and judgment to utilize it, for which the superintendent is entitled to great credit. The quarry from which it was taken was abandoned some years since and subsequently filled up. The cost of reopening it being considered too great to warrant the expenditure, the building will be completed with marble from the quarries at Tuckahoe, New Jersey, the material being of the same character, and so nearly identical that it is believed that the change cannot be detected. The former contract for the supply of marble being unsatisfactory to the Department, it gives me great pleasure to report that the contractor, Edward Learned, jr., esq., has surrendered the same, and is now furnishing the material upon conditions that are entirely satisfactory to the Government. The plans under which the building is now being constructed will, it is estimated, reduce the cost of completion $470,274 99, without detriment to its appearance, capacity, or convenience. The expenditures on this building prior to the war can be fitly characterized by the epithet of reckless extravagance, the workmanship, though fine, being apparently designed as a mere excuse for the expenditure of money. It may be worthy of remark that the management of this building, like the Boston and New Orleans custom-houses, was under a special commission.

The extension of the custom-house at Baltimore, Maryland, in order to provide accommodation for the post-office in that city, was authorized by the act of July 15, 1870, which appropriated $20,000 for the purpose. This extension is now nearly completed and will be a great improvement to the building and a relief to the over-crowded employés. The great increase of the Government business in this city demanded still further relief; it was therefore determined to utilize the large and beautiful rotunda of the building, heretofore vacant, by fitting it for customs purposes. Offices for the use of the assistant treasurer are now in course of preparation, and fire and burglar-proof vaults are now being constructed. Plans for the permanent improvement of the building have been prepared, which, if carried out, will, it is believed, provide all the accommodation that will ever be required by the Government in that city, as well as a handsome and convenient building. I strongly recommend that the necessary appropriation be obtained and the work completed as soon as practicable. I also renew the recommendation contained in my last report in regard to the purchase of the Merchants' Bank property, if it can be obtained at a fair price.

I desire you to renew the recommendations contained in former reports in regard to the unfinished marine hospital at New Orleans, Louisiana. It is situated in one of the most unsuitable and unhealthy localities that could have been selected. It was, when purchased, a palmetto swamp, and, though it has been since partially drained, is much more suitable for cemetery than hospital purposes. The building is an immense structure of cast iron, and has already cost $528,134 34. The lowest estimate of the cost of completion that can fairly be made is $200,000. A fine and convenient pavilion hospital of ample size could be erected for a sum not to exceed $75,000, exclusive of the site, which should be situated on the banks of the river, either immediately above or below the city. In my last report I recommended the transfer of Sedgwick Hospital to the marine hospital establishment, it being no longer needed for military purposes. No action having been taken by Congress, this fine and admirably arranged establishment, which cost the Government upward of $800,000, and which was in good condition, was sold at public auction and realized but the nominal sum of $9,305 75, the land on which it was erected being held on a lease, and not owned by the Government. The material in the present hospital building is valuable, and though it is yearly depreciating from neglect and decay, could undoubtedly be sold for enough to erect a suitable and commodious pavilion hospital, thereby effecting a direct saving of not less than $200,000. I strongly recommend that authority be obtained to dispose of the building and land, either together or separately, and to purchase a new site and erect a suitable building with the proceeds.

Sealed proposals for the wreck of the marine hospital at San Francisco, which has been vacant since the earthquake of October, 1868, were invited by public advertisement. The highest offer that was obtained was but $1,560 coin. This result being unsatisfactory, all the bids were rejected, and the superintendent of the new mint in that city directed a careful examination of the building, and an estimate of the value of the material it contained, with a view to wrecking the building and disposing of the material. The result of his investigation being unsatisfactory, no further action has been taken. Considerable and unfavorable comment has been elicited at the low prices offered for the old material contained in this wreck. It was not, however, entirely unexpected to me, though considerably below my estimate of its value, the bricks of which it was constructed being, as I have previously reported, of little or no value, being made with salt water, and imperfectly burned. The result fully vindicates the opinion expressed of the worthless character of the structure and the inexpediency of making any further repairs upon it. I desire to renew my recommendations in regard to the erection of a pavilion hospital on one of the Government reservations near the city, to be selected hereafter.

Plans have been prepared that will afford ample and excellent accommodation at a total cost of $58,789 56, to which sum the expenditure may be safely restricted.

The marine hospital building at Pittsburgh is in bad condition, and needs a much larger expenditure for repairs and improvements than is, in my opinion, justified by the value of the building. Since it was erected the property immediately adjoining has been occupied by iron-works, which, while increasing the intrinsic value of the property, have injured it materially for hospital purposes. The supervising surgeon recommends the sale of the property, the purchase of a more eligible site, and the erection thereon of a hospital on the pavilion system. I fully concur in this opinion, for economical as well as sanitary reasons, and feel confident that a suitable site and a convenient and satisfactory building can be purchased and erected for the value of the present property, thus saving the entire cost of the necessary repairs, which are estimated at upwards of $25,000. I also desire to renew my recommendation that the smaller marine hospitals be disposed of, and that hospitals be maintained by the Government at the principal ports only. Most of the buildings now owned by the Government were constructed at a time when little knowledge existed, and less attention was paid to sanitary construction. They were also, as a rule, cheaply constructed, and badly planned. As a consequence they are in constant need of repairs, and are, at the best, unsatisfactory and unsuitable structures. The practice of leasing is not satisfactory in the results to the buildings, and greatly increases the amount of cost for repairs. I believe the interests of the Government will be better subserved by the sale of those that are not of sufficient importance to warrant their management by the Department.

The opinions expressed in the following extract from my report of September 30, 1866, viz, " I regret to report that the custom-house building at Portland, Maine, which has been considered strictly fire-proof, was irreparably injured by the disastrous conflagration in that city, and must be rebuilt from the foundation-walls. The total destruction of its contents was only prevented by the strenuous efforts of some persons who were overtaken by the fire, and were unable to leave the building, where they barely escaped with their lives. The experience in this case has proved conclusively that stone and iron structures, however carefully constructed, offer no successful resistance to a large conflagration, and that all Government buildings should be isolated by wide streets or open spaces," have been fully sustained by the results of the late disastrous fire in Chicago. The custom-house in that city was situated on the southwest corner of Dearborn and Monroe streets, the former of which is eighty and the latter sixty-six feet in width. Its west façade, however, faced Lombard block, which was a fine structure, five stories in height, rising from fifteen to twenty feet above the top of the custom-house, from which it was separated by a narrow street only twenty-seven feet wide. The immediate cause of the destruction of the custom-house was the burning of this block, the flames from which, driven, by the fierce southwest gale prevailing at the time, against the walls of the building, soon destroyed the stone-work, warped the iron-work and shutters of the windows from their fastenings, and gave the flames free access to the interior.

The requirements of the Post-Office Department, for whose use the first story of the building was designed, made it necessary to carry the entire interior on cast-iron columns, which, of course, soon yielded to the heat and precipitated the upper floors into the cellar. It has been supposed that the destruction of the column was caused by the heat evolved from the burning furniture in the post-office. This, I am am satisfied, from a personal examination, was not the case. The columns at the south end of the building, which were not exposed to the fiery blast from the Lombard block, though in immediate contact with the wood-partitions forming the office of the postmaster, assistant postmaster and cashier, remain intact, while those at other points not directly in contact with any wood-work were entirely destroyed. The destruction of the building was, in my opinion, attributable entirely to the intense heat which was forced through the open windows like hot blasts from a smelting-furnace, and which thoroughly fused metal and glass. I feel confident that, had the iron columns been rendered fire-proof, which could readily have been done, the interior construction of the building, as well as the contents of the rooms on the east front, including the vaults of the depository, would have been saved; and had the exterior of the building been protected by fire-proof shutters its contents would have been preserved. Indeed, the contents of one room, at the south end of the building, which was the only one in the second story supported by brick walls instead of iron columns, were uninjured. Had the custom-house been isolated on all sides by streets of equal width with those first mentioned, I do not believe that it would have been seriously damaged. The property on which the building was erected was purchased in 1855 and 1857 for $60,200, and the building erected within 15 feet of the line of the Government property. In 1865 an arrangement was made with Mr. Lombard, at a cost of $8,400, by which this space was increased, as above stated, to 27 feet. At the time the building was erected there was no difficulty in obtaining all the land that was desired at a low price; and I believe that for an additional sum, not to exceed $30,000, an ample lot could have been secured and the destruction of the building in all probability averted. If this was an exceptional case some excuse might be offered for the selection of so small a lot; but it has been the rule instead of the exception. One entire side of many of the most important buildings erected prior to 1860 is practically worthless, from the absence of light, due to the smallness of the lot and the proximity of lofty buildings which entirely overshadow them and cut off the light; and under the same circumstances as at Chicago they will share a similar fate.

In this connection I would call the attention of the Department to the necessity for such legislation as will enable the Government to condemn any land that is absolutely needed for the preservation of the buildings now owned by the Government, or for the acquisition of suitable lots for those hereafter to be erected. The experience at Boston has shown that the Department is at present at the mercy of any property-owner, should he desire to use the necessities of the Government for speculative purposes, and that condemnation is the only remedy. In my last report I called attention to the fact, that although the entire space within the custom-house building at Chicago, including the cellar, had been occupied, it was still entirely inadequate for the transaction of the public business, the postal business alone in that city having increased over 80 per cent. during the past three years. The fire has been productive of a still further increase, and it would now be impossible to accommodate that department in the building, even were it desirable to attempt its reconstruction. The increase of the customs business, by reason of direct importations of dutiable merchandise from foreign countries under the provisions of the act of July 14, 1870, has been even greater, with every prospect that it will continue to augment for years to come.

26 D

Under all the circumstances I believe that the necessities of the Government require the purchase of the remainder of the block on which the custom-house building is located, and the erection thereon without delay of a building of sufficient capacity to accommodate all the branches of the Government service in that city.

The completion of the granite dock on the Battery in New York City renders a decision in regard to a new barge office imperative, as it will be of little or no practical value to the revenue department, for whose use it was principally intended, until a suitable building is erected thereon. In this connection I again call attention to the importance of securing the whole or a portion of the Battery as a site for the erection of a new custom-house, and other buildings for the use of the revenue department in that city. The present buildings are overcrowded and unsuitable, and with the increasing of business of that port cannot much longer be used. The Battery is the natural and only suitable location for such structures, and should be secured before it is too late. I respectfully suggest that authority be obtained from Congress for a full and thorough investigation of this subject.

I also desire to call attention to the importance of erecting appraisers' stores in that city. The building now occupied is not only unsuitable for the examination and appraisal of goods, or for their safety while in the custody of the Government, but for the accommodation of its officers and the public. The enormous increase in that branch of the public business can be well illustrated by a comparison of the receipts of the months of August and September, of the present year, with the corresponding period in 1869 and 1870. The number of packages received is as follows, viz:

Receipts in August, 1869, were 15,592
Receipts in September, 1869, were 14,875

                                                                       30,467
                                                                       ======

Receipts in August, 1870, were 16,873
Receipts in September, 1870, were 19,293

                                                                       36,166
                                                                       ======

Receipts in August, 1871, were 23,790
Receipts in September, 1871, were 23,427

                                                                       47,217
                                                                       ======

The total receipts for 1869 161,866
The total receipts for 1870 200,461
The total receipts for nine months of 1871 173,916

which shows an increase, during the present year, of 30½ per cent. Unless some definite action is taken soon, the rent, which amounts at present to $66,003 25 per annum, must be increased, and additional accommodations procured elsewhere. If the present system of renting is continued for the next ten years, the Government will pay more than the value of a suitable building and site, without even then obtaining facilities for the transaction of its business or any adequate security for the goods in its custody. I believe few expenditures are more urgently demanded by the necessities of the Government than this. I also desire to call special attention to the great importance of providing similar stores at the ports of Boston, Chicago, Cincinnati, and St. Louis, all of which should be fire-proof—not only in name, but in fact—which can readily be accomplished in buildings of that character, and at a moderate cost. The appraisers' stores at Philadelphia and Baltimore are located in well-constructed buildings of brick and iron, the former being, in my opinion, absolutely fire-proof, and the latter requiring nothing but the addition of fire-proof doors and shutters to make them equally so. This branch of the public service is well provided for in the custom-houses at New Orleans, Charleston, Savannah, Portland, and many minor ports.

I would again recommend the sale of the United States Mint buildings at New Orleans, Louisiana, and Charlotte, South Carolina, neither of which are required for the use of the Government. And I would again urge the passage of an act authorizing the Department in its discretion to dispose of such public property under its charge as may no longer be required for government purposes. Such a law would greatly facilitate the business of the Department, and obviate the necessity of obtaining special legislation in each case.

I also desire to call special attention to the necessity for a decision in regard to the quarantine buildings and property now owned by the Government. It appears to me that an effective quarantine by State authorities is, in the present condition of inter-communication, impossible, and that if a quarantine is to be maintained, it should be under the direction of the General Government. It needs no argument to prove that a quarantine at the port of New York, however strict, without a quarantine at the adjoining ports, would be of no avail, as infected passengers and merchandise could be landed in the adjoining States, and transported by rail to that city almost as quickly as they could pass the ordinary examination and be landed at the wharf in that city. Should it be deemed expedient to place the matter under charge of the General Government, the quarantine property should be placed in good condition, to do which will require the expenditure of a considerable sum of money. If, on the other hand, it should be deemed desirable to leave the enforcement of quarantine in the hands of the State authorities, it appears to me that they should provide proper facilities for carrying into effect their own laws, and that the Government should not be expected to bear the expense of a quarantine over which it has no control.

The change in the grade on the east front of the Treasury building necessitated the reconstruction of the sidewalks and approaches on that front, as well as the underpinning of a large portion of the building. This work is now nearly finished, and will be completed at a cost considerably within the amount of the estimate and the appropriation. I cannot refrain from expressing my regret that so much money was expended on the only portion of the building that cannot be considered permanent, convenient, or suitable. I would respectfully renew my recommendation for the condemnation of the property on the opposite side of the street, as explained in my report for the year 1868, and feel sure that the plan must ultimately be adopted, and that each year's delay but increases the value of the property that must eventually be purchased. In addition to the architectural reasons that necessitate this change, the enormous value to the Government of the Treasury building and its contents, and the irreparable loss to the country that its destruction would involve, no possible precaution for its preservation should be omitted; and, though I do not believe it probable that it will ever be subjected to the ordeal, I am by no means certain that it would escape unscathed from the effects of a conflagration on the east side of Fifteenth Street, under similar conditions as existed at Chicago, the windows and sash of the old portion of the building being of ordinary wooden construction, and the entire building without shutters.

I also desire to renew my recommendation that an appropriation be obtained for additional coal-vaults, and a sub-way for the receipt of fuel and the removal of ashes on the west front; also, the abandoning of the inclined cartway and the narrowing of the area on that front, which disfigures its magnificent façade and suggests the combination of a palace and a manufactory. These improvements would complete the north, south, and west wings in a permanent and creditable manner, and involve the expenditure of but $30,000.

I desire to call attention to the fact that it is impossible to comply with the requirements of the fifth, sixth, and seventh sections of the act of July 12, 1870, in regard to unexpended balances, as interpreted by the First Comptroller of the Treasury, who is vested by law with authority to determine the effect of its provisions. It needs no argument to prove that each suspension of work during the progress of a building costs the Government a sum of money, greater or less, in proportion to the magnitude of the undertaking. No saving can result from the application of this law to public works of any kind or description; on the contrary, it is a constant and fruitful source of embarrassment and annoyance; it multiplies the labors and responsibilities of every officer in charge of the construction or repair of public works; increases the clerical labors; complicates the accounts; and results only in an increase of cost to the Government, and a delay in the performance of the duties assigned to such officer. I fail to see any possible benefit to be derived from the application of this law to the class of expenditures to which I have alluded.

The progress and cost of the works under the supervision of this office have during the past year been satisfactory, save in a few instances. Contracts for the supplies of material have been generally made below current market rates, and the cost of the work, as a rule, kept within the estimates. The liberal appropriation made at the last session of Congress for repairs and furniture has enabled the Department to make many necessary repairs, and improve the condition of the public buildings. Expenditures have been judiciously made, and with a view to permanency as well as immediate convenience. The large number of buildings and the pressing necessity that existed for this appropriation has, however, rendered it necessary to make nothing more than temporary repairs on a considerable number, and I earnestly hope that the additional appropriation asked for will be granted. It is undoubtedly far cheaper to keep the buildings in good repair than to restore them from the condition of dilapidation, which has been too generally the case. The appropriation for the pay of janitors and custodians of public buildings has enabled the Department to protect much valuable property from injury; and by keeping its buildings in a creditable condition has greatly added to the convenience and comfort of the public as well as the officers of the Government. It is believed that the direct saving to the Government is more than the amount of the appropriation for this purpose.

I desire once more to enter my protest against the inadequate compensation of the officers, clerks, and employés of this office. The salaries are either too large or too small. If the mere object is to secure the services of persons who desire positions under the Government, they are certainly too high, as occupants for every place can be obtained at much lower rates, who will willingly draw their salary with zeal and regularity. But if the object is to obtain and retain persons who are competent to perform their duties, and whose services are valuable to the Government, they are far too low. The talents and integrity required for the proper transaction of the public business will and do command much higher rates from private individuals and corporations.

Many Government employés holding responsible positions involving large expenditures receive less pay than journeymen mechanics whose responsibilities end with each day's work. This office has, perhaps, been more embarrassed from this cause than any other, many of its employés being men of technical education, whose places cannot readily be filled. I feel it but justice to call special attention to the services rendered by the assistant supervising architect, James O. Rankin, esq., whose capacity, fidelity, and integrity cannot be too highly praised. Mr. Rankin has retained his position thus far at my personal solicitation, with the hope that justice would be done him. I cannot longer hope to retain him, unless his compensation is increased to a degree that approximates the value of the services rendered and the responsibilities of his position.

I also take great pleasure in testifying to the fidelity and industry of the clerks and draughtsmen employed in this office, and my indebtedness to them for the success that has attended my labors during the past year.

In conclusion, I desire to tender you my thanks for the cordial support and assistance, and the uniform courtesy which I have experienced at your hands, and remain,

Yours, very respectfully,

A. B. MULLETT,
Supervising Architect.

Hon. GEORGE S. BOUTWELL,
Secretary of the Treasury.

Tabular statement of custom-houses, court-houses, post-offices, mints, &c., under the charge of this office, exhibiting the cost of site, date of purchase, contract price of construction, actual cost of construction, and the total cost of the work, including site, alterations, and repairs, to June 30, 1871.

Nature and location of work	Date of purchase.	Cost of site.	Contract price of construction.	Actual cost of construction.	Total cost to June 30, 1871.	Remarks.
CUSTOM-HOUSES.						
Alexandria, Va., (old)	Nov. 25, 1820	$6,000 00		$8,246 46	$14,396 46	Sold April 8, 1871.
Alexandria, Va., (new)	May 13, 1856	16,000 00	$37,149 37	57,913 64	82,492 53	
Astoria, Oreg., (old)	Mar. 27, 1856	900 00			920 00	
Astoria, Oreg., (new)	May 7, 1868	8,000 00			48,754 47	In course of erection.
Bath, Me	Feb. 7, 1852	15,000 00	47,549 36	90,182 65	106,982 63	
Bangor, Me	June 5, 1851	15,000 00	45,584 39	103,698 13	212,562 82	
Barnstable, Mass	April 24, 1855	1,500 00	17,250 00	34,433 71	38,639 93	
Baltimore, Md	July 16, 1817	*70,000 00				Part of present building.
Baltimore, Md	Feb. 10, 1853	*110,000 00				Do.
Baltimore, Md	May 23, 1857	*207,000 00		431,672 61	915,505 75	Including both of above.
Belfast, Me	Oct. 4, 1856	5,000 00	17,500 00	34,340 25	38,630 56	
Boston, Mass	Aug. 29, 1857	180,000 00		866,658 00	1,110,816 49	
Bristol, R. I.	Mar. 12, 1856	4,400 00	17,322 00	23,952 68	28,540 88	
Buffalo, N. Y.	Jan. 22, 1855	45,000 00	117,769 05	191,764 34	292,973 43	
Burlington, Vt.	Mar. 30, 1855	7,750 00	28,238 40	40,036 96	74,834 96	
Cairo, Ill	April 28, 1866	*1,200 00			238,298 54	In course of erection; site donated.
Castine, Me	April 6, 1833				13,030 72	In course of erection.
Charleston, S. C.	July 10, 1849	130,000 00			2,220,556 49	
Cleveland, Ohio	April 9, 1856	30,000 00	83,500 00	138,236 30	190,948 73	
Cincinnati, Ohio	Sept. 1, 1851	50,000 00		242,197 23	363,911 26	
Chicago, Ill	Jan. 10, 1855	26,000 00	276,750 56	365,694 18	505,618 58	
Chicago, Ill	July 1, 1857	34,200 00		214,020 61	223,184 35	
Detroit, Mich	Jan. 26, 1865	8,400 00	103,160 66	179,095 96	199,850 51	
Detroit, Mich	Nov. 13, 1855	24,000 00	87,334 50			
Dubuque, Iowa	Feb. 17, 1857	20,000 00			45,056 20	Old building; acquired for debt.
Eastport, Me	July 17, 1830	2,780 00	30,500 00	32,509 60	26,646 42	
Ellsworth, Me	July 3, 1847	3,000 00	9,200 00	21,629 84	34,205 69	
Erie, Pa.	April 11, 1855	*29,000 00			82,138 02	
Galena, Ill	July 2, 1849	16,500 00	43,629 00	61,372 44	135,218 45	
Galveston, Tex	Mar. 24, 1857	6,000 00	94,470 74	106,339 82	67,406 29	
Georgetown, D. C.	Sept. 1, 1855	9,000 00	41,582 00	55,368 15	50,754 82	
Gloucester, Mass	Oct. 23, 1856	*1,575 00	26,596 78	40,765 11	2,346 42	
Key West, Fla.	June 6, 1855	*4,003 00			9,036 89	
Kennebunk, Me	Nov. 19, 1832	5,250 00				
Knoxville, Tenn	Mar. 3, 1871	16,000 00			96,447 50	In course of erection.
Louisville, Ky	Oct. 7, 1851	1,000 00	148,158 00	246,640 75	334,775 57	
Machias, Me	May 7, 1870				2,430 00	In course of erection.

Location	Date					Remarks
Middletown, Conn	Feb. 8, 1833	3,500 00		12,176 64	32,891 83	
Milwaukee, Wis	Feb. 16, 1855	12,500 00		161,779 61	190,818 31	
Mobile, Ala	Oct. 13, 1851	12,500 00		382,159 93	417,809 92	
Nashville, Tenn	Feb. 17, 1857	20,000 00			20,502 41	
Newark, N.J	May 30, 1855	50,000 00		109,873 00	167,761 33	
New Bedford, Mass	April 9, 1833	4,900 00		24,500 00	35,432 70	
Newburyport, Mass	Aug. 1, 1833	3,000 00		24,188 50	26,960 80	
New Haven, Conn	June 1, 1853	25,500 00		158,614 50	294,168 72	
New London, Conn	May 18, 1853	3,400 00		14,600 00	21,674 85	
New Orleans, La	Jan. 1, 1848		130,664 03		3,071,537 14	In course of erection; site donated.
Newport, R.I	Sept. 16, 1849	*1,000,000 00		9,100 00	12,926 88	Old building.
New York, N.Y	April 29, 1865	1,400 00			1,285,428 97	
Norfolk, Va	Dec. 6, 1817	9,000 00			47,002 33	
Norfolk, Va	Feb. 28, 1832	13,500 00		34,352 33	226,520 44	
Ogdensburgh, N.Y	Feb. 4, 1857	8,000 00	81,252 90	203,893 75	231,417 27	
Oswego, N.Y	Dec. 15, 1854	12,000 00	88,000 00	216,626 88	136,223 75	
Plattsburgh, N.Y	June 10, 1856	5,000 00		114,012 03	73,561 35	
Pensacola, Fla	Feb. 5, 1856	15,000 00	77,255 00	66,925 17	53,330 70	Site acquired from Spain.
Petersburgh, Va	May 8, 1851	41,000 00	51,324 94	49,177 43	117,681 43	
Pittsburgh, Pa	Aug. 27, 1844	*257,000 00	67,619 88	84,664 88	154,678 31	
Philadelphia, Pa	May 17, 1834	*2,500 00	39,666 00	99,747 00	324,612 54	
Plymouth, N.C	June 22, 1837	19,500 00			2,932 37	
Portsmouth, N.H	Oct. 4, 1838	5,500 00	62,728 96	145,046 91	179,923 34	
Portland, Me	Dec. 21, 1866	35,000 00			524,633 12	
Providence, R.I	Nov. 26, 1817	40,000 00		10,504 00	16,492 96	Old building; used as warehouse.
Providence, R.I	Oct. 9, 1854	15,000 00	151,000 00	209,841 71	262,854 24	In course of erection.
Portland, Oreg	April 6, 1868	61,000 00			114,324 79	
Richmond, Va	June 22, 1853	150,000 00	110,000 00	194,404 47	288,165 61	
San Francisco, Cal	Sept. 8, 1854	11,000 00	400,000 00	638,581 49	814,755 26	
Sandusky, Ohio	Dec. 16, 1845	20,725 00	47,560 00	64,019 41	85,658 05	
Savannah, Ga	June 23, 1818	5,000 00		156,434 35	194,817 80	
Salem, Mass	Oct. 31, 1851	37,000 00		14,271 77	35,538 89	
St. Louis, Mo	April 10, 1867	16,000 00		321,987 06	383,097 08	In course of erection.
St. Paul, Minn	May 20, 1855	*6,000 00			300,031 38	
Suspension Bridge, N.Y	Feb. 29, 1852	12,000 00			25,883 37	
Toledo, Ohio	Nov. 29, 1852	2,000 00	45,530 11	83,543 52	96,312 41	
Waldoborough, Me	Sept. 7, 1855	20,500 00	15,800 00	22,824 68	25,132 93	Destroyed by fire January, 1840.
Wheeling, W.Va	Mar. 19, 1819	*14,000 00		96,618 64	125,408 26	Built on site of above.
Wilmington, N.C	May 17, 1845	1,000 00	85,070 83		15,000 00	
Wilmington, N.C	May 27, 1843	3,500 00		42,039 75	60,325 15	
Wilmington, Del	June 20, 1868	1,800 00	29,234 00	40,146 34	55,124 21	
Wiscasset, Me			17,000 00	23,230 00	29,940 30	
MARINE HOSPITALS.						
Chelsea, Mass	July 12, 1858	50,000 00	122,185 39	223,015 31	383,554 33	
Cleveland, Ohio	Oct. 11, 1837	12,000 00	20,000 00	79,972 05	111,146 49	
Chicago, Ill	Jan. 22, 1867	10,000 00	54,637 12		207,428 16	In course of erection.
Detroit, Mich	Nov. 19, 1855	23,000 00		78,215 14	107,033 62	

* Building and site.

Tabular statement of the custom-houses, court-houses, post-offices, mints, &c.—Continued.

Nature and location of work.	Date of purchase.	Cost of site.	Contract price of construction.	Actual cost of construction.	Total cost to June 30, 1871.	Remarks.
MARINE HOSPITALS—Continued.						
Key West, Fla.	Nov. 30, 1844	$500 00		$25,600 00	$34,644 84	
Louisville, Ky.	Nov. 3, 1842	6,000 00		53,591 28	90,664 78	
Mobile, Ala.	June 20, 1838	4,000 00		51,400 00	64,540 00	
Natchez, Miss.	Aug. 25, 1837	6,000 00		59,785 37	66,785 37	
New Orleans, La.	Aug. 9, 1851	7,000 00	$29,393 79	496,162 05	528,134 34	
Ocracoke, N. C.	May 15, 1843	12,100 00		8,927 07	10,327 07	
Pittsburgh, Pa.	Nov. 7, 1842	1,100 00		50,420 32	66,976 05	
Portland, Mo.	Nov. 22, 1852	10,523 00		84,758 73	122,452 68	Portion of ground sold April, 1870.
San Francisco, Cal.	Nov. 13, 1852	11,600 00	66,200 00	224,000 00	232,471 10	
St. Louis, Mo.	Mar. 7, 1850			85,712 63	107,861 00	Site ceded by War Department.
Vicksburgh, Miss	June 25, 1853 / Feb. 28, 1856	4,500 00 / 4,700 00	57,021 02	67,525 16	76,975 16	Sold December 15, 1870.
Wilmington, N. C.	Mar. 17, 1857	6,500 00	28,968 25	37,346 04	43,897 44	Sold December 7, 1870.
COURT-HOUSES, POST-OFFICES, ETC.						
Baltimore, Md., court-house	June 6, 1859	50,000 00	112,806 04	205,176 97	263,100 66	
Boston, Mass., court house	1859	*105,000 00			123,802 30	
Boston, Mass, post-office and sub-treasury	Mar. 25, 1868 / Mar. 16, 1871	458,415 00 / 68,278 75			1,199,254 66	In course of erection.
Charleston, S. C., post-office	Feb. 14, 1818	*60,000 00			90,000 00	
Columbia, S. C., court-house, &c					339 21	Old custom-house.
Des Moines, Iowa, court-house, &c	Oct. 16, 1866	15,000 00			236,437 00	In course of erection; site donated.
Indianapolis, Ind., court-house, &c	Nov. 5, 1856	17,160 00	98,963 78	166,240 00	203,911 79	
Key West, Fla., court-house, &c	April 28, 1858	3,000 00			3,000 00	
Memphis, Tenn., court-house, &c	June 6, 1860	15,000 00			15,000 00	
Madison, Wis., court-house, &c	Mar. 25, 1867				329,388 97	
New York, N. Y., post-office, &c	April 11, 1867	500,000 00			1,975,373 51	Site donated.
New York, N. Y., post-office	Oct. 29, 1860	*200,000 00			242,683 29	In course of erection.
Omaha, Nebr. post-office, &c	May 19, 1870				41,547 44	
Portland, Me., court-house, &c	July 1849				376,816 64	
Philadelphia, Pa., court-house, &c	Oct. 6, 1860	*161,000 00			364,249 77	Site donated; in course of erection.
Raleigh, N. C., court-house, &c	Aug. 7, 1860	7,700 00			7,700 00	Built on site of old custom-house.
Rutland, Vt., court-house, &c	July 4, 1857 / May 17, 1859	1,400 00 / 500 00	55,701 75	62,897 56	74,313 09	
St. Augustine, Fla., court-house, &c	Mar. 2, 1857	6,000 00			2,000 00	Acquired from Spain.
Springfield, Ill., court-house, &c			53,258 84	285,841 03	302,291 00	
Windsor, Vt., court-house, &c	Mar. 4, 1857	4,700 00		71,347 32	92,755 41	

Mints and Assay Offices, etc.	Date					Remarks
Boisé City, assay office	July 8, 1869				68,591 31	In course of erection; site donated.
Carson City, branch mint	May 3, 1865			352,983 85	352,983 85	Including machinery; site donated.
Charlotte, branch mint	Nov. 2, 1835	1,500 00		26,000 00	36,756 65	site donated.
Dahlonega, branch mint	Aug. 3, 1835	1,050 00		69,586 33	70,638 33	Transferred to North Georgia Agricultural College, July, 1871, act of April 20, 1871.
Dalles City, branch mint	Feb. 28, 1868				103,280 00	In course of erection; site donated.
Denver City, branch mint	Nov. 25, 1862	*25,000 00			93,377 09	
New Orleans, branch mint	June 19, 1835			327,548 55	614,825 88	
New York, assay office	Aug. 21, 1854	*530,000 00			713,358 75	
New York, sub-treasury	Dec. 16, 1816 / Jan. 9, 1833	*70,000 00 / 200,000 00			1,319,505 03	Formerly custom-house.
Philadelphia, Mint	July 18, 1792 / April 30, 1829	*5,466 06		207,101 25	229,508 03	Old building.
	May 2, 1854	*31,656 67			300,000 00	In course of erection.
San Francisco, branch mint	Jan. 1, 1867	*283,925 10 / 100,000 00			860,693 36	
MISCELLANEOUS.						
Baltimore, appraisers' stores	June 10, 1833	*30,000 00			41,653 17	Sea-wall.
New York, barge office	Mar. 30, 1867	10,000 00			225,090 00	
New York, No. 21 Pine street	1859	*11,137 60			13,891 57	
New Orleans, quarantine warehouse	Sept. 23, 1858		31,984 00	39,865 12	39,865 12	Building and site donated.
Pass à l'Outre, boarding station	Feb. 1, 1856		10,900 00	12,000 00	16,361 70	Use of site granted by New Orleans.
Philadelphia, appraisers' stores	Mar. 1, 1857	*250,000 00			624,346 00	In course of erection on site of Pennsylvania Bank building.
San Francisco, appraisers' stores	Feb. 1, 1856		53,000 00	93,566 75	104,161 00	
Santa Fé, penitentiary	1854				20,000 00	Acquired by conquest.
Santa Fé, capitol					50,000 00	
Santa Fé, adobe palace					14,107 39	
Southwest Pass, boarding station	May 9, 1857	*3,500 00			7,333 70	
Washington, Treasury building					6,899,398 24	

* Building and site.

Tabular statement of appropriations for the erection or repair of public buildings, &c., under control of this office, showing available balance June 30, 1871.

Nature and location of work.	Balance available June 30, 1870.	Appropriated in 1870-'71.	Authorized and expended in 1870-'71.	Balance available June 30, 1871.
CUSTOM-HOUSES.				
Astoria, Oreg		$25,000 00	$25,000 00	
Bangor, Me	$11,582 27		8,457 45	$3,124 82
Baltimore, Md		21,000 00	20,935 42	64 58
Cairo, Ill		103,768 00	60,000 00	43,768 00
Castine, Me	600 00			600 00
Charleston, S. C	14,460 00	150,000 00	101,324 09	63,135 91
Charleston, S. C*		20,000 00	20,000 00	
Chicago, Ill		20,000 00	20,000 00	
Detroit, Mich	1,500 00	13,500 00	14,564 98	435 02
Knoxville, Tenn	101,569 10	20,000 00	85,927 69	35,640 50
Machias, Me	18,590 00		1,020 00	17,570 00
Nashville, Tenn	104,013 53			74,771 90
New Orleans, La	25,000 00	175,000 00	86,576 31	113,423 69
Ogdensburgh, N. Y		701 88	701 88	
Potersburgh, Va		10,000 00	10,000 00	
Philadelphia, Pa	167 56		166 57	
Portland, Me	655 63	95,055 99	95,711 62	
Portland, Oreg	29,849 19	140,000 00	44,173 98	125,675 21
San Francisco, Cal		10,000 00	9,067 42	932 58
Sandusky, Ohio		10,000 00	10,000 00	
St. Paul, Minn	25,000 00	194,462 38	125,051 38	94,411 00
St. Louis, Mo		300,000 00		300,000 00
Wiscasset, Me	3,166 05	4,000 00	7,017 10	148 94
MARINE HOSPITALS.				
Chelsea, Mass	2,506 36		937 16	
Chicago, Ill	100,012 73	31,539 36	45,080 10	86,471 99
COURT-HOUSES AND POST-OFFICES.				
Boston, Mass., post-office, &c	498,175 84	1,268,852 75	439,015 50	1,228,013 09
Columbia, S. C., court-house, &c	74,714 79		54 00	74,660 79
Des Moines, Iowa, court-house, &c	30,740 96	22,856 00	52,346 10	1,250 76
Madison, Wis., court-house, &c		84,082 74	84,082 74	
New York, N. Y., post-office, &c	700,199 30	2,394,897 00	702,057 22	2,393,039 08
Omaha, Nebr., post-office, &c	25,000 00	100,000 00	41,547 44	83,452 56
Portland, Me., court-house, &c		91,816 64	91,816 64	
Springfield, Ill., court-house, &c		3,000 00		3,000 00
Trenton, N. J., post-office, &c		100,000 00		100,000 00
Williamsport, Pa., court-house		3,000 00	3,000 00	
Philadelphia, Pa., court-house		15,000 00	15,000 00	
MINTS, ETC.				
Boise City, assay-office	74,115 21		67,706 52	6,408 69
Carson City, branch mint		61,920 56	60,983 85	986 71
Dalles City, branch mint	5,586 44	10,000 00	8,866 44	6,720 00
San Francisco, Cal §	131,970 10	1,000,000 00	392,663 46	739,306 64
San Francisco, Cal	45,000 00			
MISCELLANEOUS.				
Furniture and repairs of furniture for public buildings	1,130 65	225,000 00	89,261 21	136,869 44
Fuel, light, and water for public buildings	22,457 27	215,000 00	180,125 04	57,332 23
Heating apparatus for public buildings		20,000 00	20,000 00	
Lazaretto Point, Philadelphia, repairs, wharves, &c		8,000 00	8,000 00	
New York, barge-office		100,000 00	100,000 00	
Philadelphia, appraisers' stores		126,846 00	126,846 00	
Photographing, engraving, and printing plans, &c		10,000 00		10,000 00
Repairs and preservation of public buildings	13,396 17	350,000 00	185,108 36	178,287 81
Treasury building, alterations of	213 80	112,794 73	112,685 53	323 00
Treasury building, annual repairs	420 59	15,000 00	15,375 11	45 48
Treasury building, repairs of side-walk		19,816 00	19,816 00	
Treasury building, files-rooms under porticoes	1,135 10			1,135 10
Vaults, safes, and locks for public buildings		25,000 00	25,000 00	

* Repairs; old custom-house for a post-office.
† Ten per cent. contingencies. $9,215 69 carried to surplus fund June 30, 1871.
‡ Balance carried to surplus fund June 30, 1871. § Carried to surplus fund June 30, 1871.

Tabular statement of expenditures authorized and made from the appropriation for repairs and preservation of public buildings during the year ending June 30, 1871.

Nature and location of building.	Authorized and expended.	Nature and location of building.	Authorized and expended.
CUSTOM-HOUSES.		Philadelphia, Pa	$4,211 18
		Portsmouth, N. H	6,221 62
Alexandria, Va	$4,505 64	Providence, R. I	1,409 33
Bath, Me	1,258 28	Richmond, Va	736 00
Bangor, Me	6,532 17	Sandusky, Ohio	93 00
Barnstable, Mass	1,150 00	St. Louis, Mo	633 47
Baltimore, Md	828 73	Wilmington, N. C	553 45
Belfast, Me	95 74	Wilmington, Del.	8,163 00
Boston, Mass	1,394 36	Wheeling, W. Va	109 55
Bristol, R. I	243 88	Wiscasset, Me	690 30
Buffalo, N. Y	8,881 43		
Burlington, Vt	3,625 00	**MARINE HOSPITALS.**	
Cleveland, Ohio	735 91		
Cincinnati, Ohio	1,504 85	Chelsea, Mass	9,271 66
Chicago, Ill	17,275 05	Cleveland, Ohio	657 38
Detroit, Mich	154 56	Detroit, Mich	790 49
Dubuque, Iowa	77 80	Key West, Fla	3,266 71
Eastport, Me	2,000 00	Portland, Me	849 46
Erie, Pa	2,060 55	St. Louis, Mo	9,402 97
Galveston, Tex	4,203 85		
Georgetown, D. C	135 78	**COURT-HOUSES, ETC.**	
Key West, Fla	240 41		
Louisville, Ky	31,046 96	Boston, Mass	4,503 90
Milwaukee, Wis	328 37	Indianapolis, Ind	1,113 10
Mobile, Ala	2,203 17	New York, (post office,) N. Y	9,308 70
Newark, N. J	840 07	Philadelphia, Pa	1,465 66
New Bedford, Mass	253 88	Springfield, Ill.	958 81
New Haven, Conn	217 50	Windsor, Vt	6,850 08
New London, Conn	262 90		
Newport, R. I	242 00	**MISCELLANEOUS.**	
New York, N. Y	7,540 65		
Norfolk, Va	1,132 78	New York, N. Y., No. 23 Pine street.	265 00
Ogdensburgh, N. Y	636 49	New York, N. Y., sub-treasury	292 95
Oswego, N. Y	2,265 00	New Mexico, adobe palaco	387 00
Pensacola, Fla	1,509 22	San Francisco, Cal., appraisers' stores	357 05
Petersburgh, Va	4,330 10		
Pittsburgh, Pa	2,642 46	Total	185,108 36

Tabular statement of expenditures authorized and made from the appropriation for heating apparatus for public buildings during the year ending June 30, 1871.

Nature and location of building.	Authorized and expended.	Nature and location of building.	Authorized and expended.
CUSTOM-HOUSES.		Portland, Me	$2,446 17
Portland, Mo	$4,663 38	Madison, Wis	2,862 38
		Washington, D. C., Treasury build'g.	4,711 35
COURT-HOUSES, ETC.			
Des Moines, Iowa	5,316 72	Total	20,000 00

Tabular statement of expenditures authorized and made from the appropriation for furniture and repairs of furniture for public buildings during the year ending June 30, 1871.

Nature and location of building.	Authorized and expended.	Nature and location of building.	Authorized and expended.
CUSTOM-HOUSES.		Petersburgh, Va	$3, 203 14
		Pittsburgh, Pa	2, 945 77
Alexandria, Va	$848 27	Philadelphia, Pa	3, 069 54
Bath, Me	195 42	Portsmouth, N. H	2, 563 96
Bangor, Me	438 02	Providence, R. I	45 00
Baltimore, Md	2, 920 96	Richmond, Va	525 43
Boston, Mass	671 27	San Francisco, Cal	1, 860 65
Bristol, R. I	249 58	Savannah, Ga	3, 470 54
Buffalo, N. Y	1, 558 50	St. Louis, Mo	720 53
Burlington, Vt	3, 142 66	Waldoborough, Me	24 50
Charleston, S. C	586 50	Wilmington, N. C	29 75
Cleveland, Ohio	166 00	Wilmington, Del	2, 785 19
Cincinnati, Ohio	559 91		
Chicago, Ill	11, 956 04	**MARINE HOSPITALS.**	
Detroit, Mich	1, 677 70		
Dubuque, Iowa	171 56	Chelsea, Mass	523 45
Erie, Pa	496 14	St. Louis, Mo	575 81
Galena, Ill	229 65		
Galveston, Tex	253 42	**COURT-HOUSES, ETC.**	
Louisville, Ky	9, 325 27		
Milwaukee, Wis	75 00	Boston, Mass	212 31
Mobile, Ala	879 20	Indianapolis, Ind	940 96
Newark, N. J	728 88	Madison, Wis	6, 165 57
New Bedford, Mass	43 37	New York, (post office,) N. Y	3, 491 54
New London, Conn	32 80	Philadelphia, Pa	744 50
New Orleans, La	830 35	Springfield, Ill	2, 723 87
New York, N. Y	5, 848 75	Baltimore, Md., appraisers' stores	628 24
Norfolk, Va	112 51	New York, N. Y., sub-treasury	377 15
Ogdensburgh, N. Y	1, 081 67	Philadelphia, Pa., appraisers' stores	4, 013 46
Oswego, N. Y	1, 195 07	San Francisco, Cal., appraisers' stores	394 48
Plattsburgh, N. Y	156 50		
Pensacola, Fla	195 00	Total	89, 261 21

o

REPORT OF THE CHIEF OF THE BUREAU OF STATISTICS.

REPORT

OF THE

CHIEF OF THE BUREAU OF STATISTICS.

TREASURY DEPARTMENT,
Bureau of Statistics, October 31, 1871.

SIR: I have the honor to submit the following report of the operations of this Bureau during the fiscal year ended June 30, 1871 :

CLERICAL FORCE.

At the close of the year the clerical force of the Bureau consisted of thirty males and eight females, who were employed as follows :

Division.	Name of chief.	Number of clerks.		
		Males.	Females.	Total.
Examination..	J. N. Whitney........	4	1	5
Compilation	Thomas Clear.........	14	3	17
Tonnage and immigration	L. F. Ward..........	3	1	4
Registry of merchant marine......................	J. B. Parker	3	1	4
Revision, translation, and miscellaneous	A. W. Angerer	2	1	3
Publication and miscellaneous.	James Ryan	1	1	2
Library and files......................................	E. T. Peters	1	....	1
Stationery, pay, and property......................	J. D. O'Connell	1	....	1

In addition to the female clerks above designated, one has charge of the correspondence.

At the present time the clerical force consists of one chief clerk, Mr. E. B. Elliott, (who is, moreover, a member of the permanent board of civil service examiners for the Treasury Department, and also a member of the commission for improving the efficiency of the civil service of the United States,) thirty-one male and nine female clerks, one of the latter being assigned from another Bureau.

WORK OF THE BUREAU.

Owing to the peculiar and varied character of the work performed in the Bureau, it is impossible to furnish a tabular exhibit which shall indicate its nature and extent.

Examination.—In the division of examination, for example, the following work was performed :

Number of pages of letters written 5,259
Letters acknowledged 2,031
Acknowledgments of statements written 5,387
Statements examined 18,940
Statements called for.. 741
Statements corrected by correspondence 1,360

The above figures give, however, a very inadequate conception of the critical and elaborate examination of the various monthly and quarterly returns from the various custom-houses, or of the variety of work of a miscellaneous character performed in that division.

Compilation.—The same remark is applicable to the division in which the clerks are employed in the compilation of statistics of commerce. This division is subdivided into sections, embracing statistics of home consumption, indirect and intransitu trade, and warehouse statistics, of which sections Charles H. Evans, J. D. O'Connell, and Miss M. A. Spencer are the respective chiefs.

Immigration and navigation.—The statistics of navigation are now published monthly, instead of quarterly, as heretofore, involving additional labor in this division, to which is also assigned the collection and digest of the statistics of immigration. Extraordinary, and to some 'extent successful, efforts have been made during the past year to obtain and publish accurate statements of the nationality and occupation, as well as the sex, age, &c., of each immigrant. Special efforts have also been made to secure accurate statistics of the departure of emigrants from this country, a task rendered the more difficult, owing to the absence of compulsory legislation on this subject.

Numbering of vessels, tonnage, &c.—The compiling, copying, proof-reading, and distribution of the last annual list of merchant vessels occupied a large portion of the force in this division during the year. Official numbers were assigned to about 3,000 vessels, involving a considerable amount of careful labor in searching the previous records to avoid duplication of numbers, in filling up and forwarding notices to the applicants, entering the awards upon a manuscript list, and the permanent register of the office. Compilations for the monthly and annual reports of the Bureau, the preparation of various statements for Members of Congress and others, with a variety of miscellaneous work, formed part of the operations of this division.

A table exhibiting the number of vessels and amount of tonnage belonging to the several customs districts of the United States on the 30th of June, 1871, geographically classified, is appended to this report. From this it will be seen that the tonnage of the country was, in the aggregate, 4,111,412, a net increase over that at the close of the preceding fiscal year of 165,262 tons.

Revision and translation.—The vast amount of statistics compiled in the Bureau for publication, and in response to requests for information, involves a corresponding amount of labor in revision. As the statistical publications of various countries in continental Europe possess information of great value, the labor of translation previous to publication is not inconsiderable.

Publication, library, and miscellaneous.—The work performed by the chiefs of these divisions and their assistants is of too varied a character for detailed notice. It is sufficient to say that the duties of these officers are responsible and onerous.

PUBLICATIONS OF THE BUREAU.

Monthly reports of commerce and navigation.—The monthly reports of this Bureau have, during the year, been regularly published. Compiled at the earliest date possible after the receipt of the returns, they have been printed as soon thereafter as the arrangements of the Congressional Printing Office would permit. Although it is impossible to obtain and publish the returns as early as is done in England, yet it is satisfactory to know that the necessary delay in publication is compensated by the increased accuracy of these monthly reports. Widely distributed, as they are, throughout the country, and, to some extent, in Europe, it is unnecessary to append to this report the statements they contain. To render these reports increasingly valuable new features are from time to time introduced, which have hitherto met with general approval.

Annual report of commerce, immigration, and navigation.—Notwithstand ing the necessary delay in obtaining, correcting, and compiling the various statements for the annual report—the delay increased by the great amount of labor required at the printing office in the composition and printing of 800 octavo pages of rule and figure work—the volume for the fiscal year 1870 was bound and distributed three months earlier than in previous years; and had it not been for the hindrance which occurred in binding, owing to the pressure of other work, this indispensable collection of commerce and navigation statistics would have been submitted to Congress in December. In consequence of extra exertions, which have again been made, the data for 1871 have been compiled and sent to the Congressional Printing Office at a period sufficiently early to justify the belief that "said report, embracing the returns of the commerce and navigation, the exports and imports of the United States, to the close of the fiscal year, shall be submitted to Congress in a printed form on or before the first day of December," in accordance with the provisions of the act under which the Bureau was established.

List of merchant-vessels of the United States.—Agreeably to the requirements of the act of July 28, 1866, the third annual statement of "vessels registered, enrolled, and licensed under the laws of the United States, designating the class, name, tonnage, and place of registry," as well as the official number and signal letters awarded to each vessel, was prepared, and 3,000 copies published. The officers of customs, the commanders of United States war-vessels, and the largest merchant-vessels engaged in the foreign trade, as well as the principal ship-owners, have been supplied with it.

Special Report on Immigration.

This report, including information for immigrants and tables showing the cost of labor and subsistence in the United States, having been compiled during the year, was submitted to the House of Representatives at the session in March last. Congress having adjourned without taking action upon the subject the report was stereotyped, and 3,000 copies printed for distribution in Europe and in this country, at the expense of the Treasury Department.

Comparative tariff tables.—To supply a want long felt, "a comparative statement of the rates of duties and imposts under the several tariff acts from 1789 to 1870," was prepared and 1,000 extra copies printed for distribution. After the great labor involved in its preparation, it is gratifying to know that its accuracy is almost if not quite absolute, and that it is highly appreciated by those who are best qualified to judge of its value. It forms Appendix A of a "Special Report on the Customs-tariff Legislation of the United States," which will soon be submitted to you.

USEFULNESS OF THE BUREAU FOR LEGISLATIVE AND OTHER PURPOSES.

During the last two years the services of the Bureau were called into requisition to an unusual extent, and its usefulness recognized by members of both Houses of the national legislature.

While the periodical statements of the trade of the country given in the published monthly reports of the Bureau afforded reliable data for

27 F

legislative purposes, those of a miscellaneous character have also furnished a variety of important foreign statistics. The constant calls for
statistical information by members of Congress and for commercial and
other purposes have been responded to so far as the ability of the
Bureau permitted; moreover, it has been the aim of the undersigned to
anticipate and provide for the demands for such data.

INDUSTRIAL STATISTICS.

In my last annual report reference was made to the obstacles which
prevented the collection and digest of statistics of the manufactures of
the United States, which obstacles still exist. Statistics of the manufactures of the United States, giving their localities, sources of raw
material, markets, exchanges with the producing regions of the country,
transportation of products, wages, and the number of persons indirectly
as well as directly supported by the various industries, would be of great
practical utility to legislators and to the people at large. While the
other great interests, agriculture and commerce, have obtained their
due, but not undue, share of attention, manufacturing industry has not
received from the Government the consideration to which its importance
entitled it.
    As the publication of the census returns of the products of industry
may soon be expected, it is not deemed advisable at the present time to
make extraordinary efforts to obtain information similar in character
but necessarily incomplete.

TRANSPORTATION OF PRODUCTS AND MERCHANDISE.

The movement of the crops toward the sea-board and of merchandise
into the interior, whether by rail or by canal, lake or river, would, if
ascertained and published, afford information of great value. The
officers of some of the great lines of railway are convinced of the public
utility of such statistics, but in the absence of compulsory legislation
on the subject do not feel it compatible with their duty to stockholders
to incur the expense which the employment of clerical services for this
purpose would necessarily involve.
    Additional legislation will probably be necessary before full and satis-
factory information in regard to the two subjects above indicated can
be obtained.

IMMIGRATION.

The statistics of immigration for the past fifty-one years were given
and the value thereof to the country discussed, in the special report on
the subject which I had the honor to submit to you in March last. The
fact has already been stated that in consequence of the failure of Congress to authorize the printing of extra copies, upward of three thousand
have been ordered at the expense of the Treasury Department, for distribution at home and abroad. Although the number supplied to United
States consuls and others in Europe was necessarily limited, yet material
benefits have already resulted, as evidenced by the increased interest
aroused, not only in Ireland and Germany, whence the largest portion
of our immigration has been derived, but also in England, France,
Belgium, the Scandinavian countries, and to some extent in Italy. The
increase in immigration from England within the past two or three
years has been decided, reaching to 55,046 in 1869, and 59,488 in 1870,
while for the quarter ended June 31, 1871, the arrivals were 21,659.

These embraced more than the usual proportion of professional men, skilled laborers, farmers, and others, bringing with them some capital. From communications received by the undersigned, as well as from information obtained from various other sources, the fact is patent that there is among these classes an eager desire to learn what are the inducements offered by different sections of the country.

In France, owing largely to the distress occasioned by the late war, the desire to emigrate has been greatly stimulated, and many inquiries as to the advantages offered by our country have been made at our consulates. Similar interest has been awakened, and earnest inquiries made, not only in Germany, but in Belgium, Norway, Switzerland, and Italy. The demand for the translation of the report into the spoken languages of Continental Europe, more particularly into the German, Danish-Norwegian, and French, has been of the most pressing nature, not only from those who desire to emigrate, but from a number of diplomatic and consular officers of the United States, who are impressed with the conviction that great benefit would result if each person wishing to emigrate could read in his own language the information which the report embodies.

If the economical value of the immigrant to our country be even approximately so great as is indicated in the report, the expenditure necessary for printing for European distribution an adequate number of copies in the English, German, French, and Norwegian languages, would be more than compensated by the benefits resulting from the increased immigration which such a distribution would necessarily occasion.

It has been represented by the public press, and mentioned in correspondence from Europe, that the fact of the report having emanated from an officer of the National Government inspires a degree of confidence in it which is not reposed in the representations of any State officer, or of an agent of any company having lands to dispose of. This is undoubtedly true; for however honest and truthful these representations may be in regard to the advantages possessed by the particular State or locality in which such officer or agent is interested, he has no motive, and perhaps does not possess the requisite information, to make known to inquirers the advantages of other localities.

BUREAU OF IMMIGRATION.

In the special report already alluded to, at the close of a review of the advantages conferred by immigration, the question was asked, " What are the duties of the Government toward the immigrant?" In reply, it was asserted that among these duties were those of furnishing him with trustworthy information, and affording adequate protection, such services being alike called for by considerations of humanity and the dictates of sound policy. The act to encourage immigration, approved July 4, 1864, having expired by limitation, no such officer as commissioner of immigration now exists, and various duties which seemed to pertain to such an office have devolved upon the chief of this Bureau. The preparation of the information for immigrants, obtained and compiled by the undersigned, and published in the special report already referred to, furnishes a case in point; the statistics of immigration have also been regularly compiled and published by the Bureau of Statistics for a number of years past. Owing to such facts, the officer in charge of this Bureau has apparently been regarded as discharging the functions of commissioner of immigration; and correspondence from Europe, as well as from various parts of our own country, has been addressed to him in such capacity. Yielding to earnest requests, he attended, in November 1870, the National Immigration Convention at Indianapolis, and more recently, the National Commercial Convention in Baltimore, at which immigration formed a subject of careful consideration. In view of these circumstances, and of the familiarity with various important branches of the subject already acquired by the officers of this Bureau, it is pertinent to inquire whether, by an extension of its powers, it might not be made more useful in this direction; and also, whether the functions for the discharge of which the creation of a bureau of immigration has been proposed, cannot be far more economically performed by utilizing the facilities which this bureau already possesses.

SALARIES OF OFFICERS.

In bearing testimony to the industry and efficiency of the clerks, both male and female, as well as of other employés of this Bureau, I cannot close this report without directing your attention to the low salaries paid to the officers. The chiefs of division and other officers are men of ability and great industry. The duties of some of them require talents of a high order, and involve exhaustive labor. Giving, as they do, the best years of their lives to the public service, and contributing to establish the reputation of the Bureau, in furnishing to the public accurate and trustworthy information, they receive very inadequate remuneration. Some of the clerks of the fourth class, while performing their duties satisfactorily, are exempt from the cares and responsibilities which attach to chiefs of division, and yet the latter receive no greater salary than the former.

It is respectfully urged, therefore, that several of these officers receive the salary of head of division, as provided by law for the office of internal revenue.

It is not, perhaps, improper to remark that the work of the Bureau, although neither smaller in amount nor less reliable in character than in former years, is now performed by fewer clerks and at considerably less aggregate expense, as the following figures will show:

Period.	Average number of officers, clerks, and other employés.	Average monthly salaries.
Year ended March 31, 1869	60	$6,551 62
Year ended March 31, 1870	53	5,824 08
Nineteen months ended October 31, 1870	45	5,171 38

From the above statement it appears, that for the past nineteen months, as compared with the year ended March 31, 1869, there has been a reduction of the expenditure of the Bureau for salaries at the rate of $16,323 per annum; less than one-third of which sum, if applied to the increase of the existing salaries, would afford adequate remuneration, not only to the officers indicated, but also to those upon whom the chief responsibilities of the Bureau rests.

I have the honor to be, very respectfully, your obedient servant,

EDWARD YOUNG,
Chief of Bureau.

Hon. GEORGE S. BOUTWELL,
Secretary of the Treasury.

APPENDIX.

Table exhibiting the number of merchant-vessels and amount of tonnage belonging within the several customs districts and ports of the United States on the 30th of June, 1871, geographically classified.

Customs districts.	Sailing-vessels.		Steam-vessels.		Unrigged vessels.		Total.	
	No.	Tons.	No.	Tons.	No.	Tons.	Vessels.	Tons.
ATLANTIC AND GULF COASTS.								
Bangor, Me	227	37,141.87	5	666.72	......	....	232	37,808.59
Bath, Me................	248	128,045.33	10	3,437.56	......	....	258	131,482.89
Belfast, Me	353	72,965.20	....	....	......	....	353	72,965.20
Castine, Mo.............	352	24,302.20	....	....	......	....	352	24,302.20
Frenchman's Bay, Me....	286	17,496.19	3	314.19	......	....	289	17,810.38
Kennebunk, Me..........	40	3,479.92	....	....	......	....	40	3,479.92
Machias, Me	215	24,930.53	2	133.91	......	....	217	25,064.44
Passamaquoddy, Me	185	21,718.62	9	3,669.35	......	....	194	25,387.97
Portland and Falmouth, Me.	354	81,122.05	21	8,754.77	......	....	375	89,876.82
Saco, Me	23	3,870.07	3	340.02	......	....	26	4,210.09
Waldoborough, Me......	546	93,785.24	....	....	......	....	546	93,785.24
Wiscasset, Me	166	9,519.17	....	....	......	....	166	9,519.17
York, Me	15	708.12	1	15.47	......	....	16	723.59
	3,010	519,084.51	54	17,331.99	......	....	3,064	536,416.50
Portsmouth, N. H........	66	19,457.86	5	459.22	......	....	71	19,917.08
Barnstable, Mass	595	48,667.38	1	266.64	......	....	596	48,934.02
Boston and Charlestown, Mass.	796	264,827.48	61	22,866.50	......	....	857	287,693.98
Edgartown, Mass	21	2,733.85	....	....	......	....	21	2,733.85
Fall River, Mass	115	10,963.65	10	2,069.62	......	....	125	13,033.27
Gloucester, Mass........	550	28,260.10	4	191.62	......	....	554	28,451.72
Marblehead, Mass.......	63	2,703.86	....	....	......	....	63	2,703.86
Nantucket, Mass........	13	1,201.22	1	484.00	......	....	14	1,685.22
New Bedford, Mass	286	58,730.01	5	1,489.03	......	....	291	60,219.04
Newburyport, Mass......	76	11,077.17	1	15.91	......	....	77	11,093.08
Plymouth, Mass	114	4,670.52	....	....	......	....	114	4,670.52
Salem and Beverly, Mass.	94	9,110.45	....	....	......	....	94	9,110.45
	2,723	442,945.69	83	27,383.32	......	....	2,806	470,329.01
Bristol and Warren, R. I..	18	1,212.48	1	38.28	......	....	19	1,250.76
Newport, R. I	84	4,711.94	11	16,863.01	......	....	95	21,574.95
Providence, R. I.........	71	10,587.46	21	10,502.55	......	....	92	21,090.01
	173	16,511.88	33	27,403.84	......	....	206	43,915.72
Fairfield, Conn..........	150	8,533.81	7	1,932.75	6	746.82	163	11,213.38
Middletown, Conn	125	11,838.32	22	7,259.19	1	324.49	148	19,422.00
New Haven, Conn.......	132	13,720.21	9	3,513.44-	6	1,269.81	147	18,503.46
New London, Conn......	158	10,496.05	16	10,760.82	......	....	174	21,256.87
Stonington, Conn........	100	3,593.27	7	6,318.33	......	....	107	9,911.60
	665	48,181.66	61	29,784.53	13	2,341.12	739	80,307.31
New York, N. Y	2,418	467,963.80	674	307,390.40	1,862	223,952.55	4,954	999,306.75
Sag Harbor, N. Y	225	9,025.40	1	33.50	......	....	226	9,058.90
	2,643	476,989.20	675	307,423.90	1,862	223,952.55	5,180	1,008,365.65
Bridgetown, N. J........	270	13,879.51	5	1,179.87	1	879.51	285	15,938.89
Burlington, N. J........	47	3,026.34	14	2,782.90	73	6,830.70	134	12,639.94
Great Egg Harbor, N. J..	119	12,888.67	....	....	......	....	119	12,888.67
Little Egg Harbor, N. J..	54	5,764.90	....	....	......	....	54	5,764.90
Newark, N. J	65	3,077.14	26	2,754.86	33	3,771.91	124	9,603.91
Perth Amboy, N. J.......	212	10,055.75	37	14,229.61	44	7,209.42	293	31,494.78
	776	48,692.31	82	20,947.24	151	18,691.54	1,000	88,331.09
Philadelphia, Pa	766	97,631.18	238	50,052.71	1,542	149,318.67	2,546	297,002.56

Table exhibiting the number of merchant-vessels, &c., geographically classified—Cont'd.

Customs districts.	Sailing-vessels.		Steam-vessels.		Unrigged vessels.		Total.	
	No.	Tons.	No.	Tons.	No.	Tons.	Vessels.	Tons.
ATLANTIC AND GULF COASTS—Continued.								
Delaware, Del	140	9, 056. 64	15	3, 961. 64	9	775. 93	164	13, 794. 21
Annapolis, Md	82	2, 025. 10	2	81. 17			84	2, 106. 27
Baltimore, Md	753	45, 331. 07	99	38, 466. 10	514	30, 300. 79	1, 366	114, 097. 96
Eastern District, Md	556	15, 940. 85					556	15, 940. 85
	1, 391	63, 297. 02	101	38, 547. 27	514	30, 300. 79	2, 006	132, 145. 08
ATLANTIC AND GULF STATES.								
Georgetown, D. C	73	2, 009. 62	24	5, 182. 92	274	16, 612. 32	371	23, 804. 86
Alexandria, Va	82	1, 854. 18	12	517. 28	68	4, 422. 31	162	6, 782. 77
Cherrystone, Va	327	6, 826. 11	2	41. 34			329	6, 867. 45
Norfolk and Portsm'th, Va	296	4. 702. 58	31	2, 673. 63	8	567. 98	335	7, 944. 19
Petersburgh, Va	3	66. 21	1	11. 11			4	77. 32
Richmond, Va	3	76. 05	15	1, 855. 69	59	3, 388. 66	77	5, 320. 40
Tappahannock, Va	28	630. 44					28	630. 44
Yorktown, Va	93	2, 188. 29					93	2, 188. 29
	832	16, 343. 86	61	5, 094. 05	135	8, 378. 95	1, 028	29, 816. 86
Albemarle, N. C	46	860. 24	4	445. 70	5	191. 69	55	1, 497. 63
Beaufort, N. C	72	1, 022. 94					72	1, 022. 94
Pamlico, N. C	83	1, 560. 45	1	120. 02			84	1, 680. 47
Wilmington, N. C	20	493. 45	15	1, 600. 23			35	2, 093. 68
	221	3, 937. 08	20	2, 165, 95	5	191. 69	246	6, 294. 72
Beaufort, S. C	6	82. 50					6	82. 50
Charleston, S. C	134	2, 960. 75	17	2, 988. 03			151	5, 948. 78
Georgetown, S. C	6	528. 32	5	242. 64			11	770. 96
	146	3, 571. 57	22	3, 230. 67			168	6, 802. 24
Saint Mary's, Ga	18	4, 810. 55					18	4, 810. 55
Savannah, Ga	25	552. 34	21	3, 085. 14			46	4, 237. 48
	43	5, 362. 89	21	3, 685. 14			64	9, 048. 03
Apalachicola, Fla	9	115, 44	6	1, 853. 97			15	1, 969. 41
Fernandina, Fla	3	49. 22	1	183. 16			4	232. 38
Key West, Fla	92	1, 686. 09					92	1, 686. 09
Pensacola, Fla	57	1, 664. 98	10	6, 265. 19			67	2, 930. 17
Saint Augustine, Fla	2	39. 42					2	39. 42
Saint John's, Fla	2	38. 95	17	1, 670. 49			19	1, 709. 44
Saint Mark's, Fla	14	107. 07					14	107. 07
	179	3, 701. 17	34	4, 072. 81			213	8, 673. 98
Mobile, Ala	74	1, 569. 57	52	12, 113. 17	96	4, 364. 26	222	18, 047. 00
Pearl River, Miss	79	1, 582. 20	2	27. 93			81	1, 610. 13
New Orleans, La	378	12, 795. 32	172	45, 248. 59	15	1, 609. 81	565	59, 653. 72
Teche, La	15	248. 01	13	1, 065. 82	1	114. 38	29	1, 428. 21
	393	13, 043. 33	185	46, 314. 41	16	1, 724. 19	594	61, 081. 93
Brazos de Santiago, Tex	6	101. 71	3	951. 91			9	1, 053. 62
Corpus Christi, Tex	19	357. 49					19	357. 49
Saluria, Tex	39	683. 88					39	683. 88
Texas, Tex	159	3, 413. 38	29	4, 689. 27	19	2, 034. 06	207	10, 136, 71
	223	4, 556. 46	32	5, 641. 18	19	2, 034. 06	274	12, 231. 70
WESTERN RIVERS.								
Alton, Ill			4	796. 92			4	796. 92
Burlington, Iowa			10	736. 64			10	736. 64
Cairo, Ill			13	1, 768. 61			13	1, 768. 61
Cincinnati, Ohio			122	40, 614. 95	310	38, 595. 17	432	79, 210. 12
Dubuque, Iowa			20	2, 078. 00	48	2, 734. 02	68	4, 812. 02
Evansville, Ind			49	8, 222. 66	14	1, 001. 39	63	9, 224. 05
Galena, Ill			30	7, 222. 54	82	9, 314. 76	112	16, 537. 30

Table exhibiting the number of merchant-vessels, &c., geographically classified—Continued.

Customs districts.	Sailing-vessels.		Steam-vessels.		Unrigged vessels.		Total.	
	No.	Tons.	No.	Tons.	No.	Tons.	Vessels.	Tons.
WESTERN RIVERS—Cont'd.								
Keokuk, Iowa			8	802.17			8	802.17
Louisville, Ky			39	10,353.00	5	2,563.53	44	12,916.53
Memphis, Tenn			42	9,297.61			42	9,297.61
Minnesota, Minn			63	11,146.17	77	9,195.01	140	20,341.18
Nashville, Tenn			20	3,485.53			20	3,485.53
Natchez, Miss			3	135,57			3	135.57
Paducah, Ky			11	2,910.23			11	2,910.23
Pittsburgh, Pa			155	44,221.84	158	32,458.19	313	76,680.03
Quincy, Ill			9	1,441.88	12	678.82	21	2,120.70
Saint Louis, Mo			146	67,836.64	68	28,808.45	214	96,645.09
Vicksburgh, Miss			14	1,918,93			14	1,918.93
Wheeling, W. Va			51	7,436.81	42	3,554.96	93	11,011.77
Saint Joseph, Mo			5	1,149.49			5	1,149.49
			814	223,596.19	816	128,904.30	1,630	352,500.49
NORTHERN LAKES.								
Buffalo Creek, N. Y	112	38,000.67	113	51,509.00	495	57,021.02	720	146,530.69
Cape Vincent, N. Y	29	4,087.91	1	17.63			30	4,105.54
Champlain, N. Y	119	7,662.86	8	818.82	666	42,580.18	793	51,061.86
Chicago, Ill	333	64,702.26	84	6,846.30	233	23,735.39	650	95,283.95
Cuyahoga, Ohio	152	34,692.03	52	12,855.03	202	10,320.03	406	57,867.09
Detroit, Mich	199	31,088.50	120	36,829.06	46	11,183.56	365	79,101.12
Dunkirk, N. Y	3	573.23	1	545	3	350.99	7	929.87
Erie, Pa	25	4,834.31	16	2,460.44	238	8,404.23	279	15,698.98
Genesee, N. Y	11	1,390.34	4	379.15	212	26,456.85	227	28,226.34
Huron, Mich	127	11,459.29	73	9,654.38	48	10,386.34	248	31,500.01
Miami, Ohio	26	5,086.48	17	1,108.51	178	10,446.51	221	16,641.50
Michigan, Mich	96	6,009.54	65	3,891.67	14	2,890.64	175	12,791.85
Milwaukee, Wis	207	26,753.72	44	14,787.97			251	41,541.69
Niagara, N. Y	5	816.34	1	267.33	33	3,637.55	39	4,721.22
Oswegatchie, N. Y	15	1,509.72	8	267.79	3	384.23	26	2,161.74
Oswego, N. Y	75	16,110.17	15	677.96	847	90,209.44	937	106,997.57
Sandusky, Ohio	65	9,586.99	20	2,278.78			85	11,865.77
Superior, Mich	13	1,531.51	29	1,613.78			42	3,145.29
Vermont, Vt	9	572.22	6	4,760.64	8	556.65	23	5,889.51
	1621	266,468.09	677	151,029.69	3226	298,563.61	5,524	716,061.39
PACIFIC COAST.								
Alaska, Alaska	6	372.75					6	372.75
Oregon, Oreg	30	1,784.15	11	981.07	3	190.57	44	2,955.70
Puget Sound, Wash	70	21,617.68	22	2,843.73	6	91.31	98	24,552.72
San Francisco, Cal	723	78,820.40	145	51,964.13	64	8,061.48	932	138,906.01
Willamette, Oreg	5	749.77	30	7,043.24	6	334.38	41	8,127.59
	834	103,404.75	208	62,832.17	79	8,677.94	1,121	174,914.86

RECAPITULATION.

	Vessels.	Tons.
Sailing-vessels	17,071	2,167,398.54
Steam-vessels	3,499	1,049,181.94
Unrigged vessels	8,757	894,831.92
Total	29,327	4,111,412.40

SUMMARY BY STATES.

	Vessels.	Tons.
Maine	3,064	536,416.50
New Hampshire	71	19,917.08
Massachusetts	2,806	470,329.01
Rhode Island	206	43,915.72
Connecticut	739	80,307.31
New York	5,180	1.008,365.65
New Jersey	1,009	88,331.09
Pennsylvania	2,546	297,002.56
Delaware	164	13,794.21
Maryland	2,006	132,145.08
Territory of Columbia	371	23,804.86
Virginia	1,028	29,816.86
North Carolina	246	6,294.72
South Carolina	168	6,802.24
Georgia	64	9,048.03
Florida	213	8,673.98
Alabama	222	18,047.00
Mississippi	81	1,610.13
Louisiana	594	61,081.93
Texas	274	12,231.70
Western Rivers	1,630	352,500.49
Northern Lakes	5,524	716,061.39
Pacific Coast	1,121	174,914.86
Total	29,327	4,111,412.40

REPORT OF THE DIRECTOR OF THE MINT.

REPORT

OF

THE DIRECTOR OF THE MINT.

MINT OF THE UNITED STATES,
Philadelphia, September 28, 1871.

SIR: I have the honor to submit the following report of the operations of the Mint and branches for the fiscal year ending June 30, 1871:

DEPOSITS AND COINAGE.

The deposits of bullion at the Mint and branches during the fiscal year were as follows: Gold, $37,054,202 26; silver, $5,975,982 54; total deposits, $43,030,184 80. Deducting from this total the re-deposits, or bars made at one branch of the Mint and re-deposited in another for coinage, the amount will be $39,137,404 13.

For the same period the coinage was as follows: Gold coin, number of pieces, 1,120,916; value, $21,302,473; unparted and fine-gold bars, $13,101,089 42. Silver coin, pieces, 3,664,792; value, $1,955,905 25; silver bars, $3,544,180 13; nickel-copper and bronze, pieces, 11,672,750; value, $283,760; total number of pieces struck, 16,458,458; total value of coinage, $40,187,409 80.

The distribution of the bullion received and coined at the Mint and branches was as follows:

Philadelphia.—At Philadelphia, gold deposited, $3,064,733 31; gold coined, $3,206,760; fine-gold bars, $129,184 88; silver deposited and purchased, $1,557,892 50; silver coined, $1,156,255 25: silver bars, $143,647 75; nickel-copper and bronze coinage, value, $283,760; total deposits of gold and silver, $4,622,625 81; total coinage, $4,919,607 88; total number of pieces, 13,670,015.

San Francisco.—At the branch mint, San Francisco, the gold deposits were $25,521,650 56; gold coined, $24,241,006 23; silver deposited and purchased, $937,577 89; silver coined, $908,015 27; total deposits and purchases, $26,459,228 45; total coinage, $25,149,021 50; total number of pieces, 2,649,900.

New York.—The assay office in New York received during the year in gold bullion, $6,345,338 88; in silver bullion, including purchases, $2,171,120 36; total value received, $8,516,459 24; number of fine-gold bars stamped, 9,769; value, $5,461,801 10; silver bars, 10,763; value, $1,269,501 75; total value gold and silver bars stamped, $6,731,302 85.

Denver.—At the assay office, late branch mint, Denver, Colorado, the deposits for unparted bars were, gold, $1,104,147 10; silver, $18,561 63; total deposits, $1,122,708 73; an increase of deposits over the last year of $116,658 47. This is a very gratifying fact, and encourages the belief that, as the mineral resources of the district are developed, the business of this office will be correspondingly increased. It is now engaged, as last year, in melting, assaying, and stamping gold and silver bullion in unparted bars, bearing the Government stamp of weight and fineness. The assay office, in the performance of its appropriate functions, fully meets all the demands of the mining interests of Colorado.

Charlotte.—The deposits at the branch mint at Charlotte, North Carolina, have not been large, and, I regret to say, are not increasing. The deposits, as heretofore, are assayed and returned to depositors in the form of unparted bars. The deposits for bars during the year were, gold, $14,522 81; silver parted from gold, $145 31; total deposits, $14,668 12; a decrease from last year of $1,440 48.

Dahlonega and New Orleans.—The branch mints at these places are still closed. As stated in my last report, no necessity exists for their being opened again as assay offices or branch mints.

Carson City.—This branch mint has been in successful operation during the past fiscal year, and the prospects for the future are most encouraging. The deposits during the year were, gold, $1,003,809 60; gold coined, $230,715; unparted gold bars, $731,320 79; silver deposits and purchases, $1,290,684 85; silver coined, $52,875; unparted and fine bars, $1,969,645 05; total deposits and purchases, $2,294,494 45; total number of pieces, 138,543.

This statement exhibits the gratifying fact that the amount in value of the gold and silver deposits during the year has exceeded that of the past year more than $2,000,000. The superintendent, in his report, expresses full confidence in the future of that branch. A bullion fund adequate to the exigencies of the business of the Mint has been provided, and full authority has been given to melt, assay, and stamp gold and silver bullion, and return the same to depositors in unparted bars, bearing the Government stamp of weight and fineness. This has largely increased its business and added to its usefulness. The clerical force of this branch is inadequate, and should be increased. The salaries of all the officers and clerks are too small for that locality, and I earnestly recommend an increase of salary and clerical force. The policy of the Government toward this and similar institutions, in their relation to the development of the mineral wealth of our country, should be liberal and generous.

In addition to the increase of business from the assaying and stamping of unparted gold and silver bars, the superintendent in his report says : "To the increased product of the mines throughout the State may also be attributed the enlarged business of the past year. The late rich discoveries of ore at the lowest levels of the Comstock Lode, and the constantly increasing product of the country to the south and east of this city, have materially aided in adding to our business; while on the other hand a reciprocal benefit, both to produce and to the State, has been derived by the location of this institution near the mining centers, and the accuracy and promptitude of its returns."

The suggestions of the report on other subjects connected with the prosperity of this branch are worthy of consideration, and only a want of power prevents their adoption. The report is highly encouraging, and its facts and statements attest the efficiency of its management.

I again refer to the importance of the early completion of the new branch mint at San Francisco, and it is gratifying to know that the work is being prosecuted with energy.

Boise City.—The assay office at Boise City, Idaho, will soon be prepared for active operations. The building is erected, and the apparatus and appliances necessary for such an institution nearly ready. It is hoped that this office, in its appropriate work, will greatly aid and encourage the efforts made to discover and increase the production of the precious metals.

REDEMPTION OF COPPER AND NICKEL-BRONZE COINS.

The redemption of the nickel copper cents in exchange for the five-cent nickel coin, was continued, as authorized by law, until the 25th day of March, A. D. 1871, at which time the law for the general redemption of all the base or token coinage went into operation. The amount thus redeemed to the 25th day of March, 1871, was, pounds, 39,527 ; value, $38,736 46.

The amount of base coins redeemed under the act of March 3, 1871, to June 30, 1871, was, in tale or nominal value, $178,133 75. The different kinds redeemed under that law to same date are as follows, viz :

Denomination and kind.	Number of pieces.	Value.
Copper one-cent pieces	1, 005, 215	$10, 052 15
Nickel one-cent pieces	3, 645, 921	36, 459 21
Bronze one-cent pieces	3, 101, 810	31, 018 10
Bronze two-cent pieces	1, 272, 016	25, 440 32
Nickel three-cent pieces	219, 144	6, 574 32
Nickel five-cent pieces	1, 371, 793	68, 589 65
Total redemption to June 30, 1871	10, 615, 899	178, 133 75

It is worthy of remark that while the sum of $178,133 75 was redeemed during that period, orders were received during the same time for a large amount of the bronze one and two and the nickel-copper three and five cent pieces.

PROFITS.

The profits of the nickel-copper and bronze coinage paid into the Treasury of the United States during the fiscal year were $100,000.

The alloy of the minor coinage has been regularly assayed and reported by the assayer of the Mint ; and the legal proportion of the constituent metals been properly maintained.

The continued suspension of specie payments restricts the work of the Mint and the amount of the coinage. The capacity of the Mint and branch mints now in operation is more than sufficient to meet every demand for the conversion of the gold and silver deposits into coin, and consequently there is no legitimate necessity for increasing the number of branch mints. My views on this subject in connection with assay offices remain as expressed in former reports. From the discoveries and developments constantly making of the deposits of the precious metals in our western States and Territories, it is not beyond the practical and real to say that before another decade the annual production of gold and silver in the United States will be more than doubled. The reports are full of encouragement ; but at the same time care must be taken by the prudent to distinguish between the true statement and the exaggeration of the mere speculator.

DEVICES ON COINS.

This subject was referred to in my last annual report. The legends and devices on our national coinage should not be too frequently changed ; but change, when it rises to the dignity of an improvement, should be encouraged. It should not be so great as to destroy the identity of the new with the previous coinage of the country, or remove those peculiar national characteristics that have ever been recognized by the people as the stamp and certificate of the Government. Art and science are progressive. Why should not the influence of this progress be seen and marked upon the coins of the United States? Aesthetics, or the science of the beautiful in nature and art, in its cultivation not only adorns but adds strength and dignity to national greatness. Let the coinage of our country, in its devices and artistic execution, meet the improved taste and higher cultivation of our advancing civilization. I propose to have prepared such devices as may improve the general appearance of our coins, retaining their general characteristics; to be used, if approved, in the event of a change, by legislation, in our national coinage.

ABRADED COINS AS A LEGAL TENDER.

Having, as Director of the Mint, advantages of observing the defects of existing mint laws, or of such as are anticipated and pending, I beg leave respectfully to mention some points that occur to me as proper to place in an annual report:

1st. It seems a remarkable omission in our laws that there is no limit at which our coins shall cease to be a legal tender on account of *wear*. In England, the sovereign, or pound sterling, is not legally current when it has lost more than half a grain; although, by a recent examination of the state of the currency there, it appears that a large amount of coin is much lighter, especially in the countries remote from the capital. When the gold coin is offered at banking-houses, if not new, it is weighed, and received at a deduction proportionate to the loss. However, there was a time (nearly a century past) when the light gold was called in and re-coined, the loss being made good by government, to the amount of over a half million of pounds sterling. And at this day the worn silver coin is kept up to legal weight in the same way without loss to private holders.

It has not been a serious trouble in this country, from the fact that our coin is so apt to be exported. And yet it makes difficulty at the custom-houses and national treasuries, as we have had occasion to know. The collectors and treasurers hardly know what they are to do when coins much abraded are offered to them. In some sections, where gold is much used, as on the Pacific coast and in the extreme Southwest, the wear is very marked. Quarter-eagles may be met with not really worth more than $2 40; and gold dollars still more deficient in proportion. It would be well to declare, by law, that gold coin shall be a legal tender at their stamped value, so long as they weigh within one per cent. for the smaller denominations, and one-half per cent. for the larger. But then the question arises, Who shall lose the difference when the coin becomes uncurrent?

2d. This brings us to a second point of discussion—a provision for keeping up the coins to legal weight, without laying the burden upon the last holder.

Whether it is positively right that the whole country should maintain the integrity of the country's coin, is a fair question for debate. That this should be the rule in regard to fractional silver coin, on which the Government makes a small gain, is a plain case enough. In regard to the gold, that could also be undertaken without great loss to the Treasury, if the plan which has been spoken of in England be adopted, to make a small diminution of weight, and consequently a small profit in the first issue. That is to say, suppose the Mint value of standard gold continue to be $1,000 for 53¾ ounces, at which rate any person bringing gold bullion or foreign coin would be paid in fine or standard bars or coin; but the Mint would make it into $1,010, lawful coin, by a reduction of (say) 1 per cent. The difference could be reserved as a fund to enable the Mint in all future time to give out new pieces in exchange for worn and uncurrent prices, at even tale. The English idea, however, was merely to pay expense of coinage in this way. The difference would not suffice to avoid all loss, but it would materially reduce the burden.

It is to be assumed that only the loss by *abrasion* should thus be made good; not the fraudulent lightening by boring, filing, clipping, filling, or sweating. Persons who take such pieces must do so at their own cost.

There is some reason why the gross material should be of less value, weight for weight, than the articles which are made from it. But, on the other hand, it is a prolific source of confusion and misunderstanding to have a difference in the value of an ounce of gold, according as it is found in a bar or in a coin. Still, the question of loss by wear should be met, and if ever there is to be an *international* coinage, there should be a joint engagement that each nation will keep up its own coins to the standard, or within reasonable bounds.

Here it may be allowable to say that the international system should aim chiefly at a uniform *money of account*. Our coinage laws have carefully provided for "emblems of liberty," and the explanatory word "liberty" besides; and it is not likely that such coins would be welcome among peoples who are thus reminded of subjection. With us, public opinion is generally against the glorification of any man by placing his titles and effigy on the coin; and if our President, and even our Washington, is excluded, we hardly wish to have emperors and kings thus complimented among us. Still, no man will object to the occasional receipt of a gold coin of known value, be the portrait what it may, or the legend in what language soever.

This *money of account* should be based upon refined gold in bar; that is, upon a definite weight of fine gold, without reference to a standard for coin. Old names could be retained, but five dollars of account, twenty-five francs of account, and one pound sterling of account, should express the same amount. After this basis, if each country should make its coins nine-tenths fine, and in weight less than the bar rate, say, by 1 per cent., with a mutual guarantee to keep up the weight by recoinage, the coins would be passable for small sums beyond the lines; while for large transactions commercial houses would expect to pay and be paid in bar-gold. But within each country its own gold coin would be an unlimited legal tender at the stamped value; and this would tend to keep such coins at home, and secure a specie circulation as far as is desirable.

Some may think that to issue gold bars at one rate, and gold coin at a slightly different rate, would tend to check coinage. But this is not likely. The depositor of bullion would know no difference as to the tale value of his returns. The only difference would be that, if he wanted to hold specie for shipment, he would take bars; if he wanted it for home use or deposit in bank, he would take coin.

What has been said must not be taken as recommending such a system, but merely as a statement of the matter in its various bearings for further consideration. As already remarked, it does not originate here.

In general, the country's currency must always be, as it has been, chiefly in paper redeemable in gold. A perfect domestic money system, would seem to be, bank or Government notes for large payments; gold coin for occasional use in large or small; silver coins for the fraction of a dollar down to the tenth part; and an inferior alloy for smaller denominations.

Concurrently with this an issue of Treasury paper notes of one dollar, and a half dollar, always redeemable at the Treasury in silver coin, would be a great convenience for the transmission of small dues by mail, and for other purposes.

A currency of paper only, cheap and easily made, is a baseless fabric. It derives all its value from its being redeemable in the precious metals. The national scarcity of gold and silver, the difficulty of mining, and the cost of extracting and refining them, their noble qualities and their uses in various ways, give them a positive and high intrinsic value, and fit them to perform the office of money. On this point the wisdom of ages can never become foolish or obsolete.

TOKEN SILVER COINAGE.

3. A third point in which our monetary laws evidently require amendment is a reduction in weight of our silver coins, with competent guards as to the amount of issue and extent of legal tender, so as to insure us a metallic fractional currency, even if gold should ascend to a premium. This has been enlarged upon in a previous report, and need only be noticed here.

COUNTERFEIT AND IMITATION COINS.

Here it may be mentioned that an act passed June 8, 1864, supplied a real omission in the penal code, as regards the protection of the metallic currency. It provides (in brief) for the punishment of any who make or pass counterfeit coins in any metal or alloy, in the resemblance of those of the United States or of foreign countries; or who make or pass coins of "original design" for the purpose of money. This last provision might seem to be useless, on the supposition that nobody would take a coin which was not an imitation. But the fact is quite otherwise, not only in respect to the baser coin, of which great quantities of *original design* were issued more than thirty years ago, and in later times; but also in regard to the precious metals, as recent facts have proved. I refer to small pieces designated as "half dollars" and "quarter dollars," with some claim to be considered gold coins, as they really contain as much of that metal as is to be found in common jewelry. The pieces which began to be issued in San Francisco, in 1859, and perhaps have been coined more recently, may not have been actually pushed into circulation, but may rather have served as play-pieces or curiosities. However, they were sold at their pretended value, while in fact the half dollar, weighing six grains on an average, and about 425-thousandths fine, was worth eleven cents; the quarter dollar nearly in the same proportion, some pieces being actually worth six cents. No doubt they have been imposed upon ignorant persons as real money. Their shapes were various, some octagonal, some circular.

A similar case has recently occurred of a large issue of "half-dollars" from a private mint in Leavenworth, Kansas. On the obverse is a female head with thirteen stars, and the date 1871; on the reverse is a wreath inclosing the words, "Half dollar, Cal." The weight of a specimen tried here was 7.6 grains, and the fineness 520 thousandths, making a value of just seventeen cents. The case has been properly taken in hand by the judicial authorities of that district.

I may next speak of another fraud upon the gold currency, into which we have lately been making minute and extended examination. I refer to filing away the reeding on the edge or periphery, and then restoring it by a hand-tool; by which operation there is a gain of about fifty cents' worth, more or less, of gold-dust from each double eagle so dealt with. This has been done extensively on the Pacific coast, and has been punished by the courts. It requires some delicacy of touch to discover the difference; but the Treasury officers, custom-houses, and banks are very apt to check the circulation of such depreciated pieces.

The best preventive of this, probably, would be to abandon the ribbing or reeding, and substitute some other impression on the edge. This reeding was made use of from the very first on our gold coins, being heretofore considered a good safeguard against filing or clipping. It has also been impressed upon our silver coins for about thirty-five years past. Before that, the larger pieces had a periphery legend in sunken letters. Briefly to advert to the practice of some other nations, we find in England, as early as the reign of Charles the Second, the appropriate motto *Decus et Tutamen* running around the edge of the piece of five guineas, in raised letters. This was renewed in the double pound of George the Fourth. In the succeeding reign the edge of the gold coin was smooth, and during the reign of Victoria it has been uniformly reeded. In France, under the first Napoleon, the motto *Dieu Protege la France* was impressed in sunken letters. In the reign of Louis Phillippe, and since, the same legend has appeared in relief. The gold coins of Prussia also have a periphery motto, incuse. In Belgium the legend is in raised letters.

A modification of the steam-press, so as to adapt it to the segment-collar, would enable us to substitute letters for reeding, and evidently with much greater protection against the fraudulent reduction by filing, as well as against the practice of filling with a cheaper metal. The only difference would be that the press could not move so rapidly, which, in the coinage of gold, is a matter of no moment.

REFINING BY CHLORINE.

The processes of refining and separating gold and silver have received an unusual share of attention and experiment during the past year, both at the Mint and the assay office at New York. At the latter, the sulphuric acid process has been fully and successfully established, and the noxious fumes neutralized. This is a very economical operation, although it does not always leave the gold and silver in the highest state of ductility. A method of refining silver has also been originated there, by which the work is done in the ordinary melting-pot, with the aid of bone-ash as an absorbent. This is a well-contrived and economical mode, and gives very good results.

At the Mint, the reverberatory furnace, or bone-ash test, formerly in use, has been restored to meet cases of refinage growing out of the peculiar character of some of our western bullion. The presence of sulphur, antimony, lead, and arsenic, one or all, frequently makes the Nevada silver brittle and refractory.

We have also been experimenting upon a pretty large scale with the chlorine-refining of gold, recently invented and perfected in Australia, and largely employed there and in New Zealand, and also coming into use in England. It answers the double purpose of parting out the silver and of removing the last traces of base metals which prevent the perfect malleability of gold. We had the advantage of the presence and management of the inventor, F. Boyer Miller, esq., assayer of the Sydney

As the invention is a very remarkable one, and the process is likely to displace all others within the scope of its adaptation, I may briefly state that it is founded upon the eager affinity of chlorine for almost every metal, but generally less for gold than the others. The gas is generated by the action of muriatic acid on the black oxide of manganese, both very cheap materials. A current of this gas is conveyed by tubes into and down to the bottom of the melting-pot, while the mixed metals are in a state of fluidity. It seizes upon the baser metals, if any are present, and disperses them as volatile chlorides, copper forming the only exception. But in addition to that, the chlorine combines with the silver alloy, forming chloride of silver, which rises to the surface, the gold remaining in a purified condition beneath. The silver, holding the copper, if there is any, is protected from evaporation by a coating of borax on top of the melt. Absorption into the pot is also prevented by a previous coating of the same agent. The silver (argentic chloride) is taken off after the cooling in solid cakes, brought to the metallic state in a galvanic battery by an ingenious arrangement due to Mr Leihins, also of the Sydney mint.

The chlorine acts somewhat upon the gold, so that about 2 per cent. of that metal is converted into a chloride, and rises with the silver. But this difficulty is overcome by the subsequent addition of a small quantity of metallic silver, on which the chlorine fastens by a greater affinity, and liberates the gold.

The peculiar merits of this process are, that it is cheap, rapid, and makes the most ductile gold. Its economy and quickness will be better understood when it is observed that in other processes, say the sulphuric or nitric, it is necessary to add to the gold, by a preliminary melting, nearly twice its weight, or four times its bulk, of silver, and to granulate the mixture so as to enable the acid to have any action ; and then, what with the parting and the subsequent recovery of the two metals, several days are consumed in the whole operation. But in the chlorine process no such addition of silver is required, the application being direct and simple, and a few hours will finish the work. The cost of materials and labor is much less than by any other method. The fine gold resulting from it, as shown by the experiments here, assayed from 994 to 997½ thousandths, which is as high as is needed for commercial bars, and nearly as high as the results from sulphuric acid.

On the other hand, this process (chlorine) is not applicable to silver containing a small proportion of gold. So that when two kinds of bullion are presented, as is frequently the case at our mints and assay offices, namely, gold containing silver and silver containing gold, it is highly advantageous and a great saving to combine the two. In this case the sulphuric acid process is greatly to be preferred to any other. It seems desirable that we should have the benefit of both this and the chlorine; but the latter is a patented process, and, perhaps, cannot be obtained without legislative aid.

HUMID ASSAY.

The humid assay of silver, hitherto thought to be complete, has been still further perfected at the New York office, and here, by an admirable change in the mode of drawing and measuring the normal liquor. But we see no reason to take up with certain other suggestions for using the hydrobromic precipitant instead of the hydrochloric, or for working through the medium of yellow light. It is a mere affectation to carry the assay beyond the attainable degree of homogeneity in melting or nicety in weighing at the assay balance.

It is a satisfaction to find that we can now have our delicate apparatus made in this country, and partly in our own house, so that we need no longer resort to London or Paris.

TABLE OF FOREIGN COINS.

The statement of the weight, fineness, and value of foreign coins, required by law to be made annually, will be found appended to this report. We have no alterations to report in this annual statement.

Mexican silver dollars of 1871, new devices, somewhat exceed the fineness reported in our tables, but it would not be safe to assess them at a higher value than therein stated.

We are expecting specimens of new European coins, which will illustrate the great changes of government that have recently occurred there; but as yet we have only some silver pieces of France, which conform to the style formerly issued under the republic. Germany, France, Spain, and Italy will all have a new coinage to show, at least in respect to devices.

MEDAL DEPARTMENT.

This department, organized a number of years ago, under the direction and by the authority of the Secretary of the Treasury, still continues in successful operation. A large number of medals have been made for the Government in the Indian Department, and many others have been made and sold. This department is not only profitable but a credit to the Government. It should be encouraged.

THE MINT CABINET.

This cabinet of coins and medals has been visited during the past year by more than fifty thousand persons from our own and other countries. It is a place of great attraction, and well repays the visitor. The annual appropriation for this cabinet should not only be continued but increased.

STATISTICAL TABLES.

The statistics relating to the deposits of bullion and coinage at the Mint of the United States and branches will be found in the tabular statement hereto annexed. These tables have been prepared with great care, and every effort made to correct and avoid mistakes. They are believed to be trustworthy and accurate.

Very respectfully, your obedient servant,

JAS. POLLOCK, *Director.*

Hon. GEO. S. BOUTWELL,
    Secretary of the Treasury, Washington, D. C.

LIST OF TABLES IN APPENDIX.

F.—Coinage at branch mint, New Orleans, from organization to January, 1861.

G.—Coinage at branch mint at Dahlonega, Georgia, from organization to February 28, 1861:

H.—Coinage at branch mint, Charlotte, North Carolina, from organization to March 31, 1861.

I.—Coinage at assay office, New York, from organization to June 30, 1871.

K.—Coinage at branch mint, Denver, Colorado, from organization to June 30, 1871.

K¹.—Coinage at branch mint, Carson City, Nevada, from organization to June 30, 1871.

L.—Summary exhibit of coinage at Mint and branches to close of year ending June 30, 1871.

M.—Gold of domestic production deposited at the Mint of the United States to close of year ending June 30, 1871.

N.—Same at branch mint, San Francisco, to June 30, 1871.

O.—Same at branch mint, New Orleans, to January 31, 1861.

P.—Same at branch mint, Dahlonega, Georgia, to February 28, 1861.

Q.—Same at branch mint, Charlotte, North Carolina, to June 30, 1871.

R.—Same at assay office, New York, to June 30, 1871.

S.—Same at branch mint, Denver, to June 30, 1871.

T.—Summary exhibit of gold deposits at the Mint of the United States and branches to June 30, 1871.

U.—Statement of amount of silver coined at the Mint of the United States and branches at San Francisco, New Orleans, and Carson City, under act of February 21, 1853.

V. Statement of amount of silver of domestic production deposited at the Mint of the United States and branches from January, 1841, to June 30, 1871.

W.—Statement of domestic gold and silver deposited at Mint of the United States and branches, for coinage, to June 30, 1871.

X.—Statement of weight, fineness, and value of foreign gold coins.

Y.—Statement of weight, fineness, and value of foreign silver coins.

APPENDIX.

A.—*Statement of deposits at the Mint of the United States; the branch mint, San Francisco; assay office, New York; and branch mint, Denver; branch mint, Charlotte; and branch mint, Carson City, during the fiscal year ending June 30, 1871.*

Description of bullion.	Mint United States, Philadelphia.	Branch mint, San Francisco.	Assay office, New York.	Branch mint, Denver.	Branch mint, Charlotte.	Branch mint, Carson City.	Total.
GOLD.							
Fine bars	$1,932,637 02	$19,101,396 12					$21,034,033 14
Mint bars re-deposited			$761,915 66				761,915 66
United States bullion	603,393 26	6,920,493 20	4,258,120 13	$1,104,147 10	$14,522 81	$1,003,809 60	13,204,486 10
United States coin	109,444 55		16,783 10				126,227 65
Jewelers' bars	184,224 63		421,176 48				605,401 11
Foreign coin	2,225 52	131,539 50	468,675 96				602,440 98
Foreign bullion	232,808 33	68,221 74	418,667 55				719,697 62
Total gold	3,064,733 31	25,521,650 56	6,345,338 88	1,104,147 10	14,522 81	1,003,809 60	37,054,202 26
SILVER.							
Fine bars	1,172,611 95	421,009 89					1,593,651 84
Mint bars re-deposited	956 66		4,681 46				5,638 12
United States bullion	290,583 16	87,312 06	1,607,755 19	18,561 63	145 31	1,290,684 85	3,285,042 20
United States coin	30,521 61		15,677 96				66,199 57
Jewelers' bars	21,823 02		137,034 34				158,857 36
Foreign coin	30,385 65	421,447 07	340,541 51				792,374 23
Foreign bullion	1,010 45	7,778 87	65,429 90				74,219 22
Total silver	1,557,892 50	937,377 89	2,171,120 36	18,561 63	145 31	1,290,684 85	5,975,982 54
Total gold and silver	4,622,625 81	26,459,228 45	8,516,459 24	1,122,708 73	14,668 12	2,294,494 45	43,030,184 80
Less re-deposits at different institutions:							
Gold	1,952,302 37		761,915 66				
Silver	1,173,681 18		4,681 46				
Total re-deposits							3,892,780 67
							39,137,404 13

B.—Statement of gold and silver of domestic production deposited at the Mint of the United States; the branch mint, San Francisco; assay office, New York; and branch mints, Denver, Charlotte, and Carson City, during the fiscal year ending June 30, 1871.

Description of bullion.	Mint of United States, Philadelphia.	Branch mint, San Francisco.	Assay office, New York.	Branch mint, Denver.	Branch mint, Charlotte.	Branch mint, Carson City.	Total.
GOLD.							
Alabama	$5,720 60						$5,720 60
Arizona	4,039 31	$177,125 25	$1,657 24	$552 30			183,354 30
California	4,865 44	5,294,436 49	197,680 72				5,496,953 65
Colorado	12,984 87		472,378 58	982,712 70			1,468,076 15
Branch mint, Colorado	16,959 51						16,959 51
Georgia	14,451 74		29,144 92				43,596 66
Idaho	42,599 42	146,156 57	532,853 20	4,328 75			725,937 94
Montana	374,108 19	81,912 22	2,775,930 82	8,218 25			3,240,169 48
Maryland	18 85						18 85
Nebraska	965 02		2,793 65				3,758 67
Nevada	227 92	8,118 56	19,480 47			$164,888 77	182,715 02
New Mexico	15,941 40		61,794 67	97,536 25			175,272 32
North Carolina	58,308 00		20,030 78		$14,522 81		92,861 59
Branch mint, North Carolina	2,905 84						2,905 84
Oregon	2,357 10	433,502 28	8,978 81				444,838 19
South Carolina	3,043 08		1,609 78				4,652 86
Tennessee			102 85				102 85
Utah	1,564 02	1,282 18	4,951 63				7,797 83
Virginia	5,974 24		916 40				6,890 64
Wyoming Territory	2,147 40		22,630 82	798 65			25,576 87
Washington Territory		1,652 14					1,652 14
Parted from silver	6,696 62	76,307 51	105,204 79			107,600 04	295,808 96
Source unknown	27,515 39						27,515 39
Bars		19,101,396 12	761,915 66			731,320 79	20,594,638 57
Total	603,393 26	25,321,889 32	5,020,035 79	1,104,147 10	14,522 81	1,003,809 60	33,067,797 88
SILVER.							
Arizona		1,755 36		5 10			1,760 46
California	81 36		47,825 37				47,906 73
Colorado	119,802 49		230,510 19	17,085 06			367,397 74
Branch mint, Colorado	112 57						112 57
Idaho	103 59		4,711 14	41 65			4,856 38
Lake Superior	5,056 12		168,252 68				173,308 80
Montana	86 83		27,914 37	129 71			28,130 91
New Mexico	1,256 35			3,276 88			4,533 23
Nevada	137,104 90	31,813 25	1,022,832 49			50,860 29	1,242,953 93
Nebraska			23,953 41				23,953 41
North Carolina					145 31		145 31

Utah	2,836 26	....	941 60	....	....	6,925 65	3,779 80
Parted from gold	14,187 85	....	78,830 52	....	....	....	152,891 47
Wyoming	....	....	....	7 65	....	....	7 65
Source unknown	32 84	†33,743 45	....	....	....	....	32 84
Bars	....	421,039 89	4,681 46	....	....	1,233,598 91	1,659,320 26
Total	980,583 16	508,351 95	1,612,436 65	18,561 63	145 31	1,290,684 65	3,710,763 55
Total gold and silver of domestic production	883,976 42	25,830,241 27	6,632,472 44	1,122,708 73	14,608 12	2,294,494 45	36,778,561 43

* Contained in silver.   † Contained in gold.

C.—Statement of the coinage at the Mint of the United States; the branch mint, San Francisco; assay office, New York; and branch mints, Carson City, Charlotte, and Denver, during the fiscal year ending June 30, 1871.

Denomination	Mint, United States, Philadelphia Pieces	Value	Branch mint, San Francisco Pieces	Value	Assay office, New York Value	Branch mint, Denver Value	Branch mint, Carson City Pieces	Value	Branch mint, Charlotte, N.C. Value	Total Pieces	Value
GOLD.											
Double eagles	157,740	$3,134,800 00	883,000	$17,660,000 00			5,222	$104,440 00		1,045,962	$20,919,240 00
Eagles	1,640	16,400 00	8,000	80,000 00			6,685	66,850 00		16,325	163,250 00
Half eagles	2,840	14,200 00	17,000	85,000 00			11,885	59,425 00		31,725	158,625 00
Three dollars	1,340	4,020 00								1,340	4,020 00
Quarter eagles	5,360	13,400 00	16,000	40,000 00						21,360	53,400 00
Dollars	3,940	3,940 00								3,940	3,940 00
Fine bars	264	129,184 68			$5,461,465 84	$1,119,574 40			$14,322 81	264	5,605,173 53
Unparted bars				6,376,006 23	335 26						7,495,915 69
Total gold	173,124	3,335,944 88	924,000	24,241,006 23	5,461,801 10	1,119,574 40	23,792	230,715 00	14,322 81	1,190,916	34,403,564 42
SILVER.											
Dollars	657,625	657,625 00					304	304 00		657,929	657,929 00
Half dollars	941,125	470,562 50	1,444,000	722,000 00			100,417	50,208 50		2,485,542	1,242,771 00
Quarter dollars	82,997	20,524 25	30,900	7,725 00			6,890	1,722 30		119,887	29,971 75
Dimes	10,675	1,067 30	90,000	9,000 00			6,400	640 00		107,075	10,707 30
Half dimes	136,925	6,346 25	161,000	8,050 00						297,925	14,396 25
Three-cent pieces	4,325	129 75								4,325	129 75
Bars	1,369	143,647 75			1,247,232 79		15	1,735 17	145 31	1,384	1,392,761 02
Unparted bars				161,240 27	22,268 96		725	1,967,909 88		725	2,151,419 11
Total silver	1,824,141	1,299,903 00	1,725,900	908,015 27	1,269,501 75		114,751	2,022,520 05	145 31	3,664,792	5,500,085 38
COPPER.											
Five-cent pieces	3,439,000	171,950 00								3,439,000	171,950 00
Three-cent pieces	921,000	27,630 00								921,000	27,630 00
Two-cent pieces	1,105,250	22,105 00								1,105,250	22,105 00
One-cent pieces	6,207,500	62,075 00								6,207,500	62,075 00
Total copper	11,672,750	283,760 00								11,672,750	283,760 00
Total coinage	13,670,015	4,919,607 88	2,649,900	25,149,021 50	6,731,302 85	1,119,574 40	138,543	2,253,235 05	14,668 12	16,458,458	40,167,409 80

D.—*Coinage of the Mint and branches, from their organization to the close of the fiscal year ending June 30, 1871.*

MINT OF THE UNITED STATES, PHILADELPHIA.

Period.	GOLD COINAGE.						
	Double eagles.	Eagles.	Half eagles.	Three dollars.	Quarter eagles.	Dollars.	Fine bars.
	Pieces.	*Pieces.*	*Pieces.*	*Pieces.*	*Pieces.*	*Pieces.*	*Value.*
1793 to 1817...	....	132,592	845,909	....	22,197	....	....
1818 to 1837...	....	....	3,087,925	....	879,903	....	....
1838 to 1847...	....	1,227,759	3,269,921	....	345,526	....	....
1848 to 1857...	8,122,526	1,970,597	2,260,390	223,015	5,544,900	15,348,608	$33,612,140 46
1858 to 1867...	5,740,871	179,745	795,075	66,381	1,609,749	2,360,634	1,078,168 51
1868	188,540	3,050	5,750	4,900	3,650	10,550	98,848 03
1869	152,525	9,485	1,785	2,525	4,345	5,925	130,141 91
1870	137,845	2,535	4,035	3,535	4,955	6,335	171,624 97
1871	157,740	1,640	2,840	1,340	5,360	3,940	129,184 88
Total	14,500,047	3,527,403	10,273,630	301,696	8,420,585	17,736,192	35,220,108 76

Period.	SILVER COINAGE.						
	Dollars.	Half dollars.	Quarter dollars.	Dimes.	Half dimes.	Three cents.	Bars.
	Pieces.	*Pieces.*	*Pieces.*	*Pieces.*	*Pieces.*	*Pieces.*	*Value.*
1793 to 1817...	1,439,517	13,104,433	650,280	1,007,151	265,543	....	....
1818 to 1817...	1,000	74,793,560	5,041,749	11,854,949	14,463,700	....	....
1838 to 1847...	879,873	20,203,333	4,952,073	11,387,995	11,093,235	....	....
1848 to 1857...	350,250	10,691,088	41,073,080	35,172,010	34,368,520	37,778,900	$32,355 55
1858 to 1867...	758,700	12,632,830	22,955,730	6,042,330	12,995,330	4,209,330	73,552 45
1868	54,800	411,500	29,900	423,150	85,800	4,000	6,729 94
1869	231,350	387,350	16,550	49,050	10,550	5,050	92,090 12
1870	576,150	891,450	87,250	721,850	734,450	3,850	195,078 01
1871	657,025	941,125	82,097	10,075	126,925	4,325	143,647 75
Total	4,949,265	130,056,669	74,888,709	66,669,160	74,144,053	42,005,455	543,453 82

Period.	COPPER COINAGE.				
	Five cents.	Three cents.	Two cents.	One cent.	Half cent.
	Pieces.	*Pieces.*	*Pieces.*	*Pieces.*	*Pieces.*
1793 to 1817...	....	....	....	29,316,272	5,235,513
1818 to 1837...	....	....	....	46,554,830	2,205,200
1838 to 1847...	....	....	....	34,967,663	....
1848 to 1857...	....	....	....	51,449,979	544,510
1858 to 1867...	32,574,000	16,987,000	38,245,500	284,909,000	....
1868	28,902,000	3,613,000	3,066,500	9,856,500	....
1869	22,025,000	2,146,000	1,730,750	7,681,000	....
1870	9,750,000	1,423,000	1,144,500	5,636,500	....
1871	3,439,000	921,000	1,105,250	6,207,500	....
Total	96,690,000	25,090,000	45,292,500	476,979,244	7,985,223

Period.	TOTAL COINAGE.				
	Number of pieces coined.	Value of gold.	Value of silver.	Value of copper.	Total.
1793 to 1817	52,019,407	$5,610,957 50	$8,268,295 75	$319,340 28	$14,198,593 53
1818 to 1837	158,882,816	17,639,382 50	40,566,897 15	476,574 30	58,682,853 95
1838 to 1847	88,327,378	29,491,010 00	13,913,019 00	349,676 63	43,753,705 63
1848 to 1857	244,898,373	256,950,474 46	22,365,413 55	517,222 34	279,833,110 35
1858 to 1867	443,062,405	128,252,763 01	14,267,879 35	5,752,310 00	148,272,952 36
1868	46,663,500	3,963,273 03	321,479 94	1,713,385 00	5,998,137 97
1869	34,659,240	3,308,779 41	526,836 62	1,279,055 00	5,114,671 03
1870	21,328,740	2,830,752 50	1,152,960 50	611,445 00	4,595,158 00
1871	13,670,015	3,335,944 88	1,299,903 00	283,760 00	4,919,607 88
Total	1,103,511,964	451,383,337 29	102,682,684 86	11,302,708 55	565,368,790 70

E.—BRANCH MINT AT SAN FRANCISCO.

GOLD COINAGE.

Period.	Double eagles.	Eagles.	Half eagles.	Three dollars.	Quarter eagles.	Dollars.	Unparted bars.	Fine bars.
	Pieces.	Pieces.	Pieces.	Pieces.	Pieces.	Pieces.	Value.	Value.
1854	141,408	123,826	268	......	246	14,632	$5,641,504 05	$5,863 16
1855	859,175	9,000	61,000	6,600	......	...	3,270,504 93	88,782 50
1856	1,121,750	73,500	94,100	34,500	71,120	24,600	3,047,001 29	122,136 55
1857	604,500	10,000	47,000	5,000	20,000	......	......	......
1858	885,940	27,800	58,600	9,000	49,200	20,000	816,295 65	......
1859	689,140	2,0.0	9,720	.....-	8,000	15,000	......	19,871 68
1860	579,975	10,000	16,700	7,000	28,800	13,000	......	......
1861	614,300	6,000	8,000	......	14,000	......		
1862	760,000	18,000	18,000	......	30,000	......		
1863	866,423	9,000	16,500	......	4,000	......		
1864	947,320	5,000	10,000	......	8,800	......		
1865	925,160	8,700	12,000	......	8,250	......		
1866	876,500	30,500	53,420	......	46,080	......		
1867	901,000	2,000	24,000	......	26,000	......		
1868	696,750	12,500	25,000	......	26,000	......		
1869	511,805	11,800	14,000	......	38,000	......		....
1870	950,750	2,930	13,000	......	9,500	3,000	......	
1871	883,000	6,000	17,000	......	16,000	......	6,376,006 23	......
Total	14,283,151	370,256	528,308	62,100	404,002	90,232	19,151,402 15	236,653 89

SILVER COINAGE.

Period.	Dollars.	Half dollars.	Quarter dollars.	Dimes.	Half dimes.	Bars.
	Pieces.	Pieces.	Pieces.	Pieces.	Pieces.	Value.
1854						
1855		121,950	412,400			
1856		211,000	286,000			$23,609 45
1857		86,000	28,000			
1858		218,000	63,000	30,000		19,752 61
1859	15,000	463,000	172,000	90,000		29,469 87
1860	5,000	693,000	24,000	40,000		211,411 52
1861		350,000	52,000	100,000		71,485 61
1862		1,179,500	120,000	219,500		1,278 65
1863		1,542,000	43,000	291,250	100,000	224,763 68
1864		648,000	20,000	140,000	90,000	120,909 02
1865		613,000	22,000	150,000	36,000	145,235 58
1866		490,000	19,000	210,000	204,000	442,342 64
1867		1,216,000	52,000	130,000		146,048 54
1868		1,482,000	120,000	310,000	400,000	
1869		736,000	76,000	190,000		
1870		1,114,000	......	260,000	230,000	
1871		1,444,000	30,900	90,000	161,000	161,240 24
Total	20,000	12,607,450	1,540,300	2,250,750	1,221,000	1,597,547 41

TOTAL COINAGE.

Period.	No. of pieces.	Gold value.	Silver value.	Total value.
1854	280,440	$9,731,574 21	......	$9,731,574 21
1855	1,470,125	20,957,677 43	$164,075 00	21,121,752 43
1856	1,976,570	28,315,537 84	200,609 45	28,516,147 29
1857	800,500	12,490,000 00	50,000 00	12,540,000 00
1858	1,361,540	19,276,095 65	147,502 61	19,423,598 26
1859	1,463,860	13,906,271 68	327,969 87	14,234,241 55
1860	1,417,475	11,889,000 00	572,911 52	12,461,911 52
1861	1,144,300	12,421,000 00	269,485 61	12,690,485 61
1862	2,345,000	15,545,000 00	642,978 65	16,187,978 65
1863	2,872,173	17,510,960 00	1,040,638 68	18,551,598 68
1864	1,869,120	19,068,400 00	468,409 02	19,536,809 02
1865	1,775,116	18,670,840 00	474,035 58	19,144,875 58
1866	1,929,500	18,217,300 00	723,292 64	18,940,592 64
1867	2,351,000	18,225,000 00	780,048 54	19,005,048 54
1868	3,072,250	14,250,000 00	822,000 00	15,072,000 00
1869	2,006,500	18,650,000 00	406,000 00	19,056,000 00
1870	2,592,180	19,316,030 00	594,500 00	19,910,550 00
1871	2,649,900	24,241,006 23	908,015 27	25,149,021 50
Total	33,377,549	312,681,713 04	8,592,472 44	321,274,185 48

F.—BRANCH MINT, NEW ORLEANS.

Period.	GOLD COINAGE.					
	Double eagles.	Eagles.	Half eagles.	Three dollars.	Quarter eagles.	Dollars.
	Pieces.	Pieces.	Pieces.	Pieces.	Pieces.	Pieces.
1838 to 1847		1,026,342	709,925		550,528	
1848 to 1857	730,500	534,250	108,100	20,000	546,100	1,004,000
1858	47,500	21,500	13,000		34,000	
1859	24,500	4,000				
1860	4,350	8,200				
1861	9,600	5,200				
Total	816,450	1,599,492	831,025	24,000	1,130,628	1,004,000

Period.	SILVER COINAGE.						
	Dollars.	Half dollars.	Quarter dollars.	Dimes.	Half dimes.	Three cents.	Bars.
	Pieces.	Pieces.	Pieces.	Pieces.	Pieces.	Pieces.	Value.
1838 to 1847	59,000	13,509,000	3,273,600	6,473,500	2,789,000		
1848 to 1857	40,000	21,406,000	4,556,000	5,690,000	8,170,000	720,000	
1858		4,614,000	1,416,000	1,540,000	2,540,000		$334,996 47
1859	200,000	4,912,000	544,000	440,000	1,060,000		25,422 33
1860	280,000	2,212,000	388,000	370,000	1,060,000		16,818 33
1861	395,000	828,000					
Total	974,000	47,481,000	10,177,600	14,513,500	15,619,000	720,000	377,237 13

TOTAL COINAGE.

Period.	Number of pieces.	Value of gold.	Value of silver.	Total value coined.
1838 to 1847	28,390,895	$15,189,365 00	$8,418,700 00	$23,608,065 00
1848 to 1857	43,528,950	22,934,250 00	12,881,100 00	35,815,350 00
1858	10,226,000	1,315,000 00	2,942,000 00	4,257,000 00
1859	7,184,500	530,000 00	3,223,996 37	3,753,996 37
1860	4,322,550	169,000 00	1,598,422 33	1,767,423 33
1861	1,237,800	244,000 00	825,818 33	1,069,818 33
Total	94,890,695	40,381,615 00	29,890,037 03	70,271,652 03

G.—BRANCH MINT, DAHLONEGA, GEORGIA.

Period.	GOLD COINAGE.					
	Half eagles.	Three dollars.	Quarter eagles.	Dollars.	Total pieces.	Total value.
	Pieces.	Pieces.	Pieces.	Pieces.		
1838 to 1847	576,553		134,105		710,658	$3,218,017 50
1848 to 1857	478,392	1,120	60,605	60,897	601,014	2,607,729 50
1858	19,256		900	1,637	21,793	100,167 00
1859	11,404		642	6,957	19,003	65,582 00
1860	12,800		1,602	1,472	15,874	69,477 00
1861	11,876			1,566	13,442	60,946 00
Total	1,110,281	1,120	197,854	72,529	1,381,784	6,121,919 00

H.—BRANCH MINT, CHARLOTTE, N. C.

Period.	GOLD COINAGE.				
	Half eagles.	Quarter eagles.	Dollars.	Total pieces.	Total value.
	Pieces.	Pieces.	Pieces.		o
1838 to 1847	269, 424	123, 576	....	393, 000	$1, 656, 060 00
1848 to 1857	500, 872	79, 736	103, 899	684, 507	2, 807, 599 00
1858	31. 066	9, 056	....	40, 122	177, 970 00
1859	39, 500	....	5, 235	44, 735	202, 735 00
1860	23, 005	7, 469	....	30, 474	133, 697 50
1861, (to March 31)	14, 116	....	....	14, 116	70, 580 00
Total	877, 983	219, 837	109, 134	1, 206, 954	5, 048, 641 50

I.—ASSAY OFFICE, NEW YORK.

Period.	Fine gold bars.	Fine silver bars.	Total.
	Value.	Value.	Value.
1854	$2, 888, 059 18	....	$2, 888, 059 18
1855	20, 441, 813 63	....	20, 441, 813 63
1856	19, 396, 046 89	$6, 792 63	19, 402, 839 52
1857	9, 335, 414 00	123, 317 00	9, 458, 731 00
1858	21, 798, 691 04	171, 961 79	21, 970, 652 83
1859	13, 044, 718 43	272, 424 05	13, 317, 142 48
1860	6, 831, 532 01	222, 226 .11	7, 053, 758 12
1861	19, 948, 728 88	187, 078 63	20, 135, 807 51
1862	16, 094, 768 44	415, 603 57	16, 510, 372 01
1863	1, 793, 838 16	158, 542 91	1, 952, 381 07
1864	1, 539, 751 27	173, 308 64	1, 713, 059 91
1865	4, 947, 809 21	165, 003 45	5, 112, 812 66
1866	8, 862, 451 00	459, 594 00	9, 322, 045 00
1867	11, 411, 258 26	425, 155 26	11, 836, 413 52
1868	5, 567, 082 77	449, 506 54	6, 016, 589 31
1869	9, 221, 914 30	642, 100 55	9, 864, 014 85
1870	6, 656, 268 11	707, 400 04	7, 363, 668 15
1871	5, 461, 801 10	1, 269, 501 75	6, 731, 302 85
Total	185, 241, 946 68	5, 849, 516 92	191, 091, 463 60

K.—BRANCH MINT, DENVER.

Period.	Gold bars.	Silver bars.	Total.
	Value.	Value.	Value.
1864	$486, 329 97	....	$486, 329 97
1865	545, 363 00	....	545, 363 00
1866	159, 917 76	....	159, 917 76
1867	130, 559 70	....	130, 559 70
1868	360, 879 26	....	360, 879 26
1869	847, 272 32	....	847, 272 32
1870	1, 001, 984 52	....	1, 001, 984 52
1871	1, 104, 147 10	$18, 561 63	1, 104, 147 10
Total	4, 636, 453 63	18, 561 63	4, 655, 015 26

K.—BRANCH MINT AT CARSON CITY.

Period.	GOLD COINAGE.			
	Double eagles.	Eagles.	Half eagles.	Fine bars.
	Pieces.	*Pieces.*	*Pieces.*	*Value.*
1870	3, 329	3, 448	1, 890	$66 05
1871	5, 222	6, 685	11, 885	....
Total	8, 551	10, 133	13, 775	66 05

Period.	SILVER COINAGE.				
	Dollars.	Half dollars.	Quarter dollars.	Dimes.	Bars.
	Pieces.	*Pieces.*	*Pieces.*	*Pieces.*	*Value.*
1870	12, 158	12, 800	4, 940	....	......
1871	304	100, 417	6, 890	6, 400	$740
Total	12, 462	113, 217	11, 830	6, 400	740

Period.	TOTAL COINAGE.			
	Number of pieces.	Gold value.	Silver value.	Total value.
1870	38, 566	$110, 576 05	$19, 793 00	$130, 369 05
1871	138, 543	230, 715 00	2, 022, 520 05	2, 253, 235 05
Total	177, 119	341, 291 05	2, 042, 313 05	2, 383, 604 10

L.—SUMMARY EXHIBIT OF THE COINAGE OF THE MINT AND BRANCHES TO THE CLOSE OF THE YEAR ENDING JUNE 30, 1871.

Mints.	Commenced-operation of coin-age.	Gold coinage. Value.	Silver coinage. Value.	Copper coinage. Value.	Entire coinage. Pieces.	Entire coinage. Value.
Philadelphia	1793	$451,363,337 29	$102,682,694 86	$1,302,766 55	1,103,511,984	$565,368,790 70
San Francisco	1854	312,381,713 04	8,592,672 44		33,317,549	321,274,185 48
New Orleans, to January 31, 1861	1838	40,361,615 00	29,890,037 03		94,890,695	70,271,652 03
Charlotte, to March 31, 1861	1838	5,048,641 50			1,206,954	5,048,641 50
Dahlonega, to February 28, 1861	1838	6,121,919 00			1,381,784	6,121,919 00
New York	1854	185,241,946 68	5,649,516 92			191,091,463 60
Denver	1863	4,636,453 63	18,561 63			4,655,015 26
Carson City	1870	341,291 05	2,042,313 05			2,383,604 10
Charlotte, reopened	1869	33,791 81	467 92			34,259 73
Total		1,005,870,709 00	149,076,053 81	1,302,766 55	1,234,362,946	1,166,249,531 40

M.—Statement of gold of domestic production, deposited at the Mint of the United States and branches, to the close of the year ending June 30, 1871.

MINT OF THE UNITED STATES, PHILADELPHIA.

Period.	Parted from silver.	Virginia.	N. Carolina.	S. Carolina.	Georgia.	Tennessee.	Alabama.	New Mexico.	California.	Nebraska.	Wyoming Territory.
1804 to 1827			$110,000 00	$327,500 00	$1,763,900 00	$12,400 00					
1828 to 1837		$427,000 00	2,319,500 00	152,366 00	566,316 00	16,499 00					
1838 to 1847		518,294 00	1,303,636 00	55,626 00	44,577 00	6,669 00	$45,493 00				
1848 to 1857		534,401 50	469,237 00	6,156 15	129,940 00	835 88	9,451 00	$8,397 00	$226,839,521 63		
1858 to 1867	$105,070 16	77,689 48	214,453 74	1,019 11	30,675 88		530 06	9,685 33	4,095,477 30	$3,645 08	
1868	8,868 92	10,235 21	51,199 64	406 19	31,649 27		133 18	6,093 14	15,640 90	2,231 00	$153 93
1869	4,672 44	10,518 55	56,618 34	1,797 19	22,412 43	122 94	1,146 18	6,905 54	19,425 51	8,872 23	2,147 40
1870	7,239 53	11,357 52	60,929 87	3,043 08	14,451 74		2,334 22	3,361 40	28,423 31	965 02	
1871	6,696 62	5,974 24	61,213 84				5,720 00		4,665 44		
Total	132,547 67	1,595,820 30	4,646,789 43	547,973 72	2,609,922 82	36,526 82	64,848 20	190,321 89	231,013,933 44	15,713 33	2,301 33

M.—*Statement of gold of domestic production, &c.*—Continued.

MINT OF THE UNITED STATES.

Period.	Montana.	Oregon.	Colorado.	Maryland.	Arizona.	Washington Territory.	Kansas.	Idaho Territory.	Utah Territory.	Nevada.	Other sources.	Total.
1804 to 1827												$110,000 00
1828 to 1837												5,063,500 00
1838 to 1847												2,623,500 00
1848 to 1857												228,063,473 62
1858 to 1867	$3,990,940 52	$54,925 00	$5,835,150 23		$7,708 29	$26,127 55		$2,799,559 81	$4,327 11	$2,522 67	$13,200 00	17,439,227 00
1868	935,061 53	123,238 80	65,410 70		115 01			90,035 17		860 97	21,037 00	17,300,338 53
1869	935,003 94	6,680 19	26,896 36	$89 15	232 80			50,047 24		511 70	7,218 00	1,198,163 58
1870	648,660 75	4,300 70	32,695 34	18 85	4,039 31	451 22	$846 36	81,632 73	228 17		27,929 43	990,972 71
1871	374,108 19	2,357 10	29,944 38					42,599 42	1,564 02	227 22	27,515 39	603,393 26
Total	6,933,174 93	202,134 85	6,010,097 01	108 00	12,175 40	26,578 77	846 36	3,063,894 37	6,119 30	4,122 56	102,159 20	257,418,708 70

N.—BRANCH MINT, SAN FRANCISCO.

Period.	Parted from silver.	California.	Colorado.	Mexico.	Nevada.	Oregon.	Dakota.	Sitka.	Washington.	Idaho.	Arizona.	Montana.	Refined gold.	Utah.	Total.
1854		$10,842,291 23													$10,842,281 23
1855		20,860,437 20													20,860,437 20
1856		29,209,218 24													29,209,218 24
1857		12,526,896 93													12,526,896 93
1858		19,104,369 99													19,104,369 99
1859		14,098,564 14													14,098,564 14
1860		11,319,913 83													11,319,913 83
1861		12,206,382 64													12,206,382 64
1862	$522,823 01	14,629,759 95	$620 00			$666,000 00									15,754,362 96
1863	1,192,466 57	33,045,711 69	59,472 00			3,001,104 00	$3,760 00		$12,672 00	$1,257,497 50					17,244,436 56
1864	220,490 19	14,863,647 52			$3,400 00	2,139,305 00	2,000 00			3,499,281 14	$20,369 49				18,481,330 20
1865	217,935 98	11,088,974 53			43,497 28	1,103,076 34			92,460 94	2,680,203 48	30,430 68	$3,000 00	$2,398,601 49		18,560,100 09
1866	374,393 92	10,034,775 03			43,677 09	838,433 11				2,023,899 72	23,437 51	549,733 32	2,665,033 00		17,436,491 18
1867	395,158 76	8,170,771 82			37,414 56	975,974 30				867,845 43	77,639 62	576,397 80	5,715,260 40		17,906,169 40
1868	122,436 25	4,446,139 27			32,463 54	337,183 04				406,191 15	218 80	268,059 64	8,693,399 01		14,854,711 84
1869	60,582 39	5,076,785 90				464,784 63		$397 64		112,658 32	169,143 55	213,845 14	111,059,727 65		18,714,122 41
1870	66,623 24	5,016,172 38		$190 10	5,154 56	695,947 32				169,143 55	137,125 25	157,335 14	112,207,368 85		18,499,282 42
1871	*76,391 51	5,294,436 49			8,118 56	433,502 98			1,652 14	146,156 55		81,912 22	29,101,396 12	$1,282 18	25,321,889 32
Total	3,466,429 37	221,239,178 77	60,152 90	190 10	204,975 29	10,901,310 22	5,760 00	397 64	36,785 08	11,244,123 29	705,345 89	1,850,483 13	62,040,805 32	1,282 18	311,757,218 98

* Contained in silver.

O.—BRANCH MINT, NEW ORLEANS.

Period	N. Carolina	S. Carolina	Georgia	Tennessee	Alabama	California	Colorado	Other sources	Total
1838 to 1847	$741 00	$14,306 00	$37,364 00	$1,772 00	$61,903 00			$3,613 00	$119,699 00
1848 to 1857		1,911 00	2,317 00	947 00	15,379 00	$21,606,461 54		3,677 00	21,630,692 54
1858			1,560 00	164 12		448,439 84			450,163 96
1859						93,272 41			93,272 41
1860					661 53	97,135 00	$1,770 39		99,566 92
1861, (to January 31)						19,932 10	1,666 81		21,598 91
Total	741 00	16,217 00	41,241 00	2,863 12	77,943 53	22,265,240 89	3,437 20	7,290 00	22,414,993 74

P.—BRANCH MINT, DAHLONEGA.

Period	Utah	N. Carolina	S. Carolina	Georgia	Tennessee	Alabama	California	Colorado	Other sources	Total
1838 to 1847		$64,351 00	$95,427 00	$2,978,353 00	$32,175 00	$47,711 00				$3,218,017 00
1848 to 1857		28,278 82	174,811 91	1,159,420 98	9,837 42	11,918 92	$1,124,712 82		$951 00	2,509,931 87
1858			32,322 28	57,991 45	107 31		5,293 52			95,614 59
1859		2,656 88	4,610 35	57,023 12			699 19	$82 70		65,072 24
1860		3,485 70	2,004 36	35,588 92			1,097 37	2,490 86		44,667 21
1861, (to February 28)	$145 14	812 79	2,066 91	22,182 14			4,213 79	32,772 28		62,193 05
Total	145 14	99,585 19	311,242 81	4,310,459 61	42,119 75	59,629 92	1,136,016 69	35,343 84	951 00	5,995,495 95

Q.—BRANCH MINT, CHARLOTTE, NORTH CAROLINA.

Period	N. Carolina	S. Carolina	California	Total
Total				

R.—ASSAY OFFICE, NEW YORK.

Period	Parted from silver	Virginia	N. Carolina	S. Carolina	Georgia	Alabama	New Mexico	California	Montana	Wyoming
1854 to 1864	$282,975 00	$20,390 00	$252,159 07	$24,519 29	$121,338 28	$5,720 62	$13,837 00	$140,327,062 42		
1865	14,003 00		29,536 50		3,422 00	2,269 00	3,924 00	2,177,934 04	$1,217,518 00	
1866	79,304 00	1,693 00	27,354 50	713 93	11,161 00	1,135 00		4,456,392 00	3,132,370 00	
1867	42,935 50	700 74	39,706 38	587 81	8,084 31		9,616 33	5,103,602 24	4,246,410 00	
1868	12,971 90	970 18	56,893 86	594 49	15,889 05	112 41	21,299 10	2,308,861 39	2,087,756 32	
1869	33,080 23	1,847 74	24,071 95	6,754 74	23,151 24	102 49	59,939 48	4,199,736 35	2,670,499 70	
1870	40,141 65	358 66	20,030 78	1,609 78	21,017 99		79,988 77	1,559,728 45	2,931,119 97	$83,963 53
1871	105,204 79	916 40			29,144 92		61,794 67	197,680 72	2,775,930 82	22,630 82
Total	616,625 07	26,806 72	248,752 54	40,080 04	233,206 79	9,339 52	259,399 35	160,330,557 61	18,361,604 71	106,594 35

Period	Nebraska	Idaho	Colorado	Utah	Arizona	Oregon	Nevada	Vermont	Other sources	Total
1854 to 1864		$201,288 00	$4,267,237 00	$78,414 00	$22,618 00	$22,296 00	$40,920 00	$298 00	$150,168 00	$145,637,110 68
1865			938,593 00		707 00	9,876 00	949 00	316 00	364,857 00	4,734,388 04
1866		305,844 00	496,805 00			8,705 00	5,710 00		129,100 00	8,557,755 00
1867		108,467 43	657,390 69			4,377 32				10,209,652 99
1868		40,656 38	637,094 33	4,783 30	293 25	5,225 14	338 36	898 66	273 64	5,197,205 21
1869		145,479 57	830,039 47	5,517 47	5,132 33	5,750 87	8,399 67	3,508 09	8,714 26	8,058,687 23
1870		512,045 90	703,468 44	5,572 67	669 33	4,644 80	9,339 24	439 13	651 23	5,284,098 80
1871	$2,793 65	532,833 20	472,378 58	4,951 63	1,657 24	8,978 81	19,480 47		102 85	4,258,120 13
Total	2,793 65	1,746,614 44	9,023,596 53	99,239 07	31,063 15	70,853 94	85,156 74	5,459 88	653,866 98	194,937,018 08

29 F

S.—BRANCH MINT, DENVER.

Period	Colorado	Montana	Idaho	Wyoming	Oregon	New Mexico	Arizona	Total
1864	$496,329 97	$93,613 01	$71,310 49		$1,230 16			$496,329 97
1865	375,065 90	44,134 13	19,549 89		777 54		$339 48	541,559 04
1866	96,521 38	13,758 92	531 61		6,065 35			160,982 94
1867	110,203 62							130,559 70
1868	357,935 11							357,935 11
1869	795,546 38							795,566 38
1870	814,939 03	10,740 38		$4,425 75		$159,952 02		990,063 18
1871	992,712 70	8,218 25	4,348 75	798 65		97,336 25	532 50	1,104,147 10
	4,029,274 29	170,464 69	95,740 74	5,224 40	8,073 05	257,494 27	871 98	4,567,143 42

T.—Summary exhibit of the entire deposits of domestic gold at the Mint of the United States and branches, to June 30, 1871.

Mint	Parted from silver	Virginia	North Carolina	South Carolina	Georgia	Alabama	Tennessee	Utah	Nebraska	Colorado	California	Maryland	Kansas
Philadelphia	$132,547 67	$1,595,220 30	$4,846,788 43	$547,973 72	$2,609,922 82	$64,848 20	$30,536 82	$6,119 30	$15,713 33	$6,010,097 01	$231,013,933 44	$108 00	$846 36
San Francisco	3,466,429 37						3,989 12	1,282 18		60,132 00	221,239,178 77		
New Orleans			741 00	16,217 00	41,241 00	77,943 53				3,437 20	22,265,240 69		
Charlotte			4,554,522 60	460,523 34	4,310,459 61	59,629 02	42,119 75	145 14	2,793 65		87,321 01		
Dahlonega			99,585 19	311,242 81	233,203 79	9,339 32		99,239 07		35,345 84	1,136,016 69		
N. York assay office	610,625 07	28,806 72	284,752 54	40,680 04						9,023,396 53	160,330,957 61		
Denver													
Carson City	131,458 24												
Total	4,341,000 35	1,622,627 02	9,750,389 76	1,376,036 91	7,194,832 32	211,761 17	81,529 69	106,785 69	18,506 98	19,161,902 87	636,072,648 41	108 00	846 36

U.—*Statement of the silver coinage at the Mint of the United States and branches at San Francisco, Carson City, and New Orleans, under the act of February 21, 1853.*

Year.	United States Mint, Philadelphia.	Branch mint, San Francisco.	Branch mint, New Orleans, to Jan. 31, 1861.	Branch mint, Carson City.	Total.
1853.	$7, 806, 461 00		$1, 225, 000 00		$9, 031, 461 00
1854.	5, 340, 130 00		3, 246, 000 00		8, 586, 130 00
1855.	1, 393, 170 00	$164, 075 00	1, 918, 000 00		3, 475, 245 00
1856.	3, 150, 740 00	177, 000 00	1, 744, 000 00		5, 071, 740 00
1857.	1, 333, 000 .00	50, 000 00			1, 383, 000 00
1858.	4, 970, 980 00	127, 750 00	2, 942, 000 00		8, 040, 730 00
1859.	2, 926, 400 00	283, 500 00	2, 689, 000 00		5, 898, 900 00
1860.	519, 890 00	356, 500 00	1, 293, 000 00		2, 169, 390 00
1861.	1, 433, 800 00	198, 000 00	414, 000 00		2, 045, 800 00
1862.	2, 108, 951 50	641, 700 00			2, 810, 651 50
1863.	326, 817 80	815, 875 00			1, 142, 692 60
1864.	177, 544 10	347, 500 00			525, 044 10
1865.	274, 608 00	328, 800 00			603, 408 00
1866.	340, 764 50	280, 950 00			621, 714 50
1867.	295, 871 00	634, 000 00			929, 871 00
1868.	259, 950 00	822, 000 00			1, 081, 950 00
1869.	203, 396 50	406, 000 00			609, 396 50
1870.	1, 152, 960 50	594, 500 00		$7, 635 00	1, 755, 095 50
1871.	498, 630 25	746, 775 00		2, 022, 216 05	3, 267, 621 30
Total.	34, 574, 065 15	6, 974, 925 00	15, 471, 000 00	2, 029, 851 05	59, 049 841 20

V.—*Statement of the amount of silver of domestic production deposited at the Mint of the United States and branches, from January, 1841, to June 30, 1871.*

Year.	Montana.	California.	Georgia.	Idaho.	Lake Superior.	Nevada.	Arizona.	Oregon.	Parted from gold.
1841 to 1857									$2,700,728 50
1858					$15,623 00				300,849 36
1859					30,122 13				219,647 34
1860					25,880 58	$102,540 57			138,561 70
1861					13,372 71	213,420 84			364,724 73
1862					21,366 38	757,446 60			245,122 47
1863					8,765 77	856,043 27			188,394 94
1864		$8,224 00			13,111 32	311,837 01	$13,357 00		166,791 35
1865		459 18			13,671 51	335,910 42	12,280 00	$1,580 51	251,757 87
1866	$19,095 48	453 00		$38,859 49	22,913 98	340,345 87	105 00	183 68	271,888 51
1867	24,347 73	310 26		160,269 24	18,535 35	579,931 76	139 63		263,669 59
1868	16,568 77	9,196 94	$403 83	37,602 56	26,595 72	290,415 51	3,212 26		147,358 87
1869	11,502 53	13,973 30		16,339 52	25,362 44	205,380 28	6,711 29		138,259 81
1870		437 25		31,922 59	15,910 83	692,589 22	2,322 75		159,865 46
1871	28,139 91	47,906 73		4,856 38	173,308 80	2,476,209 84	1,760 46		99,299 33
Total	98,854 42	80,760 66	403 83	269,842 78	424,780 50	7,245,071 19	39,868 39	1,764 19	5,707,120 03

Year.	New Mexico and Sonora.	North Carolina.	Colorado.	Bars.	Nebraska.	Kansas.	Wyoming.	Utah.	Source unknown.	Total.
1841 to 1857	$1,200 00	$23,398 00								$2,700,728 50
1858		12,257 00								316,472 36
1859		6,233 00								273,167 47
1860										293,796 85
1861										610,011 29
1862	45 00		$419 00	$16,273 22						1,032,264 45
1863	25 84		543 78	10,709 00						1,057,549 53
1864										487,439 33
1865										631,824 82
1866		73 75	46,881 13	397,478 40						893,282 02
1867	473 56	9 57	197,678 54	168,714 73						1,056,680 39
1868	2,778 18		236,689 49	174,267 31		$68 00				986,335 46
1869	1,671 35	1,792 54	367,510 31	421,039 89	$23,953 41		$74 25			901,908 89
1870	4,533 23						7 15	$3,779 86		1,326,722 82
1871									$32 84	3,652,338 14
Total	10,727 16	43,763 86	849,722 25	1,188,487 55	23,953 41	468 00	81 40	3,779 86	32 84	16,210,582 32

W.—*Statement of domestic gold and silver deposited at the United States Mint and branches, for coinage, to June 30, 1871.*

From—	Gold.	Silver.	Gold and silver.
California	$636, 072, 648 41	$80, 760 66	$636, 153, 409 07
Montana	27, 315, 727 46	98, 854 42	27, 414, 581 88
Colorado	19, 161, 902 87	849, 722 25	20, 011, 625 12
Idaho	16, 150, 372 84	289, 842 78	16, 440, 215 62
North Carolina	9, 750, 389 76	43, 763 86	9 794, 153 62
Oregon	11, 182, 972 06	1, 764 19	11, 184, 736 25
Georgia	7, 194, 832 22	403 83	7, 195, 236 05
Virginia	1, 622, 627 02		1, 622, 627 02
South Carolina	1, 376, 036 91		1, 376, 036 91
Nevada	559, 439 60	7, 245, 971 19	7, 805, 410 79
Alabama	211, 761 17		211, 761 17
Arizona	749, 461 42	39, 868 39	789, 329 81
New Mexico	698, 405 62		698, 405 62
Utah	106, 785 69	3, 779 86	110, 565 55
Tennessee	81, 529 69		81, 529 69
Washington Territory	63, 363 85		63, 363 85
Dakota	5, 760 00		5, 760 00
Nebraska	18, 506 98	23, 953 41	42, 460 39
Vermont	5, 459 88		5, 459 88
Other sources	63, 536, 393 29	32 84	63, 536, 426 13
Parted from silver	4, 341, 060 35		4, 341, 060 35
Lake Superior		424, 780 50	424, 780 50
New Mexico and Sonora		10, 727 16	10, 727 16
Sitka	397 64		397 64
Wyoming Territory	114, 120 08	81 40	114, 201 48
Maryland	108 00		108 00
Kansas	846 36	468 00	1, 314 36
Fine bars		1, 168, 487 55	1, 188, 487 55
Parted from gold		5, 707, 120 03	5, 707, 120 03
Total	800, 320, 909 17	16, 010, 382 32	816, 331, 291 49

A statement of foreign gold and silver coins, prepared by the Director of the Mint, to accompany his annual report, in pursuance of the act of February 21, 1857.

EXPLANATORY REMARKS.—The first column embraces the names of the countries where the coins are issued; the second contains the name of the coin, only the principal denominations being given. The other sizes are proportional; and when this is not the case the deviation is stated.

The third column expresses the weight of a single piece in fractions of the troy ounce, carried to the thousandth and in a few cases to the ten thousandth of an ounce. The method is preferable to expressing the weight in grains for commercial purposes, and corresponds better with the terms of the Mint. It may be readily transferred to weight in grains by the following rules : Remove the decimal point; from one-half deduct four per cent. of that half, and the remainder will be grains.

The fourth column expresses the fineness in thousandths, *i. e.*, the number of parts of pure gold or silver in 1,000 parts of the coin.

The fifth and sixth columns of the first table express the valuation of gold. In the fifth is shown the value as compared with the legal contents or amount of fine gold in our coin. In the sixth is shown the value as paid in the Mint, after the uniform deduction of one-half of one per cent. The former is the value for any other purposes than recoinage, and especially for the purpose of comparison ; the latter is the value in exchange for our coins at the Mint.

For the silver there is no fixed legal valuation, the law providing for shifting the price according to the condition of demand and supply. The present price of standard silver is 122½ cents per ounce, at which rate the values in the fifth column of the second table are calculated. In a few cases, where the coins could not be procured, the data are *assumed* from the legal rates, and so stated.

I. Gold coins.

Country.	Denominations.	Weight.	Fineness.	Value.	Value after deduction.
		Oz. Dec.	*Thous.*		
Australia	Pound of 1852	0. 281	916. 5	$5 32. 4	$5 29. 7
Do	Sovereign of 1855-'60	0. 256. 5	916	4 85. 7	4 83. 3
Austria	Ducat	0. 112	986	2 28. 3	2 27
Do	Sovereign	0. 363	900	6 75. 4	6 72
Do	New Union coin, (assumed)	0. 357	900	6 64. 2	6 60. 9
Belgium	Twenty-five francs	0. 254	899	4 72	4 69. 8
Bolivia	Doubloon	0. 867	870	15 59. 3	15 51. 5
Brazil	Twenty milreis	0. 575	917. 5	10 90. 6	10 85. 1
Central America	Two escudos	0. 209	853. 5	3 68. 8	3 66. 9
Do	Four reals	0. 027	875	48. 8	48. 6
Chili	Old doubloon	0. 867	870	15 59. 3	15 51. 5
Do	Ten pesos	0. 492	900	9 15. 4	9 10. 8
Denmark	Ten thaler	0. 427	895	7 90	7 86. 1
Ecuador	Four escudos	0. 433	844	7 55. 5	7 51. 7
England	Pound or sovereign, new	0. 256. 7	916. 5	4 86. 3	4 83. 9
Do	Pound or sovereign, average	0. 256. 2	916	4 85. 1	4 82. 7
France	Twenty francs, new	0. 207. 5	899	3 85. 8	3 83. 9
Do	Twenty francs, average	0. 207	899	3 84. 7	3 82. 8
Germany, North	Ten thaler	0. 427	895	7 90	7 86. 1
Do	Ten thaler, Prussian	0. 427	903	7 97. 1	7 93. 1
Do	Krone, (crown)	0. 357	900	6 64. 2	6 60. 9
Germany, South	Ducat	0. 112	986	2 28. 2	2 27. 1
Greece	Twenty drachms	0. 185	900	3 44. 2	3 42. 5
Hindostan	Mohur	0. 374	916	7 08. 2	7 04. 6
Italy	Twenty lire	0. 207	898	3 84. 3	3 82. 3
Japan	Old cobang	0. 362	568	4 44	4 41. 8
Do	Old cobang	0. 289	572	3 57. 6	3 55. 8
Mexico	Doubloon, average	0. 867. 5	866	15 53	15 45. 2
Do	Doubloon, new	0. 867. 5	870. 5	15 61. 1	15 53. 3
Do	Twenty pesos, (Max.)	0. 086	875	19 64. 3	19 54. 5
Do	Twenty pesos, (Repub.)	1. 090	875	19 72	19 62. 1
Naples	Six ducacti, new	1. 245	996	5 04. 4	5 01. 9
Netherlands	Ten guilders	0. 215	899	3 99. 7	3 97. 6
New Granada	Old doubloon, Bogota	0. 868	870	15 61. 1	15 53. 3
Do	Old doubloon, Popayan	0. 867	858	15 37. 8	15 30. 1
Do	Ten pesos	0. 525	891. 5	9 67. 5	9 62. 7
Peru	Old doubloon	0. 867	868	15 55. 7	15 47. 9
Do	Twenty soles	1. 035	898	19 21. 3	19 11. 7
Portugal	Gold crown	0. 308	912	5 80. 7	5 77. 8
Prussia	New crown, (assumed)	0. 357	900	6 64. 2	6 60. 9
Rome	Two and a half scudi, new	0. 140	900	2 60. 5	2 59. 2
Russia	Five roubles	0. 210	916	3 97. 6	3 95. 7
Spain	One hundred reals	0. 208	896	4 96. 4	4 93. 9
Do	Eighty reals	0. 215	869. 5	3 86. 4	3 84. 5
Sweden	Ducat	0. 111	875	2 23. 7	2 22. 6
Do	Carolin, 10 francs	0. 104	900	1 93. 5	1 91. 5
Tunis	Twenty-five piasters	0. 161	900	2 99. 5	2 98. 1
Turkey	One hundred piasters	0. 231	915	4 36. 9	4 34. 8
Tuscany	Sequin	0. 112	999	2 31. 3	2 30. 1

Y.—Silver coins.

. Country.	Denominations.	Weight.	Fineness.	Value.
		Oz. Dec.	Thous.	
Austria	Old rix dollar	0. 902	833	$1 02. 3
Do	Old scudo	0. 836	902	1 02. 6
Do	Florin before 1858	0. 451	833	51. 1
Do	New florin	0. 397	900	48. 6
Do	New Union dollar	0. 596	900	73. 1
Do	Maria Theresa dollar, 1780	0. 895	838	1 02. 1
Belgium	Five francs	0. 803	897	98.
Bolivia	New dollar	0. 801	900	98. 1
Brazil	Double milreis	0. 820	918. 5	1 02. 5
Canada	Twenty cents	0. 150	925	18. 9
Do	Twenty-five cents	0. 187. 5	925	23. 6
Central America	Dollar	0. 866	850	1 00. 2
Chili	Old dollar	0. 864	908	1 06. 8
Do	New dollar	0. 801	900. 5	98. 2
China	Dollar, (English, assumed)	0. 866	901	1 06. 2
Do	Ten cents	0. 087	901	10. 6
Denmark	Two rigsdaler	0. 927	877	1 10. 7
England	Shilling, now	0. 182. 5	924. 5	23
Do	Shilling, average	0. 178	925	22. 4
France	Five francs, average	0. 800	900	98
Do	Two francs	0. 320	835	36. 4
Germany, North	Thaler before 1857	0. 712	750	72. 7
Do	New thaler	0. 595	900	72. 9
Germany, South	Florin before 1857	0. 340	900	41. 7
Do	New florin, (assumed)	0. 340	900	41. 7
Greece	Five drachms	0. 719	900	88. 1
Hindostan	Rupee	0. 374	916	46. 6
Japan	Itzbu	0. 279	991	37. 6
Do	New itzbu	0. 279	890	33. 8
Mexico	Dollar, new	0. 867. 5	903	1 06. 6
Do	Dollar, average	0. 866	901	1 06. 2
Do	Peso of Maximilian	0. 861	8902. 5	1 05. 5
Naples	Scudo	0. 844	830	95. 3
Netherlands	Two and a half guilders	0. 804	944	1 03. 3
Norway	Specie daler	0. 927	877	1 10. 7
New Granada	Dollar of 1857	0. 803	896	98
Peru	Old dollar	0. 866	901	1 06. 2
Do	Dollar of 1858	0. 766	909	94. 8
Do	Half dollar, 1835 and 1838	0. 433	650	38. 3
Do	Sol	0. 802	900	98. 2
Prussia	Thaler before 1857	0. 712	750	72. 7
Do	New thaler	0. 595	900	72. 9
Rome	Scudo	0. 864	900	1 05. 8
Russia	Rouble	0. 667	875	79. 4
Sardinia	Five live	0. 800	900	98
Spain	New pistareen	0. 166	899	20. 3
Sweden	Rix dollar	0. 092	750	1 11. 5
Switzerland	Two francs	0. 323	899	39. 5
Tunis	Five piasters	0. 511	898. 5	62. 5
Turkey	Twenty piasters	0. 770	830	87
Tuscany	Florin	0. 220	. 925	27. 6

Weight and value of United States silver coins.

Denominations.	Weight.	Fineness.	Weight in grains.
Dollar, (legal)	0. 859. 375	900	412. 5
Half-dollar	0. 406	900	192
Quarter-dollar	0. 200	900	96
Dime	0. 080	900	38. 4
Half-dime	0. 040	900	19. 2
Three-cent	0. 024	900	11. 52

Weight and value of United States gold coins.

Denominations.	Weight.	Fineness.	Value.	Weight in grains.
	Oz. dec.	Thous.		
Dollar, (legal)	0. 053. 75	900	$1 00	25. 8
Quarter-eagle	0. 134. 37	900	2 50	64. 5
Three-dollar	0. 161. 25	900	3 00	77. 4
Half-eagle	0. 268. 75	900	5 00	129
Eagle	0. 537. 5	900	10 00	258
Double-eagle	1. 075	900	20 00	516

REPORT OF THE COMMISSIONER OF INDIAN AFFAIRS.

REPORT

OF

THE COMMISSIONER OF INDIAN AFFAIRS.

DEPARTMENT OF THE INTERIOR,
Washington, D. C., October 26, 1871.

SIR: I have the honor to transmit herewith, for your information, a letter dated the 25th instant from the Acting Commissioner of Indian Affairs, and the accompanying "statement" showing the present liabilities of the United States to the Indian tribes.

Very respectfully, your obedient servant,

W. H. SMITH,
Acting Secretary.

The Honorable SECRETARY OF THE TREASURY.

DEPARTMENT OF THE INTERIOR,
OFFICE OF INDIAN AFFAIRS,
Washington, D. C., October 25, 1871.

SIR: I have the honor to transmit herewith a statement showing the present liabilities of the United States to Indian tribes under stipulations of treaties, &c., to be forwarded to the Secretary of the Treasury, to accompany his report on the state of finances.

Very respectfully, your obedient servant,

H. R. CLUM,
Acting Commissioner.

HON. C. DELANO,
Secretary of the Interior.

Statement showing the present liabilities of the United States to Indian tribes under stipulations of treaties, &c.—Continued.

Names of tribes.	Description of annuities, stipulations, &c.	Reference to laws: Statutes at Large.	Number of installments yet unappropriated, explanations, remarks, &c.	Annual amount necessary to meet stipulations indefinite as to time, now allowed but liable to be discontinued.	Aggregate of future appropriations that will be required during a limited number of years to pay limited annuities incidentally necessary to carry into effect the payment.	Amount of annual liabilities of a permanent character.	Amount held in trust by the United States on which five per cent. is annually paid, and amount which, invested at five per cent., would produce permanent annuities.
Apaches, Kiowas, and Comanches.	Thirty installments, provided to be expended under 10th article treaty Oct. 21, 1867.	Vol. 15, pages 581–589.	Twenty-six installments unappropriated, at $30,000 each.	$26,000 00	$780,000 00		
Do	Purchase of clothing	...do...	10th article treaty Oct. 21, 1867. (estimated.)	7,700 00			
Do	Pay of carpenter, farmer, blacksmith, miller, engineer, physician, and teacher.		14th article treaty Oct. 21, 1867; annual appropriation.				
Do	Three installments, for seeds and agricultural implements.	Vol. 15, page 584.	Three installments, at $2,500 each, still due.		7,500 00		
Arickarees, Gros Ventres, and Mandans.	Pay of second blacksmith, iron, and steel.	...do...	8th article treaty Oct. 21, 1867; 7th article treaty July 27, 1866; laws not published.	2,000 00			
	Amount to be expended in such goods, &c., as the President may from time to time determine.		7th article treaty July 27, 1866; laws not published.	75,000 00			
Assinaboines	Amount to be expended in such goods, &c., as the President may from time to time determine.		7th article treaty July 27, 1866; laws not published.	30,000 00			
Blackfeet, Bloods, and Piegans.	Amount to be expended in such goods, &c., as the President may from time to time determine.		8th article treaty Sept. 1, 1868; laws not published.	50,000 00			
Calapooias, Molallas, and Clackamas of Willamette Valley.	Five installments, 4th series, of annuity for beneficial objects.	Vol. 10, page 1114	2d article, three installments of $5,500 each, to be appropriated.		16,500 00		
Cheyennes and Arapahoes.	Thirty installments, provided to be expended under 10th article treaty Oct. 28, 1867.	Vol. 15, page 593	Twenty-six installments unappropriated, at $30,000 each.		590,000 00		
Do.	Purchase of clothing	...do...	10th article treaty Oct. 28, 1867. (estimated.)	14,500 00			
Do.	Pay of physician, carpenter, farmer, blacksmith, miller, engineer, and teacher.	Vol. 15, page 597.	13th article, treaty Oct. 28, 1867. (estimated.)	7,700 00			
Do.	Three installments, for the purchase of seeds and agricultural implements.	...do...	Three installments, at $2,500, still due.		7,500 00		

Chickasaws	Permanent annuity in goods	Vol. 1, page 619; vol. 14, p. 774.	Act of Feb. 25, 1799, per annum		$3,000 00
Chippewas—Boise Fort Band.	Twenty installments, for blacksmith and assistant, tools, iron, &c.	Vol. 14, page 706	Fourteen installments unappropriated, at $1,500 each.		21,000 00
Do	Twenty installments, for schools, instructing Indians in farming, and purchase of seeds, tools, &c.	...do...	Fourteen installments unappropriated, at $1,600 each.		22,400 00
Do	Twenty installments of annuity, in money, goods, and other articles, in provisions, ammunition, and tobacco.	...do...	Annuity, $3,500; goods, &c., $6,500; provisions, ammunition, and tobacco, $1,600; fourteen installments unappropriated.		154,000 00
Chippewas of Lake Superior.	Twenty installments, in coin, goods, implements, &c., and for education.	Vol. 10, page 1111.	Three installments unappropriated, at $19,000.		57,000 00
Do	Twenty installments, for six smiths and assistants, iron and steel.	...do...	Three installments unappropriated, at $6,360.		19,080 00
Do	Support of smith and shop, and pay of two farmers, during the pleasure of the President.	Vol. 11, p. 1112; vol. 14, p. 766.	Estimated at...	1,800 00	
Chippewas of the Mississippi.	Twenty installments for the seventh smith, &c. Money, goods, support of schools, provisions, and tobacco; 4th article treaty Oct. 4, 1842; 8th article treaty Sept. 30, 1854; and 3d article treaty May 7, 1864.	Vol. 10, page 1111; Vol. 7, page 392; vol. 10, page 111.	Five installments of $1,060 each, due. Ten installments, 2d series, at $9,000 01; five installments unappropriated.		5,300 00 45,000 05
Do	Two farmers, two carpenters, two smiths and assistants, iron and steel; same article and treaty.	...do...	Ten installments, 2d series, at $1,400; five installments unappropriated.		7,000 00
Do	Twenty installments in money of $20,000 each	Vol. 10, page 1167.	Three installments unexpended		60,000 00
Do	Twenty-six installments of $1,000 each, to be paid to the Chippewas of the Mississippi.	...do...	One installment unappropriated		1,000 00
Do	Ten installments, for support of schools, in promoting the progress of the people in agriculture, and assisting them to become self-sustaining; support of physician, and purchase of medicine.		Six installments unappropriated, at $11,500; laws not published.		69,000 00
Chippewas of the Mississippi, and Pillager & Lake Winnebagoshish bands of Chippewas.	Ten installments of 1,500 each, to furnish said Indians with oxen, log-chains, &c.	Vol. 13, page 694.	Two installments unappropriated		3,000 00
Do	Pay of two carpenters, two blacksmiths, four farm laborers, and one physician, ten years.	...do...	Two installments of $7,700 each, yet due.		15,400 00
Do	Pay for services and traveling expenses of a board of visitors, not more than five persons, to attend annuity payments, &c.	...do...	7th article treaty May 7, 1864.	480 00	
Do	To be applied for the support of a saw-mill as long as the President may deem necessary.	...do...	6th article treaty May 7, 1864; annual appropriation.	1,000 00	
Do	Pay of female teachers employed on the reservation.	...do...	13th article treaty May 7, 1864.	1,000 00	
Chippewas —Pillager and Lake Winnebagoshish bands.	Money, $10,666 66; goods, $8,000; and purposes of utility, $4,000; 3d article treaty Feb. 22, 1855.	Vol. 10, page 1168.	Thirty installments; thirteen unappropriated, at $22,666 66.		294,666 55

Statement showing the present liabilities of the United States to Indian tribes, &c.—Continued.

Names of tribes.	Description of annuities, stipulations, &c.	Reference to laws: Statutes at Large.	Number of installments yet unappropriated, explanations, remarks, &c.	Annual amount necessary to meet stipulations indefinite as to time, now allowed, but liable to be discontinued.	Aggregate of future appropriations that will be required during a limited number of years to pay limited annuities incidentally necessary to effect the payment.	Amount of annual liabilities of a permanent character.	Amount held in trust by the United States on which five per cent. is annually paid, and amounts which, invested at five per cent., would produce permanent annuities.
Chippewas — Pillager and Lake Winnebagoshish bands—Cont'd.	Purposes of education; 3d article treaty Feb. 22, 1855.	Vol. 10, p. 1168.	Twenty installments of $3,000 each; three yet due.		$9,000 00		
Chippewas of Red Lake and Pembina tribe of Chippewas.	$10,000 as annuity to be paid per capita to the Red Lake band, and $5,000 to the Pembina band, during the pleasure of the President.	Vol. 13, pages 666, 689.	3d article treaty Oct. 2, 1863, and 2d article supplementary treaty April 12, 1864; annual appropriation required.	$15,000 00			
Do	Fifteen installments of $12,000 each, for the purpose of supplying them with gilling twine, cotton maptire, linsey, blankets, &c.	Vol. 13, pages 688, 690.	Estimated for Red Lake band, $8,000; Pembina band, $4,000; seven installments unappropriated.		84,000 00		
Do	One blacksmith, physician, &c., miller, farmer; $3,900; iron and steel, and other articles, $1,500; carpentering, &c., $1,000.	Vol. 13, page 690.	Fifteen installments; seven at $6,400 yet due.		44,800 00	9,600 00	
Do	To defray the expenses of a board of visitors, not more than three persons, to attend the annuity payments.	Vol. 13, page 662.	Fifteen installments of $390 each; seven unappropriated.		2,720 00		
Choctaws	Permanent annuities	Vol. 7, pages 99, 614; vol. 11, pp. 213, 236.	2d article treaty Nov. 16, 1805, $3,000; 13th article treaty Oct. 18, 1820, $600; 3d article treaty Jan. 20, 1825, $6,000.				
Do	Provisions for smiths, &c	Vol. 7, page 212.	6th article treaty Oct. 18, 1820, and 9th article treaty Jan. 20, 1825; say $920.			920 00	
Do	Interest on $390,257 92; articles 10 and 13 treaty Jan. 22, 1855.	Vol. 11, pages 613, 614.	Five per cent. for educational purposes.			19,512 99	$390,257 90
Confederated tribes and bands in middle Oregon.	For beneficial objects, at the discretion of the President; 2d article treaty June 25, 1855.	Vol. 12, page 964.	Five installments of $4,000 each; third series; three unappropriated.		12,000 00		

Tribe	Object	Reference	Stipulation			
Do	Physician, sawyer, miller, superintendent of farming, and school teacher, for twenty years.	Vol. 12, page 965.	Eight installments unappropriated, at $5,600 each.	44,800 00		
Do	Salary of head chief for twenty years.	...do...	Eight installments unappropriated, at $500 each.	4,000 00		
Creeks	Permanent annuities	Vol. 7, pages 36, 287; vol. 11, page 700.	4th article treaty Aug. 7, 1790, $1,500; 2d article treaty June 16, 1802, $3,000; 4th article treaty Jan. 24, 1826, $20,000.		24,500 00	450,000 00
Do	Smiths, shops, &c.	Vol. 7, page 287.	8th article treaty Jan. 24, 1826, say $1,110.		1,110 00	52,200 00
Do	Wheelwright, permanent	Vol. 7, page 287; vol. 11, page 700.	6th article treaty Jan. 24, 1826, and 5th article treaty Aug. 7, 1856, say $600.		600 00	12,000 00
Do	Allowance during the pleasure of the President.	Vol. 7, pages 287, 419.	5th article treaty Feb. 14, 1833, and 8th article treaty Jan. 24, 1856.	4,310 00		
Do	Interest on $200,000, held in trust; 6th article treaty Aug. 7, 1856.	Vol. 11, page 700.	Five per centum for education		10,000 00	200,000 00
Do	Interest on $675,168, held in trust; 3d article treaty June 14, 1866.	Vol. 14, page 786.	Five per centum to be expended under direction of the Secretary of the Interior.		33,758 40	675,168 00
Crows	For supplying male persons over fourteen years of age with a suit of good, substantial woolen clothing; females over twelve years of age with a flannel skirt, or goods to make the same, a pair of woolen hose, calico and domestic; and boys and girls under the ages named such flannel and cotton goods, &c.	Vol. 15, page 651.	9th article treaty May 7, 1868, (estimated.)	22,723 00		
Do	Purchase of such articles as from time to time the condition and necessities of the Indians may indicate to be proper.	Vol. 15, page 652.	9th article treaty May 7, 1868, (estimated.)	10,000 00		
Do	Physician, carpenter, miller, engineer, farmer, and blacksmith.	Vol. 15, page 652.	10th article treaty May 7, 1868, (estimated.)	6,600 00		
Do	Twenty installments, pay of teachers, and for books, stationery, &c.	Vol. 15, page 651.	7th article treaty May 7, 1868; eighteen installments, at $3,000 each, due.	54,000 00		
Do	Blacksmith, iron and steel, and for seeds and agricultural implements.	...do...	8th article treaty May 7, 1868, (estimated.)	3,250 00		
Do	Purchase of such articles as from time to time the condition and necessities of the Indians may indicate to be proper.	Vol. 15, page 652.	9th article treaty May 7, 1868, (estimated.)	20,000 00		
Do	Four installments, to furnish said Indians with flour and meat.	...do...	11th article treaty May 7, 1868; two installments due, at $131,400; one installment at $500 due.	262,800 00		
Do	Three installments, to be expended in presents.	...do...	12th article treaty May 7, 1868; one installment at $500 due.	500 00		
Delawares	Life annuity to chiefs.		Private act to supplementary treaty Sept. 24, 1829, to treaty Oct. 3, 1818.	100 00		
Do	Interest on $46,080 at 5 per centum, being the value of thirty-six sections of land, set apart by treaty 1829, for education.	Vol. 5, page 1040.	Senate resolution Jan. 19, 1838.		2,304 00	46,050 00

Statement showing the present liabilities of the United States to Indian tribes, &c.—Continued.

Names of tribes.	Description of annuities, stipulations, &c.	Reference to laws: Statutes at Large.	Number of installments yet unappropriated, explanations, remarks, &c.	Annual amount necessary to meet stipulations indefinite as to time, now allowed, but liable to be discontinued.	Aggregate of future appropriations that will be required during a limited number of years to pay limited annuities incidentally necessary to effect the payment.
Dwamish and other allied tribes in Washington Territory.	$150,000, under the direction of the President, in twenty installments.	Vol. 12, page 928.	6th article treaty, Jan. 22, 1855; eight installments unappropriated.	....	$63,000 00
Do	Twenty installments, for an agricultural school and teacher.	Vol. 12, page 929.	14th article treaty Jan. 22, 1855; eight installments, at $3,000, unappropriated.	....	24,000 00
Do	Twenty installments, for smith and carpenter-shop and tools.	.....do......	14th article treaty Jan. 22, 1855; eight installments, at $500, unappropriated.	....	4,000 00
Do	Twenty installments, for blacksmith, carpenter, farmer, and physician.	.....do......	14th article treaty Jan. 22, 1855; eight installments, at $4,600, unappropriated.	....	36,800 00
Flatheads and other confederated tribes.	Five installments, 3d series, for beneficial objects, under the direction of the President.	Vol. 12, page 976.	4th article treaty July 16, 1855; two installments unappropriated, at $4,000 each.	....	8,000 00
Do	Twenty installments, for an agricultural and industrial school, providing necessary furniture, books, stationery, &c., and employment of suitable instructors.	Vol. 12, page 977.	5th article treaty July 16, 1855; agricultural and industrial school, &c., $300; pay of instructors, $1,800; eight installments unappropriated, at $2,100 each.	....	16,900 00
Do	Twenty installments, for two farmers, two millers, blacksmith, gunsmith, tinsmith, carpenter and joiner, and wagon and plow-maker, $7,400; and keeping in repair blacksmith's, carpenter's, and wagon and plow-maker's shops, and furnishing tools, $500.	.....do......	5th article treaty July 16, 1855; eight installments unappropriated, at $7,900 each.	....	63,200 00
Do	Twenty installments, for keeping in repair flour ...	.....do......	5th article treaty July 16, 1855;	....	4,000 00

	Object	Reference	Treaty reference				
Do	Twenty installments, for pay of physician, $1,400; keeping in repair hospital and for medicines, $300.	do	5th article treaty July 16, 1855; eight installments unappropriated, at $1,700.		13,600 00		
Do	Repairing buildings required for various employés, &c., twenty years.	do	5th article treaty July 16, 1855; eight installments unappropriated, at $300.		2,400 00		
Do	$500 per annum, for twenty years, for each of the head chiefs.	do	5th article treaty July 16, 1855; eight installments unappropriated, at $1,500.		12,000 00		
Gros Ventres	Amount to be expended in such goods, provisions, &c., as the President may from time to time determine, &c.	do	8th article treaty July 13, 1866; laws not published.	$35,000 00			
Iowas	Interest on $57,500, being the balance of $157,500.	Vol.10, page 1071.	9th article treaty May 7, 1854			$2,875 00	$57,500 00
Kansas	Interest on $200,000, at 5 per centum.	Vol. 9, page 842.	2d article treaty Jan. 1846			10,000 00	200,000 00
Kickapoos	Interest on $100,000, at 5 per centum.	Vol.10, page 1079.	2d article treaty May 18, 1854			5,000 00	100,000 00
Do	Gradual payment on $200,000.	do	2d article treaty May 18, 1854; $190 heretofore appropriated, due.		10,000 00		
Klamaths and Modocs.	Five installments of $5,000, 2d series, to be applied under the direction of the President.		2d article treaty Oct. 14, 1864; four installments unappropriated.		20,000 00		
Do	Repairing saw and flouring-mill, and buildings for blacksmiths, carpenter, wagon and plow-maker, manual-labor school and hospital, for twenty years.		4th article treaty Oct. 14, 1864; fifteen installments unappropriated, at $1,000 each.		15,000 00		
Do	For tools and materials for saw and flour-mill, carpenter's, blacksmith's, wagon and plow-maker's shops, books and stationery for manual-labor school, twenty years.		4th article treaty Oct. 14, 1864; fourteen installments unappropriated, at $1,500 each.		21,000 00		
Do	Pay of superintendent farming, farmer, blacksmith, sawyer, carpenter, and wagon and plow-maker, fifteen years.		5th article treaty Oct. 14, 1864; nine installments, of $6,000 each, unappropriated.		54,000 00		
Do	Pay of physician, miller, and two teachers, for twenty years.		5th article treaty Oct. 14, 1864; fourteen installments of $3,600, yet due.		50,400 00		
Makahs.	Ten installments, being 5th series, for beneficial objects, under the direction of the President.	Vol. 12, page 940.	5th article treaty Jan. 31, 1855; eight installments unappropriated, at $1,000 each.		8,000 00		
Do	Twenty installments for agricultural and industrial school and teacher, for smith and carpenter-shops, and tools; and for blacksmith, carpenter, farmer, and physician.	Vol. 12, page 941.	11th article treaty Jan. 31, 1855; eight installments unappropriated, at $7,600 each:		60,800 00		
Menomonees.	Fifteen installments, to pay $242,686 for cession of land.	Vol.10, page 1065.	4th article treaty May 12, 1854, and Senate amendment thereto; nine installments, of $16,170 06 each, unappropriated.		145,611 54		
Miamies of Kansas.	Permanent provision for smiths' shops, &c., and miller.	Vol. 7, pages 191, 194; vol. 10, page 1095.	5th article treaty Oct. 6, 1818; 5th article treaty Oct. 23, 1834; and 4th article treaty June 5, 1854; say $940 for shop and $600 for miller.			1,540 00	30,800 00
Do	Twenty installments upon $200,000, 3d article treaty June 5, 1854.	Vol.10, page 1094.	$150,000 of said sum payable in twenty installments of $7,500 each, eight installments unappropriated.		60,000 00		

30 F

n

Names of tribes.	Description of annuities, stipulations, &c.	Reference to laws: Statutes at Large.	Number of installments yet unappropriated, explanations, remarks, &c.	Annual amount necessary to meet stipulations indefinite as to time, now allowed, but liable to be discontinued.	Aggregate of future appropriations that will be required during a limited number of years to pay limited annuities incidentally necessary to effect the payment.	Amount of annual liabilities of a permanent character.	Amount held in trust by the United States on which five per cent. is annually paid, and amount which, invested at five per cent., would produce permanent annuities.
Miamies of Kansas—Cont'd.	Interest on $50,000, at 5 per centum	Vol.10, page 1094	3d article treaty June 5, 1854			$2,500 00	$30,000 00
Miamies of Indiana	Interest on $221,257 86, in trust	Vol.10, page 1099	Senate amendment to 4th article treaty June 5, 1854			11,062 89	221,257 86
Miamies of Eel River	Permanent annuities		4th article treaty 1795; 3d article treaty 1805; and 3d article treaty Sept. 1809; aggregate.			1,100 00	22,000 00
Molels	Pay of teacher to manual-labor school, and subsistence of pupils, &c.	Vol. 12, page 982	2d article treaty Dec. 21, 1855; amount necessary during the pleasure of the President	3,000 00			
Mixed Shoshones, Bannacks, and Sheep Eaters.	To be expended in such goods, provisions, &c. as the President may from time to time determine, &c.		6th article treaty Sept. 24, 1868; not published	35,000 00			
Navajoes	For such articles of clothing, or raw material in lieu thereof, and for seeds, farming implements, &c.	Vol. 15, page 669.	7th and 8th articles treaty June 1, 1868, for articles of clothing or raw material, $40,000; and for seeds, farming implements, &c., $35,000.	75,000 00			
Do	Purchase of such articles as from time to time the condition and necessities of the Indians may indicate to be proper, &c.	do	8th article treaty June 1, 1868	14,000 00			
Do	Pay of two teachers	do	6th article treaty June 1, 1868	2,000 00			
Nez Perces	Five installments, 3d series, for beneficial objects, at the discretion of the President.	Vol. 12, page 958.	4th article treaty June 11, 1855; three installments unappropriated, at $6,000 each.		$18,000 00		
Do	Twenty installments, for two schools, &c.; pay of superintendent teaching and two teachers; superintendent farming, two farmers, two millers, two blacksmiths, tinner, gunsmith, carpenter, wagon and plow-maker, keeping	Vol. 12, page 959.	5th article treaty June 11, 1855; eight installments, at $17,200 each, unappropriated.		137,600 00		

Tribe	Objects of expenditure	Reference to Statutes	Remarks	Amount	Amount	Amount
Do.	and furnishing medicines, &c.; repairing buildings for employés, and the shops for blacksmith, tinsmith, gunsmith, carpenter, wagon and plow-maker; providing tools therefor; and pay of local chief.	Vol. 14, page 649.	4th article treaty June 9, 1863; ten installments, of $3,000 each, unappropriated.		30,000 00	
Do.	Sixteen installments for boarding and clothing children who attend school providing school, &c., with necessary furniture, purchase of wagons, teams, tools, &c.	Vol. 14, page 650.	5th article treaty June 9, 1863	1,000 00		
Do.	Salary of two subordinate chiefs.	...do...	5th article treaty June 9, 1863; ten installments, of $2,500 each, unappropriated.		25,000 00	
Do.	Fifteen installments, for repair of houses, mills, shops, &c., and providing furniture, tools, &c.	...do...	5th article treaty June 9, 1863			
Do.	Salary of two matrons to take charge of the boarding schools, two assistant teachers, farmer, carpenter, and two millers.	...do...	5th article treaty June 9, 1863	7,600 00		
Nisqually, Puyallup, and other tribes and bands of Indians.	Payment of $32,500 in graduated payments.	Vol.10, page 1133.	4th article treaty Dec. 26, 1854; still unappropriated.		2,000 00	
Do.	Pay of instructor, smith, physician, carpenter, &c., twenty years.	Vol.10, page 1134.	10th article treaty Dec. 26, 1854; three installments, of $6,700, still due.		20,100 00	
Do.	Support of agricultural and industrial school, support of smith and carpenter-shop, and providing necessary tools therefor.	...do...	10th article treaty Dec. 26, 1854; three installments, of $1,500, still due.		4,500 00	
Northern Cheyennes and Arapahoes.	Purchase of clothing.	Vol. 15, page 657.	6th article treaty May 10, 1868, (estimated.)	15,000 00		
Do.	To be expended by the Secretary of the Interior, for Indians roaming, in the purchase of such articles as from time to time may be determined.	...do...	6th article treaty May 10, 1868, (estimated.).	18,000 00		
Do.	Four installments, to furnish flour and meat.	...do...	6th article treaty May 10, 1868; one installment due.		66,576 00	
Do.	Pay of teacher, carpenter, miller, farmer, blacksmith, engineer, and physician.	Vol. 15, page 658.	7th article treaty May 10, 1868, (estimated.)	7,700 00		
Omahas.	Fifteen installments, 3d series, in money or otherwise.	Vol.10, page 1044.	4th article treaty March 16, 1854; eleven installments, of $20,000 each, unappropriated.		220,000 00	
Do.	Ten installments, for pay of engineer, miller, farmer, and blacksmith, keeping in repair grist and saw-mill, support of blacksmith-shop, and furnishing tools.	Vol.10, page 1044; vol. 14, page 668.	8th article treaty March 16, 1854, and 3d article treaty March 6, 1865; estimated, engineer, $1,200; miller, $600; farmer, $600; blacksmith, $900; keeping in repair grist and saw-mill, and support of smiths' shop, $600; four installments, of $4,500 each, unappropriated.		18,000 00	
Osages.	Interest on $69,120, at 5 per centum, for educational purposes.	Vol. 7, page 242.	Senate resolution Jan. 19, 1838, and 6th article treaty Jan. 2, 1825.		3,456 00	69,120 00

Names of tribes.	Description of annuities, stipulations, &c.	Reference to laws: Statutes at Large.	Number of installments yet unappropriated, explanations, remarks, &c.	Annual amount necessary to meet stipulations indefinite as to time, now allowed, but liable to be discontinued.	Aggregate of future appropriations that will be required during a limited number of years to pay limited annuities incidentally necessary to effect the payment.	Amount of annual liabilities of a permanent character.	Amount held in trust by the United States on which five per cent. is annually paid, and amount which, invested at five per cent., would produce permanent annuities.
Osages—Cont'd	Interest on $300,000 at 5 per centum, to be paid semi-annually in money or such articles as the Secretary of the Interior may direct.	Vol. 14, page 687.	1st article treaty Sept. 29, 1865			$15,000 00	$300,000 00
Ottoes and Missourias.	Fifteen installments, 3d series, in money or otherwise.	Vol.10, page 1039.	4th article treaty March 15, 1854; eleven installments, of $9,000, still due.		$99,000 00	30,000 00	
Pawnees	Annuity goods, and such articles as may be necessary.	Vol. 11, page 729.	2d article treaty Sept. 24, 1857	$11,200 00			
Do	Support of two manual-labor schools and pay of two teachers.	Vol. 11, page 730.	3d article treaty Sept. 24, 1857	2,180 00			
Do	For iron and steel and other necessaries for shops, and pay of two blacksmiths, one of whom to be tinsmith and gunsmith, and compensation of two strikers or apprentices.	...do......	4th article treaty Sept. 24, 1857; for iron, steel, &c., $500; two blacksmiths, $1,200; and two strikers, &c., $460.				
Do	Farming utensils and stock, pay of farmer, miller, and engineer, and compensation to apprentices to assist in working the mill, and keeping in repair grist and saw-mills.	...do......	4th article treaty Sept. 24, 1857, (estimated.)	4,400 00			
Poncas	Ten installments, 2d series, to be paid to them or expended for their benefit.	Vol. 12, page 997.	2d article treaty March 12, 1858; two installments, of $10,000 each, unappropriated.		20,000 00		
Do	Amount to be expended, during the pleasure of the President, for aid in agricultural and mechanical pursuits.	Vol. 12, page 998.	2d article treaty March 12, 1858	7,500 00			
Pottawatomies	Life annuity to chiefs.	Vol. 7, page 379.	3d article treaty Oct. 20, 1832.	500 00			
Do	Permanent annuity, in money.	Vol. 7, pages 51, 114, 185, 317, 320, 853.	4th article treaty 1795, $413 31; 3d article treaty 1809, $200 18; 3d article treaty 1818, $1,045 87; 3d article treaty 1828, $536 60; 2d article treaty 1832, $536 60; 2d article			9,329 17	166,583 40

Tribe	Object of expenditure	Reference to treaty or law	Vol./page			
Do.	Education, during the pleasure of Congress.	3d article treaty Oct. 16, 1826; 2d article treaty Sept. 20, 1828; and 4th article treaty Oct. 27, 1832.	Vol. 7, pages 296, 318, 401.	5,000 00		
Do.	Permanent provision for three smiths.	2d article treaty Sept. 20, 1828; and 3d article treaty Oct. 16, 1826.	Vol. 7, pages 296, 318, 321.	1,179 74		
Do.	Permanent provision for furnishing salt.	2d article treaty July 29, 1829	Vol. 7, page 320.	183 03		
Do.	Interest on $286,998.17 at 5 per centum.	7th article treaty June 5 and 17, 1846.	Vol. 9, page 854.		13,449 90	266,998 17
Pottowatomies of Huron.	Permanent annuities.	2d article treaty Nov. 17, 1807.	Vol. 7, page 106.		400 00	8,000 00
Quapaws.	For education, smith and farmer, and smith's shop, during the pleasure of the President.	3d article treaty May 13, 1833; $1,000 per year for education; and $1,660 for smith, farmer, &c.	Vol. 7, page 423.	2,660 00		
Qui-nai-elto and Quil-leh-utes.	$25,000, 5th series, to be expended for beneficial objects.	4th article treaty July 1, 1855; three installments, of $1,000, still due.	Vol. 12, page 972.		3,000 00	
Do.	Twenty installments, for agricultural and industrial school; employment of suitable instructors; support of smith and carpenter-shop, and tools; pay of blacksmith, carpenter, farmer, and physician.	10th article treaty July 1, 1855; eight installments, of $7,600, still due.	do		60,800 00	
Rogue River.	Five installments, in blankets, clothing, farming utensils, and stock.	4th article treaty July 1, 1855; three installments, of $3,000, still due.	Vol. 10, page 1019		9,000 00	
River Crows.	A mount to be expended in such goods, provisions, &c., as the President may from time to time determine, &c.	7th article treaty July 15, 1866; laws not published.		35,000 00		
Sacs and Foxes of the Mississippi.	Permanent annuities.	3d article treaty Nov. 3, 1804.	Vol. 7, page 85.		1,000 00	20,000 00
Do.	Interest on $200,000 at 5 per centum.	2d article treaty Oct. 21, 1837.	Vol. 7, page 541.		10,000 00	200,000 00
Do.	Interest on $800,000 at 5 per centum.	2d article treaty Oct. 11, 1842.	Vol. 7, page 596.		40,000 00	800,000 00
Do.	Five installments, for support of physician, &c., and furnishing tobacco and salt.	10th article treaty Feb. 18, 1867 for physician, &c., $1,500, and tobacco and salt $350; two installments, of $1,850, still due.	Vol. 15, page 497.		3,700 00	
Sacs and Foxes of Missouri.	Interest on $157,400 at 5 per centum.	2d article treaty Oct. 21, 1837	Vol. 7, page 543.		7,870 00	157,400 00
Seminoles.	Interest on $11,615.25 at 5 per centum.	Treaty March 6, 1861.	Vol. 12, page 1170.		2,636 49	11,615 25
Do.	Interest on $500,000, 6th article treaty Aug. 7, 1856.	$25,000, annuities.	Vol. 11, page 702.		25,000 00	500,000 00
Do.	Interest on $70,000 at 5 per centum.	3d article treaty March 21, 1866, for support of schools, &c.	Vol. 14, page 757.		3,500 00	70,000 00
Senecas.	Permanent annuities.	4th article treaty Sept. 9, 1817, $500; 4th article treaty Sept. 17, 1817, $500.	Vol. 7, pages 161, 179.		1,000 00	20,000 00
Do.	Smith and smiths' shops, and miller.	4th article treaty Feb. 28, 1831, say	Vol. 7, page 349.	1,660 00		
Senecas of New York.	Permanent annuities.	Act Feb. 19, 1841.	Vol. 4, page 442.		6,000 00	120,000 00
Do.	Interest on $75,000 at 5 per centum.	Act June 27, 1846.	Vol. 9, page 35.		3,750 00	75,000 00

Statement showing the present liabilities of the United States to Indian tribes, &c.—Continued.

Names of tribes.	Description of annuities, stipulations, &c.	Reference to laws: Statutes at Large.	Number of installments yet unappropriated, explanations, remarks, &c.	Annual amount necessary to meet stipulations indefinite as to time, now allowed, but liable to be discontinued.	Aggregate of future appropriations that will be required during a limited number of years to pay limited annuities incidentally necessary to effect the payment.	Amount of annual liabilities of a permanent character.	Amount held in trust by the United States on which five per cent. is annually paid, and amounts which, invested at five per cent., would produce permanent annuities.
Senecas of New York—Cont'd. Senecas and Shawnees.	Interest on $43,050 transferred from Ontario Bank to United States Treasury. Permanent annuities.	Vol. 9, page 35.	Act June 27, 1846.			$2,152 50	$43,050 00
Do.	Permanent annuities.	Vol. 7, page 119.	4th article treaty Sept. 17, 1818.			1,000 00	20,000 00
Senecas, Shawnees, Quapaws, Peorias, Ottawas, Wyandottes, and others.	Support of smith and smiths' shops. Five installments, for blacksmith and assistant, shop and tools, iron and steel for shop, for Shawnees.	Vol. 7, page 352. Vol. 15, page 515.	4th article treaty July 20, 1831. 8th article treaty Feb. 23, 1867; two installments, of $300 each, unappropriated.	$1,060 00	$1,000 00		
Do.	Six installments, for blacksmith and necessary iron, steel, and tools, for Peorias, Kaskaskias, &c.	Vol. 15, page 530.	27th article treaty Feb. 23, 1867; three installments, of $1,123 29 each, unappropriated.		3,329 87		
Shawnees.	Permanent annuities, for education.	Vol. 7, pages 51, 100.	4th article treaty Aug. 3, 1795; 3d article treaty May 10, 1854; and 4th article treaty Sept. 29, 1817.			3,000 00	60,000 00
Shoshones—Western band.	Interest on $40,000 at 5 per centum. Twenty installments, of $5,000 each, under direction of the President.	Vol. 10, page 1056.	3d article treaty May 10, 1854; 7th article treaty Oct. 1, 1863; twelve installments, unappropriated.		60,000 00	2,000 00	40,000 00
Shoshones—Eastern band.	Twenty installments, of $10,000 each, under direction of the President.		5th article treaty July 2, 1863; twelve installments, unappropriated.		120,000 00		
Shoshones—Northwestern band.	Twenty installments, of $5,000 each, under direction of the President.	Vol. 13, page 663.	3d article treaty July 30, 1863; twelve installments, unappropriated.		60,000 00		
Shoshones—Goship band.	Twenty installments, of $1,000 each, under direction of the President.	Vol. 13, page 682.	7th article treaty Oct. 7, 1863; twelve installments, unappropriated.		12,000 00		
Shoshones and Bannacks.	For Shoshonies: Three installments, to purchase seeds and im-	Vol. 15, page 675.	8th article treaty July 3, 1868; two		5,000 00		

Nation	Object of appropriation	Reference	Treaty or article	Amount	Amount	Amount
Do	Purchase of clothing for men, women, and children.	Vol. 15, page 676.	9th article treaty July 3, 1868, (estimated.)	13,574 00		
Do	Purchase of such articles as may be considered proper by the Secretary of the Interior for persons roaming, &c.	...do...	9th article treaty July 3, 1868, (estimated.)	30,000 00		
Do	Pay of physician, teacher, carpenter, engineer, farmer, and blacksmith.	...do...	10th article treaty July 3, 1868, (estimated.)	6,800 00	1,000 00	
Do	Three installments, for presents	...do...	12th article treaty July 3, 1869, two installments at $500, still due.			
Do	Blacksmith, and for iron and steel, &c. For Bannacks;	Vol. 15, page 675.	6th article treaty July 3, 1869, (estimated.)	2,000 00		
Do	Purchase of clothing for men, women, and children.	...do...	9th article treaty July 3, 1868, (estimated.)	6,937 00		
Do	Purchase of such articles as may be considered proper by the Secretary of the Interior for persons roaming, &c.	...do...	9th article treaty July 3, 1866, (estimated.)	16,000 00		
Do	For seeds and agricultural implements.	...do...	8th article treaty July 3, 1868, (estimated.)	2,500 00		
Do	Pay of physician, teacher, carpenter, miller, engineer, farmer, and blacksmith.	...do...	10th article treaty July 3, 1868, (estimated.)	6,890 00	500 00	
Do	Three installments, for presents	...do...	12th article treaty July 3, 1868, one installment, of $300, still due.		4,500 00	90,000 00
Six Nations of New York.	Permanent annuities in clothing, &c.	Vol. 7, page 46.	6th article treaty Nov 11, 1794.	100,000 00		
Sisseton and Wahpeton of Lake Traverse and Devil's Lake.	Amount to be expended in such goods, provisions, and other articles as the President may from time to time determine, &c.	Vol. 15, page 509.	Senate amendment to treaty Feb. 19, 1867.	15,000 00		
Sioux of different tribes.	Purchase of seeds and agricultural implements.	Vol. 15, page 638.	10th article treaty April 29, 1868, (estimated.)	159,460 00		
Do	Purchase of clothing for men, women, and children.	...do...	10th article treaty April 29, 1868, (estimated.)	6,000 00		
Do	Blacksmith, and for iron and steel, &c.	...do...	8th article treaty April 29, 1868, (estimated.)	236,000 00		
Do	For such articles as may be considered proper by the Secretary of the Interior for persons roaming, &c.	...do...	10th article treaty April 29, 1869, (estimated.)	1,314,000 00		
Do	For 7,300,000 pounds of beef, and same quantity of flour.	...do...	10th article treaty April 29, 1868, (estimated.)	10,400 00		
Do	Physician, five teachers, carpenter, miller, engineer, farmer, and blacksmith.	...do...	13th article treaty April 29, 1868, (estimated.)		500 00	
Do	Three installments, for presents	...do...	14th article treaty April 29, 1868; one installment still due, at $300.		7,200 00	
S'Klallams.	Five installments on $60,000, fifth series	Vol. 12, page 934.	5th article treaty June 26, 1855; three installments, of $2,400, due.		56,800 00	
Do	Twenty installments, for an agricultural and industrial school, pay of teachers, blacksmith, carpenter, farmer, and physician.	Vol. 12, pages 934, 935.	11th article treaty June 26, 1855; eight installments, of $7,100, due.			
Do	Smith and carpenter shop, and tools	Vol. 12, page 935.	11th article treaty June 26, 1855.	500 00	40,000 00	
Talleqaache band of Utahs.	Ten installments of $20,000 each	Vol. 13, page 673.	8th art. treaty Oct. 7, 1863; goods, $10,000.; provisions, $10,000, two installments unappropriated.			

Statement showing the present liabilities of the United States to Indian tribes, &c.—Continued.

Names of tribes.	Description of annuities, stipulations, &c.	Reference to laws; Statutes at Large.	Number of installments yet unappropriated, explanations, remarks, &c.	Annual amount necessary to meet stipulations indefinite as to time, now allowed, but liable to be discontinued.	Aggregate of future appropriations that will be required during a limited number of years to pay limited annuities incidentally necessary to effect the payment.	Amount of annual liabilities of a permanent character.	Amount held in trust by the United States on which five per cent. is annually paid, and amounts which, invested at five per cent., would produce permanent annuities.
Tabequache band of Utahs—Cont'l.	Purchase of iron, steel, and tools for blacksmith-shop, and pay of blacksmith and assistant.	Vol. 13, page 675	10th article treaty Oct. 7, 1863; iron and steel, $220; blacksmith and assistant, $1,100.	$1,320			
Tabequache. Muache, Capote, Weennuche, Yampa, Grand River, and Uintah band of Utes.	Two carpenters, two millers, two farmers, one blacksmith, and two teachers.	Vol. 15, page 622	15th article treaty March 2, 1868	11,000 00			
Do.	For iron and steel, and the necessary tools for blacksmith-shop.	Vol. 15, page 621	15th article treaty March 2, 1868	220 00			
Do.	Thirty installments of $30,000, to be expended under the direction of the Secretary of the Interior, for clothes, blankets, &c.	Vol. 15, page 622	11th article treaty March 2, 1868; twenty-seven installments unappropriated.		$810,000 00		
Do.	Annual amount to be expended, under the direction of the Secretary of the Interior, in supplying said Indians with beef, mutton, wheat, flour, beans, &c.	....do....	15th article treaty March 2, 1868	30,000 00			
Umpquas and Calapooias of Umpqua Valley, Oregon.	Five installments, 4th series, of annuity for beneficial objects.	Vol. 10, page 1126	3d article treaty Nov. 29, 1855; three installments of $1,000, still due.		3,000 00		
Do.	Support of teachers, &c., twenty years	Vol. 10, page 1127	6th article treaty Nov. 29, 1855, still due. three installments, of $1,450.		4,350 00		
Umpquas, (Cow Creek band.)	Twenty installments of $550 each	Vol. 10, page 1027	3d article treaty Sept. 19, 1853; two installments unappropriated.		1,100 00		
Walla-Walla, Cayuse and Umatilla	Five installments, 3d series, to be expended under the direction of the President.	Vol. 12, page 946	2d article treaty June 9, 1855; three installments, of $4,000.		12,000 00		

	Object	Reference	Treaty / Terms				
Do...	farmer, superintendent of farming operations, two school teachers, physician blacksmith, wagon and plow maker, and carpenter and joiner.		eight installments of $11,200 still due.				
Do...	Twenty installments for mill fixtures, tools, medicines, books, stationery, furniture, &c.	do	4th article treaty June 9, 1855; eight installments of $3,000 still due.		24,000 00		
Do...	Twenty installments of $1,500 each for head chiefs of these bands, ($500 each.)	do	5th article treaty June 9, 1855; eight installments unappropriated.		12,000 00		
Winnebagoes	Interest on $295,493 15 at 5 per centum	Vol. 7, page 546, vol. 12, page 628	4th article treaty Nov. 1, 1837, and Senate amendment July 17, 1862.			$44,774 66	$895,493 15
Do...	Thirty installments of interest on $76,116 92.	Vol. 9, page 879	4th article treaty Oct. 13, 1846; five installments of $3,805 84 still due.		19,029 20		
Do...	Interest on $179,098 63 at 5 per centum, under the direction of the Secretary of the Interior.		Act July 15, 1870.			8,954 93	179,098 63
Wal-pah-pe tribe of Snake Indians.	Ten installments, 2d series, under the direction of the President.	Vol. 14, page 664	7th article treaty Aug. 12, 1865; still due at $1,200 each.		12,000 00		
Yankton tribe of Sioux.	Ten installments of $40,000 each, 2d series, to be paid to them or expended for their benefit.	Vol. 11, page 744	4th article treaty April 19, 1858; seven installments still due.		280,000 00		
Yakamas.	Five installments, 3d series, for beneficial objects, at the discretion of the President.	Vol. 12, page 953	4th article treaty June 9, 1855; three installments of $6,000 unappropriated.		18,000 00		
Do...	Twenty installments for two schools, one of which to be an agricultural and industrial school, keeping the same in repair, and providing books, stationery, and furniture.	do	5th article treaty June 9, 1855; eight installments of $500 unappropriated.		4,000 00		
Do...	Twenty installments for superintendent of teaching, two teachers, superintendent of farming, two farmers, two millers, two blacksmiths, tinner, gunsmith, carpenter, wagon and plow maker.	do	5th article treaty June 9, 1855; eight installments of $14,600 unappropriated.		116,800 00		
Do...	Twenty installments for keeping in repair hospital, and furnishing medicine, &c., pay of physician, repairing grist and saw mill, and furnishing necessary tools.	do	5th article treaty June 9, 1855; eight installments of $2,200 unappropriated.		17,600 00		
Do...	Twenty installments for keeping in repair buildings for employés.	do	5th article treaty June 9, 1855; eight installments of $300 unappropriated.		2,400 00		
Do...	Salary of head chief for twenty years.	do	5th article treaty June 9, 1855; eight installments of $200 unappropriated.		4,000 00		
Do...	Twenty installments for keeping in repair blacksmith's, tinsmith's, gunsmith's, carpenter's, and wagon and plow maker's shops, and furnishing tools.	do	5th article treaty June 9, 1855; eight installments of $500 unappropriated.		4,000 00		
Total				2,552,236 77	5,869,573 21	378,156 83	6,651,622 26

REPORT OF THE SUPERINTENDENT OF THE UNITED STATES COAST SURVEY.

REPORT

SUPERINTENDENT OF THE UNITED STATES COAST SURVEY.

CoAST SURVEY OFFICE,
Washington, D. C., September 22, 1871.

SIR : I have the honor to present, as usual, in advance of the detailed report, a synopsis showing the distribution of surveying parties on the coasts of the United States during the year which will end with the month of October. Two working seasons are included in that period, one at the North, and the 'other on southern sections of the coast, work generally closing on the coast of New England early in November.

. My previous detailed report includes mention of the work done in the autumn of the year 1870. The abstract now submitted will include the subsequent operations. Of these, nearly all that concern places on the Atlantic coast north of Chesapeake entrance are now in progress, and field-work in those sites will continue, as before stated, until the mouth of November.

Following with notices in the usual geographical order, a topographical and a hydrographic party are now at work in Southwest Harbor, (Mount Desert Island,) on the coast of Maine; and if practicable, Moose-a-bec Reach and Goldsborough Bay will be sounded this season. The plane-table survey is in progress on the western shore of Penobscot Bay, and on the adjacent islands, including Isleborough, Isle au Haut, and the Fox Islands, three parties are engaged. Another is sounding Isle au Haut Bay. Tidal observations have recorded each rise and fall during the year at North Haven. Farther westward the work now in hand includes topography and hydrography of the Kennebec and Androscoggin Rivers; triangulation near the primary station, Sebattis; coast topography between Saco entrance and Richmond's Island; and additional soundings at several places between Portland and Plymouth Harbor. The tides of the year have been recorded regularly at Charlestown navy yard, near Boston. Special observations have been made at Edgartown Harbor, Massachusetts, with reference to the development of the laws which bring about physical changes at port entrances along the coast of New England. Plane-table work, continued during the winter, has completed the survey of Narragansett Bay, and the same party is now on the coast westward of Point Judith; another is at work near New Haven, Connecticut, points for the plane-table survey having been determined near midsummer. The survey of Lake Champlain is in progress northward of the limits reached last year, and also the connection of that survey by triangulation with adjacent geodetic stations of the Atlantic coast. The work here referred to incidentally determines points for the State surveys of New Hampshire and Vermont, as authorized in the appropriation bill for the present fiscal year, and a party is now engaged in that service. Another is employed in reconnaissance for stations to connect the triangulation of the lake with that of Hudson River. In the vicinity of New York a party has inspected and secured the triangulation marks on the shores of Long Island Sound; another has extended soundings in Newark Bay; and observations will be continued for determining the nature of the physical changes which affect New York Harbor. Daily tidal observations have been recorded during the year at that port.

On the coast of New Jersey a topographical and a hydrographic party are engaged in the survey of Little Egg Harbor; another party is in the field for triangulation between Mount Holly and Barnegat Lighthouse. The special survey at the confluence of the Delaware and Schuylkill Rivers will be completed by the end of the present working season. Latitude and azimuth have been determined at Calvert Station, at Tangier Island; and at Wolf Trap, on Chesapeake Bay; and a party is assigned to select stations for connecting the bay triangulation with that of the Atlantic coast across the peninsula of Virginia. The survey of the estuaries of the Chesapeake has been continued, and the Broad Water north of Cape Charles has been developed. All the tides of the year at Old Point Comfort have been recorded. Magnetic observations have been repeated at the station in Washington City. Triangulation has been extended on the James River, Virginia, and the primary work passing southward of Washington, along the Blue Ridge, is in progress.

In the lower sections of the Atlantic coast the operations of the year include triangulation over Pamlico Sound, North Carolina, and the determination of latitude and azimuth at the Ocracoke base line; the topography and hydrography of Pamlico River; survey of the coast above and below Bogue Inlet, North Carolina; off-shore hydrography south of Cape Hatteras; plane-table survey and soundings, embracing parts of the Chechesse, Colleton, Maskey's, May, Cooper, Bull, and Combahee Rivers, in South Carolina; the hydrography of St. Mary's River, Georgia, and of the coast approaches southward to the mouth of St John's River, Florida, with the inland sea channels between St. Mary's and Nassau Sound; the topography of Nassau Sound and of the coast adjacent; triangulation of the eastern side of Florida south of Matanzas Inlet; hydrography of the western end of the Florida Reef north of the Tortugas and Quicksands, including the development of a large bank in that vicinity.

In the Gulf of Mexico soundings have been made near Apalachicola entrance; the triangulation and topography are complete in St. Andrew's Bay; determinations have been made there for latitude and azimuth; Santa Rosa Sound has been developed eastward from Pensacola entrance, the surveys being now continuous. To the westward the work of the year embraces the extension of the survey of Isle au Breton Sound, and of the Mississippi River above the head of the passes; soundings in Lake Pontchartrain and in the Gulf approaches to the South Pass and Southwest Pass of the Mississippi. Trinity Shoal, in the Gulf, to the westward of the Delta, has been surveyed for light-house purposes. On the coast of Texas the hydrography of Matagorda Bay and its branches has been completed.

In the vicinity of St. Louis, and in Illinois, Ohio, and Kentucky, points have been determined in the triangulation which has been authorized for connecting the survey of the Atlantic coast with that of the Pacific. This work is yet in progress.

On the western coast most of the field operations are yet in hand. The steamer under construction for service in the western sections not being yet completed, only partial observations have been practicable in the hydrographic reconnaissance between Panama and San Diego. The plans of the year, under which parties are now in the field, include the determination of latitude and longitude at Cape San Lucas; the longitude of San Diego; topography near San Pedro, California; the latitude and longitude of Santa Barbara; topography of the coast of California, near Point Conception; San Luis Obispo and San Simeon; and of the Santa Barbara Islands; reconnaissance for extending the triangulation south of Monterey; the hydrographic development of Falmouth Shoal, and of the vicinity of a rock off the Farallones, and additional soundings in San Francisco entrance; the tracing of wharf lines at Oakland; topography near Point Arena, and of the coast south of Cape Mendocino, California; the longitude of Eureka; topography near Cresent City; the latitude and longitude of Yaquinna, on the coast of Oregon; topography north and south of Columbia River entrance, and of the river shores above Three-Tree Point.

In Washington Territory the survey is in progress on the west side of Whidby Island, and on the shores of Admiralty Inlet. The hydrography in that quarter will develop, in the course of the season, Lawson Shoal and the vicinity of Belle Rock in Rosario Strait. At Seattle the longitude will be determined by the telegraphic method.

When the appropriation for the present fiscal year became available, a party, previously organized, was sent from San Francisco without delay, to make such development in hydrography and such other observations of interest and value as may be practicable in the vicinity of the Aleutian Islands, off the coast of Alaska. The party sailed in August, but time has not yet elapsed for advice of the arrival of the vessel at her destination.

Within the year laborious computations have been completed, giving final values for the longitude of points intermediate between the Atlantic and the Pacific coast. Of these the principal ones are Omaha, Salt Lake City, and San Francisco. Computations are in progress for determining the transatlantic longitude, which depends upon the observations made last year at Brest and Duxbury.

The discussion is continued of full series of tidal observations, with reference to the construction of tables of prediction.

In the Coast Survey Office the operations of the several divisions have kept pace with the field-work. Twenty new charts have been published, including three new editions of charts made needful by extensive changes. Fifty-eight charts have been in hand in the drawing division, of which nine were commenced within the year. Of the various engraved charts about ten thousand copies have been printed, and an equal number of copies distributed from the office. Of the manuscript maps on file in the archives sixty-six have been copied or traced within the year, to meet calls for information from various branches of the public service.

Tide-tables for the ports of the United States for the year 1872 have been computed and issued from the office.

In the hydrographic division special care has been taken in regard to the marked places of buoys on the published charts. Most of the sea-marks liable to shift have been carefully determined in position, and marked on the charts which admitted of such changes without detriment to the sailing directions.

In conformity with the act of Congress approved July 15, 1870, for observing the solar eclipse of December 22, 1870, in Europe, several parties were organized under my direction, and occupied stations in Sicily and in Spain. As the weather was unfavorable, generally, along the line on which the eclipse was total, it is gratifying that the sky was least obscured at the stations selected for the several observers. Full reports have been received from the leading members of the expedition, and results of much interest are expected from the discussion of the observations.

This recapitulation of the operations of the year in part explains the object of the estimates which have been submitted for continuing the survey of the coast.

Respectfully submitted.

BENJAMIN PEIRCE,
Superintendent United States Coast Survey.

Hon. GEO. S. BOUTWELL,
Secretary of the Treasury.

REPORT OF THE LIGHT-HOUSE BOARD.

31 F

OFFICERS OF THE LIGHT-HOUSE BOARD.

[Light-House Board of the United States, organized in conformity to the act of Congress approved August 31, 1852.]

LIGHT-HOUSE BOARD.

Hon. GEORGE S. BOUTWELL, Secretary of the Treasury, *ex-officio* President.

REAR-ADMIRAL W. B. SHUBRICK, United States Navy.

PROF. JOSEPH HENRY, LL. D., Secretary Smithsonian Institution.

BREVET MAJOR GENERAL A. A. HUMPHREYS, Chief of Engineers, United States Army.

BREVET MAJOR GENERAL J. G. BARNARD, Colonel of Engineers, United States Army.

REAR-ADMIRAL C. K. STRIBLING, United States Navy.

PROF. BENJ. PEIRCE, LL. D., Superintendent Coast Survey.

REAR-ADMIRAL THORNTON A. JENKINS, United States Navy.

MAJOR GEORGE H. ELLIOT, Corps of Engineers, United States Army.

CHAIRMEN OF COMMITTEES.

Finance.—GENERAL HUMPHREYS.
Engineering.—GENERAL BARNARD.
Experiments.—PROF. HENRY.

Lighting.—PROF. PEIRCE.
Floating Aids.—REAR-ADMIRAL STRIBLING.

The Chairman and Secretaries are *ex-officio* members of all committees.

MEMBERS OF THE BOARD EMPLOYED IN THE OFFICE

REAR-ADMIRAL W. B. SHUBRICK, United States Navy, Chairman.
REAR-ADMIRAL THORNTON A. JENKINS, United States Navy, Naval Secretary.
MAJOR GEORGE H. ELLIOT, Corps of Engineers, United States Army, Engineer Secretary.

CLERKS.

ARNOLD B. JOHNSON, chief clerk.
WILLIAM D. O'CONNOR, corresponding clerk.
FRANK BAKER, accountant.
BRUCE SMALL, examining clerk.

A. H. SAWYER, records clerk.
SAMUEL STONE, recording clerk.
MRS. E. J. BEARE, register clerk.
JOSEPH McMAKIN, draughtsman.

REPORT

OF

THE UNITED STATES LIGHT-HOUSE BOARD.

TREASURY DEPARTMENT,
Office Light-House Board, September 25, 1871.

SIR: By your direction the following report of the operations of this Board, during the last year, is respectfully submitted:

The detailed statements under the heads of the respective districts, based mainly upon the annual reports of the Engineers and Inspectors, embrace the work which has been done; that which has been laid out for the current year; and the present condition of all the aids to navigation, with such remarks and recommendations in regard to improvement of existing and the establishment of such new aids as seem to require the attention of Congress at this time.

The Light-houses and Light-vessels (so far as the exhibition of efficient Lights is concerned) are, it is believed, equal to any in the world, and those beacons and buoys actually in position are efficient day-marks to guide clear of the obstructions for which they were established. For those Light-stations at which extensive repairs and renovations are needed, special appropriations are recommended.

The aggregate estimates for the fiscal year ending June 30, 1873, are $45,000 in excess of the appropriations for the fiscal year ending June 30, 1872, and $358 less than the estimates of last year.

The special items in excess, in the estimates of general expenses, over the actual appropriation for the current fiscal year, are for buoyage and for expenses of Fog-signals. The sum estimated for the buoy service is the same that has been submitted for several years past, owing to the great increase in the numbers of those aids to navigation, especially on the Southern, Gulf, and Pacific coasts, and the failure to make the increased appropriation ($25,000) asked for two years since, made it necessary to apply for a deficiency appropriation, part of which was made.

The other item of increase ($20,000) "for expenses of Fog-signals," arises from the large number of those aids to navigation authorized within the last two years.

Of the large number of Lights and other aids to navigation for which appropriations have been made, such as are established on sites belonging to the Government, and those where valid titles, according to law, in cases in which land had to be purchased, have been obtained, the works have been commenced or completed. Great difficulty is experienced in perfecting titles to sites for Light-houses, and building them within the limited time appropriations are available. It not unfrequently happens that the title-papers of a site for a Light-house, costing only a few hundred dollars, remain in the hands of the law officers for many months before the validity of the title is reported upon, and then, very often, in consequence of some legal omission or informality, the papers have to be returned to the United States attorney for further investigation.

The two small sailing-vessels which have been employed for many years in delivering oil and other Light-house supplies on the Atlantic and Gulf coasts are too much decayed to be economically repaired after the present year, and an estimate for building two new vessels for that service has been submitted in the estimates for next year.

FIRST DISTRICT.

The First District extends from the northeastern boundary of the United States, (Maine,) to and including Hampton Harbor, New Hampshire.

Inspector.—Commander A. E. K. Benham, United States Navy.

Engineer.—Brevet Brigadier General J. C. Duane, Lieutenant Colonel of Engineers, United States Army.

In this district there are:

Light-houses and lighted beacons 48
Day, or unlighted beacons 50
Buoys actually in position 339
Spare buoys for relief, and to supply losses 177
Tender, steamer *Iris* 1
Tender, steam launch, *Mary* 1
Tender, (sail,) schooner *Wave* 1

The following numbers, which precede the names of stations, correspond with those of the "Light-house List of the Atlantic, Gulf, and Pacific Coasts of the United States," issued January 1, 1871.

LIGHT-HOUSES AND LIGHTED BEACONS.

Burnt-Coat Harbor, Swan's Island, coast of Maine.—In consequence of difficulty in obtaining title to the land, it will probably be impossible to complete the Light-house before the 1st of July next, and it is therefore recommended that the money may be re-appropriated.

21. *White Head.*—Repairs are being made to the main part of the keeper's dwelling; a road has been graded from the landing to the Fog-signal house; a coal-shed erected, and a wharf is being built.

Halfway Rock, Casco Bay, Maine.—On the 30th of June, 1870, the balance on hand for the construction of this work having reverted to the Treasury, the construction of the work was discontinued, and the machinery and material removed and stored. As soon as the new appropriation became available the work was resumed. The tower has been completed, and all that now remains to be done is the roofing of the lantern and the introduction of the apparatus. The station will be lighted on the 15th of August. It is proposed, during the present season, to build a substantial masonry boat-house and establish a Fog-signal.

40. *Cape Elizabeth*, coast of Maine.—The westerly tower of the two, at this Light-station, was built in 1828 of *rubble stone*, and is now in such a state as to render it necessary to rebuild it in a better manner, for which an estimate has been submitted in the annual estimates. The station is one of the most important on the eastern coast, serving the double purpose of a sea-coast Light-station, and as a mark for the entrance into Casco Bay and to Portland Harbor.

43. *Whale's Back.*—The masonry of the new tower has reached the height of twenty feet above low-water mark. The position is one of the most difficult to work upon on the coast, as the rock is covered by the

waves, except at low water, and is exposed to the full force of the Atlantic. The new structure will be a masonry tower, solid to the height of twenty feet above low-water mark, and the blocks of granite which will form a facing for the interior mass of concrete will be tied together by dove-tail joints, as is usual in similar sea structures. The diameter of the tower at the base will be twenty-seven feet, and height of focal plane above the sea will be sixty-eight feet.

4. *Portsmouth Harbor.*—A new keeper's dwelling is being erected.

At each of the following-named Light-stations there have been repairs and renovations, more or less extensive, during the year, viz:

1. *St. Croix*, on Dochet's Island, St. Croix River, Maine.
2. *West Quoddy Head*, west entrance to Passamaquoddy Bay.
3. *Little River*, west side of entrance to harbor.
4. *Libby Island*, entrance to Machias Bay.
5. *Moose Peak*, on Moosepeak Head.
6. *Nash's Island*, west end of Moosepeak Reach.
7. *Narraguagus*, entrance to Narraguagus Bay.
8. *Petit Menan*, on Petit Menan Island.
   Prospect Harbor, east side of entrance to Prospect Harbor.
9. *Winter Harbor*, west side of entrance to Winter Harbor.
10. *Mount Desert*, on Mount Desert Rock.
11. *Baker's Island*, southwest side entrance to Frenchman's Bay.
12. *Bear Island*, east side entrance to northeast harbor.
13. *Bass Harbor Head*, east side entrance to Bass Harbor.
14. *Edgemoggin*, near east end of Edgemoggin Reach.
15. *Saddleback*, in Isle au Haute Bay.
16. *Heron Neck*, west entrance to Carver's Harbor.
17. *Deer Isle*, west entrance to Thoroughfare.
18. *Eagle Isle*, west side of Isle au Haute Bay.
19. *Pumpkin Isle*, west entrance to Edgemoggin Reach.
20. *Matinicus*, off Penobscot Bay.
21. *Owl's Head*, west side of Muscle Ridge Channel, Penobscot Bay.
23. *Brown's Head*, south side of west entrance to Fox Islands Thoroughfare.
24. *Negro Island*, south side of entrance to Camden Harbor.
25. *Grindle's Point*, north side of entrance to Gilkey's Harbor.
26. *Dice's Head*, north side of entrance to Castine Harbor.
27. *Fort Point*, west side of entrance to Penobscot River.
28. *Tenant's Harbor*, south side of entrance to Tenant's Harbor.
29. *Marshall's Point*, east entrance to Herring Gut.
30. *Manheigan*, off George's Islands.
31. *Franklin Island*, on east side of west entrance to George's River.
32. *Pemaquid*, on Pemaquid Point.
33. *Burnt Island*, west side of entrance to Townsend Harbor.
34. *Hendrick's Head*, east side of entrance to Sheepscot River.
35. *Pond Island*, west side of entrance to Kennebec River.
36. *Seguin*, off Kennebec River.
37. *Cape Elizabeth*, on southwest side of Casco Bay.
38. *Portland Head*, on southwest side of entrance to Portland Harbor.
39. *Portland Breakwater*, on outer end of Breakwater, Portland Harbor.
40. *Wood's Island*, west side of entrance to Saco River.
41. *Goat Island*, east side of entrance to Cape Porpoise Harbor.
42. *Boone Island*, off York Harbor.
45. *Isle of Shoals*, on White Island, off Portsmouth.

The following-named Light-stations require repairs to be made during the current and ensuing year:

1. *St. Croix.*
2. *West Quoddy Head.*
4. *Libby Island.*
6. *Nash's Island.*
7. *Narraguagus.*
8. *Petit Menan.*
   Prospect Harbor.
9. *Winter Harbor.*
10. *Mount Desert.*
11. *Baker's Island.*
12. *Bear Island.*
13. *Bass Harbor Head.*
14. *Edgemoggin.*
15. *Saddleback.*
16. *Heron Neck.*
18. *Eagle Island.*
19. *Pumpkin Isle.*
20. *Matinicus.*
21. *White Head.*
22. *Owl's Head.*
23. *Brown's Head.*
24. *Negro Island.*
25. *Grindle's Point.*
26. *Dice's Head.*
27. *Fort Point.*
28. *Tenant's Harbor.*
29. *Marshall's Point.*
30. *Manheigan.*
31. *Franklin Island.*
32. *Pemaquid.*
33. *Burnt Island.*
34. *Hendrick's Head.*
35. *Pond Island.*
36. *Seguin.*
37. *Cape Elizabeth.*
38. *Portland Head.*
40. *Wood Island.*
41. *Goat Island.*
42. *Boone Island.*
44. *Portsmouth Harbor.*
45. *Isle of Shoals.*

DAY OR UNLIGHTED BEACONS.

Names and positions of the day or unlighted beacons in the first district:

No. 1. *Jerry's Point,* Portsmouth Harbor.—Iron beacon. In good condition.

No. 2. *South Beacon,* Portsmouth Harbor.—Stone beacon. In good condition.

No. 3. *North Beacon,* Portsmouth Harbor.—Wooden mast. In good condition.

No. 4. *Willey's Ledge,* Portsmouth Harbor.—Iron spindle. In good condition.

No. 5. *York Ledge*, off York River.—Iron spindle. In good condition.

No. 6. *Fishing Rocks*, Kennebunkport.—Iron spindle. Broken off. Spar-buoy substituted.

No. 7. *Stage Island Monument*, entrance to Saco River.—Stone tower forty feet high. In good condition.

No. 8. *Sharp's Rocks*, entrance to Saco River.—Iron socket and wooden shaft. Socket broken off. Spar-buoy placed to mark the danger.

No. 9. *Back Cove Beacon*, Portland Harbor.—Pile beacon. In good condition.

No. 10. *White Head Ledge*, in White Head passage to Portland Harbor.—Iron spindle slightly bent under the cage, in good condition otherwise.

No. 11. *Trott's Rock* in the above passage.—Iron spindle broken off within a few feet of the ledge.

No. 12. *Mark Island Monument*, Casco Bay.—Stone tower fifty feet high. In good condition.

No. 13. *Black Jack Rock*, Kennebec River.—Iron socket, wooden shaft; broken off.

No. 14. *Seal Rock*, Kennebec River.—Iron spindle with copper cylinder, painted black. In good condition.

No. 15. *Lee's Rock*, Kennebec River.—Iron and wood broken; a spar-buoy is placed to mark the danger.

No. 16. *Ram Island Ledge*, Kennebec River.—Iron socket and wooden shaft. In good condition.

No. 17. *Winslow's Rocks*, Kennebec River.—Iron socket, wooden shaft; broken off. Spar-buoy substituted.

No. 18. *Ame's Ledge*, Kennebec River.—Iron socket, wooden shaft. In good condition.

No. 19. *Beef Rock*, Kennebec River.—Iron socket, wooden shaft. In good condition.

No. 20. *Lime Rock*, Back River.—Iron socket, wooden shaft. In good condition.

No. 21. *Carleton's Ledge*, Back River.—Iron socket, wooden shaft. In good condition.

No. 22. *Clough's Rock*, Sheepscot River.—Iron socket, wooden shaft. In good condition.

No. 23. *Merrill's Ledge*, Sheepscot River.—Iron socket, wooden shaft. In good condition.

No. 24. *Yellow Ledges*, Penobscot Bay.—Iron shaft, copper cylinder. In good condition.

No. 25. *Garden Island Ledge*, Penobscot Bay.—Iron shaft, copper cylinder and one ball. Shaft good, cylinder partially broken away and ball gone.

No. 26. *Otter Island Ledge*, Penobscot Bay.—Iron shaft, copper cylinder and two balls. Shaft bent, cylinder partially broken away, and one ball gone.

No. 27. *Ash Island Point*, Penobscot Bay.—Iron socket, wooden shaft. In good condition.

No. 28. *Dodge's Point Ledge*, Penobscot Bay.—Wooden mast twelve feet long. In good condition.

No. 29. *Potters-field Ledge*, Penobscot Bay.—Stone beacon. In good condition.

No. 30. *Lowell's Rock*, Penobscot Bay.—Iron spindle and cage. In good condition.

No. 31. *Seal's Ledge*, Penobscot Bay.—Iron spindle and cage. In good condition.

No. 32. *Harbor Ledge*, Penobscot Bay.—Stone beacon. In good condition.

No. 33. *Shipyard Ledge*, Penobscot Bay.—Iron spindle; broken off. Not necessary.

No. 34. *Fiddler's Ledge*, Penobscot Bay, near west entrance to Fox Island Thoroughfare.—Stone beacon. Two or three stones of the upper course are out of place; otherwise, in good condition.

No. 35. *North Point of Northeast Ledge*, Camden Harbor.—Iron spindle. In good condition.

No. 36. *Morse's Point Ledge*, Camden Harbor.—Iron spindle. In good condition.

No. 37. *Hosmer's Ledge*, Castine Harbor.—Stone monument. In good condition.

No. 38. *Steel's Ledge*, Belfast Harbor.—Stone beacon. In good condition.

No. 39. *Fort Point Ledge*, Penobscot River.—Stone beacon. In good condition.

No. 40. *Odom's Ledge*, Penobscot River.—Stone beacon. In good condition.

No. 41. *Buck's Ledge*, Penobscot River.—Iron beacon. In good condition.

Centre Harbor Ledge, in Centre Harbor, near east end of Edgemoggin Reach, three feet out at low water.—Iron socket with wooden shaft, twenty-five feet high, and cask at top painted black, (new.) In good condition.

No. 42. *Ship and Barges*, Blue Hill Bay.—Iron socket, wooden shaft thirty feet, and cask. In good condition.

No. 43. *Bunker's Ledge*, Mount Desert.—Stone beacon. In good condition.

No. 44. *Half-tide Ledge*, Narraguagas Harbor.—Iron socket, wooden shaft and cask. In good condition.

No. 45. *Norton's Reef*, Pleasant River.—Iron tripod and shaft, ball at top. In good condition.

No. 46. *Snow's Rock*, Moosepeak Reach.—Iron socket, wooden shaft. In good condition.

No. 47. *Gilchrist Rock*, Moosepeak Reach.—Iron shaft. In good condition.

No. 48. *Moose Rock*, Moosepeak Reach.—Iron tripod. In good condition.

No. 49. *Western Bar*, Lubec Narrows.—Wooden crib filled with stone. Being rebuilt.

No. 50. *The Ledge*, St. Croix River.—Wooden crib filled with stone. In good condition.

The beacons on *Fishing Rocks*, Kennebunkport; *Sharp's Rocks*, Saco River; *Lee's Rock and Winslow's Rocks*, Kennebec River, were broken off by ice and other casualties, and their places supplied with spar-buoys.

The steam-whistles in this district are in good working order, and are highly spoken of by persons navigating this coast.

SECOND DISTRICT.

The Second District extends from Hampton Harbor, New Hampshire, to include Gooseberry Point, Massachusetts.

Inspector.—Commander John J. Walker, United States Navy.

Engineer.—Brevet Brigadier General J. C. Duane, Lieutenant Colonel of Engineers, United States Army.

In this district there are—

Light-houses and lighted beacons	58
Day or unlighted beacons	49
Light-vessels, (including one for relief)	9
Buoys actually in position	500
Spare buoys for relief and to supply losses	273
Tender (steam) *Verbena*	1

The numbers preceding the names of stations correspond with those of the "Light-house List of the Atlantic, Gulf, and Pacific Coasts of the United States," issued January 1, 1871.

LIGHT-HOUSES AND LIGHTED BEACONS.

46. *Newburyport Harbor*, Massachusetts.—The fifth-order lens has been removed and a fourth-order substituted. A new keeper's dwelling is being erected. This Light-station was first established in 1790, and the beacon-light, designed to serve as a range for entering the harbor, (or for reaching a safe anchorage at night,) was erected in 1816. The tower of the main Light is a low, octagonal wooden structure, and the beacon must necessarily be so constructed as to allow it to be moved from one side to another in front of the main Light, as changes take place on the bar and in the outer channel.

Newburyport is a place of sufficient importance to justify the establishment of a more powerful light than the present one, and the erection of buildings of better materials than wood.

It is recommended that the temporary wooden structure on which the main Light is situated be replaced by a permanent cast-iron tower, supported on a concrete base, extending below the low-water line.

Should any future change in the formation of the site require the removal of the tower, this may be effected with little more expense than that of making a new concrete base.

The citizens of Newburyport have for several years maintained by subscription two range lights to guide vessels in the inner harbor, and they have lately petitioned the Government to take charge of them. Should this petition be granted it will be necessary to erect two small structures near the sites of the present lights. As a further aid to navigation entering this difficult harbor, it is recommended that a day beacon be erected on Black Rock, near the entrance. This point is at present marked by a spindle, which will probably sooner or later be carried off by the ice; moreover it does not sufficiently mark the rock in the night.

Estimated cost of main Light-house	$50,000
Estimated cost of two range-lights	10,000
Estimated cost of day-beacon	6,000
Total	66,000

52 *Cape Ann*, Massachusetts.—A steam Fog-signal has been placed at this station. The towers are being repointed and buildings repaired.

Hospital Point, Salem Harbor, Massachusetts.—This new Light was exhibited from a temporary building on May 1, 1871. Permanent buildings are now being erected.

Fort Pickering, Salem Harbor, Massachusetts.—This new Light was exhibited on January 17, 1871.

Derby Wharf, Salem Harbor, Massachusetts.—This new Light was exhibited on January 17, 1871.

59. *Boston*, Massachusetts.—Two frame buildings for Fog-signals have been erected. The floor of the room for the storage of oil has been relaid.

60. *Narrows*, entrance to Boston Harbor, Massachusetts.—The tower platform, railing and posts, and window-shutters and doors have been thoroughly repaired and all the iron-work has been scraped and painted. The ice-breaker has also been thoroughly repaired. A fifth-order lens will be substituted for the present sixth-order.

62. *Plymouth*, "*The Gurnet*," entrance to Plymouth Harbor, Massachusetts.—These Lights are of the sixth order and are entirely too small; they may readily be mistaken for the lights in a dwelling-house, when they can be seen at all, and the distance apart, thirty-one feet, is altogether too short to afford an efficient range. It is recommended to replace them by two fourth-order Lights, separated by a proper distance for an effective range. The estimated cost is $25,000.

Duxbury Pier, entrance to Plymouth, Duxbury, and Kingston Harbors, Massachusetts.—Four sections of the tower have been erected, bringing it to a height of thirty-six feet, and the base filled with concrete to a height of twenty feet. The structure will be a tower twenty-five feet in diameter at the base, with a height of fifty feet focal plane. It is founded in two feet of water at low tide, and is of concrete, faced with iron. The run of ice is very severe from Plymouth Harbor, and to resist it, and the heavy seas by which it will be assailed, the tower will be built in one solid mass to a height of fifteen feet above the water. It is expected that the entire work will be completed by the end of the current fiscal year.

72. *Monomoy Point.*—The Light at this station, which is of the fourth order, on a tower about forty feet high, was originally intended as a guide to *Old Stage Harbor*. The harbor has been filled with sand, and cannot now be entered, and the Light is therefore of no further use for that purpose. But inasmuch as nearly all vessels (both steamers and sailing) plying between New York and the eastern ports pass this point, and have now no other guide than the Light-ships, which cannot be seen a sufficient distance, it is considered a matter of the greatest importance that this Light should be replaced by one of sufficient power to guide vessels safely through this intricate passage. For this purpose there is recommended a second-order Fixed Light, varied by red flashes, for which an estimate is submitted.

80. *Nantucket Beacon.*—Land has been purchased for a site for a keeper's dwelling, and the dwelling is now being erected. The beacon will also be removed to this lot.

At each of the following-named stations there have been repairs more or less extensive during the last year:

47. *Newburyport Beacon*, Merrimack River.
48. *Ipswich*, entrance to Ipswich Harbor.
49. *Ipswich*, beacon, Ipswich Harbor.
50. *Annisquam*, Annisquam Harbor.
51. *Straitsmouth*, Straitsmouth Island.
53. *Eastern Point*, Gloucester Harbor.
54. *Ten Pound Island*, Gloucester Harbor.
55. *Baker's Island*, Salem Harbor.
56. *Marblehead*, Marblehead Harbor.
57. *Egg Rock*, off Nahant.
58. *Minot's Ledge*, in Boston Bay.
61. *Long Island Head*, Boston Harbor.

62. *Plymouth,* entrance to Plymouth Harbor.
63. *Race Point,* Cape Cod.
64. *Long Point,* Cape Cod.
65. *Mayo's Beach,* Wellfleet Bay.
66. *Billingsgate,* entrance Wellfleet Harbor.
67. *Sandy Neck,* Barnstable Bay.
68. *Cape Cod.*
69. *Nanset Beach Beacon,* Cape Cod.
70. *Chatham,* Chatham Harbor, Cape Cod.
71. *Pollock Rip Light-vessel.*
72. *Monomoy Point,* Cape Cod.
73. *Shovelful Light-vessel.*
74. *Handkerchief Light-vessel.*
75. *Nantucket,* (Great Point.)
76. *Sankaty Head,* Nantucket.
77. *South Shoal Light-vessel.*
78. *Gay Head,* Martha's Vineyard.
79. *Brant Point,* Nantucket.
81. *Nantucket Cliff Beacons.*
82. *Bass River,* Vineyard Sound.
83. *Bishop & Clerk's,* Vineyard Sound.
84. *Hyannis,* Vineyard Sound.
85. *Cross Rip Light-vessel.*
86. *Cape Poge,* Martha's Vineyard.
87. *Succonnessett Light-vessel.*
88. *Edgartown,* Martha's Vineyard.
89. *Holmes' Hole,* Martha's Vineyard.
91. *Nobsque,* Wood's Hole.
92. *Tarpaulin Cove,* Naushon Island.
93. *Vineyard Sound Light-vessel.*
94. *Hen and Chickens Light-vessel.*
95. *Cuttyhunk,* Buzzard's Bay.
97. *Clark's Point,* New Bedford Harbor.
98. *Palmer's Island,* New Bedford Harbor.
99. *Ned's Point,* Mattapoisett Harbor.
100. *Bird Island,* Sippican Harbor.
101. *Wing's Neck,* Buzzard's Bay.

The following-named Light-stations require repairs to be made during the ensuing year:

48. *Ipswich.*
52. *Cape Ann.*
61. *Long Island Head.*
72. *Monomoy Point.*
83. *Bishop & Clerk's.*
98. *Palmer's Island.*
51. *Straitsmouth.*
57. *Egg Rock.*
63. *Race Point.*
81. *Cliff Beacons.*
96. *Dumpling Rock.*

DAY OR UNLIGHTED BEACONS.

Names and positions of the day or unlighted beacons in the Second District:

No. 1. *Old Cock,* Buzzard's Bay, iron spindle, thirty-six feet high, with cage at top.

No. 2. *Egg Island*, Buzzard's Bay.—Granite cone with iron spindle, vane at top.

No. 3. *Range Beacon*, Fairhaven Fort Point.—Boiler-iron triangular pyramid, forty feet high.

No. 4. *Cormorant Rocks*, south side of entrance to Mattapoisett Harbor, Buzzard's Bay.—Iron spindle, twenty-six feet high, with cage at top.

No. 5. *Lone Rocks*, northeast entrance to Wood's Hole.—Iron spindle, cage at top.

No. 6. *Collier's Ledge*, entrance Centreville Harbor, Vineyard Sound.—Granite base, iron spindle, ball and vane.

No. 7. *Great Rock*, west of Point Gammon, Vineyard Sound.—Iron spindle, twenty-six feet high, cage at top.

No. 8. *Hyannis Breakwater*, east end.—Wooden spindle, four arms and cask at top.

No. 9. *Sunken Pier.*—Wooden spindle, cask at top, on northeast part of Bass River Bar.

No. 10. *Spindle Rock*, entrance to Edgartown Harbor.—Iron spindle, cask at top.

No. 11. *Billingsgate Shoal*, old site.—Timber beacon, fifteen feet high, with fifteen feet masts and slats across.

No. 12. *Egg Island Rock*, entrance to Wellfleet Harbor.—Wooden spindle, cask at top.

No. 13. *Duxbury Beacon*, square, granite, with four-foot granite post on top.

No. 14. *Breakwater Beacon.*—Square open-work granite, with wooden spindle.

No. 15. *Hogshead Beacon.*—Iron spindle with arm, cask and cage at top.

No. 16. *North Beacon*, entrance Scituate Harbor.—Iron spindle with two rounds.

No. 17. *South Beacon*, entrance Scituate Harbor.—Iron spindle with two lozenges.

No. 18. *Londoner*, off Thatcher's Island, Cape Ann.—Iron spindle forty-five feet high, with cage at top.

No. 19. *Point Alderton.*—Square granite pyramid with cone at top.

No. 20. *False-Spit.*—Granite base with iron spindle and cage.

No. 21. *Spit Beacon.*—Square granite pyramid.

No. 22. *Nix's Mate.*—Square granite base with octagonal pyramid.

No. 23. *Great Farm Bar.*—Square granite base and granite cone with iron spindle and cage at top.

No. 24. *Deer Island Point.*—Square granite pyramid.

No. 25. *Bird Island Beacon*, southeast point of Bird Island.—Iron spindle with cage at top.

No. 26. *Sunken Island.*—Open-work granite base, with wooden spindle and cage at top.

No. 27. *Pig Rocks.*—Granite pyramid, ten feet square at base, twenty feet high, with wooden mast and square cage at top. (Rebuilt this season.)

No. 28. *Halftide Rock.*—Wooden shaft forty feet high, with cask at top.

No. 29. *Cat Island Beacon.*—Wooden spindle.

No. 30. *Marblehead Rock.*—Conical, granite, with wooden spindle.

No. 31. *Little Aquavitæ*, entrance Salem Harbor.—Granite, with wooden spindle and cage at top.

No. 32. *Great Aquavitæ*, entrance to Salem Harbor.—Granite, with

No. 33. *Hardy's Rock.*—Wooden spindle, with two triangles at top.

No. 34. *Bowditch Beacon.*—Triangular pyramid of granite, with wooden spindle and cage at top.

No. 35. *Halfway Rock.*—Granite beacon in ruins.

No. 36. *Little Haste.*—Wooden mast thirty-five feet high, with cask at top.

No. 37. *Abbott's Monument.*—Square, granite, with wooden mast and cage at top.

No. 38. *Monument Bar.*—Square wooden crib filled with stone, mast and cage at top.

No. 39. *Ram's Horn.*—Square wooden crib filled with stone, wooden shaft at top.

No. 40. *Lobster Rocks,* Beverly Harbor.—Stone, with wooden spindle.

No. 41. *Black Rock,* Gloucester Harbor.—Iron spindle with oblong cage at top.

No. 42. *Harbor Rock,* Gloucester Harbor.—Iron spindle, with ball cage at top.

No. 43. *Five-Pound Island,* Gloucester Harbor.—Granite base, with iron spindle and ball at top.

No. 44. *Lobster Rock,* Annisquam.—Square open-work granite beacon.

No. 45. *Lane's Point.*—Square wooden beacon.

No. 46. *Point Neck Rock.*—Iron spindle, with ball at top.

Black Rocks on starboard hand entering Merrimack River, Newburyport Harbor, rocks out at half tide.—Iron spindle twenty-three feet high, with cask at top. Erected this season.

No. 47. *North Pier.*—Newburyport harbor.—Wooden crib filled with stone.

No. 48. *South Pier,* Newburyport harbor.—Wooden crib filled with stone.

LIGHT-VESSELS.

No. 87. *Shovelful Light-vessel* No. 3.—Good order. This vessel has been taken into Hyannis, her metal repaired, &c.

No. 88. *Handkerchief Light-vessel* No. 4.—Good order. This vessel has been taken into Hyannis to have her metal and stern repaired, &c.

No. 100. *Cross Rip Light-vessel* No. 5.—This vessel has been taken into New Bedford placed on the marine railway, her metal repaired, partially recalked, her boats repaired, &c.

No. 102. *Succonnessett Light-vessel* No. 6.—This vessel is in very bad condition, and another vessel (No. 24) has been sent to the district to supply her place, but she will require some repairs before being put on the station.

No. 107. *Vineyard Sound Light-vessel* No. 7.—This vessel was taken to New Bedford last November, her upper works newly calked, decks sheathed, supplied with new foresail, new windlass, new running rigging, fifteen fathoms new chain cable, and put in thorough order.

No. 108. *Hen and Chickens Light-vessel* No. 8.—This vessel has been taken to New Bedford, placed upon the marine railway, her bottom partially refastened, recalked, remetaled, a new set of plain sails supplied, and the vessel put in thorough order generally.

RELIEF LIGHT-VESSELS.

Relief Light-vessel No. 9.—This vessel has been entirely retopped the past year, supplied with a new suit of plain sails, her water-tanks re-bottomed, furnished with new day-marks, and such new rigging as she required, and is now a most excellent vessel, suitable for occupying any station in the district.

Relief Light-vessel No. 38.—The upper works of this vessel have been recalked and painted, and the vessel is now in excellent condition, and in readiness to go to any station in the district at a moment's notice. Has been recently sent for temporary service to the Sixth District.

BUOYS.

Buoys actually in position.—All the buoys in the district (five hundred in number) have been shifted since the opening of the spring, and are now in excellent order.

TENDERS.

° The steam tender Verbena is an efficient vessel, and in good condition, but one tender is insufficient for a district having so many buoys, Light-vessels and Light-houses to visit and look after.

LIGHT-VESSEL AND BUOY-DEPOTS.

The *Buoy Depot at Gulf Island,* the place of residence of the Minot's Ledge Light-keepers, is difficult of access, as it can only be reached at high water, and it is proposed to have the buoys kept higher up in Boston Bay if a proper place can be obtained.

At the *Light-vessel and Buoy-depot* at Wood's Hole some repairs of the wharf required will soon be made under the direction of the Engineer of the district.

TENDER.

The tender authorized by the last session of Congress, designed for the use of the Engineer of the First and Second Districts, is being built under contract.

THIRD DISTRICT.

The Third District embraces all aids to navigation from Gooseberry Point, Massachusetts, to include Squam Inlet, New Jersey, as well as the Hudson River, Whitehall Narrows, and Lake Champlain.

Inspector.—Commodore James H. Strong, United States Navy.

Engineer.—Brevet Brigadier General I. C. Woodruff, Lieutenant Colonel of Engineers, United States Army.

In this district there are—

Light-house and lighted beacons	107
Day or unlighted beacons	48
Light-vessels	9
Buoys actually in position	432
Spare buoys for relief and to supply losses	458
Tenders (steam) *Cactus* and *Putnam*	2

The numbers preceding the names of stations correspond with the "Light-house Lists of the Atlantic, Gulf, and Pacific Coasts, and the Northern and Northwestern Lakes of the United States," issued January 1, 1871.

LIGHT-HOUSES AND LIGHTED BEACONS.

Castle Hill, east side of entrance to Newport Harbor, Narragansett Bay, Rhode Island.—The application of former years for a Fog-signal on *Castle Hill* is not renewed, in view of the proposed erection of a steam syren signal at *Beaver Tail* Light-station, distant only about two miles.

118. *Beaver Tail*, Rhode Island.—A steam syren will be erected at this station during this season, and it is believed that there will be no necessity for the Fog-signal at *Castle Hill* on the opposite side of entrance to Newport Harbor, which has frequently been petitioned for.

119. *Lime Rock*, Rhode Island.—The rock on which this Light-house stands is full of crevices, through which the water, during heavy rains, enters the cellar. It is proposed either to cover the rock with concrete made of Portland cement, gravel, and sand, or to endeavor to remedy it by drains. The latter has been directed to be done, (experimentally,) being less expensive.

120. *Newport Harbor*, (Goat Island,) Rhode Island.—It is recommended that a Fog-bell, operated by Stevens's striking apparatus, may be placed at this station, as an essential aid in entering the harbor. Estimated cost, $800.

123. *Poplar Point*, Narragansett Bay, Rhode Island.—The repairs and renovations which were authorized for this station have been completed, and a new lantern substituted for one of the oldest construction.

Muscle Bed Beacon, Narragansett Bay, Rhode Island.—The construction of a Light-house on *Hog Island Reef* has been petitioned for for several years, but hitherto Congress has not granted an appropriation therefor. The erection of a portable Light and a Fog-bell on the existing stone tower on the *Muscle Bed*, one-half mile distant, on the opposite side of the channel, at a cost of $3,000, will, it is believed, obviate the necessity for this Light-house, which would be a very expensive construction.

127. *Conimicut Point*, Rhode Island, entrance to Providence River, Narragansett Bay.—When the Light on the shoal off *Conimicut Point* was lighted as a substitute for the Light on the main land, at *Nayat Point*, (distant about one mile,) the only available means of attending upon it were to allow the keepers to retain the dwelling at the old Light-station, and for them to visit the new Light by boat. The land constituting the site of the old Light-station at *Nayat Point* is valuable, and would bring at public sale a good price. The old tower is not worth the cost of tearing it down, and the dwelling not having been repaired, in expectation of an appropriation for completing the buildings at *Conimicut Point*, to include a proper dwelling for the keeper, it now becomes necessary either to make considerable expenditure upon the *Nayat Point* dwelling, or ask for a special appropriation for the necessary protection pier against running ice, and for a dwelling at that Light-house. The estimated cost of the work is $30,000.

Sabine's Point, Providence River, Rhode Island.—By an act of Congress, approved March 3, 1871, an appropriation was made for the erection of a Light-house on this point. Plans and specifications have been prepared, and proposals for the construction of the work are invited by public advertisements, to be received until July 31, 1871.

128. *Pumham Rock.*

129. *Fuller's Rock.*

Sassafras Point.

The construction of these three permanent Lights in Providence River, above *Sabine's Point*, Rhode Island, authorized by an appropriation made July 15, 1870, is progressing under contracts, and will be completed this season.

130. *Point Judith*, Rhode Island.—The present Fog-signal, operated by a caloric engine, has been found insufficient for this important sta-

tion on the water-route from New York to New England. Frequently
the sound of the signal is lost in the noise of the surf, so that steamers
and vessels are left without a reliable guide off this dangerous point.
It is recommended to replace the present signal by a first-class steam
Fog-signal *whistle*, and a duplicate at a cost of $5,000, including the
housing. To distinguish it from the *Beaver Tail Syren*, a whistle should
be placed at *Point Judith*.

131. *Block Island*.—To arrest the drifting sands which created some
apprehension for the safety of the buildings, a wattling of small stakes,
driven into the sand and interlaced with brush, was recommended in a
special report to the Light-House Board, and by it approved. It is believed that willow-slips, in addition to the above wattling, will be efficient in arresting the drifts. For this object an estimate of $1,800 is
presented.

132. *Watch Hill, Connecticut.*—The repairs and renovations provided
for in the appropriation of July 15, 1870, were completed during this
season, with the exception of placing the lantern-deck and parapet,
which is now ready for shipping to the station.

133. *Montauk Point*, Long Island,. New York.—The keeper's dwelling
requires a new roof, and ceilings in the attic require replastering. This,
with other incidental repairs of the tower, &c., will cost $1,500. It is
recommended that a Fog-signal be placed at this important station, for
which, with a duplicate, $8,000 is estimated.

137. *North Dumpling*, Fisher's Island Sound.—The repairs and renovations provided for in the appropriation of July 15, 1870, are completed.
The roof on the keeper's dwelling was replaced by a Mansard roof, and
a new tower, with lantern, erected upon the dwelling. The bell-tower
was thoroughly repaired, the roof over the striking apparatus tinned,
and the whole repainted. A barn was built, and the banks of the sluice
leading into the pond, which is used as a basin for the keeper's boat,
have been protected by rough granite blocks.

140. *Race Rock*, Fisher's Island Sound, New York.—The construction
of the foundation for a new Light-house on *Race Rock*, commenced in
April last, is progressing satisfactorily, about 3,000 tons of granite having been placed in riprap foundation, in addition to which 7,000 tons
will be delivered under a contract now in operation. The entire foundation, together with a portion of the supporting pier and landing
wharf, will be put under contract and completed by the close of this
fiscal year. The original estimate of the cost for this structure is
$200,000. The amounts provided by special acts of Congress are as fol-
lows, viz:

By act approved July 15, 1870............................. $10,000
By act approved March 3, 1871............................. 150,000

Total.. 160,000

The amount of $40,000 is embraced in the estimates for continuing
this work.

141. *Little Gull Island*, Long Island Sound.—A horizontal steam-boiler
to operate a syren Fog-signal has been placed at this important point,
and is found to be very efficient in guiding vessels through "the Race"
in foggy weather. A duplicate signal, for which an appropriation was
made March 3, 1871, is in process of construction, and will be put up
as soon as completed. The bell, which had been retained for cases of
emergency, will then be removed. A suitable building for the reception

of the duplicate signal is just being completed. Cisterns have been built, and the entire pier, on which the tower and dwelling stand, was covered with concrete flagging for the purpose of collecting all the rainfall which is required for the steam Fog-signals. To complete the landing the sum of $5,000 is estimated.

142. *Gardiner's Island*, Long Island Sound.—The necessary alterations in the lantern, and the painting of the tower and keeper's dwelling, inside and out, are completed.

143. *Plum Island*, Long Island Sound.—The rebuilding of this station is completed, and a Fog-bell, operated by a Stevens's striking apparatus, placed at this station.

Oyster Pond Point, Plum Gut, Long Island Sound.—An estimate is again submitted for the erection of a stone beacon on *Oyster Pond Point Reef*, to guide vessels to and from Long Island Sound to Gardiner's Bay, New York.

144. *Long Beach Bar*, Long Island Sound.—The erection of a lighted beacon at this station was provided for by special appropriation of July 15, 1870, the plan adopted being a light on the keeper's dwelling, which is founded on screw-piles. These are protected by an ice-breaker of granite blocks placed in riprap. The entire iron and wood-work for this structure is completed, and contracts are now in operation for the erection of the Light-house, and building the ice-breaker. It is expected that the Light can be exhibited at this station by the close of this season.

148. *Brockway's Reach*, Connecticut River.—A portion of the stones which protect the foundation of this beacon having been washed away by the spring freshets, has been replaced.

149. *Devil's Wharf*, Connecticut River.—The stones, which were washed away by freshets, have been replaced.

151. *Horton's Point*, Long Island.—The repairs and renovations provided for by the appropriation of July 15, 1870, are completed. The rooms for the accommodation of the assistant keeper were added to the keeper's dwelling, and a room provided for the Light-house supplies; the keeper's dwelling was thoroughly repaired and repainted. A cast-iron lantern-deck was substituted for the stone one, which leaked. The third-order lens, which originally formed a part of a revolving apparatus, has been replaced by a third-order fixed lens; the focal plane was raised and the illuminating apparatus rendered more efficient. The entire outside brick-work of the tower and dwelling, which was found in a state of rapid decay, caused by the action of the atmosphere and frost, was covered with a coating of Portland cement-mortar. The barn has been thoroughly repaired, and the fences to a great extent renewed and repaired.

152. *Falkner's Island*, Long Island Sound.—The repairs and renovations—including rebuilding of keeper's dwelling, and substituting an iron stairway for a wooden one—authorized by the appropriation of July 15, 1870, are progressing, and will be completed during this season. A powerful steam Fog-signal is recommended for this station to prevent the frequent losses of vessels which occur in its vicinity during fogs and snow-storms. For this object an appropriation of $5,000 is asked. The bank to the eastward is slowly wearing away, the loss having been about twelve feet in the course of twenty years. It may be necessary at a day not far distant to protect the foot of the slope, near the Light-house, by riprap along a distance of about two hundred feet or more.

153. *New Haven Harbor*.—The repairs and renovations provided for by the appropriation of July 15, 1870, are completed. The caloric

engine which operated the Fog-bell being worn out, was replaced by a Stevens's striking apparatus.

155. *Stratford Point*, Long Island.—The condition of this station is very bad. The rebuilding of the tower and keeper's dwelling has been recommended for the last three years. It is now recommended that a frame building be erected, on which the lantern-tower will be placed. For this and the necessary out-buildings, an estimate of $15,000 is respectfully submitted.

157. *Bridgeport Harbor*, Connecticut.—The rebuilding of this beacon was authorized by the appropriation of July 15, 1870. The plan adopted is similar to that for *Long Beach Bar*, viz, a Light on keeper's dwelling, which is founded on screw-piles: these being protected by an ice-breaker of granite blocks placed in riprap. The entire iron and wood-work for this structure is completed, and contracts are now in operation for the erection of the Light-house, and building the ice-breaker. The Light will probably be exhibited by October next.

158. *Black Rock*, Connecticut.—The buoy-wharf and shed for storage of buoys at this station, authorized by the appropriation of $8,000, on March 3, 1871, will be built during this season, the plans being in readiness to invite proposals for its construction.

160. *Penfield Reef*, Long Island Sound.—The construction of a Light-house on *Penfield Reef*, near Bridgeport, Connecticut, authorized by appropriations made July 15, 1870, and March 3, 1871, has been commenced under contracts now in operation, and will be prosecuted with a view to its completion during the next working season.

161. *Eaton's Neck*, Long Island.—A powerful steam Fog-signal, authorized under appropriation made July 20, 1868, has been put up at this station. It is a syren, and a building for a duplicate now in process of construction, and a building for the caloric engine for pumping water for the use of the Fog-signal, have been erected.

162. *Lloyd's Harbor*, Long Island.—The damage caused to the Light-house at this station by the gale of November 22, 1870, has been repaired and a granite wall built to protect the station, at a cost of about $3,000.

Stamford Harbor, Connecticut.—An examination of the "Ledge" in this harbor was made under instructions from the Light-House Board, by the Inspector and Engineer of the district, in accordance with petition of a large number of persons interested in the trade of this port for a Light to mark the "Ledge." The report of the Inspector and Engineer recommends a day-beacon on the "Ledge" and a lighted beacon on the opposite side of the channel. The cost of the two structures will be $8,000, which amount is included in the estimates.

165. *Execution Rocks*, Long Island Sound.—The work of protecting this station against the ice and sea, authorized by the appropriation made July 15, 1870, has been completed. The damage caused by the ice during the winter has also been repaired, and the keeper's dwelling is now being repainted. The tower needs extensive repairs, pointing on the exterior, and alterations in the interior.

166. *Sand's Point*, Long Island.—The damage caused by gales during the winter to the jetties and sea-wall which protect this station have been repaired at a cost of about $3,000. The buildings require repairs, and for this purpose an estimate is submitted of $3,000.

Hart Island, Long Island Sound.—An appropriation was made in 1866 for the erection of a Light at this point. The owner of the island being unwilling to sell the requisite quantity of land for this Light-station for such a sum as the Board would have been authorized to give, proceedings were instituted, in conformity to law, for condemning the land. The award of the appraisers for five acres of land was $25,000, a sum far exceeding the entire appropriation, and, in the opinion of the board, far beyond its intrinsic money value. Having made further examinations, it is found that the south end of the island, upon which the Light would necessarily be placed, if placed on the island at all, is continually washing away, and unless it is protected by an expensive sea-wall, a Light-house could not remain there very long. The end of the reef, (in six feet water,) which runs out from the southern end of the island, would afford a good foundation and proper site for the erection of a stone structure similar to those already erected at points on the Hudson River. The estimated cost of the proposed structure and apparatus, complete in all respects, is $50,000, and is included in the annual estimates this year.

169. *Great West Bay*, Long Island.—The tower requires repointing and coating with Portland cement; the dwelling also requires repairing and painting; speaking-tubes and an alarm-bell are needed to communicate from the watch-room in the tower with the keeper's dwelling. An estimate of $500 is submitted herewith.

170. *Fire Island*, Long Island.—The outside painting on the tower is very defective, and does not appear in the color represented in the Light-house list. Many bricks are crumbled, and require to be replaced by sound ones, and the tower covered with Portland cement-wash. Speaking-tubes and an alarm-bell are also needed to communicate from the watch-room with the keeper's dwelling. An estimate of $500 is submitted herewith.

175. *East Beacon*, Sandy Hook.—A new first-class steam (syren) Fog-signal, with horizontal boiler, has been substituted for the old one with vertical boiler, the tubes of which were destroyed by corrosion. A duplicate steam Fog-signal, authorized by the appropriation of March 3, 1871, is in course of construction, and will be put up as soon as completed.

A new frame building has been erected for the new Fog-signal. The old building has been moved to the vicinity of the new one, and has been renovated to receive the duplicate signal.

A well has been dug and walled, which furnishes fresh water for the boilers of the signal. The keeper's dwelling requires repainting inside and outside, which will be done at an early period.

In the previous annual report reference was made to the abrasion of the beach, which rendered it necessary to remove the beacon building five hundred feet to the southward. The abrasion does not seem to be of a threatening character at this time, but no doubt is entertained that upon the completion of the jetties, recently commenced by the Engineer Department for the protection of the beach in front of the fort from abrasion, the accumulation of sand will be arrested, and abrasion will most likely result in the vicinity of the beacon and the new Fog-signal structures. It is hence deemed imperative to guard against such a contingency by the construction of two jetties similar to those adopted by the Engineer Department. The cost of such protection is estimated at $20,000.

It may be well to state that a further removal of the beacon and the Fog-signal to the southward is impossible, as they would, if so removed, be masked by the works of defense seaward or in the direction the sound from the signal is especially needed.

Flynn's Knoll, Lower Bay of New York.—The erection of a Light-house on *Flynn's Knoll*, in nine feet water, to form a range with *Princess Bay Light*, for the deepest water in Gedney's Channel, was recommended in last year's report and in those of former years. The great importance of a reliable guide to navigation on this dangerous shoal seems to justify the attempt to bring the subject again to the attention of Congress. The amount of $100,000 for commencing the work is embraced in the estimates.

177. *Conover Beacon,* Sandy Hook Bay.—Repairs at this station are much needed and will be made as soon as the more urgent necessities of the district admit.

178. *Chapel Hill Beacon,* New Jersey.—The out-buildings at this station, blown down during a gale, have been rebuilt, and the fences have been repaired.

181. *Elm Tree Beacon,* Staten Island.—The extension of the jetty, for which funds have been provided by the appropriation of March 3, 1871, will be built during this season.

183. *Princess Bay,* Staten Island.—The protecting wall authorized by the appropriation of July 15, 1870, is in course of construction under contract, and, it is expected, will be completed during the present season. The wood-work of the keeper's dwelling and the iron-work of the tower have been repainted.

184. *Fort Tompkins,* Staten Island.—The Light-house at this station must be removed shortly to the interior of the works of defense. Its present site is required for the purposes of a battery now in course of construction. Experimental firings are of frequent occurrence at this fort, during which the glass of the lantern is broken. As a temporary expedient a wooden frame has been made, and a light will be exhibited therefrom near to the present Light-house, at a point designated by the Engineer officer in charge of the fort. For a dwelling surmounted by a tower, at the new site of the Light-house, the sum of $8,000 is asked.

192. *Esopus Meadow,* Hudson River.—The rebuilding of this station under the appropriation of July 15, 1870, is in progress under contract, and will be completed during the present fiscal year.

194. *Saugerties,* Hudson River.—The Engineer of the district was authorized to draw up a contract for signature of the persons desiring to occupy the old Light-house pier at this station for a public wharf, in such a manner as to secure the interests of the United States. He sent the contract so prepared, but up to this time the contract has not been returned to him. One of the conditions was to remove the old dwelling-house, also requested by the petitioners for use as a store-house, to such a distance as not to endanger the new structure by fire. In case the parties do not comply with the terms of the contract the old buildings will be taken down, being of no further use to the station.

197. *Stuyvesant Light-house,* Hudson River.—The old dwelling at this station will be retained as a depot for keeping portable beacons of Hudson River during the close of navigation.

198. *New Baltimore.*

199. *Five Hook Island.*

200. *Cocyman's Bar.*

201. *Roha Hook.*

202. *Schodack Channel.*

203. *Nine-mile Tree.*

204. *Cow Island.*

205. *Parada Hook.*

206. *Van Weiss Point.*

207. *Cuyler's Dyke.*

These ten beacon-lights in the Hudson River, which were destroyed by ice and freshets, will be restored during this season, under the appro-priation of March 3, 1871, for this purpose.

White Hall Narrows, 416, 417, and 420–431 inclusive.—The portable beacons in *White Hall Narrows* are in good order. The customary removal for the winter was unnecessary, during the last winter the ice in the Narrows having melted to such a degree before it moved that no damage to the beacons was anticipated. Two stake-lights require to be replaced by portable beacons, viz:

418. *Opposite Chapman's Dock;* and
419. *South of Snoddy's Dock.*
Estimated cost $800 each.

432. *Crown Point*, Lake Champlain.—The keeper's dwelling needs repairs and repainting. A stable is much needed at this station, and has been recommended in previous reports. The recommendation is renewed. Estimated cost for repairs and for stable, $1,500.

433. *Barber's Point*, Lake Champlain.—A contract has been made for the construction of a Light-house on this point, as provided by the appropriation of July 15, 1870. The work will be commenced as soon as a certain judgment debt is removed and a valid title to the United States can be secured.

434. *Split Rock*, Lake Champlain.—Boatways and capstan authorized by the appropriation of March 3, 1871, will be supplied during this season.

435. *Juniper Island*, Lake Champlain.—The construction of a wharf and boat-house, under the appropriation of March 3, 1871, will be car-ried into effect during the present season.

436, 437. *Burlington Breakwater*, Lake Champlain.—Funds have been provided, under the appropriation of March 3, 1871, for the construc-tion of a Light on keeper's dwelling upon the north end of the break-water. The work will be commenced as soon as the extension of the breakwater is completed.

438. *Colchester Reef*, Lake Champlain.—By an act of Congress ap-proved July 15, 1870, the amount of $20,000 was provided for building a Light-house at *Colchester Point*, or in its vicinity, Lake Champlain. It was reported last year as follows: "After a careful examination and survey of the locality, it was found that the rock called 'Middle Bunch' was the proper place for the new Light-house. This rock is in the middle of the channel, with seven feet water over it at low water, and deep water on either side. With a Light thereon a vessel can pass on either side close to the rock. The work has been commenced and will be carried above water (and further, if possible) this fall, and will be completed next season."

The crib for the foundation was made in Burlington, and was towed to, placed on the reef, and filled in with concrete and rough stone. Two courses of the cut stone were also laid, and thereby the pier was brought above water. Before the work was abandoned for the season, it was ballasted with heavy blocks of stone to prevent its being moved by the ice. When the ice moved in the spring the ballast on the pier, with a part of the second course of cut stone, were shoved into the lake; the first course was found undisturbed. A few of the cut stone were found and replaced; but four hundred and eighty-one feet had to be rebuilt. After the damage had been repaired, the work on the pier was resumed and completed by the end of June.

The appropriation of $20,000 was made for a Light-house on *Colches-ter Point*, or its vicinity, which amount would have been ample for a structure on land. The necessary change in the locality for the Light from *Colchester Point* to a reef in seven feet water, required also a change in the plans of the structure. The new plans were prepared with the intention to keep the expenses within the amount of the appropriation. This, however, was frustrated by the various causes enumerated. The amount required for the completion of the Light-house on the *Middle Bunch,* (*Colchester Reef,*) Lake Champlain, in addition to the former appropriation, is $4,500. A Fog-bell will be erected at this station.

439. *Bluff Point,* Valcour Island, Lake Champlain.—The appropriation of July 15, 1870, provides for the construction of a Light-house on this point. A contract for its construction has been entered into, and work will be commenced as soon as a valid title to land is secured to the United States.

442. *Cumberland Head,* Lake Champlain:—The appropriation of March 3, 1871, provides the means for the purchase of additional land at this station for the object of removing certain trees which now obstruct the Light. The purchase will be made and the obstructions removed during this season.

444. *Isle La Motte,* Lake Champlain.—It has been recommended in previous reports to replace the present beacon-light by a Light on keeper's dwelling, and is renewed. The distance between the residence of the keeper and the beacon is too great to secure proper attendance. The estimated cost of the dwelling, surmounted by a tower, is $8,000.

At each of the following Light-stations there have been repairs and renovations more or less extensive during the year, and not alluded to in this report:

126. *Warwick Neck,* Narragansett Bay.
136. *Morgan's Point,* (Mystic,) Fishers' Island Sound.
138. *New London Harbor,* Connecticut.
145. *Cedar Island,* Gardiner's Bay.
154. *New Haven Long Wharf,* Long Island Sound.
167. *Throgg's Neck,* Long Island Sound.
174. *Sandy Hook,* entrance to New York Bay.
189. *Elbow Beacon,* Newark Bay.
440, 441. *Plattsburgh Beacons,* Lake Champlain.
443. *Point au Roche,* Lake Champlain.
445. *Windmill Point,* Lake Champlain.

The following-named stations have not been mentioned elsewhere:

121. *Rose Island,* Narragansett Bay, Rhode Island.
122. *Dutch Island,* Narragansett Bay, Rhode Island.
124. *Prudence Island,* Narragansett Bay, Rhode Island.
125. *Bristol Ferry,* entrance to Mount Hope Bay, Rhode Island.
134. *Stonington Harbor,* Connecticut.
146. *Saybrook,* mouth of Connecticut River.
147. *Calves' Island,* Connecticut River.
159. *Old Field Point,* Long Island Sound.
163. *Norwalk Island,* Long Island Sound.
164. *Great Captain's Island,* Long Island Sound.
168. *North Brother Island,* East River, New York.
172, 173. *Highlands of Navesink,* New Jersey, New York Bay.
176. *West Beacon,* Sandy Hook, New York Bay.
179. *Point Comfort Beacon,* entrance to New York Bay.
180. *Waackaack Beacon,* entrance to New York Bay.
182. *New Dorp Beacon,* Staten Island, New York Bay.
185. *Robbin's Reef,* New York Harbor.
186. *Bergen Point,* Newark Bay, New Jersey.

187. *Corner Stake*, opposite Elizabethport, New Jersey.
188. *Passaic Light*, near mouth of Passaic River, New Jersey.
190. *Stony Point*, Hudson River.
191. *West Point*, Hudson River.
193. *Rondout*, Hudson River.
195. *Four-mile Point*, Hudson River.
196. *Coxsackie*, Hudson River.

UNLIGHTED BEACONS, INCLUDING SPINDLES.

All the beacons and spindles in the following list are in good condition, unless otherwise stated.

1. *East Lime Rock*, near Newport.—A granite structure, surmounted by an iron spindle and cage.
2. *South Point*, Rose Island, Narragansett Bay.—Granite structure, surmounted by a spindle and cage.
3. *Halfway Rock*, three-fourths of a mile southward of Prudence Island Point, Narragansett Bay.—Spindle, with square cage.
4. *Bullock's Point*, Narragansett Bay.—Stone beacon, with iron spindle and day-mark.
5. *Pawtuxet Beacon*, Narragansett Bay.—Of stone.
6. *Pumham Beacon*, Providence River.—A stone beacon, with vane and ball.
7. *Muscle Bed*, east side of the channel below Bristol Ferry, Rhode Island.—A stone beacon, with iron spindle and day-mark.
8. *Borden's Flats*, opposite to Fall River.—A stone beacon, with iron column and day-mark.
9. *Castle Island*, near north end of Hog Island, Bristol Harbor.—A stone beacon, surmounted by a red ball. The foundation requires repairing and protection.
10. *Allen's Rock*, Warren River.—Stone beacon, one-eighth mile north of Adam's Point.
11. *Warwick, or Spindle Rock*, west channel of Narragansett Bay, and entrance to Greenwich Harbor, between Warwick Neck and Pojack Point.—Iron spindle, with square wooden cage.
12. *White Rock Beacon*, at the entrance of Wickford Harbor, Narragansett Bay.—Stone beacon, with iron column and day-mark.
13. *Watch Hill Spindle*, entrance to Fisher's Island Sound from Light-house southwest by south three-fourths of a mile.—Stands on a rock, which is bare at low water, and is surmounted by a cage.
14. *Sugar Reef Beacon*, Fisher's Island Sound.—Iron-pile beacon with cage-work day-mark in the form of a cone.
15. *East or Catumb Reef Spindle*, entrance to Fisher's Island Sound by Lord's Channel, one and one-fourth miles east of east point of Fisher's Island.—An iron-pile beacon, with square cage-work.
16. *West or Wiccopesset Spindle Rock*, entrance to Fisher's Island Sound by Lord's Channel.—Northwest of East Spindle two-thirds of a mile.
17. *Latimer's Reef*, Fisher's Island Sound, one mile northwest of east point of Fisher's Island, and three-fourths of a mile southeast of Eel Grass Shoal Light-vessel.—An iron spindle, bearing a square cage-work.
18. *Ellis's Reef*, Fisher's Island Sound, three-fourths of a mile northwest of Eel Grass Shoal Light-vessel.—An iron spindle, with a square cage-work.
19. *Ram Island Reef*, Fisher's Island Sound. One-half of a mile southeast of Ram Island.

20. *Spindle on the Whale*, entrance to the Mystic River.—As reported last year, this spindle was carried away by ice. It is proposed to build a beacon of stone, bearing a day-mark, at the estimated cost of $5,000.

21. *Crook's Spindle*, Mystic River.—Is an iron spindle, with a keg on top.

22. *Groton Long Point*, Fisher's Island Sound.—An iron spindle, bearing a cage-work in the form of an inverted cone.

23. *Sea-flower, or Potter's Reef Beacon*, Fisher's Island Sound, northwest of *North Dumpling Light* one mile.—Remains as reported last year. It is a very important mark in Fisher's Island Sound, and recommended for immediate reconstruction. It is proposed to build a granite structure for the purpose of upholding the spindle and cage of the old beacon. Estimated cost, $4,200.

24. *Black Ledge*, entrance to New London Harbor.—An iron shaft, bearing a cage-work day-mark, formed by two cones connected at the vertices.

25. *Saybrook Beacon*, Connecticut River.—Stone beacon, with globe on Saybrook Bar.

26. *Hen and Chickens*, Long Island Sound.—Iron spindle bearing a square cage, painted black.

27. *Branford Reef Beacon*, Long Island Sound.—Granite beacon, surmounted by an iron shaft, bearing a black day-mark.

28. *Quixe's Ledge*, entrance to New Haven Harbor, Connecticut.—An iron spindle, with a cask on top; stands on a rock which is dry at half tide.

29. *Southwest Ledge Spindle*, entrance to New Haven Harbor, Connecticut.—Marked by a second-class buoy.

30. *Stratford River Beacon*, entrance to Stratford River.—Granite beacon, with iron column and day-mark.

31. *Inner Beacon*, Bridgeport Harbor, Connecticut.—A frustum of a square pyramid of wood, surmounted by a wooden mast, with a cask, painted black.

32. *Outer Beacon*, Bridgeport Harbor, Connecticut.—The same as the inner beacon.

33. *Black Rock Beacon*, Long Island Sound.—An iron-pile beacon, with a cage on top.

34. *Southport Beacon*.—Granite beacon, with iron column and day-mark.

35. *Southport Breakwater Beacon*.—Granite beacon, with iron column and day-mark.

36. *Norwalk Beacon*, southwest of Norwalk Island, Connecticut.—A granite structure, supporting a shaft and day-mark of iron.

37. *Great Reef*, off Norwalk Island, entrance to Norwalk Harbor.—A wooden spindle, with cage day-mark, is in course of construction.

38. *Sand Spit*, on the south point of Sand Spit, Sag Harbor.—This beacon, having been destroyed by ice, is being replaced by a stone beacon, surmounted by a wooden tower.

39. *Oyster Pond Point*, Plum Gut, entrance to Gardiner's Bay.—As reported last year. A reef runs out into Plum Gut, which is bare at low water. It is proposed to erect a stone beacon upon it to guide vessels running into Gardiner's Bay clear of this danger. Estimated cost, $5,000.

40. *Success Rock*, Long Island Sound.—An iron shaft, with conical cage-work.

41. *Romer Beacon*, on the west side of Romer Shoal, entrance to the Bay of New York.—A granite structure in the form of a frustum of a cone, surmounted by a wooden mast and square cage day-mark. The

repairs authorized by the appropriation of March 3, 1871, will be made during this season.

42. *Mill Reef Beacon,* Kill Van Kull, opposite New Brighton.—This is a sheet-iron beacon, filled in with concrete, and secured to a granite base. It is conical in shape, and supports an iron shaft with an iron cage on top.

STATEN ISLAND LIGHT-HOUSE DEPOT.

Building for offices.—The work on this building, having been suspended more than one year for want of funds, has been resumed, and the structure will be completed and ready for occupation by November.

Shed and Wharf.—The work authorized by the appropriation of July 15, 1870, has been completed. The basin in front of the depot has been dredged to a depth of ten feet at low-water, and is now a safe harbor for the vessels connected with the Light-house service. Adjacent to the basin a coal bin of 800 tons capacity has been built. The depot being situated at the foot of a slope, which is full of springs, requires a system of drainage and grading. The estimated cost for this work, in addition to the expenses of keeping the depot and buildings in order, is $20,000.

LEGISLATION CEDING JURISDICTION OVER LIGHT-HOUSE SITES.

A circular letter from the Light-House Board of July 11, 1870, called for the names of such States in this district as had not passed, first, a general law ceding jurisdiction over land purchased by the United States from time to time for public uses; and, second, a general law providing for the acquirement of land by the United States in cases of disagreement with the owners. Letters were addressed to the secretaries of state of New Jersey, Vermont, Connecticut, Rhode Island, and New York, inquiring if these laws had been passed, and it was subsequently learned that none of these States had passed such general laws, the custom being uniform to pass special acts for each case, where land was required. Subsequently letters were addressed to the governors of Rhode Island, Connecticut, New Jersey, and New York asking the passage of these general laws, and the Engineer of the district personally urged their passage at the capitals of the States named. Rhode Island passed the general law, and in addition a special act, ceding the State's right over certain points in the navigable waters of the State. New York adhered to its former custom, and only passed a special act to cover certain sites named in the acts, and limiting the quantity of land. It is not known if the other States in the districts have passed any acts. The passage of these acts by the States of New York and Rhode Island was delayed until late in the session of their legislatures, and the works appropriated for in the act of Congress of July 15, 1870, dependent upon the passage of these laws ceding jurisdiction, were consequently delayed until very near the close of the last fiscal year.

Number of boxes, packages, and barrels received at and shipped from Light-house depot, Staten Island, from October 1, 1870, to June 30, 1871.

	Boxes.	Packages, cans, &c.	Barrels.	Total.	Same period of time last year.	Increase.
Received	1,840	3,775	2,809	8,424	4,996	3,428
Shipped	1,389	3,338	2,293	7,020	5,035	1,085
Total	3,229	7,113	5,102	15,444	10,931	4,513

Lens apparatus received at and shipped from Light-house depot, Staten Island, from October 1, 1870, to June 30, 1871.

	1st order.	2d order.	3d order.	3½ order.	4th order.	5th order.	6th order.	Steamer lenses.	Pressed lenses.	Canal lenses.	Totals.
Received	1		3		6	1	1	15	4		31
Shipped			2	1	6	5		9		4	27
Total	1		5	1	12	6	1	24	4	4	58

Articles manufactured and repaired in lamp-shop at Light-house depot, Staten Island, from October 1, 1870, to June 30, 1871.

	Lenses.	Lamps.	Lamp burners.	Miscellaneous articles.	Total.
Manufactured	11	70	216	485	782
Repaired	5	61	20	38	144
Total	16	131	236	543	926

FOURTH DISTRICT.

The Fourth Light-house District extends from Squam Inlet, New Jersey, to and including Metomkin Inlet, Virginia. It also includes Delaware Bay, River, and tributaries.

Inspector.—Commodore William H. Macomb, United States Navy.

Engineer.—Brevet Brigadier General I. C. Woodruff, Lieutenant Colonel of Engineers, United States Army.

In this district there are—

Light-houses and lighted beacons 18
Light-vessels 3
Buoys actually in position 104
Spare buoys for relief and to supply losses 83
Tender (steam) *Violet* 1

The numbers preceding the names of stations correspond with those of the "Light-house List of the Atlantic, Gulf, and Pacific Coast of the United States," issued January 1, 1871.

208. *Barnegat*, New Jersey.—The semi-monthly measurements along the beach near the Light-house have been continued throughout the year. During the winter a portion of the works of protection was damaged to some extent, though not seriously, part of the riprapping having slidden into deep water, allowing the sea to pass over and wash out the sand. Three stone jetties, for the protection of the former works, have been built, requiring 993 tons of stone, which will, it is believed, prove satisfactory. The fence around the building has been rebuilt.

210. *Absecum, New Jersey.*—The semi-monthly measurements along the beach in the vicinity of the Light-house have been made throughout the year. Favorable changes have taken place, and no apprehension for the safety of the station need be entertained. A store-house is now being built, and repairs to the keeper's dwelling made, which will be completed during the next month. The authorities of Atlantic City have not yet furnished the grant from the property owners, for the occupation of the land required for sites for the works of protection heretofore appropriated for by Congress, and the money still remains in the Treasury.

Hereford Inlet, on the coast of New Jersey, ten and three-fourths nautical miles north of *Cape May Light-house.*—A small light, say a fourth order, is respectfully recommended for this place, as it would be of importance to the coal trade, and to steamers navigating Delaware Bay and River, and to mark the entrance to the inlet, where there is a good harbor of refuge for small coasting vessels. Estimated cost $25,000.

Cross Ledge Light Station, Delaware Bay.—An estimate has been submitted for the erection of an iron screw-pile Light-house to take the place of the Light-vessel now occupying that station. An appropriation was made many years since for this Light-house, but it was found impracticable at that time to erect it, and the appropriation reverted to the surplus fund. Congress ordered subsequently (in 1867) a survey of this shoal. An estimate is submitted.

219. *Upper Middle or Cross Ledge Light-vessel.*—No repairs have been made to this vessel since the last report. This vessel was compelled to leave her station in the Delaware Bay January 10, on account of heavy ice; was returned to it again on the 25th, and remained until the 27th, when the ice again coming down the bay very heavily she was driven from her station, and was picked up by the city ice-boat and towed to New Castle, Delaware, where she remained until March 4, when she was returned to her station. Such absences of light is a great injury to commerce, but it may be remedied by building a Light-house on the shoal.

220. *Mahon's River*, Delaware, Delaware Bay.—The abrasion of the marsh at this station has been so great as to compel a change in the site of the Light-house. There is a good location about a quarter of a mile north of the present site, which will serve equally well the purposes of navigation. The estimate for a screw-pile building is $15,000.

223. *Reedy Island*, Delaware Bay.—Extensive repairs have been made to the bank inclosing the buildings, as follows: The earth bank has been thoroughly repaired and raised fifteen inches along the eastern side for a distance of four hundred feet, the outer slope protected with quarry stone imbedded in fresh mud, the top of the bank roughly paved with stone, a new sluice for draining, and the ditches cleaned out. A new roof has been put on the dwelling, and the plank platform repaired.

224. *Christiana*, Delaware, Delaware Bay.—Extensive operations have been going on to fit this station as a buoy depot and winter harbor for light-vessels. The upper wharf has been completed; it is thirty-two feet wide and extends into the Christiana River one hundred and sixty-

four feet to eight feet water at ordinary low tide; the piling, grillage, stone piers, and stone-work of the cistern are completed for the first or upper building. The frame and other materials are so far advanced, it is believed, that it will be ready for occupation by the 1st of next September. This building will be fifty by one hundred and forty feet in plan, two stories of eight feet each in height, the first or lower floor divided into one room fifty by sixty-three feet, the balance arranged for storing iron and spar buoys, chains, ballast balls, and sinkers. The second story, fifty by one hundred and forty feet, for storing sails, rigging, small boats, &c. The piles for the foundation of the second building are all driven, the building to be fifty by one hundred and fifty feet in plan, one story of ten feet, to admit first-class iron buoys. The piles for the second wharf are also driven; the wharf is thirty-two feet wide and extends one hundred and forty feet into the river, to eight feet water at ordinary low tide. A new sluice has been placed in the bank for draining the inclosure.

Near Chester, Pennsylvania, Delaware River.—In conformity with the instructions of the Light-House Board, accompanied by a petition from citizens of Chester for a light at that harbor, an examination has been made by the Light-house Inspector and Engineer of the district, who report that a light upon the south end of Little Tinicum Island would subserve the wants of the trade at Chester as well as the general wants of commerce of the port of Philadelphia. It would also be serviceable in marking the channel to the quarantine grounds. The structure recommended by the Inspector and Engineer is a screw-pile Light-house with a lens of the sixth order, the estimated cost of which is $17,000.

225. *Fort Mifflin*, Delaware River.—The foundation pier has been entirely rebuilt from line of low water, and the dwelling has been removed back from the southeastern front. Riprap stone has been placed around the front of the pier to prevent abrasion.

The stations not named heretofore are as follows:

209. *Tucker's Beach*, New Jersey, near Little Egg Harbor.
214. *Cape Henlopen Beacon*, entrance to Delaware Bay.
216. *Brandywine Shoal*, *screw-pile Light-house*, Delaware Bay.
221. *Cohansey*, New Jersey, Delaware Bay.
222. *Bombay Hook*, Delaware, Delaware Bay.
226. *Fenwick's Island*, sea-coast of Delaware.
227. *Assateague*, sea-coast of Virginia.

FIFTH DISTRICT.

The Fifth District extends from Metomkin Inlet, Virginia, to include New River Inlet, North Carolina, as well as Chesapeake Bay and its tributaries, and Albemarle and Pamlico Sounds.

Inspector.—Commodore F. Stanly, United States Navy.
Engineer.—Brevet Brigadier General James H. Simpson, Colonel of Engineers, United States Army, to December 10, 1870; Brevet Lieutenant Colonel Peter C. Hains, Captain of Engineers, United States Army, present Engineer.

In this district there are—

Light-houses and lighted beacons	67
Light-vessels	2
Day or unlighted beacons and stakes	72
Buoys actually in position	509
Spare buoys for relief and to supply losses	529
Tenders (steam) *Heliotrope* and *Tulip*	2
Tenders (sail) *Maggie* and *Spray*	2

The numbers preceding the names of stations correspond with the "Light-house List of the Atlantic, Gulf, and Pacific Coasts of the United States," issued January 1, 1871.

231. *The Light-house on "The Thimble,"* entrance to Hampton Roads, Virginia.—The want of a good screw-pile Light-house on the Horseshoe Bar, a shoal extending out from the main-land at Fortress Monroe, about five or six miles in a direction east by north from that place, has long been felt. This large bar is a source of danger to all vessels coming into Hampton Roads. The shoalest point of the bar has on it eleven feet of water at mean low tide, at a point called "*The Thimble,*" about two and a half miles east of the main-land. South of Horseshoe Bar, and only a little more than half a mile from it, is another long bar, running in a direction almost parallel to it, called *Willoughby's Spit.* Between these two bars there is ample water for the largest vessels afloat. A Light-vessel has been used to mark the channel between these bars and guide them clear of the dangers on either side. It is believed, however, that the same end may be attained at much less annual expense by the erection of an iron screw-pile Light-house on "*The Thimble*" of Horseshoe Bar, under the general law on the subject and out of the general appropriation, as a substitute for the Light-vessel, to be visible from the sea, at the entrance to Chesapeake Bay. The substructure will consist of seven wrought-iron screw-piles; one in the center, the other six ranged about it in the form of a hexagon and screwed into the shoal a depth of fifteen feet. The superstructure will be a frame building, hexagonal in plan, surmounted by a lantern, and will exhibit a fixed white light of the fourth order. In order to distinguish it from the light at Fortress Monroe, the latter will be changed to a red light. The position of this Light-house being very exposed, particularly to strong easterly winds, it is required to be of more than ordinary strength. It will be advisable, also, to protect the site and give more stability to the foundation by throwing in about it loose stones to a depth of about three feet. Borings, with an artesian well-boring apparatus, were made on the proposed site, when it was found that the shoal consisted of a fine light-colored sand with black specks on top and extending to a depth of ten feet. It then gradually becomes darker and finer to a depth of twenty-four feet, at which point the borings ceased. The construction will be commenced without delay, and it is hoped to have it finished by the last of December. This will render it unnecessary to retain the Light-vessel at *Willoughby Spit,* and she will be withdrawn. She is now in need of extensive repairs, the cost of which alone would almost suffice to build the Light-house, besides being very much less expensive to maintain. The completion of this Light-house and that off *Benoni's Point,* Choptank River, will complete the changes of all existing Light-vessels authorized in this district, to screw-pile Light-houses.

Lambert's Point.—In the last annual report of the Light-House Board, the attention of Congress was drawn to the fact that a Light-house had been strongly urged for the shoal off this point, and an appropriation for this purpose was made. The plans are now being prepared for a small substantial structure on six piles, similar to those at *Point of Shoals* and *White Shoals,* James River, omitting the ice-fending piles, which will not be required at this station.

235. *White Shoals,* James River, Virginia.

236. *Point of Shoals,* James River, Virginia.

The two screw-pile Light-houses authorized for *White Shoals* and *Point of Shoals* were built during the past year.

241. *York Spit Light-house.*—At the date of the last annual report the

iron-work of this structure was set up, properly coupled together and braced, staging removed, and the frame of the house in position. During the month of November the joiner's work was completed, painting finished, and the lens set up. The Light was exhibited for the first time November 15, 1870, and the Light-vessel which formerly marked this dangerous shoal was permanently withdrawn. This Light-house is built on fourteen wooden piles, incased in cast-iron sleeves, and stands in twelve feet water, near the end of the shoal at the mouth of York River, from which it derives its name.

256. *Choptank River Light-house*, Maryland.—It is designed, under the general law, to replace the Light-vessel at this place, which serves to mark the entrance to the Choptank River, by an iron screw-pile Light-house, similar in construction to those at York Spit and Wolf Trap, on the Chesapeake Bay, omitting four of the fender piles. The Light-house will stand in eleven feet water, mean tide, on a bar at the mouth of the river, distant about one and a half mile in a southwest direction from *Benoni's Point*, and marking three channels. After due public notice a contract was made in March with the lowest bidder, for the construction of this Light-house. The iron-work has been prepared and the superstructure framed. It is expected that this Light-house will be completed by the last of October, and enable the Light-vessel to be permanently withdrawn.

260. *Love Point Shoal Light-house*, mouth of Chester River, Maryland.—An appropriation of $15,000 was made by Congress for a Light-house on the shoal at the mouth of the Chester River, near the north end of Kent Island, the exact location of which was fixed at a point on the shoal in ten feet water, mean tide, distant from *Love Point* about one mile, in a northeasterly direction. The Light-house will be a duplicate of the one constructing for Choptank River. A contract was made for the construction of this work (after publicly advertising for proposals) with the lowest bidder. The contract requires the work to be finished by October 1, 1871.

Craighill Channel, in the Chesapeake Bay, at the entrance to the Patapsco River.—This channel extends from a point about one mile north-east of *Seven-foot Knoll*, where it intersects the Brewerton Channel, leading into the Patapsco River in a direction almost due south about five miles, or just beyond the Belvidere Shoals. It is now about two hundred and sixty feet wide, and, with the exception of a few places where there are lumps, is twenty-one feet deep. Congress made an appropriation last year of $50,000 for the improvement of this, together with the Brewerton Channel. It is understood that a sufficient amount of this sum is to be applied to widening the Craighill Channel to five hundred feet and deepening it to twenty-two feet, mean tide. Large vessels coming up the bay to enter the Patapsco will follow this channel until the range beacons at *Hawkins* and *Leading Points* are in line. They can then follow the Brewerton Channel without difficulty into the harbor of Baltimore. The latter channel is acknowledged to be of great benefit to navigation. It can be followed at night, by means of the range beacons above referred to, as well as by day. There seems to be no doubt but that the new channel will be of equal importance to navigation, and the urgency of making it available at night for the large commerce of the city of Baltimore is manifest. This can be done by the establishment of range beacons near the north end of the channel. This channel has the advantage of saving about five miles in distance to large vessels bound to Baltimore from the lower bay; avoids much, if not all, of the dangers usually experienced from the accumulation of ice in the lower part of the Brewerton Channel during the winter; is much easier navigated, or rather would be if range beacons were established, and, being a direct prolongation of the resultant of the united currents of the Patapsco and Chesapeake Bay, is more permanent in its character. It is an established fact that the current produced by the outflow of water from the river and bay tends to deepen the channel by washing out the material on the bottom, and there is no doubt but that this channel, once improved to a depth of twenty-two and width of five hundred feet, will always maintain at least those dimensions. There is, therefore, no doubt but that this channel will always be used for navigation purposes, and the range beacons now so much needed will always be required.

An appropriation of $40,000 for the purpose of establishing these beacons was asked during last session of Congress. It was then proposed to locate the beacons, one on the north, the other on the south side of Miller's Island, some five miles north of the upper end of the channel. This location has the advantage of being more protected from the heavy ice from the Susquehanna than any other position that could be selected, but the distance from the southern entrance to the channel is so great, being about twelve miles, that it would be necessary to use very strong lights and to place the rear one at a considerable elevation. Their value would be much enhanced by locating them some four or five miles nearer. This can readily be done by building artificial islands and protecting the banks with a riprap wall of loose stone. The material excavated by the dredges in deepening the channel can be used for the purpose of forming these islands. It is understood that the Engineer Officer in charge of this improvement has been authorized to deposit this material for that purpose at such places as may be selected. The establishment of these beacons need not increase the number of Lights in this vicinity for the reason that they will render the use of those at *North Point* unnecessary, and they can be discontinued. The estimated cost of the range beacons for this channel is $45,000, for which an appropriation is asked.

280. *Body's Island Light-house.*—An appropriation was made by Congress to re-establish this very important coast Light, the old Light-house having been destroyed during the war. A careful study of the topography of the country, and the action of the water-flow in and out of Pamlico Sound through Oregon Inlet, resulted in the abandonment of the old site on the south side of the inlet and the selection of another on the north side. This will be one of the most important Lights on the coast, and the necessity of placing it in a safe position, free from the danger of destruction by the encroachments of the sea, could not be over-estimated. The old site was subject to this danger. Previous to 1846, there was no inlet at this place, but during the early part of September of that year, heavy southerly winds banked up the waters of Albemarle and Pamlico Sounds several feet above their ordinary level. Then came northerly winds driving the water back, overflowing the narrow sand-bank which separated the waters of the ocean from those of Pamlico Sound. By this outflow of water Oregon Inlet was opened in one night. Since that time it has maintained a character of instability, sometimes widening and deepening in places, filling up in others, all the time gradually working to the south. This inlet is not now used for navigation purposes, there being only a depth of four feet of water over the bulkhead or inside bar. During the rebellion, however, the rebels built on the south side a fort called Fort Oregon. The site of

this fort can no longer be seen. It has been washed away in the gradual movement of the inlet to the south.

The site of the old Light, which at one time was a considerable distance from the inlet, is now only about four hundred yards. The testimony of residents in the vicinity confirms the fact that the inlet is working to the south, and that its progress is not slow. The old site could doubtless have been made use of by protecting it with jetties, but only at great expense. In view of these facts it was not deemed advisable to erect this important Light-house on a site so insecure. Another site, about one and a half mile farther north and on the north side of the inlet, protected on the west by Roanoke Island from the action of storms tending to drive the waters of Pamlico Sound toward the sea, was accordingly selected. The land at this place being held at a merely nominal sum, the purchase of fifteen acres was made, the perfection of a title in the United States being delayed, however, in getting the necessary act of the State of North Carolina ceding jurisdiction, and in complying with certain other legal forms. The site and plan of the Light-house having been determined on, contracts were made, after due public notice inviting proposals, with the lowest bidders for furnishing the material to be used in the structure. The tower will be one hundred and fifty feet high, exhibiting a first-class sea-coast Light, focal plane one hundred and fifty-three feet above the level of the sea, and will be visible at a distance of more than eighteen nautical miles. About the middle of June a working party was dispatched to this station with orders to erect the necessary temporary buildings for storage and quartering the workmen, build a narrow tramway over which the material can be easily transported from the water to the site, and a temporary wharf, on which to land it. It is expected that these preparations will be completed in about two months, when the work on the foundation of the tower itself will be begun. The completion of this tower will supply a want long felt by the commerce of the country. Every effort will be made to finish the Light-house the present year, but the frequency of storms in this latitude generally causes delay in the prosecution of works of this nature, and it is scarcely probable that the entire work will be completed within that time. An appropriation of $15,000 for the fiscal year 1872-'73 is asked to complete the work.

A First-class Light-house between Cape Henry and Body's Island, North Carolina.—With the completion of the Light-house at *Body's Island* there will remain only one important interval of unlighted coast on the Atlantic from the St. Croix, Maine, to about Mosquito Inlet, on the coast of Florida. That dark space will be embraced between *Cape Henry* and *Body's Island,* a distance of eighty miles and an unlighted space of forty miles, at the center of which there should be a first-order Light, so that from *Cape Henry* to *Cape Hatteras* the broad side of that long stretch of low land and dangers could not be approached within eighteen or twenty miles without seeing a warning of danger. In order to avoid the strong current of the Gulf Stream, vessels bound round *Cape Hatteras* from the northern and eastern ports run inside of the cold wall of water of that stream, within which they have a favorable current of one mile per hour on an average, and a smoother sea in bad weather; but in the absence of powerful sea-coast Lights sufficiently near each other to give warning of approach to danger, many vessels laden with valuable lives and cargoes have been lost between these points. It is now believed that the construction of this tower should be no longer delayed. A glance at the chart of the coast will show its importance. An appropriation therefor of $60,000 is accordingly submitted. An appropriation was made about ten years ago for this Light, but the money reverted to the Treasury. The Light-house should be similar to that being built at *Body's Island*, with a focal plane one hundred and fifty feet above the sea, and visible at a distance of eighteen nautical miles.

281. *Cape Hatteras*, North Carolina.—This important Light-house was well advanced toward completion at the date of last annual report. During the month of December the new lens was received and set up, and on the 16th of the same month the light from the new tower was exhibited. The lens on the old tower was then removed and sent to the Light-house depot at Staten Island, New York. The new tower has been covered with a cement wash to protect it from the effects of the weather, the upper part (projected against the sky) colored red, the lower part (projected against the foliage in the rear) colored white; all the iron-work of stairs, lantern, &c., painted, and the tower inclosed in a neat iron fence. During the month of February the old tower, being no longer of any use and in danger of falling during some heavy storm, was blown up and totally destroyed. In addition to the finishing of the new tower, a brick dwelling for the principal keeper of the Light-station was built and inclosed in a neat picket fence. The above completed the work at this station.

Hatteras Inlet, North Carolina.—A Light was authorized March 3, 1859, to be established at the Hatteras Inlet, the entrance to the sounds of North Carolina, but it was not commenced before the breaking out of the rebellion, and afterward it could not be built. This is at present the best inlet leading to and from the sounds of North Carolina, with which there is a very large trade. This inlet is fourteen miles southwest from Cape Hatteras, within the range of the influence of that cape upon the weather, and as the channel is narrow and only marked by buoys, it is dangerous to attempt to enter or pass out at night for want of a small Light. The estimated cost of this Light-house is $18,000, for which an appropriation is asked.

296. *Cape Lookout*, North Carolina.—The tower at this station has had some repairs made to it during the present year, but the keeper's dwelling is in a very dilapidated condition, and, though improved somewhat, is too old to be susceptible of the repairs it requires. There is positive danger of the building being destroyed in stormy weather. This would leave the keepers on a desolate coast without any shelter near their station. A new building is very essential to the health and comfort of the keepers, independent of the danger to which their lives are exposed in the present dwelling. An estimate of $10,000 is respectfully submitted to supply this defect.

During the year repairs and renovations, more or less extensive, have been made at each of the following-named Light-stations:

233. *Craney Island screw-pile Light-house*, Virginia, mouth of Elizabeth River.

234. *Naval Hospital Light*, on wharf at the Naval Hospital, Virginia, Elizabeth River.

237. *Deep Water Shoals screw-pile Light-house*, Virginia, James River.

238. *Jordan's Point Light*, Virginia, James River.

264. *Fort Carroll*, Maryland, Patapsco River.

266. *Hawkins' Point*, Maryland, Patapsco River, lower range beacon for the Brewerton Channel.

268. *Lazaretto Point*, Maryland, Patapsco River.

283. *Ocracoke*, North Carolina, entrance to Ocracoke Inlet.

284. *Southwest Point Royal Shoal screw-pile Light-house*, North Caro-lina, Pamlico Sound.

285. *Northwest Point Royal Shoal screw-pile Light-house*, North Caro-lina, Pamlico Sound.

286. *Harbor Island screw-pile Light-house*, between Pamlico and Core Sounds, North Carolina.

287. *Brant Island Shoal screw-pile Light-house*, North Carolina, Pam-lico Sound.

288. *Neuse River Light*, North Carolina, west side of entrance to Neuse River.

289. *Pamlico Point*, North Carolina, south side of entrance to Pam-lico River, Pamlico Sound.

290. *Long Shoal screw-pile Light-house*, North Carolina, east end of Long Shoal, Pamlico Sound.

291. *Roanoke Marshes screw-pile Light-house*, North Carolina, east side of channel connecting Pamlico and Croatan Sounds.

293. *North River screw-pile Light-house*, North Carolina, on bar at entrance to North River.

294. *Wade's Point screw-pile Light-house*, North Carolina, west side of Pasquotank River, Albemarle Sound.

295. *Roanoke River screw-pile Light-house*, North Carolina, near mouth of Roanoke River, Albemarle Sound.

The following are the names of the Light-stations in this district not mentioned elsewhere, some of which are now in need of repairs:

228. *Hog Island*, Virginia, west point of Hog Island, Great Matche-pungo Inlet.

229. *Cape Charles*, Virginia, entrance to Chesapeake Roads.

230. *Cape Henry*, Virginia, entrance to Chesapeake Bay.

232. *Old Point Comfort*, Virginia, entrance to Hampton Roads.

239. *Cherrystone*, Virginia, mouth of Cherrystone Inlet, Chesapeake Bay.

240. *Back River*, Virginia, entrance to Back River.

242. *New Point Comfort*, Virginia, entrance to Mobjack Bay, Chesa-peake Bay.

243. *Wolf Trap screw-pile Light-house*, Virginia, Wolf Trap Shoal, Chesapeake Bay.

244. *Stingray Point*, Virginia, mouth of Rappahannock River, Chesa-peake Bay.

245. *Windmill Point screw-pile Light-house*, Virginia, Windmill Point Shoals, Chesapeake Bay.

246. *Watt's Island*, Virginia, Tangier Sound, Chesapeake Bay.

247. *James' Island screw-pile Light-house*, Maryland, Tangier Sound, Chesapeake Bay.

248. *Somers' Cove screw-pile Light-house*, Maryland, Tangier Sound, Chesapeake Bay.

249. *Smith's Point screw-pile Light-house*, Virginia, mouth of Potomac River, Chesapeake Bay.

250. *Frog Point*, Maryland, Smith's Island, Chesapeake Bay.

251. *Clay Island*, Maryland, Tangier Sound, Chesapeake Bay.

252. *Point Lookout*, Maryland, entrance to Potomac River, Chesa-peake Bay.

253. *Hooper's Straits screw-pile Light-house*, Maryland, off mouth of Honga River, Chesapeake Bay.

254. *Cove Point*, Maryland, mouth of Patuxent River, Chesapeake Bay.

255. *Sharp's Island screw-pile Light-house,* Maryland, mouth of Choptank River, Chesapeake Bay.

256. *Thomas's Point,* north side of mouth of South River, Maryland, Chesapeake Bay.

258. *Greenbury Point,* Maryland, mouth of Severn River, Chesapeake Bay.

259. *Sandy Point,* Maryland, Chesapeake Bay.

261. *Seven-foot Knoll screw-pile Light-house,* Maryland, mouth of Patapsco River, Chesapeake Bay.

262. *North Point,* (lower,) Maryland, entrance to Patapsco River, Chesapeake Bay.

263. *North Point,* (upper,) Maryland, Patapsco River, Chesapeake Bay.

265. *Hawkins' Point,* (upper,) Maryland, Patapsco River.

267. *Leading Point screw-pile Light-house,* Maryland, Patapsco River.

269. *Pool's Island,* Maryland, off mouth of Gunpowder River, Chesapeake Bay.

270. *Turkey Point,* Maryland, mouth of Elk River, head of Chesapeake Bay.

271. *Fishing Battery,* Maryland, mouth of Susquehanna River, Chesapeake Bay.

272. *Havre de Grace,* Maryland, Concord Point, mouth of Susquehanna River, Chesapeake Bay.

273. *Piney Point,* Maryland, Potomac River.

274. *Blackistone's Island,* Maryland, entrance to Clement's Bay, Potomac River.

275. *Lower Cedar Point screw-pile Light-house,* Virginia, Yates Shoal, Potomac River.

276. *Upper Cedar Point screw-pile Light-house,* Maryland, off mouth of Tobacco River, Potomac River.

277. *Fort Washington,* Maryland, Potomac River.

278. *Jones' Point,* Virginia, Potomac River, near Alexandria.

279. *Bowler's Rock screw-pile Light-house,* Virginia, Rappahannock River.

292. *Croatan screw-pile Light-House,* North Carolina, Pamlico Sound.

DEPOTS.

The depot at *Lazaretto Point,* which was in a very dilapidated condition, has been placed in thorough repair. The work-shop has been painted inside, brick-work covered with cement wash, new slate-roof put on, and lightning-rods repaired. The wharf at the landing has also been repaired, and a contract made to have the stone wall around the front of the lot rebuilt. This work is now almost completed; the depot will then be in excellent order. A quantity of old, unserviceable material was gathered together and sold at auction, and the proceeds turned into the Treasury.

At the depot at *Portsmouth,* Virginia, the site for which was selected about a year ago, there has been a good wharf built, the lot inclosed in a board fence, and skids made on which to lay iron buoys and have them repaired.

The Engineer steam-tender *Tulip* was, at the date of the last annual report, very much in need of extensive repairs. A contract was made, after public advertisement in the daily papers, to have her hauled out on the ways and the necessary repairs made. This work was accomplished on the 10th of June. She is now in excellent condition for service. Previous to making the repairs, and since they were completed, she has been continually employed in transporting materials, &c., to new Light-stations, and to such old ones as required repairs, and in inspecting Light-houses in the district.

LIGHT-VESSELS.

Upon the completion of the two screw-pile Light-houses in this district, as substitutes for Light-vessels, there will be no Light-vessels in the district.

SIXTH DISTRICT.

The Sixth District extends from New River, North Carolina, to include Cape Canaveral Light-house, Florida.
Inspector.—Captain Richard T. Renshaw, United States Navy.
Engineer.—Brevet Major William J. Twining, Captain of Engineers, United States Army, until June 21, 1871; Brevet Lieutenant Colonel Peter C. Hains, Captain, Corps of Engineers, United States Army, present engineer.

In this district there are—

Light-houses and lighted beacons	27
Light-houses and lighted beacons destroyed during the rebellion and not rebuilt	14
Day or unlighted beacons and stakes	52
Light-vessels	6
Buoys actually in position	183
Spare buoys for relief and to supply losses	63
Tender (steam) *Alanthus*	1
Tender (sail) *Narragansett*	1

According to previous reports there were fifty-two unlighted beacons in this district. This number includes the staked channels of the St. John's River, Florida, and the inside coast passages. Of these day-marks the greater number were destroyed or have otherwise disappeared, and are being replaced as rapidly as they are required by navigation. Of the seven beacons in the Savannah River, the two on *Oyster Rocks* are serviceable and in good condition; of the remaining five, two have been destroyed by fire and will be rebuilt. There is at present an appropriation for two beacons on *Oyster Rocks*, which will be built at an early day.

The following numbers preceding the names of stations correspond with those of the "Light-house Lists of the Atlantic, Gulf, and Pacific Coast of the United States," published January 1, 1871.

308. *Sullivan's Island Beacon, Charleston Harbor, South Carolina.*—The present beacon-light at this place is a temporary open frame-work, wooden structure, erected upon the roof of a private residence. This light was established in its present position immediately after the surrender of Charleston in the spring of 1865, to enable the vessels of the Navy and those of commerce to navigate safely at night the channel leading from the inside of the outer bar of the main channel to the turning point near Fort Moultrie. An appropriation was made by Congress, March 3, 1859, for rebuilding the two beacon range-lights on *Sullivan's Island*, (which were destroyed during the rebellion,) and on July 20, 1868, an appropriation of $15,000 was made for rebuilding these lights; but failing to obtain valid title to the necessary land upon which to place them, and the required cession of jurisdiction by the State, the appropriation reverted to the Treasury under the operation of the fifth and sixth sections of the act approved July 12, 1870. Another appropriation of $10,000 for these beacons was made by Congress, approved March 3, 1871. The State passed a general act ceding jurisdiction to sites pur-

chased by the United States for Light-house purposes, but it is under-stood that only a title of questionable validity can be given by any citizen claiming to own land on this island. This question is now being investigated. As soon as the title to the necessary land on which to locate the keeper's dwelling is obtained, there will be no unnecessary delay in establishing these important range-lights. Their establishment will render the *Weehauken Light-vessel* now placed in the channel unnecessary, and she can be permanently withdrawn. It is understood that there is now twelve feet water over the old wreck which this Light-vessel marks, and the work of removing the same is still being carried on.

The beacons proposed for this range are detached from the keeper's dwelling. Their heights are respectively thirty-five and fifty feet from sill to focal plane. The illuminating apparatus is to be of the fifth order.

313. *Tybee Light-station*, entrance to the Savannah River, Georgia.—The recent gales, which have caused great damage along the southern coast, have so greatly damaged the Light-house tower at this important Light-station as to render it unsafe and to require the speedy erection of a new tower. The tower, which was built in 1793, is badly cracked, and may fall at any time. Its great age, (seventy-eight years,) the frequent necessary repairs to it during the time it has been standing, and its total neglect during the war of the rebellion, render it impossible to properly repair the present tower. An estimate is submitted for commencing the erection of a new tower near the present one.

Daufuskie Island, Calibogue Sound, South Carolina.—The appropriation asked for the range beacons on this island, to mark the entrance to Calibogue Sound, and to facilitate the passage from Port Royal Harbor to Savannah River, was made by act of Congress approved March 3, 1871. The plans and specifications have been made for the structures, and it only remains to secure a proper site before commencing work.

315. *Tybee Knoll*, Savannah River, Georgia.—An appropriation for erecting a screw-pile Light-house, to take the place of the Light-vessel stationed to mark this dangerous shoal, reverted to the Treasury under the act approved July 12, 1870. A screw-pile Light-house can be built at this place, which will better serve the purpose of navigation and at the same time be much less expensive to maintain than the Light-vessel. Borings show that below a thin stratum of clear, sharp sand, there is a layer of soft mud to a depth of nineteen feet at least, and perhaps considerably farther. This, though it will somewhat increase the expense, will not do so to an unwarrantable extent. The Light-house can be located in from two to five feet water, should stand on six piles, and be built somewhat similar to those in the Chesapeake Bay and sounds of North Carolina. The erection of this Light-house will insure the permanent removal of the Light-vessel now stationed at this place. An estimate is submitted.

Light on the Obstructions in Savannah River.—An ordinary steamboat-lantern is still retained to mark the obstructions in the Savannah River below the city. It is understood that an appropriation by Congress has been made for removing these obstructions. As soon as this work is completed the Light will be no longer required and will be discontinued. Until then, the present arrangement is very economical, and answers every purpose of navigation.

318. *Fig Island*, Savannah River, Georgia.—Such repairs as were necessary for the neatness and preservation of this station were made during the spring. More extensive repairs to the platforms and foundation of the dwelling are now being made.

323. *St. Simon's,* entrance to St. Simon's Sound, Georgia.—This Light-house has been under contract since the fall of 1869, and the time for completion has been extended on several occasions, but the tower is still unfinished, and has only been carried to a height of fifty-one feet above the ground. The death of the contractor, and one of his bondsmen—both of whom died at the work—has recently caused further delay. On account of the climate, work cannot be recommenced till the 1st of No-vember, when it will be taken in hand by the surviving bondsman, and, it is hoped, will be finished early next spring.

, 325. *Amelia Island, North Range,* St. Mary's Bar, Florida.—Plans and estimates have been prepared for a keeper's dwelling, and beacons for this range. As the site is on Government land, near Fort Clinch, there will probably be no delay in regard to the sites, and the work may be done during the present winter.

Dame's Point, St. John's River, Florida.—An examination of the site for this Light-house was made by the Engineer of the district. On sinking an artesian well, the underlying strata were found to consist of soft mud to a depth of sixteen feet. The borings were not carried below this depth. It is believed that a screw-pile light house can be built here, but before it is commenced further examination of the foundation will be made.

328. *St. Augustine,* north end of Anastasia Island, Florida.—An exam-ination was made by the Engineer of the district of Anastasia Island, with reference to the selection of a site for the new Light-house provided for by appropriation approved March 3, 1871. Reports have been received from time to time in regard to the cutting away of the shore line near the old Light. On the 1st of July, 1870, the distance from the angle of the dwelling to high-water mark was seventy feet, and on the 1st of November the distance had been reduced to forty-eight feet; since that time no cutting has taken place. The channel over the bar con-tinues to shift rapidly toward the north; as a result, the inner shoal covers for the present the site, and the force of the ebb-tide is expended along the shore-line to the west,

The opening, or partial closing, of Matanzas Inlet diminishes or in-creases the amount of water discharged by the Matanzas River at St. Augustine. The channel will probably continue to shift to the north, until, by the action of heavy and continued northeast winds, the accu-mulated waters are driven to seek a new outlet toward the southeast. Such changes are of constant occurrence at all the inlets on the coast of East Florida.

Much difficulty has been experienced in procuring a site for the new Light-house. The old Spanish grants and the claims of settlers are in much confusion, but it is to be hoped that the question may be settled by the law officers of the Government at an early day, and that a good title may be obtained to a site which will be safe from encroachments of the sea. The construction of the tower, which will be of the first order, one hundred and fifty feet above the sea, will be commenced as soon as title can be secured.

Mosquito Inlet, east coast of Florida.—The Engineer of the district has visited *Mosquito Inlet* for the purpose of reporting on the necessity and practicability of a Light at that point. In common with all the inlets and harbors on the east coast of Florida, this bar shifts constantly, so that no soundings can be relied on. The general effect of westerly winds is to reduce the depth of water, and that of northeasterly gales to increase it; thus the inlet may be opened or closed one or more times each year. The wrecks lying on or near the bar give a practical illustration of the uncertainty of the channel. For all practical purposes of construction of a Light-house, it may, however, be safely assumed that the material can be delivered without any very serious difficulty or delay, although additional expense would be incurred by reason of the remoteness of the station, and the small-sized vessels that would be required for transportation. As regards the necessity of a Light at this point, it is manifest that the commerce passing through the inlet would not justify an expenditure by the United States for a Light for merely local purposes, or at least that there are other points that may justly take precedence of it. But a Light-house between St. Augustine and Cape Canaveral Lights is necessary as one of a system of coast-lights, and *Mosquito Inlet* is undoubtedly the proper site, as, in the first place, the Light there would answer the double purpose of a harbor and coast guide, and in the second for a landing place, both for the original construction and subsequent supply and inspection, which could be made with more safety and certainty there than at any other point along the open sea-beach. A tower one hundred and fifty feet high, lighted by a first-order Fresnel lens, is recommended for this position, and for the commencement of its construction an estimate of $60,000 is submitted.

At each of the following-named Light-stations there have been repairs and renovations, more or less extensive, during the last year, viz:

297. *Federal Point*, North Carolina, New Inlet, Cape Fear River.
299, 300. *Oak Island*, (Range-lights,) North Carolina, mouth of Cape Fear River.
301. *Georgetown*, South Carolina, entrance to Winyaw Bay.
308. *Sullivan's Island*, Charleston Harbor, South Carolina.
309. *Fort Sumter*, Charleston Harbor, South Carolina.
310. *Castle Pinckney*, Charleston Harbor, South Carolina.
311. *Combahee Bank*, entrance to St. Helena Sound, South Carolina.
314. *Tybee Beacon*, Georgia, Tybee Island.
316. *Cockspur*, Georgia, Savannah River.
317. *Oyster Beds*, Georgia, Savannah River.
318. *Fig Island*, Georgia, Savannah River.
319. *Sapelo*, Georgia, entrance to Doboy Sound.
320. *Sapelo Beacon*, in front of main light.
321, 322. *Wolf Island*, Georgia, entrance to Doboy Sound.
325, 326. *Amelia Island*, Florida, St. Mary's Bar, Fernandina.
327. *St. John's River*, Florida.
The following are the names of Light-stations in this district not mentioned elsewhere:
302. *Cape Romain*, South Carolina.
303. *Bull's Bay*, South Carolina.
305, 306. *Morris Island Range-lights*, South Carolina, entrance to Charleston Harbor.
313. *Tybee*, Georgia, entrance to Savannah River.
324. *Little Cumberland Island*, entrance to St. Andrew's Sound, Georgia.

* LIGHT-VESSELS.

The Light-vessel belonging to the *Frying-Pan Shoals Station* was driven from her station during the winter by heavy weather, rendering it necessary to send the relief vessel which now occupies that station.

The *Frying-Pan Shoals Light-vessel* has been repaired at Charleston and sent to take the place of the *Martin's Industry Light-vessel* which was driven from her station during a recent heavy gale. This latter vessel is now at Savannah undergoing repairs, which will be very extensive and expensive.

The *Rattlesnake Shoals Light-vessel*, off Charleston Bar, having been reported leaking very badly and unsafe, has been withdrawn, and Light-vessel No. 38 (Relief) has been towed to Charleston for that station until the former is repaired.

TENDERS.

The Engineer of the district has had the schooner *Narragansett* to attend to all the repairs, and carry supplies, &c., for works of construction. The steam-tender *Dandelion* is now there, being fitted out, and will soon be ready for service.

SEVENTH LIGHT-HOUSE DISTRICT.

This Light-house District extends from south of Cape Canaveral to, and including, Cedar Keys, Florida.

Inspector.—Commander C. A. Babcock, United States Navy.

Engineer.—Brevet Colonel C. E. Blunt, Lieutenant Colonel of the Corps of Engineers, United States Army.

In this district there are—

Light-houses	11
Day or unlighted beacons	35
Stakes	18
Buoys actually in position	98
Spare buoys for reliefs	61
Tender, (tug,) *Ivy* (employed by Engineer in constructions and repairs)	1
Tender (sailing schooner) *Florida*	1

The numbers preceding the names of the Light-stations correspond with those of the Light-house List for 1871.

At each of the following-named Light-stations there have been repairs and renovations during the last year:

334. *Dry Bank*, iron-pile Light-house, Florida Reefs, off coast of Florida.

335. *Sand Key*, iron-pile Light-house, Florida Reefs, off coast of Florida.

336. *Key West*, Key West Island, Florida.

337. *Northwest Passage*, iron-pile Light-house, near Key West, Florida.

338. *Dry Tortugas*, Loggerhead Key, Florida.

339. *Dry Tortugas Harbor*, Fort Jefferson, Florida.

During the ensuing year repairs and renovations will probably be needed at the remaining stations in the district, which are —

330. *Jupiter Inlet*, east coast of Florida.

331. *Cape Florida.*

332. *Carysfort Reef*, iron-pile Light-house, Florida Reefs, off coast of Florida.

340. *Egmont*, entrance to Tampa Bay, Florida.

341. *Cedar Keys*, entrance to Cedar Keys, Florida.

Principal repairs at *Dry Bank Light-house*, scraping, painting, and coal-tarring of iron-work, lower section, &c.

At *Sand Key*, the same, (with a new boat-house.)

At *Northwest Passage*, the same.

At *Dry Tortugas*, new boat-house.

At *Dry Tortugas Harbor*, some slight repairs on keeper's dwelling and out-buildings, and on lantern.

Besides these repairs and renovations one more of the iron day-beacons, marking the line of the Florida Reefs, has been erected, viz: *Beacon D*, at Crocker's Reef.

Preparations for the erection of the iron-pile Light-house on Alligator Reef have been commenced. Indian Key, the nearest land (four miles) from the proposed site, has been selected as a depot, and the temporary buildings and wharf have been well advanced. It is expected that the work of erection will commence early next winter, (by which time the contractors will have delivered the materials at the depot,) and will be prosecuted as rapidly as the unfavorable circumstances attending all engineering operations along the Florida reefs will permit.

The erection of the day-beacons on the reefs will also be prosecuted as rapidly as possible. An additional number of beacons, which will be needed to complete the line, have been ordered at the North.

BUOYAGE.

The buoyage in this district is in excellent condition. There are at present ninety-eight buoys actually in position. It has been found necessary to put down several buoys in *Hawk Channel*, (inside the Florida reefs,) leading into *Key West Harbor*, *Tortugas Harbor*, *Calvose Entrance*, and *Cedar Keys*, Florida. To effectually mark the entrance to, and channel leading into *Cedar Keys Harbor*, extra buoys have been put down, and fifteen palmetto stakes, marked, painted, and numbered according to instructions, driven on either side of the channel.

TENDERS.

The steam-tug *Ivy* has been employed in the Engineer's Department during the past year.

The sailing schooner *Florida* has been in this district for many years, employed in looking after buoys, delivering supplies, other than annual, and for visiting the Light-stations periodically. These Lights are all at remote and isolated points, and can only be reached by a vessel.

The great extent of this sparsely populated coast, embracing the dangerous Florida coast reefs, and the great increase in the number of aids to navigation to be looked after, renders it necessary to have the use of a small steam-tender in place of the small sailing schooner, now over twenty years in service in that district, and an estimate is submitted.

EIGHTH DISTRICT.

This District extends from Cedar Keys, Florida, to the Rio Grande, Texas.

Inspector.—Commander William P. McCann, United States Navy.

Engineer.—Brevet Major A. N. Damrell, Captain of Engineers, United States Army, (east of Pearl River,) to December 4, 1870; M. F. Bonzano, esquire, (west of Pearl River,) to July 1, 1871; Brevet Brigadier General James H. Simpson, Colonel of Engineers, United States Army, present Engineer.

In this district there are—

Light-houses and lighted beacons	47
Day or unlighted beacons	15
Buoys actually in position	97
Spare buoys for relief and to supply losses	139

Light-vessels 1
Tender (steamer) *Geranium* 1
Tender (steam-tug) *General Poc* 1
Freight schooner *Magnolia* 1

The numbers preceding the names of the stations correspond with those of the Light-house list of January, 1871.

342. *St. Mark's*, Florida.—Repairs have been made to the tower, and the new dwelling for the keeper has been completed.

346, 347. *Pensacola*, Florida.—The main and beacon lights have been repaired during the year.

348. *Sand Island*, Alabama, entrance to Mobile Bay.—The new masonry tower, with focal plane one hundred and twenty feet above the sea, is in progress at this station.

350. *Mobile Harbor*, Alabama, to mark the entrance to Mobile Harbor.—The screw-pile Light-house for this station is now being prepared at the work-shops at the North under contract.

355. *Cat Island Light-station*, Mississippi Sound.—The iron screw-pile Light-house at this place is nearly completed, and the Light will be exhibited at an early day.

357. *Merril's Shell Bank Light station*, Mississippi Sound.—Repairs have been made at this Light-station during the year.

359. *East Rigolet*.—The brick tower is in good order, exhibiting a Light of the fourth order, capable of affording all desirable facilities to navigation. The dwelling-house is old and not worth the extensive repairs necessary to put it in good condition. A new frame dwelling, and new cypress cistern of three thousand gallons' capacity, should be built at this station, and an estimate is submitted.

360. *Proctorville Beacon*.—The available appropriation ($5,000) for a building on the plan of the Light-house at *Head of the Passes*, placed on a pile foundation, is insufficient, and if, on further examination, it is found best to place the Light at this point, the appropriation should be increased to $7,500.

Since the last annual report a canal has been made by a company called the "Mississippi and Mexican Gulf Canal Company," with the intention of affording a passage to vessels of ten feet draught, from the Mississippi River into Lake Borgne. The northern terminus of this canal adjoins Tower Dupré, on which the Light destined for the old site at Proctorville, the former terminus of the abandoned Mexican Gulf Railway, might be placed with much greater advantage to commerce and navigation. There would probably be made no military objection to the placing of a Light on the tower itself.

The canal, though finished the entire distance, has not yet been connected by locks with the Mississippi River, nor has it attained, at its entrance into Lake Borgne, the projected depth of ten feet. The canal is, however, useful, for light-draught vessels, from Lake Borgne, and thus furnishes a harbor of refuge, which Proctorville is not. The appropriation, though insufficient for the structure contemplated on the original site, is sufficient for establishing a serviceable Light on Tower Dupré, and it is therefore recommended that a re-appropriation should be made of the amount now available, and that the Board be empowered to place the Light at Tower Dupré or at Proctorville, as may be found advisable.

361. *West Rigolets*.—The repairs recommended in former annual reports, *i. e.*, the putting a slate roof on the house, rebuilding the wharf, plank-walk, and breakwater, should be made at an early date. The building has sustained some additional damage in the late high water.

The foundation of the cistern has settled and should be rebuilt on a larger area, as the ground is very soft; a timber platform, sunk about two feet below the surface, covered with a layer of concrete, and upon that a brick foundation rising four feet above the ground, is probably the best foundation for this locality; an estimate is submitted.

362. *Port Pontchartrain.*—A new dwelling, on a substantial pile foundation, with kitchen fifteen by thirty feet, cistern of three thousand gallons, and a plank-walk, connecting with the wharf of the Pontchartrain Railroad, was contracted for during the last season. The house was nearly completed at the expiration of the fiscal year, and but for the extensive inundation, caused by an extraordinary rise of the waters of the lake, which interrupted the progress of the work, would have been finished before that time. All the work contracted for will be finished about the 1st of August.

363. *Bayou St. John.*—The difficulty of exhibiting this Light in bad weather, by reason of the unsuitable form of the structure and the great distance of the keeper's dwelling from it, the hazardous approach to it, over an embankment and rotten wharf of the canal company, which, in heavy weather, are washed by the sea, has been brought to the notice of the Board.

The most economical, suitable, and lasting structure would be a screw-pile structure, on the plan of those recently ordered for Matagorda Bay. The rise of Lake Pontchartrain, in hurricanes, may be estimated at fully *five feet* above ordinary high water. On this assumption the floor of the new Light-house should not be less than nine feet above ordinary high water, for the reason that the sea, backed up, first, by the easterly and northeasterly hurricane winds, and then acted upon by the free sweep of the norther, or northwester, over a space of twenty-two miles, will rise in waves of prodigious height, to which severe gales, in ordinary stages of the water, afford no comparison. During the inundation of June last the water rose within a couple of inches of the storm level of 1860, the effect of gales from the eastward, which did not reach the lake itself. But for this fortunate circumstance, the destruction of the Pontchartrain Railway wharf would have been imminent, and the embankments of the new and old canal would have received severe damage. It is deemed of great importance to provide against these extraordinary storms, which, though rare, are nevertheless to be expected from time to time, by establishing structures of such strength and elevation as to render them capable of resisting the force of wind and waves, and giving the requisite security to the inmates.

364. *New Canal.*—Some slight repairs to roof, plastering and cistern, are required, as also painting inside and outside.

365. *Tchefuncti.*—During the high water in June last the sheet-planking on the edge of the water was damaged, the outside steps of the dwelling swept away. They will be repaired during the coming season.

366. *Pass Manchac.*—The breakwater appropriated for will be built during the coming winter.

367. *Chandeleur Island.*—The repairs, consisting of strengthening the screw-piles by connecting them with each other by diagonal braces, new cistern, new roof, new floors, new steps, plastering, and painting, are required. They will be executed during the coming season.

Errol Island, Louisiana.—The proximity of this outlying island to the dangerous shoals of Grande Gosier, to the northward of *Pass à Loutre* Light-house, distant twenty-three miles, and midway between the *Pass à Loutre* and *Chandeleur* Lights, marks it as the proper location for a Light to fill up the dark space in the approaches to the northern mouth

of the Mississippi River. The only structure offering a reasonable prospect of stability in a locality so exposed to wind and sea, is an iron screw-
pile tower, for the erection of which an estimate of $30,000 has been
submitted in the annual estimate for the next fiscal year.

368. *Pass à Loutre.*—Station is in very good order. The steam Fog-
signal recommended in the annual report of last year is now under
construction.

369. *South Pass,* mouth of the Mississippi, Louisiana.—The Light-
house at this, the most seaward point of the delta of the Mississippi,
and therefore of the importance of a first-class sea-coast Light, was built
in 1831, and is only a low wooden tower on the top of the keeper's
dwelling. The grave objections to a wooden structure at so distant a
point from succor in the case of fire, and one occupying so important a
position, (being only of the third-class,) have been mentioned in the several annual reports from this Board since 1867. The remarks previously
made have acquired additional force from the fact that the natural decay
of so perishable a material, and the age of the structure, render a new
tower at no distant day indispensable, even in an economical point of
view alone. An estimate of $75,000 for commencing the work is sub-
mitted.

010. *Head of the Passes.*—Slight repairs were made during the year to
the breakwater, and the house was thoroughly painted. The station is
now in excellent condition. The space inclosed by the breakwater is
still filling up with solid ground; a dense growth of young willows is
now spreading over it.

371. *Southwest Pass.*—The foundation for the new iron Light-house
was finished by the end of the month of May last, and is now ready for
the superstructure which is now being constructed under contract in
Ohio.

A steam Fog-signal has been authorized. This may be placed in the
southeast or southwest corner of the coffer-dam, where it will be very
conveniently accessible at all times. It is now being constructed at the
North.

The pile foundation for a keeper's dwelling is also in readiness to
receive the superstructure.

The old Light-house remains in the same condition as last reported.
It will last, dilapidated as it is, until the new Light is ready, and no
repairs of any kind are needed. In the event of its complete destruction, which, however, is hardly to be apprehended, a temporary Light
may be established on the wharf of the new work in a few days.

373. *Ship Shoal.*—The tower requires coating with coal-tar. The depth
of water under the tower has sensibly decreased since the screw-piles
were surrounded with a layer of stone concrete. The tower was then
thoroughly cleansed with a solution of caustic potash and coal-tarred.
The tanks, rain-leaders, pipes, &c., were coated with hot coal-tar inside.

Timbalier Island, intermediate between Nos. 342 and 343 of the Light-
house List of 1871.—An iron screw-pile Light-house, with focal plane one
hundred and twenty-five feet above the sea, will be erected at this place.
The land of the Government, upon which the old brick tower stood, has
been entirely washed away. The island being uninhabited and subject to
dangerous overflows, in fact a low, barren sand-reef, unfit for cultivation,
no difficulty in obtaining a new site is apprehended. The new Light-house
will be placed in a convenient depth of water inside the island, which, in
this case, will be an effectual breakwater. The location will also be at
some distance from the eastern point of West Timbalier Island, (toward
the west,) because the point is subject to abrasion. The bay affords

secure shelter for the vessels used in construction. The plans for this Light-house are completed, and it will be soon under contract.

Trinity Shoal, intermediate between Nos. 364 and 365.—A survey of this shoal was commenced by the United States Coast Survey in April and May, but not finished. An iron screw-pile Light-house, one hundred and twenty-five feet above the sea, will be contracted for at an early day for this shoal; the plans are completed.

Calcasieu Pass, intermediate between Trinity Shoal and Sabine Pass.— Inquiries have been made with a view to obtain possession of a suitable piece of land for the new Light-house. There seems to be much confusion in the claims of various parties, so that the only certain mode to acquire possession is by the operation of the laws passed at the last session of the legislature of Louisiana. The new Light-house authorized at this point will be erected during the next working season.

375. *Sabine Pass.*—The tower is in good order. The keeper's dwelling requires a new roof, new floors, and general repairs, which will be executed during the next season.

377. *Bolivar Point.*—An attempt was made to purchase a new site for the Light-house at such a point that the establishment of two Range Lights would have given perfect ranges over the bar and through the channel of the harbor. The negotiations failed. In consequence of the failure to obtain a new site, the Board ordered the foundation for the new tower to be placed on the old site, which was accordingly done. The foundation is complete. A dwelling for the light-keeper, on the plan of that at *Pass à Loutre*, has been finished. The iron Light-house for this place is now under construction at the North.

381. *Matagorda.*—The new Light-house authorized at this place will be constructed during the fiscal year.

383. *Swash.*—The screw-pile Light-house for this point is under construction at the North.

Decrow's Point.—The refusal of the owner to sell any land to the Government made it necessary to abandon the first plan of placing a couple of Range Lights on the land, and to substitute therefor a screw-pile Light-house, which is now under contract at the North.

385. *Brazos Island Beacon.*—A new iron structure is recommended for this point, on account of the rotten condition of the present temporary tower being subject to destruction in heavy gales. Estimates submitted.

Atchafalaya Bay.—The beacons marking the entrance to this bay are in good order.

Depot, at head of the Passes.—The buildings authorized were finished by the end of the year.

TENTH DISTRICT.

This District extends from the mouth of St. Regis River, New York, to include *Grassy Island Light-house*, Detroit River, Michigan.

Inspector.—Commodore Gustavus H. Scott, United States Navy.

Engineer.—Brevet Lieutenant Colonel George L. Gillespie, Captain of Engineers, United States Army.

In this district there are—

Light-houses and lighted beacons 55
Day or unlighted beacons 0
Buoys actually in position 72
Spare buoys for relief to supply losses 90
Tender (steamer) *Haze*, common to Tenth and Eleventh Districts................... 1

The numbers preceding the names of stations correspond with those of the "Light-house List of the Northern and Northwestern Lakes of the United States," issued January 1, 1871.

446. *Ogdensburgh*, New York, St. Lawrence River.—The renovation of this station commenced August 23, 1870, as mentioned in the last annual report, was continued during the working season and finally completed June 9, 1871. The sea-wall protecting the lot has been raised throughout its whole length; the space inclosed filled with loam and rich earth, graded and sown with grass, and shade-trees planted on the land front. The station is now in excellent condition.

453. *Sackett's Harbor*, New York, Lake Ontario.—The renovation of this station, commenced in August, 1870, and mentioned in the last annual report, was continued during the working season and finally completed April, 1871. A neat picket-fence incloses the dwelling and a small garden; shade-trees have been set out on the land side, and the old house and débris have been removed.' The grounds are now in excellent condition.

456. *Pier-Head*, Oswego, New York, Lake Ontario.—The pier-head of the west pier has been marked by a Light exhibited from a small glazed box fitted to the top of a mast, framed into the pier. The west pier is very much exposed to high seas, and at times it is impossible for the keeper to reach the pier-head. To insure the maintenance of the Light at the pier-head, two ⅜-inch galvanized wire ropes connect the top of the mast with iron bars, fastened inside the stone tower at the second window, and serve to support a lantern six inches in diameter, showing a fixed white Light, that is run upon them from the tower to the mast. The working of the device has, so far, been entirely satisfactory.

Fair Haven, New York, Little Sodus Bay.—An appropriation was made March 3, 1871, for the erection of a pier, Light-house, and dwelling for the keeper at this station. The station was visited May 26, 1871, when it was decided to mark the approach to the harbor by a frame beacon to be established on the pier on the west side of the channel, and a suitable site for the keeper's dwelling was accordingly purchased. As soon as the necessary papers vesting title in the United States shall have been submitted and approved by the Attorney General, proposals will be publicly invited for the construction of a frame dwelling for the keeper. The Light will be of the fourth order, fixed, white, in a frame tower, provided with hauling apparatus for pier-head Light. The focal plane of the Light will be forty feet above the pier.

459. *Big Sodus Bay*, Lake Ontario.—The renovation of this station commenced in August, 1870, and, as mentioned in the last annual report, was continued during the working season, and finally completed June 30, 1871. The old tower and house have been removed from the lot, and the stone and débris formed into a rough jetty extending into the lake at the west end of lot, to prevent a threatened wear of the bank. The jetty is seventy feet long, with a twenty-foot base, and extends to nine feet of water. The station is in fine order.

462. *Oak Orchard*, New York, Lake Ontario.—An appropriation was made July 15, 1870, for a Light-house at or near the mouth of Oak Orchard Creek, New York. After a careful examination of Oak Orchard Harbor, and the shore-line in the vicinity, it was deemed best to mark the approach to the harbor by a frame beacon placed upon the west pier. In accordance with this decision, one-half acre of land on the west bank of the creek, near its mouth, was purchased as a site for the keeper's dwelling. During the winter the title-papers of the lot were received and forwarded to the Attorney General, and by him examined and approved. For the supply of the necessary material for the

dwelling and beacon sealed proposals were publicly invited and contracts made. Work was commenced March 30, 1871. The dwelling is a one-story and attic frame structure, with a room especially arranged for the accommodation of the beacon supplies. The beacon was finished June 10, and the Light, which is of the fourth order, fixed, white, was exhibited for the first time on the evening of June 17, 1871. The dwelling was finished and the keeper installed June 22, 1871.

463. *Fort Niagara*, New York, mouth Niagara River.—An appropriation was made March 3, 1871, for rebuilding the Light-house at this station. Plans have been prepared for a stone tower with oil-room attached, to be placed on the extreme eastern end of the Light-house lot. Proposals are now invited for the necessary material for tower and oil-room. As soon as the material can be delivered under contract, the work will be commenced and pushed to completion. The tower will be of coursed rubble-stone, eighteen feet diameter at the base, and eleven feet at the top of the cornice. The height of the focal plane above the surface of the ground will be forty-five feet. The order of the Light will not be changed.

465. *Buffalo Breakwater*, (north end,) Buffalo, New York.—It was stated in last annual report that "an appropriation was made July 15, 1870, for a Beacon-light on each end of the breakwater in this harbor." As the breakwater is not finished, it was only possible to make arrangements for the construction of the beacon to occupy the north end. The appropriation would not admit of a very elaborate structure, and as it is difficult, if not impossible, to reach the breakwater at certain seasons of the year, in any way short of a steam-tug, it was found necessary to arrange a structure that should contain quarters for the keeper. These considerations, taken in connection with the depth of water at the site, made it imperative to use timber in the construction, on account of its cheapness. Proposals were publicly invited for the supply of the necessary material, and contracts have been made for the iron, stone, and timber, and for the framing of dwelling. On May 18, a crib forty feet square was sunk twenty feet *behind*, and twenty-three feet *from* the north end of the breakwater, and the framing carried to the surface of the water. To allow settlement to take place, work was suspended till June 15, when six more courses were added. Work was again suspended till June 24, when it was resumed. The pier of protection is twelve feet above the level of the lake, and the beacon, which will be elevated eight feet above it, will be supported by heavy upright oak timbers securely framed into the pier, the oak timber being firmly held by adjustable wrought-iron rods. On the west side of the beacon, twenty-four feet above the water, a Fog-bell will be arranged, striking three times in quick succession, at intervals of thirty seconds. The striking apparatus will occupy one of the rooms of the beacon. It is expected that this work will be completed by September 15, 1871. The Light will be of the fourth order, fixed, red, the focal plane thirty-seven feet above the level of the lake.

466. *Buffalo Breakwater*, (south end,) Buffalo, New York.—It is proposed to mark the unfinished south end of breakwater by a temporary frame beacon, with the focal plane twenty-eight feet above the lake level. For a height of ten feet above base it will be of open framework, strongly braced, to give the waves, as nearly as possible, uninterrupted passage over the breakwater. The Fog-bell for this station, which is to strike continuously at intervals of ten seconds, has been delivered.

The Light will be of the fourth order, fixed, white. The proposed length of breakwater is four thousand feet; at present only seventeen hundred and fifty feet have been built. If the usual annual appropriations are made, the residue should be built in three to, four years. In view of this distant date of completion of work, no appropriation is asked at present for the construction of the beacon to mark the south end.

467. *Buffalo*, New York, Lake Erie.—An appropriation was made March 3, 1871, for the reconstruction and improvement of the wharf in front of Light-house depot. Sealed proposals for the supply of the necessary material and for the labor were publicly invited, and contracts for the supply of the timber, stone, iron, and framing were made. Work was commenced June 10. The old crib-work has been entirely removed, and the contractor is now dredging along the front of the lot preparatory to sinking the cribs of the new pier. The pier will be two hundred and sixty-four feet long by twelve feet wide, and sunk six feet below water-level. It is expected that it will be completed by September 1, 1871.

A Lake-coast Light on the northern side of *Presqu'isle*, Lake Erie, has been petitioned for. An estimate has been submitted, accordingly, of $15,000.

475. *Conneaut*, Ohio, Lake Erie.—An appropriation was made March 0, 1871, for building a light-keeper's dwelling at this station. Plans and specifications of the dwelling have been prepared, and proposals will be invited for the construction under contract, when the title-papers of the lot purchased for the site have been examined and approved by the Attorney General of the United States.

476. *Ashtabula*, Ohio, Lake Erie.—An appropriation was made March 3, 1871, for building a light-keeper's dwelling at this station. Plans and specifications of the dwelling have been prepared, and sealed proposals will be publicly invited for the construction under contract, when the title-papers of the lot purchased for the site have been examined and approved by the Attorney-General of the United States.

477. *Grand River*, Fairport, Ohio, Lake Erie.—An appropriation was made March 3, 1871, for completing the tower upon which work had been stopped by act of July 12, 1870, and for the reconstruction of the keeper's dwelling. The new dwelling will be a one-story and attic brick structure, placed upon the site of the old one, and connected with the tower by a brick covered-way. Sealed proposals for the supply of the necessary material were publicly invited, and contracts were made for the lumber, rubble-stone, and brick. The stone for the tower being already on hand and dressed ready for laying, work was resumed on the 20th of May. The tower is now nearly finished, and it is expected that the Light can be exhibited by the 15th of August. The order of the Light will not be changed. A great part of the material for the dwelling has been delivered, and the construction has advanced above the water-table. The station will be in complete order by the 20th of September.

479. *Cleveland*, Ohio, Lake Erie.—An appropriation was made March 3, 1871, for rebuilding the Light-house at this station. Sealed proposals were publicly invited for the supply of the material necessary for the construction of a stone wall to inclose the grounds on the north and east sides, and for a third-order lantern complete, with stairs for the tower, and contracts have been made. The stone and cement were delivered early in June, and work was commenced on the 24th of June. It is recommended that the appropriation for this station be extended to June 30, 1873.

482. *Black River*, Ohio, Lake Erie.—This station has no keeper's dwelling. An appropriation of $4,000 is recommended for the construc-

tion of a dwelling similar to the one to be constructed at Ashtabula, Ohio.

483. *Vermillion*, Ohio, Lake Erie.—An appropriation was made March 3, 1871, for building a light-keeper's dwelling at this station. The station was visited May 18 for the purpose of selecting and purchasing a suitable site. No suitable vacant lot could be purchased that was easily accessible from the piers, and from which the beacon could be seen, and in consequence a purchase was made of a lot with a new house upon it, containing every convenience for a keeper's dwelling. Occupation will take place when the papers necessary for vesting title in the United States have been examined and approved by the Attorney General.

484. *Huron*, Ohio, Lake Erie.—An appropriation was made March 3, 1871, for building a light-keeper's dwelling at this station. The station was visited May 17, for the purpose of selecting and purchasing a suitable site. A purchase was made, but the owner of the lot has since refused to give a title. Further efforts will be made to obtain a suitable lot.

485. *Cedar Point*, Lake Erie, near Sandusky, Ohio.—It is proposed to establish a Fog-bell at this station before the close of the season.

490. *Turtle Island*, Lake Erie, near Toledo, Ohio.—It is proposed to establish a Fog-bell at this station before the close of the season.

491. *Maumee Outer Range*, Toledo, Ohio.—An appropriation was made March 3, 1871, to build a light-keeper's dwelling at this station. Sealed proposals were publicly invited to June 3, for the construction of the dwelling, and a contract has been made. It will be a frame dwelling, one-story and attic, placed on the west end of the range, and behind the inner range tower. It is expected that the dwelling will be ready for occupation by the 20th of September.

498. *Gibraltar*, Lake Erie, mouth of Detroit River, Michigan. An appropriation of $10,000 is recommended to rebuild the tower and keeper's dwelling at this station. The present buildings are very old, and not worth repairing.

At each of the following-named stations there have been repairs and renovations more or less during the last year:

449. *Sunken Rock*, St. Lawrence River.
450. *Rock Island*, St. Lawrence River.
452. *Galloo Island*, Lake Ontario, entrance to St. Lawrence River.
455. *Oswego*, New York, Lake Ontario.
460. *Genesee*, Charlotte, New York, Lake Ontario.
464. *Horseshoe Reef*, Buffalo, New York, Lake Ontario.
471. *Presqu'isle Beacon*, Range No. 1, Erie, Pennsylvania.
472. *Presqu'isle Beacon*, Range No. 2, Erie, Pennsylvania.
485. *Cedar Point*, Sandusky, Ohio, Lake Erie.
497. *Monroe*, Monroe, Michigan, Lake Erie.

The following-named Light-stations require repairs to be made during the ensuing year:

461. *Genesee Beacon*, Charlotte, New York, Lake Ontario.
464. *Horseshoe Reef*, Buffalo, New York.
468. *Dunkirk*, Dunkirk, New York, Lake Erie.
473. *Peninsula Beacon Range*, No. 1, Erie, Pennsylvania.
478. *Grand River*, Fairport Beacon, Fairport, Ohio, Lake Erie.
488. *Green Island*, Green Island, Lake Erie.
489. *West Sister Island*, Lake Erie.
493, 494. *Maumee Middle Range*, Toledo, Ohio.
497. *Monroe*, Monroe, Michigan, Lake Erie.
499. *Mamajuda*, Detroit River.
500. *Grassy Island*, Detroit River.

The following are the names of the Light-stations in this district not mentioned elsewhere:

447. *Cross-over Island*, St. Lawrence River.
448. *Sister Islands*, St. Lawrence River.
451. *Tibbett's Point*, entrance to St. Lawrence River.
454. *Stony Point*, Lake Ontario.
457, 458. *Big Sodus Range Beacons*, Lake Ontario.
469. *Dunkirk Beacon*, Dunkirk, New York, Lake Erie.
470. *Erie Harbor*, Erie, Pennsylvania.
471, 472. *Presqu'isle Beacon Ranges*, Nos. 1 and 2, Erie, Pennsylvania.
480. *Cleveland Beacon*, No. 1, Cleveland, Ohio.
481. *Cleveland Beacon*, No. 2, Cleveland, Ohio.
486. *Cedar Point Range*, Sandusky, Ohio.
487. *Marblehead*, Sandusky, Ohio.
495, 496. *Maumee Inner Range*, Toledo, Ohio.

An estimate is submitted for a steam-tender for the Inspector and Engineer of the Tenth Light-house District, rendered necessary by the large increase in the number of Lights requiring repairs and supplies, buoys and other aids to navigation in the Northern and Northwestern lakes since 1865, which it is found cannot be effectually attended to by the tender stationed at Detroit for Lakes St. Clair, Huron, Michigan, and Superior. The buoy service, which has heretofore, and is now, mainly performed under contract with private individuals, is not satisfactory, and can only be properly performed by a small steam-vessel.

ELEVENTH DISTRICT.

The Eleventh District embraces all aids to navigation on the Northern and Northwestern Lakes above Grassy Island Light-house, Detroit River.

Inspector.—Commodore Alexander Murray, United States Navy.
Engineers.—Brevet Brigadier General O. M. Poe, Major of Engineers, United States Army.

There are in this district—

Light-houses and lighted beacons	91
Day or unlighted beacons	2
Buoys actually in position	144
Spare buoys for relief and to supply losses	60
Tenders (steam) *Warrington* and *Haze*	2
Tender (sail) *Belle*	1

The numbers preceding the names of stations correspond with the "Light-house List of the Northern and Northwestern Lakes of the United States," issued January 1, 1871.

504, 505. *Saint Clair Flats*, new channel.—By the act of July 12, 1870, returning to the Treasury the available funds, work on these Light-houses was suspended while in full progress, and it was not until the appropriation of March 3, 1871, became available that operations could be resumed. An adequate working force is now upon the ground, and the two stations will be ready for occupancy before the close of the season. Meanwhile, temporary structures have been erected, and everything is in readiness to exhibit lights, as soon as the announcement is made that the channel is open to navigation.

506. *Fort Gratiot*, Lake Huron.—Under the provisions of the appropriation of March 3, 1871, for a Fog-signal at this station, one is now under construction, and will be in operation before the close of the season.

A Light-house between Fort Gratiot and Point Aux Barques, Lake

Huron.—The last annual report contained the following, which is again submitted, in the hope that the necessary appropriation may be made:

An additional coast Light, between *Fort Gratiot* and *Point Aux Barques*, Lake Huron, and recommended in last year's report, is very much needed.

The distance between the two places is seventy-five miles, for the whole of which vessels keep the shore well aboard while going in either direction.

The amount required for such a Light-house, including the purchase of the land, will be about $30,000.

Range-lights at the mouth of Saginaw River, Saginaw Bay, Lake Huron.—An appropriation of $12,000 for these ranges was made by act of Congress approved July 15, 1870. The title to the small portion of marsh required for these lights was so much involved that there was but little hope of its being cleared up in time to save the appropriation from reversion to the Treasury, under the provisions of the act of Congress of July 12, 1870. Moreover, the price ($2,500) asked for the few acres of swamp, impassable on foot in the summer time, was so much above its real value that application was made to the governor of Michigan for a commission to condemn the property under the State laws. The commission fixed the sum of $17,496 84 as a fair and just compensation for the site required. This amount being largely in excess of the entire appropriation, as well as greatly beyond its value, the award of the commission was promptly declined by the Board, and on the 30th June, 1871, the appropriation reverted to the Treasury. It is not recommended that any further steps be taken at present.

514. *Thunder Bay Island.*—Under the act appropriating for a Fog-signal at this station, one is now under construction. It consists of a 10-inch whistle, actuated by steam from a horizontal tubular boiler, and will be completed during the present season.

517. *Presqu'isle*, Lake Huron.—This important coast Light, which was under construction at the date of the last annual report, was unexpectedly completed, and was lighted for the first time upon the opening of navigation this season. It is of great benefit to navigation. After the new Light was exhibited the old tower at the entrance to the harbor was dismantled, and the lantern and lens are ready for use elsewhere.

Spectacle Reef, Lake Huron.—After the date of the last annual report work upon the crib-pier of protection was prosecuted at Scammon's Harbor (where a sufficient depot with dockage has been established) until the close of the season, and resumed on the opening of navigation about the 1st of April. It is expected that the entire crib, ninety-two feet square, will be ready to be placed on the reef early in July.

During the winter the coffer-dam was framed at Detroit, and after the opening of navigation it was taken to Scammon's Harbor, in readiness for use as soon as the crib shall have been completed and placed in position.

A contract for the stone required for the Light-house was made, and it was agreed to deliver granite at Scammon's Harbor, beds and builds cut, for the sum of $1 25 per cubic foot. The contractor utterly failed to furnish the stone, and, owing to the rapid advance of the season, there was not time to again advertise for proposals with any hope of completing the contracts and securing the delivery of a sufficient quantity of stone to bring the work above water before the close of the season.

In this emergency application was made for authority to purchase limestone from Marblehead, Ohio, in sufficient quantity to secure the object. The honorable the Secretary of the Treasury authorized this purchase, and it was accordingly made at a rate of $1 75 per cubic foot stone, with beds and builds cut, and $1 50 for stone in the rough.

At the time the proposals were opened under the advertisement these same persons offered to furnish the same stone for $2 25 per cubic foot, beds and builds out, or 50 cents per cubic foot higher. While these stones are not as good or durable as granite, it is still believed that they will answer the purpose and endure for ages.

The wreck of the schooner *Nightingale*, reported last year as occupying the site selected for the Light-house, was removed during the month of June.

Every preparation looking to the successful placing of the crib on the reef has been completed. The requisite tugs, among the most powerful on the lakes, have been chartered to tow the crib, as well as barges and scows of capacity sufficient to float 250 cords of stone, all of which will go out with the crib, and it is hoped and expected that, taking advantage of suitable weather, the crib will be placed on the reef and secured within twelve hours after leaving the harbor.

The requisite derricks and shears for handling the stone at the depot have been erected, and two platforms of masonry upon which to fit together the several courses of stone and drill the holes for the iron domes are under construction.

A derrick has also been ordered for use in handling the stone upon the crib and setting them in the tower.

The failure of the contractor for granite involves the loss of the balance (about $70,000) of the appropriation approved July 15, 1870, for this work, which, under the act of July 12, 1870, reverted to the Treasury on the 30th of June. It will therefore be necessary to reappropriate this amount for the fiscal year 1872–'73.

Straits of Mackinac.—The necessity for a Light to mark the passage between Round Island and the Island of Mackinac, known as the North Channel, is as great as ever, and the recommendation contained in the annual reports for the last two years, that the sum of $12,000 be appropriated for this purpose, is respectfully repeated.

522. *Detour*, Lake Huron.—The proposition contained in the last annual report to substitute a third-order lens for the fourth order then in use at this station, was carried into effect upon the opening of navigation this season, and gives great satisfaction.

Saint Helena Island, Lake Michigan.—For reasons given in the annual reports for 1868–'69 and 1870, a Light to mark the anchorage at this island is deemed important. It is again recommended that the sum of $14,000 be appropriated for this work.

Passage north of the Beaver Islands, Lake Michigan.—This passage is now much used, and the navigation through it will rapidly increase, since with certain winds it is possible to sail through it when the south passage is impracticable. Lights to mark it will soon be required, but it is proposed to defer for another year the estimates of their cost.

Little Traverse, Lake Michigan.—Attention was directed to the necessity of a Light-house to make this fine harbor of refuge available at all times, by an inquiry from the Senate Committee on Commerce.

By reference to the tracing of the lake survey detail chart of Little Traverse, and the engraved lake survey chart of the northeast end of Lake Michigan, including Big and Little Traverse Bays and the Fox and Manitou Islands, the relation of the harbor of Little Traverse to the navigation of Lake Michigan can be readily seen and appreciated. The harbor itself is excellent in every respect, easy of access, affording good anchorage and a complete shelter from all winds.

A Light-house of the fifth order, together with a Fog-bell of 600 pounds with Stevens's striking apparatus, will make the harbor available. In addition to its relation to the general commerce of Lake Michigan, the harbor has some local importance. This is increasing, and, doubtless, will continue to do so.

530. *South Manitou*, Lake Michigan.—The work of improving this station is in progress, though the working party has been temporarily withdrawn for service elsewhere. All the materials are on the ground, and by the 20th July the entire working force will be again at the station, when it is expected the work will go on uninterruptedly until its completion before the close of the season. The improvements will consist of a third-order tower founded on piles, having its focal plane one hundred feet above the surface of the lake, and a covered passage-way connecting the tower and keeper's dwelling. This improvement will be of great value to the commerce between Lake Michigan and the other lakes.

Frankfort, Lake Michigan.—As soon as the harbor piers at this place are completed a Pier-light will be required, and is estimated for under the head of "Pier Lights."

534. *Père Marquette*, Lake Michigan.—Before the close of last season a Light was established on the head of the pier at this place, under an appropriation of $6,000, approved July 15, 1870. It was also intended to erect a keeper's dwelling on shore, but it having been found impossible to perfect the title before the 30th June, the balance of the appropriation on that day reverted to the Treasury. It is respectfully recommended that the sum of $4,000 be reappropriated for the purpose in question.

Little Point Au Sable, Lake Michigan.—A Lake-coast Light of the third order is much needed at this point, as a simple inspection of the chart of Lake Michigan will show. Last year an appropriation of $35,000 for this purpose was recommended, but not made, and the recommendation is now respectfully repeated.

White River, Lake Michigan.—The appropriation of $10,000 formerly existing for a Light at this point, reverted to the Treasury June 30, 1870, under the act of July 12, 1870. It is respectfully recommended that this amount be reappropriated for the purpose indicated.

535. *Muskegon*, Lake Michigan.—The rebuilding of the main Light at this station, in progress at the date of the last annual report, was duly completed, and the Light exhibited from the new structure before the close of the season.

Muskegon Beacon.—This is to be a Pier-head Light, on the outer end of the south pier, with an elevated walk connecting it with the shore. Its erection is now in progress, and will be completed within a couple of weeks. The exhibition of the Light will be somewhat delayed for want of the required illuminating apparatus.

537. *Grand Haven*, Lake Michigan.—After the completion of the Pier-head Light at *Muskegon*, the working party will be transferred to *Grand Haven* for the purpose of erecting a beacon on the pier-head. An elevated walk starting from a point on the pier, which can be safely reached in any weather, will connect the beacon with the shore. The whole will be completed, and the Light shown early in September.

It was intended to move the Fog-signal which is located on the pier, but the performance of the machinery is quite satisfactory, and when the larger bell proposed for the station is duly hung, it is supposed it will answer all purposes.

538. *Holland*, Lake Michigan.—A Pier-head Light has been established on the outer end of the south harbor pier at this place, and was exhibited before the close of last season. The appropriation under which the work was done was intended to cover the cost of a keeper's dwelling also,

but it was not possible for the owner of the site required to make a clear title thereto in time to prevent the balance of the appropriation reverting to the Treasury on the 30th of June last, under the act of July 12, 1870. The sum of $4,000 should be reappropriated for a keeper's dwelling, and a new effort be made to obtain title.

South Haven, Lake Michigan.—An appropriation of $6,000 is available for a Beacon-light at this place, under which it is proposed to establish a Light during the present season.

Beacon at Michigan City, Lake Michigan.—The working party engaged in erecting Pier-head Lights will be transferred from *Grand Haven*, upon the completion of the work at that point, to *Michigan City*, and will complete the proposed beacon and elevated walk at this place before the close of the season.

Calumet, Lake Michigan.—After a conference by the Engineer of the district with the president of the Improvement Company, which owns the old Light-station at this point, he promised to put the title in proper shape to be submitted for the approval of the Attorney General of the United States, but he has not yet informed him of what progress is being made. As soon as the transfer to the United States is made, the work of renovating the old station will be taken in hand, under the appropriation now available, and can be completed in a very short time.

Grosse Point, Lake Michigan.—An appropriation for the removal of *Chicago* Light-house to this point is now available, and the title-papers to the land required are in course of preparation. As soon as they have been approved, the work will be taken in hand.

A Light-house at Racine Point.—The last annual report contained the following remarks:

This is a prominent point on the west coast of Lake Michigan, about three and a half miles north of Racine, and eighteen miles south of the north-cut beacon at Milwaukee. The point shuts out to the northward the *Racine* Light, which lies in a bay and is not seen by vessels coming from the north, and keeping the shore well aboard as they mostly do, until nearly abreast of it.

Frequent shipwrecks have occurred at this point for the want of a Light. For vessels coming from the south it would also be a good guide for steering clear off Racine Reef.

A Fog-signal should also be provided. For these two objects an estimate of $40,000 is submitted.

A Coast-light at Twin River Point, Lake Michigan.—The following remarks are copied from the report of last year, and are repeated as presenting a fair statement of the necessity for this Light:

This point is seven miles north of *Manitowoc*, and occupies a position on the west coast of Lake Michigan similar to *Grand Point au Sable* on the east. It is the prominent landmark for vessels navigating Lake Michigan, and should be marked by a tower one hundred feet high with an apparatus of the third order. There is an old discontinued station at the village of Twin River, but the site is too far south of the Point to answer the purposes of a coast Light.

An estimate for a proper Light at this station is submitted of $40,000.

North Bay, Lake Michigan.—By act of Congress approved July 15, 1870, an appropriation of $7,500 was made for the purpose of establishing a Light or Lights to enable vessels to enter this harbor, and a price for the land required was agreed upon. But the owner found it impracticable to clear the title before the 30th of June, when the appropriation reverted to the Treasury. Submitted for reappropriation.

A Light-house on Poverty Island, at the entrance to Green Bay.—Attention is respectfully invited to the following remarks, copied from the annual reports for the last two years. The necessity for this Light is daily increasing, the shipments of iron ore from Escanaba alone being sufficient to justify the erection of the Light:

The already large and rapidly-increasing commerce to and from the northern end of

Green Bay and lower lake ports now takes, in daylight, the northern passage from Lake Michigan into Green Bay, because of its being much shorter and more direct. To enable vessels to use the same passage in the night, a Light-house on Poverty Island is necessary.

Estimates submitted of $18,000.

A Coast-light between White Fish Point and Grand Island, Lake Superior.—In the last four annual reports this Light has been recommended. It is more needed than any other Light in the district not already provided for. The sum of $40,000 will be required to build it, and an estimate submitted.

A Light-house on Stannard's Rock, Lake Superior.—The rapid increase of the commerce between Du Luth, the eastern terminus of the Northern Pacific Railroad, and the lower lakes, will demand, at no distant day, the erection of a Light-house on this danger, so much dreaded by all vessels bound to or from points above Keweenaw Point and ports below. The case will be similar to that of Spectacle Reef, and all the costly apparatus and machinery purchased for the latter can be made available for the former, thereby greatly reducing the cost of construction.

It is not proposed, however, to do anything further at this time than to make the preliminary examinations and mature plans for the work, for which purpose an estimate of $20,000 is submitted.

L'Anse, Lake Superior.—The railroad from Escanaba and Marquette to Ontonagon passes the head of L'Anse Bay, and will, for the present, terminate there. Efforts, which will probably prove successful, are now being made to complete the road to L'Anse before the close of this season, when the place will at once become an important point for the shipment of iron ore. A good harbor is found at the head of the bay, and it should be lighted.

To establish such a Light as is needed will require an appropriation of $12,000, which amount is submitted, with estimate.

Mendota, Lake Superior.—This Light-station having been discontinued by the order of the honorable the Secretary of the Treasury, it will be dismantled when visited by the steamer Haze upon her present cruise, and the apparatus, &c., used elsewhere.

585. *Eagle Harbor,* Lake Superior.—Under an appropriation approved July 15, 1870, this station has been entirely rebuilt, and is now in excellent order.

Outer Island, Lake Superior.—The through commerce to and from the western end of Lake Superior, increasing so rapidly as the railroads having their termini at Du Luth are extended to the westward, all passes outside of the Apostle Islands, and is greatly in need of a Light-house on the northern end of Outer Island. This should be a Light of the third order, and will cost $40,000, which sum is respectfully recommended to be appropriated.

Sand Island, Lake Superior.—For reasons given in the preceding case, a Light (of a lower order, however) is demanded on the northern end of Sand Island, the most westerly of the group, for which purpose an appropriation of $18,000 is recommended.

Du Luth, Lake Superior.—The act of Congress appropriating for this Light-house provides that it shall be located at the terminus of the Northern Pacific Railway. Consequently, the Chief Engineer of that road was written to, informing him of the provision of the appropriation, and asking him to designate a site for the Light-house; also, in case the proposed site were not the property of the United States, to take the requisite steps to ascertain the owner, and, if practicable, initiate negotiations for the purchase of the site. After some delay, he replied that he had referred the communication to the president of the road, but no further answer has been received.

Passage Island.—The discovery of the silver mines on Lake Superior, and consequent sudden and remarkable increase of travel and traffic to that region, renders it desirable that a Light-house should be built on Passage Island, to mark the channel between it and Isle Royale. The island is difficult of access, and therefore any structure put there will cost more than if erected at some more accessible point.

It is respectfully recommended that an appropriation of $18,000 be made for the purpose indicated.

Pier-head Lights.—These are being erected as fast as illuminating apparatus can be supplied. That at *Muskegon* will be completed early in July, but the apparatus is not yet received. That at *Grand Haven*, as well as the one at *Michigan City*, will be completed before the close of the season, and the others provided for by the act of the 3d of March, 1871, will all be completed before the appropriations for 1871–'72 become available.

As the extension of this system of pier Lights must depend upon that of harbor improvements, it is somewhat difficult to estimate in detail until it is known just where these improvements are to be made. . Therefore the estimate for Pier-head Lights is submitted in one amount, and place it at $20,000, which will be sufficient for this district for the fiscal year.

Light-house depot at Detroit.—Work on this has progressed, though not so rapidly as was desired. A bulk-head has been built across the entire front of the lot, and the basin has been dredged out to a uniform depth of ten feet, thus giving sufficient room to accommodate all the Light-house vessels. Enough of the dredged material was deposited behind the bulk-head to fill up the low ground to the height of the bulk-head, thus forming an excellent yard for the storage of buoys and other heavy material.

The depot building, forty by sixty feet in plan, and entirely fire-proof, has been carried up to a sufficient height to admit of the completion of the second floor. The cellar for the storage of the supply of oil forms the basement of the building. It is very desirable to complete this building, so much needed. The dark room in which to test the oils delivered under contract is to be located in the story above that now completed, and the work should go on. Wherever the work is stopped now, a temporary roof must be thrown over it to protect it from the weather, which will add considerably to the cost of the building.

When the building was designed it appeared to be of ample size, but it is now plainly seen that there will be no room to spare. An estimate is submitted :

REPAIRS.

Repairs more or less extensive have been made at the following-named stations, and they are now in good order. The repairing parties are in the field, at work, and, before the close of the season, all pressing repairs will have been made.

501. *Windmill Point.*
506. *Fort Gratiot.*
508. *Tarvas.*
509. *Charity Island.*
522. *Detour.*
523. *Waugoshance.*
525. *Beaver Island Harbor.*

526. *Beaver Island.*
536. *Grand Haven.*
530. *Kalamazoo.*
543. *Chicago.*
545. *Waukegan.*
549. *Milwaukee.*
550. *Milwaukee,* (North Cut beacon.)
551. *Port Washington.*
561. *Point Peninsula.*
564. *Chamber's Island.*
580. *Manitou Island.*
581. *Gull Rock.*

FOG-SIGNALS.

Four steam Fog-signals (boilers with whistles attached) have been ordered. They are to be established as follows:

1st. Upright tubular boiler, with 10-inch whistle, at *Fort Gratiot* Light-station, Lake Huron.

2d. Horizontal (locomotive) boiler, with 10-inch whistle, at *Thunder Bay Island.*

3d. Upright tubular boiler, with 10-inch whistle, at *Detour* Light-station, Lake Huron.

4th. Horizontal (locomotive) boiler, with 10-inch whistle, at *White Fish Point,* Lake Superior.

Bells, with Stevens's striking apparatus, are to be placed at *Waugoshance, Granite Island,* and *Pottawatomie Island.*

TENDERS.

The steam-barge *Warrington* has been principally used this season in connection with the work on *Spectacle Reef.* During last winter she was strengthened by arches and additional bilge kelsons, and her deck-beams supported by stanchions, thus preparing her for carrying on her deck the heavy stones to be used in building the tower. She has also been fitted with a steam-derrick with which to handle the stone. This derrick has proved of the very greatest service already.

The hard work of the season developed such defects in her boiler that a new one was deemed necessary. Hence, in August last the tender was laid up, and a new boiler eight feet in diameter and eighteen feet long was put in, when the vessel returned to her work. As the new boiler has a larger steam capacity, it will require less coal to run it when towing in heavy weather than was required for the old one, as it will no longer be necessary to force the fires as before.

The schooner *Belle* has been, and will continue to be, used as quarters for the workmen at *Spectacle Reef.* Because of her light draught she can be moored directly on the reef, and she thus answers a purpose which very few vessels would, and indeed is of the greatest value. She is now getting old, and will need extensive repairs before long, but nothing is proposed before the close of the season.

The steam-tender Haze has been employed in delivering the light-house supplies on all the lakes, and in transporting freight and looking after the buoys.

TWELFTH DISTRICT.

This district embraces all aids to navigation on the Pacific coast of the United States, from the Mexican frontier to the boundary of Oregon.

Inspector.—Commodore Alfred Taylor, United States Navy.
Engineer.—Brevet Lieutenant Colonel R. S. Williamson, Major o
Engineers, United States Army.
There are in this district—

Light-houses... 14
Buoys actually in position.. 33
Spare buoys, for relief and to supply losses............................. 33
Tender (steam) *Shubrick* 1

The following numbers, which precede the names of stations, correspond with those of the "Light-house List of the Atlantic, Gulf, and Pacific Coasts of the United States," issued January 1, 1871.

Point Fermin, sea-coast of California, near entrance to San Pedro Harbor.—An appropriation of $25,000 is recommended to establish a fourth-order Light-house and a steam Fog-signal at this point to mark the approaches of San Pedro Harbor. The appropriation should, if possible, be made so as not to revert to the Treasury at the end of the fiscal year, for the reason that it is impossible to obtain a suitable site except by condemnation under the laws of California, which is a long and tedious process.

The number of vessels navigating near the southern coast of California, between there and San Diego, and passing through the Santa Barbara Channel, has been greatly increased within the last two years. All coast steamers stop at San Pedro, near Wilmington, the port of Los Angeles, and a Light-house and Fog-signal, as guides to the entrance of the harbor, are of great importance.

Anacapa Island, west side of southern entrance to the Santa Barbara Channel, California.—An appropriation of $70,000 is recommended for the establishment of a first-order Light-station at the eastern end of this island. The island is a barren rock about one hundred and fifty feet above the sea, destitute of verdure, and all the water and other materials necessary to prosecute the work will have to be brought from the main land.

The same reasons which make it advisable to establish a light at Point Fermin, are in still greater force with reference to *Anacapa*, which is at the south entrance of the Santa Barbara Channel, there but ten miles in width. A Fog-signal is not recommended on the island, as the coast steamers usually pass nearer the main land, and because of the high and very precipitous sides of the island, against which the waves are constantly dashing and producing a deafening noise.

Point Hueneme, sea-coast of California, east side of southern entrance to Santa Barbara Channel.—An appropriation of $10,000 is recommended for the erection of a first-class steam Fog-signal at this point, which is directly opposite *Anacapa Island*. With a first-order Light on the eastern end of *Anacapa Island*, and a steam Fog-signal on the western extremity of Point Hueneme, the southern approaches to Santa Barbara Channel will be well marked, and the navigation of the waters of that portion of California coast rendered less dangerous.

392. *Point Conception*, sea-coast of California.—An appropriation for establishing a first-class steam Fog-signal at this station was made March 3, 1871. A thorough examination and survey of this point is to be made, with a view to ascertaining the best location for the proposed signal, the supply of water, and of obtaining all other necessary information. The engine and boiler for this signal have been contracted for.

Piedras Blancas, sea-coast of California.—This point is about midway between Point Conception and Point Pinos Light-houses, distant one hundred and fifty miles from each other. But Point Pinos is only a harbor Light, and the coasting steamers take their departure from Pie-

-dras Blancas, and keep so far out that *Point Pinos Light* is not seen, and it may be considered that there is no sea-coast Light between Point Conception and Pigeon Point, which are nearly two hundred miles distant. An appropriation of $75,000 is submitted for the erection of a first-order Light and Fog-signal at Piedras Blancas.

393. *Point Pinos*, sea-coast of California, entrance to Monterey Bay.— The suit for condemnation of land, and right of way thereto, at this station, which was tried in the October term of the district court of the third judicial district of the State of California, resulted in a verdict by which the jury awarded to the owners of the land the sum of $1,280 as the value of the land, and the damage resulting by reason of taking of the same. The owners sought to obtain the value of the Light-house building and improvements, and the cost of fencing the Light-house tract and roadway. The former was denied by the court, and the latter disallowed by the jury. The owners have appealed the case to the supreme court of California, and the suit is now pending before that body.

Pigeon Point, sea-coast of California.—An appropriation of $90,000 was made March 3, 1871, for the erection of a first-class Light-house and Fog-signal at this point. The structures are to consist of a masonry tower, which is to be one hundred feet high, from base to focal plane. The elevation of the Light above mean sea-level will be one hundred and fifty-eight feet. The keeper's dwelling is to be a double two-story house, built of wood. Work on the above structures was commenced on the 9th of June. A first-class steam Fog-signal will be established at this point, and also on *Año Nuevo Island*, six miles southeast of *Pigeon Point*. It is expected that the steam Fog-signal at *Pigeon Point* will be ready for operation about the 31st of August. The steam Fog-signal for *Año Nuevo Island* may not be ready for operations until after the first rains of the coming winter, for the reason that it may be necessary to construct a water-shed and build a large cistern to collect water.

396. *Point Bonita*, entrance to San Francisco Harbor, California.—An appropriation for the establishment of a first-class steam Fog-signal at this station was made on the 3d of March last. In June of this year a thorough examination of the point was made, with a view of determining the best location for the signal, the means of supplying it with water, and the best way to get materials to this difficult site selected. A syren with its engine has been constructed for this station, and will be forwarded in a few days.

Point San Pablo, between the bays of San Francisco and San Pablo, California. An appropriation was made March 3, 1871, for the erection of a Light-house and Fog-signal at this point, as a guide through the straits of San Pablo. As it was found impossible to obtain a suitable piece of land at this point by purchase, a survey was made of the point, showing the metes and bounds of the land required, and a suit for the condemnation of the land thus surveyed has been commenced in the fifteenth judicial district of California. The court to try this case meets on the 5th of December next. The commencement of work on the proposed structures will therefore be delayed until the opening of next spring. The structures will be completed and the Light-house and Fog-signal in operation before the end of the present fiscal year.

Mare Island, entrance to the straits of Carquines, California.—An appropriation of $10,000 is recommended for the erection of a fifth-order Light at this point, to mark the approaches to Carquines Straits. The erection of a Light-house at this point has been strongly urged for many years.

399. *Point Reyes*, sea-coast of California.—The iron tower for this sta-

tion was shipped to Drake's Bay, landed there, and hauled to the top of the bluff, near the keeper's dwelling, on October 9, 1870. The work of taking the tower, lantern, and lens apparatus from the top of the bluff down to the site proposed for the tower was successfully completed shortly afterward, and its erection was commenced by the contractor. The work was completed in November, and the Light was exhibited for the first time on the night of December 1, 1870. On February 1 the work of preparing a site for the steam Fog-signal at this station was commenced. A large cistern was constructed, which, with a basin around it, will hold 100,000 gallons. A water-shed, ten thousand square feet in area, was made, from which water enough will be collected in a year to fill the cistern, even in a season in which the rain-fall will be much below the average.

The water from the cistern is conducted to the Fog-signal by means of a galvanized iron pipe, which is securely fastened to the sides of the cliff. A chute has been built from the site of the tower to the Fog-signal. This chute is constructed in the most substantial manner, and is for the purpose of conveying fuel to the Fog-signal. A winding road-way has been constructed from the cliff to the signal site. Much blast-ing was done before it was completed. The work of preparing the site for the signal-house, coal-shed, &c., was very slow, difficult, and danger-ous. Huge masses of rocks overhanging the signal site had to be blasted off, so that at the rear of the signal is a vertical wall of rock, one hun-dred feet high. An iron railing was put around the edges of the plot prepared for the signal, to keep any one from rolling off into the sea, as on all seaward sides of the signal the cliff is very steep and jagged.

On June 12 the work of taking the boiler and signal apparatus from the top of the cliff down to its position was successfully accomplished. The boiler was put in position, the apparatus fitted to it, and on June 14 the signal was tried, and found to work satisfactorily. On June 30 the work of housing the boiler and signal-apparatus was completed. The signal is now ready for operation, and can be started as soon as the rains of next winter shall have sufficiently filled the cistern with water. The work of establishing this Fog-signal has been, from the nature of the location, very expensive and dangerous.

400. *Point Arena*, sea-coast of California.—An appropriation for the establishment of a first-class steam Fog-signal at this station was made March 3, 1871. An examination of the point, with a view of determining the location for the signal and the supply of fuel and water, has been made. It is expected to complete the work and have the signal in readiness for operation November 1 next.

401. *Cape Mendocino*, sea-coast of California.—The brick dwelling-house at this station was so badly injured by an earthquake on March 2, that it was deemed necessary to pull it down, and erect in its stead a double house of wood. The place selected for the site of the new dwell-ing is on the spur of the cape on which the Light-house tower stands, and some distance above it. The spur is a rocky ledge, and has the appearance of being very permanent. The work of tearing down the old structure commenced on the 23d of June; the keepers having re-moved to a shanty near by that was fitted up as a temporary residence for them. It is expected that the new house will be finished by Novem-ber next. This structure is of the same plan as the *Cape Blanco* dwell-ing, which was built last year.

The claimants of the land at this Light-station have appealed from the decision of the judge of the eighth judicial district to the supreme court of the State, and the case is now pending before that body.

Trinidad Head, sea-coast of California.—An appropriation for the erection of a Light-house at *Trinidad Head* was approved June 20, 1860, but nothing was done toward building the structures until February of this year. The materials were purchased and the work commenced in June, and the work is now progressing favorably. The Light will be of the fourth order, fixed, varied by red flashes, and will be shown from a low, square, brick tower.

Fauntleroy Rock, Crescent City Harbor, California.—An appropriation for erecting a day-beacon on this rock was made March 3, 1871. It is to be of wrought iron, will be thirty feet high from the base of the rock, and is to be surmounted by a circular cage composed of wrought-iron rings. The work was completed on the 20th of September.

At each of the following-named stations there have been repairs and renovations, more or less extensive, made since the date of the last annual report:

391. *Santa Barbara,* coast of California, near Santa Barbara landing.

392. *Point Conception*, coast of California, west side of northern entrance to Santa Barbara Channel.

393. *Point Pinos*, coast of California, south side of entrance to Monterey Harbor.

394. *Santa Cruz*, on Point Santa Cruz, at the entrance of Santa Cruz Harbor, California.

395. *Farralones*, on the largest or southeast Farralon islet.

396. *Point Boneta*, California coast.

397. *Fort Point*, California.

398. *Alcatraz*, on Alcatraz Island, in the harbor of San Francisco, California.

399. *Point Reyes*, California.

The following are the names of the Light-stations in these districts not mentioned elsewhere:

390. *Point Loma*, California, west side of entrance to San Diego Bay.

402. *Humboldt*, California, north side of entrance to Humboldt Bay.

404. *Crescent City*, California, entrance to Crescent City Harbor.

THIRTEENTH DISTRICT.

This district embraces all aids to navigation on the Pacific coast of the United States north of the boundary between California and Oregon.

Inspector.—Commodore Alfred Taylor, United States Navy.

Engineer.—Major H. M. Robert, Corps of Engineers, United States Army.

There are in this district—

Light-houses 10
Buoys actually in position 10
Spare buoys for relief, and to supply losses 10
Tender (steam) *Shubrick*, common to Twelfth and Thirteenth Districts 1

The numbers preceding the names of the stations correspond with those of the Light-house List of January, 1871.

407. *Yaquina Bay*, Oregon.—The Light-house at this point was commenced May 1, 1871, and will be completed about September 30, 1871.

408. *Cape Foulweather*, sea-coast of Oregon.—For the erection of a first-class sea-coast Light at or near this point there was appropriated at the last session of Congress $90,000. It is proposed to erect a brick tower eighty feet from the ground to the focal plane, giving the focal plane a height of about one hundred and fifty feet above the sea level. The plans have been completed; work was commenced about September 1, and will be completed during the present fiscal year.

409. *Cape Disappointment,* mouth of Columbia River, Washington· Territory.—A new dwelling for light-keepers has been commenced, and will be completed during the present season.

411. *Cape Flattery,* entrance to Puget Sound, Washington·Territory.— A first-class steam Fog-signal has been commenced, and will be completed at this station before December next.

The following are the names of Light-stations in this district not mentioned elsewhere:

405. *Cape Blanco,* sea-coast of Oregon.
406. *Cape Arago, (Gregory,)* sea-coast of Oregon.
410. *Shoalwater Bay,* Washington Territory.
412. *Ediz Hook.*
413. *New Dungeness.*
414. *Smith's (or Blunt's) Island.*
415. *Admiralty Head.*

All of which is very respectfully submitted.

W. B. SHUBRICK,
Rear-Admiral U. S. Navy, Chairman..
THORNTON A. JENKINS,
Rear Admiral, U. S. Navy, Naval Secretary.
GEORGE H. ELLIOT,
Major Corps of Engineers, U. S. A., Engineer Secretary.

Hon. GEORGE S. BOUTWELL,
Secretary of the Treasury.

INDEX.

35 F

546 REPORT ON THE FINANCES.

O

www.ingramcontent.com/pod-product-compliance
Lightning Source LLC
Chambersburg PA
CBHW020854210326
41598CB00018B/1660